The Diversity
of Modern America

Under the Editorial Supervision of
Arthur S. Link

The Diversity
of Modern America

Essays in History
Since World War One

Edited by

David Burner

STATE UNIVERSITY OF NEW YORK
AT STONY BROOK

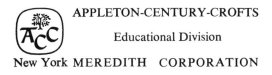

APPLETON-CENTURY-CROFTS

Educational Division

New York MEREDITH CORPORATION

To Diane and Eric
with love

Preface

The essays in this collection were chosen because they help to clarify in the understanding the nature of diverse and changing America. Some of the essays are at the crossroads of politics and social history, of literature and social science, or even of several disciplines. But politics remains at the core of this volume because to a considerable extent it shapes and reflects national values and allocates national resources. To convey to students a stronger sense of the uses of history, many of the political subjects covered here have been chosen for their relevance to the present moment. Many of the selections question established values, undermining, for example, the use of "liberal" and "conservative" as meaningful categories. Liberalism comes under attack as a kind of pushbutton reaction to events; to the New Left, for instance, liberals discourage thoroughgoing reform and think in stereotypes.

Since historical study has considerably extended its domain in recent years, the reader will find here discussions by literary and social critics as well as political and diplomatic historians, essays from periodicals as different as *Partisan Review* and the *Journal of American History*. These articles have not been endlessly reprinted and may be fresh to the teacher as well as the student. I hope the reader gains some of the same satisfaction from them that I have.

Thomas West and Robert D. Marcus have given valuable advice and encouragement. The criticisms and suggestions of Arthur S. Link and of Walter J. Green have also been invaluable. Finally, I would like to thank those authors and publishers who have allowed me to reprint their essays.

David Burner

Stony Brook, New York

Contents

The Diversity
of Modern America

Introduction: Defining Modern America

Sometime about World War One America went modern. We all recognize this change even if we cannot quite define it. Fashion designers periodically revive the short skirts, the fringes and the frills, the rosy makeup of the nineteen twenties; but the bustles and the whaleboned corsets worn by the women of the Victorian era are museum pieces. We would not feel out of place at a cocktail party of the twenties, but what would we do at a tea party of the nineties? Even those who live in country towns watch television and movies emanating from urban centers, wear clothing designed in New York, London, or Paris, even cook with recipes from the Julia Child cookbook. If we stay down on the farm, the mass media bring Broadway and much more to us. Americans pride themselves on being modern, urbane, cosmopolitan—and among the powers of the earth.

We also worry about our values and our future. Hot war, cold war, economic slumps, and bewildering change have made it difficult to believe the moral efficacy of technological progress. Perhaps a society reveals itself most by its choice of crises: the question of personal identity, although not unique to modern times, has become the American preoccupation. Certainly some suffered from this crisis before World War One, but it was not the common legacy of every man who read a book or listened to a sermon or a political speech. In short, around World War One, Americans became—or discovered that they had already become—more knowing than before, more cosmopolitan in their awareness if not in their generosities, and, by the same token, more provisional and uneasy in their beliefs. People in 1910 were more certain that they knew what was right and what was wrong, what was proper and what was not, what was possible and what was not, than people have been since. They had their own problems, as serious to them as ours are to us. But these are not our problems, and the essays in this book will discuss our problems, the concerns of Americans in the modern world of doubts, divisions, and fateful change.

Harbingers of change were visible before the First World War. Artists and writers experimented with the forms that the twenties would label "modern." Bohemians in Greenwich Village and elsewhere lived some of the styles in manner and dress that the middle class would eventually absorb. Reformers and radicals glimpsed the possibilities of utopia or disaster above and below the complacent Victorian belief in evolutionary progress. A few read Marx and a few more read Freud. American women were restless. Gallant ladies ran settlement houses in the midst of the slums, while other brave ones fought for a place in the professions or greater sexual freedom or the acceptance of birth control. Some young people began to think of themselves as a "generation" and to condemn their elders as "puritans." Some, through contact with European culture by way of books, the immigrant community, or the Grand Tour, rejected one of their society's central beliefs: the superiority of Anglo-Saxon culture. The nation was beginning to change.

It could have been a comfortably paced transformation, but World War One made it traumatically abrupt. Who could believe in progress and rationality when the most advanced nations were locked in a brutal mindless struggle? Who could see Americans as a unified and orderly society when ethnic groups angrily took sides in the European strife? Who could believe in great moral purpose when war followed President Wilson's pledges of peace, when the unjust treaty of Versailles belied Wilsonian promises of justice, when savage repression succeeded the New Freedom? If the repression shocked only some, in many ways the war and its aftermath denied the world from which all Americans had drawn their beliefs.

After the breakdown of prewar values, Americans began a search for political identity, unity, and purpose, in spite or perhaps because of their social, economic, and cultural diversity. The first great prophet of the new America, Randolph Silliman Bourne, noted this central change in American life with uncanny insight. America had become a "federation of cultures." Its population was a mixture of ethnic groups with their roots in other cultures, their life in this one, and their allegiance divided—a "dual citizenship" in which local or group allegiance was the mediating agency for participation in national life.

To the ethnic communities Bourne describes in his "Trans-National America" can be added a welter of social and economic groups that appear, change, or vanish, for America is a constantly changing conglomeration of subcultures. With its differentiations exists a half-definable stock of ideas, institutions, and traditions on which, so we think, all Americans draw; yet they believe so simply in the commonness of the heritage, in the democratic fellowship of sharing in it—or else are so angrily committed to the purity of the American past—that their divisions do not sit easily with them. A tolerance for diversity is considered part of the heritage; yet Americans are inclined to see acts of diversity—a religious argument, or some ethnic swagger—as acts of intolerance. Other nations have their focal institutions or their myths, but these are better suited to the toleration of social and cultural diversity. The British constitution accommodates equally the aristocracy and the commons, and does not demand fellowship between them; the French Revolution provides a myth that competing factions among the French may freely use against one another. But Americans feel uncomfortable in the face of their varieties and divisions. The American lives a peculiar kind of tension: he is at once American and New Englander, or American and Roman Catholic; proud of his own subculture, yet resentful when others make too pointed a reference to it; sentimentally open to the multiplicity of America, yet hostile toward his neighbor for being different and therefore less "American."

Politics in modern America has been in considerable measure a response to this tension. For several years after the First World War, a nativist segment of the American public sought to achieve the pure American heritage by the suppression of ethnic diversity. The Ku Klux Klan and some elements within both political parties sought through prohibition of alcohol, an immigrant exclusion law, and other means to reestablish the supremacy of a white Protestant America of small towns and the hinterland over the foreign-born, the Catholics, the religious modernists—over the urban twentieth century. The non-Protestant minority spoke through Governor Alfred E. Smith, whose campaign for the presidency in 1928 represented a political coming of age for Americans of immigrant stock.

Smith failed to win the White House, but as early as 1930, in another test of minority group power, labor unions together with the National Association for the Advancement of Colored People worked through Senate liberals to block the nomination of an alleged conservative to the Supreme Court. If the national politics of the nineteen twenties was a politics of mutual exclusions—with the urban wing of the Democratic party scarcely more prepared to talk to the hinterland democracy than the hinterland was prepared to listen—the nation worked during the thirties toward a coalition politics in face of the common enemy, the Great Depression. Farmers and the urban unemployed, migrants and landowners, unions, shopowners, and even elements within big business found themselves participating—sometimes in uneasy partnership—in the loose collection of programs that goes by the name of the New Deal. A few of its architects and spokesmen did have some notion that they were making a statement about America as a cooperative enterprise of peoples and classes. But these administrators and intellectuals had too bland a conviction of democratic brotherhood, or of the unity that desperation brings: many of their subsidized landowning farmers brutalized the sharecroppers and workers who lost out when the Agricultural Adjustment Administration paid for crop restrictions, and many poor whites remained vicious toward Negroes (who had a very minor voice in the coalition). Still, at its most naive, the New Deal gave us a vision of what American politics might be—as inclusive and multiple as American society, generous and comradely.

The Great Depression offered an opportunity for a statement of national ethos; international crisis has provided another. Confronting totalitarianism during the late thirties and the years of World War Two, America defined itself by the most general democratic ideals. The Cold War has led to more specific and harsher definitions. During its early days, in the late nineteen forties and early fifties, some conservatives expected good Americans to abide by an all-encompassing American anti-communist and anti-socialist ideology, nothing diluted or compromised. Now a segment of the American liberal-to-left community has asserted—partly on evidence of the Cold War, and sometimes with almost as narrow an ideological commitment as the right wing—that America is perhaps totalitarian itself and needs redemption from its military and industrial power structures.

During the decade of the fifties, a number of intellectuals and artists concerned themselves not about the differentiations in American society, but about their absence, about the washing out of individuality and the advance of conformity in American life. "Other-directedness," the sociologist David Riesman called it, a condition in which man is ruled neither by tradition nor by inner character but becomes a sort of radar receiver getting blips and charting direction from those around him. William H. Whyte's typical American was the Organization Man. What analysts of this kind thought they had discovered was not a fanatic totalitarian conformity but a bland culture of nearly compulsory happiness and good-fellowship. Few of them suggested our tradition of social and cultural pluralism as a counterforce, though Herman Wouk did so in effect when he urged American Jews not to abandon their special inheritance and identity. Riesman assumed the role not so much of critic but of detached observer; others defended the humanist patrimony of Western culture against the debasements of American mass culture.

Their worries are no longer ours. During the past few years America has heard a political oratory that states the major disharmonies rather than the surface consensus; it has witnessed the demand for a culture of spontaneity and personal style grow from the beatnik phenomenon of the fifties to achieve a major voice; it has watched spokesmen for the black ghetto turn to cultural pluralism in its most radical, separatist form. The extent to which all this means a movement toward individuality is open to question. If the decline of traditional inhibitions may suggest a more expressive sexual life, the increased use of drugs may tend to the submergence of will and reason, the death of the autonomous reasoned self. If racial separatism may provide selfhood for the black community, it may also threaten the selfhood of the black citizen.

This may suggest the real value of America's cultural pluralism. Because that pluralism hovers between extreme self-isolation of subcultures and complete surrender to some flat national consensus, it forces ambivalence and a multiple experience upon the individual. Unable to consign his will and personality completely to the keeping either of his immediate community or of some national culture, and freed from the overpowering demand that either might separately make upon him, touched by many subcultures, he can participate by an act of will in the development of selfhood.

Even though the pace of technological and social change has quickened since World War One, most of the themes of modern American history remain our substantive concerns. The continuity between past and present is sometimes difficult to discern, but still exists. For instance, mobilization for the First World War was a technique also put to use in the national effort against the depression. The war itself was repeated two decades later with the renewed outbreak of German belligerence; again followed plans for a worldwide peacekeeping organization and a second postwar reaction ensued at home. The decade of the twenties, with its accent on youth, sensual and zestful experience, and constant experimentation in modes and styles of living, suggests our own time and younger generation. But the political complacency of the prosperity decade, along with its status-consciousness, looked forward more to the nineteen fifties than the sixties; while in the thirties are to be found roots of social consciousness—and perhaps also of the violence—that flourished in the sixties.

The two world wars, the depression, and the nuclear threat of our own decades have left a pervading sense of cataclysm in America. If this is not unique to our century, it is different from previous eras insofar as we have discovered cataclysm as a circumstance not of nature but of the affairs of men, and we are therefore prepared to call upon technology as an instrument of the moral will in order to confront it.

World War One to the Great Depression: A Rich and Troubled Decade

The twenties began the modern hurried era where history is measured by decades rather than ages or generations. World War One appeared to drive a great wedge between the old and the new, marking a sharp change in styles, manners, and interests. The Jazz Age, as F. Scott Fitzgerald called it, with flappers and speakeasies, silent movies and ballyhooed sporting events, radios and mass-produced automobiles, saw the emergence of a modern urban America. This culture, tied to the new media, advertising and public relations, mass production and distribution, was the first "affluent society" of the recognizably modern type. The style of affluence not only differentiated the twenties from the semi-Victorian age preceding it, but also from the years of the locust that followed in the 1930's. The twenties came to seem like a last, spoiled adolescent party thrown by the new America before entering its grimmer maturity, an interlude between the serious worlds of the Progressive Era and the Great Depression.

This picture of the decade, which formed almost as soon as the decade was over, falls apart as soon as one touches it, turning the age from a vivid illustration—perhaps an advertisement for a new product—into a jigsaw puzzle which the historian must reassemble correctly. Of course, many more of the pieces came from the past than men of the twenties presumed. Urbanization, the power of the great corporations, the rise of a polyglot America rent with intergroup tensions were all inheritances of the previous age. Even the specifically modern culture of urban sophistication of the new literature of Fitzgerald, Sherwood Anderson, Sinclair Lewis, and Ernest Hemingway had antecedents in the small but influential knots of advanced thinkers gathered in San Francisco, Chicago, and especially in Greenwich Village.

*Similarly, the face of the twenties has remained more charac-
teristic of American life in this century than anyone in the grim
thirties would have imagined. A rising stock market, consumer
credit, and high-pressure advertising and sales of new commodities
were not part of a peculiar and irresponsible spree of the 1920's,
but rather the commercial norm of an affluent society. And the culture of the era, far from seeming trivial, and lacking in social content, has proven a permanent legacy to rank with the classic
achievements of the 1850's.*

*Nor was the era as uniform as it has sometimes been por-
trayed. The economy did not take off for the stratosphere with the
cessation of World War One: the early twenties were a depressed
period for the economy generally, and some groups, notably farmers, suffered from depressed conditions throughout the era. Nor was
the period wholly consistent in politics. The war and its aftermath
brought a brief period of political excitement and a fierce reaction
in the Red scare of 1919 before the politics of the decade fell into
relative tranquility and often unimaginative conservatism. Political
progressivism, while unsuccessful nationally, survived in many
forms, and at least one Republican, Herbert Hoover, earned a
creditable record for important innovations in governmental policy
during his lengthy tenure as Secretary of Commerce.*

*Nevertheless, the age did call itself a New Era and staked its
reputation on its economic performance. The Great Crash of 1929
ended old hopes and introduced new anxieties, starting a fresh era
in national politics and in the American way of life. Whether the
legacy of this newer age is any more permanent than that of the
twenties a historian looking at the period since must doubt. This
rich and troubled decade of the twenties remains distinctive in our
national life, even if we now hesitate to consider it unique.*

~~~~~~2

RANDOLPH BOURNE

Trans-National America

Randolph Bourne worked as the nation's conscience during World War One. He died at thirty-two in the month the war ended. Bourne's critique of the war did not rest on rhetoric about munitions makers or international bankers. Rather, he believed that during wartime art, knowledge, reason, beauty—what he called "the enhancement of life"—are "instantly and almost unanimously sacrificed." He was also sure that the war would impoverish domestic reform and that liberal intellectuals, no matter how valuable their wartime services, would have little influence in the postwar world.

It is in the context of what Bourne said about the war that his "Trans-National America" should be read. Disgusted by an Americanization that made children ashamed of their parents and that led them to contempt for their ethnic groups, Bourne sought in this essay to identify underlying democratic values that would encompass all groups. In his Whitmanesque vision of a "federation of cultures" he saw a higher ideal than the melting pot as a possibility within our grasp. Democracy for the individual meant democracy for the group and nation. In a pluralistic society ethnic and racial subgroups could educate one another out of their narrow immigrant's conservatism; each could contribute to the rich and variegated fabric of national life while retaining the best of its own culture. "Let us cease," wrote Bourne, "to think of ideals like democracy as magical qualities inherent in certain peoples. It is not what we are now that concerns us, but what this plastic next generation may become in the light of a new cosmopolitan ideal."

No reverberatory effect of the great war has caused American public opinion more solicitude than the failure of the "melting pot." The discovery of diverse nationalistic feelings among our great alien population has come to most people as an intense shock. It has brought out the unpleasant inconsistencies of our traditional beliefs. We have had to watch hard-hearted old Brahmins virtuously indignant at the spectacle of the immigrant refusing to be melted, while they jeer at patriots like Mary Antin who write about "our forefathers." We have had to listen to publicists who express themselves as stunned by the evidence of vigorous nationalistic and cultural movements in this country among Germans, Scandinavians, Bohemians, and Poles, while in the same breath they insist that the alien shall be forcibly assimilated to that Anglo-Saxon tradition which they unquestionably label "American."

As the unpleasant truth has come upon us that assimilation in this country was proceeding on lines very different from those we had marked out for it, we found ourselves inclined to blame those who were thwarting our prophecies. The truth became culpable. We blamed the war, we blamed the Germans. And then we discovered with a moral shock that these movements had been making great headway before the war even began. We found that the tendency, reprehensible and paradoxical as it might be, has been for the national clusters of immigrants, as they became more and more firmly established and more and more prosperous, to cultivate more and more assiduously the literatures and cultural traditions of their homelands. Assimilation, in other words, instead of washing out the memories of Europe, made them more and more intensely real. Just as these clusters became more and more objectively American, did they become more and more German or Scandinavian or Bohemian or Polish.

To face the fact that our aliens are already strong enough to take a share in the direction of their own destiny, and that the strong cultural movements represented by the foreign press, schools, and colonies are a challenge to our facile attempts, is not, however, to admit the failure of Americanization. It is not to fear the failure of democracy. It is rather to urge us to an investigation of what Americanism may rightly mean. It is to ask ourselves whether our ideal has been broad or narrow—whether perhaps the time has not come to assert a higher ideal than the "melting-pot." Surely we cannot be certain of our spiritual democracy when, claiming to melt the nations within us to a comprehension of our free and democratic institutions, we fly into panic at the first sign of their own will and tendency. We act as if we wanted Americanization to take place only on our own terms, and not by the consent of the governed. All our elaborate machinery of settlement and school and union, of social and political naturalization, however, will move with friction just in so far as it neglects to take into account this strong and virile insistence that America shall be what the immigrant will have a hand in making it, and not what a ruling class, descendant of those British stocks which were the first permanent immigrants, decide that America shall be made. This is the condition which confronts us, and which demands a clear and general readjustment of our attitude and our ideal.

Mary Antin is right when she looks upon our foreign-born as the people who missed the Mayflower and came over on the first boat they could find. But she forgets that when they did come it was not upon other Mayflowers, but upon a "Maiblume," a "Fleur de Mai," a "Fior di Maggio," a "Maj-blomst." These people were not mere arrivals from the same family, to be welcomed as understood and long-loved, but strangers to the neighborhood, with whom a long process of settling down had to take place. For they brought with them their national and racial characters, and each new national quota had to wear slowly away the contempt with which its mere alienness got itself greeted. Each had to make its way slowly from the lowest strata of unskilled labor up to a level where it satisfied the accredited norms of social success.

We are all foreign-born or the descendants of foreign-born, and if distinctions are to be made between us they should rightly be on some other ground than indigenousness. The early colonists came over with motives no less colonial than the later. They did not come to be assimilated in an American melting-pot. They did not come to adopt the culture of the American Indian. They had not the smallest intention of "giving themselves without reservation" to the new country. They came to get freedom to live as they wanted to. They came to escape from the stifling air and chaos of the old world; they came to make their fortune in a new land. They invented no new social framework. Rather they brought over bodily the old ways to which they had been accustomed. Tightly concentrated on a hostile frontier, they were conservative beyond belief. Their pioneer daring was reserved for the objective conquest of material resources. In their folkways, in their social and political institutions, they were, like every colonial people, slavishly imitative of the mother-country. So that, in spite of the "Revolution," our whole legal and political system remained more English than the English, petrified and unchanging, while in England law developed to meet the needs of the changing times.

It is just this English-American conservatism that has been our chief obstacle to social advance. We have needed the new peoples—the order of the German and Scandinavian, the turbulence of the Slav and Hun—to save us from our own stagnation. I do not mean that the illiterate Slav is now the equal of the New Englander of pure descent. He is raw material to be educated, not into a New Englander, but into a socialized American along such lines as those thirty nationalities are being educated in the amazing schools of Gary. I do not believe that this process is to be one of decades of evolution. The spectacle of Japan's sudden jump from mediævalism to post-modernism should have destroyed that superstition. We are not dealing with individuals who are to "evolve." We are dealing with their children, who, with that education we are about to have, will start level with all of us. Let us cease to think of ideals like democracy as magical qualities inherent in certain peoples. Let us speak, not of inferior races, but of inferior civilizations. We are all to educate and to be educated. These peoples in America are in a common enterprise. It is not what we are now that concerns us, but what this plastic next generation may become in the light of a new cosmopolitan ideal.

We are not dealing with static factors, but with fluid and dynamic generations. To contrast the older and the newer immigrants and see the one class as democratically motivated by love of liberty, and the other by mere money-getting, is not to illuminate the future. To think of earlier nationalities as culturally assimilated to America, while we picture the later as a sodden and resistive mass, makes only for bitterness and misunderstanding. There may be a difference between these earlier and these later stocks, but it lies neither in motive for coming nor in strength of cultural allegiance to the homeland. The truth is that no more tenacious cultural allegiance to the mother country has been shown by any alien nation than by the ruling class of Anglo-Saxon descendants in these American States. English snobberies, English religion, English literary styles, English literary reverences and canons, English ethics, English superiorities, have been the cultural food that we have drunk in from our mother's breasts. The distinctively American spirit—pioneer, as distinguished from the reminiscently English—that appears in Whitman and Emerson and James, has had to exist on sufferance alongside of this other cult, unconsciously belittled by our cultural makers of opinion. No country has perhaps had so great indigenous genius which had so little influence on the country's traditions and expressions. The unpopular and dreaded German-American of the present day is a beginning amateur in comparison with those foolish Anglophiles of Boston and New York and Philadelphia whose reversion to cultural type sees uncritically in England's cause the cause of Civilization, and, under the guise of ethical independence of thought, carries along European traditions which are no more "American" than the German categories themselves.

It speaks well for German-American innocence of heart or else for its lack of imagination that it has not turned the hyphen stigma into a "Tu quoque!" If there were to be any hyphens scattered about, clearly they should be affixed to those English descendants who had had centuries of time to be made American where the German had had only half a century. Most significantly has the war brought out of them this alien virus, showing them still loving English things, owing allegiance to the English Kultur, moved by English shibboleths and prejudice. It is only because it has been the ruling class in this country that bestowed the epithets that we have not heard copiously and scornfully of "hyphenated English-Americans." But even our quarrels with England have had the bad temper, the extravagance, of family quarrels. The Englishman of to-day nags us and dislikes us in that personal, peculiarly intimate way in which he dislikes the Australian, or as we may dislike our younger brothers. He still thinks of us incorrigibly as "colonials." America—official, controlling, literary, political America—is still, as a writer recently expressed it, "culturally speaking, a self-governing dominion of the British Empire."

The non-English American can scarcely be blamed if he sometimes thinks of the Anglo-Saxon predominance in America as little more than a predominance of priority. The Anglo-Saxon was merely the first immigrant, the first to found a colony. He has never really ceased to be the descendant of immigrants, nor has he ever succeeded in transforming that colony into a real nation, with a tenacious, richly woven fabric of native culture. Colonials from the other nations have come and settled down beside him. They found no definite native culture which should startle them out of their colonialism, and consequently they looked back to their mother-country, as the earlier Anglo-Saxon immigrant was looking back to his. What has been offered the newcomer has been the chance to learn English, to become a citizen, to salute the flag. And those elements of our ruling classes who are responsible for the public schools, the settlements, all the organizations for amelioration in the cities, have every reason to be proud of the care and labor which they have devoted to absorbing the immigrant. His opportunities the immigrant has taken to gladly, with almost a pathetic eagerness to make his way in the new land without friction or disturbance. The common language has made not only for the necessary communication, but for all the amenities of life.

If freedom means the right to do pretty much as one pleases, so long as one does not interfere with others, the immigrant has found freedom, and the ruling element has been singularly liberal in its treatment of the invading hordes. But if freedom means a democratic cooperation in determining the ideals and purposes and industrial and social institutions of a country, then the immigrant has not been free, and the Anglo-Saxon element is guilty of just what every dominant race is guilty of in every European country: the imposition of its own culture upon the minority peoples. The fact that this imposition has been so mild and, indeed, semi-conscious does not alter its quality. And the war has brought out just the degree to which that purpose of "Americanizing," that is, "Anglo-Saxonizing," the immigrant has failed.

For the Anglo-Saxon now in his bitterness to turn upon the other peoples, talk about their "arrogance," scold them for not being melted in a pot which never existed, is to betray the unconscious purpose which lay at the bottom of his heart. It betrays too the possession of a racial jealousy similar to that of which he is now accusing the so-called "hyphenates." Let the Anglo-Saxon be proud enough of the heroic toil and heroic sacrifices which moulded the nation. But let him ask himself, if he had had to depend on the English descendants, where he would have been living to-day. To those of us who see in the exploitation of unskilled labor the strident red *leit-motif* of our civilization, the settling of the country presents a great social drama as the waves of immigration broke over it.

Let the Anglo-Saxon ask himself where he would have been if these races had not come? Let those who feel the inferiority of the non-Anglo-Saxon immigrant contemplate that region of the States which has remained the most distinctively "American," the South. Let him ask himself whether he would really like to see the foreign hordes Americanized into such an Americanization. Let him ask himself how superior this native civilization is to the great "alien" states of Wisconsin and Minnesota, where Scandinavians, Poles, and Germans have self-consciously labored to preserve their traditional culture, while being outwardly and satisfactorily American. Let him ask himself how much more wisdom, intelligence, industry and social leadership has come out of these alien states than out of all the truly American ones. The South, in fact, while this vast Northern development has gone on, still remains an English colony, stagnant and complacent, having progressed culturally scarcely beyond the early Victorian era. It is culturally sterile because it has had no advantage of cross-fertilization like the Northern states. What has happened in states such as Wisconsin and Minnesota is that strong foreign cultures have struck root in a new and fertile soil. America has meant liberation, and German and Scandinavian political ideas and social energies have expanded to a new potency. The process has not been at all the fancied "assimilation" of the Scandinavian or Teuton. Rather has it been a process of their assimilation of us—I speak as an Anglo-Saxon. The foreign cultures have not been melted down or run together, made into some homogeneous Americanism, but have remained distinct but coöperating to the greater glory and benefit, not only of themselves but of all the native "Americanism" around them.

What we emphatically do not want is that these distinctive qualities should be washed out into a tasteless, colorless fluid of uniformity. Already we have far too much of this insipidity,—masses of people who are cultural half-breeds, neither assimilated Anglo-Saxons nor nationals of another culture. Each national colony in this country seems to retain in its foreign press, its vernacular literature, its schools, its intellectual and patriotic leaders, a central cultural nucleus. From this nucleus the colony extends out by imperceptible gradations to a fringe where national characteristics are all but lost. Our cities are filled with these half-breeds who retain their foreign names but have lost the foreign savor. This does not mean that they have actually been changed into New Englanders or Middle Westerners. It does not mean that they have been really Americanized. It means that, letting slip from them whatever native culture they had, they have substituted for it only the most rudimentary American—the American culture of the cheap newspaper, the "movies," the popular song, the ubiquitous automobile. The unthinking who survey this class call them assimilated, Americanized. The great American public school has done its work. With these people our institutions are safe. We may thrill with dread at the aggressive hyphenate, but this tame flabbiness is accepted as Americanization. The same moulders of opinion whose ideal is to melt the different races into Anglo-Saxon gold hail this poor product as the satisfying result of their alchemy.

Yet a truer cultural sense would have told us that it is not the self-conscious cultural nuclei that sap at our American life, but these fringes. It is not the Jew who sticks proudly to the faith of his fathers and boasts of that venerable culture of his who is dangerous to America, but the Jew who has lost the Jewish fire and become a mere elementary, grasping animal. It is not the Bohemian who supports the Bohemian schools in Chicago whose influence is sinister, but the Bohemian who has made money and has got into ward politics. Just so surely as we tend to disintegrate these nuclei of nationalistic culture do we tend to create hordes of men and women without a spiritual country, cultural outlaws, without taste, without standards but those of the mob. We sentence them to live on the most rudimentary planes of American life. The influences at the centre of the nuclei are centripetal. They make for the intelligence and the social values which mean an enhancement of life. And just because the foreign-born retains this expressiveness is he likely to be a better citizen of the American community. The influences at the fringe, however, are centrifugal, anarchical. They make for detached fragments of peoples. Those who came to find liberty achieve only license. They become the flotsam and jetsam of American life, the downward undertow of our civilization with its leering cheapness and falseness of taste and spiritual outlook, the absence of mind and sincere feeling which we see in our slovenly towns, our vapid moving pictures, our popular novels, and in the vacuous faces of the crowds on the city street. This is the cultural wreckage of our time, and it is from the fringes of the Anglo-Saxon as well as the other stocks that it falls. America has as yet no impelling integrating force. It makes too easily for this detritus of cultures. In our loose, free country, no constraining national purpose, no tenacious folk-tradition and folk-style hold the people to a line.

The war has shown us that not in any magical formula will this purpose be found. No intense nationalism of the European plan can be ours. But do we not begin to see a new and more adventurous ideal? Do we not see how the national colonies in America, deriving power from the deep cultural heart of Europe and yet living here in mutual toleration, freed from the age-long tangles of races, creeds, and dynasties, may work out a federated ideal? America is transplanted Europe, but a Europe that has not been distintegrated and scattered in the transplanting as in some Dispersion. Its colonies live here inextricably mingled, yet not homogeneous. They merge but they do not fuse.

America is a unique sociological fabric, and it bespeaks poverty of imagination not to be thrilled at the incalculable potentialities of so novel a union of men. To seek no other goal than the weary old nationalism,—belligerent, exclusive, inbreeding, the poison of which we are witnessing now in Europe,—is to make patriotism a hollow sham, and to declare that, in spite of our boastings, America must ever be a follower and not a leader of nations.

If we come to find this point of view plausible, we shall have to give up the search for our native "American" culture. With the exception of the South and that New England which, like the Red Indian, seems to be passing into solemn oblivion, there is no distinctively American culture. It is apparently our lot rather to be a federation of cultures. This we have been for half a century, and the war has made it ever more evident that this is what we are destined to remain. This will not mean, however, that there are not expressions of indigenous genius that could not have sprung from any other soil. Music, poetry, philosophy, have been singularly fertile and new. Strangely enough, American genius has flared forth just in those directions which are least understood [*sic*] of the people. If the American note is bigness, action, the objective as contrasted with the reflective life, where is the epic expression of this spirit? Our drama and our fiction, the peculiar fields for the expression of action and objectivity, are somehow exactly the fields of the spirit which remain poor and mediocre. American materialism is in some way inhibited from getting into impressive artistic form its own energy with which it bursts. Nor is it any better in architecture, the least romantic and subjective of all the arts. We are inarticulate of the very values which we profess to idealize. But in the finer forms—music, verse, the essay, philosophy—the American genius puts forth work equal to any of its contemporaries. Just in so far as our American genius has expressed the pioneer spirit, the adventurous, forward-looking drive of a colonial empire, is it representative of that whole America of the many races and peoples, and not of any partial or traditional enthusiasm. And only as that pioneer note is sounded can we really speak of the American culture. As long as we thought of Americanism in terms of the "melting-pot," our American cultural tradition lay in the past. It was something to which the new Americans were to be moulded. In the light of our changing ideal of Americanism, we must perpetrate the paradox that our American cultural tradition lies in the future. It will be what we all together make out of this incomparable opportunity of attacking the future with a new key.

Whatever American nationalism turns out to be, it is certain to become something utterly different from the nationalisms of twentieth-century Europe. This wave of reactionary enthusiasm to play the orthodox nationalistic game which is passing over the country is scarcely vital enough to last. We cannot swagger and thrill to the same national self-feeling. We must give new edges to our pride. We must be content to avoid the unnumbered woes that national patriotism has brought in Europe, and that fiercely heightened pride and self-consciousness. Alluring as this is, we must allow our imaginations to transcend this scarcely veiled belligerency. We can be serenely too proud to fight if our pride embraces the creative forces of civilization which armed contest nullifies. We can be too proud to fight if our code of honor transcends that of the school-boy on the playground surrounded by his jeering mates. Our honor must be positive and creative, and not the mere jealous and negative protectiveness against metaphysical violations of our technical rights. When the doctrine is put forth that in one American flows the mystic blood of all our country's sacred honor, freedom, and prosperity, so that an injury to him is to be the signal for turning our whole nation into that clan-feud of horror and reprisal which would be war, then we find ourselves back among the musty schoolmen of the Middle Ages, and not in any pragmatic and realistic America of the twentieth century.

We should hold our gaze to what America has done, not what mediæval codes of dueling she has failed to observe. We have transplanted European modernity to our soil, without the spirit that inflames it and turns all its energy into mutual destruction. Out of these foreign peoples there has somehow been squeezed the poison. An America, "hyphenated" to bitterness, is somehow non-explosive. For, even if we all hark back in sympathy to a European nation, even if the war has set every one vibrating to some emotional string twanged on the other side of the Atlantic, the effect has been one of almost dramatic harmless-ness.

What we have really been witnessing, however unappreciatively, in this country has been a thrilling and bloodless battle of Kulturs. In that arena of friction which has been the most dramatic—between the hyphenated German-American and the hyphenated English-American—there have emerged rivalries of philosophies which show up deep traditional attitudes, points of view which accurately reflect the gigantic issues of the war. America has mirrored the spiritual issues. The vicarious struggle has been played out peacefully here in the mind. We have seen the stout resistiveness of the old moral interpretation of history on which Victorian England thrived and made itself great in its own esteem. The clean and immensely satisfying vision of the war as a contest be-tween right and wrong; the enthusiastic support of the Allies as the incarnation of virtue-on-a-rampage; the fierce envisaging of their selfish national purposes as the ideals of justice, freedom and democracy—all this has been thrown with intensest force against the German realistic interpretations in terms of the struggle for power and the virility of the integrated State. America has been the intellectual battleground of the nations.

The failure of the melting-pot, far from closing the great American demo-cratic experiment, means that it has only just begun. Whatever American na-tionalism turns out to be, we see already that it will have a color richer and more exciting than our ideal has hitherto encompassed. In a world which has dreamed of internationalism, we find that we have all unawares been building up for the first international nation. The voices which have cried for a tight and jealous nationalism of the European pattern are failing. From that ideal, however valiantly and disinterestedly it has been set for us, time and tendency have moved us further and further away. What we have achieved has been rather a cosmopolitan federation of national colonies, of foreign cultures, from whom the sting of devastating competition has been removed. America is already the world-federation in miniature, the continent where for the first time in history has been achieved that miracle of hope, the peaceful living side by side, with character substantially preserved, of the most heterogeneous peoples under the sun. Nowhere else has such contiguity been anything but the breeder of misery. Here, notwithstanding our tragic failures of adjustment, the outlines are already too clear not to give us a new vision and a new orientation of the American mind in the world.

It is for the American of the younger generation to accept this cosmopolitanism, and carry it along with self-conscious and fruitful purpose. In his colleges, he is already getting, with the study of modern history and politics, the modern literatures, economic geography, the privilege of a cosmopolitan outlook such as the people of no other nation of to-day in Europe can possibly secure. If he is still a colonial, he is no longer the colonial of one partial culture, but of many. He is a colonial of the world. Colonialism has grown into cosmopolitanism, and his motherland is no one nation, but all who have anything life-enhancing to offer to the spirit. That vague sympathy which the France of ten years ago was feeling for the world—a sympathy which was drowned in the terrible reality of war—may be the modern American's, and that in a positive and aggressive sense. If the American is parochial, it is in sheer wantonness or cowardice. His provincialism is the measure of his fear of bogies or the defect of his imagination.

Indeed, it is not uncommon for the eager Anglo-Saxon who goes to a vivid American university to-day to find his true friends not among his own race but among the acclimatized German or Austrian, the acclimatized Jew, the acclimatized Scandinavian or Italian. In them he finds the cosmopolitan note. In these youths, foreign-born or the children of foreign-born parents, he is likely to find many of his old inbred morbid problems washed away. These friends are oblivious to the repressions of that tight little society in which he so provincially grew up. He has a pleasurable sense of liberation from the stale and familiar attitudes of those whose ingrowing culture has scarcely created anything vital for his America of to-day. He breathes a larger air. In his new enthusiasms for continental literature, for unplumbed Russian depths, for French clarity of thought, for Teuton philosophies of power, he feels himself citizen of a larger world. He may be absurdly superficial, his outward-reaching wonder may ignore all the stiller and homelier virtues of his Anglo-Saxon home, but he has at least found the clue to that international mind which will be essential to all men and women of good-will if they are ever to save this Western world of ours from suicide. His new friends have gone through a similar evolution. America has burned most of the baser metal also from them. Meeting now with this common American background, all of them may yet retain that distinctiveness of their native cultures and their national spiritual slants. They are more valuable and interesting to each other for being different, yet that difference could not be creative were it not for this new cosmopolitan outlook which America has given them and which they all equally possess.

A college where such a spirit is possible even to the smallest degree, has within itself already the seeds of this international intellectual world of the future. It suggests that the contribution of America will be an intellectual internationalism which goes far beyond the mere exchange of scientific ideas and discoveries and the cold recording of facts. It will be an intellectual sympathy which is not satisfied until it has got at the heart of the different cultural expressions, and felt as they feel. It may have immense preferences, but it will make understanding and not indignation its end. Such a sympathy will unite and not divide.

Against the thinly disguised panic which calls itself "patriotism" and the thinly disguised militarism which calls itself "preparedness" the cosmopolitan ideal is set. This does not mean that those who hold it are for a policy of drift. They, too, long passionately for an integrated and disciplined America. But they do not want one which is integrated only for domestic economic exploitation of the workers or for predatory economic imperialism among the weaker peoples. They do not want one that is integrated by coercion or militarism, or for the truculent assertion of a mediæval code of honor and of doubtful rights. They believe that the most effective integration will be one which coördinates the diverse elements and turns them consciously toward working out together the place of America in the world-situation. They demand for integration a genuine integrity, a wholeness and soundness of enthusiasm and purpose which can only come when no national colony within our America feels that it is being discriminated against or that its cultural case is being prejudged. This strength of coöperation, this feeling that all who are here may have a hand in the destiny of America, will make for a finer spirit of integration than any narrow "Americanism" or forced chauvinism.

In this effort we may have to accept some form of that dual citizenship which meets with so much articulate horror among us. Dual citizenship we may have to recognize as the rudimentary form of that international citizenship to which, if our words mean anything, we aspire. We have assumed unquestioningly that mere participation in the political life of the United States must cut the new citizen off from all sympathy with his old allegiance. Anything but a bodily transfer of devotion from one sovereignty to another has been viewed as a sort of moral treason against the Republic. We have insisted that the immigrant whom we welcomed escaping from the very exclusive nationalism of his European home shall forthwith adopt a nationalism just as exclusive, just as narrow, and even less legitimate because it is founded on no warm traditions of his own. Yet a nation like France is said to permit a formal and legal dual citizenship even at the present time. Though a citizen of hers may pretend to cast off his allegiance in favor of some other sovereignty, he is still subject to her laws when he returns. Once a citizen, always a citizen, no matter how many new citizenships he may embrace. And such a dual citizenship seems to us sound and right. For it recognizes that, although the Frenchman may accept the formal institutional framework of his new country and indeed become intensely loyal to it, yet his Frenchness he will never lose. What makes up the fabric of his soul will always be of this Frenchness, so that unless he becomes utterly degenerate he will always to some degree dwell still in his native environment.

Indeed, does not the cultivated American who goes to Europe practice a dual citizenship, which, if not formal, is no less real? The American who lives abroad may be the least expatriate of men. If he falls in love with French ways and French thinking and French democracy and seeks to saturate himself with the new spirit, he is guilty of at least a dual spiritual citizenship. He may be still American, yet he feels himself through sympathy also a Frenchman. And he finds that this expansion involves no shameful conflict within him, no surrender of his native attitude. He has rather for the first time caught a glimpse of the cosmopolitan spirit. And after wandering about through many races and civilizations he may return to America to find them all here living vividly and crudely, seeking the same adjustment that he made. He sees the new peoples here with a new vision. They are no longer masses of aliens, waiting to be "assimilated," waiting to be melted down into the indistinguishable dough of Anglo-Saxonism. They are rather threads of living and potent cultures, blindly striving to weave themselves into a novel international nation, the first the world has seen. In an Austria-Hungary or a Prussia the stronger of these cultures would be moving almost instinctively to subjugate the weaker. But in America those wills-to-power are turned in a different direction into learning how to live together.

Along with dual citizenship we shall have to accept, I think, that free and mobile passage of the immigrant between America and his native land again which now arouses so much prejudice among us. We shall have to accept the immigrant's return for the same reason that we consider justified our own flitting about the earth. To stigmatize the alien who works in America for a few years and returns to his own land, only perhaps to seek American fortune again, is to think in narrow nationalistic terms. It is to ignore the cosmopolitan significance of this migration. It is to ignore the fact that the returning immigrant is often a missionary to an inferior civilization.

This migratory habit has been especially common with the unskilled laborers who have been pouring into the United States in the last dozen years from every country in southeastern Europe. Many of them return to spend their earnings in their own country or to serve their country in war. But they return with an entirely new critical outlook, and a sense of the superiority of American organization to the primitive living around them. This continued passage to and fro has already raised the material standard of living in many regions of these backward countries. For these regions are thus endowed with exactly what they need, the capital for the exploitation of their natural resources, and the spirit of enterprise. America is thus educating these laggard peoples from the very bottom of society up, awakening vast masses to a new-born hope for the future. In the migratory Greeks, therefore, we have not the parasitic alien, the doubtful American asset, but a symbol of that cosmopolitan interchange which is coming, in spite of all war and national exclusiveness.

Only America, by reason of the unique liberty of opportunity and traditional isolation for which she seems to stand, can lead in this cosmopolitan enterprise. Only the American—and in this category I include the migratory alien who has lived with us and caught the pioneer spirit and a sense of new social vistas—has the chance to become that citizen of the world. America is coming to be, not a nationality but a trans-nationality, a weaving back and forth, with the other lands, of many threads of all sizes and colors. Any movement which attempts to thwart this weaving, or to dye the fabric any one color, or disentangle the threads of the strands, is false to this cosmopolitan vision. I do not mean that we shall necessarily glut ourselves with the raw product of humanity. It would be folly to absorb the nations faster than we could weave them. We have no duty either to admit or reject. It is purely a question of expediency. What concerns us is the fact that the strands are here. We must have a policy and an ideal for an actual situation. Our question is, What shall we do with our America? How are we likely to get the more creative America—by confining our imaginations to the ideal of the melting pot, or broadening them to some such cosmopolitan conception as I have been vaguely sketching?

The war has shown America to be unable, though isolated geographically and politically from a European world-situation, to remain aloof and irresponsible. She is a wandering star in a sky dominated by two colossal constellations of states. Can she not work out some position of her own, some life of being in, yet not quite of, this seething and embroiled European world? This is her only hope and promise. A trans-nationality of all the nations, it is spiritually impossible for her to pass into the orbit of any one. It will be folly to hurry herself into a premature and sentimental nationalism, or to emulate Europe and play fast and loose with the forces that drag into war. No Americanization will fulfill this vision which does not recognize the uniqueness of this trans-nationalism of ours. The Anglo-Saxon attempt to fuse will only create enmity and distrust. The crusade against "hyphenates" will only inflame the partial patriotism of trans-nationals, and cause them to assert their European traditions in strident and unwholesome ways. But the attempt to weave a wholly novel international nation out of our chaotic America will liberate and harmonize the creative power of all these peoples and give them the new spiritual citizenship, as so many individuals have already been given, of a world.

Is it a wild hope that the undertow of opposition to metaphysics in international relations, opposition to militarism, is less a cowardly provincialism than a groping for this higher cosmopolitan ideal? One can understand the irritated restlessness with which our proud pro-British colonists contemplate a heroic conflict across the seas in which they have no part. It was inevitable that our necessary inaction should evolve in their minds into the bogey of national shame and dishonor. But let us be careful about accepting their sensitiveness as final arbiter. Let us look at our reluctance rather as the first crude beginnings of assertion on the part of certain strands in our nationality that they have a right to a voice in the construction of the American ideal. Let us face realistically the America we have around us. Let us work with the forces that are at work. Let us make something of this trans-national spirit instead of outlawing it. Already we are living this cosmopolitan America. What we need is everywhere a vivid consciousness of the new ideal. Deliberate headway must be made against the survivals of the melting-pot ideal for the promise of American life.

We cannot Americanize America worthily by sentimentalizing and moralizing history. When the best schools are expressly renouncing the questionable duty of teaching patriotism by means of history, it is not the time to force shibboleth upon the immigrant. This form of Americanization has been heard because it appealed to the vestiges of our old sentimentalized and moralized patriotism. This has so far held the field as the expression of the new American's new devotion. The inflections of other voices have been drowned. They must be heard. We must see if the lesson of the war has not been for hundreds of these later Americans a vivid realization of their trans-nationality, a new consciousness of what America meant to them as a citizenship in the world. It is the vague historic idealisms which have provided the fuel for the European flame. Our American ideal can make no progress until we do away with this romantic gilding of the past.

All our idealisms must be those of future social goals in which all can participate, the good life of personality lived in the environment of the Beloved Community. No mere doubtful triumphs of the past, which redound to the glory of only one of our trans-nationalities, can satisfy us. It must be a future America, on which all can unite, which pulls us irresistibly toward it, as we understand each other more warmly.

To make real this striving amid dangers and apathies is work for a younger *intelligentsia* of America. Here is an enterprise of integration into which we can all pour ourselves, of a spiritual welding which should make us, if the final menace ever came, not weaker, but infinitely strong.

~~~~~3

STANLEY COBEN

A Study in Nativism:
The American Red Scare of 1919–1920

As World War One drew to a close, a cosmic optimism prevailed among many who had witnessed America at war. Their hopes lifted by the idealistic fervor of the times, they thought demobilization would be accomplished with the same directness employed to win the war. But demobilization was chaos, for no one expected the war to end as quickly as it did and little advance planning had been undertaken. What Congress might have done in the autumn of 1918, it shunned as socialistic or abandoned in the rage for economy. For his part, President Wilson had no wish to inflame congressional tempers at a time when he looked forward to Senate approval of his League of Nations. An air of conflict developed in 1919 as workers sought to preserve their wartime gains, farmers to maintain wartime government price supports, and Negroes to keep their improved economic status. Into this atmosphere was released an unexpended reserve of fighting spirit, now deprived of the German enemy.

In Bolshevism the aroused American found a new object for his hostility. Stories of Bolshevik cruelty replaced those of German atrocities, and of course it was rumored that Germans had instigated the Russian upheaval. Indeed, Bolshevism was the enemy in Siberia, where in February, 1919, American troops suffered casualties in an effort to please their allies, who wished to support an anti-Bolshevik regime. Conditions were ripe for the famous Red Scare of 1919. Stanley Coben has also written a biography of the incumbent Attorney General, A. Mitchell Palmer.

Reprinted with permission from the *Political Science Quarterly,* March, 1964, vol. 79, no. 1.
I am grateful to Robert D. Cross and Clyde C. Griffen for their critical reading of this article, and to Anthony F. C. Wallace and Abram Kardiner for their helpful comments on my use of anthropological and psychological material.

At a victory loan pageant in the District of Columbia on May 6, 1919, a man refused to rise for the playing of "The Star-Spangled Banner." As soon as the national anthem was completed an enraged sailor fired three shots into the unpatriotic spectator's back. When the man fell, the *Washington Post* reported, "the crowd burst into cheering and handclapping." In February of the same year, a jury in Hammond, Indiana, took two minutes to acquit the assassin of an alien who yelled, "To Hell with the United States." Early in 1920, a clothing store salesman in Waterbury, Connecticut, was sentenced to six months in jail for having remarked to a customer that Lenin was "the brainiest," or "one of the brainiest" of the world's political leaders.[1] Dramatic episodes like these, or the better known Centralia Massacre, Palmer Raids, or May Day riots, were not everyday occurrences, even at the height of the Red Scare. But the fanatical one hundred percent Americanism reflected by the Washington crowd, the Hammond jury, and the Waterbury judge pervaded a large part of our society between early 1919 and mid-1920.

Recently, social scientists have produced illuminating evidence about the causes of eruptions like that of 1919–20. They have attempted to identify experimentally the individuals most responsive to nativistic appeals, to explain their susceptibility, and to propose general theories of nativistic and related movements. These studies suggest a fuller, more coherent picture of nativistic upheavals and their causes than we now possess, and they provide the framework for this attempt to reinterpret the Red Scare.

Psychological experiments indicate that a great many Americans—at least several million—are always ready to participate in a "red scare." These people permanently hold attitudes which characterized the nativists of 1919–20: hostility toward certain minority groups, especially radicals and recent immigrants, fanatical patriotism, and a belief that internal enemies seriously threaten national security.[2]

In one of the most comprehensive of these experiments, psychologists Nancy C. Morse and Floyd H. Allport tested seven hypotheses about the causes of prejudice and found that one, national involvement or patriotism, proved to be "by far the most important factor" associated with prejudice. Other widely held theories about prejudice—status rivalry, frustration-aggres-

[1] *Washington Post*, May 7, 1919; Mark Sullivan, *Our Times, The United States 1900–1925* (New York, 1935), VI, 169; *The Nation*, CX (April 17, 1920), 510–11. The most complete account of the Red Scare is Robert K. Murray, *Red Scare, A Study in National Hysteria* (Minneapolis, 1955). But see the critical review of Murray's book by John M. Blum in *Mississippi Valley Historical Review*, XLII (1955), 145. Blum comments that Murray failed to explain "the susceptibility of the American people and of their elite to the 'national hysteria.' . . . About hysteria, after all, psychology and social psychology in particular have had considerable to say." John Higham places the postwar movement in historical perspective in his superb *Strangers in the Land, Patterns of American Nativism, 1860–1925* (New Brunswick, 1955), especially Chaps. 8 and 9.

[2] On the incidence of prejudice against minorities in the United States, see Gordon W. Allport and Bernard M. Kramer, "Some Roots of Prejudice," *Journal of Psychology*, XXII (1946), 9–39; Morris Janowitz and Dwaine Marvick, "Authoritarianism and Political Behavior," *Public Opinion Quarterly*, XVII (1953), 185–201; Bruno Bettelheim and Morris Janowitz, *Dynamics of Prejudice, A Psychological and Sociological Study of Veterans* (New York, 1950), 16, 26, and *passim*.

sion, and scapegoat hypotheses, for example,—were found to be of only secondary importance.[3] Summarizing the results of this and a number of other psychological experiments, Gordon W. Allport, a pioneer in the scientific study of prejudice, concluded that in a large proportion of cases the prejudiced person is attempting to defend himself against severe inner turmoil by enforcing order in his external life. Any disturbance in the social *status quo* threatens the precarious psychic equilibrium of this type of individual, who, according to Allport, seeks "an island of institutional safety and security. The nation is the island he selects. . . . It has the definiteness he needs."

Allport pointed out that many apprehensive and frustrated people are not especially prejudiced. What is important, he found,

> is the way fear and frustration are handled. The institutionalistic way—especially the nationalistic—seems to be the nub of the matter. What happens is that the prejudiced person defines 'nation' to fit his needs. The nation is first of all a protection (the chief protection) of him as an individual. It is his in-group. He sees no contradiction in ruling out of its beneficent orbit those whom he regards as threatening intruders and enemies (namely, American minorities). What is more, the nation stands for the status quo. It is a conservative agent; within it are all the devices for safe living that he approves. His nationalism is a form of conservatism.[4]

Substantial evidence, then, suggests that millions of Americans are both extraordinarily fearful of social change and prejudiced against those minority groups which they perceive as "threatening intruders." Societal disruption, especially if it can easily be connected with the "intruders," not only will intensify the hostility of highly prejudiced individuals, but also will provoke many others, whose antagonism in more stable times had been mild or incipient, into the extreme group.

A number of anthropologists have come to conclusions about the roots of nativism which complement these psychological studies. Since the late nineteenth century, anthropologists have been studying the religious and nativistic cults of American Indian tribes and of Melanesian and Papuan groups in the South Pacific. Recently, several anthropologists have attempted to synthesize

[3] Nancy C. Morse and F. H. Allport, "The Causation of Anti-Semitism: An Investigation of Seven Hypotheses," *Journal of Psychology,* XXXIV (1952), 197–233. For further experimental evidence indicating that prejudiced individuals are no more anxious, neurotic, or intolerant of ambiguity than those with more "liberal" attitudes, Anthony Davids, "Some Personality and Intellectual Correlates to Intolerance of Ambiguity," *Journal of Abnormal and Social Psychology,* LI (1955), 415–20; Ross Stagner and Clyde S. Congdon, "Another Failure to Demonstrate Displacement of Aggression," *Journal of Abnormal and Social Psychology,* LI (1955), 695–96; Dean Peabody, "Attitude Content and Agreement Set in Scales of Authoritarianism, Dogmatism, Anti-Semitism and Economic Conservatism," *Journal of Abnormal and Social Psychology,* LXIII (1961), 1–11.

[4] Gordon W. Allport, *The Nature of Prejudice* (Cambridge, 1955), 406; *see* Boyd C. Shafer, *Nationalism, Myth and Reality* (New York, 1955), 181.

their findings and have shown striking parallels in the cultural conditions out of which these movements arose.[5] In every case, severe societal disruption preceded the outbreak of widespread nativistic cult behavior. According to Anthony F. C. Wallace, who has gone farthest toward constructing a general theory of cult formation, when the disruption has proceeded so far that many members of a society find it difficult or impossible to fulfill their physical and psychological needs, or to relieve severe anxiety through the ordinary culturally approved methods, the society will be susceptible to what Wallace has termed a "revitalization movement." This is a convulsive attempt to change or revivify important cultural beliefs and values, and frequently to eliminate alien influences. Such movements promise and often provide participants with better means of dealing with their changed circumstances, thus reducing their very high level of internal stress.[6]

American Indian tribes, for example, experienced a series of such convulsions as the tide of white settlers rolled west. The Indians were pushed onto reservations and provided with Indian agents, missionaries, and physicians, who took over many of the functions hitherto assumed by chiefs and medicine men. Indian craftsmen (and craftswomen) were replaced by dealers in the white man's implements. Most hunters and warriors also lost their vocations and consequently their self-respect. What an anthropologist wrote of one tribe was

[5] See, especially, the works of Anthony F. C. Wallace: "Revitalization Movements," *American Anthropologist,* LVIII (1956), 264–81; "Handsome Lake and the Great Revival in the West," *American Quarterly,* IV (1952), 149–65; "Stress and Rapid Personality Change," *International Record of Medicine and General Practice Clinics,* CLXIX (1956), 761–73; "New Religions Among the Delaware Indians, 1600–1900," *Southwest Journal of Anthropology,* XII (1956), 1–21. Also, Michael M. Ames, "Reaction to Stress: A Comparative Study of Nativism," *Davidson Journal of Anthropology,* III (1957), 16–30; C. S. Belshaw, "The Significance of Modern Cults in Melanesian Development," *Australian Outlook,* IV (1950), 116–25; Raymond Firth, "The Theory of 'Cargo' Cults: A Note on Tikopia," *Man,* LV (1955), 130–32; Lawrence Krader, "A Nativistic Movement in Western Siberia," *American Anthropologist,* LVIII (1956), 282–92; Ralph Linton, "Nativistic Movements," *American Anthropologist,* XLV (1943), 220–43; Margaret Mead, *New Lives for Old* (New York, 1956); Peter Worsley, *The Trumpet Shall Sound* (London, 1957). Several sociologists and psychologists have come to conclusions about the causes of these movements that are similar in important respects to Wallace's, although less comprehensive. See Leon Festinger, *A Theory of Cognitive Dissonance* (New York, 1957); Hadley Cantril, *The Psychology of Social Movements* (New York, 1941), especially pp. 3–4, Chaps. 5, 8, and 9; Hans H. Toch, "Crisis Situations and Ideological Revaluation," *Public Opinion Quarterly,* XVIX (1955), 53–67.

[6] Wallace, "Revitalization Movements." For a recent verification of Wallace's theories see Thomas Rhys Williams, "The Form of a North Borneo Nativistic Behavior," *American Anthropologist,* LXV (1963), 543–51. On the psychological results of socially caused stress, Wallace, "Stress and Rapid Personality Change"; William Caudill, *Effects of Social and Cultural Systems in Reactions to Stress,* Social Science Research Council Pamphlet No. 14 (New York, 1958); Caudill, "Cultural Perspectives on Stress," Army Medical Service Graduate School, *Symposium on Stress* (Washington, D.C., 1953); Hans Selye, *The Stress of Life* (New York, 1956); Roland Fischer and Neil Agnew, "A Hierarchy of Stressors," *Journal of Mental Science,* CI (1955), 383–86; Daniel H. Funkenstein, Stanley H. King, and Margaret E. Drolette, *Mastery of Stress* (Cambridge, 1957); M. Basowitz *et al., Anxiety and Stress: An Interdisciplinary Study of a Life Situation* (New York, 1955).

true of many others: "From cultural maturity as Pawnees they were reduced to cultural infancy as civilized men." [7]

One of the last major religious upheavals among the Indians was the Ghost Dance cult which spread from Nevada through Oregon and northern California in the eighteen-seventies, and a similar movement along the Rocky Mountain and western plains Indians about 1890. Although cult beliefs varied somewhat from tribe to tribe, converts generally were persuaded that if they followed certain prescribed rituals, including the dance, they would soon return to their old ways of living. Even their dead relatives would be restored to life. Most Indians were too conscious of their military weakness to challenge their white masters directly. Ghost Dancers among the Dakota Sioux, however, influenced by the militant proselyter Sitting Bull, became convinced that true believers could not be harmed by the white man's bullets and that Sioux warriors would drive the intruders from Indian lands. Their dreams were rudely smashed at the massacre of Wounded Knee Creek in December 1890.[8]

The Boxer movement in China, 1898 to 1900, resembled in many respects the Indian Ghost Dance cults; however, the Boxers, more numerous and perhaps less demoralized than the Indians, aimed more directly at removing foreign influences from their land. The movement erupted first in Shantung province where foreigners, especially Japanese, British, and Germans, were most aggressive. A flood of the Yellow River had recently deprived about a million people in the province of food and shelter. Banditry was rampant, organized government ineffective. The Boxer movement, based on the belief that these tragic conditions were due almost entirely to the "foreign devils" and their agents, determined to drive the enemy out of China. Boxers went into action carrying charms and chanting incantations supposed to make them invulnerable to the foreigners' bullets. The first object of the Boxers' nativistic fury were Chinese who had converted to Christianity, the intruders' religion. The patriots then attacked railroad and telegraph lines, leading symbols of foreign influence. Finally, the Boxers turned against the foreigners themselves, slaughtering many. Not until after the Boxers carried on a two-month siege of the foreign community in Peking did American, European, and Japanese armies crush the movement.[9]

[7] Alexander Lesser, *The Pawnee Ghost Dance Hand Game. A Study of Cultural Change* (New York, 1933), 44.

[8] Cora DuBois, *The 1870 Ghost Dance,* Anthropological Records, III (Berkeley, 1946); Leslie Spier, *The Ghost Dance of 1870 Among the Klamath of Oregon,* University of Washington Publications in Anthropology, II (Seattle, 1927); Lesser, *Ghost Dance;* A. L. Kroeber, *Handbook of the Indians of California,* Bureau of American Ethnology Bulletin 78 (Washington, D.C., 1925). Anthropologists recently have argued about the origins of the Ghost Dance cults. Both sides agree, however, that whatever their origins, the cults took the form they did because of intolerable cultural conditions caused largely by white encroachments. David F. Aberle, "The Prophet Dance and Reactions to White Contact," *Southwest Journal of Anthropology,* XV (1959), 74–83; Leslie Spier, Wayne Suttles, and Melville Herskovits, "Comment on Aberle's Thesis of Deprivation," *Southwest Journal of Anthropology,* XV (1959), 84–88.

[9] The best account of the Boxer movement is Chester C. Tan, *The Boxer Catastrophe* (New York, 1955). Also, George N. Steiger, *China and the Occident,*

Other revitalization attempts proved more successful than the Boxers or Ghost Dancers. The Gaiwiio movement, for example, helped the Iroquois Indians of western New York State to retain their identity as a culture while adjusting successfully to an encroaching white civilization during the first decade of the nineteenth century. The movement implanted a new moral code among the Indians, enjoining sobriety and family stability and encouraging acceptance of Western technology, while revivifying cohesive Indian traditions.[10]

Dominant as well as conquered peoples, Ralph Linton has pointed out, undergo nativistic movements. Dominant groups, he observed, are sometimes threatened "not only by foreign invasion or domestic revolt but also by the invidious process of assimilation which might, in the long run, destroy their distinctive powers and privileges." Under such circumstances, Linton concluded, "the frustrations which motivate nativistic movements in inferior or dominated groups" are "replaced by anxieties which produce very much the same [nativistic] result" in dominant groups.[11]

Communist "brainwashers" have consciously attempted to achieve results comparable to those obtained by prophets of movements like the Ghost Dance cult and the Boxers. They create intolerable stress within individuals, not through rapid societal change, but by intentional physical debilitation and continual accusations, cross-examinations, and use of other anxiety-provoking techniques. Then they offer their prisoners an escape from the induced psychological torment: conversion to the new gospel.[12]

The similarity in the mental processes involved in "brainwashing" and in the formation of nativistic movements becomes even clearer upon examination of the Chinese Communist attempt to establish their doctrines in mainland China. Again, the Communists intentionally have created conditions like those out of which nativistic cults have arisen more spontaneously in other societies. In addition to the stress which ordinarily would accompany rapid industrialization of an economically backward society, the Chinese leaders have provoked additional anxiety through the systematic use of group confessions and denunciations and have intentionally disrupted family life. Hostility toward the American enemy has been purposely aroused and used to unify the masses, as well as to justify the repression of millions of alleged internal enemies. The whole population has been continually urged to repent their sins and to adopt wholeheartedly the Communist gospel, which has a strong nativistic component.

---

the Origin and Development of the Boxer Movement (New Haven, 1927); Peter Fleming, The Siege at Peking (New York, 1959).

[10] Wallace, "Handsome Lake." Wallace compared the Gaiwiio with a Chinese attempt to accommodate their society to Western civilization in "Stress and Rapid Personality Change." For a successful movement in the South Pacific see Mead, New Lives for Old.

[11] Linton, 237. Also, Carroll L. Riley and John Hobgood, "A Recent Nativistic Movement Among the Southern Tepehuan Indians," Southwest Journal of Anthropology, XV (1959), 355–60.

[12] Robert J. Lifton, "Thought Reform in Western Civilians in Chinese Communist Prisons," Psychiatry, XIX (1956), 173–95; Edgar H. Schein, "The Chinese Indoctrination Program for Prisoners of War, A Study of Attempted Brainwashing," Psychiatry, XIX (1956), 149–72.

As a psychologist has remarked, to a large extent the Chinese Communists provide both the disease and the cure.[13]

The ferocious outbreak of nativism in the United States after World War I was not consciously planned or provoked by any individual or group, although some Americans took advantage of the move nent once it started. Rather, the Red Scare, like the Gaiwiio and Boxer r ovements described above, was brought on largely by a number of severe social and economic dislocations which threatened the national equilibrium. The full extent and the shocking effects of these disturbances of 1919 have not yet been adequately described. Runaway prices, a brief but sharp stock market crash and business depression, revolutions throughout Europe, widespread fear of domestic revolt, bomb explosions, and an outpouring of radical literature were distressing enough. These sudden difficulties, moreover, served to exaggerate the disruptive effects already produced by the social and intellectual ravages of the World War and the preceding reform era, and by the arrival, before the war, of millions of new immigrants. This added stress intensified the hostility of Americans strongly antagonistic to minority groups, and brought new converts to blatant nativism from among those who ordinarily were not overtly hostile toward radicals or recent immigrants.

Citizens who joined the crusade for one hundred percent Americanism sought, primarily, a unifying force which would halt the apparent disintegration of their culture. The movement, they felt, would eliminate those foreign influences which the one hundred percenters believed were the major cause of their anxiety.

Many of the postwar sources of stress were also present during World War I, and the Red Scare, as John Higham has observed, was partly an exaggeration of wartime passions.[14] In 1917–18 German-Americans served as the object of almost all our nativistic fervor; they were the threatening intruders who refused to become good citizens. "They used America," a patriotic author declared in 1918 of two million German-Americans, "they never loved her. They clung to their old language, their old customs, and cared nothing for ours. . . . As a class they were clannish beyond all other races coming here."[15] Fear of subversion by German agents was almost as extravagant in 1917–18 as anxiety about "reds" in the postwar period. Attorney General Thomas Watt Gregory reported to a friend in May 1918 that "we not infrequently receive as many as fifteen hundred letters in a single day suggesting disloyalty and the making of investigations."[16]

Opposition to the war by radical groups helped smooth the transition among American nativists from hatred of everything German to fear of radical revolution. The two groups of enemies were associated also for other reasons.

[13] Edgar H. Schein, with Inge Schneier and Curtis H. Bark, *Coercive Persuasion* (New York, 1961); William Sargent, *Battle for the Mind* (New York, 1957), 150–65; Robert J. Lifton, *Thought Reform and the Psychology of Totalism* (New York, 1961); R. L. Walker, *China Under Communism* (London, 1946).

[14] Higham, 222.

[15] Emerson Hough, *The Web* (Chicago, 1919), 23. Hough was a rabid one hundred percenter during the Red Scare also.

[16] T. W. Gregory to R. E. Vinson, May 13, 1918, Papers of Thomas Watt Gregory (Library of Congress, Washington, D.C.).

High government officials declared after the war that German leaders planned and subsidized the Bolshevik Revolution.[17] When bombs blasted homes and public buildings in nine cities in June 1919, the director of the Justice Department's Bureau of Investigation asserted that the bombers were "connected with Russian Bolshevism, aided by Hun money." [18] In November 1919, a year after the armistice, a popular magazine warned of "the Russo-German movement that is now trying to dominate America. . . ." [19]

Even the wartime hostility toward German-Americans, however, is more understandable when seen in the light of recent anthropological and psychological studies. World War I disturbed Americans not only because of the real threat posed by enemy armies and a foreign ideology. For many citizens it had the further effect of shattering an already weakened intellectual tradition. When the European governments decided to fight, they provided shocking evidence that man was not, as most educated members of Western society had believed, a rational creature progressing steadily, if slowly, toward control of his environment. When the great powers declared war in 1914, many Americans as well as many Europeans were stunned. The *New York Times* proclaimed a common theme—European civilization had collapsed: The supposedly advanced nations, declared the *Times,* "have reverted to the condition of savage tribes roaming the forests and falling upon each other in a fury of blood and carnage to achieve the ambitious designs of chieftains clad in skins and drunk with mead." [20] Franz Alexander, director for twenty-five years of the Chicago Institute of Psychoanalysis, recently recalled his response to the outbreak of the World War:

> The first impact of this news is [*sic*] unforgettable. It was the sudden intuitive realization that a chapter of history had ended. . . . Since then, I have discussed this matter with some of my contemporaries and heard about it a great deal in my early postwar psychoanalytic treatments of patients. To my amazement, the others who went through the same events had quite a similar reaction. . . . It was

[17] Subcommittee of Senate Committee on the Judiciary, *Hearings, Brewing and Liquor Interests and German and Bolshevik Propaganda,* 66th Congress, 1st Session, 1919, 2669 ff.; *The New York Times,* July 7, August 11 and 29, September 15–21, 1918.

[18] *Washington Post,* July 3, 1919. Bureau Director William J. Flynn produced no evidence to back this assertion. Later he claimed to have conclusive proof that the bombers were Italian anarchists. Flynn to Attorney General Harry Daugherty, April 4, 1922, Department of Justice Records, File 202600, Sect. 5 (National Archives, Washington, D.C.).

[19] *Saturday Evening Post,* CXCII (November 1, 1919), 28. For similar assertions in other publications, Meno Lovenstein, *American Opinion of Soviet Russia* (Washington, D.C., 1941), Chap. 1, *passim.*

[20] Quoted in William E. Leuchtenburg, *The Perils of Prosperity, 1914–32* (Chicago, 1958), 13. There is no comprehensive study of the effects of the war on the American mind. For brief treatments, Henry F. May, *The End of American Innocence* (New York, 1959), 361–67; Merle Curti, *The Growth of American Thought* (New York, 1951), 687–705; Ralph Henry Gabriel, *The Course of American Democratic Thought* (New York, 1956), 387, 404; André Siegfried, *America Comes of Age* (New York, 1927), 3; Walter Lord, *The Good Years, From 1900 to the First World War* (New York, 1960), 339–41.

> an immediate vivid and prophetic realization that something irrevocable of immense importance had happened in history.[21]

Americans were jolted by new blows to their equilibrium after entering the war. Four million men were drafted away from familiar surroundings and some of them experienced the terrible carnage of trench warfare. Great numbers of women left home to work in war industries or to replace men in other jobs. Negroes flocked to Northern industrial areas by the hundreds of thousands, and their first mass migration from the South created violent racial antagonism in Northern cities.

During the war, also, Americans sanctioned a degree of government control over the economy which deviated sharply from traditional economic individualism. Again, fears aroused before the war were aggravated, for the reform legislation of the Progressive era had tended to increase government intervention, and many citizens were further perturbed by demands that the federal government enforce even higher standards of economic and social morality. By 1919, therefore, some prewar progressives as well as conservatives feared the gradual disappearance of highly valued individual opportunity and responsibility. Their fears were fed by strong postwar calls for continued large-scale government controls—extension of federal operation of railroads and of the Food Administration, for example.

The prime threat to these long-held individualistic values, however, and the most powerful immediate stimulus to the revitalistic response, came from Russia. There the Bolshevik conquerors proclaimed their intention of exporting Marxist ideology. If millions of Americans were disturbed in 1919 by the specter of communism, the underlying reason was not fear of foreign invasion —Russia, after all, was still a backward nation recently badly defeated by German armies. The real threat was the potential spread of communist ideas. These, the one hundred percenters realized with horror, possessed a genuine appeal for reformers and for the economically underprivileged, and if accepted they would complete the transformation of America.

A clear picture of the Bolshevik tyranny was not yet available; therefore, as after the French Revolution, those who feared the newly successful ideology turned to fight the revolutionary ideals. So the *Saturday Evening Post* declared editorially in November 1919 that "History will see our present state of mind as one with that preceding the burning of witches, the children's crusade, the great tulip craze and other examples of softening of the world brain." The *Post* referred not to the Red Scare or the impending Palmer Raids, but to the spread of communist ideology. Its editorial concluded: "The need of the country is not more idealism, but more pragmatism; not communism, but common sense." [22] One of the most powerful patriotic groups, the National Security League, called upon members early in 1919 to "teach 'Americanism.' This means the fighting of Bolshevism . . . by the creation of well defined National Ideals." Members "must preach Americanism and instil the

---

[21] Franz Alexander, *The Western Mind in Transition* (New York, 1960), 73–74. Also see William Barrett, *Irrational Man* (Garden City, N.Y., 1961), 32–33.
[22] *Saturday Evening Post*, CXCII (November 1, 1919), 28.

idealism of America's Wars, and that American spirit of service which believes in giving as well as getting." [23] New York attorney, author, and educator Henry Waters Taft warned a Carnegie Hall audience late in 1919 that Americans must battle "a propaganda which is tending to undermine our most cherished social and political institutions and is having the effect of producing widespread unrest among the poor and the ignorant, especially those of foreign birth." [24]

When the war ended Americans also confronted the disturbing possibility, pointed up in 1919 by the struggle over the League of Nations, that Europe's struggles would continue to be their own. These factors combined to make the First World War a traumatic experience for millions of citizens. As Senator James Reed of Missouri observed in August 1919, "This country is still suffering from shell shock. Hardly anyone is in a normal state of mind. . . . A great storm has swept over the intellectual world and its ravages and disturbances still exist." [25]

The wartime "shell shock" left many Americans extraordinarily susceptible to psychological stress caused by postwar social and economic turbulence. Most important for the course of the Red Scare, many of these disturbances had their greatest effect on individuals already antagonistic toward minorities. First of all, there was some real evidence of danger to the nation in 1919, and the nation provided the chief emotional support for many Americans who responded easily to charges of an alien radical menace. Violence flared throughout Europe after the war and revolt lifted radicals to power in several Eastern and Central European nations. Combined with the earlier Bolshevik triumph in Russia these revolutions made Americans look more anxiously at radicals here. Domestic radicals encouraged these fears; they became unduly optimistic about their own chances of success and boasted openly of their coming triumph. Scores of new foreign language anarchist and communist journals, most of them written by and for Southern and Eastern European immigrants, commenced publication, and the established radical press became more exuberant. These periodicals never tired of assuring readers in 1919 that "the United States seems to be on the verge of a revolutionary crisis." [26] American newspapers and magazines reprinted selections from radical speeches, pamphlets, and periodicals so their readers could see what dangerous ideas were abroad in the land.[27] Several mysterious bomb explosions and bombing attempts, reported

[23] National Security League, *Future Work* (New York, 1919), 6.

[24] Henry Waters Taft, *Aspects of Bolshevism and Americanism, Address before the League for Political Education at Carnegie Hall, New York, December 6, 1919* (New York, 1919), 21.

[25] U.S., *Congressional Record,* 66th Congress, 1st Session, August 15, 1919, 3892.

[26] Robert E. Park, *The Immigrant Press and Its Control* (New York, 1922), 214, 230–38, 241–45; R. E. Park and Herbert A. Miller, *Old World Traits Transplanted* (New York, 1921), 99–101; Daniel Bell, "The Background and Development of Marxian Socialism in the United States," in Donald Drew Egbert and Stow Persons, *Socialism in American Life* (Princeton, 1952), I, 334; Lovenstein, 7–50; Leuchtenburg, 67–68; Murray, 33–36.

[27] The Justice Department distributed pamphlets containing such material to all American newspapers and magazines; *Red Radicalism, as Described by Its Own Leaders* (Washington, D.C., 1920); National Popular Government League, *To the*

in bold front page headlines in newspapers across the country, frightened the public in 1919. To many citizens these seemed part of an organized campaign of terror carried on by alien radicals intending to bring down the federal government. The great strikes of 1919 and early 1920 aroused similar fears.[28]

Actually American radical organizations in 1919 were disorganized and poverty-stricken. The Communists were inept, almost without contact with American workers and not yet dominated or subsidized by Moscow. The IWW was shorn of its effective leaders, distrusted by labor, and generally declining in influence and power. Violent anarchists were isolated in a handful of tiny, unconnected local organizations.[29] One or two of these anarchist groups probably carried out the "bomb conspiracy" of 1919; but the extent of the "conspiracy" can be judged from the fact that the bombs killed a total of two men during the year, a night watchman and one of the bomb throwers, and seriously wounded one person, a maid in the home of a Georgia senator.[30]

Nevertheless, prophesies of national disaster abounded in 1919, even among high government officials. Secretary of State Robert Lansing confided to his diary that we were in real peril of social revolution. Attorney General A. Mitchell Palmer advised the House Appropriations Committee that "on a certain day, which we have been advised of," radicals would attempt "to rise up and destroy the Government at one fell swoop." Senator Charles Thomas of Colorado warned that "the country is on the verge of a volcanic upheaval." And Senator Miles Poindexter of Washington declared, "There is real danger that the government will fall." [31] A West Virginia wholesaler, with offices throughout the state, informed the Justice Department in October 1919 that "there is hardly a respectable citizen of my acquaintance who does not believe that we are on the verge of armed conflict in this country." William G. Mc-Adoo was told by a trusted friend that "Chicago, which has always been a

---

American People, Report Upon the Illegal Practices of the Department of Justice (Washington, D.C., 1920), 64–66. The staunchly anti-radical *New York Times* published translations from a large sample of foreign language radical newspapers on June 8, 1919.

[28] Murray, Chaps. 5, 7–10. Asked by a congressional committee a few weeks after the spate of bombings in June 1919 whether there was real evidence of an organized effort to destroy the federal government, Assistant Attorney General Francis P. Garvan replied, "Certainly." Garvan was in charge of federal prosecution of radicals. *Washington Post,* June 27, 1919.

[29] Theodore Draper, *The Roots of American Communism* (New York, 1957), 198–200, 302, 312–14; David J. Saposs, *Left Wing Unionism, A Study in Policies and Tactics* (New York, 1926), 49–50, 152–57; Selig Perlman and Philip Taft (eds.), *Labor Movements* in John R. Commons (ed.), *History of Labour in the United States 1896–1932,* IV (New York, 1935), 621, 431–32; Jerome Davis, *The Russian Immigrant* (New York, 1922), 114–18; Kate Holladay Claghorn, *The Immigrant's Day in Court* (New York, 1923), 363–73; John S. Gambs, *The Decline of the I.W.W.* (New York, 1932), 133; Murray, 107–10.

[30] *The New York Times,* May 1, June 3, 4, 1919.

[31] "The Spread of Bolshevism in the United States," private memorandum, dated July 26, 1919, Papers of Robert Lansing (Library of Congress, Washington, D.C.); "One Point of View of the Murders at Centralia, Washington," private memorandum, dated November 13, 1919, Lansing Papers; U.S., *Congressional Record,* 66th Congress, 1st Session, October 14, 1919, 6869; *Washington Post,* February 16, 1919; New York *World,* June 19, 1919.

very liberal minded place, seems to me to have gone mad on the question of the 'Reds.' " Delegates to the Farmers National Congress in November 1919 pledged that farmers would assist the government in meeting the threat of revolution.[32]

The slight evidence of danger from radical organizations aroused such wild fear only because Americans had already encountered other threats to cultural stability. However, the dislocations caused by the war and the menace of communism alone would not have produced such a vehement nativistic response. Other postwar challenges to the social and economic order made the crucial difference.

Of considerable importance was the skyrocketing cost of living. Retail prices more than doubled between 1915 and 1920, and the price rise began gathering momentum in the spring of 1919.[33] During the summer of 1919 the dominant political issue in America was not the League of Nations; not even the "red menace" or the threat of a series of major strikes disturbed the public as much as did the climbing cost of living. The *Washington Post* early in August 1919 called rising prices, "the burning domestic issue. . . ." Democratic National Chairman Homer Cummings, after a trip around the country, told President Woodrow Wilson that more Americans were worried about prices than about any other public issue and that they demanded government action. When Wilson decided to address Congress on the question the Philadelphia *Public Ledger* observed that the administration had "come rather tardily to a realization of what is uppermost in the minds of the American people." [34]

Then the wave of postwar strikes—there were 3,600 of them in 1919 involving over 4,000,000 workers [35]—reached a climax in the fall of 1919. A national steel strike began in September and nationwide coal and rail walkouts were scheduled for November 1. Unions gained in membership and power during the war, and in 1919 labor leaders were under strong pressure to help workers catch up to or go ahead of mounting living costs. Nevertheless, influential government officials attributed the walkout to radical activities. Early in 1919, Secretary of Labor William B. Wilson declared in a public speech that recent major strikes in Seattle, Butte, Montana, and Lawrence, Massachusetts, had been instituted by the Bolsheviks and the IWW for the sole purpose of bringing

[32] Henry Barham to Palmer, October 27, 1919, Justice Department Records, File 202600; unidentified correspondent to McAdoo, February 10, 1920, McAdoo Papers (Library of Congress, Washington, D.C.); A. P. Sanders to Palmer, November 12, 1919, Justice Department Records, File 202600; *The New York Times,* October 31, 1919.

[33] U.S. Bureau of the Census, *Historical Statistics of the United States, Colonial Times to 1952, A Statistical Abstract Supplement* (Washington, D.C., 1960), 91, 92, 126; U.S. Department of Labor, Bureau of Labor Statistics, Bulletin Number 300, *Retail Prices 1913 to December, 1920* (Washington, D.C., 1922), 4; Daniel J. Ahearn, Jr., *The Wages of Farm and Factory Laborers 1914–1944* (New York, 1945), 227.

[34] *Washington Post,* August 1, 4, 1919; *The New York Times,* July 30, August 1, 1919; Philadelphia *Public Ledger,* August 5, 1919.

[35] Florence Peterson, *Strikes in the United States, 1880–1936,* U.S. Department of Labor Bulletin Number 651 (Washington, D.C., 1938), 21. More employees engaged in strikes in 1919 than the total over the ten-year period 1923–32.

about a nationwide revolution in the United States.[36] During the steel strike of early fall, 1919, a Senate investigating committee reported that "behind this strike there is massed a considerable element of IWW's, anarchists, revolutionists, and Russian soviets. . . ." [37] In April 1920 the head of the Justice Department's General Intelligence Division, J. Edgar Hoover, declared in a public hearing that at least fifty per cent of the influence behind the recent series of strikes was traceable directly to communist agents.[38]

Furthermore, the nation suffered a sharp economic depression in late 1918 and early 1919, caused largely by sudden cancellations of war orders. Returning servicemen found it difficult to obtain jobs during this period, which coincided with the beginning of the Red Scare. The former soldiers had been uprooted from their homes and told that they were engaged in a patriotic crusade. Now they came back to find "reds" criticizing their country and threatening the government with violence, Negroes holding good jobs in the big cities, prices terribly high, and workers who had not served in the armed forces striking for higher wages.[39] A delegate won prolonged applause from the 1919 American Legion Convention when he denounced radical aliens, exclaiming, "Now that the war is over and they are in lucrative positions while our boys haven't a job, we've got to send those scamps to hell." The major part of the mobs which invaded meeting halls of immigrant organizations and broke up radical parades, especially during the first half of 1919, was comprised of men in uniform.[40]

A variety of other circumstances combined to add even more force to the postwar nativistic movement. Long before the new immigrants were seen as potential revolutionists they became the objects of widespread hostility. The peak of immigration from Southern and Eastern Europe occurred in the fifteen years before the war; during that period almost ten million immigrants from those areas entered the country. Before the anxious eyes of members of all classes of Americans, the newcomers crowded the cities and began to disturb the economic and social order.[41] Even without other postwar disturbances a nativistic movement of some strength could have been predicted when the wartime solidarity against the German enemy began to wear off in 1919.

In addition, not only were the European revolutions most successful in Eastern and to a lesser extent in Southern Europe, but aliens from these areas

---

[36] *Washington Post,* February 21, 1919. As late as April 1920, Secretary Wilson agreed with Palmer during a Cabinet meeting that the nationwide rail walkout had been caused by Communists and the IWW. Entry in Josephus Daniels' Diary for April 14, 1920, Papers of Josephus Daniels (Library of Congress, Washington, D.C.).

[37] U.S. Senate, Committee on Education and Labor, *Report, Investigation of Strike in Steel Industry,* 66th Congress, 1st Session, 1919, 14.

[38] *The New York Times,* April 25, 1920, 23.

[39] George Soule, *Prosperity Decade, From War to Depression: 1917–1929* (New York, 1947), 81–84; Murray, 125, 182–83.

[40] *Proceedings and Committees, Caucus of the American Legion* (St. Louis, 1919), 117; *The New York Times,* May 2, 1919; *Washington Post,* May 2, 1919. Ex-servicemen also played major roles in the great Negro-white race riots of mid-1919. *Washington Post,* July 20–23, 28–31.

[41] *Historical Statistics of the United States,* 56. On the causes of American hostility to recent immigrants see John Higham's probing and provocative essay "Another Look at Nativism," *Catholic Historical Review,* XLIV (1958), 147–58. Higham stresses status conflicts, but does not explain why some competitors on the crowded social ladder were much more antagonistic to the new immigrants than were others.

predominated in American radical organizations. At least ninety per cent of the members of the two American Communist parties formed in 1919 were born in Eastern Europe. The anarchist groups whose literature and bombs captured the imagination of the American public in 1919 were composed almost entirely of Italian, Spanish, and Slavic aliens. Justice Department announcements and statements by politicians and the press stressed the predominance of recent immigrants in radical organizations.[42] Smoldering prejudice against new immigrants and identification of these immigrants with European as well as American radical movements, combined with other sources of postwar stress to create one of the most frenzied and one of the most widespread nativistic movements in the nation's history.

The result, akin to the movements incited by the Chinese Boxers or the Indian Ghost dancers, was called Americanism or one hundred per cent Americanism.[43] Its objective was to end the apparent erosion of American values and the disintegration of American culture. By reaffirming those beliefs, customs, symbols, and traditions felt to be the foundation of our way of life, by enforcing conformity among the population, and by purging the nation of dangerous foreigners, the one hundred percenters expected to heal societal divisions and to tighten defenses against cultural change.

Panegyrics celebrating our history and institutions were delivered regularly in almost every American school, church, and public hall in 1919 and 1920. Many of these fervent addresses went far beyond the usual patriotic declarations. Audiences were usually urged to join a crusade to protect our hallowed institutions. Typical of the more moderate statements was Columbia University President Nicholas Murray Butler's insistence in April 1919 that "America will be saved, not by those who have only contempt and despite for her founders and her history, but by those who look with respect and reverence upon the great series of happenings extending from the voyage of the Mayflower. . . ." [44]

What one historian has called "a riot of biographies of American heroes—statesmen, cowboys, and pioneers" [45] appeared in this brief period. Immigrants as well as citizens produced many autobiographical testimonials to the superiority of American institutions. These patriotic tendencies in our literature were as short-lived as the Red Scare, and have been concealed by "debunking" biographies of folk heroes and skeptical autobiographies so common later in the nineteen-twenties. An unusual number of motion pictures about our early history were turned out immediately after the war and the reconstruction of colonial Williamsburg and of Longfellow's Wayside Inn was begun. With great

[42] Draper, 189–90; *Annual Report of the Attorney General for 1920* (Washington, D.C., 1920), 177; Higham, *Strangers in the Land,* 226–27.

[43] The word "Americanism" was used by the nativists of the eighteen-forties and eighteen-fifties. During World War I, the stronger phrase "100 per cent Americanism" was invented to suit the belligerent drive for universal conformity.

[44] Horace M. Kallen, *Culture and Democracy in the United States* (New York, 1924), Chap. 3, 154–55; Edward G. Hartman, *The Movement to Americanize the Immigrant* (New York, 1948), Chap. 9; Nicholas Murray Butler, *Is America Worth Saving? An Address Delivered Before the Commercial Club of Cincinnati, Ohio, April 19, 1919* (New York, 1919), 20.

[45] Emerson Hunsberger Loucks, *The Ku Klux Klan in Pennsylvania* (New York, 1936), 163.

fanfare, Secretary of State Lansing placed the original documents of the Constitution and the Declaration of Independence on display in January 1920, and the State Department distributed movies of this ceremony to almost every town and city in the United States.[46] Organizations like the National Security League, the Association for Constitutional Government, the Sons and the Daughters of the American Revolution, the Colonial Dames of America, with the cooperation of the American Bar Association and many state Bar Associations, organized Constitution Day celebrations and distributed huge numbers of pamphlets on the subject throughout the country.

The American flag became a sacred symbol. Legionaires demanded that citizens "Run the Reds out from the land whose flag they sully." [47] Men suspected of radical leanings were forced to kiss the stars and stripes. A Brooklyn truck driver decided in June 1919 that it was unpatriotic to obey a New York City law obliging him to fly a red cloth on lumber which projected from his vehicle. Instead he used as a danger signal a small American flag. A policeman, infuriated at the sight of the stars and stripes flying from a lumber pile, arrested the driver on a charge of disorderly conduct. Despite the Brooklyn patriot's insistence that he meant no offense to the flag, he was reprimanded and fined by the court.[48]

Recent immigrants, especially, were called upon to show evidence of real conversion. Great pressure was brought to bear upon the foreign-born to learn English and to forget their native tongues. As Senator William S. Kenyon of Iowa declared in October 1919, "The time has come to make this a one-language nation." [49] An editorial in the *American Legion Weekly* took a further step and insisted that the one language must be called "American. Why even in Mexico they do not stand for calling the language the Spanish language." [50]

Immigrants were also expected to adopt our customs and to snuff out remnants of Old World cultures. Genteel prewar and wartime movements to speed up assimilation took on a "frightened and feverish aspect." [51] Welcoming members of an Americanization conference called by his department, Secretary of the Interior Franklin K. Lane exclaimed in May 1919, "You have been gathered together as crusaders in a great cause. . . . There is no other question of such importance before the American people as the solidifying and strengthening of true American sentiment." A Harvard University official told the conference that "The Americanization movement . . . gives men a new and holy religion. . . . It challenges each one of us to a renewed consecration and devotion to the welfare of the nation." [52] The National Security League boasted, in 1919, of establishing one thousand study groups to teach teachers

[46] Kallen, Chap. 3, 154–55; Division of Foreign Intelligence, "Memorandum about Constitution Ceremonies," January 19, 1920, Lansing Papers; *The New York Times,* January 18, 1920.

[47] *American Legion Weekly,* I (November 14, 1919), 12.

[48] Sullivan, VI, 118; New York *World,* June 22, 1919.

[49] *The New York Times,* October 14, 1919.

[50] *American Legion Weekly,* I (November 14, 1919), 12.

[51] Higham, *Strangers in the Land,* 225.

[52] United States Department of the Interior, Bureau of Education, *Organization Conference, Proceedings* (Washington, D.C., 1919), 293, 345–50.

how to inculcate "Americanism" in their foreign-born students.[53] A critic of the prevailing mood protested against "one of our best advertised American mottoes, 'One country, one language, one flag,' " which, he complained, had become the basis for a fervent nationwide program.[54]

As the postwar movement for one hundred per cent Americanism gathered momentum, the deportation of alien nonconformists became increasingly its most compelling objective. Asked to suggest a remedy for the nationwide upsurge in radical activity, the Mayor of Gary, Indiana, replied, "Deportation is the answer, deportation of these leaders who talk treason in America and deportation of those who agree with them and work with them." "We must remake America," a popular author averred, "We must purify the source of America's population and keep it pure. . . . We must insist that there shall be an American loyalty, brooking no amendment or qualification." [55] As Higham noted, "In 1919, the clamor of 100 per centers for applying deportation as a purgative arose to an hysterical howl. . . . Through repression and deportation on the one hand and speedy total assimilation on the other, 100 per centers hoped to eradicate discontent and purify the nation." [56]

Politicians quickly sensed the possibilities of the popular frenzy for Americanism. Mayor Ole Hanson of Seattle, Governor Calvin Coolidge of Massachusetts, and General Leonard Wood became the early heroes of the movement.[57] The man in the best political position to take advantage of the popular feeling, however, was Attorney General A. Mitchell Palmer.[58] In 1919, especially after the President's physical collapse, only Palmer had the authority, staff, and money necessary to arrest and deport huge numbers of radical aliens. The most virulent phase of the movement for one hundred per cent Americanism came early in 1920, when Palmer's agents rounded up for deportation over six thousand aliens and prepared to arrest thousands more suspected of membership in radical organizations. Most of these aliens were taken without warrants, many were detained for unjustifiably long periods of time, and some suffered incredible hardships. Almost all, however, were eventually released.[59]

[53] National Security League, 4.

[54] *Addresses and Proceedings of the Knights of Columbus Educational Convention* (New Haven, 1919), 71. Again note the family resemblance between the attempt to protect America through absolute conformity in 1919–20 and the more drastic, centrally-planned Chinese Communist efforts at national indoctrination. A student of Chinese "coercive persuasion" described the "elaborate unanimity rituals like parades, . . . 'spontaneous' mass demonstrations and society-wide campaigns, the extensive proselytizing among the 'heretics' or the 'infidels,' the purges, programs of re-education, and other repressive measures aimed at deviants." In China, also, past national glory is invoked as evidence of present and future greatness. Schein *et al.*, 62; Lifton, *Thought Reform and the Psychology of Totalism;* Walker, *China Under Communism.*

[55] Emerson Hough, "Round Our Town," *Saturday Evening Post,* CXCII (February 21, 1920), 102; Hough, *The Web,* 456.

[56] Higham, *Strangers in the Land,* 227, 255.

[57] Murray, 62–65, 147–48, 159–60.

[58] For a full discussion of Palmer's role, Stanley Coben, *A. Mitchell Palmer: Politician* (New York, 1963).

[59] Coben, *Palmer,* Chaps. 11, 12; Claghorn, Chap. 10; Constantine Panunzio, *The Deportation Cases of 1919–1920* (New York, 1920); Zechariah Chafee, Jr., *Free Speech in the United States* (Cambridge, 1941), 204–17; Murray, Chap. 13.

After Palmer decided that he could ride the postwar fears into the presidency, he set out calculatingly to become the symbol of one hundred per cent Americanism. The Palmer raids, his anti-labor activities, and his frequent pious professions of patriotism during the campaign were all part of this effort. Palmer was introduced by a political associate to the Democratic party's annual Jackson Day dinner in January 1920 as "an American whose Americanism cannot be misunderstood." In a speech delivered in Georgia shortly before the primary election (in which Palmer won control of the state's delegation to the Democratic National Convention), the Attorney General asserted: "I am myself an American and I love to preach my doctrine before undiluted one hundred per cent Americans, because my platform is, in a word, undiluted Americanism and undying loyalty to the republic." The same theme dominated the address made by Palmer's old friend, John H. Bigelow of Hazleton, Pennsylvania, when he placed Palmer's name in nomination at the 1920 National Convention. Proclaimed Bigelow: "No party could survive today that did not write into its platform the magic word 'Americanism.' . . . The Attorney-General of the United States has not merely professed, but he has proved his true Americanism. . . . Behind him I see a solid phalanx of true Americanism that knows no divided allegiance." [60]

Unfortunately for political candidates like Palmer and Wood, most of the social and economic disturbances which had activated the movement they sought to lead gradually disappeared during the first half of 1920. The European revolutions were put down; by 1920 communism seemed to have been isolated in Russia. Bombings ceased abruptly after June 1919, and fear of new outrages gradually abated. Prices of food and clothing began to recede during the spring. Labor strife almost vanished from our major industries after a brief railroad walkout in April. Prosperity returned after mid-1919 and by early 1920 business activity and employment levels exceeded their wartime peaks.[61] At the same time, it became clear that the Senate would not pass Wilson's peace treaty and that America was free to turn its back on the responsibilities of world leadership. The problems associated with the new immigrants remained; so did the disillusionment with Europe and with many old intellectual ideals. Nativism did not disappear from the American scene; but the frenzied attempt to revitalize the culture did peter out in 1920. The handful of unintimidated men, especially Assistant Secretary of Labor Louis F. Post, who had used the safeguards provided by American law to protect many victims of the Red Scare, found increasing public support. On the other hand, politicians like Palmer, Wood, and Hanson were left high and dry, proclaiming the need for one hundred per cent Americanism to an audience which no longer urgently cared.

It is ironic that in 1920 the Russian leaders of the Comintern finally took charge of the American Communist movement, provided funds and leadership,

---

[60] Coben, *Palmer*, Chap. 13; *The New York Times*, January 9, 1920; Atlanta *Constitution*, April 7, 1920; *Official Report of the Proceedings of the Democratic National Convention, 1920* (Indianapolis, 1920), 113–14. Palmer also launched a highly publicized campaign to hold down soaring prices in 1919–20, by fixing retail prices and bringing suits against profiteers and hoarders.

[61] Bell, 334; Soule, 83–88; *Seventh Annual Report of the Federal Reserve Board for the Year 1920* (Washington, D.C., 1920), 7.

and ordered the Communist factions to unite and participate actively in labor organizations and strikes. These facts were reported in the American press.[62] Thus a potentially serious foreign threat to national security appeared just as the Red Scare evaporated, providing a final illustration of the fact that the frenzied one hundred per centers of 1919–20 were affected less by the "red menace" than by a series of social and economic dislocations.

Although the Red Scare died out in 1920, its effects lingered. Hostility toward immigrants, mobilized in 1919–20, remained strong enough to force congressional passage of restrictive immigration laws. Some of the die-hard one hundred per centers found a temporary home in the Ku Klux Klan until that organization withered away during the mid-twenties. As its most lasting accomplishments, the movement for one hundred per cent Americanism fostered a spirit of conformity in the country, a satisfaction with the *status quo,* and the equation of reform ideologies with foreign enemies. Revitalization movements have helped many societies adapt successfully to new conditions. The movement associated with the American Red Scare, however, had no such effect. True, it unified the culture against the threats faced in 1919–20; but the basic problems—a damaged value system, an unrestrained business cycle, a hostile Russia, and communism—were left for future generations of Americans to deal with in their own fashion.

[62] Draper, 244, 267–68; New York *World,* March 29, 1920.

~~~~~4

ARTHUR S. LINK

Wilson and the Great Debate over Collective Security

In what must surely be the most famous remark made by a historian on America's refusal to join the League of Nations, Thomas A. Bailey called it "the supreme act of infanticide." According to Bailey the sickly President Wilson "slew his own brainchild" by refusing to agree to certain reservations that would have won for the League the needed support of Senate moderates.

Probably Bailey is right in his analysis of responsibility for the League's defeat. But while his treatment of the episode is from the vantage point of domestic politics, Arthur Link analyzes the same story from the standpoint of what role the United States should play in world affairs. Thereby the analysis takes on greater contemporary meaning. Wilson, of course, believed there could be no effective collective security system without the League. His stand placed him in opposition to important traditions of American foreign policy— traditions not of isolationism but of freedom from binding commitments. His refusal to compromise with these largely controlling premises contributed decisively to the Senate defeat of the League.

Having helped to lay the foundations of a new world order in Paris, Wilson returned to the United States in June, 1919, to face the crucial task of winning the approval of the Senate and the support of the people for the Versailles Treaty, the principal part of the Paris settlement.

During the months following Wilson's homecoming, indeed until the election of 1920, there ensued in the United States a debate no less important than the great debate of 1787 to 1789 over the ratification of the Constitution. At stake in the latter-day discussion was the issue of American participation in a new system of collective security. To a large degree the fate of that experiment and the future peace of the world would depend upon the response that the American people gave.

Reprinted by permission of The Johns Hopkins Press.

The facts of the treaty fight are well known, so often and in such detail have historians and biographers told the story of the epic parliamentary struggle between Republicans and Democrats and of the bitter personal controversy between the President and his chief antagonist, Senator Henry Cabot Lodge of Massachusetts. I cannot ignore the forces and factors that cut the channels of the debate and perhaps decisively affected the decisions that the leaders and their followers made. My main purpose in this brief discussion, however, will be to show what has often been obscured by too much concern for dramatic details, namely, the way in which the great debate of 1919–1920 revealed differences in opinion concerning the role that the United States should play in foreign affairs, differences that were fundamental and authentic because they transcended partisanship and personality and have as much relevance for Americans of the mid-twentieth century as they had in Wilson's day.

The lines of battle over ratification of the Treaty of Versailles were first drawn, not after that treaty had been signed, but before Wilson went to Paris, as a consequence of three decisions that he made between October and December of 1918. The first was his decision to issue an appeal to the country on October 25 for the election of a Democratic Congress, and by so doing to make the forthcoming election a specific test of national confidence in his conduct of foreign affairs. The second was his decision to ignore the Senate and the Republican party in discussions of the possible terms of the settlement and in the appointment of the American delegation to the Paris conference, and to name only such men as he thought would be loyal to him and his ideals and subordinate to his direction. The third was Wilson's decision to go to Paris in person, as the head of the American commission.

The first two decisions were certainly egregious mistakes. On the other hand, Wilson was probably right in deciding that he had to go to Paris to take personal leadership in the fight for a liberal peace. However, the important point is not whether Wilson acted wisely or foolishly; it is the way in which his preparations for the peace conference predetermined the shape of the battle over the treaty that would be signed. By appealing for the election of a Democratic Congress on the ground that a Republican victory would imply a repudiation of his leadership in foreign affairs, and by appointing a peace commission composed with one unimportant exception of Democrats, Wilson made a partisan division on the issues of peace inevitable. In other words, he made it certain that Republicans would oppose and Democrats would support whatever treaty he might help to write. Moreover, by first ignoring the Senate in his appointment of the commissioners, and then by going himself to Paris, Wilson made it inevitable that the treaty fight would renew in virulent form the old conflict between the president and the upper house for control of foreign policy.

While Wilson was in Paris there were unmistakable signs at home that he would encounter bitter opposition when he returned with his peace treaty. The most ominous of these was the so-called "Round Robin" resolution that Senator Lodge presented to the upper house on March 4, 1919. Signed by thirty-seven senators, it declared that the Covenant of the League of Nations, "in the form now proposed to the peace conference," was unacceptable. At the same time, frankly isolationist opponents of the League were beginning a furious rhetorical attack in the Senate chamber.

Although there were limits beyond which Wilson would not go in compromise, as he said in a New York address on the eve of his return to France after a brief visit to the United States in late February and early March of 1919, he yielded to the advice of friends who urged him to conciliate his critics. For example, he endeavored to assuage the signers of the "Round Robin" resolution by permitting Henry White, the Republican member of the American peace delegation, to attempt to ascertain from Lodge why the Covenant was unacceptable to them. Or again, after Lodge had refused to answer specifically, Wilson took the advice of former President William Howard Taft and other Republican supporters of the League and obtained amendments to meet certain American criticisms of the Covenant.

Undertaken reluctantly at best, these measures did little to conciliate the extreme opposition or to conceal Wilson's true feelings about his senatorial critics and his growing determination to defy them. The more he had to concede at Paris during the final months of the conference, the more this determination hardened. By the time he signed the Versailles Treaty, Wilson was obviously sick of making compromises and eager to return to a political arena in which he could fight hard again, without the necessity of giving ground to opponents who had as much power as he. "I have found one can never get anything in this life that is worth while without fighting for it," he told Colonel House, who had urged him to meet the Senate in a conciliatory spirit, on the day that he left Paris.

Arriving in Washington on July 8, the President made no effort to conceal his fighting mood. When a reporter asked him on July 10 whether the Versailles Treaty could be ratified if the Senate added certain reservations, Wilson shot back, "I do not think hypothetical questions are concerned. *The Senate is going to ratify the treaty.*" To cite another example, the French Ambassador, Jules Jusserand, went to the White House at about the same time with a plan that he thought would assure the Senate's approval of the treaty. Conceived by President Nicholas Murray Butler of Columbia University and approved by a large number of Republican senators, this plan envisaged the adoption of certain reservations to the treaty to protect American sovereignty and congressional control over the war-making power. If the President would only accept the reservations, Jusserand urged, there would be no doubt about the treaty's fate in the Senate. "Mr. Ambassador," Wilson replied, "I shall consent to nothing. The Senate must take its medicine."

Wilson was, therefore, in the mood of a triumphant leader presenting his adversaries with a *fait accompli* when he presented the treaty formally to the Senate on July 10. He did not refer to the senators, as he had often done before, as his "colleagues" in the conduct of foreign relations, nor did he use his favorite phrase "common counsel" or talk about the necessity of agreement among reasonable men. On the contrary, after "informing" the senators that a world settlement had been made, he took the highest possible ground to urge prompt and unqualified approval of the treaty. The League of Nations, he exclaimed, was the hope of mankind. "Dare we reject it and break the heart of the world?" He reiterated the answer in an impromptu peroration at the end:

> The stage is set, the destiny disclosed. It has come about by no plan of our conceiving, but by the hand of God who led us into this way.

We cannot turn back. We can only go forward, with lifted eyes and freshened spirit, to follow the vision. It was of this that we dreamed at our birth. America shall in truth show the way. The light streams upon the path ahead, and nowhere else.

Many historians have been frankly puzzled by Wilson's refusal even to attempt to build support for the peace settlement in the Senate and the Republican party—among the very men who would have the power of life or death over the Treaty of Versailles. How could an authority on the American constitutional system have forgotten the Senate's jealous role in foreign affairs? How could an intelligent and astute political strategist have done the things best calculated to assure the defeat of plans upon which he thought depended the future happiness of mankind? The dilemma inherent in these hyperbolic questions is much more apparent than real. In fact, it is not too much to say that Wilson acted in the only way that it was possible for him to act, given his convictions concerning the President's control over foreign relations, his belief in party responsibility, his view of public opinion, and his own temperament.

Wilson believed that the president was a virtual sovereign, responsible only to public opinion and not to Congress, in the conduct of external affairs. In ignoring the Senate in the appointment of the peace commission, in taking personal responsibility for writing the peace treaty, and in standing defiantly in its defense, he was, therefore, simply playing the constitutional role that he thought was proper for the chief executive. Given Wilson's views of party responsibility, moreover, it was inevitable that he should have ignored the Republican opposition in the processes of peace-making, because he could not work in harmony with men whose duty he knew it would be to oppose him at every turn. Given Wilson's urge to dominate and his belief that the Republican leaders, particularly Senator Lodge, represented all the dark forces against which he was battling, it is difficult to imagine him sharing responsibility or dealing with his opponents on a give-and-take basis after his return from Paris.

These are reasons enough to explain the President's methods and his posture of defiance at the beginning of the treaty fight. There was another reason that was more important than all the rest—Wilson's supreme confidence in his own creation and in the overwhelming support of the American people. He knew not only that he was right, but that the people would know that he was right and would crush any man who dared to obstruct the fulfillment of the age-old dream of peace. That was what he meant when he told reporters that of course the Senate would ratify the Versailles Treaty, or when in private he talked about the Senate, that is, the Republican Senate, having to take its medicine.

Actually, the situation was far less simple and reassuring than Wilson imagined at the beginning of the great debate. For one thing, powerful voices were already raised in outright and violent condemnation of the treaty on various grounds. There were the idealists who had thrilled at Wilson's vision of a new world and who now drew back in disgust because the treaty failed to establish a millennial order. There were the so-called hyphenate groups—the German-Americans, who believed that the treaty was a base betrayal of the Fatherland; the Italian-Americans, who were sulking over Wilson's opposition to Italy's demands; and, most important, the several million Irish-Americans, inflamed by the civil war then raging in Ireland, who were up in arms because Wilson had refused to press the cause of Irish independence at Paris and because the treaty allegedly benefited the hated English. There was the powerful chain of Hearst newspapers, marshaling and inciting all the hyphenate protests. There were the out-and-out isolationists, who believed that American membership in the League of Nations would mean entanglement in all of Europe's rivalries and wars. They had powerful advocates in a small group of so-called irreconcilables or bitter-enders in the Senate, led by Hiram Johnson of California, William E. Borah of Idaho, and James A. Reed of Missouri, who opposed the treaty for nationalistic reasons of their own divination.

There were the major groups who opposed ratification of the treaty. In the ensuing debate they were perhaps the loudest and busiest participants of all. They were, however, a minority among the leaders of thought and political opinion, and they spoke for a minority of the people, at least before 1920 if not afterward. This is a simple point but a vital one, because in its important aspects the debate over the treaty was not a struggle between advocates of complete withdrawal on the one side and proponents of total international commitment on the other. It was, rather, a contest between the champions of a strong system of collective security and a group who favored a more limited commitment in international affairs. It was a choice between these alternatives, and not between complete isolation or complete internationalism, that the President, the Senate, and the American people eventually had to make. For this reason, therefore, I propose to let the arguments of the isolationists pass without analyzing them, and to concentrate my attention upon the two main and decisive courses of the debate.

Before we do this, it might be well to remind ourselves of the precise issues at stake. There were differences of opinion in the United States over the territorial and other provisions of the treaty, to be sure, but all of them were insignificant as compared to the differences evoked by the Covenant of the League and its provisions for universal collective security. Those provisions were clear and for the most part unequivocal. There was, of course, Article 10, which guaranteed the political independence and territorial integrity of every member nation throughout the world. There were, besides, Articles 11, 12, 13, 15, 16, and 17, which established the machinery of arbitration for all international disputes susceptible to that procedure and decreed that an act of war against one member nation should *"ipso facto* be deemed to . . . [be] an act of war against all the other Members" and should be followed automatically by an economic blockade against the aggressor and by Council action to determine what military measures should be used to repel the aggression. These were almost ironclad guarantees of mutual security, meant to be effective and unencumbered by the right of any nation involved in a dispute to veto action by the League's Council. Whether such a world-wide system could work, and whether the American people were prepared at this stage of their development to support such a system even if it did—these were the two main issues of the great debate of 1919–1920.

The decisive opposition to the Versailles Treaty came from a group of men who to a varying degree gave negative answers to both these questions. This group included some of the most distinguished leaders in the Senate and out, men like Senator Frank B. Kellogg of Minnesota, Nicholas Murray Butler, former Secretary of State Elihu Root, Charles Evans Hughes, and Herbert Hoover. Most of them were Republicans, because few Democrats active in politics dared to incur the President's wrath by opposing him. They were not isolationists, but limited internationalists who in a varying degree believed that the United States should play an active role in preserving the peace of the world. Most of them favored, for example, arbitration, the establishment of something like a World Court to interpret and codify international law, and international agreements for disarmament, economic co-operation, and the like. Some of them even supported the idea of alliances with certain powers for specific purposes.

On the other hand, all the limited internationalists opposed any such approval of the treaty as would commit the United States unreservedly to such a system of collective security as the Covenant of the League had created. Their arguments might be summarized as follows:

First, a system of collective security that is world-wide in operation is not likely either to work or to endure the strains that will inevitably be put upon it, because in practice the great powers will not accept the limitations that the Covenant places upon their sovereignty, and no nation will go to war to vindicate Article 10 unless its vital interests compel it to do so. Such sweeping guarantees as the Covenant affords are, therefore, worse than no guarantees at all because they offer only an illusory hope of security.

Second, the Covenant's fundamental guarantee, embodied in Article 10, is impossible to maintain because its promise to perpetuate the *status quo* defies the very law of life. As Elihu Root put it:

> If perpetual, it would be an attempt to preserve for all time unchanged the distribution of power and territory made in accordance with the views and exigencies of the Allies in this present juncture of affairs. It would necessarily be futile. . . . It would not only be futile; it would be mischievious. Change and growth are the law of life, and no generation can impose its will in regard to the growth of nations and the distribution of power, upon succeeding generations.

Third, the American people are not ready to support the Covenant's sweeping commitments and in fact should not do so unless their vital interests are involved in a dispute. They would and should be ready to act to prevent the outbreak of any conflict that threatened to lead to a general war, but it is inconceivable that they would or should assume the risk of war to prevent a border dispute in the Balkans, or to help maintain Japanese control of the Shantung Province or British supremacy in Ireland and India. Unconditional ratification of the treaty by the United States would, therefore, be worse than outright rejection, for it would mean the making of promises that the American people could not possibly honor in the future.

Fourth, unqualified membership in the League will raise grave dangers to American interests and the American constitutional system. It will menace American control over immigration and tariff policies, imperil the Monroe Doctrine, increase the power of the president at the expense of Congress, and necessitate the maintenance of a large standing army for the fulfillment of obligations under the Covenant.

Fifth, and most important, full-fledged participation in such a system of collective security as the Covenant establishes will spell the end of American security in foreign affairs, because it will mean transferring the power of decision over questions of peace and war from the president and Congress to an international agency which the United States could not control.

Voicing these objections day in and out as the great debate reached its crescendo in the autumn of 1919, the limited internationalists made their purposes and program indelibly clear. They would accept most of the provisions of the treaty unrelated to the League and acquiesce in the ones that they did not like. They would also sanction American membership in the League of Nations. But they would also insist upon reserving to the United States, and specifically to Congress, the power of decision concerning the degree of American participation in the League; and they would make no binding promise to enforce collective security anywhere in the future.

This was also the position of Senator Lodge, the man who devised and executed the Republican strategy in the upper house during the parliamentary phase of the treaty struggle. Personally, Lodge had little hope for the success of the League, a profound personal contempt for Wilson, and almost a sardonic scorn for the President's international ideals. The Massachusetts senator was an ardent nationalist, almost a jingoist, no isolationist, but a believer in a strong balance of power. His solution would have been harsh terms, including dismemberment, for Germany and the formation of an Anglo-Franco-American alliance as the best insurance for future peace. But as chairman of the Foreign Relations Committee and leader of his party in the Senate, it was his duty to sublimate his own strong feelings and to find a common ground upon which most Republicans could stand. That common ground, that program acceptable to an overwhelming majority of Republicans inside the Senate and out, was, in brief, to approve the treaty and accept membership in the League, subject to certain amendments and reservations that would achieve the objectives of the limited internationalists.

Debated all through the late summer of 1919, these amendments and reservations were embodied in the report that the Republican majority of the Foreign Relations Committee presented to the upper house on September 10. During the following weeks the Senate rejected the amendments and adopted most of them in the form of reservations, fourteen in all. Most of them were unimportant, but there was one that constituted a virtual rejection of the system of collective security that Wilson had constructed. It was Reservation 2, which declared that the United States assumed no obligations to preserve the territorial integrity or political independence of any other country, unless Congress should by act or joint resolution specifically assume such an obligation. In addition, the preamble to the reservations provided that American ratification of the treaty should not take effect until at least three of the four principal Allied powers had accepted the reservations in a formal exchange of notes.

This, then, was the program to which most of Wilson's opponents stood committed by the time that the Senate moved toward a formal vote on the Versailles Treaty. Whether Lodge himself was an irreconcilable who desired the defeat of the treaty, or whether he was merely a strong reservationist is an important question, but an irrelevant one at this point. The significant fact is that he had succeeded in uniting most Republicans and in commiting them to a program that affirmed limited internationalism at the same time that it repudiated American support of collective security for virtually the entire world.

Meanwhile, despite his earlier show of intransigence, Wilson had been hard at work in preparation for the impending struggle. In an effort to split the Republican ranks, he held a series of conferences in late July with eleven moderate Republican senators who were called mild reservationists because they favored approval of the treaty after the adoption of a few interpretive reservations. On August 19 the President met the Foreign Relations Committee at the White House for a three-hour grilling on all phases of the settlement. In spite of these overtures, there were unmistakable signs that Wilson had failed to win the support of any large number of Republican senators and that the strong reservationists and isolationists were rapidly gaining ground in the debate that was now proceeding in full fury throughout the country.

In response, Wilson made one of the most fateful decisions of his career. It was, as he put it, to go to the people and purify the wells of public opinion that had been poisoned by the isolationists and opponents of unreserved ratification. He was physically weakened by his labors at Paris, and his physician warned that a long speaking tour might endanger his life. Even so, he insisted upon making the effort to rally the people, the sources of authority, who had always sustained him in the past.

Leaving Washington on September 3, 1919, Wilson headed for the heartland of America, into Ohio, Indiana, Missouri, Iowa, Nebraska, Minnesota, and the Dakotas—into the region where isolationist sentiment was strongest. From there he campaigned through the Northwest and the major cities of the Pacific Coast. The final leg of his journey took him through Nevada, Utah, Wyoming, and Colorado, where the tour ended after Wilson's partial breakdown on September 25 and 26. In all he traveled 8,000 miles in twenty-two days and delivered thirty-two major addresses and eight minor ones. It was not only the greatest speaking effort of Wilson's career, but also one of the most notable forensic accomplishments in American history.

Everywhere that he went Wilson pleaded in good temper, not as a partisan, but as a leader who stood above party strife and advantage. He made his tour, he explained, first of all so that the people might know the truth about the Treaty of Versailles and no longer be confused by the misrepresentations of its enemies. As he put it at Oakland and at Reno:

> One thing has been impressed upon me more than another as I have crossed the continent, and that is that the people of the United States have been singularly and, I some times fear deliberately, misled as to the character and contents of the treaty of peace.
> Some of the critics . . . are looking backward. . . . Their power to divert, or to pervert, the view of this whole thing has made it necessary for me repeatedly on this journey to take the liberty that I am going to take with you to-night, of telling you just what kind of a treaty this is.

In almost every speech, therefore, Wilson explicitly described and defended the major provisions of the treaty and the purposes of its framers. He defended the severity of the articles relating to Germany, on the ground that her crimes against civilization demanded stern punishment. He answered the critics of the Shantung settlement, first by frankly admitting that he did not like the provisions for Japanese control and next by declaring that he had obtained the only possible settlement that offered any hope for China's eventual recovery of the province. In a similar manner he tried to answer other criticisms, and he concluded, not by denying that there were imperfections in the treaty, but by declaring that they were more than counterbalanced by the constructive achievements.

Wilson's supreme purpose was, of course, not to explain the controverted provisions of the treaty relating to territories, colonies, and reparations, but rather to defend the League of Nations against its traducers, to explain the system of collective security that its Covenant had established, and to call the American people to the world leadership that he said history now demanded of them.

He began usually by telling how the League of Nations was the fulfillment of an old American dream of peace, how it was an attempt to apply the principles of the Monroe Doctrine to the world at large, how the suggestion of such an organization had come in recent times as much if not more from Republicans than from Democrats, and how he had simply translated American ideas and proposals into statutory form and insisted that they be embodied in the treaty.

The President then proceeded to describe the provisions of the Covenant for collective security, to show how they would work in actual practice, and to attempt to prove that they afforded a system for peace instead of for war. Article 10, he was fond of emphasizing, was the heart of the Covenant and the foundation of the new world order. "Article X," he said at Indianapolis, "speaks the conscience of the world." "Article X," he added at Reno,

> is the heart of the enterprise. Article X is the test of the honor and courage and endurance of the world. Article X says that every member of the League, and that means every great fighting power in the world, . . . solemnly engages to respect and preserve as against external aggression the territorial integrity and existing political independence of the other members of the League. If you do that, you have absolutely stopped ambitious and aggressive war . . . , [for] as against external aggression, as against ambition, as against the desire to dominate from without, we all stand together in a common pledge, and that pledge is essential to the peace of the world.

In answer to critics who had argued that unconditional affirmation of Article 10 would involve the United States perpetually in war, Wilson replied by attempting to demonstrate that future wars would be virtually impossible and almost unnecessary if the collective security provisions of the Covenant implementing Article 10 were observed and enforced by the members of the League. To begin with, nations engaged in a dispute that might lead to war were bound to submit their controversy either to arbitration, the World Court, or the Council of the League. Should any nation go to war in violation of these promises, then all the other members of the League would automatically institute a total blockade, "financial, commercial, and personal," against the aggressor.

As Wilson explained at Kansas City:

> We absolutely boycott them [the aggressors]. . . . There shall be no communication even between them and the rest of the world. They shall receive no goods; they shall ship no goods. They shall receive no telegraphic messages; they shall send none. They shall receive no mail; no mail will be received from them. The nationals, the citizens, of the member states will never enter their territory until the matter is adjusted, and their citizens cannot leave their territory. It is the most complete boycott ever conceived in a public document, and I want to say to you with confident prediction that there will be no more fighting after that.

It was possible, of course, Wilson admitted, that war would occur in spite of all these precautions. "Nobody in his senses claims for the Covenant . . . that it is certain to stop war," he said at Indianapolis. If an aggressor flaunted the provisions of the Covenant, and if economic measures did not suffice to stop the aggression, then war would probably occur. If it were a major conflagration, then the United States could not remain neutral in any event. If it were a minor controversy far removed from the Western Hemisphere, then the United States would not be directly involved. Enemies of the League had charged that membership in that body would mean American involvement in every dispute everywhere in the world. "If you want to put out a fire in Utah," the President replied at Salt Lake City,

> you do not send to Oklahoma for the fire engine. If you want to put out a fire in the Balkans, if you want to stamp out the smoldering flame in some part of central Europe, you do not send to the United States for troops. The Council of the League selects the powers which are most ready, most available, most suitable, and selects them only at their own consent, so that the United States would in no such circumstances conceivably be drawn in unless the flame spread to the world.

To the charge that membership in the League would impair American sovereignty and require the fulfillment of unpleasant duties, Wilson replied that the contention was, of course, true in part. "The only way in which you can have impartial determinations to this world is by consenting to something you do not want to do," he said at Billings, Montana.

> Every time you have a case in court one or the other of the parties has to consent to something he does not want to do. . . . Yet we regard that as the foundation of civilization, that we will not

fight about these things, and that when we lose in court we will take our medicine.

It seemed almost superfluous, Wilson added, to argue the necessity of American membership in the League of Nations. There was the obvious fact, he declared at Des Moines, that American isolation had ended,

> not because we chose to go into the politics of the world, but because by the sheer genius of this people and the growth of our power we have become a determining factor in the history of mankind, and after you have become a determining factor you cannot remain isolated, whether you want to or not.

The only question confronting the American people was, therefore, whether they would exercise their influence in the world, which could henceforth be profound and controlling, in partnership with the other powers or in defiance of them. Standing alone, he warned, meant defying the world; defying the world meant maintaining a great standing army and navy; and such militarism and navalism meant the end of democracy at home.

There was the additional fact that without American participation and leadership the League of Nations would become merely another armed alliance instead of a true concert of power. "It would be an alliance," Wilson declared at St. Louis,

> in which the partnership would be between the more powerful European nations and Japan, and the . . . antagonist, the disassociated party, the party standing off to be watched by the alliance, would be the United States of America. There can be no league of nations in the true sense without the partnership of this great people.

Without American participation and leadership, therefore, the League would fail. Without the League there could be no effective collective security system. Without collective security, wars would come again. American participation was, therefore, essential to peace, the most vital and elemental interest of the United States. This became increasingly the main theme of Wilson's addresses as he journeyed deeper into the West. Over and over he cried out warnings like these:

> Ah, my fellow citizens, do not forget the aching hearts that are behind discussions like this. Do not forget the forlorn homes from which those boys went and to which they never came back. I have it in my heart that if we do not do this great thing now, every woman ought to weep because of the child in her arms. If she has a boy at her breast, she may be sure that when he comes to manhood this terrible task will have to be done once more. Everywhere we go, the train when it stops is surrounded with little children, and I look at them almost with tears in my eyes, because I feel my mission is to save them. These glad youngsters with flags in

their hands—I pray God that they never have to carry that flag upon the battlefield!

Why, my fellow citizens, nothing brings a lump into my throat quicker on this journey I am taking than to see the thronging children that are everywhere the first, just out of childish curiosity and glee, no doubt, to crowd up to the train when it stops, because I know that if by any chance we should not win this great fight for the League of Nations it would be their death warrant. They belong to the generation which would then have to fight the final war, and in that final war there would not be merely seven and a half million men slain. The very existence of civilization would be in the balance. . . . Stop for a moment to think about the next war, if there should be one. I do not hesitate to say that the war we have just been through, though it was shot through with terror of every kind, is not to be compared with the war we would have to face next time. . . . Ask any soldier if he wants to go through a hell like that again. The soldiers know what the next war would be. They know what the inventions were that were just about to be used for the absolute destruction of mankind. I am for any kind of insurance against a barbaric reversal of civilization.

Who were the enemies of the League and of the future peace of the world? They were, Wilson declared, the outright isolationists and the men who would destroy the charter of mankind by crippling reservations. They were little Americans, provincials, men of narrow vision. "They are ready to go back to that old and ugly plan of armed nations, of alliances, of watchful jealousies, of rabid antagonisms, of purposes concealed, running by the subtle channels of intrigue through the veins of people who do not dream what poison is being injected into their systems." "When at last in the annals of mankind they are gibbeted, they will regret that the gibbet is so high."

One by one Wilson answered the specific criticisms of the Covenant relating to the Monroe Doctrine, the right of members to withdraw, and the question whether the League had any jurisdiction over the domestic affairs of member nations. He told how he had obtained revision of the Covenant to satisfy American doubts about its first draft. These amendments, he continued, were embodied in the Covenant and were written in language as explicit as he knew how to devise. He would not object to reservations that merely clarified the American understanding of these questions. Reservations that in any way changed the meaning of the Covenant were, however, more serious, because they would require the re-negotiation of the treaty.

There remained the greatest threat of all to the integrity of the Covenant, the challenge of the Lodge reservations to Article 10. This reservation, Wilson warned, would destroy the foundations of collective security, because it was a notice to the world that the American people would fulfill their obligations only when it suited their purposes to do so. "That," the President exclaimed at Salt Lake City, "is a rejection of the Covenant. That is an absolute refusal to carry any part of the same responsibility that the other members of the League carry." "In other words, my fellow citizens," he added at Cheyenne, what this proposes is this: That we should make no general promise, but leave the nations associated with us to guess in each instance what we were going to consider ourselves bound to do and what we were not going to consider ourselves bound to do. It is as if you said, "We will not join the League definitely, but we will join it occasionally. We will not promise anything, but from time to time we may coöperate. We will not assume any obligations." . . . This reservation proposes that we should not acknowledge any moral obligation in the matter; that we should stand off and say, "We will see, from time to time; consult us when you get into trouble, and then we will have a debate, and after two or three months we will tell you what we are going to do." The thing is unworthy and ridiculous, and I want to say distinctly that, as I read this, it would change the entire meaning of the treaty and exempt the United States from all responsibility for the preservation of peace. It means the rejection of the treaty, my fellow countrymen, nothing less. It means that the United States would take from under the structure its very foundations and support.

The irony of it all was, Wilson added, that the reservation was actually unnecessary, *if the objective of its framers was merely to reserve the final decision for war to the American government.* In the case of all disputes to which it was not a party, the United States would have an actual veto over the Council's decision for war, because that body could not advise member nations to go to war except by unanimous vote, exclusive of the parties to the dispute. Thus, the President explained, there was absolutely no chance that the United States could be forced into war against its will, unless it was itself guilty of aggression, in which case it would be at war anyway.

These were, Wilson admitted, legal technicalities, and, he added, he would not base his case for American participation in the League of Nations upon them. The issue was not who had the power to make decisions for war, but whether the American people were prepared to go wholeheartedly into the League, determined to support its collective system unreservedly, and willing to make the sacrifices that were necessary to preserve peace. Wilson summarized all his pleading with unrivaled feeling at the Mormon capital, as follows:

Instead of wishing to ask to stand aside, get the benefits of the League, but share none of its burdens or responsibilities, I for my part want to go in and accept what is offered to us, the leadership of the world. A leadership of what sort, my fellow citizens? Not a leadership that leads men along the lines by which great nations can profit out of weak nations, not an exploiting power, but a liberating power, a power to show the world that when America was born it was indeed a finger pointed toward those lands into which men could deploy some of these days and live in happy freedom, look each other in the eyes as equals, see that no man was put upon, that no people were forced to accept authority which was not of their own choice, and that out of the general generous impulse of the human genius and the human spirit we were lifted along the levels of civilization to days when there should be wars no more, but men should govern themselves in peace and amity and quiet. That is the leadership we said we wanted, and now the world offers it to us. It is inconceivable that we should reject it.

We come now to the well-known tragic sequel. Following his address at Pueblo, Colorado, on September 25, 1919, the President showed such obvious signs of exhaustion that his physician canceled his remaining engagements and sped the presidential train to Washington. On October 2 Wilson suffered a severe stroke and paralysis of the left side of his face and body. For several days his life hung in the balance; then he gradually revived, and by the end of October he was clearly out of danger. But his recovery was only partial at best. His mind remained relatively clear; but he was physically enfeebled, and the disease had wrecked his emotional constitution and aggravated all his more unfortunate personal traits.

Meanwhile, the Senate was nearing the end of its long debate over the Treaty of Versailles. Senator Lodge presented his revised fourteen reservations on behalf of the Foreign Relations Committee to the upper house on November 6, 1919. Senator Gilbert M. Hitchcock of Nebraska, the Democratic minority leader, countered with five reservations, four of which Wilson had approved in substance before he embarked upon his western tour. They simply sought to make clear the American understanding of Article 10 and other provisions of the treaty. The issue before the Senate was, therefore, now clear— whether to approve the treaty with reservations that did not impair the American obligation to enforce collective security, or whether to approve the treaty with reservations that repudiated all compelling obligations and promised American support for only a limited international system.

Lodge beat down the Hitchcock reservations with the help of the irreconcilables and then won adoption of his own. Now the President had to choose between ratification with the Lodge reservations or running the risk of the outright defeat of the treaty. He gave his decision to Hitchcock in a brief conference at the White House on November 17 and in a letter on the following day: Under no circumstances could he accept the Lodge reservation to Article 10, for it meant nullification of the treaty. When the Senate voted on November 19, therefore, most of the Democrats joined the irreconcilables to defeat ratification with the Lodge reservations by a count of thirty-nine ayes to fifty-five nays. Hoping to split the Republican ranks and win support of the "mild reservationists," the Democratic leaders then moved unconditional approval of the treaty. This strategy, upon which Wilson had placed all his hopes, failed, as a firm Republican majority defeated the resolution with the help of the irreconcilables by a vote of thirty-eight ayes to fifty-three nays.

It was not the end, for during the following months an overwhelming majority of the leaders of opinion in the United States refused to accept the Senate's vote as the final verdict. In the absence of any reliable indices, it is impossible to measure the division of public opinion as a whole; but there can be little doubt that an overwhelming majority of thoughtful people favored ratification with some kind of reservations, and even with the Lodge reservations, if that were necessary to obtain the Senate's consent.

There was, consequently, enormous pressure upon the leaders in both parties for compromise during the last weeks of 1919 and the early months of 1920. Prominent Republicans who had taken leadership in a nonpartisan campaign for the League, including former President Taft and President A. Lawrence Lowell of Harvard University; scores of editors and the spokesmen of various academic, religious, and labor organizations; and Democratic leaders who dared oppose the President, like William J. Bryan and Colonel House, begged Lodge and Wilson to find a common ground. Alarmed by the possibility of American rejection of the treaty, spokesmen for the British government declared publicly that limited American participation in the League would be better than no participation at all.

Under this pressure the moderate leaders in both camps set to work in late December and early January to find a basis for agreement. Even Lodge began to weaken and joined the bipartisan conferees who were attempting to work out an acceptable reservation to Article 10. But the Massachusetts senator and his friends would not yield the essence of their reservation, and it was Wilson who had to make the final choice. By January he had recovered sufficient physical strength to manage his forces in the upper house. All the while, however, his intransigence had been compounded by personal bitterness and by the growing conviction that rejection of the treaty was preferable to a dishonorable ratification. Consequently, between January and March, 1920, when the final debates and maneuvers were in progress, he rejected all suggestions of yielding on Article 10. Instead, he apparently began to make fantastic plans to run again for the presidency in a campaign that would decide the fate of the treaty. "If there is any doubt as to what the people of the country think on this vital matter," he wrote in a letter to the Democratic party on January 8, 1920, "the clear and single way out is to submit it for determination at the next election to the voters of the Nation, to give the next election the form of a great and solemn referendum."

Thus the parliamentary phase of the struggle moved to its inexorable conclusion when the Senate took its second and final vote on the treaty on March 19, 1920. The only hope for approval lay in the chance that enough Democrats would defy the President, as many friends of the League were urging them to do, to obtain a two-thirds majority for ratification with the Lodge reservations. Twenty-one Democrats did follow their consciences rather than the command from the White House, but not enough of them defected to put the treaty across. The treaty with the Lodge reservations failed by seven votes.

There was a final sequel. The Democratic presidential and vice-presidential candidates, James M. Cox and Franklin D. Roosevelt, tried hard to make the election of 1920 a "great and solemn referendum" on the League. But the effort failed, because so many other issues were involved, because the Republican candidate, Warren G. Harding, equivocated so artfully that no one knew where he stood, and because virtually all the distinguished leaders of the G.O.P. assured the country that a Republican victory promised the best hope of American membership in the League. These promises were obviously not honored. One of the new President's first official acts was to repudiate the idea of membership in the League; one of the new administration's first foreign policies was to conclude a separate peace with Germany.

Virtually all historians now agree that Wilson's refusal to permit his followers in the Senate to approve the treaty with the Lodge reservations was an error of tragic magnitude. Having built so grandly at Paris, having fought so magnificently at home for his creation, he then proceeded by his own hand to remove the cornerstone of his edifice of peace. Why? Were there inner demons of pride and arrogance driving him to what one historian has called "the supreme infanticide"? Did his illness and seclusion prevent him from obtaining a realistic view of the parliamentary situation, or so disarrange him emotionally that he became incompetent in the tasks of statesmanship? Or was he simply an idealist who would make no compromises on what he thought were fundamental principles?

The historian, who sees through a glass darkly when probing the recesses of the mind, is not able to give final answers to questions like these. Wilson, for all his high-mindedness and nobility of character, was headstrong and not much given to dealing graciously or to compromising with men whom he distrusted and disliked. Once before, in a violent dispute at Princeton over control of the graduate school, he had revealed these same traits and suffered defeat because he could not work with men whom he did not trust. The sympathetic biographer would like to believe that it was his illness, which aggravated his bitterness and his sense of self-righteousness, that drove Wilson to his fatal choice. Perhaps this is true. He had not always been incapable of compromise: perhaps he would have yielded in the end if disease had not dethroned his reason.

These attempts to extenuate ignore the fact that there were fundamental and vital issues at stake in the controversy over the treaty—whether the United States would take leadership in the League of Nations without hesitations and reservations, or whether it would join the League grudgingly and with no promises to help maintain universal collective security. To Wilson the difference between what he fought for and what Lodge and the Republicans would agree to was the difference between the success or failure and the life or death of man's best hope for peace. This he had said on his western tour, at a time when his health and reasoning faculties were unimpaired. This he believed with his heart and soul. It is, therefore, possible, even probable, that Wilson would have acted as he did even had he not suffered his breakdown, for it was not in his nature to compromise away the principles in which he believed.

If this is true, then in this, the last and greatest effort of his life, Wilson spurned the role of statesman for what he must have thought was the nobler role of prophet. The truth is that the American people were not prepared in 1920 to assume the world leadership that Wilson offered them, and that the powers of the world were not yet ready to enforce the world-wide, universal system of collective security that the President had created.

Collective security failed in the portentous tests of the 1930's, not because the League's machinery was defective, but because the people of the world, not merely the American people alone, were unwilling to confront aggressors with the threat of war. As a result a second and more terrible world conflict came, as Wilson prophesied it would, and at its end the United States helped to build a new and different league of nations and took the kind of international leadership that Wilson had called for. But events of the past decade have not fully justified Wilson's confidence in international organization; the only really promising systems of collective security, the regional ones like NATO, have been of a kind that Wilson fervently denounced; and only the future can reveal whether his dream of a universal system can ever be made a reality.

And so it was Wilson the prophet, demanding greater commitment, sacrifice, and idealism than the people could give, who was defeated in 1920. It is also Wilson the prophet who survives in history, in the hopes and aspirations of mankind and in whatever ideals of international service that the American people still cherish. One thing is certain, now that men have the power to sear virtually the entire face of the earth: The prophet of 1919 was right in his larger vision; the challenge that he raised then is today no less real and no less urgent than it was in his own time.

F. SCOTT FITZGERALD

The Jazz Age

One of Fitzgerald's great achievements was his ability to perceive and describe the evolution of modern American culture. This Side of Paradise (*1920*), The Beautiful and the Damned (*1922*), *and* The Great Gatsby (*1925*) *catch the glitter and frantic pursuit of youth and pleasure we have come to associate with the twenties. Because he so accurately evokes the quality of the decade, the essay reprinted here is particularly valuable to those who did not live through the era.*

Clearly the breathless new culture that Fitzgerald describes is far more like our own than was the Victorianism it replaced or the cheerless depression days of the thirties. The twenties were not only the expensive orgy a chastened Fitzgerald looked back on in the thirties; they were the beginning of our own modern age of affluence, doubt, social division, violence, and fear. His themes are subjects of most of the novels and plays of the years since: the personal hardships of living in a world where standards have evaporated, where violence lurks below the surface of pleasure, and the matter-of-fact demands of earning a living no longer dominate the national psychology. Fitzgerald still speaks to a nation learning how to live with leisure and affluence.

It is too soon to write about the Jazz Age with perspective, and without being suspected of premature arteriosclerosis. Many people still succumb to violent retching when they happen upon any of its characteristic words—words which have since yielded in vividness to the coinages of the underworld. It is as dead as were the Yellow Nineties in 1902. Yet the present writer already looks back to it with nostalgia. It bore him up, flattered him and gave him more money than he had dreamed of, simply for telling people that he felt as they did, that something had to be done with all the nervous energy stored up and unexpended in the War.

The ten-year period that, as if reluctant to die outmoded in its bed, leaped to a spectacular death in October, 1929, began about the time of the May Day riots in 1919. When the police rode down the demobilized country boys gaping at the orators in Madison Square, it was the sort of measure bound to alienate the more intelligent young men from the prevailing order. We didn't remember anything about the Bill of Rights until Mencken began plugging it, but we did know that such tyranny belonged in the jittery little countries of South Europe. If goose-livered business men had this effect on the government, then maybe we had gone to war for J. P. Morgan's loans after all. But, because we were tired of Great Causes, there was no more than a short outbreak of moral indignation, typified by Dos Passos' "Three Soldiers." Presently we began to have slices of the national cake and our idealism only flared up when the newspapers made melodrama out of such stories as Harding and the Ohio Gang or Sacco and Vanzetti. The events of 1919 left us cynical rather than revolutionary, in spite of the fact that now we are all rummaging around in our trunks wondering where in hell we left the liberty cap—"I know I *had* it"—and the moujik blouse. It was characteristic of the Jazz Age that it had no interest in politics at all.

It was an age of miracles, it was an age of art, it was an age of excess, and it was an age of satire. A Stuffed Shirt, squirming to blackmail in a lifelike way, sat upon the throne of the United States; a stylish young man hurried over to represent to us the throne of England. A world of girls yearned for the young Englishman; the old American groaned in his sleep as he waited to be poisoned by his wife, upon the advice of the female Rasputin who then made the ultimate decision in our national affairs. But such matters apart, we had things our way at last. With Americans ordering suits by the gross in London, the Bond Street tailors perforce agreed to modernize their cut to the American long-waisted figure and loose-fitting taste, something subtle passed to America, the style of man. During the Renaissance, Francis the First looked to Florence to trim his leg. Seventeenth-century England aped the court of France, and fifty years ago the German Guards officer bought his civilian clothes in London. Gentleman's clothes—symbol of "the power that man must hold and that passes from race to race."

We were the most powerful nation. Who could tell us any longer what was fashionable and what was fun? Isolated during the European War, we had begun combing the unknown South and West for folkways and pastimes and there were more ready to hand.

The first social revelation created a sensation out of all proportion to its novelty. As far back as 1915 the unchaperoned young people of the smaller cities had discovered the mobile privacy of that automobile given to young Bill at sixteen to make him "self-reliant." At first petting was a desperate adventure even under such favorable conditions, but presently confidences were exchanged and the old commandment broke down. As early as 1917 there were references to such sweet and casual dalliance in any number of the *Yale Record* or the *Princeton Tiger*.

But petting in its more audacious manifestations was confined to the wealthier classes—among other young people the old standards prevailed until after the War, and a kiss meant that a proposal was expected, as young officers in strange cities sometimes discovered to their dismay. Only in 1920 did the veil finally fall—the Jazz Age was in flower.

Scarcely had the staider citizens of the republic caught their breaths when the wildest of all generations, the generation which had been adolescent during the confusion of the War, brusquely shouldered my contemporaries out of the way and danced into the limelight. This was the generation whose girls dramatized themselves as flappers, the generation that corrupted its elders and eventually overreached itself less through lack of morals than through lack of taste. May one offer in exhibit the year 1922! That was the peak of the younger generation, for though the Jazz Age continued, it became less and less an affair of youth.

The sequel was like a children's party taken over by the elders, leaving the children puzzled and rather neglected and rather taken aback. By 1923 their elders, tired of watching the carnival with ill-concealed envy, had discovered that young liquor will take the place of young blood, and with a whoop the orgy began. The younger generation was starred no longer.

A whole race going hedonistic, deciding on pleasure. The precocious intimacies of the younger generation would have come about with or without prohibition—they were implicit in the attempt to adapt English customs to American conditions. (Our South, for example, is tropical and early maturing—it has never been part of the wisdom of France and Spain to let young girls go unchaperoned at sixteen and seventeen.) But the general decision to be amused that began with the cocktail parties of 1921 had more complicated origins.

The word jazz in its progress toward respectability has meant first sex, then dancing, then music. It is associated with a state of nervous stimulation, not unlike that of big cities behind the lines of a war. To many English the War still goes on because all the forces that menace them are still active—Wherefore eat, drink and be merry, for to-morrow we die. But different causes had now brought about a corresponding state in America—though there were entire classes (people over fifty, for example) who spent a whole decade denying its existence even when its puckish face peered into the family circle. Never did they dream that they had contributed to it. The honest citizens of every class, who believed in a strict public morality and were powerful enough to enforce the necessary legislation, did not know that they would necessarily be served by criminals and quacks, and do not really believe it to-day. Rich righteousness had always been able to buy honest and intelligent servants to free the slaves or the Cubans, so when this attempt collapsed our elders stood firm with all the stubbornness of people involved in a weak case, preserving their righteousness and losing their children. Silver-haired women and men with fine old faces, people who never did a consciously dishonest thing in their lives, still assure each other in the apartment hotels of New York and Boston and Washington that "There's a whole generation growing up that will never know the taste of liquor." Meanwhile their granddaughters pass the well-thumbed copy of "Lady Chatterley's Lover" around the boarding-school and, if they get about at all, know the taste of gin or corn at sixteen. But the generation who reached maturity between 1875 and 1895 continue to believe what they want to believe.

Even the intervening generations were incredulous. In 1920 Heywood Broun announced that all this hubbub was nonsense, that young men didn't kiss but told anyhow. But very shortly people over twenty-five came in for an intensive education. Let me trace some of the revelations vouchsafed them by reference to a dozen works written for various types of mentality during the decade. We begin with the suggestion that Don Juan leads an interesting life ("Jurgen," 1919); then we learn that there's a lot of sex around if we only knew it ("Winesburg, Ohio," 1920), that adolescents lead very amorous lives ("This Side of Paradise," 1920) that there are a lot of neglected Anglo-Saxon words ("Ulysses," 1921), that older people don't always resist sudden temptations ("Cytherea," 1922), that girls are sometimes seduced without being ruined ("Flaming Youth," 1922), that even rape often turns out well ("The Sheik," 1922), that glamorous English ladies are often promiscuous ("The Green Hat," 1924), that in fact they devote most of their time to it ("The Vortex," 1926), that it's a damn good thing too ("Lady Chatterley's Lover," 1928), and finally that there are abnormal variations ("The Well of Loneliness," 1928, and Sodome and Gomorrhe," 1929).

In my opinion the erotic element in these works, even "The Sheik" written for children in the key of "Peter Rabbit," did not one particle of harm. Everything they described, and much more, was familiar in our contemporary life. The majority of the theses were honest and elucidating—their effect was to restore some dignity to the male as opposed to the he-man in American life. ("And what is a 'He-man'?" demanded Gertrude Stein one day. "Isn't it a large enough order to fill out to the dimensions of all that 'a man' has meant in the past? A *'He*-man'!") The married woman can now discover whether she is being cheated, or whether sex is just something to be endured, and her compensation should be to establish a tyranny of the spirit, as her mother may have hinted. Perhaps many women found that love was meant to be fun. Anyhow the objectors lost their tawdry little case, which is one reason why our literature is now the most living in the world.

Contrary to popular opinion the movies of the Jazz Age had no effect upon its morals. The social attitude of the producers was timid, behind the times and banal—for example no picture mirrored even faintly the younger generation until 1923, when magazines had already been started to celebrate it and it had long ceased to be news. There were a few feeble splutters and then Clara Bow in "Flaming Youth"; promptly the Hollywood hacks ran the theme into its cinematographic grave. Throughout the Jazz Age the movies go no farther than Mrs. Jiggs, keeping up with its most blatant superficialities. This was no doubt due to the censorship as well as to innate conditions in the industry. In any case the Jazz Age now raced along under its own power, served by great filling stations full of money.

The people over thirty, the people all the way up to fifty, had joined the dance. We graybeards (to tread down F.P.A.) remember the uproar when in 1912 grandmothers of forty tossed away their crutches and took lessons in the Tango and the Castle-Walk. A dozen years later a woman might pack the Green Hat with her other affairs as she set off for Europe or New York, but

Savonarola was too busy flogging dead horses in Augean stables of his own creation to notice. Society, even in small cities, now dined in separate chambers, and the sober table learned about the gay table only from hearsay. There were very few people left at the sober table. One of its former glories, the less sought-after girls who had become resigned to sublimating a probable celibacy, came across Freud and Jung in seeking their intellectual recompense and came tearing back into the fray.

By 1926 the universal preoccupation with sex had become a nuisance. (I remember a perfectly mated, contented young mother asking my wife's advice about "having an affair right away," though she had no one especially in mind, "because don't you think it's sort of undignified when you get much over thirty?") For a while bootleg negro records with their phallic euphemisms made everything suggestive, and simultaneously came a wave of erotic plays— young girls from finishing schools packed the galleries to hear about the romance of being a Lesbian and George Jean Nathan protested. Then one young producer lost his head entirely, drank a beauty's alcoholic bath-water and went to the penitentiary. Somehow his pathetic attempt at romance belongs to the Jazz Age, while his contemporary in prison, Ruth Snyder, had to be hoisted into it by the tabloids—she was, as *The Daily News,* hinted deliciously to gourmets, about "to cook, *and sizzle, AND FRY!"* in the electric chair.

The gay elements of society had divided into two main streams, one flowing toward Palm Beach and Deauville, and the other, much smaller, toward the summer Riviera. One could get away with more on the summer Riviera, and whatever happened seemed to have something to do with art. From 1926 to 1929, the great years of the Cap d'Antibes, this corner of France was dominated by a group quite distinct from that American society which is dominated by Europeans. Pretty much of anything went at Antibes—by 1929 at the most gorgeous paradise for swimmers on the Mediterranean no one swam any more save for a short hangover dip at noon. There was a picturesque graduation of steep rocks over the sea and somebody's valet and an occasional English girl used to dive from them but the Americans were content to discuss each other in the bar. This was indicative of something that was taking place in the homeland —Americans were getting soft. There were signs everywhere: we still won the Olympic games but with champions whose names had few vowels in them— teams composed, like the fighting Irish combination of Notre Dame, of fresh overseas blood. Once the French became really interested the Davis Cup gravitated automatically to their intensity in competition. The vacant lots of the Middle-Western cities were built up now—except for a short period in school we were not turning out to be an athletic people like the British after all. The hare and the tortoise. Of course if we wanted to we could be in a minute; we still had all those reserves of ancestral vitality, but one day in 1926 we looked down and found we had flabby arms and a fat pot and couldn't say boop-boop-a-doop to a Sicilian. Shades of Van Bibber!—no utopian ideal, God knows. Even golf, once considered an effeminate game, had seemed very strenuous of late—an emasculated form appeared and proved just right.

By 1927, a wide-spread neurosis began to be evident, faintly signalled, like a nervous beating of the feet, by the popularity of cross-word puzzles. I remember a fellow expatriate opening a letter from a mutual friend of ours, urging him to come home and be revitalized by the hardy, bracing qualities of the native soil. It was a strong letter and it affected us both deeply, until we noticed that it was headed from a nerve sanitarium in Pennsylvania.

By this time contemporaries of mine had begun to disappear into the dark maw of violence. A classmate killed his wife and himself on Long Island, another tumbled "accidentally" from a skyscraper in Philadelphia, another purposely from a skyscraper in New York. One was killed in a speak-easy in Chicago; another was beaten to death in a speak-easy in New York and crawled home to the Princeton Club to die; still another had his skull crushed by a maniac's axe in an insane asylum where he was confined. These are not catastrophes that I went out of my way to look for—these were my friends; moreover, these things happened not during the depression but during the boom.

In the spring of '27, something bright and alien flashed across the sky. A young Minnesotan who seemed to have had nothing to do with his generation did a heroic thing, and for a moment people set down their glasses in country clubs and speak-easies and thought of their old best dreams. Maybe there was a way out by flying, maybe our restless blood could find frontiers in the illimitable air. But by that time we were all pretty well committed; and the Jazz Age continued; we would all have one more.

Nevertheless, Americans were wandering ever more widely—friends seemed eternally bound for Russia, Persia, Abyssinia and Central Africa. And by 1928 Paris had grown suffocating. With each new shipment of Americans spewed up by the boom the quality fell off, until toward the end there was something sinister about the crazy boatloads. They were no longer the simple pa and ma and son and daughter, infinitely superior in their qualities of kindness and curiosity to the corresponding class in Europe, but fantastic neanderthals who believed something, something vague, that you remembered from a very cheap novel. I remember an Italian on a steamer who promenaded the deck in an American Reserve Officer's uniform picking quarrels in broken English with Americans who criticised their own institutions in the bar. I remember a fat Jewess, inlaid with diamonds, who sat behind us at the Russian ballet and said as the curtain rose, "Thad's luffly, dey ought to baint a bicture of it." This was low comedy but it was evident that money and power were falling into the hands of people in comparison with whom the leader of a village Soviet would be a gold-mine of judgment and culture. There were citizens travelling in luxury in 1928 and 1929 who, in the distortion of their new condition, had the human value of pekinese bivalves, cretins, goats. I remember the Judge from some New York district who had taken his daughter to see the Bayeux Tapestries and made a scene in the papers advocating their segregation because one scene was immoral. But in those days life was like the race in "Alice in Wonderland," there was a prize for every one.

The Jazz Age had had a wild youth and a heady middle age. There was the phase of the necking parties, the Leopold-Loeb murder (I remember the time my wife was arrested on Queensborough Bridge on the suspicion of being the "Bob-haired Bandit") and the John Held Clothes. In the second phase such phenomena as sex and murder became more mature, if much more conventional. Middle age must be served and pajamas came to the beach to save fat thighs and flabby calves from competition with the one-piece bathing-suit.

Finally skirts came down and everything was concealed. Everybody was at scratch now. Let's go—

But it was not to be. Somebody had blundered and the most expensive orgy in history was over.

It ended two years ago, because the utter confidence which was its essential prop received an enormous jolt and it didn't take long for the flimsy structure to settle earthward. And after two years the Jazz Age seems as far away as the days before the War. It was borrowed time anyhow—the whole upper tenth of a nation living with the insouciance of grand ducs and the casualness of chorus girls. But moralizing is easy now and it was pleasant to be in one's twenties in such a certain and unworried time. Even when you were broke you didn't worry about money, because it was in such profusion around you. Toward the end one had a struggle to pay one's share; it was almost a favor to accept hospitality that required any travelling. Charm, notoriety, mere good manners, weighed more than money as a social asset. This was rather splendid but things were getting thinner and thinner as the eternal necessary human values tried to spread over all that expansion. Writers were geniuses on the strength of one respectable book or play; just as during the War officers of four months' experience commanded hundreds of men, so there were now many little fish lording it over great big bowls. In the theatrical world extravagant productions were carried by a few second-rate stars, and so on up the scale into politics where it was difficult to interest good men in positions of the highest importance and responsibility, importance and responsibility far exceeding that of business executives but which paid only five or six thousand a year.

Now once more the belt is tight and we summon the proper expression of horror as we look back at our wasted youth. Sometimes, though, there is a ghostly rumble among the drums, an asthmatic whisper in the trombones that swings me back into the early twenties when we drank wood alcohol and every day in every way grew better and better, and there was a first abortive shortening of the skirts, and girls all looked alike in sweater dresses, and people you didn't want to know said "Yes, we have no bananas," and it seemed only a question of a few years before the older people would step aside and let the world be run by those who saw things as they were—and it all seems rosy and romatic to us who were young then, because we will never feel quite so intensely about our surroundings any more.

$\sim\!\sim\!\sim\!\sim\!6$

HERBERT HOOVER

American Individualism

Herbert Hoover's career is significant in its relation to a number of economic and administrative crises of the twentieth century. As head of the Commission for Relief in Belgium, Food Administrator in the United States, and director of the postwar European relief program, he discovered the difficulties and opportunities a representative government faces in the attainment of efficiency under stress of war. Hoover's jobs conditioned him for various kinds of emergency mobilization; he endorsed government regulation of the railroads and supervised the ordering of the wartime economy. His progressive stewardship of the Department of Commerce under the Harding and Coolidge administrations was a repudiation of laissez-faire. Broader problems of economic mobilization are revealed in the efforts of the Hoover administration to cope with the depression. Much has to be learned about the important processes of decision making that prevailed during Hoover's administration and their effectiveness as means for the ordering of the economy; the degree to which various pressures of tradition binding Hoover himself or the nation at large may have interfered with his efforts to combat the depression; the range of alternatives that were open or closed to him and the extent to which these may be open or closed today.

Hoover's thinking in economic and political questions is important in its attempt to achieve an enlightened statement of an American ethos. Especially as Secretary of Commerce, he worked toward a rationale for business—or for America itself, which was deriving so many of its material and psychological symbols from business. In Hoover the American entrepreneurial ideal found one of its most humanely articulate spokesmen at perhaps the last moment of its full sway. In American Individualism *he calls for "pioneers" to invade "continents of human welfare of which we have penetrated only the coastal plain."*

The individualism of responsibility and service that Hoover preached, the striking of "that fine balance which links the future with the past," contained a major contradiction. In the twenties Americans were learning, as never before, to work with collectivities even while they drew on a rhetoric of individual initiative. For example, the stock market attracted the small investor to throw in his lot with a collective private enterprise, and beyond this, with the projected growth of an entire collective economy, and think himself an individualist for doing it. In Henry Ford's insistence that a technologically advanced factory put unprecedented demands on the skill and intelligence of the worker is an acceptance of a collectively organized activity as a sphere within which individual effort is supposedly fulfilled. Then there were the private agricultural cooperatives, flourishing as never before, to which Hoover gave his blessing. During Hoover's presidency, in fact, his own Farm Board provided loans for collectivities organized to impose order on agricultural purchase and marketing. That Hoover encompassed within his own life and thought so much of individualist doctrine, and so much of the American achievement in organization, makes him an interesting study in a major irony of recent American history.

We have witnessed in this last eight years the spread of revolution over one-third of the world. The causes of these explosions lie at far greater depths than the failure of governments in war. The war itself in its last stages was a conflict of social philosophies—but beyond this the causes of social explosion lay in the great inequalities and injustices of centuries flogged beyond endurance by the conflict and freed from restraint by the destruction of war. The urgent forces which drive human society have been plunged into a terrible furnace. Great theories spun by dreamers to remedy the pressing human ills have come to the front of men's minds. Great formulas came into life that promised to dissolve all trouble. Great masses of people have flocked to their banners in hopes born of misery and suffering. Nor has this great social ferment been confined to those nations that have burned with revolutions.

Now, as the storm of war, of revolution and of emotion subsides there is left even with us of the United States much unrest, much discontent with the surer forces of human advancement. To all of us, out of this crucible of actual, poignant, individual experience has come a deal of new understanding, and it is for all of us to ponder these new currents if we are to shape our future with intelligence.

Even those parts of the world that suffered less from the war have been partly infected by these ideas. Beyond this, however, many have had high hopes of civilization suddenly purified and ennobled by the sacrifices and services of the war; they had thought the fine unity of purpose gained in war would be carried into great unity of action in remedy of the faults of civilization in peace. But from concentration of every spiritual and material energy upon the single purpose of war the scene changed to the immense complexity and the many purposes of peace.

Thus there loom up certain definite underlying forces in our national life that need to be stripped of the imaginary—the transitory—and a definition should be given to the actual permanent and persistent motivation of our civilization. In contemplation of these questions we must go far deeper than the superficials of our political and economic structure, for these are but the products of our social philosophy—the machinery of our social system.

Nor is it ever amiss to review the political, economic, and spiritual principles through which our country has steadily grown in usefulness and greatness, not only to preserve them from being fouled by false notions, but more importantly that we may guide ourselves in the road of progress.

Five or six great social philosophies are at struggle in the world for ascendency. There is the Individualism of America. There is the Individualism of the more democratic states of Europe with its careful reservations of castes and classes. There are Communism, Socialism, Syndicalism, Capitalism, and finally there is Autocracy—whether by birth, by possessions, militarism, or divine right of kings. Even the Divine Right still lingers on although our lifetime has seen fully two-thirds of the earth's population, including Germany, Austria, Russia, and China, arrive at a state of angry disgust with this type of social motive power and throw it on the scrap heap.

All these thoughts are in ferment today in every country in the world. They fluctuate in ascendency with times and places. They compromise with each other in daily reaction on governments and peoples. Some of these ideas are perhaps more adapted to one race than another. Some are false, some are true. What we are interested in is their challenge to the physical and spiritual forces of America.

The partisans of some of these other brands of social schemes challenge us to comparison; and some of their partisans even among our own people are increasing in their agitation that we adopt one or another or parts of their devices in place of our tried individualism. They insist that our social foundations are exhausted, that like feudalism and autocracy America's plan has served its purpose—that it must be abandoned.

There are those who have been left in sober doubt of our institutions or are confounded by bewildering catchwords of vivid phrases. For in this welter of discussions there is much attempt to glorify or defame social and economic forces with phrases. Nor indeed should we disregard the potency of some of these phrases in their stir to action.—"The dictatorship of the Proletariat," "Capitalistic nations," "Germany over all," and a score of others. We need only to review those that have jumped to horseback during the last ten years in order that we may be properly awed by the great social and political havoc that can be worked where the bestial instincts of hate, murder, and destruction are clothed by the demagogue in the fine terms of political idealism.

For myself, let me say at the very outset that my faith in the essential truth, strength, and vitality of the developing creed by which we have hitherto lived in this country of ours has been confirmed and deepened by the searching experiences of seven years of service in the backwash and misery of war. Seven years of contending with economic degeneration, with social disintegration, with incessant political dislocation, with all of its seething and ferment of individual and class conflict, could but impress me with the primary motivation of social forces, and the necessity for broader thought upon their great issues to humanity. And from it all I emerge an individualist—an unashamed individualist. But let me say also that I am an American individualist. For America has been steadily developing the ideals that constitute progressive individualism.

No doubt, individualism run riot, with no tempering principle, would provide a long category of inequalities, of tyrannies, dominations, and injustices. America, however, has tempered the whole conception of individualism by the injection of a definite principle, and from this principle it follows that attempts at domination, whether in government or in the process of industry and commerce, are under an insistent curb. If we would have the values of individualism, their stimulation to initiative, to the development of hand and intellect, to the high development of thought and spirituality, they must be tempered with that firm and fixed ideal of American individualism—*an equality of opportunity*. If we would have these values we must soften its hardness and stimulate progress through that sense of service that lies in our people.

Therefore, it is not the individualism of other countries for which I would speak, but the individualism of America. Our individualism differs from all others because it embraces these great ideals: *that while we build our society upon the attainment of the individual, we shall safeguard to every individual an equality of opportunity to take that position in the community to which his intelligence, character, ability, and ambition entitle him; that we keep the social solution free from frozen strata of classes; that we shall stimulate effort of each individual to achievement; that through an enlarging sense of responsibility and understanding we shall assist him to this attainment; while he in turn must stand up to the emery wheel of competition.*

Individualism cannot be maintained as the foundation of a society if it looks to only legalistic justice based upon contracts, property, and political equality. Such legalistic safeguards are themselves not enough. In our individualism we have long since abandoned the laissez faire of the 18th Century—the notion that it is "every man for himself and the devil take the hindmost." We abandoned that when we adopted the ideal of equality of opportunity—the fair chance of Abraham Lincoln. We have confirmed its abandonment in terms of legislation, of social and economic justice,—in part because we have learned that it is the hindmost who throws the bricks at our social edifice, in part because we have learned that the foremost are not always the best nor the hindmost the worst—and in part because we have learned that social injustice is the destruction of justice itself. We have learned that the impulse to production can only be maintained at a high pitch if there is a fair division of the product. We have also learned that fair division can only be obtained by certain restrictions on the strong and the dominant. We have indeed gone even further in the 20th Century with the embracement of the necessity of a greater and broader sense of service and responsibility to others as a part of individualism.

Whatever may be the case with regard to Old World individualism (and we have given more back to Europe than we received from her) the truth that is important for us to grasp today is that there is a world of difference between the principles and spirit of Old World individualism and that which we have developed in our own country.

We have, in fact, a special social system of our own. We have made it ourselves from materials brought in revolt from conditions in Europe. We have lived it; we constantly improve it; we have seldom tried to define it. It abhors autocracy and does not argue with it, but fights it. It is not capitalism, or socialism, or syndicalism, nor a cross breed of them. Like most Americans, I refuse to be damned by anybody's word-classification of it, such as "capitalism," "plutocracy," "proletariat" or "middle class," or any other, or to any kind of compartment that is based on the assumption of some group dominating somebody else.

The social force in which I am interested is far higher and far more precious a thing than all these. It springs from something infinitely more enduring; it springs from the one source of human progress—that each individual shall be given the chance and stimulation for development of the best with which he has been endowed in heart and mind; it is the sole source of progress; it is American individualism.

The rightfulness of our individualism can rest either on philosophic, political, economic, or spiritual grounds. It can rest on the ground of being the only safe avenue to further human progress.

PHILOSOPHIC GROUNDS

On the philosophic side we can agree at once that intelligence, character, courage, and the divine spark of the human soul are alone the property of individuals. These do not lie in agreements, in organizations, in institutions, in masses, or in groups. They abide alone in the individual mind and heart.

Production both of mind and hand rests upon impulses in each individual. These impulses are made of the varied forces of original instincts, motives, and acquired desires. Many of these are destructive and must be restrained through moral leadership and authority of the law and be eliminated finally by education. All are modified by a vast fund of experience and a vast plant and equipment of civilization which we pass on with increments to each succeeding generation.

The inherited instincts of self-preservation, acquisitiveness, fear, kindness, hate, curiosity, desire for self-expression, for power, for adulation, that we carry over from a thousand of generations must, for good or evil, be comprehended in a workable system embracing our accumulation of experiences and equipment. They may modify themselves with time—but in terms of generations. They differ in their urge upon different individuals. The dominant ones are selfish. But no civilization could be built or can endure solely upon the groundwork of unrestrained and unintelligent self-interest. The problem of the world is to restrain the destructive instincts while strengthening and enlarging those of altruistic character and constructive impulse—for thus we build for the future.

From the instincts of kindness, pity, fealty to family and race; the love of liberty; the mystical yearnings for spiritual things; the desire for fuller expression of the creative faculties; the impulses of service to community and nation, are moulded the ideals of our people. And the most potent force in society is its ideals. If one were to attempt to delimit the potency of instinct and ideals, it would be found that while instinct dominates in our preservation yet the great propelling force of progress is right ideals. It is true we do not realize the ideal; not even a single person personifies that realization. It is therefore not surprising that society, a collection of persons, a necessary maze of compromises, cannot realize it. But that it has ideals, that they revolve in a system that makes for steady advance of them is the first thing. Yet true as this is, the day has not arrived when any economic or social system will function and last if founded upon altruism alone.

With the growth of ideals through education, with the higher realization of freedom, of justice, of humanity, of service, the selfish impulses become less and less dominant, and if we ever reach the millennium, they will disappear in the aspirations and satisfactions of pure altruism. But for the next several generations we dare not abandon self-interest as a motive force to leadership and to production, lest we die.

The will-o'-the-wisp of all breeds of socialism is that they contemplate a motivation of human animals by altruism alone. It necessitates a bureaucracy of the entire population, in which, having obliterated the economic stimulation of each member, the fine gradations of character and ability are to be arranged in relative authority by ballot or more likely by a Tammany Hall or a Bolshevist party, or some other form of tyranny. The proof of the futility of these ideas as a stimulation to the development and activity of the individual does not lie alone in the ghastly failure of Russia, but it also lies in our own failure in attempts at nationalized industry.

Likewise the basic foundations of autocracy, whether it be class government or capitalism in the sense that a few men through unrestrained control of property determine the welfare of great numbers, is as far apart from the rightful expression of American individualism as the two poles. The will-o'-the-wisp of autocracy in any form is that it supposes that the good Lord endowed a special few with all the divine attributes. It contemplates one human animal dealing to the other human animals his just share of earth, of glory, and of immortality. The proof of the futility of these ideas in the development of the world does not lie alone in the grim failure of Germany, but it lies in the damage to our moral and social fabric from those who have sought economic domination in America, whether employer or employee.

We in America have had too much experience of life to fool ourselves into pretending that all men are equal in ability, in character, in intelligence, in ambition. That was part of the claptrap of the French Revolution. We have grown to understand that all we can hope to assure to the individual through government is liberty, justice, intellectual welfare, equality of opportunity, and stimulation to service.

It is in maintenance of a society fluid to these human qualities that our individualism departs from the individualism of Europe. There can be no rise for the individual through the frozen strata of classes, or of castes, and no stratification can take place in a mass livened by the free stir of its particles. This guarding of our individualism against stratification insists not only in preserving in the social solution an equal opportunity for the able and ambitious to rise from the bottom; it also insists that the sons of the successful shall not by any mere right of birth or favor continue to occupy their fathers' places of power against the rise of a new generation in process of coming up from the bottom. The pioneers of our American individualism had the good sense not to reward Washington and Jefferson and Hamilton with hereditary dukedoms and fixtures in landed estates, as Great Britain rewarded Marlborough and Nelson. Otherwise our American fields of opportunity would have been clogged with long generations inheriting their fathers' privileges without their fathers' capacity for service.

That our system has avoided the establishment and domination of class has a significant proof in the present Administration in Washington. Of the twelve men comprising the President, Vice-President, and Cabinet, nine have earned their own way in life without economic inheritance, and eight of them started with manual labor.

If we examine the impulses that carry us forward, none is so potent for progress as the yearning for individual self-expression, the desire for creation of something. Perhaps the greatest human happiness flows from personal achievement. Here lies the great urge of the constructive instinct of mankind. But it can only thrive in a society where the individual has liberty and stimulation to achievement. Nor does the community progress except through its participation in these multitudes of achievements.

Furthermore, the maintenance of productivity and the advancement of the things of the spirit depend upon the ever-renewed supply from the mass of those who can rise to leadership. Our social, economic, and intellectual progress is almost solely dependent upon the creative minds of those individuals with imaginative and administrative intelligence who create or who carry discoveries to widespread application. No race possesses more than a small percentage of these minds in a single generation. But little thought has ever been given to our racial dependency upon them. Nor that our progress is in so large a measure due to the fact that with our increased means of communication these rare individuals are today able to spread their influence over so enlarged a number of lesser capable minds as to have increased their potency a million-fold. In truth, the vastly greater productivity of the world with actually less physical labor is due to the wider spread of their influence through the discovery of these facilities. And they can arise solely through the selection that comes from the free-running mills of competition. They must be free to rise from the mass; they must be given the attraction of premiums to effort.

Leadership is a quality of the individual. It is the individual alone who can function in the world of intellect and in the field of leadership. If democracy is to secure its authorities in morals, religion, and statesmanship, it must stimulate leadership from its own mass. Human leadership cannot be replenished by selection like queen bees, by divine right or bureaucracies, but by the free rise of ability, character, and intelligence.

Even so, leadership cannot, no matter how brilliant, carry progress far ahead of the average of the mass of individual units. Progress of the nation is the sum of progress in its individuals. Acts and ideas that lead to progress are born out of the womb of the individual mind, not out of the mind of the crowd. The crowd only feels: it has no mind of its own which can plan. The crowd is credulous, it destroys, is consumes, it hates, and it dreams—but it never builds. It is one of the most profound and important of exact psychological truths that man in the mass does not think but only feels. The mob functions only in a world of emotion. The demagogue feeds on mob emotions and his leadership is the leadership of emotion, not the leadership of intellect and progress. Popular desires are no criteria to the real need; they can be determined only by deliberative consideration, by education, by constructive leadership.

SPIRITUAL PHASES

Our social and economic system cannot march toward better days unless it is inspired by things of the spirit. It is here that the higher purposes of individualism must find their sustenance. Men do not live bread alone. Nor is individualism merely a stimulus to production and the road to liberty; it alone admits the universal divine inspiration of every human soul. I may repeat that the divine spark does not lie in agreements, in organizations, in institutions, in masses or in groups. Spirituality with its faith, its hope, its charity, can be increased by each individual's own effort. And in proportion as each individual increases his own store of spirituality, in that proportion increases the idealism of democracy.

For centuries, the human race believed that divine inspiration rested in a few. The result was blind faith in religious hierarchies, the Divine Right of Kings. The world has been disillusioned of this belief that divinity rests in any special group or class whether it be through a creed, a tyranny of kings or of proletariat. Our individualism insists upon the divine in each human being. It rests upon the firm faith that the divine spark can be awakened in every heart. It was the refusal to compromise these things that led to the migration of those religious groups who so largely composed our forefathers. Our diversified religious faiths are the apotheosis of spiritual individualism.

The vast multiplication of voluntary organizations for altruistic purposes are themselves proof of the ferment of spirituality, service, and mutual responsibility. These associations for advancement of public welfare, improvement, morals, charity, public opinion, health, the clubs and societies for recreation and intellectual advancement, represent something moving at a far greater depth than "joining." They represent the widespread aspiration for mutual advancement, self-expression, and neighborly helpfulness. Moreover, today when we rehearse our own individual memories of success, we find that none gives us such comfort as memory of service given. Do we not refer to our veterans as service men? Do not our merchants and business men pride themselves in something of service given beyond the price of their goods? When we traverse the glorious deeds of our fathers, we today never enumerate those acts that were not rooted in the soil of service. Those whom we revere are those who triumphed in service, for from them comes the uplift of the human heart and the uplift of the human mind.

While there are forces in the growth of our individualism which must be curbed with vigilance, yet there are no less glorious spiritual forces growing within that promise for the future. There is developing in our people a new valuation of individuals and of groups and of nations. It is a rising vision of service. Indeed if I were to select the social force that above all others has advanced sharply during these past years of suffering, it is that of service—service to those with whom we come in contact, service to the nation, and service to the world itself. If we examine the great mystical forces of the past seven years we find this great spiritual force poured out by our people as never before in the history of the world—the ideal of service.

Just now we are weakened by the feeling of failure of immediate realization of the great ideas and hopes that arose through the exaltation of war. War by its very nature sets loose chaotic forces of which the resultants cannot be foretold or anticipated. The insensitiveness to the brutalities of physical violence, and all the spiritual dislocations of war, have left us, at the moment, poorer. The amount of serenity and content in the world is smaller.

The spiritual reaction after the war has been in part the fruit of some illusions during those five years. In the presence of unity of purpose and the mystic emotions of war, many men came to believe that salvation lay in mass and group action. They have seen the spiritual and material mobilization of nations, of classes, and groups, for sacrifice and service; they have conceived that real human progress can be achieved by working on "the psychology of the people"—by the "mass mind"; they yielded to leadership without reservation; they conceived that this leadership could continue without tyranny; they have forgotten that permanent spiritual progress lies with the individual.

ECONOMIC PHASES

That high and increasing standards of living and comfort should be the first of considerations in public mind and in government needs no apology. We have long since realized that the basis of an advancing civilization must be a high and growing standard of living for all the people, not for a single class; that education, food, clothing, housing, and the spreading use of what we so often term nonessentials, are the real fertilizers of the soil from which spring the finer flowers of life. The economic development of the past fifty years has lifted the general standard of comfort far beyond the dreams of our forefathers. The only road to further advance in the standard of living is by greater invention, greater elimination of waste, greater production and better distribution of commodities and services, for by increasing their ratio to our numbers and dividing them justly we each will have more of them.

The superlative value of individualism through its impulse to production, its stimulation to invention, has, so far as I know, never been denied. Criticism of it has lain in its wastes but more importantly in its failure of equitable sharing of the product. In our country these contentions are mainly over the division to each of his share of the comforts and luxuries, for none of us is either hungry or cold or without a place to lay his head—and we have much besides. In less than four decades we have added electric lights, plumbing, telephones, gramophones, automobiles, and what not in wide diffusion to our standards of living. Each in turn began as a luxury, each in turn has become so common-place that seventy or eighty percent of our people participate in them.

To all practical souls there is little use in quarreling over the share of each of us until we have something to divide. So long as we maintain our individual-ism we will have increasing quantities to share and we shall have time and leisure and taxes with which to fight out proper sharing of the "surplus." The income tax returns show that this surplus is a minor part of our total production after taxes are paid. Some of this "surplus" must be set aside for rewards to saving for stimulation of proper effort to skill, to leadership and invention—therefore the dispute is in reality over much less than the total of such "surplus." While there should be no minimizing of a certain fringe of injustices in sharing the results of production or in the wasteful use made by some of their share, yet there is vastly wider field for gains to all of us through cheapening the costs of production and distribution through the eliminating of their wastes, from increasing the volume of product by each and every one doing his utmost, than will ever come to us even if we can think out a method of abstract justice in sharing which did not stifle production of the total product.

It is a certainty we are confronted with a population in such numbers as can only exist by production attuned to a pitch in which the slightest reduction of the impulse to produce will at once create misery and want. If we throttle the fundamental impulses of man our production will decay. The world in this hour is witnessing the most overshadowing tragedy of ten centuries in the heart-breaking life-and-death struggle with starvation by a nation with a hundred and fifty millions of people. In Russia under the new tyranny a group, in pur-suit of social theories, have destroyed the primary self-interest impulse of the individual to production.

Although socialism in a nation-wide application has now proved itself with rivers of blood and inconceivable misery to be an economic and spiritual fallacy and has wrecked itself finally upon the rocks of destroyed production and moral degeneracy, I believe it to have been necessary for the world to have had this demonstration. Great theoretic and emotional ideas have arisen before in the world's history and have in more than mere material bankruptcy deluged the world with fearful losses of life. A purely philosophical view might be that in the long run humanity has to try every way, even precipices, in finding the road to betterment.

But those are utterly wrong who say that individualism has as its only end the acquisition and preservation of private property—the selfish snatching and hoarding of the common product. Our American individualism, indeed, is only in part an economic creed. It aims to provide opportunity for self-expression, not merely economically, but spiritually as well. Private property is not a fetich in America. The crushing of the liquor trade without a cent of compen-sation, with scarcely even a discussion of it, does not bear out the notion that we give property rights any headway over human rights. Our development of individualism shows an increasing tendency to regard right of property not as an object in itself, but in the light of a useful and necessary instrument in stimulation of initiative to the individual; not only stimulation to him that he may gain personal comfort, security in life, protection to his family, but also because individual accumulation and ownership is a basis of selection to leadership in administration of the tools of industry and commerce. It is where dominant private property is assembled in the hands of the groups who control the state that the individual begins to feel capital as an oppressor. Our American demand for equality of opportunity is a constant militant check upon capital becoming a thing to be feared. Out of fear we sometimes even go too far and stifle the reproductive use of capital by crushing the initiative that makes for its creation.

Some discussion of the legal limitations we have placed upon economic domination is given later on, but it is desirable to mention here certain potent forces in our economic life that are themselves providing their own correction to domination.

The domination by arbitrary individual ownership is disappearing because the works of today are steadily growing more and more beyond the resources of any one individual, and steadily taxation will reduce relatively excessive individual accumulations. The number of persons in partnership through division of ownership among many stockholders is steadily increasing—thus 100,000 to 200,000 partners in a single concern are not uncommon. The overwhelmingly largest portion of our mobile capital is that of our banks, insurance companies, building and loan associations, and the vast majority of all this is the aggregated small savings of our people. Thus large capital is steadily becoming more and more a mobilization of the savings of the small holder—the actual people themselves—and its administration becomes at once more sensitive to the moral opinions of the people in order to attract their support. The directors and managers of large concerns, themselves employees of these great groups of individual stockholders, or policy holders, reflect a spirit of community responsibility.

Large masses of capital can only find their market for service or production to great numbers of the same kind of people that they employ and they must therefore maintain confidence in their public responsibilities in order to retain their customers. In times when the products of manufacture were mostly luxuries to the average of the people, the condition of their employees was of no such interest to their customers as when they cater to employees in general. Of this latter, no greater proofs need exist than the efforts of many large concerns directly dependent upon public good will to restrain prices in scarcity— and the very general desire to yield a measure of service with the goods sold. Another phase of this same development in administration of capital is the growth of a sort of institutional sense in many large business enterprises. The encouragement of solidarity in all grades of their employees in the common service and common success, the sense of mutuality with the prosperity of the community are both vital developments in individualism.

There has been in the last thirty years an extraordinary growth of organizations for advancement of ideas in the community for mutual coöperation and economic objectives—the chambers of commerce, trade associations, labor unions, bankers, farmers, propaganda associations, and what not. These are indeed variable mixtures of altruism and self-interest. Nevertheless, in these groups the individual finds an opportunity for self-expression and participation in the moulding of ideas, a field for training and the stepping stones for leadership.

The number of leaders in local and national life whose opportunity to service and leadership came through these associations has become now of more importance than those through the direct lines of political and religious organization.

At times these groups come into sharp conflict and often enough charge each other with crimes against public interest. They do contain faults; if they develop into warring interests, if they dominate legislators and intimidate public officials, if they are to be a new setting of tyranny, then they will destroy the foundation of individualism. Our Government will then drift into the hands of timorous mediocrities dominated by groups until we shall become a syndicalist nation on a gigantic scale. On the other hand, each group is a realization of greater mutuality of interest, each contains some element of public service and each is a school of public responsibility. In the main, the same forces that permeate the nation at large eventually permeate these groups. The sense of service, a growing sense of responsibility, and the sense of constructive opposition to domination, constantly recall in them their responsibilities as well as their privileges. In the end, no group can dominate the nation and a few successes in imposing the will of any group is its sure death warrant.

Today business organization is moving strongly toward coöperation. There are in the coöperative great hopes that we can even gain in individuality, equality of opportunity, and an enlarged field for initiative, and at the same time reduce many of the great wastes of overreckless competition in production and distribution. Those who either congratulate themselves or those who fear that coöperation is an advance toward socialism need neither rejoice or worry. Coöperation in its current economic sense represents the initiative of self-interest blended with a sense of service, for nobody belongs to a cooperative who is not striving to sell his products or services for more or striving to buy from others for less or striving to make his income more secure. Their members are furnishing the capital for extension of their activities just as effectively as if they did it in corporate form and they are simply transferring the profit principle from joint return to individual return. Their only success lies where they eliminate waste either in production or distribution—and they can do neither if they destroy individual initiative. Indeed this phase of development of our individualism promises to become the dominant note of its 20th Century expansion. But it will thrive only in so far as it can construct leadership and a sense of service, and so long as it preserves the initiative and safeguards the individuality of its members.

The economic system which is the result of our individualism is not a frozen organism. It moves rapidly in its form of organization under the impulse of initiative of our citizens, of growing science, of large production, and of constantly cheapening distribution.

A great test of the soundness of a social system must be its ability to evolve within itself those orderly shifts in its administration that enable it to apply the new tools of social, economic, and intellectual progress, and to eliminate the malign forces that may grow in the application of these tools. When we were almost wholly an agricultural people our form of organization and administration, both in the governmental and economic fields, could be simple. With the enormous shift in growth to industry and commerce we have erected organisms that each generation has denounced as Frankensteins, yet the succeeding generation proves them to be controllable and useful. The growth of corporate organizations, of our banking systems, of our railways, of our electrical power, of our farm coöperatives, of our trade unions, of our trade associations, and of a hundred others indeed develops both beneficent and malign forces. The timid become frightened. But our basic social ideas march through the new things in the end. Our demagogues, of both radical and standpat breed, thrive on demands for the destruction of one or another of these organizations as the only solution for their defects, yet progress requires only a guardianship of the vital principles of our individualism with its safeguard of true equality of opportunity in them.

POLITICAL PHASES

It is not the primary purpose of this essay to discuss our political organization. Democracy is merely the mechanism which individualism invented as a device that would carry on the necessary political work of its social organization. Democracy arises out of individualism and prospers through it alone.

Without question, there exists, almost all over the world, unprecedented disquietude at the functioning of government itself. It is in part the dreamy social ferment of war emotion. It is in part the aftermath of a period when the Government was everything and the individual nothing, from which there is much stimulation to two schools of thought: one that all human ills can be cured by governmental regulation, and the other that all regulation is a sin.

During the war, the mobilization of every effort, the destruction of the normal demand and the normal avenues of distribution, required a vast excursion over the deadline of individualism in order that we might secure immediate results. Its continuation would have destroyed the initiative of our people and undermined all real progress. We are slowly getting back, but many still aspire to these supposed short cuts to the millennium.

Much of our discontent takes the form of resentment against the inequalities in the distribution of the sacrifies of war. Both silently and vocally there is complaint that while some died, others ran no risk, and yet others profited. For these complaints there is adequate justification. The facts are patent. However, no conceivable human intelligence would be able to manage the conduct of war so as to see that all sacrifices and burdens should be distributed equitably. War is destruction, and we should blame war for its injustices, not a social system whose object is construction. The submergence of the individual, however, in the struggle of the race could be but temporary—its continuance through the crushing of individual action and its inequities would, if for no other reason, destroy the foundations of our civilization.

Looked at as the umpire in our social system, our Government has maintained an equality before the law and a development of legal justice and an authority in restraint of evil instincts that support this social system and its ideals so far as the imperfections of developing human institutions permit. It has gone the greatest distance of any government toward maintaining an equality of franchise; an equality of entrance to public office, and government by the majority. It has succeeded far beyond all others in those safeguards of equality of opportunity through education, public information, and the open channels of free speech and free press. It is, however, much easier to chart the course of progress to government in dealing with the abstract problems of order, political liberty, and stimulation to intellectual and moral advancement than it is to chart its relations to the economic seas. These seas are new and only partly discovered or explored.

Our Government's greatest troubles and failures are in the economic field. Forty years ago the contact of the individual with the Government had its largest expression in the sheriff or policeman, and in debates over political equality. In those happy days the Government offered but small interference with the economic life of the citizen. But with the vast development of industry and the train of regulating functions of the national and municipal government that followed from it; with the recent vast increase in taxation due to the war; —the Government has become through its relations to economic life the most potent force for maintenance or destruction of our American individualism.

The entrance of the Government began strongly three decades ago, when our industrial organization began to move powerfully in the direction of con-solidation of enterprise. We found in the course of this development that equality of opportunity and its corollary, individual initiative, was being throttled by the concentration of control of industry and service, and thus an economic domination of groups builded over the nation. At this time, particu-larly, we were threatened with a form of autocracy of economic power. Our mass of regulation of public utilities and our legislation against restraint of trade is the monument to our intent to preserve an equality of opportunity. This regulation is itself proof that we have gone a long way toward the abandonment of the "capitalism" of Adam Smith.

Day by day we learn more as to the practical application of restrictions against economic and political domination. We sometimes lag behind in the correction of those forces that would override liberty, justice, and equality of opportunity, but the principle is so strong within us that domination of the few will not be tolerated. These restraints must keep pace with the growing complexity of our economic organization, but they need tuning to our social system if they would not take us into great dangers. As we build up our powers of production through the advancing application of science we create new forces with which men may dominate—railway, power, oil, and what not. They may produce temporary blockades upon equality of opportunity.

To curb the forces in business which would destroy equality of opportunity and yet to maintain the initiative and creative faculties of our people are the twin objects we must attain. To preserve the former we must regulate that type of activity that would dominate. To preserve the latter, the Government must keep out of production and distribution of commodities and services. This is the deadline between our system and socialism. Regulation to prevent domination and unfair practices, yet preserving rightful initiative, are in keeping with our social foundations. Nationalization of industry or business is their negation.

When we come to the practical problems of government in relation to these economic questions the test lies in two directions: Does this act safeguard an equality of opportunity? Does it maintain the initiative of our people? For in the first must lie the deadline against domination, and in the second the deadline in preservation of individualism against socialism. Excluding the temporary measures of the war, the period of regulation has now been long enough with us to begin to take stock of its effect upon our social system. It has been highly beneficial, but it has also developed weaknesses in the throttling of proper initiative that require some revision. We have already granted relief to labor organizations and to agriculture from some forms of regulation. There is, however, a large field of coöperative possibilities far outside agriculture that are needlessly hampered.

The most important of considerations in any attempt to pass judgment upon social systems is whether we maintain within them permanent and continuous motivation toward progress. These forces must be of two orders, one spiritual and the other economic.

We may discover the situation in our own social system either by an analysis of the forces that are today in motion or by noting the strides of progress over the century or over the last ten years. By a consideration of the forces that move us we can see whether our system shows signs of decay, whether its virility is maintained; and by the touchstone of time we can find out whether these forces have been powerful enough to overcome the malign influences that would lessen the well-being of our system.

If we should survey the fundamentals of our civilization from the point of view of its progress by the test of time, we can find much for satisfaction and assurance. It is unnecessary to recount the values of economic individualism in stimulation to invention; large constructive vision; intensity in production with decreased physical effort; our increased standards of living and comfort. It is of course easy to enumerate our great economic progress, but the progress of the social forces that will sustain economic progress is infinitely more important—for upon them depends the real future of our people. Education in its many phases has made much advance. The actual equipment, the character of instruction, the numbers reached, period of instruction—show improvement with every decade. Public opinion has become of steadily increasing potency and reliability in its reaction. The great strides in development of processes and equipment for production and distribution are being followed by increasing devotion to the human factors in their execution. Moral standards of business and commerce are improving; vicious city governments are less in number; invisible government has greatly diminished; public conscience is penetrating deeper and deeper; the rooting up of wrong grows more vigorous; the agencies for their exposure and remedy grow more numerous, and above all is the growing sense of service. Many people confuse the exposure of wrongs which were below the surface with degeneration; their very exposure is progress. Some accredit the exposures of failure in our government and business as evidence of standards of a lower order than in some other nations. A considerable experience leads me to the conviction that while we do wash our dirty linen in public most others never wash it.

It is easy to arraign any existing institution. Men can rightly be critical because things have happened that never ought to happen. That our social system contains faults no one disputes. One can recite the faulty results of our system at great length; the spirit of lawlessness; the uncertainty of employment in some callings; the deadening effect of certain repetitive processes of manufacture; the

12-hour day in a few industries; unequal voice in bargaining for wage in some employment; arrogant domination by some employers and some labor leaders; child labor in some states; inadequate instruction in some areas; unfair competition in some industries; some fortunes excessive far beyond the needs of stimulation to initiative; survivals of religious intolerance; political debauchery of some cities; weaknesses in our governmental structure. Most of these occur locally in certain regions and certain industries and must cause every thinking person to regret and to endeavor. But they are becoming steadily more local. That they are recognized and condemned is a long way on the road to progress.

One of the difficulties in social thought is to find the balance of perspective. A single crime does not mean a criminal community. It is easy to point out undernourished, overworked, uneducated children, children barred from the equality of opportunity that our ideals stand for. It is easy to point out the luxurious petted and spoiled children with favored opportunity in every community. But if we take the whole thirty-five millions of children of the United States, it would be a gross exaggeration to say that a million of them suffer from any of these injustices. This is indeed a million too many, but it is the thirty-four million that tests the system with the additional touchstone of whether there are forces in motivation which are insistently and carefully working for the amelioration of the one million. Its by-products of endowed loafers, or hoodlums, at respective ends of the economic scale, are indeed spectacular faults. Yet any analysis of the 105,000,000 of us would show that we harbor less than a million of either rich or impecunious loafers. If we measure our people by scales of other civilized peoples, we also find consolation. We have a distaste for the very expression of "class," but if we would use European scales of "classes" we would find that above their scale of "lower classes" we have in equivalent comfort, morality, understanding, and intelligence fully eighty percent of our native-born whites. No European state will lay claim to thirty percent of this order. Does this not mean that we have been gaining something?

I do not conceive that any man, or body of men, could ever be capable of drafting a plan that would solve these multiple difficulties in advance. Moreover, if we continue to advance we will find new difficulties and weaknesses as the by-product of progress—but to be overcome.

THE FUTURE

Individualism has been the primary force of American civilization for three centuries. It is our sort of individualism that has supplied the motivation of America's political, economic, and spiritual institutions in all these years. It has proved its ability to develop its institutions with the changing scene. Our very form of government is the product of the individualism of our people, the demand for an equal opportunity, for a fair chance.

The American pioneer is the epic expression of that individualism, and the pioneer spirit is the response to the challenge of opportunity, to the challenge of nature, to the challenge of life, to the call of the frontier. That spirit need never die for lack of something for it to achieve. There will always be a frontier to conquer or to hold as long as men think, plan, and dare. Our American individualism has received much of its character from our contacts with the forces of nature on a new continent. It evolved government without official emissaries to show the way; it plowed and sowed two score of great states; it built roads, bridges, railways, cities; it carried forward every attribute of high civilization over a continent. The days of the pioneer are not over. There are continents of human welfare of which we have penetrated only the coastal plain. The great continent of science is as yet explored only on its borders, and it is only the pioneer who will penetrate the frontier in the quest for new worlds to conquer. The very genius of our institutions has been given to them by the pioneer spirit. Our individualism is rooted in our very nature. It is based on conviction born of experience. Equal opportunity, the demand for a fair chance, became the formula of American individualism because it is the method of American achievement.

After the absorption of the great plains of the West came the era of industrial development with the new complex of forces that it has brought us. Now haltingly, but with more surety and precision than ever before and with a more conscious understanding of our mission, we are finding solution of these problems arising from new conditions, for the forces of our social system can compass and comprise these.

Our individualism is no middle ground between autocracy—whether of birth, economic or class origin—and socialism. Socialism of different varieties may have something to recommend it as an intellectual stop-look-and-listen sign, more especially for Old World societies. But it contains only destruction to the forces that make progress in our social system. Nor does salvation come by any device for concentration of power, whether political or economic, for both are equally reversions to Old World autocracy in new garments.

Salvation will not come to us out of the wreckage of individualism. What we need today is steady devotion to a better, brighter, broader individualism— an individualism that carries increasing responsibility and service to our fellows. Our need is not for a way out but for a way forward. We found our way out three centuries ago when our forefathers left Europe for these shores, to set up here a commonwealth conceived in liberty and dedicated to the development of individuality.

There are malign social forces other than our failures that would destroy our progress. There are the equal dangers both of reaction and radicalism. The perpetual howl of radicalism is that it is the sole voice of liberalism—that devotion to social progress is its field alone. These men would assume that all reform and human advance must come through government. They have forgotten that progress must come from the steady lift of the individual and that the measure of national idealism and progress is the quality of idealism in the individual. The most trying support of radicalism comes from the timid or dishonest minds that shrink from facing the result of radicalism itself but are devoted to defense of radicalism as proof of a liberal mind. Most theorists who denounce our individualism as a social basis seem to have a passion for ignorance of its constructive ideals.

An even greater danger is the destructive criticism of minds too weak or too partisan to harbor constructive ideas. For such, criticism is based upon the distortion of perspective or cunning misrepresentation. There is never danger from the radical himself until the structure and confidence of society has been undermined by the enthronement of destructive criticism. Destructive criticism can certainly lead to revolution unless there are those willing to withstand the malice that flows in return from refutation. It has been well said that revolution is no summer thunderstorm clearing the atmosphere. In modern society it is a tornado leaving in its path the destroyed homes of millions with their dead women and children.

There are also those who insist that the future must be a repetition of the past; that ideas are dangerous, that ideals are freaks.

To find that fine balance which links the future with the past, whose vision is of men and not of tools, that possesses the courage to construct rather than to criticize—this is our need. There is no oratory so easy, no writing so trenchant and vivid as the phrase-making of criticism and malice—there is none so difficult as inspiration to construction.

We cannot ever afford to rest at ease in the comfortable assumption that right ideas always prevail by some virtue of their own. In the long run they do. But there can be and there have been periods of centuries when the world slumped back toward darkness merely because great masses of men became impregnated with wrong ideas and wrong social philosophies. The declines of civilization have been born of wrong ideas. Most of the wars of the world, including the recent one, have been fought by the advocates of contrasting ideas of social philosophy.

The primary safeguard of American individualism is an understanding of it; of faith that it is the most precious possession of American civilization, and a willingness courageously to test every process of national life upon the touchstone of this basic social premise. Development of the human institutions and of science and of industry have been long chains of trial and error. Our public relations to them and to other phases of our national life can be advanced in no other way than by a willingness to experiment in the remedy of our social faults. The failures and unsolved problems of economic and social life can be corrected; they can be solved within our social theme and under no other system. The solution is a matter of will to find solution; of a sense of duty as well as of a sense of right and citizenship. No one who buys "bootleg" whiskey can complain of gunmen and hoodlumism.

Humanity has a long road to perfection, but we of America can make sure progress if we will preserve our individualism, if we will preserve and stimulate the initiative of our people, if we will build up our insistence and safeguards to equality of opportunity, if we will glorify service as a part of our national character. Progress will march if we hold an abiding faith in the intelligence, the initiative, the character, the courage, and the divine touch in the individual. We can safeguard these ends if we give to each individual that opportunity for which the spirit of America stands. We can make a social system as perfect as our generation merits and one that will be received in gratitude by our children.

~~~~~7

DAVID BURNER

The Brown Derby Campaign

Not so long ago American history held forth many men of an exalted and heroic cast. But a more critical reading of the nation's past has uncovered noteworthy defects in even its greatest leaders. Andrew Jackson, once portrayed as a forerunner of Franklin Roosevelt, is now seen not so much as a great democrat but as a representative of new exploitive economic groups eager to share in the spoils of American life. The reputation of Abraham Lincoln, a name traditionally invoked by campaign orators of both parties, has been tarnished by the exhumation of his conservative views on the Negro. Franklin Roosevelt himself conserved much more of the capitalist order than he remade. All of these men continue to deserve much admiration and respect, but except in elementary school they are no longer heroes.

Similarly, Al Smith, so this writer believes, is in need of reappraisal. To remember him as the urban, Roman Catholic, immigrant-stock martyr to the prejudices of the electorate that rejected him as President in 1928 is to ignore his own conduct of his campaign. Smith's eastern, urban provincialism rivaled the hinterland provincialism that cast its vote against him; what remarks he did address to smalltown and rural America were close to disdainful. After the election he dismissed the opposition to him as bigotry, but later in his life he virtually acknowledged that he had not gone far enough toward understanding the frustrations and pride of the hinterland.

In his early years in the New York State Assembly Smith was merely the servant of Tammany Hall, which often opposed reform; and he later opposed the New Deal. But his progressive commitment had been effective, and much of it independent of Tammany. He earned the praise liberals have given him for his social progressivism: as leader of the Assembly he persuaded Charles Murphy's Tammany to support educational and factory reform; as governor he won the passage of a moderate amount of social welfare legislation.

Reprinted by permission of the New York State Historical Association, Cooperstown, N.Y.

To call Smith to task for 1928 is to say no more than that he was a prisoner of his own time and place. The American majority of the twenties was not prepared for a man who bore the ethnic stamp Smith carried so proudly, and his urban immigrant community had not yet learned enough of the art of national politics— or lost enough of its own identity—to succeed. Possibly it is asking too much to expect Al Smith to have overlooked the bigots and contended with his more rational Protestant critics. But he did not; and his failure is as much the story of 1928 as is the prejudice of his most inflamed opponents.

A President must, without compromising his integrity of origin and manner, show that he is broadly representative of the nation over which he has been placed, and toward which he stands in so peculiarly symbolic a relationship. The task of squaring a social, ethnic, or regional with a national identity need not be an overwhelming one: Harry Truman and John Kennedy, both deeply stamped by their divergent breedings and places of origin, succeeded admirably. But some presidential candidates never transcend the political image that served them in local politics. To this category belongs Governor Alfred E. Smith of New York.

In studying the 1928 campaign, analysts have quite properly concentrated their attention upon the scurrilous tactics of Protestant bigots; almost by default, the New Yorker has emerged as a liberal martyr sacrificed to religious prejudice and prohibitionist morality. But this view of Al Smith is more myth than fact. It is now commonly recognized that any study of the 1928 campaign must begin upon the assumption that whatever the more flamboyant issues, economic prosperity probably predestined the success of the party in power. As Richard Hofstadter has observed: "There was not a Democrat alive, Protestant or Catholic, who could have beaten Hoover in 1928." More serious, however, has been the reluctance to examine the strategy within the Smith camp—to gauge the response on the part of the candidate and his lieutenants to the charge that his background ill fitted him to represent the whole American people, rural as well as urban, Protestant as well as Roman Catholic. Such an examination will reveal that Al Smith was less than successful, and at moments less than tactful, in presenting his case to that portion of American society which lay outside his immediate cultural experience.

The failure of Smith to present himself as a national candidate—reflected in his choice of a brown derby as a campaign symbol—was also a mark of his party's failure to unify itself. In 1928 the Democrats thrust upon the whole nation the same conflict that had caused them internal chaos four years earlier at their national convention in New York City. But no longer was Smith's political opposition solely a fundamentalist rural America under the leadership of William Jennings Bryan and his protégé William Gibbs McAdoo. While this rural element undoubtedly contributed to his defeat, Smith now faced in Herbert Hoover a powerful antagonist who could command the respect of politically sophisticated Americans having little in common with the narrow ruralists of 1924. And the whole controversy surrounding Smith's candidacy has since obscured the solid appeal of his opponent almost as much as it has romanticized the New Yorker himself.

To gain a deeper understanding of the campaign, we may first call to mind the background of the 1928 Democratic nominee: his big-city upbringing, and his political rise; and then examine the campaign itself, in order to discover the kind of presidential image the Smith forces created for their candidate, and the nature of their reply to the assaults of Protestantism, nativism, and rural politicians.

Smith's birthplace, now in the shadow of Brooklyn Bridge, stood in sharp contrast to President Coolidge's homestead in Vermont or Hoover's Quaker village in Iowa. Nor were both of Smith's parents American-born; his father was a native of Manhattan, but his mother's birthplace, according to Smith himself, was in West Meath County, Ireland. Smith's boyhood was shaped to a pattern unprecedented among major presidential candidates. In place of the swimming hole, he had the East River; he attended not the one-room schoolhouse of rural nostalgia but the city's Roman Catholic parochial schools. He married Katie Dunn of the lower East Side, who bore him five children, all of whom attended the same church schools. And Smith's later career as governor in upstate New York never took him far from the mode of life he knew in the city.

Smith was born in 1873; his formal education was ended before he completed the ninth grade when his father died leaving young Al, age fifteen, to help support the family. Graduating, as he later would say, from the Fulton Street Fish Market, where he was a bookkeeper in a commission house, Smith entered ward politics at an age when boys from families of higher income entered college. In 1902 he was elected to the New York State Assembly and served there with increasing prominence until 1915. After distinguishing himself in that year's state constitutional convention, he became Sheriff of New York County and then President of the Board of Aldermen of New York City. Smith went on to win the governorship of New York in 1918. He lost in 1920, but won again in 1922, 1924, and 1926; altogether he served four terms, a record unequalled since the administration of George Clinton. Smith's career exclusively in New York politics led William Allen White to stigmatize him as a "town-lot Sir Galahad who never fared afield." H. L. Mencken, who voted for and frequently defended him, observed that Smith's world "begins at Coney Island and ends at Buffalo." Mencken wrote of Smith still more caustically: "Not only is he uninterested in the great problems facing the nation, but he has never heard of them."

The governor had gotten his political start as the favorite of Charles Murphy of Tammany Hall. But though at first he was of necessity obedient to the political bosses of New York City—his record came under attack from the Citizens' Union of Manhattan—Smith later overshadowed them and developed his own independent Democratic organization. In affairs at Albany Smith depended not primarily on Murphy, but on advisers such as Mrs. Belle Moskowitz and Judge Joseph Proskauer. Mrs. Moskowitz in particular encouraged the governor to promote welfare legislation that actually helped to diminish the influence of Tammany Hall, since it made voters less dependent on local politicians for favors. The governor also gained considerable power within the increasingly important Democratic machines in Brooklyn and the Bronx. After Murphy's death in 1924, Smith's following was powerful enough to name as his successor George W. Olvany. Yet this victory is itself evidence of Smith's ambivalent relationship toward Tammany Bossism; while sufficiently strong and autonomous to be able to dictate terms to the organization, the Smith forces nevertheless found it necessary to support, in Olvany, a man whose ethics seem to have been in the Tammany vein. Smith's own integrity is certain, but he could never shake the stigma of Tammany; it remained a nettle to his rural and small-town opponents. Smith's association with the Wigwam put the Democrats in a defensive position in 1928, much as that in which the Teapot Dome oil scandals had earlier placed the Republicans.

Smith drank in defiance of prohibition and won for himself the epithet "Alcohol Al." In the summer of 1923 he was presented with a bill repealing the state's prohibition-enforcement law. Franklin Roosevelt advised a veto; instead, the governor—in conformity to his own conscience as well as to the demands of Charles Murphy—signed the bill and issued a declaration that wine and beer should be legalized. When Smith stepped beyond state politics, his stand against prohibition became a major political liability, especially in the South and West. That same year Smith made an off-the-record remark to some newspapermen, which was widely quoted as: "Wouldn't you like to have your foot on the rail and blow the foam off some suds?" Early in 1924, in a letter to Franklin Roosevelt, a nervous Louis Howe remarked: "I took lunch today with some of the Albany boys and they told me in some ways at least Smith is much drier than he used to be. How long he has sworn off for this time, God knows. Let us trust until after the national convention." Even at the Executive Mansion in Albany, Edward Flynn recalled, "a cocktail or highball, in fact, was always available."

The question of Smith's own conduct during prohibition days was to persist. "Does 'Al' drink and does he drink too much?" asked a correspondent of Oswald Garrison Villard, editor of *The Nation,* in 1927. "I am reliably informed," wrote Villard in reply, "that he drinks every day, and the number of his cocktails and highballs is variously estimated at from four to eight." The liberal editor was to regret the remark, for it was widely quoted, but later he assured Lillian Wald: "I am certain that it is true, or was true before the campaign began." A friend of William Allen White insisted: "I am told that he drinks regularly. If this is true, how does he get his liquor? He must be either violating the law or knowing that someone else does. If this is true he is not a fit man to be either Governor or President."

The behavior of Smith, in face of national prohibition, during these years prior to 1928 provides one of the more startling instances of an urban provincialism or perhaps a mere personal stubbornness on his part. What was at issue here, of course, was not Smith's legitimate opposition to the prohibition laws but the manner of his opposition. Certainly it would be no great crime for a private citizen to engage in genial defiance of a law that appeared both senseless and obtrusive; Smith regarded the prohibitionist cause, moreover, as a covert attack on the immigrant and his culture, and he thought it hypocritical to camouflage his personal life. But Smith was no private citizen; he was occupant of one important position of public trust and aspirant to another, in which he would become the highest of the sworn defenders of the Constitution, the representative of the whole people. One of the most recent additions to the fundamental national law embodied a principle close to the heart of small-town American Protestantism; and the blatant refusal of Smith to submit to prohibition could be interpreted as a cocky defiance, almost a contempt for that considerable part of the nation that made the law. Having scorned one of our enactments, which of our remaining hopes will this man choose to dash if he becomes our President and representative? So might the query have come from the America that lay west of the Alleghenies and south of Staten Island.

The question of Smith's religion, too, was far from non-existent long before the presidential campaign of 1928. Smith embraced his church, simply and deeply. He took great pride in outward tokens of his faith; in the Executive Mansion in Albany, for instance, he displayed a portrait of Pope Pius XI autographed in 1924. And Katie Smith exhibited on the religious issue a similar openness. In 1925 Louis Howe was fidgeting over the loquacity of the governor's wife, who had just returned from a European trip that included a papal audience. "Mrs. Smith is back from Europe," Howe wrote to Roosevelt:

> and complains to your "Missus" that there were too many ruins in Rome. She is talking too much for Al's good, describing with much gusto and detail their special audience with the Pope and how he referred to Al as his son and the great knowledge he showed in the political campaign. One of her stories is particularly delicious. She says that the Pope turned to McCooey [John H. McCooey, Brooklyn Democratic leader], who was with them and said, "I know how hard you have worked for my beloved son, Governor Smith, but next time you must work even harder." She also is announcing that she brought back a photograph of the Pope personally inscribed "To my beloved son, Alfred E. Smith."

During the 1928 campaign, snobbery was unleashed against Mrs. Smith. When complimented by an ambassador's wife on her gown, for example, Mrs. Smith would supposedly reply: "You said a mouthful."

Before 1928, Smith had also become innocently involved in a number of incidents that anti-Catholics could use against him. In 1915 he had offered a highly controversial amendment to the Commissioner of Education at the New York State Constitutional Convention. The measure proposed to strike out of the constitution a clause prohibiting the state from making direct appropriations to denominational schools. Actually, Smith had not pressed his resolution and later explained that he had introduced it to counter another amendment providing for the taxation of church property. Smith's record as governor might have seemed invulnerable to attacks on religious grounds. But his opponents pointed out that New York City, with Smith's approval, paid as much as $4 million in one year to parochial schools. Though a long-standing practice, it rebounded, of course, against Smith. Joe Tumulty warned the governor in 1927: "You must flatly, once and for all, dispose of the notion that the Pope will be the Colonel House of your administration"; and before the 1928 presidential race got under way, Smith settled to his own satisfaction the "problem" of his religion. He did so by taking advantage of an invitation offered him by Ellery Sedgwick, editor of the *Atlantic Monthly* and a supporter of McAdoo in 1924. Sedgwick had persuaded Smith to clear the air by replying to an Episcopal lawyer, Charles Marshall, who in an article published in Sedgwick's magazine had alleged a conflict between the American Constitution and the "Two Powers" dogma of the Roman Church, and had assembled evidence to try to show that American Catholics would have at best a divided allegiance between church and state. The draft of Smith's reply was written by Judge Joseph Proskauer with the approval of two priests, Francis P. Duffy and Francis J. Spellman; yet the sentiments were patently Smith's own. If religious questions arose, he said, he would follow the dictates of his own conscience. The governor also pointed to his own career as a pragmatic testament that theological controversies did not bind the judgment of Catholic statesmen. In fact, as governor of New York he had approved a bill providing for an extension of the grounds for divorce that the Catholic Church specifically opposed; and he objected emphatically to most forms of public censorship. "I believe," he wrote, "in the absolute separation of church and state. . . ." But other events were to show that ammunition far more powerful than a single magazine article would be necessary in the face of the religious issue. Later, Michael Williams, editor of *Commonweal,* remarked on Charles Marshall's letter to Smith and his subsequent book, *The Roman Catholic Church in the Modern State* (New York, 1928): "We called him a variety of names. We accused him of misquotation and bad faith. But the point is we did not reply to his book."

Those voters who were prepared to look beyond Smith's religion and his stand on prohibition to his political and economic philosophy could ascertain that though he had won a well-deserved campaign reputation as a progressive, he was in a deeper and more lasting sense a conservative. Here he contrasted with Bryan, who remained an economic radical to the end. In 1924 Smith promised, if elected President, to reassert states' rights and to halt the expansion of federal taxes, laws, and commissions; "We must stop the dangerous over-centralization of Federal power," he wrote during Coolidge's first year in the White House. As presidential aspirant in 1928, as well as in 1924, Smith chose to advertise himself as a Jeffersonian. He instructed the Houston convention to build a platform on "unflinching application of Jeffersonian principles to the problems of the day." Rexford Tugwell admonished the candidate in the *New Republic:* "Cannot Governor Smith understand that—ridiculous as it sounds —the stronghold of Jeffersonianism has shifted from the South to the Northeast and that its latter day prophet is Coolidge?" The testimony of friends and critics alike suggests that Smith's later opposition to New Deal reform may not have been the about-face that is so often portrayed. Walter Lippmann in 1925 called Smith "the most powerful conservative in urban America." His remark is echoed and expanded upon in dozens of commentaries, including ones by Henry F. Pringle, Robert Moses, Edward Flynn, Mrs. Franklin D. Roosevelt, John Gunther, Bernard Bellush, Richard Neuberger, and George Mowry.

Set against all this, to be sure, is a remarkably progressive streak in Smith's thinking. His gubernatorial administration made some major legislative and executive advances in education and factory labor; a "mildly humanitarian" program, the historian George Mowry calls it, but for its own day a very impressive program indeed. And he completely reorganized the state government, following to a certain extent the example of Governor Frank Lowden of Illinois. The reformist and the conservative tendencies in Smith are in any case quite compatible; it is possible to find their common source in his upbringing and early manhood. The city streets had schooled him in the facts of economic hardship and the plight of the ghetto; they had also set him forth upon a self-made career—and the economic individualism of the self-made is a matter of common record.

As a self-made man Smith had experienced in his own person some of the privations of the urban poor; and this was the grounds of a progressivism that is less moral and evangelistic than practical, addressed to specifics. And because he was a politician, and as long as he remained active in politics on the city and state level, Smith had to take major account of the problems of his constituents, and could not have taken on the hard, arrogant indifference of some of the self-made who go into business; as a politician, moreover, he had the kind of constant contact with the urban poor, at least at second or third hand, that would have kept his sympathies genuinely alive, his memories fresh. And since he was not a businessman, he did not need to undergo those painful encounters with labor unions or socially inspired taxation that can make an entrepreneur, risen from the streets or the backwater farm, turn his back upon those who must continue to endure the hardships he has overcome. The complexity and technical nature of urban problems and the sophisticated structure of the urban political machines also conduce to a pragmatic reform rather than one of an ideological origin. The machine in particular may in its demand for loyalty offset the more humane impulses of its workers and protégés—even if one of its members gets as far up as a legislative seat, he will not find it to his advantage to support clean-government legislation, or to oppose business interests allied to a Tammany.

But Smith's background may have had its even deeper effect. He grew up in the atmosphere of moral conservatism, of endangered values carefully preserved, so vividly portrayed by Oscar Handlin in *The Uprooted;* and his traditionalist attitude toward some issues of social and moral conduct is striking. For all his apparent hostility to the blue-law temperament, he signed the so-called Padlock Bill of 1927, a Draconic measure that would close a theater for one year if any play it presented should be declared indecent by the courts. This came about after he mistakenly attended a broadway play depicting Lesbianism. He reacted to Edward Bourdet's classic by asking the city police to take action against theaters not only when formal complaints were made, but also to anticipate what productions might be violating the law. His devotion to civil liberties had its limits. The principles he upheld in denouncing the Red-baiting Lusk Committee he abandoned in signing a bill that almost outlawed the Ku Klux Klan. He also refused to speak against a clean literature bill, supported by the Catholic Church, which would place the definition of obscenity in the hands of a jury and declare irrelevant the testimony of literary critics. He was notably hostile to woman suffrage; he relied heavily on the political advice of a woman, it is true, but one who believed in the mental inferiority of her sex. A conservatism of this sort, nurtured within the ordered community, would leave its mark upon economic as well as moral considerations; concretely sensitive to the special economic needs of the community, it would at the same time react instinctively whenever the pace of reform seemed to threaten the traditions and the orthodoxies.

In sum, the man the Democrats nominated in 1928 possessed a peculiar mixture of characteristics, some as yet new to national politics, and some as old as American statesmanship; a breeding and a religion foreign to Jackson, Lincoln, and Theodore Roosevelt; a conservatism cut in part to a conventional American mold.

As the Democratic Convention got under way at Houston in June of 1928, Smith had little competition. Edwin T. Meredith of Iowa had inherited some of McAdoo's strength but died ten days before the balloting commenced; the wet Maryland Governor Albert Ritchie was impeded by the relative obscurity of his name. Cordell Hull of Tennessee and Senator Walter F. George of Georgia were also mentioned as possible nominees. But Senator Thomas J. Walsh, a dry Catholic from Montana, was the only figure other than Smith who might have been a formidable candidate. Democrats remembered Walsh as the investigator of Teapot Dome and as chairman of the 1924 convention. Because he was a dry, Walsh found himself acceptable as a candidate to the Methodist Board of Temperance, Prohibition, and Public Morals. His supporters urged that he was uniquely qualified to be at once the candidate of the dry, Protestant, rural South and the wet, Catholic, urban North. Unlike Smith, however, Walsh had no large personal following who would support him in the election, and after suffering a severe defeat in the California primary he withdrew weeks before the convention opened. Walsh believed that southerners could have escaped the charge of religious bigotry had they supported him against Smith. But in spite of help from McAdoo, Walsh gained negligible southern support. The McAdoo group made a last-ditch effort to stop Smith by supporting Senator James A. Reed of Missouri, who had recently visited twenty-eight states and entered several primaries without winning any. Reed was a former wet, and it was disastrous for the McAdoo element to pin its hopes on him.

Smith and his supporters made a conscious effort at the 1928 Democratic Convention to eradicate the poor impression that lingered in the minds of those who had attended the 1924 conclave in New York. At that time, James J. Hoey, a Smith man, had kept the galleries full of unruly crowds who infuriated the McAdoo and Bryan supporters, and a host of Catholic clergy had by their presence antagonized the rural delegates. After his defeat in the New York convention, Smith had not bothered to hide his resentment. In an address to the convention, he had told the skeptical delegates that New York was the greatest city in the world; the speech had a self-congratulatory and arrogant tone. But in 1928 the Smith contingent had mellowed and matured its tactics. Two upstate Democrats, George R. Van Namee, State Democratic Chairman, and Franklin Delano Roosevelt, led the floor fight for the governor, and the more urban politicians stayed sober and respectable. Senator Thomas J. Walsh remarked that "there was no finer looking, better dressed, more polite, less demonstrative delegation in the convention than the delegates sent by Tammany Hall." Some New Yorkers carried books of poetry with them, others tomes written in a foreign language. In the selection of the New York delegates, preference had been given to those born in the South. Heeding the advice of Joe Tumulty to "let the demands for your election come from elsewhere in America," Smith made certain that speeches seconding his nomination be representative of all regions. In addition, he had given up his fight for repeal of the two-thirds rule; repeal would have denied the South a veto that its politicians had decided not to use on Smith. Finally, the governor assured the delegates that the lengthy deliberations of the 1924 convention would not recur, and promised to withdraw if as many as ten ballots had to be taken.

At the convention "things went off like clockwork," remarked Franklin Roosevelt. The proceedings that opened on June 26 closed on June 29, and except for a fist fight among the Mississippi delegates and another skirmish over the prohibition plank, the Democrats behaved like an assembly of Republicans. Roosevelt, who one day would bring to the party the surface harmony that Smith had not achieved, nominated the governor as "one who has the will to win —who not only deserves success but commands it. Victory is his habit—the happy warrior, Alfred E. Smith." Although street-corner evangelists predicted that God would intervene to avert the catastrophe, and a local Baptist church held all-day and all-night fundamentalist prayer meetings, it was to no avail; the governor of New York was nominated when Ohio switched its vote at the end of the first ballot. The delegates refused to name him by acclamation, but it was an impressive victory, astounding in contrast to the previous convention. Smith was joined on the ticket by Senator Joseph T. Robinson, an Arkansas dry. A southern seminary head described the pairing of Smith and Robinson as an attempt to carry fire and water in the same bucket. Robinson—who earlier had been reported "unalterably opposed" to Smith's candidacy—was the first southerner, aside from Woodrow Wilson, to have a place on the national ticket since the Civil War.

A fortnight before Smith won the Democratic nomination, Herbert Hoover was awarded that of the Republican party. A great success in far-flung engineering projects, Hoover had gone on to acquire an even wider reputation as a result of European relief work. And in bringing to several high federal posts, during and after the Great War, a vision and an administrative skill acquired in big business, he won solid acclaim as a progressive. Beginning in 1921 Hoover served as Secretary of Commerce, strengthening his department so that its many functions visibly served the business community. On the important issue of prohibition, his background was that of a teetotaler, although in early June 1918, he had urged Wilson to veto the wartime prohibition act. On the religious question, Hoover occupied unassailable ground. "By blood and conviction," the Quaker candidate could say in 1928, "I stand for religious tolerance both in act and spirit." He spoke during the campaign neither of Smith's religion nor his affiliation with Tammany. And while the jovial Smith permitted countless photographs of himself with a cigar in one hand and his brown derby in the other, the meticulous Republican candidate refused even to allow pictures to be taken while he smoked a pipe. By any measure, Hoover's candidacy seemed ideal for the Republicans.

In his speeches during the 1928 campaign, Hoover gave body to the promise of his wartime career. Far more than Smith, the Republican candidate looked forward to a material fulfillment for America: to the day, when, in the words of his acceptance address, "poverty will be banished from this nation." Hoover continued: "There is no guarantee against poverty equal to a job for every man. That is the primary purpose of the economic policies we advocate." In the same speech, delivered at his alma mater, Stanford University, Hoover called for a shorter workday and greater purchasing power for labor, for ending the abuse of the injunction, and for collective bargaining; more public works, greater educational opportunity publically financed, and the spending of "hundreds of millions" of dollars for farm relief. A week later he declared against the national-origins principle of the immigration law, complaining of its favoritism toward Great Britain and Ireland, and still later he called for a "humanizing" of the law. While endorsing a limited number of reforms, Smith in his acceptance speech complained of the proliferation of government agencies and their rising costs; insisted that "Government should interfere with as little as possible with business" and at the same time noted that a few corporations were making outrageous profits; advocated putting the tariff on "a strictly business basis"; and called for "fearless application of Jeffersonian principles." Neither candidate sought any general revision of taxes.

Only on the matter of public power did Smith appear more progressive than Hoover. But as Norman Thomas, the Socialist candidate, put it: "He [Smith] accepts Hoover's general philosophy and reduces the battle between them to the comparatively insignificant question of power at Muscle Shoals and Boulder Dam." Elsewhere, Thomas criticized Smith for not having carried out his earlier proposals for regulating utilities. Hoover, on the other hand, tried to stand by his commitment not to let the government compete with private enterprise, but later in the campaign he did agree to public development of Muscle Shoals. And he had been a most active supporter of the proposed St. Lawrence Seaway, Boulder Dam, and the deepening of the Mississippi River. Smith's own willingness as governor to permit utility companies to contract for the transmission of power further narrowed the divergence between the two candidates on the question, yet Hoover condemned Smith's position as one of state socialism.

On the issue of farm relief, Smith endorsed the "principle" of McNary-Haugen but not the equalization fee, and he was unspecific about possible remedies. During the campaign, Hoover dismissed the whole plan as unpromising—as indeed it was; it had earlier been rejected in the Republican Convention by a vote of 807 to 277. Instead, he proposed a special session of Congress —if the one ending in December 1928, should offer no solution—to set up a Federal Farm Loan Board, which would provide initial funds for a farmer-owned stabilization agency to offset "seasonal" and "periodic" surpluses. Speaking of the farm situation as the "most urgent economic problem in our nation today," Hoover hoped for the achievement of better than pre-war standards of agricultural prosperity, and his acceptance speech impressed Governor Frank Lowden of Illinois, although he still opposed Hoover on the farm issue. Understandably, farm support was divided between the two candidates.

Hoover was more definite and more positive in his formulation of economic policy; he was, indeed, the more explicitly progressive candidate—enough so that Coolidge's Secretary of the Treasury Andrew Mellon fiercely opposed his presidential candidacy. Of sixty-six local workers who responded to a pro-

Smith campaign letter from Lillian Wald, forty-five declared for Hoover. Add to his progressivism a personal identity with the business community, a magnificently successful and splendidly humanitarian career, both public and private, and a manner and background appealing alike to urban and provincial voters; the Republican candidate would have presented an awesome challenge to any democratic opponent.

The conservative—or, at most, thinly progressive—cast of the Democratic campaign was reflected in its programs and personnel. The platform adopted at Houston was significant in its omissions and could be read as a passive endorsement of the status quo. A low tariff, one clearly traditional bulwark of the Democratic party, went unchampioned in a campaign financed by industrialists protected by Republican high tariffs. Reference to the League of Nations and the World Court was also omitted, while regard was paid to the isolationist sentiment of "freedom from entangling alliances." Newton Baker remarked of the platform that McKinley could have run on the tariff plank and Lodge on the one dealing with international relations. The convention gave only vague endorsement to the McNary-Haugen agricultural plan. Finally, the platform stressed economy, protection of states' rights, and "businesslike methods in Government."

The governor's conservative strain, as well as his stubbornness, also revealed itself in his choice of John J. Raskob as National Chairman of the Democratic party. Raskob, in the manner of a Horatio Alger hero, had been born poor and had risen to the top as a secretary to Pierre S. DuPont; and this background appealed to Smith. In 1919 Raskob had acquired prominence as a business delegate at President Wilson's National Industrial Conference in Washington, where the position of the business representatives for the open shop and against labor's unimpeded right to organize and to bargain collectively brought the meeting to a halt. By 1928 Raskob was vice president of E. I. DuPont de Nemours and chairman of the finance committee of General Motors. He also served as a director of the Bankers Trust, American Surety, and County Trust companies. In the then current *Who's Who* he accurately listed himself as a capitalist; William Leuchtenburg describes him as an "arch reactionary."

Raskob, like Smith, was a devout Catholic and an ardent wet. He had contributed more than a million dollars to the church, and in recognition of loyalty Pope Pius XI made him a Knight of the Order of Saint Gregory the Great. Raskob saw the Pope in 1927 and again in 1928 when the industrialist received a special benediction and was made a private chamberlain in the papal household. George Van Namee, who had served in the complementary position of a preconvention manager, was also a Catholic, as were a number of state chairmen, like that of Iowa. As for prohibition, Raskob pronounced it a "damnable affliction," and on receiving his appointment he called it the "chief issue" of the campaign. He was, in a way, a counterpart of the professional dry, for lately he had spent a large part of his time and energy as a director of the Association Against the Prohibition Amendment; and when he took on the job of National Chairman, he did so knowing that the Democratic party would serve the interests of the Association, which he energetically promoted until his retirement in 1932. In 1928 his remarks on the liquor issue were stronger even than those of Smith himself, and on this subject, at least,

Raskob's influence surpassed that of Belle Moskowitz, one of Smith's long-standing advisers.

Raskob was not a man to attract either organized labor or the hinterland; and as if this were not enough, southerners could not have found it to their liking that in the 1928–9 edition of *Who's Who* he had listed himself as a Republican. "I do not know Mr. Raskob personally," wrote Walter Lippmann after seeing him in action for three years, "but from watching his brief political career I have the impression that in politics he is an innocent lamb." The choice of Raskob, which was made against the objection of his closest advisers, foreshadowed the way in which in the course of the campaign Smith would react to the charges of his opponents. He seemed determined to flaunt what was most controversial about his candidacy.

During the convention a measure of peace had been maintained between North and South; the very choice of Houston as the convention city had been aimed at appeasing southern Democrats, for not since 1860 had a Democratic convention met in the South. But even before appointing Raskob, Smith shattered the harmony that prevailed at Houston when he sent an important telegram to the adjourning delegates declaring for "fundamental changes in the present provisions of national prohibition." The statement was taken as a rejection of the more moderate platform plan. Franklin Roosevelt later wrote of that "fool telegram," Josephus Daniels called it "unnecessary and ill-timed," and the Anti-Saloon League reacted by an immediate endorsement of Hoover—the first candidate the League had ever officially supported. Actually, it was not clear what course Smith would pursue with regard to prohibition should he achieve the presidency. Walter Lippmann predicted that he would follow a moderate policy of law enforcement; certainly, Lippmann observed, the Democrats could do no worse job of it than the Republicans had been doing. To other commentators, "fundamental change" suggested repeal. As the campaign progressed, Smith's meaning became clearer. In August he took an advanced stand when he called for state control of liquor, and later he said he would lead a nationwide fight for a change in the prohibition law.

The good fellowship of the convention was dissolved by the Smith telegram and the Raskob appointment. The campaign would henceforth take on a new tone, but nowhere more emphatically than in the South. Bishop James Cannon, Jr., of the Methodist Episcopal Church, South, and Dr. Arthur J. Barton, Chairman of the Committee on Social Service of the Southern Baptist Convention, met in Asheville, North Carolina, in July to form an anti-Smith group. Cannon in particular worked indefatigably in directing the *ad hoc* association in its mission of defeating the New Yorker; he raised ample funds, some of them donated by the Republican National Committee, to spread propaganda into every area of the South.

Through the Anti-Smith Democrats and other organizations the South was encouraged to refuse Smith its traditional hospitality when he made a campaign trip there—he had first visited the region in April of 1928. Newspapers patronizingly reported that at the town of Biltmore, North Carolina, Smith had said to a cheering crowd: "I hope to meet yez-all personally." In his autobiography, Smith wrote that in Louisville a policeman accused him of being drunk, the whole police force was rude, and someone turned the heat too high in the auditorium where he delivered a speech. John E. Sullivan,

Smith's physician who accompanied him on the campaign, recalled that when the candidate's bodyguard, William Roy, went down to the steamroom to see what the matter was, he found a cordon of policemen protecting the engineers who were stoking the furnace. After a series of discourtesies on October 11, Smith was "solemn, silent and sullen." It appeared that although most of the southern politicians had accepted Smith in the convention the majority of voters would not support him. "Of the Southern delegates who voted for Smith," wrote one observer, "not one reflected the real wishes of his constituents."

While it was most pronounced in the South, the denominational attack on Smith was national in scope. A large contingent of ministers, including the popular Billy Sunday, fought Smith by every means available. Sunday called himself the "Ambassador of God" out "to defy the forces of hell—Al Smith and the rest of them." Sunday called Smith's male supporters "the damnable whiskey politicians, the bootleggers, crooks, pimps and business men who deal with them." After the election Vice President Charles Curtis sent Sunday a letter thanking him for his "valued assistance" and "good work in the South." One of the most intemperate of the churchmen who opposed Smith came not from the South but from the Calvary Baptist Church in New York City: in a speech in Dallas, John Roach Straton announced that "Smith is the nominee of the worst forces of hell." And in Riverside Park, New York, Dr. Ed Bywater delivered his popular sermon "To Hell with the Pope." A Methodist paper with countrywide circulation declared: "Governor Smith has a constitutional right to run for President, even though a Catholic. This we confess. And we have a constitutional right to vote against him because he is a Catholic. This we assert." The Moral Welfare Department of the Presbyterian Church of America adopted a resolution denouncing any prospective wet candidate. And the leaders of four million Baptists voted in convention to warn the Democratic party against a Catholic candidate. Dr. Mordecai Ham of the First Baptist Church, the largest in Oklahoma City, made the penalty for voting Democratic clear enough: "If you vote for Al Smith, you're voting against Christ and you'll all be damned." Lutherans were most emphatic in opposing Smith for his religion. Even the Unitarian leader, Dr. Alfred C. Dieffenbach, called to mind the Roman Catholic persecution of Unitarians in other countries and declared that no Catholic should be elected to the presidency. Bishop Warren A. Candler of Emory University, among others, ventured the hope that his fellow Methodists would not bring their church into politics. One later scholar noted that "the people seemed to have one thing in their minds—Al Smith's religion."

Such was the denominational opposition to Smith; the nationwide attack it fostered was in most cases the least fair of the campaign, for it was the most difficult to combat. Smith was accused of all the crimes of the Spanish inquisition and the medieval popes. Bishop Edwin Mouzon of the Methodist Episcopal Church, South, compiled in the North Carolina *Christian Advocate* a list of "Catholic crimes" in Mexico and England. In the same periodical Mouzon suggested topics for political-religious sermons. In New Jersey a confectioner sent along with his invoices copies of "The Inquisitorial Horrors of the Roman Catholic Church, as Described by an Officer in Napoleon's Army." The fundamentalist *Fellowship Forum* caricatured Smith driving a beer truck bearing the sign "Make America 100 percent Catholic, Drunk, and Illiterate," and another cartoon, showing a buxom woman giving a cup to a reclining cleric, bore the caption "The Pope Converted the Vatican into a House of Ill Fame." The flavor of the *Fellowship Forum* is caught in its advertisement for an "eye-opening" ten-cent pamphlet: "Can a Bobbed-Haired Woman Go to Heaven?" The *Forum* and other such publications gave wide circulation to a spurious Knights of Columbus oath: "I will spare neither sex, age nor condition, and [I swear] that I will hang, waste, boil, flay, strangle and burn alive these infamous heretics [Protestants]; rip up the stomachs and wombs of their women and crush infants' heads against the wall, in order to annihilate forever their execrable race. Then when the same cannot be done openly, I will secretly use the poison cup, the strangulation cord, the steel of the poniard, or the leaden bullet [and so forth]."

Senator Thomas Heflin of Alabama delivered some of the most vitriolic anti-Catholic attacks on record. Initially he used the floor of the Senate to denounce Smith and the Pope, and to urge the deportation of all Catholics; but in 1928 he carried his message throughout the country. In that year as before, one of the groups to pay his speaking expenses was the Ku Klux Klan. With Heflin, anti-Catholicism became a mania, growing into a conviction that the Catholics were planning to murder him. The Cincinnati *Catholic Telegram* said of the Alabamian—who slept with a gun under his pillow—that he had "strangely overlooked what is probably the most striking proof of the papal invasion of the United States. The telegraph pole bears the form of the cross from one end of the country to the other. . . . The plan was devised by none but a mastermind." A Holy Name Society sent Heflin a check for $250 "in appreciation of aid to the Catholic church," and a fellow senator described Heflin's delusion as "the airiest bubble that had ever found lodgment in an empty head."

With a co-religionist as a major presidential candidate for the first time in the nation's history, American Catholics were naturally on the defensive in 1928. A study of Catholic periodicals has shown that few openly urged the election of Smith. Many Catholics thought that only when one of their number became President could they achieve full social status in America, and they did not choose to forfeit their opportunity by confirming the fears of Protestants. Ellery Sedgwick of the *Atlantic Monthly* complimented the Catholic clergy on its good manners and restraint. Their discretion in the campaign contrasted with the behavior of many Protestant ministers who chose not to respect the principle for which they spoke, the separation between religion and politics. In Ohio two thousand of them willingly heard Mrs. Mabel Walker Willebrandt, Assistant Attorney General of the United States, urge them to use their pulpits and clerical influence against Smith. Mrs. Willebrandt spoke at the request of the Republican National Committee. "There are 2,000 pastors here," she said. "You have in your churches more than 600,000 members of the Methodist Church in Ohio alone. That is enough to swing the election." A public outburst would have greeted a comparable appeal for Smith before an assembly of Catholic priests.

Could there be a well-founded suspicion of Smith on religious grounds? Some Catholic leaders, it is true, had indicated a willingness to bring the church into politics. In 1922, for example, two priests, John A. Ryan—the New Deal liberal of a later day—and Moorhouse F. X. Millar had published *The State and the Church,* a work that might offend many Protestants too sophisticated to base their thinking upon stories of the inquisitorial atrocities of other lands and centuries. Ryan and Millar used as one of their texts the famous 1895 Encyclical of Pope Leo, which stated in part that "it would be very erroneous to draw the conclusion that in America is to be sought the type of the most desirable status of the Church. . . . She would bring forth more abundant fruits if, in addition to liberty, she enjoyed the favor of the laws and the patronage of public authority." In one of his essays included in the book, Ryan argued that "the State should officially recognize the Catholic religion as the religion of the Commonwealth. . . . Should [non-Catholics] be permitted to practice their own form of worship?" he asked. "If these are carried on within the family, or in such an inconspicuous manner as to be an occasion neither of scandal nor of perversion to the faithful. . . ." Ryan insisted that in America the Church would never be so recognized and that tolerance was a precious part of the American Catholic heritage; but he added that "error has not the same rights as truth." Catholic churchmen, it should be noted, had insisted upon the separation of Church and State even if Catholics someday predominate.

It was not alone the autocratic remarks of individual priests that antagonized many intelligent Protestants toward the presidency of a Roman Catholic. The example of several European and Latin American countries, where the Catholic Church had inexorably attempted to control political as well as spiritual affairs, was particularly disturbing. As Catholics became more numerous, might not the same fate befall America? At an International Eucharistic Congress held in Chicago during the summer of 1926, Smith was kept forward as the major lay figure; and before attending the meeting he had held a reception for eight cardinals at City Hall in New York, knelt before two of the visiting prelates, and kissed the ring of the papal legate, Cardinal Banzano. The Vatican itself made known that it would rejoice to see a Catholic President of the United States. Rome, apparently, was interested, and it is not odd that some Protestants —even though the threat of papal control was absurd—believed they had ample reason to take offense at this interest. Smith's unequivocal stand in the *Atlantic Monthly* in 1927 was not enough to dispel these fears.

Here again, the conduct of Smith requires commentary. A Catholic both loyal and stalwart in the assertion of his faith, Smith had before 1928 engaged in many small expressions of his Catholicism remarkable for a hardened politician aiming for national election, and as constitutional delegate and governor had taken political actions perhaps reflective of his religion. During the presidential campaign of 1928 he continued to follow the path he had always trod, making no apparent concessions to the instinctive revulsion shared by much of America against the symbols of Catholicism. In September he even volunteered to serve as an acolyte during a New Jersey church service. Smith's conduct on the matter of religion must, it is true, be judged on grounds somewhat different from those by which his defiance of prohibition is tested. In showing at least some respect for the law of the constitution and for that large segment of the people who called for the prohibition amendment, Smith would have combined good politics with good morals. But with regard to the religious question, morality and political strategy had to diverge; the minutest compromise of religious faith and observance would have been as morally questionable as it would be politically shrewd. Of course, it may be pointed out that the display of an autographed picture of the Pope in Smith's Albany office, for example, falls outside the scope of religious duty. Yet even here, Al Smith's conscience might have equated the least coyness in the affirmation of his faith with moral cowardice.

But all this does not free Smith from the charge of provincialism on the religious issue. For if he could not shirk his religion itself, or modify the slightest symbolic act of allegiance, he could at least have addressed himself more fully to the fears in which so many of his fellow Americans had been reared. Even assuming that the Smith forces may at first have pinned their hopes on the *Atlantic Monthly* article—which the governor had been reluctant to write—and reasoned that further reference on their part to the religious controversy would only more inflame the issue, it should have become apparent during the course of the campaign that nothing could have worsened the situation as it already stood. Smith might have acknowledged the occasional alliance between Latin Catholicism and political tyranny and then pointed to the historical American tradition of religious harmony, as embodied in Lord Baltimore; he and his supporters might even have made explicit contrast between their position, along with the position of countless of their fellow religionists in the United States, and that of Catholic reactionaries; he might have sought out the support of Protestant clergymen or outstanding laymen; he might have increased the Protestant contingent in his campaign committee.

Senator Burton K. Wheeler, Democrat of Montana, asked that prominent Norwegians and Swedes be enlisted in his state to defend Smith on the religious issue: "The need for that kind of approach ought to be pounded into the heads of those simple-minded people in New York who think the whole world revolves around that section of the country east of the Hudson River. The Smith forces may be playing fine politics as far as the East is concerned, but they did not display very much intelligence thus far with reference to the West in the selection of their advisers." Lynn Haines, a journalist who wrote an unpublished manuscript, "Al Smith and Certain Soothsayers," added to Wheeler's criticisms with a warning for Smith: "He must go west—not merely west of Broadway, not west of the Hudson, but west of the Alleghanies [sic]. From Ohio west and northwest and southwest, clear to the coast, is electoral territory ripe for Smith conquest. The key to the situation is the great agricultural depression—that plus a fighting progressive slant to the whole campaign. . . . Governor Smith will be nominated; if he goes far enough west of Broadway—in understanding and sympathy and spirit and purpose—he will easily be elected." In short, Smith might have acted as though he were aware of the anxiety, however silly or bigoted, that was felt by much of rural American Protestantism, as one who shared with it a sense of America's role in preserving religious liberty. A provincial Protestant ruralism and a provincial Catholic urbanism stared at each other in uncomprehending hostility, and with the single exception of Smith's article of 1927, neither attempted to break the impasse with a liberal word or gesture.

The contrast between Al Smith's handling of the religious question and John Fitzgerald Kennedy's is compelling. Smith discussed the issue once during the campaign. In his speech at Oklahoma City he lashed out angrily at a hostile audience, whom he attacked for hiding under the cloak of antiprohibition. He overpersonalized the religious debate and used explosive gesticulations to match his words. Kennedy, on the other hand, spoke often and directly to critics of his religion. "My experience . . . shows it is a matter of great concern," he said. "I am delighted to answer any questions about it. . . . There is nothing improper in discussing it." In a speech to the Greater Houston Ministerial Association, he gave his audience the benefit of the doubt for opposing him. He was specific, moreover, in his remarks about what worried that audience: "No church or church school," he said, should be granted "public funds or political preference." Kennedy asserted his opposition to state control of religion; and on the matter of birth control he promised to follow his own conscience without regard to outside religious pressures. Nor had Kennedy compounded the religious problem by politically amateurish appointments. As National Chairman, for example, he named Senator Henry M. Jackson of Washington, after passing over a prominent Catholic congressman. Undoubtedly, Kennedy had profited from Smith's mistakes, as he had also profited from the liberalization of his church.

Smith's religion did not stand alone as an issue in the campaign; opponents saw it as but one of a complex of characteristics that marked the New Yorker as a personality alien to the American grain. Smith was not merely a wet; he was a "Bowery wet," and his position toward alcohol, like his faith, affronted not only the most ignorant but also Americans of a genteel, middle-class tradition —offended their gentility or their conception of Americanness as much or more than their morals. As a social liability, Smith's wet position vied with a number of mannerisms that stamped him as a Gotham Cockney. Over the radio, then a new and impressive contribution to presidential campaigns, Smith's voice could be heard only with difficulty, for he spoke indistinctly and insisted on dashing from one side of the microphone to the other. His speeches themselves lacked grace and symmetry. He employed "ain't" and "he don't," and changed "work" to "woik"—forms of speech defended by the Johns Hopkins philologist Kemp Malone. His language, gestures, and physical appearance, all of which the new motion-picture newsreels conveyed, stamped him as an intruder in national politics. Even the two spittoons in Smith's Albany office seemed to speak loudly of his social origins. His eighth-grade education was insufficient, critics insisted, to equip him to face national and world problems, and on more than one occasion Smith himself admitted that he was interested only in the concrete and did not read books. When Smith visited Lincoln's birthplace in Kentucky, he bought a corncob pipe at the souvenir stand and immediately stuck it between his teeth. On another occasion, he joked with reporters about the needs of the states west of the Mississippi: "What states *are* west of the Mississippi?" he asked. When he met Babe Ruth, Smith—who had signed bills legalizing boxing and Sunday baseball—remarked: "Say, I read in a paper somewhere that in some place—I think Pennsylvania—somebody wouldn't let the series be announced on Sunday. Well, I'd like to see that place," mused the Governor, "it must be a hot one." He did not even hesitate to make a potentially abrasive public demonstration of fellowship with Tammany Hall, that embodiment of big-city politics and values. Before the national convention Smith visited Tammany, where, after a two-years absence from the annual ceremonies, he was reinstated as an honorary Sachem. Because Tammany Hall had lasted a century, he said, it must be "all right."

In sum, the matter of Smith's Catholicism, his obliviousness to Tammany's bad name, and his intransigence toward the Eighteenth Amendment blended with other characteristics less explicitly reflective of Smith's political outlook, yet combining to create a total impression of the man. A Florida Democrat told Roosevelt that "the sidewalks of New York didn't synchronize with my thought . . . of the dignity of the job." One woman wrote to Roosevelt:

> There were vast numbers who did not regard him as a fit man, either by birth, culture, dignity, or breadth of vision, to fill the great office of President of the United States. One who had never until middle life traveled beyond the counties of his native state could not possibly have other than a provincial viewpoint. His superficial knowledge of nationwide affairs, hastily acquired, could not give him the understanding or sympathetic outlook necessary in dealing with great national and international problems.

Another correspondent of Roosevelt identified a mélange of reasons for voting Republican; this is one of many "know-nothing" letters written to political figures in 1928:

> Mr. Roosevelt: Birds of a feather flock together, and if you uphold Smith and help him get in it is obvious you are in Tammany's pay. Of course he may be better than the ordinary man but Tammany has not become honest. . . . Everyone knows that Tammany uses Public School surplus to supply parochial schools so god knows what they will do when he gets to be President. . . . If you ever heard the Knights of Columbus oath I am sure you a Protestant would be through with [Roman Catholics]. They say it is all right to steal or cut out the bellies (the exact words used) of Protestants. . . . Why people are saying that he will make us have war with Mexico and he will so he can kill off some Protestants. . . . We can't trust them, don't you know that their church and the Pope come first, and they will be subject as it was to them first, and to America and her ideals second. . . . You ought to know the corruption there is in New York with Smith having a private telegraph wire to Tammany Hall, so of course he'll have a private wire to Tammany if he is made President. . . . An eyewitness saw him carried on the train dead drunk after his mother's funeral. He'd make a fine President, getting the Protestants drunk like he did when he was speaker or leader of the floor, in Albany, just so they would vote his way. And everyone knows his sons had to get married. And what kind of a woman would that be in the White House. Some difference from Mrs. Coolidge, who is educated and refined and cultured. Mrs. Smith's father was a saloon keeper, and kept Prostitute Houses and yet you'd help those kind of people get in. Well, all I can say is God help you and all of us, if they do get in.

> From an American who wants an American President who
> will protect America's Ideals, first, last, and always.

Even in his choice of an executive committee, Smith displayed a lack of sensitivity toward the touchy social and ethnic issues of the campaign. The selection of Raskob has already been mentioned; the rest of the committee came principally from New York and was largely composed of first- or second-generation Jews and Irish Catholics. Some of them were adept at urban politics and most had no connection with Tammany, but in general they showed the limited outlook of their candidate. One of Smith's closest advisers was James J. Hoey, the man who led the raucous galleries at the 1924 convention as they cheered "Oil! Oil!" to embarrass McAdoo. Joe Cohn of the tabloid New York *Evening Graphic,* Smith's press contact man, was another bad choice; as Smith himself observed in an interview some ten years later, his snappy clothes and overbearing manner made it almost impossible for him to win over conservative, middle-aged newspapermen of the West and South. Conversely, Smith ignored advice from most western and southern* Democrats. As early as May 1927, Joe Tumulty had criticized him for failing to consult out-of-state Democrats traveling through New York. Franklin Roosevelt, who was definitely not a member of Smith's inner circle, objected vigorously to the way Smith ran his presidential campaign, especially to the publicity organization, which he described as a combination of Mrs. Moskowitz and the advertising section of General Motors. In complaining of Smith's tactics to Harry Byrd of Virginia, Roosevelt said: "Things depend so much on the way they are put." On his campaign train Smith took with him Tammany judges and other New Yorkers; the only noneasterners to accompany him for very long were J. Bruce Kremer, the conservative Montanian closely associated with the Anaconda Copper Company, and former Senator Gilbert Hitchcock, who had voted against the prohibition amendment in 1920. Senator Robinson, the southern vice presidential candidate, who considered Raskob's acceptance remarks "inadvisable and unnecessary," did not hear from Smith for almost two weeks after the notification ceremonies.

Are the Smith forces free of responsibility for the misunderstandings and antagonisms of the campaign? In answer, we may first acknowledge that no amount of political skill on their part, no conceivable effort at conciliation could have obliterated the bigotry with which they had to contend. But it was not bigotry alone that ruled the emotions of the campaign; was there not a legitimate concern, on the part of some of the anti-Smith voters, at the possibility that the kind of America they had known might cease to find its symbol in the Executive Mansion—a concern that need not have been unduly aroused by Smith's candidacy, had he only taken the proper steps to still it? Failing this, a candidate can hardly complain if voters sense the mutual estrangement.

Three years prior to the 1928 campaign, Walter Lippmann wrote:

> The older American stocks in the South and the West, and in the
> East, too, are not all Ku Kluxers, and the Governor's more hasty
> friends show an intolerance when they believe that Al Smith is the
> victim of purely religious prejudice. Quite apart from the sincere

opposition of the prohibitionists, the objection to Tammany, the sectional objection to New York, there is an opposition to Smith which is as authentic and, it seems to me, as poignant as his support. It is inspired by the feeling that the clamorous life of the city should not be acknowledged as the American ideal. . . . The Ku Kluxers may talk about the Pope to the lunatic fringe, but the main mass of the opposition is governed by an instinct that to accept Al Smith is to certify and sanctify a way of life that does not belong to [their America].

In 1928, a special responsibility rested upon Smith to harmonize his America with that beyond the Hudson. For at that time, America had only begun to recognize that the "urban frontier," as well as the rural, had composed the substance of her past; she had not had time fully to absorb that more teeming frontier—of which Smith is today almost a folk hero—into her self-image. Smith might have tried to make 1928 a year of reconciliation between the two American cultures, but to do so he would have had to reach out, beyond the eastern city, to rural and small-town Protestant America, address it and show that he understood its feelings as well as the feelings of the lower East Side and the Bowery.

Instead he sometimes displayed during his candidacy an exclusionist provinciality unequalled even during the bids of William Jennings Bryan. His taste for the Sunday manner of New York was laudable; his sniping at the Protestant blue laws of small-town Pennsylvania was not good politics. His identification with the sidewalks of New York was of course legitimate; his reluctance to campaign in the South—against the advice of his strategists—and his jocular reference to "the states west of the Mississippi" made him doubly vulnerable to the charge of remaining a provincial New Yorker. To oppose prohibition was his prerogative; flagrantly to defy it was not. In fact, it may be suggested that had Smith entered the White House, rural America—and genteel urban Protestants as well—would have had as much cause to suffer a sense of alienation from the Presidency as would H. L. Mencken, for example, at the election of Bryan. Smith was at once a victim of prejudice and of his own clinging loyalty to his special environment. In 1932 he blamed his defeat on "bigotry"; but in an interview in May of 1937, he admitted that he had lacked a sensitivity to the social and cultural condition of those Americans he should have addressed.

JOHN KENNETH GALBRAITH

The Great Crash

The economists who study the business cycle evidently think that they can control it, but can they really? Even if they know what to do to restrain inflation or to revive a lagging economy, can they influence government policy swiftly enough and to a sufficient extent to avert danger? Is stock market speculation even now properly regulated? Are the market's fluctuations genuinely related to the health of the economy?

John Kenneth Galbraith is a Harvard economist closely identified with the advanced liberal wing of the Democratic party. Possessed of a dry wit, he is scarcely an alarmist. It is then a fearsome story he tells about some testimony he gave in 1955 before a congressional investigating committee, shortly before the publication of his book on the Great Depression.

I testified at the morning session of the stock market hearings on Tuesday, March 8, 1955. Several witnesses from the financial world, including Mr. G. Keith Funston and a bevy of vice-commissars of the New York Stock Exchange, had preceded me. The market had reacted to their testimony with admirable equanimity perhaps because they had said nothing although they had said it very well. Nor was my testimony sensational. I had brought along the proofs of this book; I drew on them to tell what had happened twenty-five years before, in 1928 and 1929. Toward the end I suggested that history *could* repeat itself, although I successfully resisted all invitations to predict when. I did urge a stiff tightening of margin requirements as a precautionary step. Similar action to minimize the use of credit for speculation had been taken during the war when the speculative enthusiasm was much less. Through it all the newspapermen sat gazing with partly open mouths at the ceiling of the Senate caucus chamber or looking down briefly to scribble a random note. An aide appeared occasionally, sidling along the wall behind the Committee, to pass a note to one of the Senators. The audience, I knew from waiting my turn on earlier occasions, was following me closely and, on occasion, exchanging a critical aside on my facts, logic, or diction. As the testimony gave way to questions, more Senators came in. This is perhaps the most trying time of any hearing. Each in his turn apologizes graciously for being late and then asks the question that has occurred to him on the way over. The question is always the same; and the Senator does not know that it has been asked before:

> SENATOR ROBERTSON: Well, Professor, we have been told by all the witnesses so far that present stock prices are not too high. What is your view on that?
>
> SENATOR IVES: You do not think we are faced with a bust, do you?
>
> SENATOR MONRONEY: I am wondering if there is any substance to the oft-repeated reason for the new high levels . . . That the stock market is merely catching up with the inflationary boom. . . .
>
> SENATOR PAYNE: I am sorry I came in late . . . would you want to indicate whether or not some of these increases have perhaps more truly reflected the true value of stocks in relation to their earnings?

The experienced witness observes that the question, though it bears a resemblance to some already asked, has been formulated in a novel way. Then he gives an answer which is the same in substance but decently different in form from those offered before. The audience is especially appreciative of able handling of such details.

Toward the end of the morning, interest appeared to increase. First one and then several photographers appeared. Then a newsreel camera or two. Through the weariness that develops with even so modest a sojourn in the public eye, I thought I sensed a certain tension. I remember noticing that the normal attrition of the Committee—which on a subject such as economics can leave one in a matter of an hour or so with only the Chairman and a precautionary member of the opposition—was not taking place. All Senators were staying. And soon I was the only one in the room who did not know the reason. The stock market was taking a nasty plunge.

I still did not know the reason when the hearing recessed at 12:57, just as a harried man from CBS came dashing into the chamber followed by two beasts of burden carrying a vast poundage of electronic marvels. He had been off in another room photographing Dulles. The real history had passed him by. In response to his almost tearful plea, I repeated several minutes of my testimony to an open window. The substitution of this for the Senators led to a considerable release from inhibition. I rather let myself go with the gestures— at times grave and statesmanlike, at others perhaps a trifle flamboyant. . . .

I still did not realize what had happened until someone handed me a paper with a big headline. The *New York Times* industrials went off 7 points on the day. Stocks lost $3 billion in value on the New York Stock Exchange. . . . (From the Author's Introduction to the Second Edition [1961].)

It is hard to say when the stock market boom of the nineteen-twenties began. There were sound reasons why, during these years, the prices of common stocks should rise. Corporate earnings were good and growing. The prospect seemed benign. In the early twenties stock prices were low and yields favorable.

In the last six months of 1924, the prices of securities began to rise, and the increase was continued and extended through 1925. Thus at the end of May 1924, the *New York Times* average of the prices of twenty-five industrial stocks was 106; by the end of the year it was 134.[1] By December 31, 1925, it had gained very nearly another 50 points and stood at 181. The advance through 1925 was remarkably steady; there were only a couple of months when values did not show a net gain.

During 1926 there was something of a setback. Business was off a little in the early part of that year; it was thought by many that values the year before had risen unreasonably. February brought a sharp fall in the market, and March a rather abrupt collapse. The *Times* industrials went down from 181 at the beginning of the year to 172 at the end of February, and then dropped by nearly 30 points to 143 at the end of March. However, in April the market steadied and renewed its advance. Another mild setback occurred in October, just after the hurricane blew away the vestiges of the Florida boom, but again recovery was prompt. At the end of the year values were about where they had been at the beginning.

In 1927 the increase began in earnest. Day after day and month after month the price of stocks went up. The gains by later standards were not large, but they had an aspect of great reliability. Again in only two months in 1927 did the averages fail to show an increase. On May 20, when Lindbergh took off from Roosevelt Field and headed for Paris, a fair number of citizens were unaware of the event. The market, which that day was registering another of its small but solid gains, had by then acquired a faithful band of devotees who spared no attention for more celestial matters.

In the summer of 1927 Henry Ford rang down the curtain on the immortal Model T and closed his plant to prepare for Model A. The Federal Reserve index of industrial production receded, presumably as a result of the Ford shutdown, and there was general talk of depression. The effect on the market was imperceptible. At the end of the year, by which time production had also turned up again, the *Times* industrials had reached 245, a net gain of 69 points for the year. . . .

In June of 1928 the market retreated a parasang or two—in fact, the losses during the first three weeks were almost as great as the March gains. June 12, a

[1] Throughout I have used the *New York Times* industrial averages as the shorthand designation of the level of security prices. This series is the arithmetical, unweighted average of the prices of twenty-five of what the *Times* describes as "good, sound stocks with regular price changes and generally active markets." The selection of the *Times* averages in preference to the Dow-Jones or other averages was largely arbitrary. The *Times* averages are the ones I have watched over the years; they are somewhat more accessible to the non-professional observer than the Dow-Jones averages. Also, while the latter are much better known, they carry in their wake a certain lore of market theory which is irrelevant for present purposes. The industrial rather than the railroad or combined average is cited because industrial stocks were the major focus of speculation and displayed the widest amplitude of movement. Unless there is indication to the contrary, values given are those at the close of the market for the date indicated.

day of particularly heavy losses, was a landmark. For a year or more, men of vision had been saying that the day might come when five million shares would be traded on the New York Stock Exchange. Once this had been only a wild conversational gambit, but for some time it had shown signs of being overtaken by the reality. On March 12, the volume of trading had reached 3,875,910 shares, an all-time high. By the end of the month such a volume had become commonplace. On March 27, 4,790,270 shares were traded. Then on June 12, 5,052,790 shares changed hands. The ticker also fell nearly two hours behind the market; Radio dropped 23 points, and a New York paper began its accounts of the day's events, "Wall Street's bull market collapsed yesterday with a detonation heard round the world."

The announcement of the death of the bull market was as premature as any since that of the death of Mark Twain. In July there was a small net gain, and in August a strong upsurge. Thereafter not even the approach of the election caused serious hesitation. People remained unperturbed when, on September 17, Roger W. Babson told an audience in Wellesley, Massachusetts, that "if Smith should be elected with a Democratic Congress we are almost certain to have a resulting business depression in 1929." He also said that "the election of Hoover and a Republican Congress should result in continued prosperity for 1929," and it may have been that the public knew it would be Hoover. In any case, during the same month reassurance came from still higher authority. Andrew W. Mellon said, "There is no cause for worry. The high tide of prosperity will continue."

Mr. Mellon did not know. Neither did any of the other public figures who then, as since, made similar statements. These are not forecasts; it is not to be supposed that the men who make them are privileged to look farther into the future than the rest. Mr. Mellon was participating in a ritual which, in our society, is thought to be of great value for influencing the course of the business cycle. By affirming solemnly that prosperity will continue, it is believed, one can help insure that prosperity will in fact continue. Especially among businessmen the faith in the efficiency of such incantation is very great.

Hoover was elected in a landslide. This, were the speculators privy to Mr. Hoover's mind, should have caused a heavy fall in the market. In his memoirs Mr. Hoover states that as early as 1925 he became concerned over the "growing tide of speculation." During the months and years that followed this concern gradually changed to alarm, and then to something only slightly less than a premonition of total disaster. "There are crimes," Mr. Hoover said of speculation, "far worse than murder for which men should be reviled and punished." As Secretary of Commerce he had sought nothing so much as to get the market under control.

Mr. Hoover's attitude toward the market was, however, an exceptionally well-kept secret. People did not know of his efforts, uniformly frustrated by Coolidge and the Federal Reserve Board, to translate his thoughts into action. The news of his election, so far from causing a panic, set off the greatest increase in buying to date. On November 7, the day after the election, there was a "victory boom," and the market leaders climbed 5 to 15 points. Volume reached 4,894,670 shares, or only a little less than the all-time record of June 12, and this new level was reached on a rising, not a falling market. On November 16, a further wave of buying hit the market. An astonishing 6,641,250 shares changed hands—far above the previous record. The *Times* industrial averages made a net gain of 4½ points on the day's trading—then considered an impressive advance. Apart from the afterglow of the election, there was nothing particular to incite this enthusiasm. The headlines of the day told only of the sinking of the steamship *Vestris* and the epic achievements of the officers and crew in shouldering aside the women and children and saving their own lives. November 20 was another huge day. Trading—6,503,230 shares—was fractionally smaller than on the sixteenth, but by common agreement it was much more frantic. The following morning the *Times* observed that "for cyclonic violence yesterday's stock market has never been exceeded in the history of Wall Street."

December was not so good. Early in the month there was a bad break, and, on December 8, Radio fell a ghastly 72 points in one day. However, the market steadied and then came back. Over the whole year of 1928 the *Times* industrial average gained 86 points, or from 245 to 331. During the year Radio went from 85 to 420 (it had never paid a dividend); Du Pont went from 310 to 525; Montgomery Ward from 117 to 440; Wright Aeronautic from 69 to 289. During the year 920,550,032 shares were traded on the New York Stock Exchange, as compared with a record-breaking 576,990,875 in 1927. But there was still another and even more significant index of what was happening in the market. That was the phenomenal increase in trading on margin.

As noted, at some point in the growth of a boom all aspects of property ownership become irrelevant except the prospect for an early rise in price. Income from the property, or enjoyment of its use, or even its long-run worth are now academic. As in the case of the more repulsive Florida lots, these usufructs may be non-existent or even negative. What is important is that tomorrow or next week market values will rise—as they did yesterday or last week—and a profit can be realized.

It follows that the only reward to ownership in which the boomtime owner has an interest is the increase in values. Could the right to the increased value be somehow divorced from the other and now unimportant fruits of possession and also from as many as possible of the burdens of ownership, this would be much welcomed by the speculator. Such an arrangement would enable him to concentrate on speculation which, after all, is the business of a speculator.

Such is the genius of capitalism that where a real demand exists it does not go long unfilled. In all great speculative orgies devices have appeared to enable the speculator so to concentrate on his business. In the Florida boom the trading was in "binders." Not the land itself but the right to buy the land at a stated price was traded. This right to buy—which was obtained by a down payment of 10 percent of the purchase price—could be sold. It thus conferred on the speculators the full benefit of the increase in values. After the value of the lot had risen he could resell the binder for what he had paid plus the full amount of the increase in price.

The worst of the burdens of ownership, whether of land or any other asset, is the need to put up the cash represented by the purchase price. The use of the binder cut this burden by 90 percent—or it multiplied tenfold the amount of acreage from which the speculator could harvest an increase in value. The buyer happily gave up the other advantages of ownership. These included the current income of which, invariably, there was none and the prospect of permanent use in which he had not the slightest interest.

The stock market also has its design for concentrating the speculative energies of the speculator, and, as might be expected, it improves substantially on the crudities of the real estate market. In the stock market the buyer of securities on margin gets full title to his property in an unconditional sale. But he rids himself of the most grievous burden of ownership—that of putting up the purchase price—by leaving his securities with his broker as collateral for the loan that paid for them. The buyer again gets the full benefit of any increase in value—the price of the securities goes up, but the loan that bought them does not. In the stock market the speculative buyer also gets the earnings of the securities he purchased. However, in the days of this history the earnings were almost invariably less than the interest that was paid on the loan. Often they were much less. Yields on securities regularly ranged from nothing to 1 or 2 percent. Interest on the loans that carried them was often 8, 10, or more percent. The speculator was willing to pay to divest himself of all of the usufructs of security ownership except the chance for a capital gain.

The machinery by which Wall Street separates the opportunity to speculate from the unwanted returns and burdens of ownership is ingenious, precise, and almost beautiful. Banks supply funds to brokers, brokers to customers, and the collateral goes back to the banks in a smooth and all but automatic flow. Margins—the cash which the speculator must supply in addition to the securities to protect the loan and which he must augment if the value of the collateral securities should fall and so lower the protection they provide—are effortlessly calculated and watched. The interest rate moves quickly and easily to keep the supply of funds adjusted to the demand. Wall Street, however, has never been able to express its pride in these arrangements. They are admirable and even wonderful only in relation to the purpose they serve. The purpose is to accommodate the speculator and facilitate speculation. But the purposes cannot be admitted. If Wall Street confessed this purpose, many thousands of moral men and women would have no choice but to condemn it for nurturing an evil thing and call for reform. Margin trading must be defended not on the grounds that it efficiently and ingeniously assists the speculator, but that it encourages the extra trading which changes a thin and anemic market into a thick and healthy one. At best this is a dull by-product and a dubious one. Wall Street, in these matters, is like a lovely and accomplished woman who must wear black cotton stockings, heavy woolen underwear, and parade her knowledge as a cook because, unhappily, her supreme accomplishment is as a harlot.

However, even the most circumspect friend of the market would concede that the volume of brokers' loans—of loans collateraled by the securities purchased on margin—is a good index of the volume of speculation. Measured by this index, the amount of speculation was rising very fast in 1928. Early in the twenties the volume of brokers' loans—because of their liquidity they are often referred to as call loans or loans in the call market—varied from a billion to a billion and a half dollars. By early 1926 they had increased to two and a half billions and remained at about that level for most of the year. During 1927 there was another increase of about a billion dollars, and at the end of the year they reached $3,480,780,000. This was an incredible sum, but it was only the beginning. In the two dull winter months of 1928 there was a small decline and then expansion began in earnest. Brokers' loans reached four billion on the first of June 1928, five billion on the first of November, and by the end of the year they were well along to six billion. Never had there been anything like it before.

People were swarming to buy stocks on margin—in other words, to have the increase in price without the costs of ownership. This cost was being assumed, in the first instance, by the New York banks, but they, in turn, were rapidly becoming the agents for lenders the country over and even the world around. There is no mystery as to why so many wished to lend so much in New York. One of the paradoxes of speculation in securities is that the loans that underwrite it are among the safest of all investments. They are protected by stocks which under all ordinary circumstances are instantly salable, and by a cash margin as well. The money, as noted, can be retrieved on demand. At the beginning of 1928 this admirably liquid and exceptionally secure outlet for non-risk capital was paying around 5 percent. While 5 percent is an excellent gilt-edged return, the rate rose steadily through 1928, and during the last week of the year it reached 12 percent. This was still with complete safety.

In Montreal, London, Shanghai, and Hong Kong there was talk of these rates. Everywhere men of means told themselves that 12 percent was 12 percent. A great river of gold began to converge on Wall Street, all of it to help Americans hold common stock on margin. Corporations also found these rates attractive. At 12 percent Wall Street might even provide a more profitable use for the working capital of a company than additional production. A few firms made this decision: instead of trying to produce goods with its manifold headaches and inconveniences, they confined themselves to financing speculation. Many more companies started lending their surplus funds on Wall Street.

There were still better ways of making money. In principle, New York banks could borrow money from the Federal Reserve Bank for 5 percent and re-lend it in the call market for 12. In practice they did. This was, possibly, the most profitable arbitrage operation of all time. . . . In the accepted history of these times, the Federal Reserve authorities are held to be not so much unaware or unwilling as impotent. They would have liked to stop the boom, but they lacked the means. This puts far too elaborate a face on matters. And it largely disguises the real nature of the dilemma which the authorities faced.

The classic instruments of control were indeed largely useless. These, as almost every college sophomore knows, are two: open market operations and the manipulation of the rediscount rate. Open market sales of government securities by the Federal Reserve bring to the vaults of the Reserve Banks the cash which is paid for the securities. There it remains sterile and harmless. Had it stayed in the commercial banks it would have been loaned to the public in multiple volume and particularly in those days to people who were buying common stocks.

If such a policy is to succeed, the Federal Reserve System rather obviously must have securities to sell. One of the inestimable blessings of the years of depression, war, and deficit-financing since 1930 is a spacious inventory of government debt in the Reserve Banks. In 1929 the Banks were not so well endowed. At the beginning of 1928, holdings were $617 million. During the first half of the year there were heavy sales as part of an effort to dry up the supply of funds that was feeding the market. Although sales were discontinued in the latter part of the year in the highly erroneous belief that the policy had succeeded and that the boom was under control, they couldn't have been continued much longer in any case. By the end of 1928 the inventory of government securities of the Federal Reserve System amounted only to $228 million. Had these all been dropped into the market, they might possibly have had some effect. But the Board was not given to any such drastic behavior which, incidentally, would also have largely denuded the Reserve Banks of earning assets. Sales were made a few millions at a time in the early months of 1929, but the effect was inconsequential. Moreover, even in following this feeble policy the Board worried lest, in denying funds to the stock market, it might put a pinch on "legitimate" business. The Reserve Banks continued to buy acceptances—the security that emerges in the course of financing ordinary non-speculative trade—and, relieved of the need to carry this paper, the commercial banks happily loaned more money in the stock market.

The other instrument of Federal Reserve policy was the rediscount rate. This is the rate at which member commercial banks borrow from the Reserve Banks of their district so that they may accommodate more borrowers than their own resources permit. In January 1929, the rediscount rate at the New York Federal Reserve Bank was 5 percent. The rate on brokers' loans ranged from 6 to 12 percent. Only a drastic increase would have made it unprofitable for a bank to borrow at the Federal Reserve in order to lend the proceeds, directly or indirectly, in the stock market. Apart from the general aversion to drastic action, such an increase would also have raised rates to ordinary businessmen, consumers, and farmers. In fact, higher interest rates would have been distressing to everyone but the speculator. A man who paid, say, an average of 10 percent to carry his holdings of Radio through 1928 would not have been either deterred or much disturbed had the rate been twice that high. During the same year, he made 500 percent on the appreciation in the value of his investment.

On February 14, 1929, the New York Federal Reserve Bank proposed that the rediscount rate be raised from 5 to 6 percent to check speculation. The Federal Reserve Board in Washington thought this a meaningless gesture which would only increase rates to business borrowers. A long controversy ensued in which President Hoover sided with the Board against the Bank. The rate was not increased until late in the summer.

There was another circumstance which gave the Reserve authorities an admirable excuse for inaction. That was the previously noted flow of funds from corporations and individuals to the market. During 1929, Standard Oil of New Jersey contributed a daily average of $69 million to the call market; Electric Bond and Share averaged over $100 million. A few corporations—Cities Service was one—even sold securities and loaned the proceeds in the stock market. By early 1929, loans from these non-banking sources were approximately equal to those from the banks. Later they became much greater. The Federal Reserve authorities took for granted that they had no influence whatever over this supply of funds.

In fact, the Federal Reserve was helpless only because it wanted to be. Had it been determined to do something, it could for example have asked

Congress for authority to halt trading on margin by granting the Board the power to set margin requirements. Margins were not low in 1929; a residue of caution had caused most brokers to require customers to put up 45 to 50 percent of the value of the stocks they were buying in cash. However, this was all the cash numerous of their customers had. An increase in margins to, say, 75 percent in January 1929, or even a serious proposal to do so, would have caused many small speculators and quite a few big ones to sell. The boom would have come to a sudden and perhaps spectacular end. (The power to fix margin requirements was eventually given to the Federal Reserve Board by the Securities Exchange Act in 1934, a year in which the danger of a revival of speculation about equaled that of a renascence of prohibition.)

Actually, not even new legislation, or the threat of it, was needed. In 1929, a robust denunciation of speculators and speculation by someone in high authority and a warning that the market was too high would almost certainly have broken the spell. It would have brought some people back from the world of make-believe. Those who were planning to stay in the market as long as possible but still get out (or go short) in time would have got out or gone short. Their occupational nervousness could readily have been translated into an acute desire to sell. Once the selling started, some more vigorously voiced pessimism could easily have kept it going.

The very effectiveness of such a measure was the problem. Of all the weapons in the Federal Reserve arsenal, words were the most unpredictable in their consequences. Their effect might be sudden and terrible. Moreover, these consequences could be attributed with the greatest of precision to the person or persons who uttered the words. Retribution would follow. To the more cautious of the Federal Reserve officials in the early part of 1929 silence seemed literally golden. . . .

Thursday, October 24, is the first of the days which history—such as it is on the subject—identifies with the panic of 1929. Measured by disorder, fright, and confusion, it deserves to be so regarded. That day 12,894,650 shares changed hands, many of them at prices which shattered the dreams and the hopes of those who had owned them. Of all the mysteries of the stock exchange there is none so impenetrable as why there should be a buyer for everyone who seeks to sell. October 24, 1929, showed that what is mysterious is not inevitable. Often there were no buyers, and only after wide vertical declines could anyone be induced to bid.

The panic did not last all day. It was a phenomenon of the morning hours. The market opening itself was unspectacular, and for a while prices were firm. Volume, however, was very large, and soon prices began to sag. Once again the ticker dropped behind. Prices fell farther and faster, and the ticker lagged more and more. By eleven o'clock the market had degenerated into a wild, mad scramble to sell. In the crowded boardrooms across the country the ticker told of a frightful collapse. But the selected quotations coming in over the bond ticker also showed that current values were far below the ancient history of the tape. The uncertainty led more and more people to try to sell. Others, no longer able to respond to margin calls, were sold out. By eleven-thirty the market had surrendered to blind, relentless fear. This, indeed, was panic.

Outside the Exchange in Broad Street a weird roar could be heard. A crowd gathered. Police Commissioner Grover Whalen became aware that something was happening and dispatched a special police detail to Wall Street to insure the peace. More people came and waited, though apparently no one knew for what. A workman appeared atop one of the high buildings to accomplish some repairs, and the multitude assumed he was a would-be suicide and waited impatiently for him to jump. Crowds also formed around the branch offices of brokerage firms throughout the city and, indeed, throughout the country. Word of what was happening, or what was thought to be happening was passed out by those who were within sight of the board or the Trans-Lux. An observer thought that people's expressions showed "not so much suffering as a sort of horrified incredulity." Rumor after rumor swept Wall Street and these outlying wakes. Stocks were now selling for nothing. The Chicago and Buffalo Exchanges had closed. A suicide wave was in progress, and eleven well-known speculators had already killed themselves.

At twelve-thirty the officials of the New York Stock Exchange closed the visitors gallery on the wild scenes below. One of the visitors who had just departed was showing his remarkable ability to be on hand with history. He was the former Chancellor of the Exchequer, Mr. Winston Churchill. It was he who in 1925 returned Britain to the gold standard and the overvalued pound. Accordingly, he was responsible for the strain which sent Montagu Norman to plead in New York for easier money, which caused credit to be eased at the fatal time, which, in this academy view, in turn caused the boom. Now Churchill, it could be imagined, was viewing his awful handiwork.

There is no record of anyone's having reproached him. Economics was never his strong point, so (and wisely) it seems most unlikely that he reproached himself.

In New York at least the panic was over by noon. At noon the organized support appeared.

At twelve o'clock reporters learned that a meeting was convening at 23 Wall Street at the offices of J. P. Morgan and Company. The word quickly passed as to who was there—Charles E. Mitchell, the Chairman of the Board of the National City Bank, Albert H. Wiggin, the Chairman of the Chase National Bank, William C. Potter, the President of the Guaranty Trust Company, Seward Prosser, the Chairman of the Bankers Trust Company, and the host, Thomas W. Lamont, the senior partner of Morgan's. According to legend, during the panic of 1907 the elder Morgan had brought to a halt the discussion of whether to save the tottering Trust Company of America by saying that the place to stop the panic was there. It was stopped. Now, twenty-two years later, that drama was being re-enacted. The elder Morgan was dead. His son was in Europe. But equally determined men were moving in. They were the nation's most powerful financiers. They had not yet been pilloried and maligned by New Dealers. The very news that they would act would release people from the fear to which they had surrendered.

It did. A decision was quickly reached to pool resources to support the market. The meeting broke up, and Thomas Lamont met with reporters. His manner was described as serious, but his words were reassuring. In what Frederick Lewis Allen later called one of the most remarkable understatements of all time, he told the newspapermen, "There has been a little distress selling on the Stock Exchange." He added that this was "due to a technical condition of the market" rather than any fundamental cause, and told the newsmen that things were "susceptible to betterment." The bankers, he let it be known, had decided to better things.

Word had already reached the floor of the Exchange that the bankers were meeting, and the news ticker had spread the magic word afield. Prices firmed at once and started to rise. Then at one-thirty Richard Whitney appeared on the floor and went to the post where steel was traded. Whitney was perhaps the best-known figure on the floor. He was one of the group of men of good background and appropriate education who, in that time, were expected to manage the affairs of the Exchange. Currently he was vice-president of the Exchange, but in the absence of E. H. H. Simmons in Hawaii he was serving as acting president. What was much more important at the moment, he was known as floor trader for Morgan's and, indeed, his older brother was a Morgan partner.

As he made his way through the teeming crowd, Whitney appeared debonair and self-confident—some later described his manner as jaunty. (His own firm dealt largely in bonds, so it is improbable that he had been much involved in the turmoil of the morning.) At the Steel post he bid 205 for 10,000 shares. This was the price of the last sale, and the current bids were several points lower. In an operation that was totally devoid of normal commercial reticence, he got 200 shares and then left the rest of the order with the specialist. He continued on his way, placing similar orders for fifteen or twenty other stocks.

This was it. The bankers, obviously, had moved in. The effect was electric. Fear vanished and gave way to concern lest the new advance be missed. Prices boomed upward.

The bankers had, indeed, brought off a notable coup. Prices as they fell that morning kept crossing a large volume of stop-loss orders—orders calling for sales whenever a specified price was reached. Brokers had placed many of these orders for their own protection on the securities of customers who had not responded to calls for additional margin. Each of these stop-loss orders tripped more securities into the market and drove prices down farther. Each spasm of liquidation thus insured that another would follow. It was this literal chain reaction which the bankers checked, and they checked it decisively.

In the closing hour, selling orders continuing to come in from across the country turned the market soft once more. Still, in its own way, the recovery on Black Thursday was as remarkable as the selling that made it so black. The *Times* industrials were off only 12 points, or a little more than a third of the loss of the previous day. Steel, the stock that Whitney had singled out to start the recovery, had opened that morning at 205½, a point or two above the previous close. At the lowest it was down to 193½ for a 12-point loss. Then it recovered to close at 206 for a surprising net gain of 2 points for this day. Montgomery Ward, which had opened at 83 had gone to 50, came back to 74. General Electric was at one point 32 points below its opening price and then came back 25 points. On the Curb, Goldman Sachs Trading Corporation opened at 81, dropped to 65, and then came back to 80. J. I. Case, maintaining a reputation for eccentric behavior that had brought much risk capital into the threshing machine business, made a net gain of 7 points for the day. Many had good reason to be grateful to the financial leaders of Wall Street.

Not everyone could be grateful to be sure. Across the country people were only dimly aware of the improvement. By early afternoon, when the market started up, the ticker was hours behind. Although the spot quotations on the bond ticker showed the improvement, the ticker itself continued to grind out the most dismal of news. And the news on the ticker was what counted. To many, many watchers it meant that they had been sold out and that their dream—in fact, their brief reality—of opulence had gone glimmering, together with home, car, furs, jewelry, and reputation. That the market, after breaking them, had recovered was the most chilling of comfort.

It was eight and a half minutes past seven that night before the ticker finished recording the day's misfortunes. In the boardrooms speculators who had been sold out since morning sat silently watching the tape. The habit of months or years, however idle it had now become, could not be abandoned at once. Then, as the final trades were registered, sorrowfully or grimly, according to their nature, they made their way out into the gathering night.

In Wall Street itself lights blazed from every office as clerks struggled to come abreast of the day's business. Messengers and boardroom boys, caught up in the excitement and untroubled by losses, went skylarking through the streets until the police arrived to quell them. Representatives of thirty-five of the largest wire houses assembled at the offices of Hornblower and Weeks and told the press on departing that the market was "fundamentally sound" and "technically in better condition than it has been in months." It was the unanimous view of those present that the worst had passed. The host firm dispatched a market letter which stated that "commencing with today's trading the market should start laying the foundation for the constructive advance which we believe will characterize 1930." Charles E Mitchell announced that the trouble was "purely technical" and that "fundamentals remained unimpaired." Senator Carter Glass said the trouble was due largely to Charles E. Mitchell. Senator Wilson of Indiana attributed the crash to Democratic resistance to a higher tariff.

On Friday and Saturday trading continued heavy—just under six million on Friday and over two million at the short session on Saturday. Prices, on the whole, were steady—the averages were a trifle up on Friday but slid off on Saturday. It was thought that the bankers were able to dispose of most of the securities they had acquired while shoring up the market on Thursday. Not only were things better, but everyone was clear as to who had made them so. The bankers had shown both their courage and their power, and the people applauded warmly and generously. The financial community, the *Times* said, now felt "secure in the knowledge that the most powerful banks in the country stood ready to prevent a recurrence [of panic]." As a result it had "relaxed its anxiety."

Perhaps never before or since have so many people taken the measure of economic prospects and found them so favorable as in the two days following the Thursday disaster. The optimism even included a note of self-congratulation. Colonel Ayres in Cleveland thought that no other country could have come through such a bad crash so well. Others pointed out that the prospects for business were good and that the stock market debacle would not make them any less favorable. No one knew, but it cannot be stressed too frequently, that for effective incantation knowledge is neither necessary nor assumed.

Eugene M. Stevens, the President of the Continental Illinois Bank, said, "There is nothing in the business situation to justify any nervousness." Walter

Teagle said there had been no "fundamental change" in the oil business to justify concern; Charles M. Schwab said that the steel business had been making "fundamental progress" toward stability and added that this "fundamentally sound condition" was responsible for the prosperity of the industry; Samuel Vauclain, Chairman of the Baldwin Locomotive Works, declared that "fundamentals are sound"; President Hoover said that "the fundamental business of the country, that is production and distribution of commodities, is on a sound and prosperous basis." President Hoover was asked to say something more specific about the market—for example, that stocks were now cheap —but he refused.

Many others joined in. Howard C. Hopson, the head of Associated Gas and Electric, omitted the standard reference to fundamentals and thought it was "undoubtedly beneficial to the business interests of the country to have the gambling type of speculator eliminated." (Mr. Hopson, himself a speculator, although more of the sure-thing type, was also eliminated in due course.) A Boston investment trust took space in *The Wall Street Journal* to say, "S-T-E-A-D-Y Everybody! Calm thinking is in order. Heed the words of America's greatest bankers." A single dissonant note, though great in portent, went unnoticed. Speaking in Poughkeepsie, Governor Franklin D. Roosevelt criticized the "fever of speculation."

On Sunday there were sermons suggesting that a certain measure of divine retribution had been visited on the Republic and that it had not been entirely unmerited. People had lost sight of spiritual values in their single-minded pursuit of riches. Now they had had their lesson.

Almost everyone believed that the heavenly knuckle-rapping was over and that speculation could be now resumed in earnest. The papers were full of prospects for next week's market.

Stocks, it was agreed, were again cheap and accordingly there would be a heavy rush to buy. Numerous stories from the brokerage houses, some of them possibly inspired, told of a fabulous volume of buying orders which was piling up in anticipation of the opening of the market. In a concerted advertising campaign in Monday's papers, stock market firms urged the wisdom of picking up these bargains promptly. "We believe," said one house, "that the investor who purchases securities at this time with the discrimination that is always a condition of prudent investing, may do so with utmost confidence." On Monday the real disaster began. . . .

It was another terrible day. Volume was huge, although below the previous Thursday—nine and a quarter million shares as compared with nearly thirteen. But the losses were far more severe. The *Times* industrials were down 49 points for the day. General Electric was off 48; Westinghouse, 34; Tel and Tel, 34. Steel went down 18 points. Indeed, the decline on this one day was greater than that of all the preceding week of panic. Once again a late ticker left everyone in ignorance of what was happening, save that it was bad.

On this day there was no recovery. At one-ten Charles E. Mitchell was observed going into Morgan's, and the news ticker carried the magic word. Steel rallied and went from 194 to 198. But Richard Whitney did not materialize. It seems probable in light of later knowledge that Mitchell was on the way to float a personal loan. The market weakened again, and in the last hour a phenomenal three million shares—a big day's business before and ever since—changed hands at rapidly falling prices.

At four-thirty in the afternoon the bankers assembled once more at Morgan's, and they remained in session until six-thirty. They were described as taking a philosophical attitude, and they told the press that the situation "retained hopeful features," although these were not specified. But the statement they released after the meeting made clear what had been discussed for the two hours. It was no part of the bankers' purpose, the statement said, to maintain any particular level of prices or to protect anyone's profit. Rather the aim was to have an orderly market, one in which offers would be met by bids at some price. The bankers were only concerned that "air holes," as Mr. Lamont had dubbed them, did not appear.

Like many lesser men, Mr. Lamont and his colleagues had suddenly found themselves overcommitted on a falling market. The time had come to go short on promises. Support, organized or otherwise, could not contend with the overwhelming, pathological desire to sell. The meeting had considered how to liquidate the commitment to support the market without adding to the public perturbation.

The formula that was found was a chilling one. On Thursday, Whitney had supported prices and protected profits—or stopped losses. This was what people wanted. To the man who held stock on margin, disaster had only one face and that was falling prices. But now prices were to be allowed to fall. The speculator's only comfort, henceforth, was that his ruin would be accomplished in an orderly and becoming manner.

There were no recriminations at the time. Our political life favors the extremes of speech; the man who is gifted in the arts of abuse is bound to be a notable, if not always a great figure. In business things are different. Here we are surprisingly gentle and forebearing. Even preposterous claims or excuses are normally taken, at least for all public purposes, at their face value. On the evening of the 28th no one any longer could feel "secure in the knowledge that the most powerful banks stood ready to prevent a recurrence" of panic. The market had reasserted itself as an impersonal force beyond the power of any person to control, and, while this is the way markets are supposed to be, it was horrible. But no one assailed the bankers for letting the people down. There was even some talk that on the next day the market might receive organized support.

Tuesday, October 29, was the most devastating day in the history of the New York stock market, and it may have been the most devastating day in the history of markets. It combined all of the bad features of all the bad days before. Volume was immensely greater than on Black Thursday; the drop in prices was almost as great as on Monday. Uncertainty and alarm were as great as on either.

Selling began as soon as the market opened and in huge volume. Great blocks of stock were offered for what they would bring; in the first half hour sales were at a 33,000,000-a-day rate. The air holes, which the bankers were to close, opened wide. Repeatedly and in many issues there was a plethora of selling orders and no buyers at all. The stock of White Sewing Machine Company, which had reached a high of 48 in the months preceding, had closed at

11 the night before. During the day someone—according to Frederick Lewis Allen it was thought to have been a bright messenger boy for the Exchange—had the happy idea of entering a bid for a block of stock at a dollar a share. In the absence of any other bid he got it. Once again, of course, the ticker lagged—at the close it was two and a half hours behind. By then, 16,410,030 sales had been recorded on the New York Stock Exchange—some certainly went unrecorded—or more than three times the number that was once considered a fabulously big day. The *Times* industrial averages were down 43 points, canceling all of the gains of the twelve wonderful months preceding.

The losses would have been worse had there not been a closing rally. Thus Steel, for which Whitney had bid 205 on Thursday, reached 167 during the course of the day, although it rallied to 174 at the close. American Can opened at 130, dropped to 110, and rose to 120. Westinghouse opened at 131 —on September 3 it had closed at 286—and dropped to 100. Then it rallied to 126. But the worst thing that happened on this terrible day was to the investment trusts. Not only did they go down, but it became apparent that they could go practically to nothing. Goldman Sachs Trading Corporation had closed at 60 the night before. During the day it dropped to 35 and closed at that level, off by not far short of half. Blue Ridge, its offspring once removed, on which the magic of leverage was now working in reverse, did much worse. Early in September it had sold at 24. By October 24 it was down to 12, but it resisted rather well the misfortunes of that day and the day following. On the morning of October 29 it opened at 10 and promptly slipped to 3, giving up more than two thirds of its value. It recovered later but other investment trusts did less well; their stock couldn't be sold at all.

The worst day on Wall Street came eventually to an end. Once again the lights blazed all night. Members of the Exchange, their employees, and the employees of the Stock Exchange by now were reaching the breaking point from strain and fatigue. In this condition they faced the task of recording and handling the greatest volume of transactions ever. All of this was without the previous certainty that things might get better. They might go on getting worse. In one house an employee fainted from exhaustion, was revived and put back to work again.

In the first week the slaughter had been of the innocents. During this second week there is some evidence that it was the well-to-do and the wealthy who were being subjected to a leveling process comparable in magnitude and suddenness to that presided over a decade before by Lenin. The size of the blocks of stock which were offered suggested that big speculators were selling or being sold. Another indication came from the boardrooms. A week before they were crowded, now they were nearly empty. Those now in trouble had facilities for suffering in private.

The bankers met twice on the 29th—at noon and again in the evening. There was no suggestion that they were philosophical. This was hardly remarkable because, during the day, an appalling rumor had swept the Exchange. It was that the bankers' pool, so far from stabilizing the market, was actually selling stocks! The prestige of the bankers had in truth been falling even more rapidly than the market. After the evening session. Mr. Lamont met the press with the disenchanting task of denying that they had been liquidating securities

—or participating in a bear raid. After explaining again, somewhat redundantly in view of the day's events, that it was not the purpose of the bankers to maintain a particular level of prices, he concluded: "The group has continued and will continue in a co-operative way to support the market and has not been a seller of stocks." In fact, as later intelligence revealed, Albert H. Wiggin of the Chase was personally short at the time to the tune of some millions. His co-operative support, which if successful would have cost him heavily, must have had an interesting element of ambivalence.

So ended the organized support. The phrase recurred during the next few days, but no one again saw in it any ground for hope. Few men ever lost position so rapidly as did the New York bankers in the five days from October 24 to October 29. The crash on October 24 was the signal for corporations and out-of-town banks, which had been luxuriating in the 10 percent and more rate of interest, to recall their money from Wall Street. Between October 23 and October 30, as values fell and margin accounts were liquidated, the volume of brokers' loans fell by over a billion. But the corporations and the out-of-town banks responded to the horrifying news from New York—although, in fact, their funds were never seriously endangered—by calling home over two billions. The New York banks stepped into the gaping hole that was left by these summer financiers, and during that first week of crisis they increased their loans by about a billion. This was a bold step. Had the New York banks succumbed to the general fright, a money panic would have been added to the other woes. Stocks would have been dumped because their owners could not have borrowed money at any price to carry them. To prevent this was a considerable achievement for which all who owned stocks should have been thankful. But the banks received no credit. People remembered only that they had bravely undertaken to stem the price collapse and had failed.

Despite a flattering supposition to the contrary, people come readily to terms with power. There is little reason to think that the power of the great bankers, while they were assumed to have it, was much resented. But as the ghosts of numerous tyrants, from Julius Caesar to Benito Mussolini will testify, people are very hard on those who, having had power, lose it or are destroyed. Then anger at past arrogance is joined with contempt for present weakness. The victim or his corpse is made to suffer all available indignities.

Such was the fate of the bankers. For the next decade they were fair game for congressional committees, courts, the press, and the comedians. The great pretensions and the great failures of these days were a cause. A banker need not be popular; indeed, a good banker in a healthy capitalist society should probably be much disliked. People do not wish to trust their money to a hail-fellow-well-met but to a misanthrope who can say no. However, a banker must not seem futile, ineffective, or vaguely foolish. In contrast with the stern power of Morgan in 1907, that was precisely how his successors seemed, or were made to seem, in 1929. . . .

In mid-November 1929, at long, long last, the market stopped falling—at least, for a while. The low was on Wednesday, November 13. On that day the *Times* industrials closed at 224 down from 452, or by almost exactly one half since September 3. They were also by then down 82 points—about one quarter—from the close on that day barely two weeks before when John D.

Rockefeller had announced that he and his son were buying common stocks. On November 13 there was another Rockefeller story: it was said that the family had entered a million-share buying order to peg Standard Oil of New Jersey at 50. During the rest of November and December the course of the market was moderately up.

The decline had run its course. However, the end coincided with one last effort at reassurance. No one can say for sure that it did no good. One part was the announcement by the New York Stock Exchange of an investigation of short selling. Inevitably in the preceding weeks there had been rumors of bear raids on the market and of fortunes being made by the shorts. The benign people known as "they," who once had put the market up, were now a malign influence putting it down and making money out of the common disaster. In the early days of the crash it was widely believed that Jesse L. Livermore, a Bostonian with a large and unquestionably exaggerated reputation for bear operations, was heading a syndicate that was driving the market down. So persistent did these rumors become that Livermore, whom few had thought sensitive to public opinion, issued a formal denial that he was involved in any deflationary plot. "What little business I have done in the stock market," he said, "has always been as an individual and will continue to be done on such basis." As early as October 24, *The Wall Street Journal,* then somewhat less reserved in its view of the world than now, complained that "there has been a lot of short selling, a lot of forced selling, and a lot of selling to make the market look bad." Such suspicions the Exchange authorities now sought to dispel. Nothing came of the study.

A more important effort at reassurance was made by President Hoover. Presumably he was still indifferent to the fate of the stock market. But he could not be indifferent to the much publicized fundamentals, which by now were behaving worse each week. Prices of commodities were falling. Freight-car loadings, pig iron and steel production, coal output, and automobile production were also all going down. So, as a result, was the general index of industrial production. Indeed, it was falling much more rapidly than in the sharp postwar depression of 1920–21. There were alarming stories of the drop in consumer buying, epecially of more expensive goods. It was said that sales of radio sets in New York had fallen by half since the crash.

Mr. Hoover's first step was out of the later works of John Maynard Keynes. Precisely as Keynes and Keynesians would have advised, he announced a cut in taxes. The rate on both individuals and corporations was cut by one full percentage point. This reduced the income tax of a head of a family with no dependents and an income of $4000 by two-thirds. The man with $5000 got a similar reduction. The tax of a married man with no dependents and an income of $10,000 was cut in half. These were dramatic reductions, but their effect was sadly mitigated by the fact that for most people the taxes being cut were already insignificant. The man with $4000 had his annual tax burden reduced from $5.63 to $1.88. The man with $5000 got a cut from $16.88 to $5.63. For the man with $10,000 the reduction in annual tax was from $120 to $65. The step, nonetheless, was well received as a contribution to increased purchasing power, expanded business investment, and a general revival of confidence.

Mr. Hoover also called a series of meetings on the state of the economy. The leading industrialists, the leading railway executives, the heads of the large utilities, the heads of the important construction companies, the union leaders, and the heads of the farm organizations met in turn with the President during the latter part of November. The procedure in the case of each of the meetings was the same. There was a solemn session with the President, those attending had their picture taken with the President, and there was a press interview at which the conferees gave the press their opinion on the business prospect. The latter, without exception, was highly favorable. After the meeting of the industrial leaders on November 21, which was attended by, among others, Henry Ford, Walter Teagle, Owen D. Young, Alfred P. Sloan, Jr., Pierre du Pont, Walter Gifford, and Andrew Mellon, the expressions of confidence were so robust that Julius Rosenwald, who also attended, said he feared there might soon be a bad labor shortage.

The utility, rail, and construction executives were equally hopeful. Even the heads of the farm organizations were less misanthropic than normal for that time. They said afterward that they had told the President that "the morale of their industry was better than it had been for years."

This was organized reassurance on really a grand scale, and it attracted some of the most enthusiastic comment of the period. A Wall Street financial writer began his story of the sessions: " 'Order up the Moors!' was Marshal Foch's reply at the first battle of the Marne . . . 'Order up the business reserves,' directed President Hoover as pessimistic reports flowed in from all quarters following the stock market crash." The *Philadelphia Record* was led to describe the President as "easily the most commanding figure in the modern science of 'engineering statesmanship.' " The *Boston Globe* said that the nation is now aware "that it has at the White House a man who believes not in the philosophy of drift, but in the dynamics of mastery."

Yet to suppose that President Hoover was engaged only in organizing further reassurance is to do him a serious injustice. He was also conducting one of the oldest, most important—and, unhappily, one of the least understood—rites in American life. This is the rite of the meeting which is called not to do business but to do no business. It is a rite which is still much practiced in our time. It is worth examining for a moment.

Men meet together for many reasons in the course of business. They need to instruct or persuade each other. They must agree on a course of action. They find thinking in public more productive or less painful than thinking in private. But there are at least as many reasons for meetings to transact no business. Meetings are held because men seek companionship or, at a minimum, wish to escape the tedium of solitary duties. They yearn for the prestige which accrues to the man who presides over the meetings, and this leads them to convoke assemblages over which they can preside. Finally, there is the meeting which is called not because there is no business to be done, but because it is necessary to create the impression that business is being done. Such meetings are more than a substitute for action. They are widely regarded as action.

The fact that no business is transacted at a no-business meeting is normally not a serious cause of embarrassment to those attending. Numerous formulas have been devised to prevent discomfort. Thus scholars, who are great devotees of the no-business meeting, rely heavily on the exchange-of-ideas justification. To them the exchange of ideas is an absolute good. Any meeting at which ideas are exchanged is, therefore, useful. This justification is nearly ironclad. It is very hard to have a meeting of which it can be said that no ideas were exchanged.

Salesmen and sales executives, who also are important practitioners of the no-business gathering, commonly have a different justification and one that has strong spiritual overtones. Out of the warmth of comradeship, the interplay of personality, the stimulation of alcohol, and the inspiration of oratory comes an impulsive rededication to the daily task. This meeting pays for itself in a fuller and better life and the sale of more goods in future weeks and months.

The no-business meetings of the great business executives depend for their illusion of importance on something quite different. Not the exchange of ideas or the spiritual rewards of comradeship, but a solemn sense of assembled power gives significance to this assemblage. Even though nothing of importance is said or done, men of importance cannot meet without the occasion seeming important. Even the commonplace observation of the head of a large corporation is still the statement of the head of a large corporation. What it lacks in content it gains in power from the assets back of it.

The no-business meeting was an almost perfect instrument for the situation in which President Hoover found himself in the autumn of 1929. The modest tax cut apart, the President was clearly adverse to any large-scale government action to counter the developing depression. Nor was it very certain, at the time, what could be done. Yet by 1929 popular faith in laissez faire had been greatly weakened. No responsible political leader could safely proclaim a policy of keeping hands off. The no-business meetings at the White House were a practical expression of laissez faire. No positive action resulted. At the same time they gave a sense of truly impressive action. The conventions governing the no-business session insured that there would be no embarrassment arising from the absence of business. Those who attended accepted as a measure of the importance of the meetings the importance of the people attending. The newspapers also cooperated in emphasizing the importance of the sessions. Had they done otherwise they would, of course, have undermined the value of the sessions as news.

In recent times the no-business meeting at the White House—attended by governors, industrialists, representatives of business, labor, and agriculture —has become an established institution of government. Some device for simulating action, when action is impossible, is indispensable in a sound and functioning democracy. Mr. Hoover in 1929 was a pioneer in this field of public administration.

As the depression deepened, it was said that Mr. Hoover's meetings had been a failure. This, obviously, reflects a very narrow view.

In January, February, and March of 1930 the stock market showed a substantial recovery. Then in April the recovery lost momentum, and in June there was another large drop. Thereafter, with few exceptions the market dropped week by week, month by month, and year by year through June of 1932. The position when it finally halted made the worst level during the crash seem memorable by contrast. On November 13, 1929, it may be recalled, the *Times* industrials closed at 224. On July 8, 1932, they were 58. This value was not much more than the net by which they dropped on the single day of October 28, 1929. Standard Oil of New Jersey, which the Rockefellers were believed to have pegged at 50 on November 13, 1929, dropped below 20 in April 1932. On July 8 it was 24. U.S. Steel on July 8 reached a low of 22. On September 3, 1929, it had sold as high as 262. General Motors was a bargain at 8 on July 8, down from 73 on September 3, 1929. Montgomery Ward was 4, down from 138. Tel and Tel was 72, and on September 3, 1929, it had sold at 304. Anaconda sold at 4 on July 8. *The Commercial and Financial Chronicle* observed that "the copper shares are so low that their fluctuations are of little consequence."

However, comparatively speaking, values in these staple stocks had been well maintained. Things were far worse with the investment trusts. Blue Ridge during the week ending July 8, 1932, was 63 cents, and Shenandoah was 50 cents. United Founders and American Founders were both around 50 cents as compared with 70 and 117 (dollars, needless to say) on September 3, 1929. The fears of November 1929 that the investment trusts might go to nothing had been largely realized. . . .

~·~·~·~·~9

RICHARD L. WATSON, Jr.

The Defeat of Judge Parker:
A Study in Pressure Groups and Politics

The Senate decision in 1930 to reject President Hoover's appoint-
ment of Judge John J. Parker to the Supreme Court not only re-
flected the rise of dynamic pressure groups, but also foreshadowed
the political realignment under the Presidency of Franklin Roose-
velt. Beneath the surface of national politics in the nineteen twen-
ties, the American power structure had undergone important
changes. The transition from a rural to an urban society strength-
ened economic, ethnic, and racial interest groups that characteris-
tically find their largest constituencies in the cities. The collapse of
stock market prices in 1929 and 1930 gave a further militant edge
to partisan conflict.

Liberal Republican Senators, renewing a longstanding conflict
between that branch of Congress and the Presidency, gladly led the
anti-Parker drive. Earlier in the decade they had mounted symbolic
attacks on much more conservative nominees, but the mood of the
twenties blocked their efforts; now the depression contributed to the
confidence and momentum of their assault. Two special facts de-
termined their strategy. A ruling upholding an injunction that
Parker made as a federal judge seemed to range him behind the
yellow dog contract—a hiring agreement committing workers
not to join a union—and set the AFL against him. And Parker's
remark, in a speech of 1920 in North Carolina, that "the Negro as
a class does not desire to enter politics," drew the fire of the NAACP.
Liberals used the statements of these two increasingly powerful or-
ganizations to evoke a sense of widespread opposition to Parker.
The episode was a prelude to the politics of the nineteen thirties and
the great urban-based coalition of liberals, trade unionists, and mi-
nority groups that later constituted the political support of Franklin
Roosevelt's new Democratic Party. Not until 1969 was another
Presidential selection for the Supreme Court rejected by the United
States Senate.

Reprinted from the *Journal of American History* (September, 1963), 213–34, by
permission of the Organization of American Historians.

On March 8, 1930, Associate Justice Edward Terry Sanford of the United States Supreme Court died. Since Sanford had been the only southerner on the Court, it was a logical assumption that President Hoover would appoint another southerner to succeed him. Hoover's choice was Judge John J. Parker, a forty-four year old North Carolinian. A judge of the Fourth Circuit Court since 1925, Parker, Phi Beta Kappa and president of his class at the University of North Carolina, had entered politics as a Republican shortly after his graduation; he was successively defeated—as Republicans in North Carolina usually were—in races for the United States House of Representatives in 1910, for state attorney general in 1916, and for governor in 1920. In the 1920 election he polled 230,000 votes, more than any other Republican gubernatorial candidate had ever received in North Carolina. By this time he was one of the state's most distinguished lawyers, and in 1923 and 1924 he served as special assistant to the attorney general of the United States in the investigation, during Harding's administration, of alleged war frauds. In 1925, President Coolidge appointed him to the Circuit Court.

Hoover's nomination of Parker to the Supreme Court seemed appropriate, and one that the Senate would promptly confirm. Just two months after his name was presented, however, the Senate turned him down. Since the Senate rarely rejects a president's appointee to the Supreme Court, the episode is, for that reason alone, worth study. But other factors make the rejection even more historically significant. It symbolized labor's resurgence in the 1930's; it was one of the first important victories of the National Association for the Advancement of Colored People; it reflected a growing opposition to the predominant philosophy of the Supreme Court, an opposition which would reach a climax in 1937; it raised fundamental questions as to the role of pressure groups in a democracy; and it demonstrated how an apparently routine appointment can become a personal and a partisan campaign for office.

Within a few hours of Sanford's death, Charles Jonas, Republican national committeeman from North Carolina, had decided that Parker should be Sanford's successor. As a first move, he planned to present Parker's name to Hoover as soon after Sanford's funeral as it could properly be done. In the meantime, he suggested to Parker that the bar and judiciary launch a "non-partisan" campaign in support of the nomination prior to an endorsement by the party organization. Parker was more than receptive to this suggestion and immediately sought advice as to what tactics to follow. He rounded up friends to join a delegation to see Hoover in person, and he suggested to others that he would appreciate their writing letters of recommendation for him. At the same time, Republican State Chairman Brownlow Jackson presented Parker's name to Hoover while Jonas sought support in the Senate.

Meanwhile, North Carolina Democrats were marshaling their forces in support of Chief Justice Walter P. Stacy of the state supreme court. The two key men in this campaign were the veteran North Carolina Senators Furnifold M. Simmons and Lee S. Overman. Simmons was senior senator in point of service, and Overman was the ranking Democrat on the Senate's Judiciary Committee. Both favored Stacy, but both realized that the chance of Hoover's appointing a Democrat was small, and hence, as good North Carolinians, they were ready to support Parker. Josephus Daniels, editor of the partisan Democratic Raleigh

News and Observer, likewise supported Stacy, but said that if "Hoover insists upon making a political job of the Supreme Court Bench," an acceptable nominee would be Parker.

Senator Simmons personally talked with Hoover, on March 13, and urged upon him the appointment of one or the other of the two men. On the same day Overman formally presented Stacy's name to Hoover, with the support of the entire North Carolina congressional delegation. Shortly thereafter, a radio broadcast announced Stacy's nomination, and congratulatory messages began to pour in upon the surprised justice. A telegram from Simmons ended the unfounded rumor, but telegrams of recommendation continued to reach the offices of Simmons and Overman. Apparently the four associate justices of the North Carolina supreme court endorsed Stacy, as did numerous local bar associations. The support for Parker was also intense, and it gathered momentum when Cameron Morrison, who had defeated Parker for governor in 1920, led a bipartisan delegation of North and South Carolinians to Washington to support his former opponent.

Hoover apparently thought that Parker's nomination was a safe one. Apprehensive because of the fight that had developed over his recent nomination of Charles Evans Hughes to the Supreme Court, he had ordered Attorney General William D. Mitchell to study the more than one hundred decisions written by Parker on the Federal bench, and Mitchell had given assurances that the decisions were sound; Senator George W. Norris, chairman of the Judiciary Committee, was reported to be favorably inclined; and the North Carolina delegation was willing. Consequently, on March 21, Hoover nominated Parker, and the Senate promptly sent the nomination to the Judiciary Committee. North Carolina Republicans were delighted, although there were those who feared that a Democrat would replace Parker on the Circuit Court, an appointment which, Parker was informed, would spoil "the stimulating effect which your appointment has had on the Republicans in North Carolina."

Actually, there was not complete agreement that Parker was the best of all possible candidates. The immediate editorial reaction of the *New Republic* was to praise the style and organizations of his opinions as being "decisive and orderly," but it criticized some of them for showing little awareness of "new currents of thought" and for relying too much upon "traditional legal conceptions." It concluded by pointing out that being only forty-four years old, Parker was not too old to learn, but questioned whether Hoover was picking a "great judge or a conspicuous Southerner."

One point mentioned in the *New Republic,* almost in passing, was that one of Parker's decisions had allowed "the West Virginia non-union mines to enjoin the United Mineworkers from interfering with their business on the grounds of a restraint of interstate commerce." By the time these comments had been published it had become clear that this decision of Parker's would have a very real effect upon his confirmation. In fact, on March 25, the American Federation of Labor requested that the Senate Judiciary Committee investigate Parker's decision in the case of the *United Mine Workers v. Red Jacket Coal and Coke Company.* The issue, it appeared, would involve fighting words from the point of view of organized labor, for both "injunctions" and "yellow dog contracts" were involved.

The case had grown out of violence in the non-union coal fields of Logan and Mingo counties in West Virginia in 1921. Bloody battles had occurred as a result of an organizing campaign carried out by the United Mine Workers in spite of the fact that many workers had signed yellow dog contracts. Federal troops had halted the civil war, but the Red Jacket Company and some three hundred other non-union companies asked for a permanent injunction forbidding any "union and its officers and members from interfering with the company's employees by violence, threats, intimidation, picketing . . . or by procuring them to breach their contracts with the plaintiff." The District Court granted the injunction, but the UMW made a test case of it, and appealed to the Circuit Court, consisting of Judge Parker and two other justices. The decision upholding the District Court, read by Parker on April 18, 1927, stated in part:

> . . . There can be no doubt of the right of defendants to use all lawful propaganda to increase their membership. On the other hand, however, this right must be exercised with due regard to the right of the complainants. To make a speech or to circulate an argument under ordinary circumstances dwelling upon the advantages of union membership is one thing. To approach a company's employees, working under a contract not to join a union while remaining in the company's service, and induce them, in violation of their contracts, to join the union and go on a strike for the purpose of forcing the company to recognize the union or of impairing its power of production, is another and very different thing.[1]

To the leaders of the American Federation of Labor, the issue was clear. Parker had upheld the use of the injunction and he had accepted the yellow dog contract as a legitimate device. Thus on March 28, 1930, William Green announced that the AFL would oppose the nomination. His opposition was nicely timed, for a strong move had been developing in the Senate since the Red Jacket decision to outlaw both the use of the injunction in labor disputes and the yellow dog contract. Parker's nomination had been referred to a subcommittee, of which Senator Overman was chairman, and one of the committeemen, Senator William E. Borah, had at various times vigorously attacked the yellow dog contract.[2]

In the meantime, opposition came from another direction. The National Association for the Advancement of Colored People had become increasingly active in the 1920's in fighting cases involving the rights of Negroes through to the Supreme Court. Any new appointee was therefore scrutinized with care to discover any facts in his background which might indicate his attitude toward

[1] It should be noted that the Red Jacket case was appealed to the Supreme Court, but the Supreme Court refused to grant the appeal.

[2] Senator Felix Hebert of Rhode Island was the other member of the subcommittee. Note that T. A. Wilson, head of the North Carolina branch of the American Federation of Labor, made no objections at first to the nomination, but then promptly expressed his opposition when told of the Red Jacket case. By the first week in April protests from labor unions in many North Carolina towns were reaching the two North Carolina senators.

Negroes. The search in Parker's case was not difficult, for many North Carolina Negroes undoubtedly still remembered their irritation at a speech that Parker had made in his campaign for governor in 1920. In that campaign, the racial issue had been raised in the Democratic primary; and the Democrats were quite ready to use it against the Republicans in the election. Parker, perhaps for the loftiest of motives, did not wish to stir up racial animosities; consequently, in accepting the Republican nomination for governor he said:

> I have attended every state convention since 1908 and I have never seen a Negro delegate in any convention that I attended. The Negro as a class does not desire to enter politics. The Republican party of North Carolina does not desire him to do so. We recognize the fact that he has not yet reached the stage in his development when he can share the burdens and responsibilities of government. This being true, and every intelligent man in North Carolina knows that it is true, the attempt of certain petty Democratic politicians to inject the race issue into every campaign is most reprehensible. I say it deliberately, there is no more dangerous or contemptible enemy of the state than the man who for personal or political advantage will attempt to kindle the flame of racial prejudice or hatred.

Walter White, executive secretary of the NAACP, telegraphed Judge Parker on March 26, 1930, inquiring if he had actually made the statement, and if so whether he still held the same views. Although Parker thought that the NAACP would not oppose him if it understood the circumstances of his speech in 1920, he apparently did not answer the telegram, and thus the NAACP launched a vigorous campaign against Parker's confirmation.[3] The NAACP was aided by some two hundred Negro newspapers and the National Association of Colored Women. The official protest was filed with the Senate Judiciary Committee, and the senators were bombarded with telephone calls, telegrams, letters, petitions, and visitations.

Thus what had first appeared to be a routine appointment had developed into a tense battle in which economic, racial, political, and sectional issues were involved. The hearing on April 5 before the subcommittee gave both the labor unions and the NAACP an opportunity to put their views on the record.

They were agreed on the most important point: that Parker did not have the qualifications desirable for a Supreme Court Justice. The principal testimony was given by William Green, representing not only the AFL but also the railway brotherhoods. He argued that Parker had upheld the injunction and the yellow dog contract. He admitted that in upholding the injunction Parker could have been simply following a precedent established by the Supreme Court in the Hitchman case,[4] but he stated that labor's objection to Parker was based

---

[3] The NAACP checked with the telegraph company to be sure the message was delivered.

[4] *Hitchman Coal Company v. Mitchell* (1917) sweepingly upheld the legality of the so-called yellow dog contract and supported an injunction to prevent activity designed to "compel plaintiff, through fear of financial loss, to consent to the unionization of the mine" in spite of the contracts of employment known to be in force there,

upon what it considered his sympathetic attitude toward "the legal and economic policy embodied in the injunction." Green insisted, moreover, that numerous judicial decisions could be cited as precedents for not following the ruling in the Hitchman case. In short, what Parker should have done, according to Green, was to interpret the law in the light of changing conditions. Labor opposition was based upon "his judicial attitude" toward "great modern-day economic problems," those that "arise out of human relations in industry."

The National Association for the Advancement of Colored People based its opposition on Parker's comment in 1920 about the Negro in politics. Walter White argued that no one who favored keeping the Negro out of politics, as Parker seemed to have done in 1920, could approach Fourteenth Amendment questions with that "dispassionate, unprejudiced, and judicial frame of mind which would enable him to render a decision according to the Constitution." By this time, Parker was becoming increasingly concerned about the possibility that he might not be confirmed. He hesitated to defend his position on the racial question publicly as he thought that such a defense might be considered unbecoming a nominee to the Court. He wrote out a complete defense, however, and asked David H. Blair, a North Carolina Republican leader, to convey the substance of it to friends in the Senate.

Actually, Negro leadership was not unanimously opposed to Parker. James E. Shepard, able president of North Carolina College in Durham, had endorsed Parker, and thus was accused by the New York *Amsterdam News,* a leading Negro weekly, of being "unfitted for the position he holds." But Shepard did not withdraw his support.[5] In fact, he threw himself into the battle for Parker, urging his friends to send strong letters to the appropriate senators. When the NAACP publicly questioned Shepard's loyalty, he promptly replied that "in every fight for the manhood of my race, I have stood with them." In this case, however, he described himself as a "Republican supporting a Republican nominated by a Republican president." He was sure, he concluded, that Parker was qualified and would be fair to all groups.

Since two members of the subcommittee, Overman and Felix Hebert of Rhode Island were known to favor the appointment, it was a foregone conclusion that the recommendation would be for approval. The third member, Senator Borah, had not committed himself, and thus both sides tried to help him make up his mind. John L. Lewis asked why it was necessary for the Senate to confirm the nomination of Parker, the Judge who in the Red Jacket injunction suit "delivered fifty thousand free Americans into indentured servitude." Walter White bombarded Borah and others with affidavits and letters from prominent

---

and stated that to induce employees to break these contracts, and to use "misrepresentation, deceptive statements, and threats of pecuniary loss" were "unlawful and malicious methods" employed by the organizers.

Brandeis, supported by Holmes and Clarke, dissented. Brandeis actually did not argue that the yellow dog contract was illegal. He simply insisted that it was perfectly legal to attempt to unionize the plant. If enough employees should indicate an interest in so doing, they might strike in order to compel the employers to change their contracts. Their contract merely said that they should not both be in the employ of the Hitchman Company and be a member of a union simultaneously.

[5] Willis Briggs, Raleigh lawyer, made an affidavit that Judge Parker carried the two Negro wards in Raleigh in 1920 while Governor Gardner carried them in 1928.

North Carolina Negroes against the confirmation.[6] On the other hand, Edwin Y. Webb, who had served as a district judge in Parker's circuit for a number of years, said that Parker would have made "himself ridiculous by deliberately overruling" a Supreme Court decision. He claimed that Parker's opinions were "just and fair." Republican Committeeman Jonas urged Borah to put the Negro issue in the perspective of North Carolina politics. The Democratic party had profited from the Negro issue since the Civil War, and that issue received a new lease on life with woman suffrage. In the Democratic gubernatorial primary of 1920, according to Jonas, O. Max Gardner, who favored woman suffrage, was portrayed going to the polls arm in arm with two Negro women, and was defeated by Cameron Morrison who opposed woman suffrage. In the election, the threat of the racial issue persuaded Parker to try to eliminate that question from the campaign; thus he made the controversial statement, which was simply designed to deny any interest in the Negro vote. Parker's statement was, according to Jonas, a service to the Negroes. Defeat Parker's nomination, Jonas warned, and you will "sound the death knell of Republican hopes in North Carolina and states bordering."

On April 14, the subcommittee did the expected and by a two to one vote recommended approval by the full Judiciary Committee. But the Republican leadership was worried. Negroes in key states such as Kentucky, Illinois, West Virginia, New Jersey, Kansas, Ohio, New York, Missouri, and Indiana might play a decisive role in elections. In these same states the labor issue also might be important. B. G. Voorhees, Republican state chairman in Missouri, warned the Missouri senators that the confirmation of Parker would mean "that the Republican party might just as well say good-bye to Missouri for the next two or three elections at least. It will be the first great affront given by a Republican Senate to the Negro race since the days of Abraham Lincoln."

It was quite clear that a substantial number of Republican senators would vote against Parker, and hence Majority Leader James E. Watson, and possibly Vice-President Charles Curtis, urged Hoover either to withdraw the nomination or get some sort of disclaimer from Parker that he had uttered anything that reflected on the Negro race. Hoover stood firm, however, praising Parker's legal qualifications; at the same time his Department of Justice defended the Red Jacket opinion, saying that Parker "was dealing with 'points which had been settled by the Supreme Court, which he was bound, under his oath of office to follow.'"

By this time Parker supporters were quite willing to put aside any fear of accusations of impropriety, and they suggested the possibility of Parker's testifying personally before the full Judiciary Committee. Hoover was said to favor the move, and Overman, therefore, on April 21 moved in committee to invite Parker to testify. A vigorous debate followed, and the division went ten to four against issuing the invitation, then in a "swift and unexpected action," the committee voted by a ten to six margin to report the nomination adversely. Those favoring the appointment were Daniel O. Hastings of Delaware, Felix Hebert

---

[6] Walter White claimed that Shepard was the only influential North Carolina Negro who supported Parker, "and he is President of a school supported wholly by state funds." A number of other distinguished Negroes did, however, support the appointment.

of Rhode Island, Frederick H. Gillett of Massachusetts, and Charles W. Waterman of Colorado, Republicans; and Overman of North Carolina and Hubert D. Stephens of Mississippi, Democrats.[7]

In the meantime, Parker's friends were quietly mobilizing in his support. David Blair, Charles Jonas, and Marion Butler, Republican politicians, Edwin Y. Webb of the Federal District Court and Elliott Northcott of the Circuit Court, Walter A. Hildebrand, Washington correspondent of the Greensboro *Daily News,* and Thomas W. Davis, a nationally known North Carolina attorney, were among those most actively working. They were keeping in constant touch with Parker, who himself was "absolutely overwhelmed" in carrying on a determined fight to secure his own confirmation.

The principal aim of the campaign was to secure the endorsement of the American Bar, and to use that endorsement to influence undecided senators. Davis, who for more than twenty years had been active in the North Carolina Bar Association, sent telegrams to prominent lawyers in almost every state asking them to wire Overman and to get others to wire him. Kenneth Royall, president of the North Carolina Bar Association, urged the presidents of the other state bar associations to come to Parker's support. Wade H. Cooper, president of the Commercial National Bank of Washington, D.C., wrote to twenty or more leading newspapers in the East and South. He also communicated, as he put it, with the "controlling influences of certain Senators, which," he said, "I happen to know will be effective."

An important part of the strategy was to concentrate on undecided senators, particularly southerners. Although Senator Ellison D. Smith of South Carolina was in a hospital, a friend of Parker's visited him, impressed upon him "the seriousness of the attack being made" on Parker, especially by "the Negro opposition," and secured a promise of a favorable pair to prevent "an outrage of the South." Parker was particularly interested in securing the support of the Alabama and Georgia senators, and Thomas Davis stirred up friends in those states to use their influence. Since the Ku Klux Klan was reputed to have been responsible for Senator Hugo L. Black's election in Alabama, Black was informed that Parker "seems to have been a lily-white Republican," and thus a desirable addition to the Court. At the same time, Parker was warned that Black might be even more effectively influenced by his labor constituents to vote against Parker. Parker himself telephoned a friend in Georgia asking him to see to it that the Georgia senators were properly acquainted with the issues in the case, and likewise informed a lawyer friend in Detroit that "if your Michigan Senators will support me it will certainly help the situation wonderfully." Parker was indeed keeping up the fight "as strenuously as possible" for his own confirmation.

On the eve of the Senate debate on the appointment, the Parker supporters

[7] Those opposed were Borah of Idaho, Blaine of Wisconsin, Deneen of Illinois, Norris of Nebraska, Robinson of Indiana, and Steiwer of Oregon, Republicans; and Caraway of Arkansas, Dill of Washington, and Walsh of Montana, Democrats. Hoover did not help Overman out at all in this fight—indeed he let it be known that he had not requested Overman to invite Parker, although he did not oppose it. Borah, Blaine, Norris, Walsh, and Dill might be considered "progressives" and thus opposed to conservative nominees; Deneen and Robinson came from states where the Negro vote was considerable. Caraway was alleged to have been partial toward labor.

made their strongest appeal. In the first place, Overman released a letter written by Parker himself in his own defense. The letter stated positively that he had had "no latitude of discretion" in following earlier decisions in the Red Jacket case. On the Negro issue, he asserted that his now famous statement of 1920 was designed to remove the racial issue from the campaign. In fact, he said, "I have no prejudice whatever against the colored people." Parker carefully did not deny that he had favored the North Carolina constitutional amendment which had restricted Negro suffrage. He feared that such a denial "might lead the Southern Senators to think that [he] was hostile to the amendment, and . . . afraid that some of them might not like it." At the same time, Senator Henry J. Allen of Kansas, in a statement thought to be inspired by the administration, emphasized the fact that as recently as January, Parker had declared a segregation ordinance in Richmond unconstitutional. "Why have those who have fulminated a racial issue against the confirmation of Judge Parker," queried Allen, "deliberately ignored this proof of his unswerving fidelity to the Constitution?" [8]

Considerable negotiation was actually taking place behind the scenes on the racial issue. Robert G. Taylor, chairman of the Committee on Race Relations of the Society of Friends, sympathized with Parker's position and apparently hoped that he could persuade Parker to come out strongly against the views which he had expressed in 1920. Indeed there is some evidence that Taylor worked with Parker in drafting a letter describing the latter's position. This letter persuaded a number of NAACP leaders that their opposition to Parker should be withdrawn. Walter White, however, saw "no direct repudiation of lilywhitism," and Taylor himself was convinced that Parker still believed what he had said in 1920. Consequently neither the NAACP nor the Friends committee withdrew their protests against Parker's confirmation.

The debate on Parker's nomination was scheduled for Monday afternoon, April 28. The question attracted full galleries. High society, led by Mrs. Nicholas Longworth, was there, as well as a number of labor leaders. Representative Oscar DePriest, the only Negro congressman, was also there. Overman first made an unsuccessful effort to delay consideration of the appointment to give his colleague Simmons a chance to return from North Carolina; but the Senate had scheduled the debate by unanimous consent and any change would also require unanimous consent. Senator Borah objected on the grounds that Simmons would be back before the vote was taken, so the debate was launched. Overman, as the North Carolinian on the Judiciary Committee, had been given the responsibility of introducing the minority's recommendation for Parker's confirmation. Convinced that the fight on Parker was a kind of conspiracy on the part of Socialists, labor unions, and northern Negroes to destroy the independence of the Court, Overman was sincerely for Parker's confirmation. Yet

---

[8] The NAACP telegraphed Senator Allen that in the Richmond case Parker was simply following the precedent of the unanimous Supreme Court decision. Walter White was quite aware of the irony of his position: "Those who are supporting Judge Parker and who regard him blameless in the so-called 'Yellow Dog' Contract decision because, in their opinion, Judge Parker merely followed Supreme Court precedents, will of necessity realize that Judge Parker's action in the Richmond Segregation Case . . . upholding Judge Groner's decision was obligatory and in no way indicates that he is free from bias against the Negro."

he was quite willing that the Republican regulars assume the main burden for the defense,[9] and he made only a brief, straightforward presentation of the case for Parker.

Then Borah, representing the committee majority, arose "from behind a mass of Supreme Court Reports and other documents" to lead the attack against Parker. He based his argument on the grounds that "the Red Jacket decision demonstrated that he [Parker] sympathized with the principles of the yellow dog contract." Borah argued that Parker did not have to uphold the legality of the yellow dog contract, that Judge Benjamin Cardozo of the New York Court of Appeals had repudiated the principle, as had the Supreme Court of Kansas, and thus that it could not be said that such a contract had been "embedded in our jurisprudence." Borah asserted that he would not condemn an injunction if it were designed to restrain threats or intimidation, but that this particular injunction, was "too broad in that it enjoined peaceful persuasion, peaceful discussion, peaceful communication." The Hitchman case, Borah reasoned, did not provide a good precedent because in that case the union was enjoined because it had employed "deceit and misrepresentation." Indeed, he concluded, the Tri-City case (1921) had specifically ruled that the Hitchman decision had been based upon "deception and misrepresentation," and that normally "peaceful persuasion" was legitimate.

The Parker forces rallied, however, on Tuesday, April 29. Indeed, Senator Gillett of Massachusetts forcefully developed a point which Borah had some difficulty in answering. Gillett claimed that Borah's argument was invalid since it did not point out that the Tri-City case differed fundamentally from the Red Jacket case in that the Court in the latter was "not simply ordering the defendants not peacefully to persuade men to leave their employment but they were forbidden peacefully to persuade men to break their legal contract." The only justification that Borah could actually sustain for not using the Hitchman case, according to Gillett, would be that a yellow dog contract, though legal, was "unconscionable." Senator Simeon D. Fess then injected a point which had been in the background of the debate. After a great forensic display of historical knowledge about the Court, he argued that the real motive behind the opposition to Parker was to undermine the independence of the judiciary. Such a motive must have a source somewhere, concluded Fess, and this source was in Socialism.

Others besides Fess, including apparently Parker himself, were suspicious of the source of the opposition. Fess found the NAACP infiltrated with radicals —opponents of the obviously saner group of Negroes formerly led by Booker T. Washington. W. E. B. Du Bois was a "self-confessed" Bolshevik; William Pickins had "visited Communist Russia" and was "a communist . . . as well as

[9] On June 18, 1929, the Senate changed one of its rules by which presidential nominations "were considered in executive session." The new rule made it possible for such nominations to be "considered in open executive session, unless the Senate should otherwise determine in a closed executive session and by a majority vote." Charles E. Hughes was the first nominee to the Supreme Court to confront an open debate. William Starr Myers and William H. Newton concluded that Parker's nomination would not have been defeated "without the publicity accompanying the extended open executive session."

an ardent advocate of social equality," Mary White Overton was "a Socialist"; John Haynes Holmes was "an extremely radical preacher" who had said that no religious man can conscientiously be a soldier; Felix Frankfurter had been denounced by Theodore Roosevelt as "engaged in excusing men precisely like the Bolsheviki in Russia."

It became obvious as the debate progressed that the division would be close. Hoover would clearly not be able to count on enough Republican senators to bring him victory. He would need strong Democratic support. With Overman and Simmons wholeheartedly in support and with the southern predisposition to agree with Parker's views on the Negro, Hoover certainly expected that southern Democrats would be overwhelmingly for the nominee. Moreover, some northern opponents of Parker may have lost a few southern votes for their cause. Senator Robert F. Wagner of New York, for example, linked the Parker of the Red Jacket case with the Parker of the political speech in 1920, saying that Parker's sympathies apparently flowed to those on top whether economically or racially. "From the contributions to its development by the Negro as well as the white man," said Wagner, "the state of New York has grown to the position it holds today." While Wagner was talking, southern senators, already irritated at the prominent place Representative DePriest regularly occupied in the Senate chamber during the debate, took a walk.

If Wagner's speech gained southern support for Parker, another revelation undoubtedly balanced that gain. Senator Kenneth McKellar of Tennessee found in the files of the Senate Judiciary Committee a letter from Joseph M. Dixon, a North Carolina Republican, then First Assistant Secretary of the Interior, to Walter H. Newton, one of Hoover's secretaries. This letter, written five days after Justice Sanford's death, urged Parker's nomination on the grounds of political expediency. "North Carolina gave President Hoover 65,000 majority . . . it carries more hope of future permanent alignment with the Republican Party than any other of the Southern states," wrote Dixon. "The naming of Judge Parker . . . would appeal mightily to State pride. It would be the first distinctive major appointment made from the South. . . . [It] would be a master political stroke at this time."

The publication of this letter undoubtedly shook southern Democratic senators. Overman "was plainly perturbed." The *News and Observer* made much of the episode; Josephus Daniels, now definitely opposed to confirmation, editorialized that the Republican forces in the state had been mobilized by David Blair, "the North Carolina Mark Hanna," and that Dixon's letter was the first written move in the campaign. Parker's opponents were delighted. Many disliked Hoover and welcomed any opportunity to pick flaws in his administration, even though Attorney General Mitchell denied that Hoover had ever seen the letter.

Tempers were obviously becoming increasingly sensitive as the debate continued. Anti-Parker senators absent from Washington were finding it difficult to get pairs, and so hurry calls went out to Robert M. La Follette, Jr., and John J. Blaine of Wisconsin and William H. McMaster of South Dakota to get back to the Senate in time to cast their votes. Simmons wired Senator J. Thomas Heflin, absent in Alabama, that Parker's confirmation "was of vital importance to our section," and begged him to be paired in favor.[10] Several senators announced that their offices had been ransacked. Rumors were common that patronage was being offered to those senators who would vote for confirmation. Senator Henry F. Ashurst, one of Parker's most outspoken foes, announced that "men with Judge Parker's consent are being offered Federal Judgeships and other appointments to office if they will vote for this nominee." "Call the Lobby Committee together," Ashurst shouted, "and see what strange fish you will bring up from the depths that are working to put over the Parker nomination." Ashurst said specifically that a senator had been offered a judgeship.

Ashurst's accusations roused a storm in the Senate, and numerous senators demanded an investigation. Apparently, he himself was somewhat abashed at what he had said because he cut out of the *Congressional Record* the phrase beginning, "men with Judge Parker's consent are being offered Federal Judgeships." Indeed, he denied that he had used the phrase. Senator Allen demanded that Ashurst reveal the name of the senator to whom a bribe offer had allegedly been made, and Ashurst then named "my learned friend, the junior Senator from Washington, Mr. Dill." It soon became apparent, however, that Ashurst had been unduly impetuous in making the accusation. Dill's explanation of the incident in question was simple: a Republican friend had said that undoubtedly the administration would be willing to reward those who voted for confirmation. Dill in a jocular fashion had said that he had no further interest in running for office, whereupon his friend had mentioned a judgeship. Dill then had said he would "rather be a private citizen than a judge." His friend had had no political influence, and that remark had ended it so far as Dill was concerned.

The Ashurst explosion was the last dramatic episode in the Parker fight, and the climax was reached on Wednesday, May 7, when the vote was taken. The galleries were packed. Representatives lined the walls of the Senate chamber three deep. The chamber itself was uncharacteristically silent as the roll was called. The result was not clear until the final vote was tallied, and, for one of the comparatively few occasions, every senator had his vote recorded. The final vote, if pairs are counted, stood at 49 against the appointment and 47 for confirmation, or 41 to 39 without the pairs. The President's nominee had been rejected.

President Hoover maintained a dignified silence after his defeat. He later recorded in his memoirs, however, that it was largely the result of the desertion of Republican senators who ran "like white mice when confronted" with "lobbies" of labor and the NAACP. Parker, although so disappointed that he found it "hard to maintain [his] equanimity," publicly expressed no bitterness, and within a few days put in an appearance on Capitol Hill to thank Hoover for appointing him and those senators who had supported him.

Both Hoover and Parker would have been more than human, however, had they not been bitter and disillusioned about American politics. Parker had been formally endorsed by two United States circuit judges, ten United States district

---

[10] Frank A. Hampton, Simmons' secretary, told Heflin, a notorious white supremacist who had opposed Smith in 1928, that anti-Parker senators opposed Parker's white supremacy views and wished to punish North Carolina for having voted against Smith in 1928.

judges, many state judges, the then president and five former presidents of the American Bar Association, and twenty-two presidents of state and county bar associations. No one had raised any serious question concerning his character, although the New York *Times* did complain that he had appeared too anxious, "too much like a candidate for the office of sheriff." Indeed he did act like a candidate for the office.

More concern was shown about his experience and ability as a judge. In spite of the efforts on the part of his supporters to emphasize his effectiveness on a circuit court, no one could yet make the forty-four year old jurist a distinguished judge. His various defeats in running for political office, not unusual for a southern Republican, apparently made an impression. His participation, as assistant to Attorney General Harry M. Daugherty, in the abortive war frauds investigations of the Harding administration irritated Democrats and did not impress Republicans. In fact his conduct in these investigations had received some criticism. Hoover's reasoning that a southern appointment was desirable at this time was sound, and under normal circumstances would have gone through smoothly. But these were not normal circumstances for a judicial appointment. Hoover's political antennae were not particularly sensitive, but he had had a sharp warning in the only-too-recent debate over Hughes's confirmation that his judicial appointments were not going to be taken lightly. Hughes was a man of distinction; yet 12 out of 56 Republican senators and 16 out of 39 Democrats voted against him.

Four issues were primarily responsible for complicating the Parker appointment. Probably the most important of these was the one principally responsible for the opposition to Hughes—the determination on the part of a substantial number of Democratic and Republican senators that the appointee should have liberal leanings. There were probably thirteen nominal Republicans and perhaps four or five Democrats who were in this category.[11] All of these, except Senator Bronson Cutting of New Mexico, who did not vote in the Hughes case, and Senators Wagner and Thomas D. Schall who voted for Hughes, were against both Hughes and Parker. Norris frankly admitted that he opposed Parker because he opposed Parker's ideas. "Everyone who ascends to that holy bench should have in his heart and mind the intention of looking after the liberties of his fellow citizens . . . of discarding if necessary the old precedents of barbarous days and construing the Constitution and the laws in the light of a modern day." Robert M. La Follette, Jr., suspecting that the North Carolina Republican party was dominated by the "Duke Tobacco Trust," the water power interests, and mill owners, considered Parker's appointment as "packing the Supreme Court with the advocate of great monopoly interests and with 'lame duck' politicians." Clearly a strong minority of Congress hoped to strengthen that wing of the Court consisting of Holmes, Brandeis, and Stone.

The attitude of these "liberals" was strengthened by the injection of the

[11] These were Blaine of Wisconsin, Borah of Idaho, Couzens of Michigan, Cutting of New Mexico, Frazier of North Dakota, Howell of Nebraska, Johnson of California, La Follette of Wisconsin, McNary of Oregon, Norris of Nebraska, Nye of North Dakota, Brookhart of Iowa, and McMaster of South Dakota (Republicans); possibly Black of Alabama, Dill of Washington, Walsh and Wheeler of Montana (Democrats), and Shipstead of Minnesota (Farmer-Labor).

yellow dog contract and racial issues. A significant fact is that, as Senator Borah said in his closing attack on Parker, "no man has soiled his lips by defending the contract involved in this controversy." To the progressives, the labor issue was important in confirming their views about Parker's lack of liberalism, and no amount of argument regarding precedent could persuade them that a yellow dog contract could be justified. What they wanted was someone willing to defy precedent, and they were convinced that such defiance was not only desirable but in this case easily justified.

The racial issue was certainly important in the urban states of the North and possibly in Kansas. Senator Arthur H. Vandenberg of Michigan found it exceedingly difficult to decide how to vote. He wanted to believe in Parker's "independence and fidelity." Yet he doubted whether a human being could "shake off all predilections." Even if he could shake them off, Vandenberg reasoned, "the authority of the Supreme Court depends upon the measure of public confidence which it enjoys. Therefore if 18,000,000 colored citizens of the United States have a basis for feeling that Judge Parker is prejudiced against their political rights, it is impossible to ask of them that they still give him their confidence in respect to these constitutional questions." The NAACP saw to it that key senators were kept informed of the views of their Negro constituents. Public meetings sponsored by the NAACP in Chicago and Detroit late in April resulted in several hundred telegrams addressed to Senators Deneen and Glenn of Illinois and Vandenburg and Couzens of Michigan; all four voted against Parker and all four were Republicans. The Negro issue was also important in Indiana; here another Republican, Senator Arthur R. Robinson, refused to support Hoover's nominee.

In spite of the Republican spilt, Hoover might logically have expected enough Democratic votes to win the confirmation. Parker was a southerner, and the hostile attitude of the NAACP undoubtedly helped him among southern senators. Yet to some southern Democrats, nothing was much worse than a southern Republican politician, and the Dixon letter made it quite clear that, regardless of Parker's status, Republican politicians expected to profit from Parker's confirmation, and even Negro-hating Senator Heflin could not be convinced by his friend Senator Simmons that it was desirable to give aid and comfort to the Republicans. Fourteen southern senators voted against Parker, of whom John M. Robsion of Kentucky was a Republican, "scared to death for fear he will lose the Negro vote" in his campaign for re-election.[12] Eleven southern Democrats voted to confirm Parker. These included the Mississippi senators, Stephens and Harrison; the two Virginia senators, Glass and Swanson; the two South Carolina senators, Smith and Blease, who considered Parker "the South's only hope"; the two Louisiana senators, Broussard and Ransdell; and Fletcher of Florida. The last three, according to the Washington *Post,* would always vote with the Republicans when a tariff bill was pending. Although it may be that

[12] Robsion was defeated in the fall election. Southern Democrats who voted or were paired against Hughes were: Barkley of Kentucky, Black of Alabama, Connolly and Sheppard of Texas, Harris and George of Georgia, McKellar of Tennessee, Blease and Smith of South Carolina, Glass of Virginia, and Overman and Simmons of North Carolina. Of these, Blease, Smith, Simmons, Overman, and Glass supported Parker.

Parker won as many votes as he lost by the racial issue, there seems little question that the campaign was good for the Negro "political consciousness."

Jonas, one of the leaders in the Parker campaign, blamed Parker's defeat on the Communists, Reds, "the sons of the Wild Jackass," Negroes, Josephus Daniels, and certain southern senators, "who traded the representation of a great Southland on the highest Court" for partisan advantage. Parker himself blamed "radical Senators" for having put the "labor people" and the NAACP, "a quasi-socialistic organization," up to encouraging unions and Negro groups to influence their senators. Still, he concluded that he would have won had it not been for southern senators playing "small politics in hitting at the Administration." As one friend told him, the blunder "that killed us was the Dixon letter. How in the name of all that is holy such a *faux pas* could have been made passes all human understanding."

When one evaluates Parker's record as Circuit Court judge especially in the twenty-five years after his failure to reach the Supreme bench, one might wish that he had been confirmed. Probably few would differ with the conclusion that he became "one of the most distinguished jurists on the Federal bench." In 1946, the *American Bar Association Journal,* surveying Parker's record of twenty years on the Circuit Court, called the Senate's refusal to confirm the "most regrettable combinations of error and injustice that has ever developed as to a nomination to the great court." At the time, Harlan F. Stone disagreed heartily with the Senate's action and favored confirmation. Owen Roberts, who just one week after Parker's defeat was promptly accepted as Sanford's successor without a record vote, wrote: "It will always be a matter of regret to me that I could not have waited a later chance for elevation to the bench and then gone upon it with you as a colleague."

One might wonder, however, whether Stone and Roberts would have expressed the same sentiments had they been aware of the highly organized campaign waged for Parker's confirmation. Activities of pressure groups in favor of a confirmation may be as proper as pressure from the opposition. The question is whether it was appropriate for the nominee to a high judicial office himself to participate actively in what was for some a partisan, political campaign.

The Great Depression to 1945: Consensus in Face of Depression and War

The years from 1933 to 1945 form a definable unit: they were an age of continual crisis and they were preeminently the age of Franklin D. Roosevelt, who dominated these years as few men have ever dominated an era. A remarkably shrewd politician and a gifted speaker, Roosevelt possessed a rare willingness to experiment. His success as leader of a political party, persuader of the public, and initiator of new policies is very likely unmatched in American history. On the other hand, he was seriously lacking in administrative skills, only casually acquainted with economics, and hardly an astute diplomatist. His gigantic virtues and defects marked this age of depression and war, leaving a legacy of achievement and failure historians will wrestle with for generations.

Roosevelt approached both the depression and the rise of totalitarianism as enemies against which a united America had to wage relentless war. In some ways, his greatest achievement was in maintaining a consensus behind his leadership as the nation struggled with these enemies. For all the acrimony of some segments of business and of movements to the left of his New Deal, and for all the quarreling over diplomatic policy that marked the hesitant American response to the rise of the dictatorships, Roosevelt in the end succeeded in building solid support behind both his major efforts, largely by blurring his policies to meet the widest possible range of demands.

In his New Deal, Roosevelt aimed to save capitalism by discarding some of its traditional baggage—such as laissez-faire, a free market in agricultural products, opposition to unions, and hostility to social welfare schemes. This modernization of the American economy brought together business, labor, and government in successful agreement on a loosely planned economy;

135

providing governmental support, maintaining a large measure of group initiative, and clearly leaving corporate enterprise in its traditional position dominating the economy. The poor received benefits from New Deal economic and welfare programs that were an improvement by previous standards although hopelessly inadequate from the perspective of today. Roosevelt's domestic success was not in recovery from the depression, which did not come until the war effort boosted the economy, but in laying the groundwork for the modern welfare capitalist economy under which we have lived ever since, and in spurring the reform tradition that eventuated in the New Frontier and Great Society programs of the 1960's.

In foreign policy, Roosevelt succeeded not only in uniting the nation behind the allied war effort, but also committing it to internationalism after the war. The particular horror with which fascism struck most Americans and the collapse of the Allied cause on the European continent in 1940 were crucial to achieving this consensus against Hitler, while the American people, reminded of the League of Nations' failure, knew they could not again withdraw from European affairs without the risk of renewed war. On the other hand, Roosevelt forged the consensus on foreign policy by muting almost all domestic controversy and by a genial vagueness about war aims obscured by the rhetoric of unconditional surrender. As a result, when the much-loved President died in 1945 just before the end of the war, both the shape of postwar domestic affairs and our relations with our allies—including the Soviet Union—were in a state of uncertainty. Even the most sympathetic historians must concede that the Age of Roosevelt left a wondrously mixed legacy to posterity.

WILLIAM E. LEUCHTENBURG

The New Deal and the Analogue of War

In the Roosevelt administration an easy transition took place from waging war on the depression to waging war on the axis powers; "Dr. New Deal," in the President's words, became "Dr. Win-the-War." Both Hoover and Roosevelt had drawn on the experiences of World War One in combatting the depression; new agencies such as the Reconstruction Finance Corporation drew their structure and personnel in part from wartime counterparts, and employed the imagery of war in their public statements.

Why this urge for war in America's national rhetoric? Is it a necessity of objective circumstance or a compulsion from within? The idea of waging war against the depression is infinitely extensible: war on vice, war on poverty, or war on "the cancerous enemy at home," domestic communism. The metaphor of war is suggestive of a nation's needs when under pressure, or its inability to find unity except under war rhetoric. In actual war the Great Depression was solved and wars since that time have helped to sustain prosperity. In fact, America has not tested whether prosperity can be maintained without fueling up some kind of war machine. In this essay, William E. Leuchtenburg finds that during the Great Depression the analogy to war provided argument for suppressing normal procedures and for overriding many sensibilities.

Can the state prosper without a cultural equivalent of war? According to Randolph Bourne, "war is the health of the state. . . . In a nation at war, every citizen identifies himself with the whole, and feels immensely strengthened in that identification . . . the individual becomes almost identical with his society." Perhaps Bourne's observations explain one of the most mystifying puzzles of American politics during the depression: why more voters did not favor socialist and communist nostrums for the nation's ills. If the citizen under the spell of wartime rhetoric senses the rightness of his country and its history, he will not wish to experiment with essentially foreign ideologies.

The metaphors a nation employs reveal much about how it perceives reality. The unconscious choice of symbols bares the bedrock of its beliefs. Moreover, the words people use are not neutral artifacts; they shape ideas and behavior. Just as the psychoanalyst listens for slips of the tongue or strange incongruities of ideas to help him understand the patient, or the literary critic studies the symbols in a poem or novel, so the historian finds it rewarding to explore the imagery a particular period has used, consciously or unconsciously, to interpret its experience.

In the months and years that followed the stock market crash of 1929, America searched for some way to make comprehensible what was happening. Sometimes people thought of the Great Depression as a breakdown of a system, sometimes as the product of the machinations of evil or stupid men, sometimes as the visitation of a plague like the Black Death. But from the very first, many conceived the depression to be a calamity like war or, more specifically, like the menace of a foreign enemy who had to be defeated in combat. Occasionally, the analogue of war was a general one, more often it referred specifically to World War I. When President Hoover summoned the leading industrialists to meet in Washington, one financial journal commented: " 'Order up the Moors!' was Marshal Foch's reply at the first battle of the Marne. . . . 'Order up the business reserves,' directed President Hoover as pessimistic reports flowed in from all quarters, following the stock market crash."

For the rest of his years in office, Hoover resorted constantly to the imagery of war to describe the depression. In one of his addresses, he claimed that the country had just won its "battle of Chateau-Thierry" and must "reform [its] forces for the battle of Soissons." "Again and again he used military terms in describing the struggle in which he was engaged," recalled one of his aides. "He was the commanding officer at general headquarters, so visualized himself." Hoover's advisers perceived the crisis in the same terms. In June, 1931, after the President unfolded his reparations plan, Secretary of State Henry Stimson confided to his diary: "We have all been saying to each other the situation is quite like war."

In addition to employing the metaphor of war to explain the meaning of the depression, the 1930's drew on the experience of the economic mobilization of World War I for instrumentalities to combat hard times. These are two discrete themes. Some who resorted to the analogue of war had no interest in the precedent of the wartime mobilization, and a few who turned to the example of the mobilization did not employ the imagery of war. Hence, it would be possible to examine these strands separately. But so closely did most Americans associate the metaphor of war with the specific legacy of the war mobilization that it has seemed more fruitful to discuss both these themes in a single context.

In the New Deal years, the two strands were inseparable. As early as his "forgotten man" speech in the 1932 campaign, Franklin Roosevelt manipulated the analogue of war to his advantage. In that same address, he referred to the specific operations of the war mobilization, a heritage he was to acknowledge on many occasions after his election to the presidency. But the legacy of the war was to prove a mixed blessing. Useful as a justification for New Deal actions, it also served to limit and divert the reformers in ways that had not been anticipated.

In tracing the genealogy of the New Deal, historians have paid little attention to the mobilization of World War I. Instead, they have centered their interest on two movements: populism and progressivism. Both were important antecedents—a reasonably straight line may be drawn from the Populist sub-treasury plan to the Commodity Credit Corporation, from the Pujo committee to the Securities and Exchange Commission. Yet in concentrating on populism and progressivism, writers have given too little attention to the influence of the wartime mobilization, which may have been as great as the example of the Progressive era and certainly was more important than populism.

Much of the experience of the Progressive era proved irrelevant to the task facing Roosevelt in 1933. Very little in the Populist and Progressive periods offered a precedent for massive federal intervention in the economy. Many of the reforms of the prewar generation were modest ventures in regulation or attempts to liberate business enterprise rather than ambitious national programs of economic action. Moreover, in these years, reformers thought the state and the city more important arenas than the national capital.

World War I marked a bold new departure. It occasioned the abandonment of laissez faire precepts and raised the federal government to director, even dictator, of the economy. The War Industries Board mobilized production; the War Trade Board licensed imports and exports; the Capital Issues Committee regulated investment; the War Finance Corporation lent funds to munitions industries; the Railroad Administration unified the nation's railways; the Fuel Administration fixed the price of coal and imposed "coal holidays" on eastern industry; and the Food Administration controlled the production and consumption of food. The Lever Food and Fuel Control Act of 1917 gave the President sweeping powers: to take over factories and operate them, to fix a maximum price for wheat, and to license businesses in necessaries. By a generous interpretation of its powers, the War Industries Board supervised pricing, compelled corporations to accept government priorities, and forced companies to obey federal edicts on how to dispose of their products. "This is a crisis," a War Industries Board representative scolded steel-industry leaders, "and commercialism, gentlemen, must be absolutely sidetracked." Actions of this character, as well as the proliferation of public corporations ranging from the United States Housing Corporation to the Spruce Production Corporation, proved important precedents for New Deal enterprises fifteen years later.

The field of labor relations may serve as a single example of the difference in importance of the Populist and Progressive experience and that of World War I. Prior to the war, no serious attempt had ever been made to empower the federal government to uphold the right of collective bargaining. Federal action was limited to peripheral areas. When class lines were drawn in labor disputes, progressives frequently aligned themselves against the unions. But in World War I, the War Labor Board proclaimed its support of union rights and, to the discomfiture of businessmen, enforced these rights. Many of the labor policies pursued in the war months would have been inconceivable a short while before. When the Smith & Wesson Arms Company of Springfield, Massachusetts, insisted on its prerogative to require workers to sign yellow-dog contracts, the War Department commandeered the plant, even though the Supreme Court had upheld the legality of such contracts. The government even dared to seize Western Union when the president of the firm denied his employees the right to join the Commercial Telegraphers Union. The panoply of procedures developed by the War Labor Board and the War Labor Policies Board provided the basis in later years for a series of enactments culminating in the Wagner National Labor Relations Act of 1935.

The war gave a home to the new class of university-trained intellectuals which had emerged in the generation before the war. While some of them had found a career in public service in state governments before 1917, few had worked in the national government, chiefly because there was so little in Washington for them to do. After the United States intervened, Washington swarmed with professors, until, one writer noted, "the Cosmos Club was little better than a faculty meeting of all the universities." In all countries, he observed, professors "fought, and they managed affairs, thus refuting the ancient libellous assumption that they constituted an absent-minded third sex. . . ."

Public administrators of this type represented a new force in American politics. They were advisers and technicians but, more than that, men of influence and even of power. At a time when class conflicts were sharpening, they did not reflect particular classes so much as the thrust for power of *novi homines* who had a significant role to play on the national stage. Some like Gifford Pinchot had made their appearance in Washington before the war, and still more like Charles McCarthy had been active in such reform capitals as Madison and Albany, but it was the war which offered them an unparalleled opportunity. Randolph Bourne noted perceptively the "peculiar congeniality between the war and these men. It is as if the war and they had been waiting for each other." Phenomena almost wholly of the twentieth century, they came by the 1930's to have a crucial part in shaping legislation and in manning the new agencies which their legislation developed. The passage of the Wagner Act in 1935, for example, resulted less from such traditional elements as presidential initiative or the play of "social forces" than from the conjunction of university-trained administrators like Lloyd Garrison within the New Deal bureaucracy with their counterparts on senatorial staffs like Leon Keyserling in Senator Wagner's office.

This new class of administrators, and the social theorists who had been advocating a rationally planned economy, found the war an exciting adventure. The *New Republic* liberals rejoiced that the war produced a novel kind of democratic state which was creating a radical new order based on the democratization of industry. ". . . During the war we revolutionized our society," the *New Republic* boasted. These liberals distinguished themselves sharply from the New Freedom reformers who aimed only to achieve minor changes in the nineteenth-century tradition. Nationalists and collectivists, they looked toward a centralized state which would use its powers to reshape the economy in the interests of labor and other disadvantaged groups.

Many progressives believed that Wilson's war measures signified both a fulfillment of Progressive hopes and a happy augury for the future. Enormously impressed by "the social possibilities of war," John Dewey observed that in every warring country, production for profit had been subordinated to production for use. "The old conception of the absoluteness of private property has received the world over a blow from which it will never wholly recover." Thorstein

Veblen, who worked for the Food Administration in 1918, thought the war created new possibilities for far-reaching social change. Economists viewed the War Industries Board as "a notable demonstration of the power of war to force concert of effort and collective planning," and anticipated that lessons from the war could be applied in times of peace. When Wesley C. Mitchell closed his lectures at Columbia University in May, 1918, he remarked that peace would bring new problems, but "it seems impossible that the countries concerned will attempt to solve them without utilizing the same sort of centralized directing now employed to kill their enemies abroad for the new purpose of reconstructing their own life at home." "What we have learned in war we shall hardly forget in peace," commented Walter Weyl. "The new economic solidarity, once gained, can never again be surrendered."

The end of the war left the administrators with a sense of incompletion. One writer noted unmistakable shadows of annoyance at the Cosmos Club when "the dark cloud of peace" lowered in October, 1918. After the war, to the chagrin of the planners, the economic machinery was quickly dismantled, but the lesson that the war had taught—that the federal government could mobilize the nation's resources in a planned economy—was not forgotten. Throughout the 1920's, the more advanced Progressives looked back fondly toward the war mobilization which seemed to have drawn a blueprint for America's future. In 1927, Rexford Tugwell lauded the war as "an industrial engineer's Utopia." He wanted to co-ordinate the economy as it had been under the War Industries Board in "America's war-time socialism." "We were on the verge of having an international industrial machine when peace broke," he wrote ruefully. ". . . Only the Armistice," he lamented, "prevented a great experiment in control of production, control of price, and control of consumption."

The fascination the war example held for the Progressives was a consequence of the fusion of nationalism and reform in the previous generation. Heralded by Bismarck in Germany and Joseph Chamberlain in Great Britain, this conjunction appeared in America in the martial fantasies of Edward Bellamy, in Francis Walker's critique of classical economics, in the "industrial armies" of men like Jacob Coxey, in the military forms of the Salvation Army, and in the response of certain reformers to the imperialist issues of the 1890's. In the Progressive era, this association was starkly revealed in the career of Theodore Roosevelt who thought social justice and military preparedness to be two aspects of a common program.

While the confluence of nationalism and reform fascinated a number of progressive theorists, notably Brooks Adams, it was Herbert Croly who, in his seminal *The Promise of American Life,* explored the relationship most extensively. Croly set down the deep dissatisfaction of the Progressives with the quality of life in America. The homogeneity of the early republic, he wrote, had been fragmented by a century of individualism run riot. So long as the market place determined values, so long as each individual or interest was permitted to pursue its own ends with no commitment to a common ideal, the result could not help but be unsatisfying, Croly reasoned. Reform had foundered because it lacked a sense of national purpose. "In this country," he observed, "the solution of the social problem demands the substitution of a conscious social ideal for the earlier instinctive homogeneity of the American nation."

The war offered just such a "conscious social ideal." Through war priorities, as Bernard Baruch later explained, the economy could be "made to move in response to a national purpose rather than in response to the wills of those who had money to buy." The nationalistic demands of war denied, if only for a time, the claims of the profit system. ". . . When production and distribution became really a matter of life and death, immediate and dramatic, every warring nation, after a few months of appalling waste, threw laissez-faire out of the window," noted Stuart Chase. "Wars must be won, and it was painfully obvious that laissez-faire was no help in winning them." The individualistic, competitive economy of the prewar years had to submit to the discipline of conscious government direction. Not business profit but the national interest was to determine how resources were to be allocated. The old system of competition, Rexford Tugwell wrote jubilantly, "melted away in the fierce new heat of nationalistic vision."

When the stock market crash of 1929 precipitated the Great Depression of the 1930's, progressives turned instinctively to the war mobilization as a design for recovery. The War Industries Board, Stuart Chase pointed out, had, like the Soviet *Gosplan,* demonstrated that "super-management" could replace "industrial anarchy." George Soule contended that the war had shown that planning was neither beyond human capacity nor alien to American values. "Many of those who now advocate economic planning have been doing so, in one way or another, ever since the experiences of 1917–18, and mainly as result of the possibilities which those experiences suggested for better performance in times of peace." The same "deliberate collective effort" which had made possible a tremendous expansion of production could be turned to peacetime ends, he argued. "If that military and industrial army had been mobilized, not to kill, burn and shatter, but to substitute garden cities for slums, to restore soil fertility and reforest our waste regions, to carry out flood control, to increase the necessities of life available for those in the lower income groups, we could have achieved in a short time a large number of really desirable objectives," Soule claimed.

Such men as Gerard Swope of General Electric, a veteran of the war mobilization, and Otto T. Mallery, the leading advocate of public works in the War War I era, recommended floating large federal bond issues like Liberty Bonds to finance a massive public-works program. Swope wrote President Hoover: "If we were faced with war, the President would immediately call a special session of Congress to declare war and to raise armies. This unemployment situation in many ways is more serious even than war. Therefore it is suggested that an extra session of Congress be called and the President request it to issue a billion dollars of bonds, bearing a low interest rate, and that then a campaign be organized to sell these bonds, much as the Liberty Bond campaigns were organized when we entered the war thirteen years ago." The Wisconsin economist Richard T. Ely went a step farther. He proposed the creation of a peacetime army which, when a depression struck, could be expanded by recruiting from the ranks of the unemployed. Under the direction of an economic general staff, the army, Ely urged, "should go to work to relieve distress with all the vigor and resources of brain and brawn that we employed in the World War."

By the middle of 1931, both businessmen and politicians were calling on President Hoover to adopt the procedures of the War Industries Board to pull the country out of the depression. When William McAdoo, who had headed the wartime Railroad Administration, proposed a Peace Industries Board in June, 1931, he found ready support. The War Industries Board, one correspondent wrote McAdoo, "accomplished wonders during the war, and there is no question but that a board established now to coordinate things in our national industries will also do wonders. This historical precedent is a great asset and ought to guide us in our national planning for the benefit of all." A month later, Charles Beard urged the creation of a National Economic Council with a Board of Strategy and Planning which would follow the pattern of "the War Industries Board and other federal agencies created during the titanic effort to mobilize men and materials for the World War." The following month, Representative Chester Bolton of Ohio advanced a similar proposal. "If we could have another body like the old War Industries Board," he wrote the head of Hoover's voluntary relief agency, "I believe the situation today could be greatly bettered." In September, 1931, Gerard Swope came forth with the most influential of all the pre-New Deal proposals: the "Swope Plan" to stabilize employment and prices through a constellation of trade associations under a national economic council. Early in 1932, a group of more than a hundred businessmen requested Hoover to declare a two-year truce on destructive competition and urged him "to consider a return to war-time experience by bringing into existence A National Economic Truce Board."

The cornucopia of proposals included suggestions with widely differing ideological implications. Some called on the war example to support radical recommendations for national planning; others used the war precedent simply as a stratagem to free business of the encumbrance of the trust laws. Most of them had in common a demand for greater initiative by the federal government, and many of them—especially the public-works proposals—called for a sharp increase in government spending.

Such proposals ran far ahead of anything President Hoover and his followers would countenance. Most businessmen seemed chary of taking the War Industries Board as a model for peacetime. The President himself gave little indication of a readiness to have the federal government assume a larger role. To be sure, he signed an Employment Stabilization Bill in 1931, and gave a major share of credit for the measure to Mallery. But he deplored recommendations for lavish federal spending. Ventures of this sort, the President protested, would unbalance the budget and destroy business confidence in public credit.

These doctrines received small credence from men who recalled the war expenditures. "If it is permissible for government to expend billions in wartime in the organization of production, it is no less legitimate for government in a great emergency of peacetime to do what it is also impossible for private individuals to accomplish," reasoned the distinguished economist Edwin R. A. Seligman. The popular economic writer William Trufant Foster scolded:

> If any one still doubts that our economic troubles are mainly mental, let him consider what would happen if the United States declared war today. Everybody knows what would happen. Congress

would immediately stop this interminable talk and appropriate three billion dollars—five billion—ten billion—any necessary amount. . . .

Some day we shall realize that if money is available for a blood-and-bullets war, just as much money is available for a food-and-famine war. We shall see that if it is fitting to use collective action on a large scale to kill men abroad, it is fitting to use collective action on an equally large scale to save men at home.

Although Hoover rejected the demand that he draw on the war legacy to mount a program of public works, he could not resist for long the clamor for government initiative to expand relief to the jobless. By the summer of 1931, the number of unemployed totaled eight million. William Allen White wrote: "Hundreds of thousands of men, women and children are going to suffer terribly this winter in spite of all that the natural laws of economic change can do, however soon change may start, however rapidly it may move. Yet the situation is not hopeless, for if we can recreate the dynamic altruism outside of government which moved us during the war, we can harness forces that will bring relief and make us a better and nobler people." If Hoover could arouse the "latent altruism" of the people, White believed, great sums could be raised for relief "as we raised the Liberty Loan, Red Cross and Y drive funds during the war."

On August 19, 1931, President Hoover named Walter S. Gifford, president of the American Telephone and Telegraph Company, to head the President's Organization on Unemployment Relief. A week later Newton Baker, a member of the Advisory Committee of the POUR, noted that Gifford seemed to be planning to organize the country along the lines of the Council of National Defense, and added: "I am going a step farther and suggest that as far as possible men with military experience in the World War be used. They have had lessons in effective and disciplined action which will be valuable." That fall, the Gifford committee launched a "mobilization" to win support for local fund-raising drives. National advertisements proclaimed: "Between October 19 and November 25 America will feel the thrill of a great spiritual experience." A few weeks later, when Senator Edward Costigan of Colorado questioned the advisability of employing such techniques, Gifford responded: "We certainly did it in the war. I do not know that I like it, but, as I say, it is more or less the established practice. . . ."

President Hoover made much more forceful use of the war precedent to meet the financial crisis of the autumn of 1931. In December, 1931, Hoover asked Congress to create a Reconstruction Finance Corporation frankly modeled on the War Finance Corporation. The proposal apeared to originate at about the same time in the minds of several different men: Hoover, Federal Reserve Governor Eugene Meyer, who had been managing director of the WFC, Louis Wehle, who had been the WFC's general counsel, and Senator Joseph Robinson of Arkansas. All drew their inspiration from the WFC. "The RFC was a revival of the War Finance Corporation, that's all, but with expanded powers," Meyer recalled. Observers were astonished by the speed with which Congress approved the RFC bill. "It puts us financially on a war basis," noted the *New Republic*. When the RFC began operations, it employed many of the WFC's old staff, followed its pattern and that of the wartime Treasury in financing, and even took over, with slight modifications, the old WFC forms for loan applications.

The RFC, declared one periodical, was to be the "spearhead of the economic A.E.F." But Hoover and his aides insisted that the intervention of the RFC be held to a minimum. Hoover's reluctance to use the RFC as an agency in a new kind of mobilization suggested that the war analogy meant different things to different men and that it could be turned to conservative purposes as readily as to those envisaged by the progressives. While the progressives thought of the war as a paradigm for national planning, Hoover remembered it as a time when the government had encouraged a maximum of voluntary action and a minimum of disturbance of the profit system. He wished the crucial decisions to be made, as they had been in wartime, by corporation leaders. He employed the metaphor of war to serve a conservative function: that of draining internal antagonisms onto a common national enemy. In his address to the Republican national convention in 1932, the permanent chairman, Bertrand Snell, declared in defense of Hoover: "He solidified labor and capital against the enemy."

New York's Governor Franklin D. Roosevelt sought to reap political advantage from these different perceptions of the war experience. In his campaign for the Democratic presidential nomination in 1932, Roosevelt contrasted Hoover's performance with the achievements of the war mobilization. In his "forgotten man" address in Albany on April 7, 1932, Roosevelt declared that American success in the war had been due to leadership which was not satisfied with "the timorous and futile gesture" of sending a small army and navy overseas, but which "conceived of a whole Nation mobilized for war, economic, industrial, social and military resources gathered into a vast unit." The United States in 1932, Roosevelt asserted, faced "a more grave emergency than in 1917," and in meeting that emergency the Hoover administration had neglected "the infantry of our economic army." "These unhappy times," the Governor observed, "call for the building of plans that rest upon the forgotten, the unorganized but the indispensable units of economic power, for plans like those of 1917 that build from the bottom up and not from the top down, that put their faith once more in the forgotten man at the bottom of the economic pyramid." Less than two weeks later, at the Jefferson Day Dinner at St. Paul on April 18, Roosevelt repeated that the nation faced an emergency "more grave than that of war" and once more derided Hoover's efforts to meet the crisis. He added pointedly:

> Compare this panic-stricken policy of delay and improvisation with that devised to meet the emergency of war fifteen years ago.
>
> We met specific situations with considered, relevant measures of constructive value. There were the War Industries Board, the Food and Fuel Administration, the War Trade Board, the Shipping Board and many others.

The 1932 election brought the Democrats to power for the first time since Wilson's war administration. It was "only natural," as Swisher has observed, "that some of the World-War leaders should return to federal office and that others should become unofficial advisers of the administration. They, like the

President, thought in terms of the dramatic concentration of power in the federal government which they had helped to bring about for the defeat of a foreign enemy. It is not surprising that modes of procedure were carried over from one period to the other." In the interregnum between Roosevelt's election in November, 1932, and his inauguration in March, 1933, war recollections became even more compelling. The whole political system seemed doomed to self-asphyxiation. The discords of party, the deadlock in Congress, the maxims of the classical economists, the taboos of the Constitution all seemed to inhibit action at a time when action was desperately needed. In contrast, the war was remembered as a time of movement and accomplishment.

During the interregnum, the country debated a series of new proposals for utilizing the war experience to vanquish the depression. Daniel Roper, who would soon be Roosevelt's Secretary of Commerce, suggested a few days after the election that the new President "appoint one 'super" secretary with the other secretaries assistant to him and organize under this 'super' secretary the plan of the National Council of Defense composed of, say 21 men working without compensation as they did in War times." Many believed the crisis could be met only by vesting in the President the same arbitrary war powers that Woodrow Wilson had been given. The depression, declared Alfred E. Smith on February 7, 1933, was "doing more damage at home to our own people than the great war of 1917 and 1918 ever did." "And what does a democracy do in a war?" Smith asked. "It becomes a tyrant, a despot, a real monarch. In the World War we took our Constitution, wrapped it up and laid it on the shelf and left it there until it was over." Four days later, Republican Governor Alf Landon of Kansas inquired: "Why not give the President the same powers in this bitter peacetime battle as we would give to him in time of war?"

As early as the spring of 1932, weeks before Roosevelt had even been nominated, his brain trust had requested Joseph D. McGoldrick and Howard L. McBain to prepare a memorandum on presidential war powers, for they anticipated Roosevelt would need them as authority for emergency acts. Early in January, 1933, the President-elect asked Rexford Tugwell to explore the possibility that the Trading with the Enemy Act of 1917 might provide the basis for an edict embargoing gold exports. Tugwell's research quickly involved him in a comedy of errors in which the New Dealers sought both to obtain the necessary information without letting the Hoover Administration learn what they were up to and at the same time to persuade themselves that a statute that had been amended many times gave them the legal authority to do what they intended to do anyway. Governor Roosevelt's legal aides could not have been more cooperative. Senator Thomas Walsh, Roosevelt's choice to be Attorney General, promised that, if the President-elect found he needed the powers, he would quiet his doubts and rule that the old statute gave him the authority he required. When, after Walsh's death, Roosevelt picked Homer Cummings for the post, he turned over to him the folder on the Trading with the Enemy Act. Cummings obligingly found the statute was still alive.

As the day of Roosevelt's inauguration approached, the epidemic of bank failures drove governors in state after state to proclaim bank holidays and raised fears that the economic system was on the verge of collapse. "A blight has fallen over all American industry," declared the Akron *Beacon-Journal* on

March 3. "A foreign invader making easy conquest of our shores could do no worse." As Roosevelt took the oath of office, the atmosphere in Washington, wrote Arthur Krock, was like that "in a beleaguered capital in war time."

Roosevelt's inaugural address on March 4, 1933 reflected the sense of wartime crisis. The nation, he resolved, must move "as a trained and loyal army willing to sacrifice for the good of a common discipline." He would ask Congress to adopt his legislative program, but if Congress failed to act and the emergency continued, the new President announced: "I shall not evade the clear course of duty that will then confront me. I shall ask the Congress for the one remaining instrument to meet the crisis—broad executive power to wage a war against the emergency, as great as the power that would be given to me if we were in fact invaded by a foreign foe."

During the "Hundred Days," President Roosevelt sought to restore national confidence by evoking the mood of wartime: the feeling of national unity above any claim of partisan or private economic interest because the very existence of the country was imperiled. The opposition press suspended criticism of the President; business corporations, labor unions, and farm organizations pledged their co-operation; and Republican leaders urged the country to rally around the Democratic chief executive. Governor Landon declared: "If there is any way in which a member of that species, thought to be extinct, a Republican Governor of a mid-western state, can aid [the President] in the fight, I now enlist for the duration of the war."

The New Deal hoped to arouse the same sense of devotion to the nation and the same spirit of sacrifice that had been displayed in the war. "It is important," wrote Rexford Tugwell, "that we should again explore the possibilities of what William James called 'the moral equivalents' of war." "The ordeal of war," he told Dartmouth students, "brings out the magnificent resources of youth. . . . The ordeal of depression ought to try your mettle in similar ways. . . . The feeling which shook humanity during the War and which after the War reshaped the entire civilization of mighty nations is called for again."

When the planners of the thirties looked back at the war, they were most impressed by how much had been accomplished once the nation had been unified by allegiance to a common purpose. Writers like Rexford Tugwell and George Soule argued that the effective functioning of "a regime of industrial democracy" required the same spirit of "loyalty to larger aims" that the War Industrial Board had exploited. Nationalistic to the core, unabashedly patriotic, they believed that if the country could once again give fealty to a transcendent ideal, the depression would be conquered as once the armies of the Kaiser had been. Charles Beard proposed a "heroic national effort" that would leave people "richer in goods—and still more important, in patriotic spirit." Many conceived the New Deal not simply as a new kind of economic mobilization but also, as the war had been, a venture in "nation-saving." One of the New Deal experiments was later to be lauded because it had led to "a new baptism of patriotism and an increased consciousness of national unity."

Roosevelt's first important official act was to use the authority of the Trading with the Enemy Act of 1917 to proclaim a national bank holiday. When he sent his banking bill to Congress, the House received it with much the same ardor as it had greeted Woodrow Wilson's war legislation. Speaker Rainey said the situation reminded him of the late war when "on both sides of this Chamber the great war measures suggested by the administration were supported with practical unanimity. . . . Today we are engaged in another war, more serious even in its character and presenting greater dangers to the Republic." After only thirty-eight minutes debate, the House passed the Administration's banking bill, sight unseen.

On March 10, Roosevelt sent his second message to Congress, a plea for plenary powers to slash government spending. To the dismay of progressive Republicans and liberal Democrats, Roosevelt proved to be as orthodox on fiscal matters as his predecessor. When Senator Tom Connally of Texas talked to Roosevelt in December, 1932, the President-elect had stressed the importance of balancing the budget by cutting federal spending and had dwelt upon the constitutional limitations of the President. "If it was constitutional to spend forty billion dollars in a war," Connally told Roosevelt angrily, "isn't it just as constitutional to spend a little money to relieve the hunger and misery of our citizens?" The President-elect brushed aside such remonstrances and chose instead to heed the counsel of his conservative choice for Budget Director, Lewis Douglas. After studying the wartime authority Congress had granted Woodrow Wilson, Roosevelt decided to ask the new Congress to renew those powers in order to enable the President to balance the budget.

The spirit of war crisis speeded through the economy bill. "It is true this bill grants a great deal of power," conceded Representative John McDuffie of Alabama, "but this country is in a state of war—not against a foreign enemy but war against economic evils that demand some sacrifice on your part and mine." Representative John Young Brown of Kentucky spoke even more bluntly when he scolded fellow Democrats:

> . . . I may say to you that we are at war today, and the veterans of this country do not want you, in their name, to desert the standards of the President of the United States.
>
> I had as soon start a mutiny in the face of a foreign foe as start a mutiny today against the program of the President of the United States. [Applause.] And if someone must shoot down, in this hour of battle, the Commander in Chief of our forces, God grant that the assassin's bullet shall not be fired from the Democratic side of this House. [Applause]

Many Congressmen disliked the Administration's economy bill, but feared to oppose the President. When Senator Wallace H. White, Jr., spoke out against the proposal, a Maine constituent warned him that he was "riding out to certain death." He agreed that White's position was logically sound, yet he cautioned that since "a state of war does exist," the Senator would be foolish to sacrifice himself by disregarding the war spirit. After only two days debate, Congress voted the Economy Act. Senator Henry Fountain Ashurst of Arizona explained: "The conditions are as serious as war and we must follow the flag."

There was scarcely a New Deal act or agency that did not owe something to the experience of World War I. The Tennessee Valley Authority—the most ambitious New Deal experiment in regional planning—grew out of the creation of a government-operated nitrate and electric-power project at Muscle Shoals during and after the war. In his message asking for creation of the TVA, President Roosevelt concluded: "In short, this power development of war days leads logically to national planning. . . ." When the TVA bill was introduced in April, 1933, it seemed appropriate to refer it to the House Military Affairs Committee. Although war considerations played an inconsequential part in the birth of the Authority, the TVA Act of 1933 stipulated that in case of war or national emergency, any or all of the property entrusted to the Authority should be available to the government for manufacturing explosives or for other war purposes. The original World War I nitrate plant, which was turned over to the TVA, was to be held as a standby which might be needed in a future war. When foes of the TVA challenged it in the courts, Chief Justice Charles Evans Hughes found constitutional authority for the construction of the Wilson Dam by resting his ruling, in part, on the war power. The TVA was only one of a number of resources operations—from soil conservation to public power development—that employed the war rhetoric or drew from the World War I experience.

The public-housing movement of the thirties had first come of age during the war. In World War I, Congress authorized the Emergency Fleet Corporation and the United States Housing Corporation to provide housing for war workers. The war established the principle of federal intervention in housing, and it trained architects like Robert Kohn, who served as chief of production of the housing division of the U.S. Shipping Board. After the armistice, Kohn observed: ". . . The war has put housing 'on the map' in this country." In 1933, President Roosevelt named Kohn to head the New Deal's first public-housing venture.

Imaginative wartime experiments with garden-city ideas paved the way for the greenbelt towns of the thirties, while the rural resettlement and subsistence homestead projects of the New Deal reaped the harvest of seeds planted by Elwood Mead and Franklin K. Lane in the war years. Roy Lubove has pointed out:

> In such residential communities as Yorkship Village (New Jersey), Union Park Gardens (Delaware) and the Black Rock and Crane Tracts (Bridgeport, Connecticut), the Emergency Fleet Corporation and the United States Housing Corporation offered American architects and planners their first opportunity to apply garden city principles in comprehensive fashion: curvilinear street systems and street sizes adapted to function; park and play facilities; row-house design; the skillful spacing of mass and volume for maximum aesthetic effect and maximum sunlight and ventilation. The memory of the federal war-housing program persisted over the next two decades, a reminder of the potentialities of non-speculative, large-scale site planning for working-class housing.

The New Deal's program of farm price supports owed something to the wartime Food Administration and even more to a decade of proselytization by George Peek, a hard-bitten farm-belt agitator who had served as "a sort of generalissimo of industry" under the War Industries Board. Peek's war experience with the ways government could benefit industry had led him to argue that the government should give the same measure of aid to the distressed farmer. Frustrated in the twenties by Republican presidents in his campaign to win support for McNary-Haugenism, Peek pinned his hopes on the election of Franklin Roosevelt in 1932. "It looks to me as though in the campaign for Roosevelt for President we are in the last line of trenches and if he is not elected that agriculture is doomed to peasantry," Peek wrote. Roosevelt's victory touched off a serious debate over how to curb farm surpluses which, after months of wrangling, ended in the passage of the Agricultural Adjustment Act in the spring of 1933. To head the new Agricultural Adjustment Administration, Roosevelt named George Peek. "To him, with his war experience, this whole thing clicks into shape," Peek's wife noted, "and some of the fine men of the country are coming to his call as they did in 1917, and with the same high purpose."

Consciously devised to provide the moral equivalent to war that men like Tugwell sought, the Civilian Conservation Corps aimed to install martial virtues in the nation's youth. When the CCC enlisted its first recruits, it evoked memories of the mobilization of the AEF. "By the fifteenth of July we shall have 275,000 people all actually at work in the woods," Roosevelt reported a few weeks after Congress adopted the CCC proposal. "It is a pretty good record, one which I think can be compared with the mobilization carried on in 1917." "America has a new army and has sent it to war," observed one writer that summer. "In two brief months 300,000 men have enlisted, been trained, transferred to the front, and have started the attack. The battle is on in earnest."

While the agency was under civilian direction, the Army ran the camps. CCC recruits convened at army recruiting stations; traveled to an Army camp where they were outfitted in World War I clothing; were transported to the woods by troop-train; fell asleep in army tents to the strain of "Taps" and woke to "Reveille." A stanza of a poem by a CCC worker made clear the Army's role:

> Uncle, he says to his Army,
> "You did a good job before
> When you took three million rookies
> And polished 'em up for war,
> Now if you can handle the civvies
> Like the Doughboys and the Gob,
> And stiffen their ranks till they're tough as the yanks
> I'll give 'em a great big job."

The CCC newspaper, frankly modeled on *Stars and Stripes,* offered a prize for the best nickname for a CCC worker: "You know—some word that has caught on in your camp—the way the word 'doughboy' was used to describe the American soldier in France." *Happy Days* recounted the work of the "Tree Army" in the language of military communiques: "Company 217 at Beachy Bottoms, N.Y. has been filled to full Gypsy-moth-fighting strength," or, in Montana, "Depression Warriors Holding Western Front." On July 1, *Happy Days* reported:

The big drive has begun. Uncle Sam has thrown his full C.C.C. strength into the front lines of the forest. . . . The entire reforestation army has landed in the woods—and has the situation well in hand.

In all sectors the reforestation troops are moving ahead. Battle lines of the Gypsy moth are beginning to crack and fall back in New York and New England. Yellow pine beetles are retreating from the mountains of Colorado and California before the onslaught of the C.C.C. Forest fires . . . are being repulsed on all flanks the moment they show their smudgy red heads through the trees.

Of all the New Deal agencies, the CCC was probably the most popular, because it united two objectives: "the conservation of America's natural resources and the conservation of its young manhood." Many observers believed that the "forestry army" embodied James's proposal for an army of youth enlisted in a "warfare against nature," although Roosevelt himself may not have been directly affected by James. The Corps, it was claimed, had rescued young men from meaninglessness, rebuilt bodies and character, and given men a soldier's pride of accomplishment. Speaker Rainey wrote: "They are also under military training and as they come out of it they come out improved in health and developed mentally and physically and are more useful citizens and if ever we should become involved in another war they would furnish a very valuable nucleus for our army."

While the CCC, the AAA, the TVA, housing, economy, and banking legislation all shared in the war legacy, it was the National Recovery Administration that was the keystone of the early New Deal, and the NRA rested squarely on the War Industries Board example. The National Industrial Recovery bill, modeled on WIB procedures, wove together a series of schemes for government-business co-ordination of the kind that had prevailed in the war. One of the most influential recovery designs, sponsored by Meyer Jacobstein, a Rochester (New York) banker, and H. G. Moulton, president of the Brookings Institution, recommended the creation of "a National Board for Industrial Recovery, with powers similar to those so effectively utilized during the World War by the War Industries Board." When the President commissioned Raymond Moley to frame legislation for industrial recovery, Moley asked General Hugh Johnson, who in World War I had functioned as a liaison between the Army and the War Industries Board, to take over for him. "Nobody can do it better than you," Moley coaxed. "You're familiar with the only comparable thing that's ever been done—the work of the War Industries Board." The recovery bill, drafted by Johnson and others, won Senate approval by only the narrowest of margins; conservatives foresaw that the measure would enhance the power of the state and progressives believed the proposal would encourage cartelization. Franklin Roosevelt was more sanguine. When the President signed the recovery act of June 16, he commented: "Many good men voted this new charter with misgivings. I do not share these doubts. I had part in the great co-operation of 1917 and 1918 and it is my faith that we can count on our industry once more to join in our general purpose to lift this new threat. . . ."

Before labor would agree to the industrial-recovery program, it insisted on the same degree of government recognition of the right to organize as it had enjoyed in World War I. In December, 1932, shortly after he learned that Frances Perkins would be the new Secretary of Labor, Sidney Hillman sent her a memorandum which urged the government to pursue the kinds of policies the War Labor Board had initiated. In framing the recovery bill, W. Jett Lauck, who had been secretary of the War Labor Board, served as spokesman for John L. Lewis's United Mine Workers. Lauck, who sponsored a plan for "a national board composed of labor modeled after the War Labor Board," played a prominent part in shaping the labor provisions of the legislation. When the national industrial-recovery bill emerged from the drafting room, it incorporated the pivotal section 7(a) which granted labor's demand for recognition of the right of collective bargaining. The essential provisions of 7(a), noted Edwin Witte, were "but restatements" of principles first recognized by the National War Labor Board.

Franklin Roosevelt had not only had a prominent part in framing World War I labor policies, but had, as Gerald Nash has pointed out, "sketched out the blueprint for the War Labor Policies Board which was modeled on his directive." To staff the National Labor Board of 1933, the President named men he had first encountered in developing war labor programs. William Leiserson, executive secretary of the board, had been Roosevelt's personal adviser on labor affairs in 1918. In formulating labor policy—from interpreting 7(a) through the adoption and administration of the Wagner Act—Roosevelt and his lieutenants drew heavily on war precedents. The war agencies had established the basic principles of the New Deal labor program: that workers had the right to unionize, that they must not be discharged for union activity, and that presidential boards could restrain employers from denying such rights. More than this, they had evolved the procedure of plant elections to determine bargaining representatives which was to be the crucial instrumentality employed by Roosevelt's labor boards.

To head the NRA Roosevelt named the fiery General Johnson, who could boast pertinent experience not only with the War Industries Board but in organizing the draft. In mid-July, Johnson launched a national campaign dramatized by the symbol of the Blue Eagle. "In war, in the gloom of night attack, soldiers wear a bright badge on their shoulders to be sure that comrades do not fire on comrades," explained the President. "On that principle, those who cooperate in this program must know each other at a glance. That is why we have provided a badge of honor for this purpose. . . ."

Cabinet members greeted with skepticism Johnson's proposal for a mass movement to enlist the nation behind the NRA. Homer Cummings pointed out that the country was not at war, and it might be difficult to get everyone to sign a pledge. Johnson replied that he felt it could be put over, for the depression was more real than the war had been to most Americans. "Almost every individual has either suffered terribly, or knows of friends and relatives who have; so there is waiting here to be appealed to what I regard as the most fertile psychology that you could imagine. . . . I think this has anything that happened during the War backed off the board."

To enforce the Blue Eagle, Johnson enlisted the housewives of the country. "It is women in homes—and not soldiers in uniform—who will this time save our country," he proclaimed. "They will go over the top to as great a victory as the Argonne. It is zero hour for housewives. Their battle cry is 'Buy now under the Blue Eagle!' " By kindling the spirit of the Liberty Loan drives and the draft registration of World War I, Johnson kept alive the intense spirit of the Hundred Days through another season. "There is a unity in this country," declared Franklin Roosevelt, "which I have not seen and you have not seen since April, 1917. . . ."

The Recovery Administration conceived of the depression as, in part, a crisis in character. The New Dealers hoped that businessmen would place the public weal above their private interests, just as the copper magnates had responded to Baruch's appeal in 1917 by supplying metal to the army and navy at less than half the market price. In 1933, businessmen were asked to accept as a patriotic duty the assignment to raise wages and agree to a "truce" on price-cutting. The recovery drive, it was argued, would succeed only if it aroused the same kind of "spiritual" fervor that World War I had awakened. Morris Cooke wrote:

> Conversations with a good many different kinds of people convince me that there is needed to expedite industrial recovery a talk by the President in which he would read into our 57 varieties of effort an ethical and moral quality and call on us individually and collectively to put our shoulders to the wheel just as if we were at war. . . .
>
> Everywhere I get the impression of our people wanting to be told that the main purpose of the Recovery Administration is not exclusively the rehabilitation of our material wellbeing but a reaffirmation of the spiritual values in life.

To man the New Deal agencies, Roosevelt turned to the veterans of the war mobilization. Top NRA officials included Johnson's chief of staff, John Hancock, who had managed the War Industries Board's naval industrial program; Charles F. Horner, the genius of the Liberty Loan drive; Leo Wolman, who had headed the section on production statistics of the War Industries Board; and Major General Clarence Charles Williams, who had been Chief of Ordnance in charge of the vast war purchasing. Many other New Dealers had had their first taste of government service during the war. The first Administrator for Public Works, Colonel Donald H. Sawyer, had built cantonments; Felix Frankfurter had chaired the War Labor Policies Board; Captain Leon Henderson of Ordnance had served with the War Industries Board; and Senator Joseph Guffey had worked in the War Industries Board on the conservation of oil. For many, the summer of 1933 seemed like old times. "Washington is a hectic place," wrote Isador Lubin in August. "The hotels are filled, and the restaurants remind me very much of war times. One cannot go into the Cosmos Club without meeting half a dozen persons whom he knew during the war."

The commandants of New Deal agencies thought of themselves as soldiers in a war against depression. The young men who came to Washington said they had "volunteered in peacetime." Some even claimed they were conscripts. When Holger Cahill expressed reluctance to accept a bid to head the new Federal Art Project, an associate advised him he had no alternative. "An invitation from the

Government to a job like that is tantamount to an order. It's like being drafted." This theme quickly became commonplace. From his "general headquarters in Washington, D.C.," reported one writer, "General" Harry L. Hopkins had organized the Federal Emergency Relief Administration as "only one division of the 'American Army' in the War on Want." One of Hopkins' "noncoms," a relief worker in northern Michigan, observed: "We were like an army, drafted into service during a war." She wrote of the FERA Field Director: ". . . He had been in the front-line trenches with the rest of us when the battle raged at its worst. . . ." When the FERA gave way to the Works Project Administration late in 1935, her staff was broken up. "At this time," she commented, "I lost the other two members of my shock troops. . . ."

The processes of New Deal government owed much to the war legacy. The war provided a precedent for the concentration of executive authority, for the responsibility of government for the state of the economy, and for the role of Washington as the arbiter among social groups. It originated the practice of shunting aside the regular line agencies and creating new organizations with dramatic alphabetical titles. When the RFC, the first of the new agencies, was established, one periodical reported: "R.F.C., of course, is Reconstruction Finance Corporation, and the newspapers have fallen into the war-time habit of using the simple initials instead of the rather cumbersome full name of this anti-hard-times organization." The war offered a precedent, too, for setting up coordinating bodies like the National Emergency Council headed by Frank Walker. Not least in importance, the war experience was used to justify the New Deal's emergency legislation in the courts.

The war example saw service too as a way to refute opponents of the President's economic policies. When critics objected that the country could not "afford" New Deal reforms, Roosevelt's supporters responded with the now familiar retort that if the country could spend as it had in war, it could spend in this new emergency. "When people complain to me of the amount of money that the government has been borrowing," commented Thomas Lamont of the House of Morgan, "I always answer it by saying: 'Well, if the country was willing to spend thirty billion dollars in a year's time to try to lick the Germans, I don't see why people should complain about spending five or six billion dollars to keep people from starving.'" By 1936, when Roosevelt returned to Forbes Field in Pittsburgh, where, four years before, he had promised to slash Hoover's reckless spending, the President concluded that the argument now offered the best reply to critics who accused him of a profligate disregard of campaign promises. "National defense and the future of America were involved in 1917. National defense and the future of America were also involved in 1933," Roosevelt asserted. "Don't you believe that the saving of America has been cheap at that price?"

Roosevelt's argument would have been more compelling if he had spent at anywhere near the rate that both he and his conservative foes implied he had. For a time in the winter of 1933–34, the Administration gave a fillip to the economy when it embarked on lavish spending through the Civil Works Administration, but early in 1934, the President, alarmed by mounting deficits, decreed the death of the CWA. Distressed by Roosevelt's verdict, Senator Robert LaFollette, Jr., of Wisconsin inquired: "In 1917, Mr. President, what Senator would have dared to rise on the floor of the Senate and suggest that we could not fight the war against Germany and her allies because it would unbalance the Budget?" *The Nation* voiced a similar protest: "The country is confronted with a vastly greater crisis than it had to meet in the World War but has not yet extended itself financially as it did at that time." Progressives warned that unless the President began to spend at a wartime pace the country might take years to pull out of the depression. The progressive Cassandras proved correct. The New Deal mobilization of 1933–34, from which so much had been expected, brought disappointing economic returns.

The crux of the difficulty lay in the fact that the metaphor of war was, in more than one way, inapt. As a model for economic action, World War I was unsatisfactory, for the problems confronting Roosevelt in 1933 were quite unlike those Woodrow Wilson had been called on to meet in 1917. As the Harvard economist Edwin Gay wrote: "War stimulates the full expansion of productive energy, but the deep depression cripples every economic process and discourages even the most sanguine business leaders." Some who recalled the war experience hoped that it could provide a prototype for the same kind of impressive increases in output that had been achieved in 1917–18. But the aims of the New Deal mobilization were not the same as those of the war; General Johnson even called for "an armistice on increasing producing capacity." Frank Freidel has pointed out:

> Unlike wartime measures, the new agencies were to reduce output in most areas rather than raise it, and encourage price increases rather than restrain them. Thus, waging a war on the depression was in some ways the reverse of waging one on a foreign foe.

John M. Clark has made a similar point. The war, Clark noted, provided precedents for emergency controls, deficit spending, and expanded powers for the Federal Reserve System, but the problems of war and of depression "were radically different; in fact, they were in some respects opposite to one another." The question of determining priorities in a war economy, Clark observed, was not at all the same as that of reinvigorating sick industries. Clark concluded:

> All the machinery for allocating limited supplies of essential resources among conflicting uses, which played so large a part in the wartime controls, had no application to the depression. Where the actuating motives of private industry fail and the result is partial paralysis, the problem is essentially opposite to that of war.

These misgivings were not simply the result of hindsight. In the midst of the Hundred Days, the economist Paul Douglas warned that the country did not face the wartime task of rationing scarce resources but the quite different problem of stimulating production. "Industry must get some business before it can proceed to ration it out," Douglas gibed. He was disconcerted by the New Deal's obsession with the menace of overproduction when the critical question was how to increase purchasing power. Douglas noted: "Certainly those who are arguing from the analogy of the War Industries Board miss the point. That body had behind it the gigantic purchasing power of the government, and with this weapon it was able to instill some order in the industrial system. But unless the government creates such purchasing power in the present emergency, the regulatory body will be operating in a void."

The war analogy proved michievous in an even more significant respect. The Tugwells thought of the war as a time when the intellectuals had exercised unprecedented power over the economy, and when the feasibility of a planned society had been brilliantly demonstrated. Yet, although the intellectuals did wield power, agencies like the War Industries Board had, after all, been run chiefly by business executives. If they learned anything from the war, it was not the virtues of collectivism but the potentialities of trade associations, the usefulness of the state in economic warfare with the traders of other nations, and the good-housekeeping practices of eliminating duplication and waste. The immediate consequence of the war was not a New Jerusalem of the planners but the Whiggery of Herbert Hoover as Secretary of Commerce. While the war mobilization did establish meaningful precedents for New Deal reforms, it was hardly the "war socialism" some theorists thought it to be. Perhaps the outstanding characteristic of the war organization of industry was that it showed how to achieve massive government intervention without making any permanent alteration in the power of corporations.

The confusion over the meaning of the war experience helped conceal the ambiguities of the so-called "First New Deal." The architects of the early New Deal appeared to be in fundamental agreement, since they united in rejecting the New Freedom ideal of a competitive society in favor of business-government co-ordination in the 1917 style. In fact, they differed sharply. Tugwell hoped that the co-ordination authorized by the NRA would enable the Recovery Administration to become an agency for centralized government direction of the economy, a possibility insured in part by the NRA's licensing power. Most of the other "First New Dealers," however, meant by business-government co-ordination an economy in which businessmen would make the crucial decisions. As administrator of the NRA, General Johnson gave small scope to the government direction Tugwell had envisaged. He never used the licensing power, but relied instead on negotiation with business and on the force of social pressure. Like Moley and Richberg and the President, Johnson placed his faith not in a planned economy but in voluntary business co-operation with government.

The New Deal administrators shared, too, the conviction of the war bureaucrats that progress would be achieved not through worker or farmer rebellions, but through government programs, conceived and executed by agency officials. A month after the armistice, Wesley Mitchell had voiced the need for "intelligent experimenting and detailed planning rather than for agitation or class struggle." The war approach which the New Dealers adopted rejected both mass action and socialist planning, and assumed a community of interest of the managers of business corporations and the directors of government agencies. Roosevelt's lieutenants believed that the great danger to such an experiment lay not in the opposition of the conservatives, who were discredited, but in the menace of antiplutocratic movements. Yet in damping the fires of popular dissent, they also snuffed out support they would need to keep the reform spirit alive.

The New Dealers, distrustful of the policies of group conflict, sought to effect a truce like that of 1917 when class and sectional animosities abated. Perhaps no other approach could have accomplished so much in the spring of 1933, yet it was a tactic which had obvious perils for the cause of reform. By presenting the depression not as the collapse of a system but as a personalized foreign enemy, Roosevelt as much as Hoover sought to mend the social fabric. In doing so, Roosevelt, like his predecessor, deflected blame away from business leaders whom many thought responsible for hard times, and diverted attention from the fact that the depression was not the consequence of an assult by a foreign foe but evidence of internal breakdown.

Even more important, the New Dealers, in the interest of national solidarity, tried to suppress anti-business expressions of discontent. President Roosevelt warned the AF of L convention in 1933: "The whole of the country has a common enemy; industry, agriculture, capital, labor are all engaged in fighting it. Just as in 1917 we are seeking to pull in harness; just as in 1917, horses that kick over the traces will have to be put in a corral." General Johnson left no doubt of the intent of the President's words: "Labor does not need to strike under the Roosevelt plan. . . . The plain stark truth is that you cannot tolerate strikes. Public opinion . . . will break down and destroy every subversive influence." Far from operating a "labor government," as conservatives charged, the New Dealers in 1933 deeply resented strikes as acts of "aggression" which sabotaged the drive for recovery. Frances Perkins recalls that Johnson believed that "during the period when NRA was attempting to revive industry no stoppage of work could be tolerated under any circumstances. It was like a stoppage of work in war time. Anything had to be done to prevent that."

An administrator who spurned direct government sanctions but who was determined to have his way soon found that he was either resorting to bluster or encouraging vigilantism. Such had been the pattern in World War I. On one occasion, the War Industries Board's price-fixing committee had warned a producer to co-operate, or become "such an object of contempt and scorn in your home town that you will not dare to show your face there." Ray Lyman Wilbur, chief of the conservation division of the Food Administration, recalled: "Indiana I found the best organized state for food conservation that I had yet seen. The people were approaching rapidly the stage where violations of wheatless days, etc., were looked upon as unpatriotic enough to require that inquiries as to the loyalty of the guilty citizen, baker or hotel-keeper be made."

If the New Dealers never ran to such excesses of vigilantism, they were not beyond employing this kind of social coercion, and they matched the war administrators in the technique of bluster. "I have no patience with people who follow a course which in war time would class them as slackers," declared Attorney-General Homer Cummings of the alleged hoarders of gold. "If I have to make an example of some people, I'll do it cheerfully." When Frances Perkins hit out at the effort of the steel industry to dodge the intent of section 7(a) by setting up company unions, she denounced these unions as "war bridegrooms," the popular epithet for matrimonial draft-dodging during the war. When the economist Oliver W. M. Sprague resigned in protest at the Administration's gold-buying policy, Hugh Johnson accused him of "deserting with a shot in the flank of the army in which he had enlisted." During the Blue Eagle drive, Donald Richberg insisted that in a time of crisis there could be "no honorable excuse for the slacker who wastes these precious moments with doubting and debate—who palsies the national purpose with legalistic arguments."

Such statements infuriated the conservatives. Senator Carter Glass of Virginia found particularly galling Richberg's denunciation of NRA opponents as "slackers who deserved to have white feathers pinned on them by the women of the country." Glass wrote of Richberg's war record: "He never heard a percussion cap pop; he did not know the smell of gun powder; he did not even reach a training camp to learn the difference between 'Forward March' and 'Parade Rest.' When asked by a responsible newspaperman to give his war record in justification of his vituperative assault on other people, he could do no better than allege he had helped sell some Liberty bonds." Glass's resentment was shared by other conservative critics. "The man who lives well within his income," protested Lewis Douglas, "has come to be regarded as unpatriotic and as a slacker in the fight against the depression."

If the rhetoric of coercion disturbed the conservatives, it troubled some of the New Dealers even more. In the summer of 1933, a group of AAA officials protested:

> General Johnson, in picturing the results of his campaign, has frequently used the analogy of the war-time 'gasless Sundays.' Then, General Johnson recalls, if a man drove a car on Sunday, his neighbors pushed the car into the ditch. Popular opinion at that time was so inflamed that it expressed itself by violence.
>
> General Johnson's analogy is profoundly significant and disturbing. If his program is adopted, professional drive organizations will soon reappear in full force. Agitators may take advantage of the possible resulting hysteria to set group against group, such as farmers against wage earners, and thus defeat the real progress toward cooperation already made by the Roosevelt Administration.

Some even thought they detected in Johnson's administration of the NRA the glimmerings of a corporate state. If such was Johnson's purpose—and the grounds for such a supposition are unsubstantial—the General received no encouragement from the President. Roosevelt moved quickly to squelch signs of militarism. When Harry Woodring, Assistant Secretary of War, wrote early in 1934 that the Army stood prepared to organize the CCC, veterans of World War I, and relievers into a corps of "economic storm troops," the White House reprimanded him. In late 1934, the authoritarian-minded Johnson was let go. That same year, Henry Wallace, seeking to pursue a "middle course," wrote: "There is something wooden and inhuman about the government interfering in a definite, precise way with the details of our private and business lives. It suggests a time of war with generals and captains telling every individual exactly what he must do each day and hour."

Most of all, the Brandeisian faction of the New Dealers objected to the crisis spirit. Felix Frankfurter wrote Louis Brandeis: "Much too much of 'slacker' talk & old coercions." For the Brandeisians, the "enemy" was not "depression" but "business." They welcomed the breakup of the nation in 1934 and 1935 from the national interest into class and group interests. The early New Dealers had emphasized the war spirit of cooperation, co-ordination, and exhortation, because they feared that the bonds that held society together might be snapped. By 1935, it was clear that the crisis had been weathered, and the mood of war seemed inappropriate. Brandeisians felt free to assault business interests, other New Dealers lost faith in their ability to convert businessmen, and business groups increasingly viewed Roosevelt as their enemy. As in wartime, the first enthusiasm as the troops paraded to the front had given way to the realization that the army was not invincible, the casualty lists would be long, and the prospect of early victory was no longer promising. Yet the danger of annihilation had been averted too, and as the sense of urgency lessened, the spirit of national solidarity slackened. "The enemies who began to emerge in the eyes or the imagination of men," Paul Conkin has observed of the end of the "wartime effort" in 1935, "were not such as could demand the hostility of all Americans, for these enemies were not natural, or providential, or foreign, but human and native. A class and group consciousness was forming."

Yet the rhetoric of war persisted, even when such agencies of mobilization as NRA died. In the summer of 1935, Representative Robert L. Doughton of North Carolina observed: "Of course in every War, if it has a chance at all to be successful, there must be a leader, and this Administration and the Congress have been engaged in a war on hunger, destitute [sic], unemployment, bankruptcy and every evil incident to the economic life of our people." In his 1936 campaign, Franklin Roosevelt told a Massachusetts crowd that, like Marshal Joffre at the First Battle of the Marne, he bore the blame for victory or defeat in war. "Three and a half years ago we declared war on the depression," the President asserted. "You and I know today that that war is being won." But he was quick to point out that the war had not yet been won. The country still needed the services of its commander-in-chief. In his Franklin Field address, when he accepted renomination in June, 1936, Roosevelt declared: "I accept the commission you have tendered me. I join with you. I am enlisted for the duration of the war." But by then references to war had become purely rhetorical. When, that very year, the Administration explored the possibility of using the war power, and especially the precedent of Wilson's War Labor Policies Board, to justify federal regulation of the hours of labor, it concluded that the idea was not feasible.

Only the New Dealers committed to a planned economy held fast to the earlier vision. As late as the summer of 1939, Rexford Tugwell looked back wistfully toward the war collectivism. Tugwell pleaded for a reorientation of progressive thought away from the traditional emphases on freedom for business, a change that only a crisis like that of 1917 or 1929 would produce. Of the two, Tugwell thought that war offered the best hope, for 1929 had yielded only "atomistic reforms" while 1917 had resulted in "national organization on a unitary scheme." "How different it was in 1917!" Tugwell wrote. "It was possible . . . to make immense advances toward industrial unity. . . . That great wartime release of energy was achieved by freeing men's minds. Quantities and qualities could be thought of rather than profits." No sane person would wish a war in order to bring about a "purposive national organization," he observed.

"Yet the fact is that only war has up to now proved to be such a transcending objective that doctrine is willingly sacrified for efficiency in its service."

If the references to war in the later Roosevelt years were largely rhetorical, the rhetoric was often revealing. In his Franklin Field speech, Roosevelt insisted that the nation was waging "not alone a war against want and destitution and economic demoralization" but "a war for the survival of democracy." "We are fighting to save a great and precious form of government for ourselves and for the world," the President declared. With each passing year, the challenge of the Fascist powers was more defiant, and the demands of foreign affairs came to supersede the claims of domestic issues. New Deal agencies increasingly directed their attention to preparing for the eventuality of war with the Axis. In 1938, the TVA boasted it was "developing the power necessary for the large-scale operation of war industries in this well-protected strategic area." The furnaces at Muscle Shoals, the Authority reported, were being utilized to turn out phosphorus, a material "used in war for smoke screens and incendiary shells," and the TVA's electric furnaces, the agency foresaw, "might be converted to the electrolytic manufacture of aluminum or of chlorine—used in war gases. . . ."

Henry Wallace had long believed that the AAA was an "adjustment" program whose machinery could be used to increase output as well as to limit it. If there were a conflict beyond the ocean, a prospect he dreaded, the United States, he observed in 1934, could, through the Triple A, "provision a war . . . with far less of that plunging, uninformed and altogether unorganized overplanting which got us into so much trouble during and after the last great war." A week before the outbreak of the European war in September, 1939, Wallace wrote the President that if war came the government might consider developing plans modeled on the Food Administration with which Wallace had worked in World War I. "When we set up County Committees in AAA in 1933, I couldn't help thinking what a splendid mechanism we would have, if we ever got into a war, to meet the food problem. . . . Again when we set up the Ever Normal Granary System, I thought how marvelously this mechanism with its reserve supplies would help the country in case of war."

In 1939, James V. Forrestal tried to persuade New Dealers that the way to put across their program was to sell it as preparedness rather than reform; after all, the TVA had had its start in the Defense Act of 1916. He won few converts—most liberals refused to adopt a stratagem that surrendered the theology of liberalism—but when the war in Europe led to a new emphasis on defense, the New Dealers were quick enough to adapt themselves. A month after war began in Europe, Roosevelt phoned Wallace to call all bureau chiefs and ask what their experience had been in World War I, and how the new emergency would affect their present position. Many soon found themselves running the new defense agencies. Leon Henderson controlled prices, AAA Administrator Chester Davis coordinated agriculture with defense requirements, and Brehon Somervell, who had directed the WPA in New York, took charge of military construction.

The NYA began to train aircraft mechanics; CCC workers developed target ranges and airports for the Army; TVA dams produced the power for aluminum needed in bomber production; and the REA turned out the electricity for army camps and naval installations. New Dealers charged with developing defense and war labor policies turned repeatedly to the War Labor Board's precedents. When war came, Schlesinger writes, it "almost seemed an NRA reunion. The child of the War Industries Board, NRA was the father of the War Production Board. Leon Henderson, Donald Nelson, Sidney Hillman, Averell Harriman, William H. Davis, Isador Lubin, Edward R. Stettinius, Jr.—all had their training in national mobilization in the breathless days of 1933 and 1934." Many of these men, it might be added, had first entered government service in World War I.

Precisely as the Keynesians had foreseen, defense and war demands sparked an economic boom. In the summer of 1940, Keynes noted that the United States had failed to achieve recovery, because the volume of investment had been "hopelessly inadequate." The "dreadful experience" of war might teach the United States what it had failed to learn in peacetime. He predicted: "Your war preparation, so far from requiring a sacrifice, will be the stimulus, which neither the victory nor the defeat of the New Deal could give you, to greater individual consumption and a higher standard of life." Keynes observed sadly: "It is, it seems, politically impossible for a capitalistic democracy to organize expenditure on the scale necessary to make the grand experiment which would prove my case—except in war conditions."

Keynes's remark was to the point. The "grand experiment" of the New Deal had achieved much. But it had not created, or indeed in any serious sense even attempted to create, a new model for American society. The New Dealers resorted to the analogue of war, because in America the sense of community is weak, the distrust of the state strong. Up to a point, the metaphor of war and the precedent of World War I proved invaluable. They helped provide a feeling of national solidarity which made possible the New Deal's greatest achievement: its success in "nation-saving," in mending the social fabric. The heritage of World War I justified the New Deal's claim to represent an overarching national interest to which business and other parochial interests must conform. The war proved that, at a time of crisis, the power of private individuals with money to turn the nation's resources to their own benefit could be limited by the prior claim of providing a "social minimum." Since the war mobilization had brought to fruition much of progressivism, it offered a useful example for the New Dealers, and since the wartime control of industry went much further than earlier efforts in recognizing the place of the twentieth-century state, it was especially pertinent for some of the problems the New Deal confronted.

Yet in other respects the war analogue proved either treacherous or inadequate. The very need to employ imagery which was so often inappropriate revealed both an impoverished tradition of reform and the reluctance of the nation to come to terms with the leviathan state. Only in war or in a crisis likened to war was it possible to put aside inhibiting doctrines, create a sense of national homogeneity, and permit the government to act in the national interest. But once the war ended, or the sense of crisis dissipated, traditional doctrines once again prevailed. The country had yet to find a way to organize collective action save in war or its surrogate. Nor had it faced up to the real problems of the relation of order to liberty which the power of the twentieth-century state creates.

World War II rescued the New Deal from some of its dilemmas and obscured others. In the war years, many of the New Deal programs were set aside

—the WPA, Roosevelt said, had earned an "honorable discharge." The New Dealers turned their talents to "manning the production line." The AAA helped increase farm production instead of restricting crops; the new industrial agencies sought to speed factory output rather than curtail it. Perhaps the greatest irony of the New Deal is the most familiar. Only in war was recovery achieved. Only in war did the country finally rescue that one-third of a nation ill-housed, ill-clad and ill-nourished. Only in war was the "army of the unemployed" disbanded.

~~~~11

PAUL K. CONKIN

F. D. R. and the Irony of the New Deal

*Paul K. Conkin's critique of the New Deal, published early in 1967,
came at a predictable time. Studies that appeared during the previous dozen years rejected much of America's liberal heritage as
inadequate to deal with the problems of this and future decades. In
the hands of various historians the Populist leaders became an
irrational group and the Progressive movement a businessmen's
attempt to control and inhibit social reform. Such revisions led
inevitably to reexamination of Franklin Roosevelt's New Deal. A
number of younger New Deal scholars arrived at a more skeptical
evaluation of Roosevelt's accomplishments. For most of them the
blame lay in considerable part with Roosevelt himself; the President
seemed unwilling to go beyond a narrow set of experiments well
within the capitalist framework.*

*As Conkin argues in the first part of this essay, far from being
a pragmatist or even an opportunist, Roosevelt apparently believed
in a set of assumptions, more restricting than liberating, based on
Christianity, aristocracy, and capitalism. Conkin then explores the
welfare state as it developed between 1934 and 1936. After defining
the term and distinguishing it from socialism and other ideologies,
he investigates the motives, contingencies, and frustrations of its
architects and measures its promise against its delivery. The nation
made some gains under the New Deal, but according to Conkin
many of them were merely symbolic. Social Security would one day
develop into a program of enormous scope and great value, but
it started with a modest program. The Negro won government
recognition of his needs, but almost no concrete help. Nothing in
Roosevelt's leadership, Conkin concludes, could create the liberals'
dream: "The story of the New Deal is a sad story, the ever recurring
story of what might have been."*

*Does this judgment rest on an approach to history that, as one
critic has charged, is ahistorical, unhistorical, or anti-historical?*

Paul K. Conkin: THE NEW DEAL. Copyright © 1967 by Thomas Y. Crowell
Company.

Does it violate an essential rule of historical craftsmanship: that while the present may ask questions of the past, the past must still be evaluated in its own context and cannot be blamed for a present whose needs and demands it could not possibly have perceived? Conkin might well respond to this criticism with the last words of his book: "Only with trepidation will the student of history try to sum up the results of the New Deal. He will not do it with a sense of heartless criticism. Not only would it be unfair, but too much is involved. But judge he must, not to whip the past but to use it. His rightful criticism is directed at himself, his country, his institutions, his age. If so directed, his evaluation must be just, thorough, and honest; otherwise, he practices only self-deceit."

1. ROOSEVELT

The New Deal was an exceedingly personal enterprise. Its disparate programs were unified only by the personality of Franklin D. Roosevelt. Every characterization, every evaluation of the governmental innovations from 1933 to 1938 terminates and often flounders in this personality. Characterization is ever hazardous; least so of men who construct a coherent, articulate system of beliefs, most so of men who, like Roosevelt, operate within conventional, unarticulated beliefs and, in addition, retain a disarming simplicity. Even in the best circumstances, biography reflects the catalyzing influence of the biographer and thus reveals only the often fascinating chemical compound of two interacting personalities.

Today only a minority of Americans remember Franklin Roosevelt, at least with more than vague images of childhood. Unswayed by his vital presence, ever less impressed by his recorded speeches, unmoved by his increasingly irrelevant political concerns, young Americans are mainly baffled by the continued passion of their parents, by the subdued fervor of professors, by all oldsters who still dare confess their love or who even yet vent their hate. They note the touch of reverence in the voice of Lyndon B. Johnson, the ill-concealed worship of Arthur M. Schlesinger, Jr., the adulation of an aged or departed court—Rosenman, Tully, Tugwell, Perkins, Morgenthau. Even more, they note the unbelievable bitterness of right-wing critics, who identify an almost unbearably conventional Roosevelt with both domestic and foreign treason. Surely the sympathetic portraits are more revealing. Hate is a poor vehicle for communicating personality. But even the best portraits, conceived in love, may still seem unlovely to another generation.

Roosevelt, as President, gave millions of Americans a transfusion of courage. They still remember. From his confidence, his optimism, they gleaned bits of hope in times of trouble and confusion. This was Roosevelt's only unalloyed success as President. It was a pervasive part of the New Deal, yet tied to no policies and no programs. It was the magic of a man, based as much on illusion as on reality. There was much to fear in 1933, as there is today. Only fools or gods believed otherwise.

Roosevelt's unusual and politically invaluable self-assurance was the legacy of an unconventional childhood. The bounds were set by a rigid, possessive, but loving mother (Sarah Delano); an elderly, increasingly ill, indulgent father (James Roosevelt); a large farm estate, with trees and gardens; nurses, tutors, and loneliness for other children; a patterned, almost regimented tempo of life; and such victorian virtues as duty, honesty, and fair play. An only child of this marriage, breastfed, with no competitors for a mother's love, catered to by innumerable servants and relatives, indulged by gifts and toys and pets, young Franklin was secure and happy, reflecting a vitality and commanding presence often observed in single children. The world was his opportunity; there was nothing to fear, so much to master. The focus of his secure world was the carefully managed estate at Hyde Park, with its planted and tended forests, sleek herds of cattle, and carefully cultivated fields. Less serious but more important to a boy, there were hunting, fishing, riding to hounds, bird watching, and, joy of joys, sailing on the Hudson. Along with stamp collecting, birds and boats were to be lifelong hobbies. Conservation of natural resources, a near-romantic love of trees, concern with agricultural problems were deep commitments always colored by happy memories.

Roosevelt's boyhood security depended on wealth, but wealth securely fitted into traditional family values. Even in the late nineteenth century, few families could afford an ample mansion, tutors, servants, books and music, and yearly trips to European bathing places. In both the Roosevelt and Delano families, financial security was a product of several generations of effort, mostly in commercial and navigational enterprises and, in the more distant past, in early Hudson Valley land grants. James Roosevelt, at least in his later years, appeared to be an English country gentleman, supervising his estate and serving mankind through local Democratic politics and as vestryman in the Episcopal Church. This was the life he loved. But he was also a financier, with several speculative ventures in his past and always enough conservative investments to safeguard his chosen way of life. He served on corporate boards, invested heavily in coal and railroads, and had participated in business deals looking toward monopoly. The competitive, challenging, acquisitive, often brutal world of corporate enterprise provided a sharp contrast to gentleman farming, even as New York City sharply contrasted with Hyde Park. But to James Roosevelt, and to his young son, the real world was always Hyde Park. All else was done in behalf of it. The avocation was really the vocation. Business was a game that had to be played, but it lacked any but purely instrumental purposes. Adequate wealth was a social necessity, not an appropriate goal.

Young Franklin loved competition. He loved to win. He wanted to be in the center of things, in command if at all possible. Games gave an outlet to his love of power and mastery. Yet his boyhood was protected from more vital competition for wealth, parental approval, social standing, even grades. His person was invulnerable. He played all games to win, no holds barred. But he never had to fight for dignity, for a livelihood, for a constant input of love to compensate for a horrible lack of self-respect.

For this reason, he never quite understood a driving, acquisitive society. He always saw the world as a country squire. He disliked cities unless they could be planned to look like country estates. He always trusted farmers and believed with Jefferson in the generative impulses of soil and woodland. In the nineteen twenties he was boldly speculative in a series of financial endeavors but never displayed the grasping, predaceous impulse of so many less secure investors or corporate directors. Throughout the life he would be disarmingly casual about personal finances and about the common necessities of life. He played the stock market as he played ball—to win. He wanted other men to play the economic game as he did and never quite understood the vast majority of economic men who, driven by personal insecurity or controlled by the habits of the market-place, sought economic power as an end, struggled for advantage with deadly seriousness, tried to gain and maintain privileges of all sorts, and above all did not live up to a gentlemen's code. In disbelief, in shocked indignation, in mis-understanding, Roosevelt later denounced such men as economic royalists, traitors to their class, betrayers of their position in the community, and sinful trustees of their inheritance. But at times of deepest political involvement, he played the political game with all the seriousness, and all the cunning, of the most fervent business tycoon and identified his political ambitions with the inter-est of all the people.

The same self-assurance insulated Roosevelt from intimate involvements with people. Yet few men were ever more attuned to people and less attuned to ideas. Few men ever possessed a greater art of breaking down barriers in others. The very lack of intimacy, of a compelling emotional need to possess or love another, contributed to his ease in developing a friendly comradeship with multitudes of people. He loved the adoration and attention of people, even when elementary privacy was violated. With consummate art, he played for his audiences and won their plaudits. Some grew to love him and projected onto him their hopes and joys and deepest longings. They invested so much in the relationship; he invested so little and invested so broadly.

This unequal relationship prevailed even in his own family. While a law student at Columbia University, he married Eleanor Roosevelt, his distant cousin and a niece of Theodore Roosevelt. In so many ways his opposite, she fascinated him, and to an extent always did. He idealized and admired her; probably to the limits of his ability he loved her. But not as she loved him. Reserved, shy, lacking self-confidence, sure that she was unattractive, extremely sensitive to the feelings of others, she yet radiated a beauty of character and a charming seriousness in outlook. Her childhood had been extremely unhappy. Cursed with an alcoholic father, an unintentionally cruel mother, orphaned by ten, reared by a stern grandmother, immersed in an exciting but neurotic house-hold, she only slowly gained any sense of self worth. Much of this she gained from friendships, or by charitable efforts in New York City. The attention of a gay, handsome, confident Franklin was a great flattery and promised a haven of security. Eleanor never forgot.

Yet to a great extent she was shut out of her husband's life. Self-centered and insensitive, he remained largely unaware of most of her tribulations. Sarah Roosevelt not only tried to dominate Franklin (he evaded her efforts) but for years did dominate her daughter-in-law. As the five children came in rapid order, Eleanor, with easily more perception and sensitivity than Franklin, had to wait years before she could gain a clear sense of personal identity. Then she moved confidently into the world on her own. In their whole married life, Franklin never showed any compelling need for intimacy, and never shared his most important thoughts. In a now overly-publicized indiscretion, he apparently permitted his admiration for a gifted and attractive lady to develop, not only into a lasting friendship, but also into a serious and embarrassingly conspicuous flirtation. Otherwise, he remained loyal and, in his way, dutiful.

The children adored and enjoyed their father but suffered from his lack of involvement. For discipline or understanding they had to turn to their mother. At critical family junctures, he might be out playing poker with cronies or enjoying a fishing and sailing holiday. Franklin was like a gay uncle who periodically entertained the children by play or some adventure. They loved him all the more, for he was identified only with pleasure. In the same sense as he accepted his wife and children, Roosevelt accepted others into an enlarged family circle. There was never anything exclusive about him. Louis Howe, his political manager, and Marguerite (Missy) LeHand, his secretary, gave him the same devotion and loyalty, even to the point of adulation. Just as with Eleanor, he accepted them, used them, flattered them, but never reciprocated in kind. As a self-assured, godlike person, he allowed all devoted disciples to bask in his charm, draw strength from his surety, and eventually share in his fame. Maybe he needed them to shore up some jealously hidden fears. But to have revealed the need would have broken the bond. They flocked to him because of their own insecurity and need and his supreme strength.

Most biographers have speculated about the effect on Roosevelt of poliomyelitis, its crippling aftereffect, and years of effort to restore his legs to more normal use. Roosevelt was protected from the worst facts until recovery was under way. Eleanor may well have suffered as much mental anguish as he. By the time he accepted the worst, if he ever did, his buoyant optimism took over and nourished false hopes of near complete recovery. With all his competitive zeal, he tried to win this game, too, and came closer than weaker men could have. He never lacked this type of courage. Yet there was no evident, long-term effect on his personality. He was the same person in 1928 as he had been in 1921. In many ways his legs became a major political asset, appealing to all who suffered, who had calamities, and who aspired to overcome them. Polio made an aristocratic Roosevelt into an underdog. For him it replaced the log cabin. It also brought him to Warm Springs and helped create his sincere and flattering interest in the South and to insure him a strong Southern following.

Insulated from fear, Roosevelt was also free of doubt. Intellectually, as socially, he exuded confidence. As long as he eloquently asserted, in very broad outlines, the more conventional and traditional beliefs of Americans, he could inspire this same confidence in others and strengthen them by his sense of certainty. But searching inquiry is a product of doubt. Roosevelt never doubted important beliefs. At times he seemed unable to perceive crucial issues or to make careful distinctions. His curiosity was unlimited, but also undisciplined. His keenness in judging and directing subordinates was totally absent when it came to a judgment between abstract concepts. This is not to ignore, much less to deny, the beliefs of Roosevelt but to put them into the correct perspective.

Much scholarly effort has been devoted to Roosevelt's ideas. Futility has marked many such efforts. Thomas H. Greer's *What Roosevelt Thought* (East Lansing, 1958), for example, is superficial and trite. An excellent effort, by Daniel R. Fusfeld [*The Economic Though of Franklin D. Roosevelt and the Origin of the New Deal* (New York, 1956)], documents many of his lifelong commitments but focuses more on developed policies than on basic beliefs. Frank Freidel, the only thorough biographer of the prepresidential Roosevelt, does not try to turn Roosevelt into a thinker. In the three completed volumes of his biography [*Franklin D. Roosevelt: The Apprenticeship; . . . The Ordeal;* and . . . *The Triumph* (Boston, 1952–56)], he recognizes Roosevelt's intellectual acuity but shows that he had no capacity or inclination for pressing forward into the subtleties and perplexities of a theoretic life. His interest in most subjects reached its saturation point when the broader results and more general themes had been reached. This prepared him for his forte—the active and fighting side of life.

This characteristic bent for action, so typical of many politicians, makes it very difficult to probe Roosevelt's most basic commitments. But it in no sense precludes such commitments. All men have beliefs. That is, all men have predispositions to act in certain ways given the opportunity. By abstraction, these predispositions can be stated as beliefs. But active men, such as Roosevelt, seldom try carefully to articulate them or to make them consistent or to criticize them even when glaringly inconsistent or contrary to accepted knowledge. Other men (the very opposite of Roosevelt) become so entangled in conceptualization, in the problems of consistency and correctness, that they impart intellectual indecision into their actions and suffer terrible anxiety with every difficult choice. Roosevelt did talk about certain commitments, such as to democracy, but in such vague and general terms as to be almost meaningless except as a type of verbal assurance. But however vague, however inarticulate he may have been in expressing them, his basic beliefs were firm and constant. Only Rexford G. Tugwell, in a few articles and his *The Democratic Roosevelt* (Garden City, 1957), has come close to defining these.

As Freidel so effectively shows, Roosevelt's unswerving commitments developed in his childhood at Hyde Park, solidified in his years at Groton and Harvard, and never changed during the rest of his life. Groton gently led him away from his protective family but not into a new intellectual world. Episcopal, English in inspiration, simple to austere in habit, it apotheosized his already acquired virtues of honor, fairness, and service. The headmaster, Endicott Peabody, firm and awesome in direct contrast to a tolerant father, remained for Roosevelt a lifelong symbol of authority, a type of commanding conscience. The Groton curriculum was classical, with manners, taste, and moral habits more esteemed goals than sheer intellectual attainment. The moral tenor was high, the theological sophistication very low. Somewhat out of place in America, Groton was thoroughly Anglican and Tory, shaped for an almost nonexistent aristocracy, honorable, broadly but sincerely Christian, tradition-bound, by very responsible. Roosevelt fitted Groton far better than the sons of most industrialists or the sons of older Bostonian Puritans, whose sharp intellects could never safely absorb the unquestioned verities of Peabody. No student more completely or enthusiastically absorbed the values of Groton—*noblesse oblige,* mainly Christianity, civic duty, and love of God, country, and Groton.

At both Groton and Harvard, Roosevelt displayed a characteristic love for athletics, for physical vigor, and for fraternity. He showed much less respect for academic achievement. This valuation was not a product of youthful ir-responsibility, but a lifelong affinity. He certainly, even with his poor to average grades at Harvard, was more gifted as a student than as an athlete. He never made any varsity teams, but he always loved the strenuous life, competition, and comradeship. Team athletics and fraternal organizations gave outlet for his love of power, his desire for leadership, his preference for people over ideas. He did fall in love with books, but usually not to read. These joined his earlier love of stamps and boats as collector's items. He turned his one great achieve-ment at Harvard—editor of the *Crimson*—into support for the football team and an increased school spirit. He gained from Groton and Harvard a veneer of academic sophistication. He learned European languages and achieved some knowledge of ancient classics. He picked up the typically broad and random smattering of information and ideas found in undergraduate courses, and would always be sufficiently agile to learn quickly when need required it. Yet, except for Peabody, no single teacher made a significant or lasting impression, and no courses reoriented his beliefs or, for that matter, even touched them.

Roosevelt lived in the comforting perspective of an undoubted God and in the easy, almost lazy assurance of the Church. Since he never discussed religion, and apparently never thought deeply about it, both concepts were never expressed in other than hopelessly vague terms. Here, surely, rested much of his optimism, his sense of destiny and purpose. God was synonymous with a meaningful universe in which human effort had cosmic significance. Likewise, he loved the vast panorama of America in the same fervent and unquestioning way that he backed Harvard's teams or loved the trees at Hyde Park. The problem was how to do God's will, not to define or justify Him, and how to serve America or aid the team, not whether such devotion was justified. His attach-ment to the land, to property, to a vague "democracy," was equally firm but ill-defined and ill-supported. But simplistic and conventional as they often were, his beliefs limited his actions and focused his lifelong commitments. Exempt from formal philosophic inquiry, from serious intellectual probing, he never questioned these affirmations or defined them very well. As persistently as most other American politicians, he refused to carry on a disciplined dialogue be-tween policies and fundamental beliefs. By clever rhetoric, he always equated the two.

Roosevelt's intellectual stance combined the attitudes of a country gentle-man and a stereotyped athlete. God, country, college, estate, family, party, team—all were revered. Honor, loyalty, dutiful service were proffered to each. The established rules and codes were obeyed so long as they were fair. This often formal, traditional outlook was supported by Roosevelt's antiquarian interests, his collections and memorabilia, concern with genealogy, alumni sup-port, and competitive partisanship. Here were the unquestioned verities. He labored for them and within them. So, in roughly similar fashion, did most people. When general in conception and when clothed in persuasive rhetoric, his simple commitments proved invaluable political assets. In times of depres-sion, war, despair, cynicism, such elementary loyalty, unburdened by doubt or disturbing questions, communicated an assurance so deplorably absent in events. His faith could preserve a society at a time when courage was more needed than penetrating insight.

Roosevelt's beliefs, though broad and unexamined, were never equivocal. In fact, few men have exhibited as complete a continuity of belief as Roosevelt. Not only did he refuse to accept new systems of belief, but he rarely understood them fully. When he applauded Christians and democrats, he assumed everyone, at his best, was included. He sincerely commended both Jefferson and Jesus, without trying to understand the complexity of either man. Atheism was beyond his ken. New political ideologies surely reflected evil instead of possible alternatives. His opponents were either won over by persuasion or dismissed as traitors. He simply never had the type of intellectual discrimination to understand fundamental but subtle philosophical differences. But his beliefs, so ill-defined, so lacking in structure, were generously assumed to include almost anyone. He never concerned himself with nuances, with careful definitions. But he was not so generous at the level of power. Here he could be as ruthless and as intolerant as the occasion demanded, since he always too easily felt that he worked in behalf of the vast majority of righteous people. . . .

2. THE IRONY OF THE NEW DEAL

By 1936 the depression should have been over. "Ifs" abound: *If* businessmen in particular had understood New Deal policies and had responded in confidence rather than unreasonable fear. *If* Roosevelt had not, by 1936, turned in devastating fury upon business and thus fanned resentment and increased confusion. *If* Roosevelt, rather than using business leaders as scapegoats and merely badgering the corporations with diversionary but essentially harmless policies, had really turned toward increased federal direction and ownership. Or *if* the government, in spite of early promises of economy, had pumped such enormous sums of borrowed money into the economy that it had to respond.

By 1936 the last strategy was the going fad among intellectuals. Keynes had just published his epochal *General Theory of Employment, Interest and Money,* in which he plotted in mathematical exactitude the multiplying effects of central banking, tax, and budgetary policies on a market economy. But even large government investments were only stimulants. They could be resisted by countervailing factors that inhibited private spending. It seemed that between 1933 and 1937 the New Deal floundered between ever more daring banking and budgetary measures on one hand and ever more uncertain and stubborn business leaders on the other. Every new economic stimulant acted as a depressant on the minds of the affluent. This was aggravated by the almost total lack of dialogue between the government and business.

By 1936 the New Deal was submerged in irony. To understand this is to get at the heart of the history of the thirties and to get a much better perspective on the welfare state. At the national level, Roosevelt emerged in the clothing of a great progressive reformer. From his early attempts to understand the economic issues, from the tutelage of the brain trust, or even of the gold faddists, he moved to a firm posture—against bigness, against unearned privileges, against economic selfishness; and for the little man, for the exploited, for good and unselfish people everywhere. To Raymond Moley, this class appeal represented a damaging radicalism. To Tugwell, it represented a false smoke screen, or a political sideshow, for concealing a turn to a very conservative economic philosophy, and with it a permanent rejection of real planning.

Both were correct. Roosevelt did move away from economic realities and into the lair of the demagogue. Of course most leaders of large businesses were selfish. But small businessmen were also selfish and by all odds more so than large ones. So were labor leaders, and, believe it or not, even farmers. The label is meaningless. Of course many selfish and shortsighted businessmen, particularly small businessmen, did what they could without punishment in the pursuit of profits, even in some cases where the law forbade. So do most men. They even did it with full assurance that it was right, that the whole country gained from their daring enterprise. Not only did they do it, they would continue to do it, unless stripped of the power to do it or converted to a whole new world view that prevented it (an unlikely answer in spite of Roosevelt's sermons). But Roosevelt kept preaching his denunciatory sermons. He fanned the resentment of good, as well as of selfish and jealous, Americans without power and of far-sighted or politically loyal ones with power. He stimulated righteous indignation and the atmosphere of a moral crusade. But the crusade could do nothing except take punitive action: divide a holding company, threaten but never collect progressive taxes, or use welfare measures to uplift the downtrodden victims of evil men.

The crusade almost always ended in some degree of futility. The battle for the "people" had to eventuate in legislation, had to pass through Roosevelt and the Congress, and then stand up in the courts. In Roosevelt's terms, every New Deal "reform" was a generous act by good men of power against bad men of power. In fact, it was usually a confused compromise by an indistinguishable mixture of good and bad men of power, with Roosevelt (abetted by many historians) generally finding most Republican politicians, conservative Southern Democrats, and at least four Supreme Court judges to be bad men of power, allied to numerous bad men throughout the country. But neither bad men nor good men saw much beyond the evident selfishness of their opponents. Thus, instead of recognizing real devils, or contemplating major but almost impossible changes in American institutions or in the real power structure (not the party structure), the good men either tried some mild detergent in futile efforts to clean up the existing system or tried to appease and care for those who were suffering because of its inadequacies. The good men of power were as much a part of the system as the bad men of power. They could not see that monopoly was a natural and not always harmful end result of a private market system, that negative regulation in behalf of competition would not, could not, and probably should not work, and that more biting, more stringent positive controls would be truly revolutionary, that is, would force a shift of economic and political control, and thus often threaten their own privileged positions. Even when Roosevelt, conventional in beliefs but pleasingly archaic in his gentlemanly *noblesse oblige,* or his academic advisers (presumably good men without power) framed legislation that had some bite, such as a pure food and drugs act or a tax reform bill, it rarely survived Congress. When an ambiguous, potentially radical program did survive, or was sneaked in by executive order, it was usually neutralized by administrators, nullified by the courts, endlessly frustrated in its day-by-day operations, or eventually destroyed or emasculated for political reasons.

The story of most New Deal frustration remains untold. The thirties was indeed a reform decade, a period when sensitivity to injustice, to vast structures of privilege, to the terribly empty life of most people, prevailed as never before. Much of the concern remained outside government, in critics of the New Deal, in radical political movements, in artists of varied mediums, in a few philosophers. But many reformers worked in or with New Deal agencies, particularly the relief agencies. They were always in the minority and had to fight an unending battle within their own agencies. But the outside battle was the main one. As they struggled to carry out their programs, dealing directly with the exploited people who loved Roosevelt, they often found their task impossible. The economic and social institutions of a Democratic South, as an example, presented one tremendous source of frustration. Blocked at every turn, they learned anew the ever-relevant lesson of Lincoln Steffens. Those who effectively frustrated their efforts also loved Roosevelt and were on the side of the angels. They were also powerful. The devils could be dealt with, but not the angels. Mrs. Roosevelt knew their plight, and they loved her for knowing. On occasion, F. D. R. knew also and, when political realities permitted, tried to help his loyal good men without power. But there was nothing in his leadership capable of transforming the desires of these loyal reformers into a new structure of political power. It may have been impossible, even had he tried. Master of politics, he was also captive to politics. Thus the story of the New Deal is a sad story, the ever recurring story of what might have been. Perhaps only Tugwell among major historians has shown a vague appreciation of this sadness, but even he quickly returned to the charisma of an adored leader.

Since the New Deal failed to fulfill even the minimal dream of most reformers, why did all the evil men of power, plus millions of Republican dupes, oppose it? To Roosevelt, the answer was simple: they were evil. Economic royalists, with a monopoly of power, they were not content with a repaired and honest capitalism. Instead, they wanted to drive on with their plutocracy and bring down upon the heads of the good men of power the inevitable revolution. Then good bankers would suffer and good businessmen might lose the management of their corporations. But this answer, although in part true, was too simple. The opponents of Roosevelt misconstrued the direction of the New Deal. Many believed Roosevelt's class rhetoric. They really thought America was losing its "free" capitalist soul to some type of socialism. In their praise of freedom lurked some valuable criticism of the New Deal. Also, many Americans, perhaps particularly the monied classes, never trusted Roosevelt, much less some of his advisers. The New Deal was indeed a mixed company, a type of political bohemia, frequented by many of the better sort, but still dangerous. Roosevelt was a puzzling creature. Even when he served conservative causes, he preached an alien gospel. Let us have anything but a righteous gentleman in Washington. Even a Marxist would have made more sense to them. Finally, almost no one thought in terms of vast economic expansion, and thus no one could see welfare as other than a permanent liability, somehow drawn from the ledger of profits or high incomes, either directly by taxes or indirectly by government deficits and inflation. The threat to earnings, the inhibition to investment, seemed the central issue, more important than declining fears of revolution, humane concern, or an occasional recognition of the importance of purchasing power.

But the supreme irony is here. The enemies of the New Deal were wrong. They should have been friends. Security was a prime concern of the insecure thirties. It cut across all classes. Businessmen, by their policies, desperately sought it in lowered corporate debts and tried to get the government to practice the same austerity. Even when ragged and ill-housed, workers opened savings accounts. The New Deal, by its policies, underwrote a vast apparatus of security. But the meager benefits of Social Security were insignificant in comparison to the building system of security for large, established businesses. But like stingy laborers, the frightened businessmen did not use and enjoy this security and thus increase it. The New Deal tried to frame institutions to protect capitalism from major business cycles and began in an unclear sort of way to underwrite continuous economic growth and sustained profits. Although some tax bills were aimed at high profits, there was no attack on fair profits or even on large profits. During the thirties, as all the way up to the sixties, there was no significant leveling by taxes. The proportionate distribution of wealth remained. Because of tax policies, even relief expenditures were disguised subsidies to corporations, since they were in large part paid by future taxes on individual salaries or on consumer goods. Thus, instead of higher wages creating a market, at the short-term expense of profits, the government subsidized the businessman, without taking the cost out of his hide as he expected and feared.

Even at the local level there was no significant shift of the economic and social structure. Negroes, politically purchased by relief or by the occasional concern of bureaucrats or Mrs. Roosevelt, remained a submerged and neglected caste. Service and farm labor, including migratory, received slight succor. Millions continued in desultory enslavement to immediate needs. Thus the people of power gained added security and lost only two commodities: undisciplined freedom and a degree of popular respect. The last they regained quickly. Most of all, the individual farmer lost some entrepreneurial freedom and accepted a degree of central planning, albeit through democratic procedures. Even manufacturing industries had to accept new procedural limitations—labor laws, added regulatory agencies, new taxes, and minimum wage and maximum hours. But these were necessary for security and for ordered growth. Even without government action, many restraints were developing within large corporations, even in the twenties, and some were simply part of a rationalizing process in business. Security demanded procedural rules, a degree of uniformity in practice, and even a formalized relationship with organized labor. Only small, aggressive adventurers or promoters suffered from the new procedural limitations. The only leveling, and the only real bite, hit the middle income groups and some small businesses. Perhaps the Chambers of Commerce were correct in condemning Roosevelt in 1935. The National Association of Manufacturers was not.

Government spending in behalf of multiplied private spending, the strongest weapon of Eccles and Keynes, was to be the final and most complete insurance policy for American capitalism. After 1937, even Roosevelt reluctantly swallowed this pill. Keynes was the last great classical economist, in the tradition of Adam Smith, Ricardo, the Mills, Marx, and Marshall. A British Liberal, formal, analytical, he tried to devise the minimal government devices necessary to maintain most of the free aspects of a market system. At the beginning of this greatest economic tradition, Adam Smith tried to get the freedom. At the end, Keynes tried to keep as much as possible. He wanted to set up safeguards to prevent serious depressions, to maintain full employment, and at the same time provide all the welfare measures required by human concern. He wanted to avoid socialist ownership and bureaucratic management on one hand and the severe controls of a corporate state on the other. His complex arguments had small influence on the New Deal, but his general prescription eventually prevailed.

The magic in Keynes, at least for an interval, was the magic of growth itself, which springs from new knowledge but is implemented through political economy. Growth can raise a whole society, with rising profits matching rising wages and rising government income supporting rising welfare measures. Business, so fearful of new welfare, never realized that it could be paid for by government credit and that public debts could be maintained (or repaid) without extra tax rates and without a significant redistribution of income or wealth. Roosevelt wanted some redistribution. Like Keynes, he had social as well as economic goals. But he rarely achieved these—witness again the congressional compromises and the frustrated bureaucrats on the moral battlefield. During World War II, when massive spending purchased unbelievable growth, Roosevelt had to suspend social goals and let the public subsidize plant expansion, profits, and, above all, future profits. By then he had no political alternative. Full employment, plus overtime, reduced the welfare burden, while growth and temporarily high taxes helped pay the cost of war. Some temporary leveling actually occurred. After the war the large government subsidy to business continued—in huge defense purchases, in contracts awarded in behalf of corporate survival, in research, in tax relief, in a flexible use of antitrust laws, in enough welfare increases to soothe the discontented, in a tacit acceptance of administered prices, and increasingly even in an unwillingness to antagonize the business community (even Democrats learned the old Hoover bit about confidence).

The battle between economic leaders and the New Deal was never complete. Some businessmen and many large farmers (historians generally call them enlightened) supported Roosevelt throughout the thirties. Many more, if they had understood Roosevelt's purposes, would surely have backed him. In the same sense, Roosevelt, considering his objectives, his willingness to retain and strengthen a private economy, should have worked more at understanding and communicating with businessmen, for their choices had more to do with the success of the New Deal than anything else. Yet, there was a real issue dividing the two. Simply, it was a matter of power. Roosevelt was powerful and could not be controlled by anyone or by any group. In this sense he was incorruptible, perhaps as much so as any President in American history. For two years even intense lobbying could not block his control over the legislative process. As

Tugwell always believed, there was the potentiality of a major shift in the government of the country, with Roosevelt responding to academic advisers and effecting policies which would seriously invade the managerial prerogatives of major private interests. Instead of a limited socialization of product via welfare, Roosevelt could have socialized management or even the plant. He never did this; seemingly, he never wanted to, but until 1937 he seemed to have the political power and never gave enough assurances to convince businessmen that he might not. For a while, normal channels of power in the federal government were circumvented, particularly in 1933–34. This is why the courts became the heroes of conservative groups. But even as Roosevelt secured great political power, and thus potential economic power, the power of economic decision making remained perilously in private hands, less secure and less potent than ever before. The tense situation could not endure.

The shift to welfare policies and then to Keynesian recovery policies took away most of the threat and left private interests shaken but more secure than ever. Nationalization and economic planning became dead issues. Through banking and budgetary policies the government's resources were to be used to protect, support, and occasionally discipline private producers. This meant a helping hand for private industry, but with too many obligations, too many secure guarantees, and too many restrictions for many old-fashioned industrialists. Security does reduce freedom.

But the government had, more clearly than ever in the past, committed itself to national economic goals. This was one of the enduring achievements of the New Deal. Since it rejected planning (except to a degree in agriculture) and refused to do its own producing, it had no alternative but to rely on the major corporations and to subsidize them if necessary to insure its goals of rapid growth, high levels of employment, and low welfare needs. Even a slight increase in private economic activity can do more to benefit the country than vast welfare programs. Precluded from direct economic action, the government had to use indirect controls and incentives, plus persuasion, bribes, or, if politically possible, threats and punitive measures. In this situation, high profits rightfully became desirable public policy, since they increased the total economic activity and the level of national prosperity. In spite of all the ridicule, nothing was now truer than the quip: "What is good for General Motors is good for the country." Under the emerging system, the welfare of both were inseparable.

The dependence was mutual. The large corporations, protected by a generous government against the insecurity of the past (when politicians could safely allow depressions) and also against their own worst mistakes and abuses, were tied to government policies. The national budget was almost as important as their corporate budgets. The action of the Federal Reserve Board, or even random pronouncements by government officials, could wreck their best-laid plans. Welfare spending became a small but marginally vital part of the total market for goods, forcing some business acquiescence even here. In a few areas, such as low-rent housing, welfare programs became the major support for very profitable businesses. Later, defense spending would completely support large companies and provide the margin of profit for hundreds. Increasingly, business and government were linked in more subtle ways, particularly by a common economic orthodoxy and a common need for certain skills. Bureaucrats moved from Ivy League campuses to corporations and on to Washington. The situation invited, in fact necessitated, co-operation, or a truly joint enterprise. Roosevelt cleared the way for such co-operation, but he never desired it or achieved it and probably never perceived its inescapable logic. Unlike most politicians, he was never a good businessman, nor could he share power easily.

The old, individualistic capitalist did not fit the new picture. Mavericks were taboo. But neither did reformers fit. The new partnership, with greater government participation and greater benefits (the welfare state for business), left room for tension, even bitter conflict, as between mutually dependent husband and wife. Always, one or the other partner could try to gain too much power and upset the partnership. There was an overlapping but never identical constituency. Generally, with time and enough advice from Keynesian counselors, the two settled into almost blissful matrimony. Lyndon Johnson finally illustrated what a beautiful and happy home is possible when both sides can sit down and reason together. What about the constituency? For business, the shareholders have profited. Dividends have been large and capital accumulation even larger. For government, the larger constituency presents a much more variegated pattern. But most able and fortunate people, if they have been loyal, have received well in material returns and have profited from the general benevolence and good will of both the private and government bureaucrats who look out for them

But the economic magic of sustained growth and the political magic of welfare can be irrelevant to moral and religious vision, which may also demand a just community. For the more sensitive New Dealers, or outside critics, Keynes provided a technique for priming the economic pump but no means of purifying the water. They thirsted after the pure product. Growth could simply intoxicate the affluent minority (or majority), blunt their sensitivity, and leave them in satiated lethargy, full but unfulfilled. Welfare could do the same for the poor. Growth could lead to vast production, to an enormous gross national product, but also to ugliness and spiritual poverty everywhere. It might even lead to full employment and undreamed-of security (goals not attained because of too small a government investment), yet to a society bereft of meaningful work, of personal involvement, even of democratic participation. It might suggest the blessing of leisure but bring only the curse of idleness. Finally, it would surely conceal injustice and leave the exploited to the tender and prejudiced mercy of local conscience. During the war the disturbing reformers dropped from view and did not emerge again until the sixties. Then, to the profound surprise of all good men of power, the one-third ill-fed and ill-housed, and the two-thirds alienated and desperate, still existed. In spite of the New Deal and in spite of all that welfare!

WILLIAM E. LEUCHTENBURG

The Roosevelt Reconstruction

William E. Leuchtenburg is at pains to present a balanced account of the New Deal. In this concluding chapter to Franklin D. Roosevelt and the New Deal, 1932–1940, *he tries to negotiate between historians who see the New Deal as an extension of the Populist-Progressive tradition and those who find in its tone and concerns a sharp break with the past. Those who find the New Deal to be an evolutionary fulfillment of the earlier reform movements stress the rapidity of Roosevelt's legislative accomplishments as conveying the false appearance of revolution. Moreover, the ideology of the New Deal is not dramatically new; it draws heavily on the varieties of progressive thought embodied in Theodore Roosevelt, Woodrow Wilson, Robert La Follette, and William Jennings Bryan. Even such seemingly radical measures as TVA and social security originated in earlier times.*

On the other hand, it can be argued that although there are no discontinuities in history the central problem of the New Deal, the Great Depression, was without precedent and therefore required a new governmental philosophy. The principal enemies of the old reform movements, the trusts and the political machines, entered into a kind of partnership with government. New immigrant support and an urban, lower-middle-class base for the Roosevelt coalition also gave the New Deal a distinctive hue. Finally, its opponents, such as Herbert Hoover, argued that Roosevelt broke the power of the states and moved the country in a totalitarian direction toward a centralized planned economy.

Leuchtenburg does not commit himself on this long-standing dispute about the New Deal, but he presents the evidence on which students can draw their own conclusions. His larger purpose remains that of writing a concise summary of the period.

In eight years, Roosevelt and the New Dealers had almost revolutionized the agenda of American politics. "Mr. Roosevelt may have given the wrong answers to many of his problems," concluded the editors of *The Economist*. "But he is at least the first President of modern America who has asked the right questions." In 1932, men of acumen were absorbed to an astonishing degree with such questions as prohibition, war debts, and law enforcement. By 1936, they were debating social security, the Wagner Act, valley authorities, and public housing. The thirties witnessed a rebirth of issues politics, and parties split more sharply on ideological lines than they had in many years past. "I incline to think that for years up to the present juncture thinking Democrats and thinking Republicans had been divided by an imaginary line," reflected a Massachusetts congressman in 1934. "Now for the first time since the period before the Civil War we find vital principles at stake." Much of this change resulted simply from the depression trauma, but much too came from the force of Roosevelt's personality and his use of his office as both pulpit and lectern. "Of course you have fallen into some errors—that is human," former Supreme Court Justice John Clarke wrote the President, "but you have put a new face upon the social and political life of our country."

Franklin Roosevelt re-created the modern Presidency. He took an office which had lost much of its prestige and power in the previous twelve years and gave it an importance which went well beyond what even Theodore Roosevelt and Woodrow Wilson had done. Clinton Rossiter has observed: "Only Washington, who made the office, and Jackson, who remade it, did more than [Roosevelt] to raise it to its present condition of strength, dignity, and independence." Under Roosevelt, the White House became the focus of all government—the fountainhead of ideas, the initiator of action, the representative of the national interest.

Roosevelt greatly expanded the President's legislative functions. In the nineteenth century, Congress had been jealous of its prerogatives as the law-making body, and resented any encroachment on its domain by the Chief Executive. Woodrow Wilson and Theodore Roosevelt had broken new ground in sending actual drafts of bills to Congress and in using devices like the caucus to win enactment of measures they favored. Franklin Roosevelt made such constant use of these tools that he came to assume a legislative role not unlike that of a prime minister. He sent special messages to Congress, accompanied them with drafts of legislation prepared by his assistants, wrote letters to committee chairmen or members of Congress to urge passage of the proposals, and authorized men like Corcoran to lobby as presidential spokesmen on the Hill. By the end of Roosevelt's tenure in the White House, Congress looked automatically to the Executive for guidance; it expected the administration to have a "program" to present for consideration.

Roosevelt's most important formal contribution was his creation of the Executive Office of the President on September 8, 1939. Executive Order 8248, a "nearly unnoticed but none the less epoch-making event in the history of American institutions," set up an Executive Office staffed with six administrative assistants with a "passion for anonymity." In 1939, the President not only placed obvious agencies like the White House Office in the Executive Office but made the crucial decision to shift the Bureau of the Budget from the

Treasury and put it under his wing. In later years, such pivotal agencies as the Council of Economic Advisers, the National Security Council, and the Central Intelligence Agency would be moved into the Executive Office of the President. Roosevelt's decision, Rossiter has concluded, "converts the Presidency into an instrument of twentieth-century government; it gives the incumbent a sporting chance to stand the strain and fulfill his constitutional mandate as a one-man branch of our three-part government; it deflates even the most forceful arguments, which are still raised occasionally, for a plural executive; it assures us that the Presidency will survive the advent of the positive state. Executive Order 8248 may yet be judged to have saved the Presidency from paralysis and the Constitution from radical amendment."

Roosevelt's friends have been too quick to concede that he was a poor administrator. To be sure, he found it difficult to discharge incompetent aides, he procrastinated about decisions, and he ignored all the canons of sound administration by giving men overlapping assignments and creating a myriad of agencies which had no clear relation to the regular departments of government. But if the test of good administration is not an impeccable organizational chart but creativity, then Roosevelt must be set down not merely as a good administrator but as a resourceful innovator. The new agencies he set up gave a spirit of excitement to Washington that the routinized old-line departments could never have achieved. The President's refusal to proceed through channels, however vexing at times to his subordinates, resulted in a competition not only among men but among ideas, and encouraged men to feel that their own beliefs might win the day. "You would be surprised, Colonel, the remarkable ideas that have been turned loose just because men have felt that they can get a hearing," one senator confided. The President's "procrastination" was his own way both of arriving at a sense of national consensus and of reaching a decision by observing a trial by combat among rival theories. Periods of indecision—as in the spring of 1935 or the beginning of 1938—were inevitably followed by a fresh outburst of new proposals.

Most of all, Roosevelt was a successful administrator because he attracted to Washington thousands of devoted and highly skilled men. Men who had been fighting for years for lost causes were given a chance: John Collier, whom the President courageously named Indian Commissioner; Arthur Powell Davis, who had been ousted as chief engineer of the Department of the Interior at the demand of power interests; old conservationists like Harry Slattery, who had fought the naval oil interests in the Harding era. When Harold Ickes took office as Secretary of the Interior, he looked up Louis Glavis —he did not even know whether the "martyr" of the Ballinger-Pinchot affair was still alive—and appointed him to his staff.

The New Dealers displayed striking ingenuity in meeting problems of governing. They coaxed salmon to climb ladders at Bonneville; they sponsored a Young Choreographers Laboratory in the WPA's Dance Theatre; they gave the pioneer documentary film maker Pare Lorentz the opportunity to create his classic films *The Plow That Broke the Plains* and *The River*. At the Composers Forum-Laboratory of the Federal Music Project, William Schuman received his first serious hearing. In Arizona, Father Berard Haile of St. Michael's Mission taught written Navajo to the Indians. Roosevelt, in the face of derision from professional foresters and prairie states' governors, persisted in a bold scheme to plant a mammoth "shelterbelt" of parallel rows of trees from the Dakotas to the Panhandle. In all, more than two hundred million trees were planted—cottonwood and willow, hackberry and cedar, Russian olive and Osage orange; within six years, the President's visionary windbreak had won over his former critics. The spirit behind such innovations generated a new excitement about the potentialities of government. "Once again," Roosevelt told a group of young Democrats in April, 1936, "the very air of America is exhilarating."

Roosevelt dominated the front pages of the newspapers as no other President before or since has done. "Frank Roosevelt and the NRA have taken the place of love nests," commented Joe Patterson, publisher of the tabloid New York *Daily News*. At his very first press conference, Roosevelt abolished the written question and told reporters they could interrogate him without warning. Skeptics predicted the free and easy exchange would soon be abandoned, but twice a week, year in and year out, he threw open the White House doors to as many as two hundred reporters, most of them representing hostile publishers, who would crowd right up to the President's desk to fire their questions. The President joshed them, traded wisecracks with them, called them by their first names; he charmed them by his good-humored ease and impressed them with his knowledge of detail. To a degree, Roosevelt's press conference introduced, as some observers claimed, a new institution like Britain's parliamentary questioning; more to the point, it was a device the President manipulated, disarmingly and adroitly, to win support for his program. It served too as a classroom to instruct the country in the new economics and the new politics.

Roosevelt was the first president to master the technique of reaching people directly over the radio. In his fireside chats, he talked like a father discussing public affairs with his family in the living room. As he spoke, he seemed unconscious of the fact that he was addressing millions. "His head would nod and his hands would move in simple, natural, comfortable gestures," Frances Perkins recalled. "His face would smile and light up as though he were actually sitting on the front porch or in the parlor with them." Eleanor Roosevelt later observed that after the President's death people would stop her on the street to say "they missed the way the President used to talk to them. They'd say 'He used to talk to me about my government.' There was a real dialogue between Franklin and the people," she reflected. "That dialogue seems to have disappeared from the government since he died."

For the first time for many Americans, the federal government became an institution that was directly experienced. More than state and local governments, it came to be *the* government, an agency directly concerned with their welfare. It was the source of their relief payments; it taxed them directly for old age pensions; it even gave their children hot lunches in school. As the role of the state changed from that of neutral arbiter to a "powerful promoter of society's welfare," people felt an interest in affairs in Washington they had never had before.

Franklin Roosevelt personified the state as protector. It became commonplace to say that people felt toward the President the kind of trust they would normally express for a warm and understanding father who comforted them in their grief or safeguarded them from harm. An insurance man reported: "My mother looks upon the President as someone so immediately concerned with her problems and difficulties that she would not be greatly surprised were he to come to her house some evening and stay to dinner." From his first hours in office, Roosevelt gave people the feeling that they could confide in him directly. As late as the Presidency of Herbert Hoover, one man, Ira Smith, had sufficed to take care of all the mail the White House received. Under Roosevelt, Smith had to acquire a staff of fifty people to handle the thousands of letters written to the President each week. Roosevelt gave people a sense of membership in the national community. Justice Douglas has written: "He was in a very special sense the people's President, because he made them feel that with him in the White House they shared the Presidency. The sense of sharing the Presidency gave even the most humble citizen a lively sense of belonging."

When Roosevelt took office, the country, to a very large degree, responded to the will of a single element: the white, Anglo-Saxon, Protestant property-holding class. Under the New Deal, new groups took their place in the sun. It was not merely that they received benefits they had not had before but that they were "recognized" as having a place in the commonwealth. At the beginning of the Roosevelt era, charity organizations ignored labor when seeking "community" representation; at the end of the period, no fund-raising committee was complete without a union representative. While Theodore Roosevelt had founded a lily-white Progressive party in the South and Woodrow Wilson had introduced segregation into the federal government, Franklin Roosevelt had quietly brought the Negro into the New Deal coalition. When the distinguished Negro contralto Marian Anderson was denied a concert hall in Washington, Secretary Ickes arranged for her to perform from the steps of Lincoln Memorial. Equal representation for religious groups became so well accepted that, as one priest wryly complained, one never saw a picture of a priest in a newspaper unless he was flanked on either side by a minister and a rabbi.

The devotion Roosevelt aroused owed much to the fact that the New Deal assumed the responsibility for guaranteeing every American a minimum standard of subsistence. Its relief programs represented an advance over the barbaric predepression practices that constituted a difference not in degree but in kind. One analyst wrote: "During the ten years between 1929 and 1939 more progress was made in public welfare and relief than in the three hundred years after this country was first settled." The Roosevelt administration gave such assistance not as a matter of charity but of right. This system of social rights was written into the Social Security Act. Other New Deal legislation abolished child labor in interstate commerce and, by putting a floor under wages and a ceiling on hours, all but wiped out the sweatshop.

Roosevelt and his aides fashioned a government which consciously sought to make the industrial system more humane and to protect workers and their families from exploitation. In his acceptance speech in June, 1936, the President stated: "Governments can err, Presidents do make mistakes, but the immortal Dante tells us that divine justice weighs the sins of the cold-blooded and the sins of the warm-hearted in different scales.

"Better the occasional faults of a Government that lives in a spirit of charity than the constant omission of a Government frozen in the ice of its own indifference." Nearly everyone in the Roosevelt government was caught up to some degree by a sense of participation in something larger than themselves. A few days after he took office, one of the more conservative New Deal administrators wrote in his diary: "This should be a Gov't of humanity."

The federal government expanded enormously in the Roosevelt years. The crisis of the depression dissipated the distrust of the state inherited from the eighteenth century and reinforced in diverse ways by the Jeffersonians and the Spencerians. Roosevelt himself believed that liberty in America was imperiled more by the agglomerations of private business than by the state. The New Dealers were convinced that the depression was the result not simply of an economic breakdown but of a political collapse; hence, they sought new political instrumentalities. The reformers of the 1930's accepted almost unquestioningly the use of coercion by the state to achieve reforms. Even Republicans who protested that Roosevelt's policies were snuffing out liberty voted overwhelmingly in favor of coercive measures.

This elephantine growth of the federal government owed much to the fact that local and state governments had been tried in the crisis and found wanting. When one magazine wired state governors to ask their views, only one of the thirty-seven who replied announced that he was willing to have the states resume responsibility for relief. Every time there was a rumored cutback of federal spending for relief, Washington was besieged by delegations of mayors protesting that city governments did not have the resources to meet the needs of the unemployed.

Even more dramatic was the impotence of local governments in dealing with crime, a subject that captured the national imagination in a decade of kidnapings and bank holdups. In September, 1933, the notorious bank robber John Dillinger was arrested in Ohio. Three weeks later, his confederates released him from jail and killed the Lima, Ohio, sheriff. In January, 1934, after bank holdups at Racine, Wisconsin, and East Chicago, Indiana, Dillinger was apprehended in Tucson, Arizona, and returned to the "escape-proof" jail of Crown Point, Indiana, reputedly the strongest county prison in the country. A month later he broke out and drove off in the sheriff's car. While five thousand law officers pursued him, he stopped for a haircut in a barber shop, bought cars, and had a home-cooked Sunday dinner with his family in his home town. When he needed more arms, he raided the police station at Warsaw, Indiana.

Dillinger's exploits touched off a national outcry for federal action. State and local authorities could not cope with gangs which crossed and recrossed jurisdictional lines, which were equipped with Thompson submachine guns and high-powered cars, and which had a regional network of informers and fences in the Mississippi Valley. Detection and punishment of crime had always been a local function; now there seemed no choice but to call in the federal operatives. In July, 1934, federal agents shot down Dillinger outside a Chicago theater. In October, FBI men killed Pretty Boy Floyd near East Liverpool, Ohio; in November they shot Baby Face Nelson, Public Enemy No. 1, near Niles Center, Illinois. By the end of 1934, the nation had a new kind of hero: the G-man Melvin Purvis and the chief of the Division of Investigation of the Department of Justice, J. Edgar Hoover. By the end of that year, too, Congress had stipulated that a long list of crimes would henceforth be regarded as federal offenses, including holding up a bank insured by the Federal Deposit Insurance Corporation. The family of a kidnaped victim could call in the federal police simply by phoning National 7117 in Washington.

Under the New Deal, the federal government greatly extended its power over the economy. By the end of the Roosevelt years, few questioned the right of the government to pay the farmer millions in subsidies not to grow crops, to enter plants to conduct union elections, to regulate business enterprises from utility companies to air lines, or even to compete directly with business by generating and distributing hydroelectric power. All of these powers had been ratified by the Supreme Court, which had even held that a man growing grain solely for his own use was affecting interstate commerce and hence subject to federal penalties. The President, too, was well on his way to becoming "the chief economic engineer," although this was not finally established until the Full Employment Act of 1946. In 1931, Hoover had hooted that some people thought "that by some legerdemain we can legislate ourselves out of a world-wide depression." In the Roosevelt era, the conviction that government both should and could act to forestall future breakdowns gained general acceptance. The New Deal left a large legacy of antidepression controls—securities regulation, banking reforms, unemployment compensation—even if it could not guarantee that a subsequent administration would use them.

In the 1930's, the financial center of the nation shifted from Wall Street to Washington. In May, 1934, a writer reported: "Financial news no longer originates in Wall Street." That same month, *Fortune* commented on a revolution in the credit system which was "one of the major historical events of the generation." "Mr. Roosevelt," it noted, "seized the Federal Reserve without firing a shot." The federal government had not only broken down the old separation of bank and state in the Reserve system but had gone into the credit business itself in a wholesale fashion under the aegis of the RFC, the Farm Credit Administration, and the housing agencies. Legislation in 1933 and 1934 had established federal regulation of Wall Street for the first time. No longer could the New York Stock Exchange operate as a private club free of national supervision. In 1935, Congress leveled the mammoth holding-company pyramids and centralized yet more authority over the banking system in the federal government. After a tour of the United States in 1935, Sir Josiah Stamp wrote: "Just as in 1929 the whole country was 'Wall Street-conscious' now it is 'Washington-conscious.' "

Despite this encroachment of government on traditional business prerogatives, the New Deal could advance impressive claims to being regarded as a "savior of capitalism." Roosevelt's sense of the land, of family, and of the community marked him as a man with deeply ingrained conservative traits. In the New Deal years, the government sought deliberately, in Roosevelt's words, "to energize private enterprise." The RFC financed business, housing agencies underwrote home financing, and public works spending aimed to revive the construction industry. Moreover, some of the New Deal reforms were Janus-faced. The NYA, in aiding jobless youth, also served as a safety valve to keep young people out of the labor market. A New Deal congressman, in pushing for public power projects, argued that the country should take advantage of the sea of "cheap labor" on the relief rolls. Even the Wagner Act and the movement for industrial unionism were motivated in part by the desire to contain "unbalanced and radical" labor groups. Yet such considerations should not obscure the more important point: that the New Deal, however conservative it was in some respects and however much it owed to the past, marked a radically new departure. As Carl Degler writes: "The conclusion seems inescapable that, traditional as the words may have been in which the New Deal expressed itself, in actuality it was a revolutionary response to a revolutionary situation."

Not all of the changes that were wrought were the result of Roosevelt's own actions or of those of his government. Much of the force for change came from progressives in Congress, or from nongovernmental groups like the C.I.O., or simply from the impersonal agency of the depression itself. Yet, however much significance one assigns the "objective situation," it is difficult to gainsay the importance of Roosevelt. If, in Miami in February, 1933, an assassin's bullet had been true to its mark and John Garner rather than Roosevelt had entered the White House the next month, or if the Roosevelt lines had cracked at the Democratic convention in 1932 and Newton Baker had been the compromise choice, the history of America in the thirties would have been markedly different.

At a time when democracy was under attack elsewhere in the world, the achievements of the New Deal were especially significant. At the end of 1933, in an open letter to President Roosevelt, John Maynard Keynes had written: "You have made yourself the trustee for those in every country who seek to mend the evils of our condition by reasoned experiment within the framework of the existing social system. If you fail, rational change will be gravely prejudiced throughout the world, leaving orthodoxy and revolution to fight it out." In the next few years, teams of foreigners toured the TVA, Russians and Arabs came to study the shelterbelt, French writers taxed Léon Blum with importing "Rooseveltism" to France, and analysts characterized Paul Van Zeeland's program in Belgium as a "New Deal." Under Roosevelt, observed a Montevideo newspaper, the United States had become "as it was in the eighteenth century, the victorious emblem around which may rally the multitudes thirsting for social justice and human fraternity."

In their approach to reform, the New Dealers reflected the tough-minded, hard-boiled attitude that permeated much of America in the thirties. In 1931, the gangster film *Public Enemy* had given the country a new kind of hero in James Cagney: the aggressive, unsentimental tough guy who deliberately assaulted the romantic tradition. It was a type whose role in society could easily be manipulated; gangster hero Cagney of the early thirties was transformed into G-man hero Cagney of the later thirties. Even more representative was Humphrey Bogart, creator of the "private eye" hero, the man of action who masks his feelings in a calculated emotional neutrality. Bogart, who began as the cold desperado Duke Mantee of *Petrified Forest* and the frightening Black Legionnaire, soon turned up on the right side of anti-Fascist causes, although he never surrendered the pose of noninvolvement. This fear of open emotional commitment and this admiration of toughness ran through the vogue of the "Dead End Kids," films like *Nothing Sacred,* the popularity of the St. Louis Cardinals' spike-flying Gas House Gang, and the "hardboiled" fiction of writers like James Cain and Dashiell Hammett.

Unlike the earlier Progressive, the New Dealer shied away from being thought of as sentimental. Instead of justifying relief as a humanitarian measure, the New Dealers often insisted it was necessary to stimulate purchasing power or to stabilize the economy or to "conserve manpower." The justification for a better distribution of income was neither "social justice" nor a "healthier national life," wrote Adolf Berle. "It remained for the hard-boiled student to work out the simple equation that unless the national income was pretty widely diffused there were not enough customers to keep the plants going." The reformers of the thirties abandoned—or claimed they had abandoned—the old Emersonian hope of reforming man and sought only to change institutions. This meant that they did not seek to "uplift" the people they were helping but only to improve their economic position. "In other words," Tugwell stated bluntly, "the New Deal is attempting to do nothing to *people,* and does not seek at all to alter their way of life, their wants and desires."

Reform in the 1930's meant *economic* reform; it departed from the Methodist-parsonage morality of many of the earlier Progressives, in part because much of the New Deal support, and many of its leaders, derived from urban immigrant groups hostile to the old Sabbatarianism. While the progressive grieved over the fate of the prostitute, the New Dealer would have placed Mrs. Warren's profession under a code authority. If the archetypical progressive was Jane Addams singing "Onward, Christian Soldiers," the representative New Dealer was Harry Hopkins betting on the horses at Laurel Race Track. When directing FERA in late 1933, Hopkins announced: "I would like to provide orchestras for beer gardens to encourage people to sit around drinking their beer and enjoying themselves. It would be a great unemployment relief measure." "I feel no call to remedy evils," Raymond Moley declared. "I have not the slightest urge to be a reformer. Social workers make me very weary. They have no sense of humor."

Despite Moley's disclaimer, many of the early New Dealers like himself and Adolf Berle did, in fact, hope to achieve reform through regeneration: the regeneration of the businessman. By the end of 1935, the New Dealers were pursuing a quite different course. Instead of attempting to evangelize the Right, they mobilized massive political power against the power of the corporation. They relied not on converting industrial sinners but in using sufficient coercion. New Dealers like Thurman Arnold sought to ignore "moral" considerations altogether; Arnold wished not to punish wrongdoers but to achieve price flexibility. His "faith" lay in the expectation that "fanatical alignments between opposing political principles may disappear and a competent, practical, opportunistic governing class may rise to power." With such expectations, the New Dealers frequently had little patience with legal restraints that impeded action. "I want to assure you," Hopkins told the NYA Advisory Committee, "that we are not afraid of exploring anything within the law, and we have a lawyer who will declare anything you want to do legal."

In the thirties, nineteenth-century individualism gave ground to a new emphasis on social security and collective action. In the twenties, America hailed Lindbergh as the Lone Eagle; in the thirties, when word arrived that Amelia Earhart was lost at sea, the *New Republic* asked the government to prohibit citizens from engaging in such "useless" exploits. The NRA sought to drive newsboys off the streets and took a Blue Eagle away from a company in Huck Finn's old town of Hannibal, Missouri, because a fifteen-year-old was found driving a truck for his father's business. Josef Hofmann urged that fewer musicians become soloists, Hollywood stars like Joan Crawford joined the Screen Actors Guild, and Leopold Stokowski canceled a performance in Pittsburgh because theater proprietors were violating a union contract. In New York in 1933, after a series of meetings in Heywood Broun's penthouse apartment, newspapermen organized the American Newspaper Guild in rebellion against the disspiriting romanticism of Richard Harding Davis. "We no longer care to develop the individual as a unique contributor to a democratic form," wrote the mordant Edgar Kemler. "In this movement each individual sub-man is important, not for his uniqueness, but for his ability to lose himself in the mass, through his fidelity to the trade union, or cooperative organization, or political party."

The liberals of the thirties admired intellectual activity which had a direct relation to concrete reality. Stuart Chase wrote of one government report: "This book is live stuff—wheelbarrow, cement mixer, steam dredge, generator, combine, power-line stuff; library dust does not gather here." If the poet did not wish to risk the suspicion that his loyalties were not to the historic necessities of his generation, wrote Archibald MacLeish, he must "soak himself not in books" but in the physical reality of "by what organization of men and railroads and trucks and belts and book-entries the materials of a single automobile are assembled." The New Dealers were fascinated by "the total man days per year for timber stand improvement," and Tugwell rejoiced in the "practical success" of the Resettlement Administration demonstrated by "these healthy collection figures." Under the Special Skills Division of the RA, Greenbelt was presented with inspirational paintings like *Constructing Sewers, Concrete Mixer,* and *Shovel at Work.* On one occasion, in attempting to mediate a literary controversy, the critic Edmund Wilson wrote: "It should be possible to convince Marxist critics of the importance of a work like 'Ulysses' by telling them that it is a great piece of engineering—as it is." In this activist world of the New Dealers, the aesthete and the man who pursued a life of contemplation, especially the man whose interests centered in the past, were viewed with scorn. In Robert Sherwood's *The Petrified Forest,* Alan Squier, the ineffectual aesthete, meets his death in the desert and is buried in the petrified forest where the living to turn to stone. He is an archaic type for whom the world has no place.

The new activism explicitly recognized its debt to Dewey's dictum of "learning by doing" and, like other of Dewey's ideas, was subject to exaggeration and perversion. The New Deal, which gave unprecedented authority to intellectuals in government, was, in certain important respects, anti-intellectual. Without the activist faith, perhaps not nearly so much would have been achieved. It was Lilienthal's conviction that "there is almost nothing, however fantastic, that (given competent organization) a team of engineers, scientists, and administrators cannot do today" that helped make possible the successes of TVA. Yet the liberal activitists grasped only a part of the truth; they retreated from conceptions like "tragedy," "sin," "God," often had small patience with the force of tradition, and showed little understanding of what moved men to seek meanings outside of political experience. As sensitive a critic as the poet Horace Gregory could write, in a review of the works of D. H. Lawrence: "The world is moving away from Lawrence's need for personal salvation; his 'dark religion' is not a substitute for economic planning." This was not the mood of all men in the thirties—not of a William Faulkner, an Ellen Glasgow —and many of the New Dealers recognized that life was more complex than some of their statements would suggest. Yet the liberals, in their desire to free themselves from the tyranny of precedent and in their ardor for social achievement, sometimes walked the precipice of superficiality and philistinism.

The concentration of the New Dealers on public concerns made a deep mark on the sensibility of the 1930's. Private experience seemed self-indulgent compared to the demands of public life. "Indeed the public world with us has *become* the private world, and the private world has become the public," wrote Archibald MacLeish. "We live, that is to say, in a revolutionary time in which the public life has washed in over the dikes of private existence as sea water breaks over into the fresh pools in the spring tides till everything is salt." In the thirties, the Edna St. Vincent Millay whose candle had burned at both ends wrote the polemical *Conversation at Midnight* and the bitter "Epitaph for the Race of Man" in *Wine From These Grapes.*

The emphasis on the public world implied a specific rejection of the values of the 1920's. Roosevelt dismissed the twenties as "a decade of debauch," Tugwell scored those years as "a decade of empty progress, devoid of contribution to a genuinely better future," Morris Cooke deplored the "gilded-chariot days" of 1929, and Alben Barkley saw the twenties as a "carnival" marred by "the putrid pestilence of financial debauchery." The depression was experienced as the punishment of a wrathful God visited on a nation that had strayed from the paths of righteousness. The fire that followed the Park Avenue party in Thomas Wolfe's *You Can't Go Home Again,* like the suicide of Eveline at the end of John Dos Passos' *The Big Money,* symbolized the holocaust that brought to an end a decade of hedonism. In an era of reconstruction, the attitudes of the twenties seemed alien, frivolous, or—the most cutting word the thirties could visit upon a man or institution—"escapist." When Morrie Ryskind and George Kaufman, authors of the popular *Of Thee I Sing,* lampooned the government again in *Let 'em Eat Cake* in the fall of 1933, the country was not amused. The New York *Post* applauded the decision of George Jean Nathan and his associates to discontinue the *American Spectator:* "Nihilism, dadaism, smartsetism—they are all gone, and this, too, is progress." One of H. L. Mencken's biographers has noted: "Many were at pains to write him at his new home, telling him he was a sophomore, and those writing in magazines attacked him with a fury that was suspect because of its very violence."

Commentators on the New Deal have frequently characterized it by that much-abused term "pragmatic." If one means by this that the New Dealers carefully tested the consequences of ideas, the term is clearly a misnomer. If one means that Roosevelt was exceptionally anti-ideological in his approach to politics, one may question whether he was, in fact, any more "pragmatic" in this sense than Van Buren or Polk or even "reform" Presidents like Jackson and Theodore Roosevelt. The "pragmatism" of the New Deal seemed remarkable only in a decade tortured by ideology, only in contrast to the rigidity of Hoover and of the Left.

The New Deal was pragmatic mainly in its skepticism about utopias and final solutions, its openness to experimentation, and its suspicion of the dogmas of the Establishment. Since the advice of economists had so often been wrong, the New Dealers distrusted the claims of orthodox theory—"All this is perfectly terrible because it is all pure theory, when you come down to it," the President said on one occasion—and they felt free to try new approaches. Roosevelt refused to be awed by the warnings of economists and financial experts that government interference with the "laws" of the economy was blasphemous. "We must lay hold of the fact that economic laws are not made by nature," the President stated. "They are made by human beings." The New Dealers denied that depressions were inevitable events that had to be borne stoically, most of the stoicism to be displayed by the most impoverished, and they were willing to explore novel ways to make the social order more stable and more humane. "I am for experimenting . . . in various parts of the country, trying out schemes which are supported by reasonable people and see if they work," Hopkins told a conference of social workers. "If they do not work, the world will not come to an end."

Hardheaded, "anti-utopian," the New Dealers nonetheless had their Heavenly City: the greenbelt town, clean, green, and white, with children playing in light, airy, spacious schools; the government project at Longview, Washington, with small houses, each of different design, colored roofs, and gardens of flowers and vegetables; the Mormon villages of Utah that M. L. Wilson kept in his mind's eye—immaculate farmsteads on broad, rectangular streets; most of all, the Tennessee Valley, with its model town of Norris, the tall transmission towers, the white dams, the glistening wire strands, the valley where "a vision of villages and clean small factories has been growing into the minds of thoughtful men." Scandinavia was their model abroad, not only because it summoned up images of the countryside of Denmark, the beauties of Stockholm, not only for its experience with labor relations and social insurance and currency reform, but because it represented the "middle way" of happy accommodation of public and private institutions the New Deal sought to achieve. "Why," inquired Brandeis, "should anyone want to go to Russia when one can go to Denmark?"

Yet the New Deal added up to more than all of this—more than an experimental approach, more than the sum of its legislative achievements, more than an antiseptic utopia. It is true that there was a certain erosion of values in the thirties, as well as a narrowing of horizons, but the New Dealers inwardly recognized that what they were doing had a deeply moral significance however much they eschewed ethical pretensions. Heirs of the Enlightenment, they felt themselves part of a broadly humanistic movement to make man's life on earth more tolerable, a movement that might someday even achieve a co-operative commonwealth. Social insurance, Frances Perkins declared, was "a fundamental part of another great forward step in that liberation of humanity which began with the Renaissance."

Franklin Roosevelt did not always have this sense as keenly as some of the men around him, but his greatness as a President lies in the remarkable degree to which he shared the vision. "The new deal business to me is very much bigger than anyone yet has expressed it," observed Senator Elbert Thomas. Roosevelt "seems to really have caught the spirit of what one of the Hebrew prophets called the desire of the nations. If he were in India today they would probably decide that he had become Mahatma—that is, one in tune with the infinite." Both foes and friends made much of Roosevelt's skill as a political manipulator, and there is no doubt that up to a point he delighted in schemes and stratagems. As Donald Richberg later observed: "There would be times when he seemed to be a Chevalier Bayard, *sans peur et sans reproche,* and times in which he would seem to be the apotheosis of a prince who had absorbed and practiced all the teachings of Machiavelli." Yet essentially he was a moralist who wanted to achieve certain humane reforms and instruct the nation in the principles of government. On one occasion, he remarked: "I want to be a *preaching President*—like my cousin." His courtiers gleefully recounted his adroitness in trading and dealing for votes, his effectiveness on the stump, his wicked skill in cutting corners to win a point. But Roosevelt's importance lay not in his talents as a campaigner or a manipulator. It lay rather in his ability to arouse the country and, more specifically, the men who served under him, by his breezy encouragement of experimentation, by his hopefulness, and—a word that would have embarrassed some of his lieutenants—by his idealism.

The New Deal left many problems unsolved and even created some perplexing new ones. It never demonstrated that it could achieve prosperity in peacetime. As late as 1941, the unemployed still numbered six million, and not until the war year of 1943 did the army of the jobless finally disappear. It enhanced the power of interest groups who claimed to speak for millions, but sometimes represented only a small minority. It did not evolve a way to protect people who had no such spokesmen, nor an acceptable method for disciplining the interest groups. In 1946, President Truman would resort to a threat to draft railway workers into the Army to avert a strike. The New Deal achieved a more just society by recognizing groups which had been largely unrepresented—staple farmers, industrial workers, particular ethnic groups, and the new intellectual-administrative class. Yet this was still a halfway revolution; it swelled the ranks of the bourgeoisie but left many Americans—sharecroppers, slum dwellers, most Negroes—outside of the new equilibrium.

Some of these omissions were to be promptly remedied. Subsequent Congresses extended social security, authorized slum clearance projects, and raised minimum-wage standards to keep step with the rising price level. Other shortcomings are understandable. The havoc that had been done before Roosevelt took office was so great that even the unprecedented measures of the New Deal did not suffice to repair the damage. Moreover, much was still to be learned, and it was in the Roosevelt years that the country was schooled in how to avert another major depression. Although it was war which freed the government from the taboos of a balanced budget and revealed the potentialities of spending, it is conceivable that New Deal measures would have led the country into a new cycle of prosperity even if there had been no war. Marked gains

had been made before the war spending had any appreciable effect. When recovery did come, it was much more soundly based because of the adoption of
the New Deal program.

Roosevelt and the New Dealers understood, perhaps better than their
critics, that they had come only part of the way. Henry Wallace remarked:
"We are children of the transition—we have left Egypt but we have not yet
arrived at the Promised Land." Only five years separated Roosevelt's inauguration in 1933 and the adoption of the last of the New Deal measures, the Fair
Labor Standards Act, in 1938. The New Dealers perceived that they had done
more in those years than had been done in any comparable period in American
history, but they also saw that there was much still to be done, much, too, that
continued to baffle them. "I believe in the things that have been done," Mrs.
Roosevelt told the American Youth Congress in February, 1939. "They helped
but they did not solve the fundamental problems. . . . I never believed the
Federal government could solve the whole problem. It bought us time to think."
She closed not with a solution but with a challenge: "Is it going to be worth
while?"

"This generation of Americans is living in a tremendous moment of history," President Roosevelt stated in his final national address of the 1940 campaign.

"The surge of events abroad has made some few doubters among us ask:
Is this the end of a story that has been told? Is the book of democracy now to
be closed and placed away upon the dusty shelves of time?

"My answer is this: All we have known of the glories of democracy—its
freedom, its efficiency as a mode of living, its ability to meet the aspirations of
the common man—all these are merely an introduction to the greater story of
a more glorious future.

"We Americans of today—all of us—we are characters in the living book
of democracy.

"But we are also its author. It falls upon us now to say whether the
chapters that are to come will tell a story of retreat or a story of continued
advance."

~·~·~·~·13

GRANVILLE HICKS

How Red Was the Red Decade?

*Quite a number of American intellectuals went through a brief flir-
tation with communism in the nineteen thirties, but only a few continued as members of the party during and after World War Two.
The extent of their influence in the thirties has been disputed.
Eugene Lyons in* The Red Decade *holds that it was widespread and
dangerous, and Irving Kristol, in "McCarthyism and Civil Liberties,"
p. 278, agrees. Here Granville Hicks speaks with special authority
because he was himself a member of the Communist party, which
he quit in disgust after the prewar German-Russian alliance. Hicks's
view of the fifties is certainly colored by his experience, but his
analysis of the thirties seems remarkably dispassionate.*

An acquaintance of mine, who joined the Communist party at an early age
and wrote for its publications under his own name, left the party in 1939. A
year or so later he was drafted into the Army. Toward the end of the war,
when he had achieved fairly righ rank and was in a responsible position, a
newspaper reporter exposed his erstwhile party connections, and he was flown
to Washington to be interviewed by an important government official. "Is it
true," the official asked him, "that you once wanted to overthrow the government of the United States by force and violence?" "I guess so," X said, and
then added, "but that was only one of a lot of foolish ideas I had when I was
young." As if wondering what further depths the iniquity were to be revealed,
the official inquired apprehensively, "What ideas?" "Well," X said, "for a good
many years I was perfectly convinced that sooner or later I would sleep with
Greta Garbo."

A letch for a movie star, like many other indiscretions, can be easily forgotten, but not, as things are today, membership in the Communist party. Some
of the leading citizens of the town in which I live were members of the Ku

Reprinted from *Harper's Magazine,* CCVII (July, 1953), 56–61, by permission
of Russell and Volkening, Inc.

Klux Klan in the nineteen-twenties. Personally I think it is more honorable to have belonged to the Communist party than to have belonged to the Klan, but I quite understand that that isn't the issue. The Klan is dead, and the party, unhappily, isn't. No Klansman has been exposed as an agent of a hostile foreign power, and the wearing of a white sheet has come, with the passage of time, to seem as ridiculous and innocuous as a passion for Greta Garbo.

The irreducible facts behind the present turmoil over communism are the danger of a war with the Soviet Union and the proven activity of some American Communists in the Soviet cause. Some liberals, in their dismay over the rise of McCarthyism, seem to overlook these facts, and that may be why they have been losing their fight against McCarthy. The majority of Americans are determined, quite rightly, to defend themselves against the Communists, and if they have accepted the leadership of McCarthy, that is in part because liberal leadership often seems blind to fundamental realities.

When, however, the reality of the Communist danger has been admitted, we must go on to say that the nature and extent of that danger are being grossly misconceived. For four or five years the basic misconception, as Alistair Cooke pointed out in *A Generation on Trial,* has been the equating of communism, 1935–39, with communism, 1948–53. At bottom, I now have no doubt, the party was the same in the thirties as in the forties and fifties, but what most Communists and fellow-travelers thought about the party in the earlier period was very different from what most people, including most of those who were members and sympathizers at that time, are thinking about the party today. In the first hearings on communism in education of the House Committee on un-American Activities, I listened to the testimony of Robert Gorham Davis, while waiting my turn, and I confess that I felt amazement—and some slight nostalgia—as he talked about the little band of Harvard Communists to which he and I had belonged in 1938–39. Even I had forgotten the way it was.

Today that qualitative misconception, if I may call it such, is being compounded by a quantitative misconception. A year or so ago *Commentary* published an article on civil liberties by Irving Kristol, now executive secretary of the American Committee for Cultural Freedom, an anti-Communist organization to which I belong. In the course of the article, which made many valid points, Mr. Kristol asked:

> Did not the major segment of American liberalism, as a result of joining hands with Communists in a Popular Front, go on record as denying the existence of Soviet concentration camps? Did it not give its blessing to the "liquidation" of millions of Soviet "kulaks"? Did it not apologize for the mass purges of 1936–38, and did it not solemnly approve the grotesque trials of the Old Bolsheviks? Did it not applaud the massacre of the non-Communist left by the GPU during the Spanish Civil War?

I know that the answer is supposed to be, "Yes," but to each of these questions I am obliged to reply, "No." Some liberals did some of these things, but I think it can be demonstrated that "the major segment of American "liberalism" never did any of them.

Mr. Kristol, I imagine, is not old enough to have taken part in the events of the thirties, and I think he is being misled by a group of individuals who ought to know better. These persons were anti-Communists, or at any rate anti-Stalinists, in the later thirties—*i.e.,* at a time when the Stalinists were in a position to talk back. There may have been some excuse then for their exaggerating the influence of the Communists, for they were on the receiving end. As the years have gone by, however, it seems as if they should have revised their estimates. Actually they have piled exaggeration upon exaggeration, until a myth has taken shape.

To be specific, I will quote from an article by John Chamberlain in the *Freeman:*

> Long before Communist Harold Ware . . . planted his cell in the Department of Agriculture in Washington . . . the Communists were busy with Objective No. 1, which was the capture of New York, the word capital of the United States. This job was pulled off in the thirties. . . . In time, the infiltrees achieved a wide amount of power to give and withhold jobs, to accept and to refuse manuscripts, and to exalt or to sabotage books and articles. . . . By their oblique control of writing in the thirties and early forties, the Communists managed to poison the intellectual life of a whole nation—and the poison has lingered on.

This is now what might be called standard opinion in certain anti-Communist circles. I have heard a prominent Socialist speak of "the Red stranglehold on the moving pictures and radio." A magazine editor recently told me that "the American educational system has not yet recovered from the way it was debauched when dominated by the Communists." Again and again the assumption is made that the Communists did in fact dominate American intellectual life for a period of ten or fifteen years. And this myth has spawned another myth: the myth of the persecution of the anti-Communists. W. H. Chamberlin, also writing in the *Freeman,* gave it definitive expression:

> It is highly probable that, if a fair, honest count were made of persons who were victimized during the war and immediate postwar period because they were "premature anti-Communists" and of those who have been called to account for real or alleged proCommunist leanings, the number of cases in the first category would exceed the number in the second.

The basic document in the creation of a distorted view of the thirties is *The Red Decade,* which Eugene Lyons, another disillusioned sympathizer with communism, published in 1941. So far as facts go, the book is largely reliable, but the impression it gives is false. My response to the book may be conditioned by my distaste for the names Lyons calls me—for those I deserve even more than for those I don't. This is all part of my past, and my attitude is likely to be biased. But when I summon to mind all I know about communism in the thirties, I cannot square my recollections with Lyons' picture.

As a Communist in the thirties, I felt, and rejoiced to feel, that I belonged to a movement that was growing in power. Thanks to the Depression, the party had greatly increased its membership and, even more greatly, its influence, and its influence continued to grow during the entire period, 1935–39, in which I was a member. Yet as a writer, a publisher's adviser, and a teacher, I was never conscious of the kind of power in the intellectual world that John Chamberlain attributes to the Communists. Far from capturing "the word capital of the United States," we won only small and precarious victories.

Let me tell of what I know, beginning with the publishing business. I suppose that in the thirties almost every publishing house in the country had at least one Communist or Communist sympathizer on its staff. In many instances the political views of these men and women were known to their colleagues and superiors; in others they were suspected; in others they were more or less successfully kept secret.

It is also true that many books sympathetic to communism were published in these years, and frequently, I am sure, it was a Communist editor who brought in a Communist book. It is fatuous, however, to conclude that these books were always, or even as a general rule, "put over" by these editors. What some people are able to forget is that there was a market for left-wing books in the thirties. One need not postulate a Communist conspiracy, for example, to explain why Covici Friede published John Strachey's *The Coming Struggle for Power;* in the atmosphere of 1933 the book was bound to be popular. The firm of John Day, co-operating with the *New Masses* in offering a prize for the best proletarian novel, was a victim not of a conspiracy but of an illusion that proletarian novels would sell. When Harper & Brothers published the early books of Richard Wright, when Harcourt Brace published Ella Winter's *Red Virtue,* when Doubleday Doran published *Red Medicine* by Sir Arthur Newsholme and John A. Kingsbury, when Random House published Angelo Herndon's *Let Me Live,* when Knopf published Agnes Smedley's books on China, these eminent firms were simply behaving like publishers.

The Macmillan Company published my book, *The Great Tradition,* in in 1933, with full awareness that it purported to be a Marxist study of American literature. In 1935 they not only brought out a revised edition that was even more explicitly Communist but brought it out in co-operation with International Publishers, the official Communist publishing house. In 1936 Macmillan published my *John Reed,* a biography of a Communist by a Communist, and were happy to have it selected by the Book Union, a book club whose Communist leanings were obvious to everyone. And during all this time the president of the company was an outspoken conservative, and none of the editors, so far as I ever discovered, was a Communist or a Communist sympathizer.

I know something about the situation at Macmillan in the thirties, for I was one of the firm's literary advisers. Naturally my judgments were influenced by the fact that I was a Communist, and this was taken for granted by the editors. It was so definitely taken for granted that I couldn't have put anything over. I recommended a certain number of books that were sympathetic to communism, but I recommended them for what they were and on the grounds that they would sell. I also recommended, on the same grounds, some anti-Communist books, including Arthur Koestler's first novel, *The Gladiators.* On the other hand, the company published at least one Communist book— Henri Barbusse's *Stalin*—that I never saw until it was in print.

The policy that I followed in my work for Macmillan was, I like to think, a matter of integrity, but it was also plain common sense. After all, an editor or adviser who recommends a series of unsuccessful books, whether out of bias or out of bad judgment, doesn't last long. For that reason, Communists in other publishing firms were obliged to adhere generally to the same policy, whether they liked it or not. "Infiltrees," as John Chamberlain calls them, were prob- ably responsible for some of the pro-Communist books published in the thirties, but they accomplished less than he thinks—and less, I am sure, than they thought at the time.

As people forgot then and forget now, it is one thing to get a book pub- lished and another to get it read, as the fantastic story of Modern Age Books shows. This firm, which was founded to publish both reprints and original books in paper-bound editions, was financed by Richard S. Childs, who, to the best of my belief, was not a party member but was scarcely a militant anti-Communist. Its pioneering experiment in publishing paper-bound books, an enterprise that became so spectacularly successful in other hands, proved a failure, partly be- cause there wasn't sufficient study and preparation but also because the Com- munists took the firm over.

Modern Age did a lot for the Communists. Heaven knows how many it employed in one capacity or another, and some substantial advances fell into Communist hands. Moreover, many party-line books were published. Some of these, including my own *I Like America,* did fairly well, but the majority were flops. Even when the party pushed them for all it was worth, they would not move. Childs poured in money, but the firm tottered and fell, and a lot of loyal Communists went looking for jobs.

The story of Modern Age is in some ways comic, but it has, in my nostrils, a bad odor. When I think of the indignation that would have convulsed me in the thirties if there had been a publishing house staffed by Fascists and devoted to Fascist books, I cannot feel complacent about Modern Age and the part I played in its operations. If there were such a house in existence today, I would denounce it as promptly and as heartily as I would have denounced a Fascist concern in 1939—or would denounce one today. Yet it would be easy to ex- aggerate the evil that Modern Age was able to accomplish. If some of its books may have had a wide influence, most of them, I believe, were bought almost exclusively by people who were already convinced Communists. And the com- pany was ruined, in no great length of time, by its Communist activities.

In *The Red Decade* Eugene Lyons has a chapter called "Intellectual Red Terror," in which he argues that pressure was used to prevent the publication of anti-Communist books and that such books, if they appeared, were attacked and vilified. I know of only one attempt to suppress a book, and Mr. Lyons mentions only one, and they happen to be the same: a concerted effort, in which I refused to take part, was made to try to persuade Viking Press not to publish Benjamin Stolberg's *Story of the C.I.O.* It failed. Perhaps there were other attempts that succeeded, but the fact remains that many anti-Communist books were published in the thirties, none more successfully than Mr. Lyons'

Assignment in Utopia. All the writers he mentions as victims of the intellectual red terror—John Dewey, Max Eastman, Ben Stolberg, James Farrell, John Dos Passos, William Henry Chamberlin, etc.—found publishers in the thirties. Nor was Lyons the only writer who was able to express his disillusionment with the Soviet Union; he himself speaks of Andrew Smith, Fred Beal, Jan Valtin, Freda Utley, and the Tchernavins.

Of course these books were attacked in the Communist press, in language as virulent as that employed by Mr. Lyons. And in the heyday of the Popular Front there were, as he says, strategically placed reviewers who, if not Communists, tended to reflect the Communist line. But it was not my impression then, and it is not my impression now, that the Communists had things their own way. I wrote an article for the *New Masses* of October 2, 1934, in which I argued, with considerable evidence, that the *New York Times Book Review* assigned almost all books on Russia to anti-Communists, usually Russian enemies of the Soviet regime. I further pointed out that the editor and several of the principal reviewers consistently went out of their way to sneer at and belittle American writers known to be sympathetic to communism. Mr. Lyons can call my article part of the "intellectual red terror" if he wants to, but no one will deny that the *Times* had more influence in the world of books than the *New Masses.*

Some time later (December 7, 1937) I wrote an article on the book reviews in the *Nation.* Both the *Nation* and the *New Republic* had played a part in the leftward swing of the intellectuals, and in the later thirties both adopted editorial positions that were in general agreement with the Popular Front line. The *Nation's* book section, however, was under the direction first of Joseph Wood Krutch and then of Margaret Marshall, both of whom were anti-Communists. Miss Marshall drew a large share of her reviewers from the rapidly expanding group of men and women who, after some contact with Stalinism, had grown disillusioned. A number of them were Trotskyites. Pro-Communist books, I pointed out, were given to such reviewers as Abram Harris, Edmund Wilson, Ben Stolberg, Louis Hacker, Sterling Spero, Suzanne LaFollette, Anita Brenner, James Rorty, Philip Rahv, Sidney Hook, and James Burnham, all of whom could be counted on not to like them. The *Nation's* book review section was an organ for those anti-Communists who, according to Mr. Lyons, had such a bad time.

We felt—make no mistake about it—that we were the victims, that we were the ones who were being persecuted. The big magazines, those that paid good money, were notoriously hostile not only to communism and the Soviet Union but to virtually all the ideas advocated by the Popular Front. An individual writer for one of these magazines might be a Communist sympathizer, but he was both smart and lucky if he got away with any propaganda. Kyle Crichton, for instance, a staff writer for *Collier's,* saved his radical ideas for the articles he wrote for the *New Masses* under the name of Robert Forsythe; he did not try to put them over in *Collier's.*

In fact, communism scarcely made a dent on any of the mass media—the popular magazines, the movies, the radio. Congressional investigations have revealed that some Hollywood writers and actors were Communists or fellow-travelers at one time or another. The investigations, however, have not shown that these Communists influenced in any significant way the content of the moving pictures. I remember back in the thirties how excited we were over advance reports on "Blockade," which, we were told, was going to strike a great blow for the Loyalist cause in Spain. But when the picture appeared, it did not even indicate on which side the hero was fighting. During the war a couple of pictures appeared that were favorable to the Soviet Union, but no more favorable than our official policy at that time. The Hollywood Communists have no doubt been useful to the party, to which they have given large sums of money and which they may have helped in other ways, but I am still waiting for someone to point out to me an American movie that actually contains Communist propaganda. And if there ever has been any propaganda, it has been a tiny drop in a large bucket running over with traditional American sentiments.

The same thing is true of radio. There were commentators in the thirties who seemed to accept the Popular Front ideology, but most of them were exceedingly cautious. As a rule, the Communists in radio who have been exposed have been actors or script writers—as unable to influence policy as their Hollywood brethren. The Communists in the radio industry may have exerted a malign influence, particularly in the unions, but they have not been able to get away with much propaganda.

The black picture that Lyons paints hasn't much relation to the reality that I recall. Speaking of "the intellectual and moral red terror," he says, "It could bar you from house parties on Park Avenue, jobs in Hollywood, places on the relief rolls of your city, fair treatment in the columns of great conservative papers, a hearing before supposedly broad-minded public lecture forums, access to federal projects." Perhaps Communists did all these things at one time or another in one place or another, but the suggestion that they could do them all the time and everywhere is ridiculous.

If we need further proof that Lyons exaggerates the Red influence, he furnishes it for us. In the spring of 1939 a group of men and women, calling itself the Committee for Cultural Freedom, endorsed a statement that Lyons had prepared, denouncing totalitarianism as it existed in Germany, Italy, Spain, Japan, *and Russia.* "More than 140 men and women in intellectual pursuits had signed this statement by the time it was made public in May," Lyons says. "Scores of additional adhesions to this basic formulation of free men's faith came in from all over the country." And this in spite of the intellectual red terror!

There was, of course, a Communist counter-attack—an open letter protesting against "attempts to bracket the Soviet Union with the Fascist states." Mr. Lyons gets a good deal of understandable amusement from the fact that this letter appeared just nine days before the Soviet-Nazi nonaggression pact, which made a lot of those of us who signed it feel silly—and worse than silly. But perhaps the important thing to notice about the pro-Soviet letter is that its signers seem rather less distinguished than the signers of the anti-Soviet statement. Comparing the two lists, one gets the impression that anti-communism —and this was anti-communism, not just non-communism—was the dominant intellectual force. If it was not on August 14, 1939, it certainly was a fortnight later.

It is also important to observe that five of the signers of the Committee for Cultural Freedom statement had been among the fifty-two intellectuals who had endorsed the Communist candidate for President back in 1932, and that at least half a dozen more had been in some sense fellow-travelers. Even in the thirties, when communism seemed to be so powerful, it was constantly losing adherents among the intellectuals. The party used the intellectuals for all they were worth, but it was aware, as most people today are not, that there were limits beyond which most of them could not be used. To say this is no kind of defense of myself or anybody else, nor is it intended as one, but the fact has to be taken into account.

This fact is particularly important when we turn to another field, the teaching profession. Many teachers, especially college teachers, were Communists or sympathizers in the thirties. Like other intellectuals, they saw the Great Depression as proof of the collapse of capitalism. They had, moreover, some special grievances against the status quo. Not only had they been badly paid even before the Depression; many of them had been considerably pushed around by the business men who dominated the boards of trustees of the private colleges. Teachers were constantly being told about the glories of freedom of thought and speech, but in practice they discovered that discretion was essential to professional advancement. In an article that I wrote after being dismissed from Rensselaer Polytechnic Institute, I called teaching "the timid profession," and the phrase still seems apt. But if most teachers conformed, a certain number rebelled.

Again it is hard to remember how much the atmosphere has changed. Today Communist teachers are charged with disloyalty to the government, with conspiracy in the interests of a foreign power, and with the surrender of intellectual integrity. In the thirties, however, Communists were charged, quite simply, with being anti-capitalists. Week after week in the spring of 1935 Acting-President Edwin C. Jarrett of Rensselaer Polytechnic Institute maintained to all comers that my dismissal was purely a matter of economy. But in speaking to the alumni at Commencement time, Jarrett said: "We were founded by a capitalist of the old days. We have developed and prospered under the capitalist regime. The men we have sent forth and who have become industrial leaders have, in their generosity and for the benefit of the youth of the country, richly endowed us. . . . If we are condemned as the last refuge of conservatism, let us glory in it."

That same June Silas H. Strawn, former president of the American Bar Association, was the Commencement orator at Middlebury College in Vermont. After saying, "One of the guarantees of the federal Constitution is the freedom of speech," he continued: "Recently we have heard much about 'red' activities in the colleges and universities of the country. I am unable to sympathize with the elastic conscience of those who inveigh against the capitalistic system while on the payroll of a college or university whose budget, or whose existence, is due to the philanthropic generosity of those whose industry and frugality have enabled them to make an endowment."

No member of the Middlebury faculty was likely to miss the point, for earlier that spring each of them had received a letter from President Paul D. Moody, significantly headed, "Don't rock the boat." "We do not want our students to be thoughtless," President Moody informed his teachers, "nor do we want to tell them what to think. But we do not want them to go off at half cock. Least of all do we want them to go out of class quoting us as anarchists,

Communists, atheists, free-lovers, as, I regret to say, now and then some student does. In all that is said about capital and labor, public utilities and government ownership thereof, marriage and divorce, social customs, the liquor question and a dozen and one other matters, we cannot be too guarded." He concluded: "I should feel justified in requesting, in these days as I might not in others, the resignation of any who are unwilling or unable to subordinate their private views to the interests of the College. . . . I hope that what I have said will not be regarded as in any way a desire to dictate what you shall think, or to interfere with your private views."

Such outspoken attacks on academic freedom cannot justify the acceptance of a system that denies to teachers even a vestige of freedom and that punishes even accidental divagations not with dismissal but with execution; but they help to explain why some teachers were in a mood to adopt desperate remedies. Most of the teachers who turned to communism refused to admit the extent of Soviet tyranny, but, whatever excuses they invented to salve their consciences, they did know that academic freedom was sharply restricted in Russia. What they told themselves was that academic freedom was also restricted in the United States, and that one had to choose between communism and real or incipient fascism. The second proposition was false, but the truth of the first gave it a certain plausibility.

The number of teachers who were Communists or fellow-travelers was never, of course, more than a tiny fraction of the teachers in the country. The vital question, however, is how much influence they were able to exert. The other day, speaking at a college for teachers, I was asked whether, if I were a college president, I would permit Communists to teach. I replied that this was a problem on which my views had changed more than once. At the moment, I said, I was inclined to feel that I would retain, or even hire, an avowed Communist who was competent in his field, but that I would fire anyone who had concealed his Communist affiliation. I put this forward not as a solution of much practical importance but as a way of indicating that I saw little reason to be afraid of communism when it was in the open.

My answer shocked a young woman, who drew a startling picture of a Communist teacher, luring his students on with his pleasant manners, winning great popularity among them, and seducing vast numbers to their eternal damnation. When she had finished, I could only say, "You don't have much faith in the other teachers." Her kind of argument, which I have heard again and again in a variety of forms, always assumes that Communist teachers are phenomenally persuasive—and non-Communist teachers phenomenally dumb.

My own situation at RPI was not unlike the situation the young woman and I conjured up. My position as fellow-traveler was well known, for, writer-fashion, I had recorded my conversion, step by step, in the public press, and from January 1, 1934, on, I was on the editorial staff of the *New Masses*. Because my position was known, I had to behave in my teaching job as I behaved in my Macmillan job: I leaned over backward to keep my biases out of the classroom, and I called attention to them when they forced their way in. But even if I had done my level best to convert my students, how much headway could I have made against the several hundred members of the faculty who were thoroughly committed to the capitalist system? The exponents of capitalism, moreover, felt perfectly free to express their views in the classroom—this was not at all the kind of thing Acting-President Jarrett had in mind when he deplored the raising of "controversial" issues—whereas I, whatever my wishes, had to be restrained.

Later, for one year, I was a Councellor in American Civilization at Harvard College, and I was a member of a Communist party branch made up of faculty members. It was this branch that was investigated last February by the House Committee on un-American Activities, and testimony indicated that its maximum membership was fifteen. As I pointed out to the committee, fifteen Communists, all in the lower academic grades, is not an impressive proportion of a large faculty—1,878 teachers, according to the *World Almanac* for 1939 —especially at a time when the intellectual atmosphere was favorable to communism and the party's Popular Front line was supposed to be especially appealing to teachers.

After I had been subpoenaed by the House Committee, I tried to recall as much as I could about the meetings of that branch. We discussed many different subjects: Marxism, the Soviet Union and the way it was maligned in the capitalist press, the dangers of Fascism, the Spanish Civil War, the policies of the university administration, our plans for the Teachers Union, and the manifold and exhausting activities that were part of the Popular Front movement. But I could not remember that we had ever talked about how we could carry on Communist propaganda in the classroom. The testimony of the other witnesses completely confirmed my impression. The point is, I think, that, although we were or believed ourselves to be convinced Communists, and were anxious to win converts, we knew there were limits. Some of us felt there were limits beyond which we should not go; all of us felt there were limits beyond which we could not go.

Many Communist teachers, I am sure, went just as far as they could in presenting the Communist view of their subjects, but few of them were so situated that they could go very far. How much influence they had on their students is anybody's guess, except that it was much less than is supposed by those who, like the young woman I just mentioned, have swallowed the myth of the irresistibility of the Communist arts of seduction. There were many students in the thirties who joined the Young Communist League or belonged to one or another of the party fronts. Some of them, I am sure, were influenced by Communist teachers, but for the most part they were responding to the same influences as the teachers were. Communism was in the air, and a certain number of people were bound to catch it.

And again one must take account of the operations of disillusionment. Of the Communist teachers I knew, the majority broke with the party a long time ago. The others, I may say, have mostly been driven out of academic life, some because they were exposed as Communists, others because their dogged fidelity to the shifting party line rendered them obviously incompetent as teachers.

Disillusionment is a phenomenon that has not been sufficiently examined. As I have pointed out, most of the men who are responsible for the myth of the Red Decade—and most of the highly articulate anti-Communists in general—were themselves, for at least brief periods, under Communist influence. They recovered, and so did a larger proportion of their associates than they are willing to admit. I have already observed that five of the fifty-two signers of the 1932 Manifesto for Foster and Ford were ardent anti-Communists even before the Soviet-Nazi pact. Many of the others joined the anti-Communist ranks shortly thereafter. When the Cultural and Scientific Conference for World Peace was held at the Waldorf-Astoria in 1949, the list of sponsors included nine of the names that had appeared on the 1932 Manifesto. To me it is appalling that there could be nine so-called intellectuals who could follow the party line for seventeen years. But, statistically speaking, nine out of fifty-two isn't much of a showing.

The significance of disillusionment, moreover, is not merely statistical. The fact that so many intellectuals have been disillusioned suggests that a lot of them were not very good Communists to begin with. The public has been educated by extracts from the writings of Lenin and Stalin to an understanding of what membership in the Communist party is supposed to mean, and the autobiographies of such persons as Whittaker Chambers and Elizabeth Bentley, who tried hard to be good Communists, have helped to create a picture of the perfectly disciplined party member, ready to obey without hesitation any command his superiors may give him. That is unquestionably the party ideal, but it is an ideal to which many Communists do not measure up, and in the later thirties, when it was seeking a respectable façade, the party did not even attempt to impose this ideal upon the intellectuals. Therefore, even if it can be shown that there were so many party members at such and such a time in such and such an institution, it does not follow that there were that many docile agents of the Soviet Union. Some of these people, if the party had tried to use them as agents, would have quit on the spot, and the party knew it.

To say all this is not to extenuate the mistakes made by the intellectuals, myself included, who swallowed communism. I am saying that we were suckers, and to a great extent we were, but it is no defense whatever for an intellectual to say that he was duped, since that is what, as an intellectual, he should never allow to happen to him. We were taken in by ideas we should have seen through and people we should have suspected. And, being writers and publicists, we proceeded to take in other people, which is why the party was willing to bother with us in the first place. There is no telling how much damage I may have done, and though I have tried hard in the past fourteen years to undo it, I am by no means sure that I have succeeded.

Nor am I suggesting that communism should be taken lightly today. Communism has never been so thoroughly discredited in the United States as it is right now, and if we could think purely in national terms, it would be nothing to worry about, but we have to think in terms of the world situation, and Communists as actual or potential agents of a hostile power are a danger not to be scoffed at. We must constantly be on the alert to meet their propaganda, and, as a nation, we must be able to combat their espionage and sabotage. If the danger is sometimes exaggerated, it is nevertheless a danger.

All I am trying to do is to destroy a myth. In his contribution to *Socialism and American Life,* one of the most careful students of the subject, Daniel Bell, writes: "Although communism *never* won a mass following in the United States, it did have a disproportionate influence in the cultural field. At one time, from 1936 to 1939, through the fellow-travelers in the publishing houses, radio, Hollywood, the magazines, and other mass media, it exercised influence on public opinion far beyond the mere number of party members." That, I think, is absolutely true, but although the influence of the party undoubtedly was disproportionate to its membership, it was not unlimited. The notion that communism dominated American culture in the thirties is false.

The notion has to be corrected, not only to keep the record straight but also to counteract the damage the myth of the Red Decade is doing to our national morale. Every time somebody says, "Boy, the Reds nearly got us in the thirties," his listeners shiver, thinking, "It might happen again." The significant, the hopeful point, as Frederick Lewis Allen suggests in *The Big Change,* is that it never did happen. Even in the early thirties, when millions of people were hungry and desperate, the Communists barely polled 100,000 votes. Even in the later thirties, when the Popular Front had captured the allegiance of many intellectuals, they made little impression on the solid anti-communism of the great majority of the American people. Even when it tried to disguise itself as twentieth-century Americanism, communism could not count more than a few hundred thousand sympathizers. A hundred thousand disciplined Communists might be something to think twice about, but most sympathizers were as far from the Leninist ideal as most churchgoers are from the Christian ideal, and they soon found plenty of reason for backsliding.

That communism should seem thoroughly evil to most Americans today is natural enough. What is encouraging is that it seemed highly unattractive to all but a handful fifteen and twenty years ago, when our system appeared to be on the skids and when much less was known and is known now about Communist tyranny and aggression. Fifteen years ago I would have asserted that the American attitude towards communism was a result of misinformation and prejudice, and certainly it wasn't a purely rational thing. But it wasn't wholly irrational either. Most people felt that, however terrible the crisis was, we could figure out some way of meeting it. They didn't see any sense in tearing up the system, no matter how badly it was working, and trying one that looked good on paper. And they viewed with what turns out to be fully justified suspicion the Russian denial of national self-interest. In short, if we were suckers, most people weren't, and it seems to me that that happy fact deserves to be publicized.

~~~~~~*14*

DAVID F. TRASK

The Twentieth-Century War

In his essay on the twentieth-century war (1914–45), David F. Trask argues that the political order crucial to world stability was never restored after World War One. The Congress of Vienna of 1815, which followed the Napoleonic wars, had established a durable balance of power, but the Treaty of Versailles of 1919 did not. After the World War the balance collapsed at both ends of the Eurasian continent, and new powers, including the United States, Soviet Russia, and Japan, arose to fill the vacuum in international politics.

Once the European colonial system had become untenable, nationalistic aspirations and rivalries in the Middle East, Southeast Asia, and China would create the tensions that are still unresolved today. To restore a power balance in the world at large comparable to the one that worked so well for Europe in the nineteenth century is a formidable task.

The problem of maintaining international order is a theme of both this essay and the earlier one by Arthur Link on Wilson's failure to win approval for his League of Nations. It could even be claimed that President Wilson predicted the twentieth-century war when he warned of another war in a generation if the League were not approved.

If the imperial interlude launched America on its voyage into world history, the events of 1914–1918 and after completed the passage. At just the moment when the Americans prepared to reap the benefits of their nineteenth-century accomplishments, they found themselves inextricably tangled in that pattern of plenary violence which has become the most significant hallmark of world history in our time—the Twentieth Century War. The hostilities of 1914 began a cycle of warfare which continued until 1945, and its aftermath still lingers. The collapse of the European balance after a hundred years of stability inaugu-

203

rated patterns of world-historical change still far from complete. Historians still argue endlessly about the origins and causes of that breakdown, giving particular stress to factors like nationalism, militarism, imperialism, and industrialization. The century turned into one of those terrible eras of violence which usually mark the disruption of the established order and herald the beginning of new departures.

The jumbled history of our times often seems impossible to organize and interpret; the confusion of so much that was new and different constantly defeats efforts to unravel the labyrinth of recent events. And yet, our limited perspective permits at least a few broad generalizations. Certainly the great conflict of 1914–1918 which began the Twentieth Century War so shattered Europe, and indeed the entire western world, that it made unlikely an early escape from vast instability. The very intensity of World War I sowed the seeds of further conflict. And then, again, the very debility of the West—immensely weakened by nothing less than an international civil war, if the western world is considered a quasi-political entity—encouraged aggression by nonwestern powers in Asia, paticularly Japan until 1945 and China in more recent years. Finally, the destruction of all the great European imperial powers allowed nationalist movements in the old colonial world of Africa and Asia to acquire commanding strength. For almost five hundred years, the West had dominated the rest of the globe. That dominance came to a fiery end in the flames of the Twentieth Century War.

Each principal phase of the Twentieth Century War—the First Conflict of 1914–1918, the Long Armistice from 1919 to 1939, the Second Conflict of 1939–1945, and the troubled Aftermath of recent years—made more apparent the consequence of these developments. Europe was less and less the center of world affairs. If the locus of power shifted for the time being to the great outlying powers of the western world, the United States and Soviet Russia, the recovery of independence in ancient Asian societies such as China, India, and Araby confirmed the redemption of power in regions being victimized by western imperial exploitation. It seemed entirely possible that the revivified eastern societies might ultimately surpass the greatest countries of the western world.

What engendered the pervasive violence of the age? Was it, perhaps, the superannuation of that system of nation-states which had emerged at the dawn of modern history? There were new things under the sun in the twentieth century. Novel complexities wrought by profound intellectual and technological innovations were increasingly difficult to accommodate within the conventional order of power. If this reality was difficult to comprehend, it was because of the prior beatitudes of nation-state organization. That grand tradition seemed too effective to question. Most people thought that the complexities of the new age could be accommodated by adjustment of the international *status quo* rather than its displacement. They all too easily assumed that the nation-state was the final stage of world-political evolution, an ultimate expression of political genius.

From time immemorial, humanity has condemned itself to pandemic violence because it refused to recognize the imperatives of change. The city-state organization of the ancient Mediterranean world had seemed entirely sufficient for all time to those who benefited from its accomplishment, but a long season of warfare ensued when it became obsolescent. The universal empire of the Romans, which replaced the older city-state system, seemed to be an ultimate political accomplishment, but it also succumbed to time, the destroyer of all human pretension, and another term of violence was visited upon civilization. Only the invention of the nation-state system brought Europe out of a thousand years of political stagnation. The achievements of the national idea were so imposing that it is easy to understand why our present commitment to it is so overwhelming. Nevertheless, even before the twentieth century, forces were in motion comparable in their disruptive effect to those which had undermined the ancient Greek and Roman orders of things. As in the past, those who benefited from the ongoing system tended either to defend it *in toto* or to urge reform from within. It was almost impossible to believe that the nation was as replaceable as the cave, the village, or the city as the prime center of political organization and loyalty.

More sensitive spirits thought they discovered a necessity to adopt supranational political organization—sovereign authority beyond the nation—in order to resolve modern international tensions by means short of violence. Of course, supranational polity by no means required the destruction of nations. It meant simply that they must recede in importance. National loyalties would have to be subordinated to a more comprehensive faith, as fealty to the city-state had been subordinated to the imperial ideal of Rome two thousand years before. All too often, prophets of a new political order were dismissed as Utopians. The scoffers failed to weigh the odds against survival within the established order of things. Admittedly, it was one thing to recognize the necessity for change but another to determine effective means of accomplishing it.

The United States was suddenly exposed to a world of change which slowly repudiated the political order within which the newest of the powers had come to maturity. If the foreign policy of the United States before 1914 matured successfully in the congenial atmosphere of the long peace following the Congress of Vienna, the crowning accomplishment of the nation-state system, it ran its later course in the highly inhospitable context of the Twentieth Century War. That war presaged the passing of the old accustomed statecraft. All too often historians extol the wisdom of early American statesmen, particularly the generation of the Founders, and condemn the follies of their successors. This invidious comparison scouts the difficulties of the revolutionary changes which took place during the earlier decades of the twentieth century. It was the fortune of American statesmen from the time of Woodrow Wilson to cope with truly unprecedented waves of profound change. Latter-day change was far more complex than that of the late eighteenth century and certainly far less favorable to American security.

It is easy enough to detail the failings of modern American statecraft, but they were human failings which proceeded from kinder intentions and greater dedication than some of their critics seem to realize. Intellectual integrity commands a detailed criticism of American foreign policy during the Twentieth Century War, but not because those who presided over the destiny of the Republic were always stupid or selfish. They were as confused as everyone else by the arcane outcomes of an unexampled era of change. In the circumstances, the story of American leadership during the half-century just past is a tale of courage and fortitude as well as a catalog of error.

As the Twentieth Century War began its grisly course, the Republic found itself in a fundamentally satiate condition. America had attained its growth; it was comparable in its development to Rome at the time of Caesar Augustus. This condition did not mean that no worlds to conquer remained to the American people, but it did mean that as of about this time they became more concerned with exploiting the national territorial legacy than in expanding it. Few desired further national adventurism in the pattern of 1898. Those who have are naturally inclined to the preservation of the going order. Those in want or concerned about want favor reform or revolution according to the degree of their alienation from the established conditions. The burden of affluence dictated a pervasive American tendency to act in support of the international *status quo*—to adopt conserving policy with respect to world affairs.

The imperatives of the age required at least a tremendous alteration within the established order; they probably demanded even more. Many men and women of this century elsewhere in the world believed that the established order was totally inadequate to contend with the complexities of the new age. They argued that only a complete retooling would permit the survival of the race. In America, few radicals raised their voices effectively. Basic debate on questions of American foreign policy during this century has taken place largely between reformers who hoped to purify the ongoing international system and those who preferred to support it without change.

Those Americans who urged reform drew inspiration from the historic national tradition of faith in progress. If the United States was sated by success as of 1914, it continued to respond to a markedly progressive ideology—an ideology born during its earliest years and nurtured into principles of democratic society and polity which in its essentials went generally unquestioned by practically all meaningful factions within the relatively narrow range of domestic political controversy. Those clear distinctions which differentiated European radicals and reactionaries, or even liberals and conservatives, were largely absent from the American scene. If the United States possessed a viable conservative tradition, it differed vastly from that of Europe. America was born free, and the great national bounty insured plenty to all those with sufficient energy and imagination to draw upon it, given the felicitous state of international affairs. The domestic political outcome was a pervasive consensus, a liberal or progressive commitment shot through almost the entire polity. With some notable exceptions like Hamilton and Calhoun, those in the American past who called themselves conservatives were usually pale reflections of their liberal enemies.

So it was that despite their affluence—their undeniable presence in the House of Have—the Americans embodied political sympathies and ideas which made them peculiarly sensitive to those who continued in the House of Want. If those who possess never fully understand the meaning of poverty, they can mitigate the eternal conflict of have and have not by embracing a reformist ideology and maintaining a reform temper. Recognition of these requirements inspired that internationalist departure in American foreign policy which found its inception in the mind and heart of Woodrow Wilson during the initial phases of the Twentieth Century War. Wilsonian internationalism has survived into our own time, considerably altered as well as chastened by the tribulations of a violent age. It remains to be seen whether that tradition, however noble, is sufficient unto the day.

The United States entered into the maelstrom of the Twentieth Century War as a satiate-progressive nation, its citizens basically desiring the maintenance of the international *status quo* but receptive to reforms within the going order to benefit peoples less fortunate than themselves. At times, of course, especially when it seemed that all their fine enterprises went unappreciated by others, they gave full rein to their satiety and relapsed into lethargy. If Wilson reflected the progressive instincts of the American people applied to global politics in perhaps their finest form, a generation of successors including the early Franklin D. Roosevelt concerned themselves with national interests to the exclusion of international responsibility. The later Franklin D. Roosevelt revived and built upon the Wilsonian tradition, and his successors generally continued the pattern, deprived of the advantageous circumstances which had allowed evasion of international obligations in the wake of the Wilsonian debacle.

If America's progressive outlook has produced much that is truly admirable, it is open to certain criticisms in its international applications. What is good for Americans is not necessarily good for others. The isolated condition of America in its formative years united with unparalleled national accomplishment during a protected childhood to inculcate in American minds a sense of perfection which was hardly legitimate. It is hard to admit that national commitments which have worked splendidly at home are less than universally applicable. It is of great significance that over time the American people have gradually learned at least parts of this lesson, although frequent backsliding sometimes seems to undo all that has been done to broaden their horizons. It remains to be seen whether the lesson can be fully absorbed in time to help in avoiding still another cataclysm far more destructive than the two violent phases of the Twentieth Century War which have gone before.

Indeed, it remains to be seen whether American ideas of international peace and justice, however noble in conception, are in fact fully applicable to the revolutionized condition of the world today and tomorrow. We see through the glass darkly, but it is the part of wisdom as well as virtue to grasp what is necessary for the well-being of others. As in that mundane world of getting and spending to which we are all eternally condemned, it is well to remember that a larger community of interest transcends all lesser dissensions.

With these considerations in mind, it is time to resume the narrative of American foreign policy, a narrative of its evolution to the present day in the context of unparalleled violence and cruelty—the Twentieth Century War.

After five or six years of difficulties in the wake of the peace treaties, the world seemed to recover momentum; it appeared that gloomy predictions of impending disaster issued by intellectuals, artists, and even public men had been premature. Right after World War I Russia and Poland fought a bitter war in eastern Europe. Greece and Turkey followed suit in the eastern Mediterranean. German problems were not resolved; continuing difficulties precipitated a French occupation of the Rhineland in 1923. These untoward events finally resolved themselves; by 1924 or 1925 things seemed to have returned to something like an even keel. The early activity of the League greatly encouraged Europe, and the Locarno accords of 1925 brought Germany back to the councils of the continent. German membership in the League marked a symbolic end to the bitterness of the early postwar years. The relative prosperity and stability of the late Twenties drowned all thought of another great war. If writers like Ernest Hemingway rejected the ongoing society, preferring to live by personal codes rather than public standards in order to endure a world they never made, other folk threw themselves vigorously into the task of rebuilding their lives and fortunes along more conventional lines with considerable success.

And yet, however encouraging the overt trend of things, forces were at work to reverse the hopeful reconstruction of the postwar decade. The most telling problems were economic in character. Never properly resolved, they finally pecipitated social and political crises of the gravest magnitude. The war had indeed delivered a tremendous shock to Europe in all respects. The great international collapse of 1929–1930 finally exposed the weakness of the postwar settlement. The structure of international peace rapidly fell apart as the vast economic stagnation of the early Thirties fed the appetite of European totalitarianism, most especially in Germany, where Adolph Hitler rose from the depths to the pinnacle of power and set in motion a national aggrandizement leading ultimately to another general war.

The evanescent reconstruction of Europe seemed to confirm the wisdom of the American decision largely to withdraw from European politics and the international community in general—at least on the cooperative basis envisioned by Woodrow Wilson. The American people were caught up in a "success-exhaustion syndrome." After all, the war had been won, and Yankee intervention had insured victory. In the short run, the triumph of 1918 had brought profound national security in its train. The postwar debility of Europe seemed to guarantee that no dangers to the western hemisphere could emanate from across the sea for a long time to come. The Pacific appeared more likely to become the seat of postwar difficulties.

The people were tired of international involvement. Disillusioned by the outcome of World War I, they sought release from the terrible pressures of responsibility, especially when it appeared that their security would not be threatened by repudiating the Wilsonian scheme of things. If they had been exhausted by the crusade of 1914–1918, they had stored up a considerable interest in turning their energies directly to the satisfaction of personal desires. People wanted a good time, and they often succeeded during the Twenties, that Era of Wonderful Nonsense. They also sought filthy lucre, and in this aspiration, too, many of them succeeded. The war built a pent-up demand for consumer goods which underwrote economic success well into the Twenties. It also opened markets elsewhere in the world, contributing considerably to national prosperity. If the business cycle of the era was far less steady than many now realize, and if a good number of significant economic groups like the farmers never took part in the boom, it was undeniably a "new era," as prophets of the boom psychology liked to call it. In this manner, the recovery of optimism in Europe found its counterpart in the United States.

The success-exhaustion syndrome in America contributed to a general repudiation of international responsibility. The nation by no means reverted entirely to the policies and practices of the nineteenth century, or even of the years just preceding the Great War, but certainly it refused to contemplate anything like the degree of engagement its role as the world's first power imposed upon it. American security was at stake, as well as that of the entire world, but who in the heady Twenties could have predicted the unspeakable outcome of retreat from international duty? If the imperial interlude had ushered the United States into world politics and the World War had brought the nation fully into its complexities, the national mood of frustration at war's end produced a season of tragic error in foreign policy.

As long as prosperity abided, all things seemed to conspire to national security and progress; once again people cultivated the delusion that the world ran best with the United States in general political repose. As it happened, the United States contributed unwittingly to the maturation of those deep-lying forces which eventually undermined reconstruction and precipitated the instability of the Thirties. The onset of the second great violent phase of the Twentieth Century War in 1939 revealed that the World had failed to settle those tensions causing World War I. Instead, that struggle merely intensified them. Had the United States adopted a more responsible course during the 1920s, the outcome might have been much different. The world desperately needed American leadership, but that nation refused the burdens of power—a decision which brought to the American people and to the entire world a portion of tragedy far beyond anything experienced earlier.

The Republicans who took power in 1921—unkind antagonists called them the "Ohio gang"—realized that a prime source of unrest was the Pacific-East Asian region. There, Japan was restive and China remained weak. Harding and his associates repudiated the internationalist Wilson and all his works, but they sincerely hoped to make a contribution to security in the Pacific and to the great principle of disarmament. The result was the Washington Naval Conference of 1921–1922. It produced a series of treaties which seemed at the time a major contribution to peace and security. Like the United States, Great Britain worried about the Far East, particularly hopeful of escaping the bonds of its Japanese alliance. Secretary of State Charles Evans Hughes, one of the two stars in the rather tawdry crown of Harding's cabinet (Herbert Hoover of the Department of Commerce was the other), saw an opportunity to accomplish a number of diplomatic objectives. One was naval disarmament, a means of reducing defense expenditures, and the other was a general security system for the Pacific.

When the representatives of invited nations convened in Washington, Hughes started off things in unprecedented fashion by making a number of concrete disarmament proposals which at once shocked and intrigued the statesmen of the world. Energetic negotiations produced a "five-power treaty" establishing a ratio of $5 : 5 : 3 : 1.67 : 1.67$ for the capital-ship tonnage of the British, American, Japanese, French, and Italian navies. The agreement did not cover lesser craft, but it required several nations to destroy existing vessels, certainly a striking event. Nothing like it had ever been achieved before.

The Pacific settlement came in two other treaties and several related agreements. A "nine-power treaty" pledged the conferees to the traditional open door principles. A fine gesture, it lacked substantive significance because the treaty included no enforcement procedures. A "four-power treaty" between Britain, Japan, France, and the United States established consultative machinery to settle quarrels arising among the signatories in the Pacific. It also required non-fortification of numerous holdings in the Pacific, but failed to include enforcement procedures. Side agreements arranged Japanese withdrawal from the Shantung, the abrogation of the Anglo-Japanese alliance, and American cable rights on the lonely isle of Yap.

Widely heralded at the time and defended since as the best settlement that could have been obtained, the Pacific settlements lacked important elements. The most obvious omission was effective means of insuring that signatory powers adhered to their engagements. Less obvious, but of great significance later, was the fact that the settlement gave international sanction to Japanese gains in East Asia and also enhanced their naval power, especially in waters adjacent to the home islands. The combined Anglo-American fleet would outnumber Japan's by more than three times in capital ships at treaty limits, but Japan had to worry only about the western Pacific, whereas Britain and the United States had worldwide commitments. If men were angels, arrangements like those made at Washington would be entirely commendable. As it was, the Pacific treaty system worked well during the relatively calm Twenties, but when political instability returned to the western world during the next decade, providing another opportunity for Japanese aggression in East Asia, the partial settlement was exposed for what it really was—a jerry-built structure far less contributory to Pacific security in times of crisis than in periods of general international calm.

China failed to gain stability during the Twenties and the United States did relatively little to stimulate improvement. The rise of Chiang Kai-shek during the latter years of the postwar decade seemed to insure new departures in the Middle Kingdom, but domestic gains would be more than offset in the next few years by instability in the western world. In 1924 the United States infuriated the entire Orient by excluding immigration on racial grounds under the National Origins Act, a classic example of the way in which immoral legislation leads to grave consequences. This insult deepened Japanese conviction that the United States would never accept the racial equality of Orientals. Russo-Japanese quarrels over Manchuria boded ill for the future, as did the failure of the United States to maintain its fleet at treaty strength. A naval conference at Geneva in 1927 failed to achieve much, but the disarmament negotiations at London in 1930 extended the principles of Washington by bringing lesser naval craft into the ratio system. These arrangements seemed justified at the time, but they confirmed the weakness of the original treaty by providing no means of enforcement.

If the Pacific remained a cause of some concern, its problems seemed distant to most Americans, who were much more interested in the western hemisphere. The trend away from unilateral intervention in the Caribbean-Latin American region continued during the Twenties, despite provocations that in earlier years would easily have sent the Marines on Caribbean excursions. The events of 1917–1918 had shown that nonintervention did not jeopardize North American interests in the hemisphere. The outcome of the war insured against European adventurism in the Caribbean, depriving the Roosevelt Corollary of its *raison d'être*. Businessmen finally realized that intervention was actually hard on profits, and many Americans criticized it on sound moral and legal grounds. The result was a series of developments which preceded the greater breakthrough of the Thirties.

All the Republican Presidents and secretaries of state during the New Era lent important assistance to the emergence of an inter-American system that could substitute for police actions by the United States. Several conciliation and arbitration treaties came into being, accepted with increasing alacrity by United States delegates to inter-American conferences. In addition, the United States took tentative steps to withdraw from its various protectorates in the Caribbean. Marines left the Dominican Republic permanently in 1924. They also quit Nicaragua temporarily in 1925, but when civil conflict disturbed that unhappy country in 1927, President Calvin Coolidge sent Henry L. Stimson to mediate. He achieved a considerable success, precluding intervention by the United States, but perhaps the best examples of restraint by the United States occurred in its Mexican policy. In 1923 the two nations signed the Bucareli agreements, settling various controversies over title to land and subsoil rights caused by the Mexican constitution of 1917. When additional tensions developed later in the decade, Coolidge sent Dwight Morrow to Mexico as ambassador, and he managed a definite relaxation of tensions caused by the land, oil, and anticlerical policies of President Plutarco Calles.

The noticeable improvement in United States-Latin American relations during the Twenties was a proof that wise restraint paid dividends. If the Good Neighbor policy was not born during the Twenties, it was certainly foreshadowed; what followed later was built on the useful foundations of earlier years. The most striking public act of the era, perhaps, was the issuance of the "Clark memorandum" by the State Department in 1930. If it did not repudiate the T.R. Corollary in so many words, it argued that the original Monroe Doctrine provided no warrant for unilateral intervention, a further sign of impending change in policy. The only remaining step was overt acceptance of nonintervention, and that departure lay in the immediate future.

By various expedients the United States moved in both the Pacific and the western hemisphere to improve on the past, but European policy undermined accomplishment elsewhere during the Twenties. Throughout the Jazz era, the United States studiously avoided political participation in the affairs of Europe. Although it sent "observers" to the seat of the League at Geneva, the country never wavered in its general anti-League policy. Great efforts by protagonists of American participation in the World Court, an adjunct of the Geneva organization, failed to gain sufficient senatorial support. The only multilateral treaty signed by the United States involving Europe during the Republican ascendancy, other than the Washington Pacts, was the Paris Peace Pact. It supposedly outlawed war as an instrument of national policy. When first proposed by the Frenchman Aristide Briand, the principal architect of European harmony at the time, it was actually an effort by France to secure something like a guarantee of American support. At first Secretary of State Frank Kellogg was uninterested— even opposed. When the idea of including many nations in a general treaty came to the fore, Kellogg changed his tune and became an enthusiastic supporter of the pact. When fifteen nations signed the Kellogg-Briand treaty in August 1928, it had been reduced to a fine gesture.

Gestures are often of great importance to international relations; they sometimes precede further negotiations on critical subjects, but it is a mistake to regard them as anything other than beginnings. Otherwise they arouse false expectations. The Kellogg-Briand pact has become a classic example of the futility of unenforceable pledges to assist in keeping the peace when the chips are down. It was honored principally during the Thirties by the practice of waging "undeclared wars" to give spurious color to the claim that it had not been violated. As an indication of good intent, the Paris pact was useful; as a means of preventing wars it was entirely useless.

If the failure of the United States to assume a responsible role in European politics was its principal act of omission during the Twenties, its leading sin of commission lay in the realm of economic policy. Shortly after the war, the United States began to raise its tariff barriers. This policy precluded Europe from earning dollars by selling goods in the United States. The result was what became known in later years as a "dollar gap." Europe needed dollars not only to make needed purchases in the United States but also to repay the "war debts" incurred during the wartime emergency. A complicating element was that the United States became a "creditor nation" during World War I. It was owed more than it owed overseas for the first time in its history. The result was a "favorable balance of trade," in that American exports exceeded imports. A shortage of dollars in Europe with which to buy American goods and to meet war-debts payments led to the use of gold in making international payments to the United States, the reason for the great build-up of that precious metal at Fort Knox.

Every President including Wilson insisted upon European repayment of over $10 billion in war debts, although the pernicious effect of the debts resulted in several efforts to reduce them. The requirement of war-debts repayment was one of the reasons why the victorious powers insisted upon huge reparations from the defeated powers, especially Germany. A clear connection between war debts and reparations developed in the wake of the war. The similarity between the size of reparations payments and war-debts remittances aroused increasing interest among economists. Although the United States never officially accepted the fact of the intimate tie between the two, American negotiators gave their names to European settlements in 1924 (the Dawes plan) and in 1928 (the Young plan) decreasing the burden of reparations on Germany, and a war-debt commission in the United States reduced the obligations of the principal European debtors to America.

Constructive in intent, neither of these approaches went far enough. What was required was a renunciation of war debts by the United States in return for an end to reparations payments in Europe. Had the United States considered war debts as part of their contribution to victory rather than a conventional international loan, the problem could have been disposed of easily. As it was, the war debt-reparations tangle unsettled international finance throughout the Twenties and contributed a great deal to the failure of the international economy to recapture full efficiency. The United States erred seriously in not following policies to enhance the total volume of international trade. It may have gained in the short run from high-tariff policies and rigid loan requirements, but the long-run consequences more than outweighed the temporary benefits. An aggressive search for overseas markets obscured the adverse consequences of economic nationalism for awhile, but in the long pull, difficulties would not be ended.

After about 1924 a curious relationship developed between war debts, reparations, and American private investments in Germany. The American boom provided capitalists with excess funds; they began to sink their dollars into profitable German securities. Capital flowing to Germany moved on to the Allies as reparations. The Allies then returned it to the United States as payments on war-debt accounts. Europe lacked the ability to pay either reparations or war debts, given the general economic dislocation engendered by World War I and the costs of reconstruction at home after the war. The United States could have contributed immeasurably to European recovery by canceling the debts and extending large loans on easy terms, but this concept never gained the slightest currency during the Twenties. What would happen if something interrupted the flow of capital in the war debt-reparations-investment cycle? The answer came after 1929, when the Great Depression forced an abrupt end to American investment in Germany. That country ultimately ceased to pay reparations and the Allies defaulted their debts.

Unsound American policies on tariffs and debts contributed to Europe's underlying economic malaise during the Twenties. To be sure, Europe also pursued unwise policies, but two wrongs do not make a right. Had the United States assumed constructive leadership in the international economy after the war, the terrible strains on the world's business might have been relieved sufficiently either to prevent or mitigate the catastrophe of 1929 and after. The enhanced economic power of the United States conferred upon it not only the ability but also the responsibility to exercise constructive leadership. For its lapse, the United States reaped a bitter harvest during the Thirties.

The world depression began in the United States; it followed the crash of the American securities market in October 1929. If many domestic policies pursued by the business-dominated administrations of the dollar decade helped breed the depression, so did their international economic practices. Production outran demand and triggered a recession in the United States not only because reckless monetary and fiscal procedures dried up the home market but also because equally reckless tariff and debt policies closed out overseas markets. The United States learned too late that prosperity at home depends on international economic cooperation as well as intelligent domestic measures.

The Americans also divined too late what they might have recognized at war's end, that international prosperity was an essential precondition of general political stability. The Depression opened a veritable chamber of political horrors across both the Atlantic and the Pacific. If the American diplomacy of the Twenties reflected the success-exhaustion syndrome in the domestic body politic, the diplomacy of the Thirties flowed directly from the economic crisis at home and the break-up abroad. A continuing element in foreign policy was the persistent refusal of the United States to mend its irresponsible ways. For reasons different from those of the Twenties, the United States continued to avoid international duties and thereby multiplied the crisis wrought largely by the errors of the previous decade. The recession of 1929 and after turned national energies inward; times of domestic crisis such as depressions usually have this effect. It happened elsewhere as well, particularly in western Europe. Socialist regimes weathered the depression more efficiently than capitalist countries because their governments possessed sufficient power to fight the depression effectively. The autarchic tendencies of the capitalistic democracies produced a failure of international cooperation among them, a circumstance made to order for aggressive totalitarian regimes.

Less than two years after the crash of the American stock exchange, the Depression bred its first great international crisis; Japan resumed its conquests in East Asia. Faced with economic problems at home, a moderate Japanese government fell victim to military adventurism in Manchuria. Once again, western preoccupation with events close to home created opportunities for Japanese aggression. The fragility of democratic institutions in Japan usually became apparent at such moments, and 1931 was no exception. When opportunities for mainland expansion presented themselves, reactionary elements, especially in the army and navy, usually seized power. American statesmen did not appreciate this pattern; they tended to proceed cautiously in Far Eastern crises, hoping by this method to support moderate factions in Japanese politics. However inadvertently, this well-meaning tactic usually strengthened the elements it sought to undermine. On September 18, 1931 an incident on the South Manchurian Railway at Mukden offered a pretext for an occupation of all Manchuria. Straitened China was in no position to resist this blatant violation of the open door principles, once again exposed as useless in adverse circumstances. In January 1932, Japanese troops engaged the Chinese at Shanghai, and another force occupied the province of Jehol. The Manchurian adventure and its offshoots violated numerous international obligations, including the four-power and nine-power treaties, the covenant of the League, and the Kellogg-Briand pact, but these engagements did not deter Japan.

When the League of Nations failed to make a vigorous response, the United States undertook a unilateral effort to force Japanese withdrawal, but it turned into a mere gesture when President Hoover placed strict limits on the "Stimson doctrine" advocated by his secretary of state, Henry L. Stimson. The Secretary announced to the world in January 1932 that the United States would refuse to recognize conquests violative of the open door principles, a new version of Bryan's initiative of 1915. Although the League indorsed the Stimson doctrine, it had little or no effect on the Japanese. Neither the United States nor the international organization was prepared to enforce the statement. It was another expression of support for sound principles, but moral suasion by itself was hardly sufficient to bring Japan in line.

Late in 1932 the League finally condemned Japan as an aggressor, but that nation simply gave its required two years' notice of withdrawal and left Geneva, never to return. In 1934 the Japanese foreign office issued the "Amau statement," a document claiming for Japan a predominant influence in East Asia comparable to that exercised by the United States in the western hemisphere under the Monroe doctrine. Thus began the official elaboration of what ultimately became the concept of the "Greater East Asia Co-Prosperity Sphere." If Japanese expansionists finally withdrew the force at Shanghai and generally found it expedient to remain quiescent for a few years after 1931–1932, the Manchurian initiative had attained great success. A puppet state of Manchukuo provided a vehicle through which Japan dominated the region. The aggression of 1931 was the first in a long train of similar abuses which took place as the Thirties ran their sad course.

In 1936, military extremists again resumed control of the Japanese government after assassins murdered a number of moderate politicians who had recently defeated right-wing candidates in a parliamentary election. This gruesome feat preceded the signature of the Anti-Comintern Pact with Nazi Germany in November 1936, inaugurating the Berlin-Tokyo axis, and the beginning of the "China incident" in July 1937. An episode at the Marco Polo bridge near Peking precipitated undeclared war between China and Japan. The Japanese rapidly occupied most of China's coastal regions. After unsuccessful stands at Peking, Nanking, and Shanghai, Chiang Kai-shek's government withdrew deep into the Chinese interior and established itself at Chungking.

These events finally aroused the United States government. President Franklin D. Roosevelt journeyed to Chicago to send up a trial balloon in the very heart of isolationist territory. The President argued that international lawlessness, like contagious disease, must be subjected to quarantine. He also mentioned the need for "positive endeavors" to deal with aggressors like Japan, probably a euphemism for economic sanctions. The reaction, while often favorable, did not seem to warrant more advanced policies, and Roosevelt was forced to trim his sails, even after Japanese aircraft sank an American gunboat, the *Panay,* on the Yangtze River. In November an attempt to arrange collective international action at a conference held at Brussels came to naught. Japan sabotaged the gathering by the simple device of refusing to appear, and the United States contributed to the failure by refusing to consider Soviet proposals for joint action by the western nations. American businessmen launched a "moral embargo" on shipments of strategic materials to Japan, and the government began limited economic assistance to China, but these measures did not halt the Japanese armies.

By the outbreak of World War II in September 1939, the danger of Japan had alarmed the American people, but an effective deterrent had not been matured. In fact, the Tydings-McDuffie Act of 1934, which guaranteed independence for the Philippines in 1946, was of a piece with its predecessor, the Jones Act, in reflecting a general desire to liquidate American interests in the western Pacific and get out of harm's way. The rise of Hitler's Germany in Europe drew attention away from the Orient. Nationalist China survived only because Chiang wisely adopted a general military strategy of trading space for time, a departure creating a kind of stalemate in the undeclared Sino-Japanese war, with the Chinese retaining much of the interior, although Japan dominated the coastal regions.

If the American people and their leaders hesitated to act effectively against Japan, they were much more responsive to new departures in the western hemisphere. Roosevelt and his secretary of state, Cordell Hull, vigorously elaborated the Good Neighbor policy in Latin America, culminating the repudiation of unilateral intervention and the tendency toward an effective inter-American system. In two inter-American meetings, at Montevideo in 1933 and Buenos Aires in 1936, the United States finally abjured the practice of unilateral intervention. During the same period it continued to liquidate protectorates in the Caribbean, abrogating the Platt amendment for Cuba in 1934 after adopting circumspect policy during a rebellion against the Machado regime. Troops were also withdrawn from Haiti and Nicaragua and improved arrangements were made with Panama. Another contribution to better relations in the hemisphere was the Reciprocal Trade Agreements Act. It allowed the President on his own initiative to negotiate bilateral trade agreements with other nations, reducing tariffs by as much as fifty percent in return for parallel concessions. Reciprocal trade agreements were signed most frequently with Latin American countries; they made a measurable contribution to the success of the Good Neighbor policy.

The most impressive proof of the changed attitude of the United States came in 1938, when President Lazaro Cárdenas of Mexico expropriated foreign oil companies who refused to accept demands made on them by striking Mexican laborers. In the days of T.R. and Wilson, this deed would have provoked instant intervention, but in the late Thirties it led to a policy of caution by the United States. The oil companies complained bitterly but ultimately accepted compensation. In this instance the United States adhered strictly to international law. It authorizes expropriation under certain conditions, usually with the proviso that the expropriating nation provide reasonable compensation to property owners affected by the expropriation decree. If F.D.R. followed a sensible policy, it was because his actions accorded with the Good Neighbor policy and because the United States, given the crises then developing in Europe and Asia, hoped to avoid hemispheric troubles.

The final innovation in Latin American policy during the Thirties was the elaboration of collective hemispheric defense. At Buenos Aires in 1936 and then at Lima in 1938, a system of consultation came into being to preclude external dangers to the hemisphere. Behind this development was growing recognition of the degree to which events had gotten out of hand in Eurasia. The Declaration of Lima, committing the American Republics to act together against common dangers, accomplished nothing less than the multilateralization of the Monroe Doctrine. In the future, the principles of Monroe would be enforced by collective hemispheric action rather than by unilateral action from the United States.

The repudiation of unilateral intervention and the multilateralization of the Monroe Doctrine were distinct improvements on the past, but from the perspective of today they seem a little less impressive than at the time. The doctrine of unilateral intervention had to go; it was unsound and unnecessary from its inception. The difficulty was that nonintervention by itself did not insure the futures of most Latin Americans. The great majority found little or no surcease from oppression by local reactionary elites. The policy of hemispheric defense led by degrees to considerable arms assistance for Latin American governments from the United States, an infusion tending to accomplish what intervention had done before, i.e., shore up exploitative regimes. Fulgencio Batista of Cuba was one of the great beneficiaries of the Good Neighbor Policy. So was Rafael Trujillo of the Dominican Republic.

There remained still another problem; the concept of hemisphere defense strengthened the illusion that the United States could ride out great general wars in Eurasia. Isolationists generally supported efforts to improve hemispheric defense; it merely extended what later became known as Fortress America into

Fortress Interamericana. Collective security in the hemisphere proceeded on the assumption that it would provide a sufficient defense against involvement in the wars of Europe and Asia, a myth disproven almost as soon as it was born. The idea of collective defense was certainly constructive, but it would make its greatest contribution to national security only if integrated into a larger system of defense taking into consideration the setting at either end of Eurasia as well as the unlikely possibility of incursions in the western hemisphere.

American policy in Asia and Latin America during the Depression matured against the ominous background of another collapse in the European balance. Perhaps the most tragic event of the Long Armistice in Europe was the disintegration of the German Weimar Republic. The struggling governments at Weimar never obtained a really good opportunity to consolidate German democracy. During the Twenties they had to cope with the inroads of the Treaty of Versailles. During the early Thirties they faced the world depression. The combined impact of these blows eventually undermined the regime. Certainly historic as well as contemporary influences worked against the emergence of truly democratic institutions in German government and society after World War I, but had there been a better result from the settlements of 1919 and had there been no depression, the Weimar regime might have accomplished its goals. As it was, Germany succumbed to the totalitarian leadership of the Nazi party and its fanatical leader, Adolph Hitler. A fascist government had flourished in Italy since 1922, and several clerical-fascist governments had come to power in smaller European countries, but only the rise of German totalitarianism with all its bestial features insured that the immediate future would be inordinately influenced by the malfeasances of right-wing dictators in Europe.

In the early years of his regime, Hitler concentrated largely on consolidating his domestic power, but by 1936 he was prepared to begin recovery of territories lost in 1919. His ultimate objective was hegemony in Europe. First violating the disarmament provisions of the Versailles Treaty, Hitler then defied the victors of 1919 by occupying the demilitarized Rhineland in March 1936. The spirit of Locarno fostered during the 1920s was now completely dissipated; France attempted to invoke the guarantees included in the accords of 1925 but found no support elsewhere, and so the German *coup* was allowed to stand. The League was in no position to act. It had failed to control Japanese aggression in Asia. More recently it had collapsed in the face of Italian aggression against Ethiopia. France allowed the brazen Mussolini to aggrandize successfully; it feared an Italo-German *rapprochement* unless it condoned concessions. Britain failed to resist because it feared dangers to its communications through the Mediterranean to colonial holdings in Asia. The inability of the western democracies to form a common front against totalitarian aggression was largely a function of their failure to establish effective cooperation during the decade of prosperity after the Great War, a tendency only exacerbated after 1929 by the domestic economic distractions caused by the world depression. Another significant factor was the growing belief that a strong German state in central Europe erected a desirable buffer against the spread of Bolshevism from Soviet Russia.

As these dangerous events transpired in Europe, the United States looked to its own interests. Almost entirely preoccupied by the struggle against the domestic recession, both the Republican Herbert Hoover and the Democrat Franklin D. Roosevelt did little to influence the decisions of Europe during the depression decade. Hoover, of course, was a declared isolationist. F.D.R. had been a strong Wilsonian, but domestic political exigencies seemed to require abstinence from political entanglements abroad while the New Deal crusaded against the Depression. The consequence was a continuation of the pattern of international irresponsibility inaugurated during the affluent Twenties.

Shortly after the onset of the Depression, Hoover tried to resolve the war debts-reparations problem. In 1931, he declared a year's moratorium of debt payments, although he steadfastly refused to consider cancellation. In June 1932 the European powers met at Lausanne and reduced German reparations to a mere $700 million, hoping that the United States would respond by forgiving the war debts. When Hoover and his successor refused to take this step, the European countries one by one defaulted on payments, all except Finland, whose obligations were minimal. Greatly irritated, Congress passed the Johnson Act in 1934, forbidding private loans to countries in default of war-debt payments, a policy preventing needy European countries from borrowing in the United States to finance economic reconstruction. The American legislation contributed notably to the appeal of the rising totalitarian dictatorships. Thus ended ingloriously one of the most tangled episodes in the history of international finance.

If the war debts-reparations problem had been settled by negotiation, it probably would not have corrected the sad consequence of Hoover's tariff policy. In 1930 Congress passed the Smoot-Hawley tariff, raising schedules precipitately. Other countries naturally retaliated by raising their levies; the result was a further decline in international trade, deflationary in its effect, at a time when all efforts should have been dedicated to expanding its volume. These episodes fully confirmed the United States in its economic nationalism. Washington took little or no effective action to relieve the international economic collapse by intergovernmental cooperation.

Hoover attempted one noteworthy project in international cooperation; he supported a World Economic Conference scheduled for 1933 to reach multilateral agreement, among other things, on comprehensive currency stabilization. When the negotiators foregathered, Hoover had been retired by the American people. Roosevelt gave signs of supporting the stabilization scheme, but he suddenly repudiated the conference and turned to a unilateral policy of devaluing the dollar. The New Deal had continued the general trend toward economic nationalism, thereby lessening the effectiveness of antirecessionary policies. The President has been roundly criticized ever since for this action. Certainly his unilateral devaluation gave only temporary support to the dollar; other currencies followed suit and the initial advantage was soon canceled out.

There are, of course, good grounds for arguing that international currency stabilization would not have accomplished much in 1933. Monetary manipulation was only one of a number of international activities needed; the most critical economic task was to increase consumer purchasing power. The situation did not call for stabilization but for controlled inflation along with measures to encourage investment. The absence of effective international institutions to combat the worldwide recession made the task of recovery that much more difficult.

Water brigades cannot put out five-alarm fires. Roosevelt wisely reversed Hoover's tariff policies, but his effort was too little and too late to make a measurable contribution to general economic recovery, much less to the return of political stability in Europe.

A large number of hopeful international projects died aborning in those desperate years. In 1934 a land disarmament conference sponsored by the League and attended by the United States adjourned without accomplishing anything. At the same time Soviet Russia began to urge unity against the fascist dictators, but massive distrust of Stalin and Bolshevism prevented significant accomplishment along this line. After seventeen years of pretending that the Russian revolution had not taken place, the United States finally recognized the Soviet Union in 1933, but the action contributed little to international life. In France, intransigent opposition to all political programs from the Left was summarized in the slogan, "Better Hitler than Blum," a reaction against the socialist leader of a "popular front" movement seeking to unite liberals and radicals of all complexions against the rise of the Right. Distrust of Soviet intent constantly inhibited constructive measures against Nazi Germany during the remainder of the Long Armistice. The Soviet Union joined the League of Nations in 1934, but Germany's departure canceled out the Russian initiative. In 1935, another naval disarmament conference broke up in failure, and the high optimism of 1921–1922 was entirely dissipated. A great armaments race developed at an enormous pace in Europe and elsewhere as nations looked to their own interests.

By 1935, events in Europe had created enough concern in the United States to require some response; it came in the form of congressional reversion to a radical reincarnation of the old neutrality. Three Neutrality Acts in the period 1935–1937 attempted to forestall American involvement in another foreign war as the United States presumably had been drawn into World War I. In 1934 a sensational congressional investigation headed by Senator Gerald P. Nye of North Dakota probed the munitions industry, concentrating particularly on its operations during the period 1914–1917. The result was the untenable thesis that American munitions manufacturers—"merchants of death"—had arranged the American entry into the Great War in order to maximize their profits. An example of the "paranoid style" of politics at its worst, the accusation gained wide currency and contributed immensely to the psychology producing the neutrality legislation. It allowed the President to embargo arms shipments to belligerent powers, to issue a proclamation warning travelers on neutral ships that they did so at their own risk and to ban travel on all ships owned by belligerents, and finally to restrict private loans to belligerents.

The neutrality laws all too often played into the hands of aggressors by penalizing friendly nations who might have benefited from American aid and comfort. When Mussolini attacked Ethiopia, the United States stood by helplessly. During the Spanish Civil War (1936–1939) Congress embargoed arms shipments to Spain, thereby denying help to the loyalist troops and strengthening the insurgent forces under General Francisco Franco who received aid from Italy and Germany. Russian supplies to the Spanish Republic fell far short of what was needed to prevent Franco's victory. Britain and France contributed to the end of democracy in Spain by attempting to isolate the civil conflict so that it would not turn into a general war. Congress relented somewhat from its advanced position only when interest groups complained that absolute embargoes interfered with business as usual. It passed a "cash and carry" proviso allowing belligerents to purchase certain goods in the United States for cash if they transported their purchases in their own vessels. This provision hardly helped landlocked Ethiopia and Republican Spain. F.D.R. did take advantage of loopholes in the legislation to send some help to China, but the amount was too limited to make a decisive contribution to Chiang's resistance.

By 1937, Roosevelt had to recognize the dangers to the Republic inherent in the aggressions of the Rome-Berlin-Tokyo axis, an arrangement completed when Italy adhered to the Anti-Comintern Pact in that year. Ostensibly aimed at Soviet Russia, the loose association of the dictators turned by degrees into a coalition bent on dominating both ends of the Eurasian land mass. The quarantine speech was clear indication of Roosevelt's desire to reorient American policy, but he was hoist by his own petard, his administration having acquiesced in a pattern of neutrality legislation encouraging the public delusion that the United States could escape involvement if another general war broke out in Europe. This circumstance caused the United States for the most part to stand by idly during the critical years from 1937 to 1939 as the crisis in Europe finally erupted into war.

The purposes of Hitler and Mussolini were abundantly clear, but Britain and France chose the path of appeasement. Appeasement was a product of many influences. A mistaken policy from the first, it nevertheless seemed plausible to many in the confusion of the late Thirties. The inability of the great democratic nations to act together led them down the primrose path of least resistance. Internal political conflicts within the several countries, especially France, inhibited joint action against the dictators. An influential contemporary argument for appeasement was the claim that a strong Germany in the heart of Europe would restore the historic central European barrier to Russian expansion, a prospect particularly alarming after the Russian revolution. A final rationale for appeasement was that Germany was merely seeking to recover what was rightfully its own. Hitler himself said so, and this argument played effectively on guilt feelings in Europe, rampant because of the severity of the Versailles Treaty, called a *Diktat* by the Nazis. Behind all this was the memory of the Great War. Europeans were willing to go to great lengths in order to avoid its repetition. Ironically, appeasement contributed a great deal to just such another violent season.

Appeasement worked itself out in three phases during 1938–1939. It was applied by implication when Hitler carried out the *Anschluss,* forced union of Austria and Germany, early in 1938. Hitler's next target was the Sudetenland, a part of Czechoslovakia adjacent to the Third Reich largely populated by German-speaking people. After a long crisis, the powers met at Munich on September 30, 1938, where Prime Minister Neville Chamberlain of Britain and his French counterpart, Edouard Daladier, achieved what they hoped was "peace for our time" by accepting all that Hitler asked of them. Czechoslovakia was required to yield up the Sudetenland. The folly of this concession became apparent in March 1939, when the German army swallowed up the remaining districts of Czechoslovakia—Bohemia and Moravia. Hitler had pledged that the Sudetenland was his last territorial demand, but further aggression against

Czechoslovakia revealed his larger intentions. Appeasement was then exposed for what it was, but it continued to influence France and Britain to the very end of the last peaceful summer.

The next obvious step was the conquest of Poland, but the fly in the ointment was Soviet Russia. An invasion of Poland might plunge Germany into war with Poland's French and British allies in the West and Russia in the East, a repetition of the mistake of 1914. Once again Chamberlain and Daladier saved Hitler a peck of trouble. They made only a half-hearted attempt to negotiate a settlement with Russia during the summer of 1939 in order to protect Poland. Stalin naturally suspected that the Anglo-French combine hoped for a Russo-German war to weaken both of their European enemies. In late August the Nazi foreign minister, Joachim von Ribbentrop, flew to Moscow and there negotiated a nonaggression pact with Vyacheslav Molotov. This accomplishment fell like a thunderbolt on the world; the two countries had been sworn enemies. Hitler's Anti-Comintern Pact with Japan and Italy had answered Stalin's attempt to form a united front against the fascist powers. Apologists for Stalin argued later that he accepted the Ribbentrop-Molotov pact only to gain time. His critics alleged that he hoped for a war between the other great European powers in order to create opportunities for later Soviet aggressions.

The outcome of the agreement of August 23rd was the destruction of the Polish state. On September 1st, Germany invaded Poland from the west. Three days later, Britain and France finally turned their backs on appeasement and went to the defense of Poland—the beginning of World War II. Two weeks later, when the German *Blitzkrieg* had practically destroyed Polish resistance, Stalin moved into the country from the east. For his pains, Stalin acquired eastern Poland and also, a little later, was able to make territorial gains at the expense of Finland and to extinguish the sovereignty of the Baltic provinces made independent after World War I—Latvia, Estonia, and Lithuania. Germany acquired the Polish corridor, the free city of Danzig, and the western districts of Poland. In this fashion the two powers who had been penalized most severely in 1919 recovered lost territories in eastern Europe.

The nations of Europe had not expected the United States to enter actively into its affairs during this critical time, and this estimate proved entirely accurate. The course of American policy from the time of the repudiation of Woodrow Wilson offered ample evidence that the United States would refuse to take a stand. If President Roosevelt launched the beginnings of American rearmament in 1938, he failed to secure changes in the neutrality legislation before the war began in Europe. The only American initiative after the conquest of Czechoslovakia was to suggest a ten-year moratorium on attack against some thirty-one countries by the dictators in Berlin and Rome. As before World War I the United States in 1939 failed to commit its power to effective diplomatic endeavors for peace with honor. It preferred to watch the beginnings of a catastrophic conflict certain to threaten its security as never before during its history.

The second violent phase of the Twentieth Century War followed directly from the failure to make a satisfactory settlement in the wake of its first phase. Wars always create complications more imposing than those precipitating them; the first phase of the Twentieth Century War provides a classic example of this maxim. Wars also have unintended and unexpected outcomes; World War II offers an equally sufficient example of this truth. Twenty-seven months after the outbreak of World War II, the United States once again was drawn into a great modern war of nations in arms, requiring of it a much greater sacrifice of blood and treasure than the intervention of 1917. The price of irresponsibility was a burden of tragedy far surpassing anything that might have followed from constructive exercise of its imposing power during the Long Armistice. The war of 1939–1945 further undermined the foundations of the established international system. Its outcome made it less likely than before that the established statecraft, even of the most skillful kind, could keep the peace indefinitely.

The second violent phase of the Twentieth Century War further undermined Woodrow Wilson's grand conceptions—the maintenance of the nation-state system by various international expedients. Above all, Woodrow Wilson was an American nationalist. His plans and purposes were always consistent with the interests and aspirations of America the Beautiful, that satiate-progressive anomaly, although unlike alternative nationalist programs, they held forth great promise to less fortunate nations. From a national point of view, Wilson's diplomatic execution was far more open to criticism than his intent.

Ironically, the Second World War sold the American people as never before on the importance of accepting vast international obligations and responsibilities. They may have learned too late; the proper time to grasp this lesson was 1919 and before. Soldiers often wage war with information gained during the last conflict, ignoring the changes of the interim. Peoples all too frequently compound the miiltary error by attempting to make peace the way it should have been done the last time. World War II vastly transformed and complicated the international setting; its consequences demanded truly innovative statecraft, a species of novelty that few societies could be expected to embrace in the best of circumstances. That is the nature of war; it imposes truly difficult, sometimes insurmountable, tasks upon those who would restore peace with justice.

Once the second conflict began, it was right and appropriate that the United States should take part, if only because the circumstances permitted no other course. The tragedy was that the American people had missed an opportunity to help construct an international order in 1919 and after that might have precluded another great war. As it was, the great Republic helped sow the fields of Mars; in common with other nation-states it reaped a whirlwind of war. . . .

World War II was very different from World War I; it was at once more global and more total than its predecessor. Many nations were engaged in numerous theaters. They were also deeply implicated. If the first phase of the Twentieth Century War approached something like totality in its final year or so, the second phase was a death struggle from the very beginning. In the nature of things, World War II had to end in something closely approximating complete victory for one side and complete defeat for the other. It was bound to consume much more blood and treasure than World War I, and equally certain to produce an even more difficult and unexpected aftermath.

These elements prevented the belligerent nations from fighting entirely in terms of the famous dictum of Clausewitz, that war is a continuation of politics and should always be fought in terms of political ends. The great German theorist argued persuasively that strategy should always remain subordinate to policy. Woodrow Wilson managed a striking application of Clausewitz' dictum during 1917–1918 precisely because the earlier Armageddon was less global and less total than World War II. The desperate military situation confronting F.D.R. in December 1941 required intense preoccupation with mere survival. The enemy had to be met where he was and engaged in fierce combat. The truly devastating nature of total warfare provided much less area for political maneuver than World War I. The struggle of 1939–1945 developed its own inherent tragedy which human error might compound but not alter. The conduct and consequences of World War I had made it difficult indeed to avoid another conflict. A second war was bound to generate unmatched instability. By 1939 the world was once again on the horns of an insoluble dilemma. Neither peace nor war promised much; tragedy was bound to flow from whatever decisions were made by the nations facing totalitarian aggression.

Those who fought World War II often interpreted it in ideological terms. Ideology is, first, a function of power; it reflects the national condition. Democracy is peculiarly suitable to essentially satisfied and stable societies, just as totalitarianism is often relevant to dissatisfied and unstable societies. Nevertheless, ideology takes on life of its own and becomes an independent force. Men do not fight for bread alone; the sacrifices of combat require higher justification. The antihegemonial coalition inevitably advertised itself as a "peace-loving" bloc set out to insure a just and lasting peace. Its opponents relied on the age-old maxim that victory is the portion of the mighty; superior strength justifies any means to power. Ideological heat is often a dependent variable, which is to say that it is frequently altered in intensity by events, particularly changing power relationships. The course of World War II provides a case in point; the enormous ideological gulf separating Communist Russia from its Anglo-American allies before 1941 was quickly bridged during the joint war against the fascist coalition.

The Grand Alliance temporarily composed its ideological differences sufficiently to insure victory over the hegemonizing powers. Nothing makes friends of former enemies like common dangers. Once danger dissipates, temporary alliances fade as new conflicts of interest revive ideological tension. Politics is rarely a function either of pure ideological conflict or of naked power. It is usually a function of both. The task of those who study politics is to sort out the various interrelated strands of ideology and power. The clarity of analysis inevitably suffers by the effort, but the advantage is a certain maturity denied to those who persist in the lesser arts of more simplistic interpretation.

The elaboration of the Twentieth Century War constantly narrowed the political alternatives open to those who waged it; historians must recognize this immutable trend. Peace constantly mothers political alternatives; warfare aborts them. The web of ideology and power becomes ever more entangling as violence proliferates. All too often across the ironic history of mankind, only exhaustion has allowed the race to unravel that web and begin anew its quixotic progress to permanent peace and justice for all. War gives play to primitive instincts, undermining civility. The unparalleled exercise of violence from 1939 to 1945 was the greatest reproach to civilization within human recall. It seemed unlikely that humanity could survive another recourse to general warfare. . . .

The return of peace did not bring the new day hoped and planned for by many during the war. Almost six years of total warfare had left the world in vast disarray, to a much greater degree even than after World War I. The war of 1939–1945 completed a series of trends inaugurated in 1914–1918. Two great superpowers dominated the world in the wake of World War II, the Soviet Union and the United States. All other great powers suffered temporary or permanent eclipse. Great vacuums of power existed at both ends of the Eurasian land mass, insuring serious political instability in those regions for an indefinite period to come. The war had awakened colonial peoples everywhere; it created an unparalleled opportunity for them to regain independence. All the old colonial empires were doomed after 1945. Anticolonial leaders blossomed everywhere to guide movements of national emancipation and regeneration.

Over the heads of all brooded the enormous mushroom cloud produced by the atomic bomb, a massive symbol of potential doom for the entire human family. Never before had peace brought troubles to compare with those of September 1945 and after. But then, never before had the peoples of the world engaged in such plenary warfare. The price of victory was a legacy of international instability far beyond anything ever before bequeathed to humanity in the wake of general warfare. It was clear that the world could not endure another harvest of death, certain as it was that nuclear conflict would wreak destruction far beyond anything experienced even during the most destructive of wars just past. Despite this awareness, no one could be sure in 1945 that the Twentieth Century War had reached its conclusion.

~~~~~~~15

ROBERTA WOHLSTETTER

Surprise Attack at Pearl Harbor: Who to Blame?

For many years the charge was current that President Franklin Roosevelt deliberately planned Pearl Harbor. Wanting to galvanize public support for American participation in the World War, the argument goes, he let U.S. ships sit in Pearl Harbor inviting Japanese attack. The highest officials of the government knew the attack would be forthcoming, for they had broken important Japanese codes. This is a devil theory of war, not unrelated to a conspiratorial theory of history. In our analysis of history, should we find explanations in the evil machinations of human beings or the "limitations to perception and communication" which Mrs. Wohlstetter discusses?

If our intelligence system and all our other channels of information failed to produce an accurate image of Japanese intentions and capabilities, it was not for want of the relevant materials. Never before have we had so complete an intelligence picture of the enemy. And perhaps never again will we have such a magnificent collection of sources at our disposal.

To review these sources briefly, an American cryptanalyst, Col. William F. Friedman, had broken the top-priority Japanese diplomatic code, which enabled us to listen to a large proportion of the privileged communications between Tokyo and the major Japanese embassies throughout the world. Not only did we know in advance how the Japanese ambassadors in Washington were advised, and how much they were instructed to say, but we also were listening to top-secret messages on the Tokyo-Berlin and Tokyo-Rome circuits, which gave us information vital for conduct of the war in the Atlantic and Europe. In the Far East this source provided minute details on movements connected with the Japanese program of expansion into Southeast Asia.

Besides the strictly diplomatic codes, our cryptanalysts also had some success in reading codes used by Japanese agents in major American and foreign ports. Those who were on the distribution list for MAGIC had access to much of what these agents were reporting to Tokyo and what Tokyo was demanding of them in the Panama Canal Zone, in cities along the east and west coasts of the Americas from northern Canada as far south as Brazil, and in ports throughout the Far East, including the Philippines and the Hawaiian Islands. They could determine what installations, what troop and ship movements, and what alert and defense measures were of interest to Tokyo at these points on the globe, as well as approximately how much correct information her agents were sending her.

Our naval leaders also had at their disposal the results of radio traffic analysis. While before the war our naval radio experts could not read the content of any Japanese naval or military coded messages, they were able to deduce from a study of intercepted ship call signs the composition and location of the Japanese Fleet units. After a change in call signs, they might lose sight of some units, and units that went into port in home waters were also lost because the ships in port used frequencies that our radios were unable to intercept. Most of the time, however, our traffic analysts had the various Japanese Fleet units accurately pinpointed on our naval maps.

Extremely competent on-the-spot economic and political analysis was furnished by Ambassador Grew and his staff in Tokyo. Ambassador Grew was himself a most sensitive and accurate observer, as evidenced by his dispatches to the State Department. His observations were supported and supplemented with military detail by frequent reports from American naval attachés and observers in key Far Eastern ports. Navy Intelligence had men with radio equipment located along the coast of China, for example, who reported the convoy movements toward Indochina. There were also naval observers stationed in various high-tension areas in Thailand and Indochina who could fill in the local outlines of Japanese political intrigue and military planning. In Tokyo and other Japanese cities, it is true, Japanese censorship grew more and more rigid during 1941, until Ambassador Grew felt it necessary to disclaim any responsibility for noting or reporting overt military evidence of an imminent outbreak of war. This careful Japanese censorship naturally cut down visual confirmation of the decoded information but very probably never achieved the opaqueness of Russia's Iron Curtain.

During this period the data and interpretations of British intelligence were also available to American officers in Washington and the Far East, though the British and Americans tended to distrust each other's privileged information.

In addition to secret sources, there were some excellent public ones. Foreign correspondents for *The New York Times, The Herald Tribune,* and *The Washington Post* were stationed in Tokyo and Shanghai and in Canberra, Australia. Their reporting as well as their predictions on the Japanese political scene were on a very high level. Frequently their access to news was more rapid and their judgment of its significance as reliable as that of our Intelligence officers. This was certainly the case for 1940 and most of 1941. For the last few weeks before the Pearl Harbor strike, however, the public newspaper accounts were not very useful. It was necessary to have secret information in order to know what was happening. Both Tokyo and Washington exercised very tight control over leaks during this crucial period, and the newsmen accordingly had to limit their accounts to speculation and notices of diplomatic meetings with no exact indication of the content of the diplomatic exchanges.

The Japanese press was another important public source. During 1941 it proclaimed with increasing shrillness the Japanese government's determination to pursue its program of expansion into Southeast Asia and the desire of the military to clear the Far East of British and American colonial exploitation. This particular source was rife with explicit signals of aggressive intent.

Finally, an essential part of the intelligence picture for 1941 was both public and privileged information on American policy and activities in the Far East. During the year the pattern of action and interaction between the Japanese and American governments grew more and more complex. At the last, it became especially important for anyone charged with the responsibility of ordering an alert to know what moves the American government was going to make with respect to Japan, as well as to try to guess what Japan's next move would be, since Japan's next move would respond in part to ours. Unfortunately our military leaders, and especially our Intelligence officers, were sometimes as surprised as the Japanese at the moves of the White House and the State Department. They usually had more orderly anticipations about Japanese policy and conduct than they had about America's. On the other hand, it was also true that State Department and White House officials were handicapped in judging Japanese intentions and estimates of risk by an inadequate picture of our own military vulnerability.

All of the public and private sources of information mentioned were available to America's political and military leaders in 1941. It is only fair to remark, however, that no single person or agency ever had at any given moment all the signals existing in this vast information network. The signals lay scattered in a number of different agencies; some were decoded, some were not; some traveled through rapid channels of communication, some were blocked by technical or procedural delays; some never reached a center of decision. But it is legitimate to review again the general sort of picture that emerged during the first week of December from the signals readily at hand. Anyone close to President Roosevelt was likely to have before him the following significant fragments.

There was first of all a picture of gathering troop and ship movements down the China coast and into Indochina. The large dimensions of this movement to the south were established publicly and visually as well as by analysis of ship call signs. Two changes in Japanese naval call signs—one on November 1 and another on December 1—had also been evaluated by Naval Intelligence as extremely unusual and as signs of major preparations for some sort of Japanese offensive. The two changes had interfered with the speed of American radio traffic analysis. Thousands of interceptions after December 1 were necessary before the new call signs could be read. Partly for this reason American radio analysts disagreed about the locations of the Japanese carriers. One group held that all the carriers were near Japan because they had not been able to identify a carrier call sign since the middle of November. Another group believed that they had located one carrier division in the Marshalls. The probability seemed to be that the carriers, wherever they were, had gone into radio silence; and past experience led the analysts to believe that they were therefore in waters near the Japanese homeland, where they could communicate with each other on wavelengths that we could not intercept. However, our inability to locate the carriers exactly, combined with the two changes in call signs, was itself a danger signal.

Our best secret source, MAGIC, was confirming the aggressive intention of the new military cabinet in Tokyo, which had replaced the last moderate cabinet on October 17. In particular, MAGIC provided details of some of the preparations for the move into Southeast Asia. Running counter to this were increased troop shipments to the Manchurian border in October. (The intelligence picture is never clear-cut.) But withdrawals had begun toward the end of that month. MAGIC also carried explicit instructions to the Japanese ambassadors in Washington to pursue diplomatic negotiations with the United States with increasing energy, but at the same time it announced a deadline for the favorable conclusion of the negotiations, first for November 25, later postponed until November 29. In case of diplomatic failure by that date, the Japanese ambassadors were told, Japanese patience would be exhausted, Japan was determined to pursue her Greater East Asia policy, and on November 29 "things" would automatically begin to happen.

On November 26 Secretary Hull rejected Japan's latest bid for American approval of her policies in China and Indochina. MAGIC had repeatedly characterized this Japanese overture as the "last," and it now revealed the ambassadors' reaction of consternation and despair over the American refusal and also their country's characterization of the American Ten Point Note as an "ultimatum."

On the basis of this collection of signals, Army and Navy Intelligence experts in Washington tentatively placed D-day *for the Japanese Southeastern campaign* during the week end of November 30, and when this failed to materialize, during the week end of December 7. They also compiled an accurate list of probable British and Dutch targets and included the Philippines and Guam as possible American targets.

Also available in this mass of information, but long forgotten, was a rumor reported by Ambassador Grew in January, 1941. It came from what was regarded as a not-very-reliable source, the Peruvian embassy, and stated that the Japanese were preparing a surprise air attack on Pearl Harbor. Curiously the date of the report is coincident roughly with what we now know to have been the date of inception of Yamamoto's plan; but the rumor was labeled by everyone, including Ambassador Grew, as quite fantastic and the plan as absurdly impossible. American judgment was consistent with Japanese judgment at this time, since Yamamoto's plan was in direct contradiction to Japanese naval tactical doctrine.

On the basis of this rapid recapitulation of the highlights in the signal picture, it is apparent that our decisionmakers had at hand an impressive amount of information on the enemy. They did not have the complete list of targets, since none of the last-minute estimates included Pearl Harbor. They did not know the exact hour and date for opening the attack. They did not have an accurate knowledge of Japanese capabilities or of Japanese ability to accept very high risks. The crucial question then, we repeat, is, If we could enumerate accurately the British and Dutch targets and give credence to a Japanese attack against them either on November 30 or December 7, why were we not expecting a specific danger to *ourselves?* And by the word "expecting," we mean expecting in the sense of taking specific alert actions to meet the contingencies of attack by land, sea, or air.

There are several answers to this question that have become apparent in the course of this study. First of all, it is much easier *after* the event to sort the relevant from the irrelevant signals. After the event, of course, a signal is always crystal clear; we can now see what disaster it was signaling, since the disaster has occurred. But before the event it is obscure and pregnant with conflicting meanings. It comes to the observer embedded in an atmosphere of "noise," i.e., in the company of all sorts of information that is useless and irrelevant for predicting the particular disaster. For example, in Washington, Pearl Harbor signals were competing with a vast number of signals from the European theater. These European signals announced danger more frequently and more specifically than any coming from the Far East. The Far Eastern signals were also arriving at a center of decision where they had to compete with the prevailing belief that an unprotected offensive force acts as a deterrent rather than a target. In Honolulu they were competing *not* with signals from the European theater, but rather with a large number of signals announcing Japanese intentions and preparations to attack Soviet Russia rather than to move southward; here they were also competing with expectations of local sabotage prepared by previous alert situations.

In short, we failed to anticipate Pearl Harbor not for want of the relevant materials, but because of a plethora of irrelevant ones. Much of the appearance of wanton neglect that emerged in various investigations of the disaster resulted from the unconscious suppression of vast congeries of signs pointing in every direction except Pearl Harbor. It was difficult later to recall these signs since they had led nowhere. Signals that are characterized today as absolutely unequivocal warnings of surprise air attack on Pearl Harbor become, on analysis in the context of December, 1941, not merely ambiguous but occasionally inconsistent with such an attack. To recall one of the most controversial and publicized examples, the winds code, both General Short and Admiral Kimmel testified that if they had had this information, they would have been prepared on the morning of December 7 for an air attack from without. The messages establishing the winds code are often described in the Pearl Harbor literature as Tokyo's declaration of war against America. If they indeed amounted to such a declaration, obviously the failure to inform Honolulu of this vital news would have been criminal negligence. On examination, however, the messages proved to be instructions for code communication after normal commercial channels had been cut. In one message the recipient was instructed on receipt of an execute to destroy all remaining codes in his possession. In another version the recipient was warned that the execute would be sent out "when relations are becoming dangerous" between Japan and three other countries. There was a different code term for each country: England, America, and the Soviet Union.

There is no evidence that an authentic execute of either message was ever intercepted by the United States before December 7. The message ordering code destruction was in any case superseded by a much more explicit code-destruction order from Tokyo that was intercepted on December 2 and translated on December 3. After December 2, the receipt of a winds-code execute for code destruction would therefore have added nothing new to our information, and code destruction in itself cannot be taken as an unambiguous substitute for a formal declaration of war. During the first week of December the United States ordered all American consulates in the Far East to destroy all American codes, yet no one has attempted to prove that this order was equivalent to an American declaration of war against Japan. As for the other winds-code message, provided an execute had been received warning that relations were dangerous between Japan and the United States, there would still have been no way on the basis of this signal alone to determine whether Tokyo was signaling Japanese intent to attack the United States or Japanese fear of an American surprise attack (in reprisal for Japanese aggressive moves against American allies in the Far East). It was only after the event that "dangerous relations" could be interpreted as "surprise air attack on Pearl Harbor."

There is a difference, then, between having a signal available somewhere in the heap of irrelevancies, and perceiving it as a warning; and there is also a difference between perceiving it as a warning, and acting or getting action on it. These distinctions, simple as they are, illuminate the obscurity shrouding this moment in history.

Many instances of these distinctions have been examined in the course of this study. We shall recall a few of the most dramatic now. To illustrate the difference between having and perceiving a signal, let us consider the case of Colonel Fielder. Though he was an untrained and inexperienced Intelligence officer, he headed Army Intelligence at Pearl Harbor at the time of the attack. He had been on the job for only four months, and he regarded as quite satisfactory his sources of information and his contacts with the Navy locally and with Army Intelligence in Washington. Evidently he was unaware that Army Intelligence in Washington was not allowed to send him any "action" or policy information, and he was therefore not especially concerned about trying to read beyond the obvious meaning of any given communication that came under his eyes. Colonel Bratton, head of Army Far Eastern Intelligence in Washington, however, had a somewhat more realistic view of the extent of Colonel Fielder's knowledge. At the end of November, Colonel Bratton had learned about the winds-code setup and was also apprised that the naval traffic analysis unit under Commander Rochefort in Honolulu was monitoring 24 hours a day for an execute. He was understandably worried about the lack of communication between this unit and Colonel Fielder's office, and by December 5 he finally felt that the matter was urgent enough to warrant sending a message directly to Colonel Fielder about the winds code. Now any information on the winds code, since it belonged to the highest classification of secret information, and since it was therefore automatically evaluated as "action" information, could not be sent through normal G-2 channels. Colonel Bratton had to figure out another way to get the information to Colonel Fielder. He sent this message: "Contact Commander Rochefort immediately thru Commandant Fourteenth Naval District regarding broadcasts from Tokyo reference weather." Signal Corps records establish that Colonel Fielder received this message. How did he react to it? He filed it. According to his testimony in 1945, it made no impression on him and he did not attempt to see Rochefort. He could not sense any urgency behind the lines because he was not expecting immediate trouble, and his expectations determined what he read. A warning signal was available to him, but he did not perceive it.

Colonel Fielder's lack of experience may make this example seem to be an exception. So let us recall the performance of Captain Wilkinson, the naval officer who headed the Office of Naval Intelligence in Washington in the fall of 1941 and who is unanimously acclaimed for a distinguished and brilliant career. His treatment of a now-famous Pearl Harbor signal does not sound much different in the telling. After the event, the signal in question was labeled "the bomb-plot message." It originated in Tokyo on September 24 and was sent to an agent in Honolulu. It requested the agent to divide Pearl Harbor into five areas and to make his future reports on ships in harbor with reference to those areas. Tokyo was especially interested in the locations of battleships, destroyers, and carriers, and also in any information on the anchoring of more than one ship at a single dock.

This message was decoded and translated on October 9 and shortly thereafter distributed to Army, Navy, and State Department recipients of MAGIC. Commander Kramer, a naval expert on MAGIC, had marked the message with an asterisk, signifying that he thought it to be of particular interest. But what was its interest? Both he and Wilkinson agreed that it illustrated the "nicety" of Japanese intelligence, the incredible zeal and efficiency with which they collected detail. The division into areas was interpreted as a device for shortening the reports. Admiral Stark was similarly impressed with Japanese efficiency, and no one felt it necessary to forward the message to Admiral Kimmel. No one read into it a specific danger to ships anchored in Pearl Harbor. At the time, this was a reasonable estimate, since somewhat similar requests for information were going to Japanese agents in Panama, Vancouver, Portland, San Diego, San Francisco, and other places. It should be observed, however, that the estimate was reasonable only on the basis of a very rough check on the quantity of espionage messages passing between Tokyo and these American ports. No one in Far Eastern Intelligence had subjected the messages to any more refined analysis. An observer assigned to such a job would have been able to record an increase in the frequency and specificity of Tokyo's requests concerning Manila and Pearl Harbor in the last weeks before the outbreak of war, and he would have noted that Tokyo was not displaying the same interest in other American ports. These observations, while not significant in isolation, might have been useful in the general signal picture.

There is no need, however, to confine our examples to Intelligence personnel. Indeed, the crucial areas where the signals failed to communicate a warning were in the operational branches of the armed services. Let us take Admiral Kimmel and his reaction to the information that the Japanese were destroying most of their codes in major Far Eastern consulates and also in London and Washington. Since the Pearl Harbor attack, this information has frequently been characterized by military experts who were not stationed in Honolulu as an "unmistakable tip-off." As Admiral Ingersoll explained at the congressional hearings, with the lucidity characteristic of statements after the event:

> If you rupture diplomatic negotiations you do not necessarily have to burn your codes. The diplomats go home and they can pack up

their codes with their dolls and take them home. Also, when you
rupture diplomatic negotiations, you do not rupture consular relations. The consuls stay on.

Now, in this particular set of dispatches that did not mean a
rupture of diplomatic negotiations, it meant war, and that information was sent out to the fleets as soon as we got it. . . .

The phrase "it meant war" was, of course, pretty vague; war in Manila,
Hong Kong, Singapore, and Batavia is not war 5000 miles away in Pearl Harbor.
Before the event, for Admiral Kimmel, code burning in major Japanese consulates in the Far East may have "meant war," but it did not signal danger of
an air attack on Pearl Harbor. In the first place, the information that he received was not the original MAGIC. He learned from Washington that Japanese
consulates were burning "almost all" of their codes, not all of them, and Honolulu was not included on the list. He knew from a local source that the Japanese
consulate in Honolulu was burning secret papers (not necessarily codes), and
this back yard burning had happened three or four times during the year. In
July, 1941, Kimmel had been informed that the Japanese consulates in lands
neighboring Indochina had destroyed codes, and he interpreted the code burning in December as a similar attempt to protect codes in case the Americans or
their British and Dutch allies tried to seize the consulates in reprisal for the
southern advance. This also was a reasonable interpretation at the time, though
not an especially keen one.

Indeed, at the time there was a good deal of evidence available to support
all the wrong interpretations of last-minute signals, and the interpretations appeared wrong only *after* the event. There was, for example, a good deal of evidence to support the hypothesis that Japan would attack the Soviet Union from
the east while the Russian Army was heavily engaged in the west. Admiral
Turner, head of Navy War Plans in Washington, was an enthusiastic adherent
of this view and argued the high probability of a Japanese attack on Russia up
until the last week in November, when he had to concede that most of Japan's
men and supplies were moving south. Richard Sorge, the expert Soviet spy who
had direct access to the Japanese Cabinet, had correctly predicted the southern
move as early as July, 1941, but even he was deeply alarmed during September
and early October by the large number of troop movements to the Manchurian
border. He feared that his July advice to the Soviet Union had been in error,
and his alarm ultimately led to his capture on October 14. For at this time he
increased his radio messages to Moscow to the point where it was possible for
the Japanese police to pinpoint the source of the broadcasts.

It is important to emphasize here that most of the men that we have cited
in our examples, such as Captain Wilkinson and Admirals Turner and Kimmel
—these men and their colleagues who were involved in the Pearl Harbor disaster—were as efficient and loyal a group of men as one could find. Some of
them were exceptionally able and dedicated. The fact of surprise at Pearl Harbor has never been persuasively explained by accusing the participants, individually or in groups, of conspiracy or negligence or stupidity. What these
examples illustrate is rather the very human tendency to pay attention to the
signals that support current expectations about enemy behavior. If no one is

listening for signals of an attack against a highly improbable target, then it is very difficult for the signals to be heard.

For every signal that came into the information net in 1941 there were usually several plausible alternative explanations, and it is not surprising that our observers and analysts were inclined to select the explanations that fitted the popular hypotheses. They sometimes set down new contradictory evidence side by side with existing hypotheses, and they also sometimes held two contradictory beliefs at the same time. We have seen this happen in G-2 estimates for the fall of 1941. Apparently human beings have a stubborn attachment to old beliefs and an equally stubborn resistance to new material that will upset them.

Besides the tendency to select whatever was in accord with one's expectations, there were many other blocks to perception that prevented our analysts from making the correct interpretation. We have just mentioned the masses of conflicting evidence that supported alternative and equally reasonable hypotheses. This is the phenomenon of noise in which a signal is embedded. Even as its normal level, noise presents problems in distraction; but in addition to the natural clatter of useless information and competing signals, in 1941 a number of factors combined to raise the usual noise level. First of all, it had been raised, especially in Honolulu, by the background of previous alert situations and false alarms. Earlier alerts, as we have seen, had centered attention on local sabotage and on signals supporting the hypothesis of a probable Japanese attack on Russia. Second, in both Honolulu and Washington, individual reactions to danger had been numbed, or at least dulled, by the continuous international tension.

A third factor that served to increase the natural noise level was the positive effort made by the enemy to keep the relevant signals quiet. The Japanese security system was an important and successful block to perception. It was able to keep the strictest cloak of secrecy around the Pearl Harbor attack and to limit knowledge only to those closely associated with the details of military and naval planning. In the Japanese Cabinet only the Navy Minister and the Army Minister (who was also Prime Minister) knew of the plan before the task force left its final port of departure.

In addition to keeping certain signals quiet, the enemy tried to create noise, and sent false signals into our information system by carrying on elaborate "spoofs." False radio traffic made us believe that certain ships were maneuvering near the mainland of Japan. The Japanese also sent to individual commanders false war plans for Chinese targets, which were changed only at the last moment to bring them into line with the Southeastern movement.

A fifth barrier to accurate perception was the fact that the relevant signals were subject to change, often very sudden change. This was true even of the so-called static intelligence, which included data on capabilities and the composition of military forces. In the case of our 1941 estimates of the infeasibility of torpedo attacks in the shallow waters of Pearl Harbor, or the underestimation of the range and performance of the Japanese Zero, the changes happened too quickly to appear in an intelligence estimate.

Sixth, our own security system sometimes prevented the communication of signals. It confronted our officers with the problem of trying to keep information from the enemy without keeping it from each other, and, as in the case of MAGIC, they were not always successful. As we have seen, only a very few key individuals saw these secret messages, and they saw them only briefly. They had no opportunity or time to make a critical review of the material, and each one assumed that others who had seen it would arrive at identical interpretations. Exactly who those "others" were was not quite clear to any recipient. Admiral Stark, for example, thought Admiral Kimmel was reading all of MAGIC. Those who were not on the list of recipients, but who had learned somehow of the existence of the decodes, were sure that they contained military as well as diplomatic information and believed that the contents were much fuller and more precise than they actually were. The effect of carefully limiting the reading and discussion of MAGIC, which was certainly necessary to safeguard the secret of our knowledge of the code, was thus to reduce this group of signals to the point where they were scarcely heard.

To these barriers of noise and security we must add the fact that the necessarily precarious character of intelligence information and predictions was reflected in the wording of instructions to take action. The warning messages were somewhat vague and ambiguous. Enemy moves are often subject to reversal on short notice, and this was true for the Japanese. They had plans for canceling their attacks on American possessions in the Pacific up to 24 hours before the time set for attack. A full alert in the Hawaiian Islands, for example, was one condition that might have caused the Pearl Harbor task force to return to Japan on December 5 or 6. The fact that intelligence predictions must be based on moves that are almost always reversible makes understandable the reluctance of the intelligence analyst to make bold assertions. Even if he is willing to risk his reputation on a firm prediction of attack at a definite time and place, no commander will in turn lightly risk the penalties and costs of a full alert. In December, 1941, a full alert required shooting down any unidentified aircraft sighted over the Hawaiian Islands. Yet this might have been interpreted by Japan as the first overt act. At least that was one consideration that influenced General Short to order his lowest degree of alert. While the cautious phrasing in the messages to the theater is certainly understandable, it nevertheless constituted another block on the road to perception. The sentences in the final theater warnings—"A surprise aggressive move in any direction is a possibility" and "Japanese future action unpredictable but hostile action possible at any moment"—could scarcely have been expected to inform the theater commanders of any change in their strategic situation.

Last but not least we must also mention the blocks to perception and communication inherent in any large bureaucratic organization, and those that stemmed from intraservice and interservice rivalries. The most glaring example of rivalry in the Pearl Harbor case was that between Naval War Plans and Naval Intelligence. A general prejudice against intellectuals and specialists, not confined to the military but unfortunately widely held in America, also made it difficult for intelligence experts to be heard. McCollum, Bratton, Sadtler, and a few others who felt that the signal picture was ominous enough to warrant more urgent warnings had no power to influence decision. The Far Eastern code analysts, for example, were believed to be too immersed in the "Oriental point of view." Low budgets for American Intelligence departments reflected the low prestige of this activity, whereas in England, Germany, and Japan, 1941 budgets reached a height that was regarded by the American Congress as quite beyond reason.

In view of all these limitations to perception and communication, is the fact of surprise at Pearl Harbor, then, really so surprising? Even with these limitations explicitly recognized, there remains the step between perception and action. Let us assume that the first hurdle has been crossed: An available signal has been perceived as an indication of imminent danger. Then how do we resolve the next questions: What specific danger is the signal trying to communicate, and what specific action or preparation should follow?

On November 27, General MacArthur had received a war warning very similar to the one received by General Short in Honolulu. MacArthur's response had been promptly translated into orders designed to protect his bombers from possible air attack from Formosan land bases. But the orders were carried out very slowly. By December 8, Philippine time, only half of the bombers ordered to the south had left the Manila area, and reconnaisance over Formosa had not been undertaken. There was no sense of urgency in preparing for a Japanese air attack, partly because our intelligence estimates had calculated that the Japanese aircraft did not have sufficient range to bomb Manila from Formosa.

The information that Pearl Harbor had been attacked arrived at Manila early in the morning of December 8, giving the Philippine forces some 9 or 10 hours to prepare for an attack. But did an air attack on Pearl Harbor necessarily mean that the Japanese would strike from the air at the Philippines? Did they have enough equipment to mount both air attacks successfully? Would they come from Formosa or from carriers? Intelligence had indicated that they would have to come from carriers, yet the carriers were evidently off Hawaii. MacArthur's headquarters also pointed out that there had been no formal declaration of war against Japan by the United States. Therefore approval could not be granted for a counterattack on Formosan bases. Furthermore there were technical disagreements among airmen as to whether a counterattack should be mounted without advance photographic reconnaissance. While Brereton was arranging permission to undertake photographic reconnaissance, there was further disagreement about what to do with the aircraft in the meantime. Should they be sent aloft or should they be dispersed to avoid destruction in case the Japanese reached the airfields? When the Japanese bombers arrived shortly after noon, they found all the American aircraft wingtip to wingtip on the ground. Even the signal of an actual attack on Pearl Harbor was not an unambiguous signal of an attack on the Philippines, and it did not make clear what response was best.

FRED L. ISRAEL

Military Justice in Hawaii, 1941–1944

The question of whether the peacetime freedoms of speech and press should exist in wartime is complex. Fred L. Israel's article explores some of the larger problems faced by a nation at war. In World War Two, a war against facism, the American government should have been vigilant against adopting the tactics of the enemy; it was, except in a few cases. The treatment of the Japanese-Americans, of whom the nation had an irrational fear, was the outstanding exception.

Three hours after the Japanese attack on Pearl Harbor, Hawaii's Territorial Governor Joseph B. Poindexter proclaimed martial law. He delegated to the military commander of the Hawaiian area all of his executive authority plus "powers normally exercised by judicial officers . . . until the danger of invasion is removed." General Walter Short tersely informed the Hawaiian people that he had assumed the position of military governor with complete control of the territorial government. All civil and criminal court proceedings were immediately suspended, and, before that memorable day expired, Short established military tribunals to try all cases involving any offense committed against "the laws of the United States, the laws of the Territory of Hawaii, or the rules, regulations, orders or policies of the military authorities."

For the next two years, ten months, and seventeen days—long after the invasion danger had passed—martial law remained in effect in the Hawaiian Islands with trial by jury and writ of habeas corpus, as well as other fundamental civil liberties, suspended for "the common good." Complete military rule lasted to March 10, 1943, when, at the insistence of certain territorial and federal officials, modifications were adopted. Not until October 24, 1944, however, was martial law finally terminated. Never before in American history had

© 1967 by the Pacific Coast Branch, American Historical Association. Reprinted from PACIFIC HISTORICAL REVIEW, vol. 36, no. 3, pp. 243–267, by permission of the Branch.

I wish to thank the American Philosophical Society and the City University of New York Research Fund for their grants which facilitated my research work.

citizens been subject to military rule for so prolonged a period. Never before had the civil liberty guarantees of the Constitution received such an overt challenge.

The general scheme for martial law and the suspension of habeas corpus in the Hawaiian Islands had been completed some eighteen months prior to the Japanese attack as army and navy planners contemplated strategic courses necessary to meet any war contingency. The master draft placed paramount importance on holding Oahu Island as the main outlying Pacific base. Oahu, with its Pearl Harbor naval fortress, maintained a primary position in the military structure of the United States before and during World War II. The defense of Oahu was to be accomplished by concentrating a highly mobile force there, capable of repulsing all attacks and of suppressing local Japanese uprisings. Military intelligence reports questioned the allegiance of Japanese-Americans and predicted civilian revolts and massive sabotage, recommending complete control of Hawaii's polyglot population. By the summer of 1940, convinced that Japanese strategy envisioned an eventual Hawaiian invasion via Midway, army policymakers, relying on Federal Bureau of Investigation evaluations, had formulated detailed plans for total civilian control through martial law. When the Japanese attacked, General Short, with presidential approval, assumed direction of every civil activity down to the most petty municipal details. Through a series of orders, the general erected a military government with total power over the inhabitants and their property. "We cannot be too legalistic," Interior Secretary Harold Ickes cabled Poindexter shortly after Pearl Harbor. "The Department would understand too much zeal better than it would too great deliberation."

Martial law means government by a military commander's orders which encompass all legislative, judicial, and executive functions. To be effective, martial law must include the power to punish. "The tempo of war," reasoned army intelligence,

> cannot be hampered by the normal delays existent in time of peace. Justice must be prompt and certain; the civilian courts lack the necessary flexibility. The formalities and delay of presentment, indictment and trial by jury restricted by technical rules created to protect the individual cannot be allowed to obstruct the defense of the nation.

Since intelligence evaluations doubted the loyalty of Hawaii's Japanese-American population, some system had to be devised which would eliminate persons of Japanese ancestry, both aliens and citizens, from participating in local government. Hence, army strategists, concerned with making the territory impregnable, endorsed strict imposition of martial law as well as the confinement of known Japanese agents. "Subversive activities would be a major problem," wrote Secretary of War Henry Stimson in dismissing the constitutional safeguards enunciated in *Ex parte Milligan,* "and whether or not martial law is essential is primarily a matter of vital national interest." President Roosevelt and Secretary of the Navy Frank Knox insisted on still stronger action. Through the spring of 1943, both favored complete evacuation of all Japanese-American citizens and aliens to the mainland or to some less strategic island. Only strong protests from startled army field commanders who feared a catastrophic loss of their principal labor force delayed mass evacuation. "I do not worry about the constitutional question," explained the president. "The whole matter is one of immediate and present war emergency."

Beginning with the first arrival of white men through the transition from the monarchy to the republic to territorial status, strife had marred Hawaii's political and economic life. For decades, sugar and pineapple monopolies dominated the territorial economy, clashing with powerful labor unions as Caucasians provided the capital and a high grade technology, while those of different color supplied the necessary brawn. Contract Japanese laborers had been imported into the islands until 1906 under terms which differed from slavery only in degree. Even as free laborers, thousands lived in abject poverty, exploited by both capitalists and aggressive labor leaders. In 1940, one of every eight permanent residents was a Japanese national, and some 45 percent could claim both Japanese and American citizenship. On December 7, the commanding general found himself the military governor of a community far from tranquil. Under the circumstances—danger of another attack, the large number of Japanese, the need for controlling labor, the urgency for strict military security—all civil activities had military significance. As time passed, the Japanese population amply demonstrated their loyalty to the United States, but in the emergency presented by Pearl Harbor special problems had to be met in special ways. The measures taken in Hawaii were unprecedented, but so was the danger which called them into being. Perhaps the most unprecedented measures involved the administration of justice.

Throughout the territory, from easterly Kauai Island to Hawaii in the west, from small townships to Honolulu, civilian judges found themselves replaced by military officers who now assumed responsibility for justice. Overwhelmed with strategic planning, the military governor delegated administrative responsibility to his executive officer. Through March, 1943, Colonel Thomas Green held that position. Colonel Green actually ruled Hawaii through stern orders issued in the name of the military governor. To Green's thorough satisfaction, the quiescent 72-year-old territorial governor had virtually abdicated, completely surrendering all responsibility and authority. Green, therefore, broadly interpreted his new powers and, using security as the justification, regulated every phase of Hawaiian life. Relying on plans drawn up earlier in the year, he promptly substituted a rather simple military judiciary for the civil system. A commission tried capital offenses while several provost courts, each with a single officer, heard lesser criminal cases. No jury trials were permitted. "The administration of criminal justice is an essential element of martial law," firmly declared General Delos Emmons, who replaced Short as army commander and military governor on December 17, 1941. "The police power is not sufficient as it must have with it the power to punish the offender speedily."

Strict censorship prevented discussion of martial law in the mass media. At cabinet meetings, however, Secretary of the Interior Harold Ickes, whose department supervised the territory, doubted the wisdom of army rule almost from its outset. "I had an excellent opportunity to score a hit on the Secretary of War," boasted Ickes:

He had been trying to explain to the President just what his school was at Charlottesville, Virginia, where the Army is training people for the administration of conquered territories. The President had interposed to say that his idea was that, as soon as the civil authorities were in a position to take over they should do so. At this point I interjected myself. I commended this point of view and asked the President whether, if the military should yield to civilians in conquered territory, what their attitude should be with respect to the civil authorities in American territory.

Roosevelt evaded Ickes' question. But, with the exception of American occupation of enemy lands, no civilian precedent existed for the military commission and the fifteen provost courts instituted in Hawaii. Consisting of six army officers, the commission tried only the most serious cases, carefully following special courts martial rules. All commission sentences were automatically reviewed by a special legal board appointed by the military governor. In its entire operation, the commission tried but eight cases—three of murder and one each of attempted murder, manslaughter, espionage, robbery, and a sex offense. By far though, the provost courts were the most vexatious aspect of military justice.

Designed to be "informal and speedy," these provost courts broadly interpreted their mandate in evolving unique regulations which even army records describe as "questionable" and "not well organized." At a trial, which usually occurred on the same day as the arrest, an armed military prosecutor recited the charges against the prisoner. (In military law, one is presumed guilty until proven innocent.) All witnesses stood in semi-circle before the judge, often without any legal training, who peremptorily questioned them. Cross examination was held to a minimum. When the officer felt that sufficient evidence had been heard, he rendered an immediate decision and imposed sentence—rarely did a trial exceed twenty minutes. Appeals were not permitted, although the legal section of the military governor's office eventually reviewed all sentences —not innocence or guilt. These reviews happened arbitrarily and often months after the start of a prison term. Furthermore, the legal section could only make recommendations to the military governor who exercised final judgment. Lawyers hired by defendants generally proved ineffectual as army judges repeatedly declared in open court their oposition to civilian legal assistance. ("It has come to my attention that Honolulu lawyers think I am prejudiced against them," remarked one provost judge. "Why, I've got nothing whatever against lawyers. They're welcome in my court any time—just so long as they present their case in two minutes and get out.")

"An orderly trial was practically unknown," reported army intelligence. Except for Honolulu, provost transactions remained secret—and proceedings most probably have been destroyed. Honolulu records listed the defendant's name, his residence, nationality, age, occupation, race, the names of witnesses as well as the charge, plea, finding, and sentence. Brief summaries substituted for the usual legally required details—hence, complete trial records contain but terse statements: "theft of goods," "fraudulent bank drawing." During 1942, the three Honolulu provost courts heard 22,480 cases—all but 359, or a little more than one percent, were found guilty. Of the 1,454 people appearing before the courts in November, not one was acquitted. "Defendants," admitted the army, "were from time to time convicted upon very meager evidence [but] many who were guilty and who might have escaped judgment did not escape because of the prompt trials."

On the surface, sentences imposed by provost courts seem inconsistent from court to court and day to day—the maximum penalty being a $5,000 fine and five years imprisonment. The military governor insisted civilians be awed with the need for prompt obedience, thus justifying harsh sentences. A wholly unprecedented situation had been created by the Pearl Harbor attack; considering the constant invasion threat posed by Japan and the never-relenting fear of massive sabotage as well as Hawaii's extreme importance in over-all defense strategy, army officials agreed that civilians had to give strict obedience to military authority.

Available records amply illustrate the sternness of military justice. Fines for drunkenness, for example, jumped from the normal five dollars to one hundred dollars plus a suspended six-month sentence. If the high fine could not be paid, the prisoner worked for the county. According to Green's scale, a two-dollar fine equalled one day's work—hence, it took fifty days to pay for a normal drunkenness conviction. "It is better than that he wander around the streets in an intoxicated condition," reasoned the military governor. In addition to regular penalties, Honolulu provost judges imposed forced blood donations to the community blood bank as an additional sentence. Executive Officer Green extended this practice by allowing "credit" for all donations, with each pint equal to fifteen prison days or thirty dollars. Not infrequently, military police rounded up the Sunday night drunks who were rapidly sentenced the following morning to give a pint of their blood. This unusual penalty remained in force until September 3, 1942. Likewise, provost judges devised sentences which required prisoners to purchase United States War Bonds which the court marked "to be held for the duration of the war." These ownership limitations posed a redemption problem for local banks. Finally, the Bank of Hawaii appealed to the treasury department for a ruling on whether the provost stamp nullified the solemn United States promise to pay on demand. After months of delay, a perplexed treasury official advised the bank to ignore the provost order. Subsequent legal points raised by the treasury secretary caused the military governor to prohibit this sentence after January 28, 1943.

In reviewing Hawaii's years under martial law, the territorial army intelligence section acknowledged: "Sentences were imposed which would scarcely be declared consistent with the best practices of the English common law." Official records abound with cases involving unorthodox punishments which substantiate the army's admission. Honolulu's provost courts, especially during the first months of martial law, violated the very basic rights of the accused—the few cases cited here are by no means atypical. One Honolulu provost, for example, imposed a $1,500 fine and forfeited the license of a leading surgeon for writing a medical liquor prescription, and another sentenced an unemployed eighteen-year-old mechanic to two years at hard labor for stealing "a blanket and several foodstuffs." Honolulu's provost records confirm that non-Caucasians received harsher sentences—two years at hard labor was common for petty thefts committed by whites, while Filipinos and Japanese drew three years for the same offenses. Court-assigned infantry officers imposed the severest sentences—one lieutenant colonel ordered an eighteen-year-old Hawaiian to serve one year at hard labor for tampering with an electric meter. Judge advocate general's officers, on the other hand, tried to be more understanding, often asking former district magistrates for guidance. Homosexuals received the most extreme penalties—terms of five years plus a $2,000 fine for first offenders, with appeals denied. Army officials, aware of inconsistency in sentencing, felt that provosts should not be "shackled" but permitted to "call the shots as they saw them." Finally, as abuses became glaring, on July 15, 1943, the military governor ordered a twelve-part provost code adopted, and the following February his office issued a judicial manual.

Military sentences were severe, especially when compared to the usual civilian penalty for comparable offenses. But, in all fairness to the army, it is necessary to look beyond the actual sentence imposed to the penalty actually served. An analysis of "net" sentences—that is, after any reduction or clemency—reveals the striking fact that, with very few exceptions, "net" sentences were in line with those imposed by mainland civilian courts. Although no appeal could be made from a provost decision, the military governor's legal section eventually checked all charge sheets. If a sentence seemed excessive, the legal officer recommended a reduction or suspension. In addition, many provost judges later granted clemency. As the war situation improved, attempts were made to keep sentences similar to those of civilian courts. On October 24, 1944, the official termination of martial law, only sixteen prisoners convicted by provost courts remained incarcerated in territorial prisons.

There is no convincing proof to show Hawaiians opposed military justice. Honolulu's mayor even praised the "lenient" provost judges for "winning the confidence of the public by the sound common sense they apply to law." Content with the unprecedented wartime boom, business and labor leaders likewise lauded the provost judges and complacently accepted military rule. A study made by the office of strategic services noted that large agricultural and corporate business organizations had been "outstandingly cooperative." Martial law, wrote the president of Honolulu's chamber of commerce, "is safest and best during the emergency." "The exception to the rule," stated business tycoon Walter Dillingham, "was a feeling amongst some of our legal fraternity that we ought to say, 'By God, we ought to maintain the rights of American citizens' and all that sort of hooey that nobody cared a damn about." Hawaiian press reaction to martial law is difficult to evaluate as rigid censorship prevailed; therefore, local editorials should be judged with caution. On September 4, 1942, for example, the Honolulu *Advertiser* commented:

> Hawaii has been a test tube and a guinea pig for what might happen on the mainland. It does not mind the role. It is proud that it has had the opportunity to serve in this humble way. . . . The public has accepted military rule as a fact that is to be with us for no short time. It does not ask its abolition or that Washington turn over all of the duties of the military government to civilian authority.

But, even though Executive Officer Green reviewed this editorial as well as all others, there is very little evidence—either written during or after the war—demonstrating that Hawaiians condemned martial law. In August, 1943, Roger Baldwin of the American Civil Liberties Union attributed the very few complaints received by his office from Hawaii to rigid censorship—there is also the possibility that few were filed. Practical and strategic circumstances precluded normal civilian liberties, and the Hawaiian population apparently understood.

Pearl Harbor confronted the interior department with the most serious challenge in its four-decade administration of the Hawaiian Islands. Congress had vested in the department responsibility for general territorial supervision, and the fiery crusading Harold Ickes, who as a young lawyer had undertaken civil liberties cases without fee and who had rebuked American Fascist and Nazi sympathizers before World War II, now found a major crisis within his own administration. In discussions with the army chief of staff prior to the war, Ickes had not questioned the general martial law proclamations being prepared in the event of a Japanese attack, but now the secretary realized that a Pandora's box had been opened where his concept of martial law sharply differed from the army's interpretation. Once the immediate invasion threat subsided, Ickes and his staff reluctantly cooperated with the new military government but also simultaneously worked for the complete revocation of martial law. "I believe," wrote Ickes, "that the primary responsibility of the military authorities is for the security of the islands, and that the judicial and executive functions affecting civilian affairs can best be carried on by the regularly constituted civil authorities acting in full cooperation with the Commanding General."

"Governor Poindexter has never been anything to cheer about," Harold Ickes noted shortly before Pearl Harbor. And with the crisis, the secretary bypassed Poindexter, who had turned over his powers to the military, by dispatching his personal representative and confidant with a $15 million emergency grant to supervise interior department responsibilities. "Since arrival," reported Benjamin Thoron,

> I have conferred at length with the military and civilian authorities. The basic premises upon which all their actions are based are that the entire Territory is a theater of military operations and that all activities must recognize this situation. The conclusion is drawn that all activity over civil, as well as military, life must reside in the Military Governor.

Recognizing that the army's power superseded Interior's authority, Ickes condescended when Executive Officer Thomas Green stubbornly insisted on the military governor's sole right to allocate civilian emergency funds. If Interior did not agree, threatened Green, he would "take over the territorial treasury." Protest, the secretary instructed Thoron, but "yield if impasse is reached."

Thoron's lengthy uncensored reports stressed the illegal authority assumed by the military in the name of security, detailing wholesale procedural denials of civil liberties by the provost courts. Assuring the Washington office that Hawaiians remained capable of administering their own judiciary, Thoron implored Ickes to help restore civil government before the army further strengthened its control. Ickes' trusted adviser related stories of secret trials—including the death sentence imposed on a civilian who had been denied legal counsel—as well as of other arbitrary military actions. As the Interior staff gathered increasing evidence of military encroachments, Ickes, now convinced Governor Poindexter had erred in his hasty surrender of civil authority, pledged to resist the "repugnant" military—"repugnant to every principle for which we are fighting." The whole thing, he told Assistant Secretary of War John McCloy, "is bad business."

The interior department appealed directly to Green for provost court modifications, but to no avail as the dogmatic General insisted that the military control every phase of civilian life. Polite protests to the war department were rebuffed by McCloy's blunt statement: "Martial law exists in Hawaii and under it the Military Commander has full authority." (McCloy had recently returned from Hawaii where he commended Green for his efficient work, recommending his promotion to brigadier general.) Thoron, convinced the military administration had needlessly exceeded legal bounds, advised his chief to consult with "the highest authority—implemented by the greatest degree of tact." Ickes directed First Assistant Ebert Burlew to prepare the department's formal protest, and with the secretary's endorsement, Burlew and Thoron presented their legally buttressed "thoughts" to McCloy. "The duly constituted civil authorities are ready and able to perform not only their ordinary functions," Burlew reasoned, "but also to undertake the administration of any emergency controls which may be necessary. . . . There is every reason to restore the jurisdiction of the criminal courts and to infringe as little as possible on constitutional guarantees." McCloy received Interior's arguments five days before the air and naval battle of Midway Island (June 3–6, 1942). Midway, 1,100 miles from Honolulu and part of the Hawaiian chain, may well have been the turning point in the Pacific war, but the long road to victory had just begun. Between June 12–21, the Japanese occupied Attu and Kiska islands in the westernmost Aleutians, and on June 21, the Oregon coast was shelled. The assistant secretary of war now cited national security and declined to discuss Hawaii with Interior officials. "The Commanding General," he responded, "is greatly absorbed in the tactical defense at the present time."

Pressed by Interior, the army sought opinions from the field commanders on the necessity for continuing total martial law. General Delos Emmons, Hawaiian theater commander and territorial military governor, vigorously replied that the racially mixed population necessitated complete military control. Defending the fairness of his judiciary, Emmons cabled "my most urgent recommendation that nothing be done that will in any way limit the effectiveness of the military forces in Hawaii." Admiral Chester Nimitz, commander of the Pacific fleet, advised: "The Japanese capacity to inflict damage in this area is still very great. I, therefore, recommend that the Navy Department oppose any change in status quo or any limitations of the authority of the Military Governor." Admiral Ernest King, chief of naval operations, strongly endorsed Nimitz's views. Secretary of the Navy Frank Knox added his

> very grave concern over the menace which is presented in Oahu by
> the large number of unquestionably pro-Japanese who are still at

large. . . . The assumption that the war in the Pacific is already practically won and that there is no longer any menace of significant proportions to the security of Hawaii is, to my view, extremely dangerous and unjustified. I sincerely hope that the powers now given to the Military Governor of Hawaii will not be relaxed at the present time.

Justice Owen Roberts, who had conducted an investigation of the Pearl Harbor disaster, had also cautioned Secretaries Stimson and McCloy of the "great menace" and "potential danger" posed by Hawaii's Japanese population, both citizen and alien, especially if "a pinch came in our fortunes." McCloy now informed Interior officials that tampering with the military government would create confusion.

Nevertheless, undaunted civil libertarian Interior officials relentlessly continued their demands for martial law modifications. Martial law struck Ickes as a synonym for evil. Philosophically opposed to any army rule, he often confused stern and extra-legal measures with severity. Perhaps a more reasonable and less excitable man would have been more understanding of the real problems posed by the geographic location of Hawaii. Ickes questioned General Emmons' claim to judicial fairness by itemizing irrational provost judgments in a lengthy letter to Stimson.

Even the limits that the Articles of War place upon the penalties which courts-martial of a character similar to his Provost Courts and military commissions may impose on soldiers for military offenses were jettisoned, to say nothing of the maximum penalties provided by law for various crimes. . . . I do not think that the records of the War Department will disclose—and I know that no history or military text does—an American "Military Commander" in a martial law area who abolished jury trials, closed courts and assumed civil powers because, in his opinion, it was "better for the people."

Ickes was further incensed because support for martial law came from the "Big Five," a tightly knit oligarchy which had dominated Hawaii's economic and political life since the turn of the century. Throughout his tenure, the secretary fought these powerful interests, championing Hawaiian labor unions in attempts to break their economic grip. ("This group thinks that it is exploiting the Islands by divine right," quipped Ickes. "The 'five families' are descendants of the missionaries who originally went over to save souls and win the natives to Christianity. They soon became more interested in saving other things than souls.")

Determined to oppose the military, Ickes strengthened his staff with the appointment of Abe Fortas as undersecretary on June 18, 1942. Fortas, a brilliant thirty-two-year-old Tennessee lawyer who had been a protégé of William Douglas on the securities and exchange commission, was assigned the problem of restoring civilian government to the Hawaiian people—rapidly. In addition to Fortas, Ickes requested President Roosevelt to nominate Judge Ingram Stainback to be territorial governor. Before accepting though, Stainback received

Ickes' promise that under no circumstances would he be "a mere figure-head with the Commanding General the real Governor." Stainback received his appointment in August, 1942, and this sharp-tongued fifty-nine-year-old aggressive former district judge provided a marked contrast to the physically infirm and elderly Poindexter. In Stainback, Ickes found an administrator who fully agreed with his stand against the military. Finally, as protests from Interior increased, Secretary Stimson yielded to an "exploratory" conference.

The conferences held August 11–20, 1942, between Interior and the war department, and joined by observers of the attorney general, became the first in a prolonged series which lasted until President Roosevelt finally suspended martial law in October, 1944. Throughout, Interior argued, as Ickes phrased it, "the business before us is the emancipation of Hawaii," while army officials stoutly held that national security required complete military control. Ickes argued for the immediate return of all civilian functions to the territorial government. General Emmons demanded that final authority remain with the military governor. Attributing the Midway victory to smooth command functioning, the general feared Ickes' changes would jeopardize all future Pacific operations. Only after Stimson intervened did Emmons even consent to send Green to Washington "to talk things over." The first meetings ended on August 20 when, after considerable prodding by Interior and Justice officials, General Green acquiesced to simultaneous proclamations by Territorial Governor Stainback and General Emmons which, for all practical purposes, restored criminal jurisdiction to the Hawaiian civil courts on a trial basis. ("I feel that I should have done better," confided Green. "It was a tough go. It could be worse, I think, especially since all minds were made up before my arrival.") Ickes was jubilant at the "trial" victory as he wrote Stainback of the "considerable work to get the military to agree." But, when Green returned to Hawaii, and away from the pressures of Washington, he backed out, insisting security necessitated the military's right to try "offenses against the Government" as well as "violations in connection with the war effort." Cabled Stainback, who matched Ickes' flair for the dramatic: "We are worse than a conquered territory."

Infuriated at General Green's turnabout, Ickes unleashed his wrath at the army. Exposing his associates to a string of epithets that only he could muster, the secretary demanded Green's immediate replacement—"and I assure you that I am not going to smile until this happens." "I believe the whole thing to be a tempest in a teapot," commented Green. The army's reversal, though, served to rally the more cautious civil libertarians—Attorney General Francis Biddle, who had exercised moderation and restraint in the dispute, now joined with his more outspoken assistant, James Rowe, Jr., in protesting "this unjustified stern administration of justice." Wrote Rowe: "I am beginning to suspect that we are just sissies. I suspect this because General Green is still riding high, wide and handsome." Even McCloy, who thought the trial agreement "satisfactory," seemed bewildered at Green's "gyrations" which he "didn't like a bit." Understandably, Governor Stainback, the holder of an office shorn of power, was livid with rage as he deluged Ickes with details of army

> stupidity and bungling . . . General Green has complete control of the press; nothing can be published without his approval. . . . General Green has attempted to obtain from the post office copies of

> my official correspondence to you. . . . The Army and Navy are seriously considering the indefinite continuation of military government in Hawaii, even after the war.

After reading these alarming dispatches, Fortas recommended that the military "should be brought out in the open, and should be presented to the President."

On October 7, 1942, Secretary Ickes and Attorney General Biddle, following Fortas' advice, signed a joint letter to President Roosevelt relating the unilateral action of the military authorities in the territory. In sentences wrought with indignation at the total power assumed by the army, the two cabinet members, concerned with the philosophy of martial law rather than with military justification, enumerated examples of the summary legal system "which exceeds in severity that applied to military personnel," concluding that "this stern administration of justice is not required or justified by any need of security or of military necessity." Fortas also suggested delaying the letter if war department officials agreed to reopen negotiations—and when apprised of the contents, McCloy promptly agreed. For the next three months, Ickes, Biddle, Stimson, Fortas, McCloy, and Rowe, plus their assistants and advisers, regularly met to explore the entire military justice procedure—but, with the exception of McCloy's concession that "unilateral promulgation was unfortunate," little was accomplished.

In December, Generals Emmons and Green joined the discussions along with Governor Stainback and Hawaii's Attorney General Garner Anthony. Position papers changed as did the locale of meetings, but the fundamental differences remained. Interior and Justice objected to the military's intrusions in civil affairs with their usurpation of civilian authority while the army, as McCloy repeatedly explained, was "absolutely opposed" to the administration of any phase of martial law by a civilian governor. As Assistant Secretary of War, McCloy, although personally inclined to relax the more stringent military regulations, had to support the field commanders' evaluations that to maintain Hawaii as a bastion required control over the population. General Emmons, for example, emphasized the strategic importance of Oahu in defending the Pacific coast, Canada, and the Panama Canal. Citing supporting statements from General MacArthur and Admiral Nimitz, Emmons predicted a disaster at Oahu "might result in our losing the war to Japan. Admiral Nimitz and I are both firmly of the opinion that the status of martial law should be continued in Hawaii for military reasons of great moment." (General Emmons had briefed the war council and the joint chiefs of staff on the overriding necessity to keep "the ultimate authority in the Islands." Both of these planning groups fully agreed, with several members stressing "an important additional element in the existence of about 90,000 [sic] people of Japanese ancestry in Oahu, an unknown quantity of whom are of doubtful loyalty.") McCloy finally conceded to Francis Biddle,

> I told Abe Fortas yesterday that I found after a long talk with General Emmons that there was a fundamental difference and one which I think raises an issue that we cannot avoid raising [with the President] no matter how much goodwill or effort is made by each side.

The rush to the President was on. Stimson met with Roosevelt on December 27, declaring

> if he [Roosevelt] wanted the fortress of Hawaii to be defended he must give power to the people who are charged with its defense; if he wanted to abolish martial law and give Harold Ickes control, Harold Ickes must take the responsibility of defense; that the man having that responsibility must have the last say on all vital questions. He agreed perfectly. . . . He seemed entirely on our side.

Likewise Ickes, who personally considered Stimson "entirely ignorant of the situation," gained the president's ear. Biddle put his comments in "a strong memorandum." Roosevelt, as Stimson indicated, agreed with the war department—he also told Biddle he agreed with Interior and Justice. The presidential solution was an immediate conference between Secretaries Ickes, Biddle, Stimson, and Knox with instructions to reach an agreement. In his diary, Stimson recorded the confrontation which occurred on December 28: "The meeting today at first bade fair to end in an impasse because Ickes and Biddle were pretty stubborn . . . but after patient discussion we evolved a formula which I think will satisfy them. . . . But, it took time and patience." Actually, Stimson was being optimistic as it took a month of hard negotiating by subordinates to detail the broad principles agreed to by the cabinet members. And, considering the adamant statements made by the military commanders, any compromise was, indeed, a commendable accomplishment.

Embodied in two proclamations issued concurrently on February 8, 1943, by the military governor and the territorial governor, the compromise continued modified martial law. The writ of habeas corpus remained suspended, but the civilian government resumed control of the territory, except in labor regulations and defense matters. Hawaiian courts were given jurisdiction over all violations of civil laws, excluding military personnel. But, provost courts continued to try civilians for violations of general orders, which the military governor could issue "as he deems the military security of the Territory to require." The proclamations became effective on March 10, 1943. "Stainback is off for Hawaii with all sorts of instructions from us to cooperate and with solemn assurances on his part that he will buy every member of the military government a drink, will kiss everybody on both cheeks, and will generally be a good boy," a relieved Abe Fortas penned to John McCloy.

In addition to the demarcation line between civil and military authorities, Stimson conceded to Ickes' demand for the immediate transfer of General Green. Interior and Justice urged a "sympathetic" executive officer, suggesting Charles Poletti, then special assistant to Stimson. The army, however, delayed in replacing Green, much to Ickes' annoyance—especially as dispatches indicated the controversial general was still "bossing" Hawaii. After Ickes continued to press Stimson and McCloy, Green was finally relieved of his post at the end of March, succeeded by his assistant, Colonel William Morrison. The army promptly gave Green the distinguished service medal and promoted him to assistant judge advocate general of the United States Army. "Has it ever struck you that 'face-saving' is no longer an occidental institution?" quipped Ickes.

"There are a lot of faces in these parts that ought to be smashed rather than saved, but we go on saving them."

Martial law was modified, and the military administration of justice curbed —but, for Interior officials, only one step had been accomplished in fulfilling Ickes' pledge to restore civilian control of all civil affairs. Ickes, with his deep abiding faith in democracy, cringed at any military-administered government which, he claimed, sacrificed the precious virtues of democracy for efficiency. Brazen and often contemptuous of his fellow cabinet members, Ickes zealously dedicated himself to a full revocation of martial law: "I have agreed to the compromise," he told Stimson, "only because of my reluctance to carry another difficult controversy to the overburdened desk of the President." Throughout 1943 and 1944, Ickes never lost an opportunity to use some alleged violation of civil liberties by the Hawaiian command as evidence for his cause. When General Robert Richardson, Jr., succeeded Emmons as commanding general on June 1, 1943, Ickes protested his assuming the additional title of military governor. "There would be much more reason for some general to anoint himself as 'Military Governor of Alaska,'" he wrote McCloy. "And yet soldiers up there seem to be content to be soldiers. I hope that you can persuade these 'Military Governors' to put their resonant, if assumed, titles away in mothballs." And, as Governor Stainback furnished the secretary with fresh evidence showing how army regulations adversely affected sound employee-employer relations, Ickes used the material to denounce the entire military control of Hawaiian labor. To Ickes, neither a labor shortage nor national security justified regimentation of free workers by edicts enforced by military tribunals—"It smacks of slave labor to me." Secretary Stimson remained extremely unsympathetic to Ickes' pleas, often disdainfully lecturing him on "the lessons of history" and the need for an adequate defense system:

> I would like to sit down with you over the fire and discuss historical cases of military government in our American history with which I happen to be personally familiar, namely the governments of Cuba, Porto Rico, and the Philippines immediately following and arising out of the Spanish war. . . . To me [this] is one of the brightest pages of enlightened administration in all our American history.

McCloy, always more sympathetic and unruffled by Ickes' temper, justified the remaining military controls by citing field commanders' apprehensions over Hawaiian defense precautions for the Pacific campaigns. Unlike Stimson, McCloy spoke encouragingly about relinquishing all controls as soon as security permitted. Regardless of the explanations though, Ickes steadfastly held to his convictions.

Ickes' protests and Governor Stainback's overdramatic reports—"This is only an example of what we must put up with—how long, oh Lord, how long?" —probably did not hasten revocation of martial law. The successful Pacific campaigns were the main reason for termination. During 1943 and 1944, the allies seized the initiative as naval and amphibious forces boldly struck against Japanese-held islands in the South and Central Pacific—the Solomons, the Gilberts, the Marshalls, and the Marianas. By mid-June, 1944, only 1,300 miles separated American bases from the Japanese mainland, and invasion forces readied for the return to the Philippines. After these epic victories, the war department recommended to the president that martial law in Hawaii terminate. At the request of the White House, Interior officials prepared the necessary proclamation and a presidential covering letter. "The time has come," sighed Ickes. On October 24, 1944, the very day the Battle of Leyte Gulf assured American control of Philippine waters, martial law in Hawaii ended with the writ of habeas corpus restored. Hawaii was now designated as a "military area," the same as other strategic parts of the United States. "At the least sign of any change in the situation for the worse," the president assured Stimson, "I would promptly reestablish martial law."

On February 24, 1944, Lloyd Duncan, a civilian navy department employee, assaulted two marine sentries at the main gate of the Pearl Harbor naval base. Summoned before a provost court, he was found guilty and sentenced to serve six months in the Honolulu county jail. Upon petition, the United States District Court for the Hawaiian territory granted a writ of habeas corpus and heard arguments beginning April 5. Since a case testing the constitutionality of martial law appeared in the making, the justice department dispatched Special Assistant Edward Ennis to defend the military authorities. A lengthy trial record was accumulated; the military, attempting to prove the strategic necessity for martial law, called Admiral Nimitz and General Richardson as expert witnesses—Richardson asserted that the Japanese could still launch an invasion of Hawaii—while Duncan's attorney introduced contrary evidence, contending that victory at Midway in June, 1942, and the March, 1943, proclamations had negated the need for military trials of civilians. Duncan's innocence or guilt remained irrelevant as the presiding judge ruled martial law unconstitutional. "Congress may give the Territory of Hawaii any form of government it may see fit," wrote Judge Delbert Metzger, "but no one in the War Department has such lawful power." Therefore, the provost court which tried Duncan had acted illegally, as it lacked lawful authority over civilians. The writ was sustained, and Duncan discharged.

The day after Duncan's release, Harry E. White filed for a writ of habeas corpus in the same district court. On August 20, 1942, military police had arrested White, a Honolulu stockbroker. Two days later, White, an American citizen and a civilian not connected with the armed forces, was brought before a provost judge and orally charged with embezzlement. White's attorney promptly entered a written plea questioning the court's jurisdiction. The plea was overruled, whereupon White demanded a jury trial. The demand was denied. White then moved for a continuance, citing insufficient time to prepare a defense and the ill health of his attorney. The court also refused this motion, and over White's objection, the trial proceeded. On August 25, after a brief trial during which White was not asked to plead to the charge, the provost judge convicted White and sentenced him to five years in prison. Martial law did not allow an appeal, but an administrative review by the military governor's legal staff reduced White's sentence to four years without assigning any reason.

In White's petition for release on habeas corpus, he claimed the provost court had deprived him of the rights guaranteed by the Fifth and Sixth Amendments. The court granted the writ and began to take evidence. White contended that in August, 1942, no military emergency existed in Hawaii to justify the military trial of civilians for violations of territorial laws. The provost court, therefore, had unlawfully deprived him of his constitutional rights—a proper grand jury trial and the right to call witnesses on his behalf. The army, on the other hand, questioned the issuance of the writ, as martial law had been approved by the president and White had lost his normal constitutional rights. Judge Metzger ruled martial law imposed on Hawaii was itself unconstitutional and, therefore, White had been denied his lawful rights. The court ordered his immediate release.

The government appealed both the *Duncan* and *White* decisions to the Ninth Circuit Court of Appeals which disposed of them *en banc* on November 1, 1944, with three opinions reversing the district court. Substantially, the judges argued martial law had been legally imposed on the territory, warranted by the large Oriental population which "posed a continuous threat to public safety." Likewise, military security justified summary punishment to discourage crimes which endangered the over-all war effort. At the time of the White trial in August 1942, "the civil courts were disabled from functioning," and "the situation necessitated his trial by the military." In the *Duncan* case, however, the judges were confronted with the March 10, 1943, proclamations which substantially restored civil authority. The proclamations, they held, omitted violations of military orders from civilian jurisdiction. Since assaulting a military officer violated military orders, the provost court had tried Duncan legally. "In emergencies arising out of total war," observed the court, "there are fields in which civilian conduct is necessarily impinged upon by regulations of the military, even in areas which are not regarded as part of the theatre of actual warfare." The judgment of the lower court in both cases was reversed. This decision surprised war department officials who, after the lower court ruling, were dismayed at a reversal and began to plan for complete termination of martial law.

Counsel for Duncan and White petitioned the Supreme Court for a writ of certiorari. Citing *Ex parte Milligan* (1866), he posed the same question if, whether in time of war, with civilian courts open and capable of functioning, their powers could be scrapped and military trials substituted. The Supreme Court granted certiorari, and the *Duncan* and *White* cases were argued on December 7, 1945, exactly four years after Pearl Harbor. (In the meantime, the presidential proclamation had formally terminated martial law on October 24, 1944.)

The court delivered four opinions. In a 6 to 2 decision, the Supreme Court reversed the Court of Appeals and declared the army had so exceeded its authority in Hawaii as "to warrant this Court's complete and outright repudiation of the action." Justice Hugo Black wrote for the majority. Chief Justice Harlan Stone and Justice Frank Murphy delivered concurring opinions, while Justice Harold Burton dissented, joined by Justice Felix Frankfurter. Although the term martial law carries no precise meaning and has been used in various ways at different times, reasoned Justice Black, civilian courts and their procedural safeguards are indispensable to our system of government. The president's approval of martial law authorized the military to defend the islands against a rebellion or invasion and did not sanction the suppression of civil courts for military tribunals.

We believe that when Congress passed the Hawaiian Organic Act [1900] and authorized the establishment of "martial law" it had in mind and did not wish to exceed the boundaries between military and civilian power, in which our people have always believed, which responsible military and executive officers had heeded, and which had become part of our political philosophy and institutions prior to the time Congress passed the Organic Act.

Black challenged the army's audacity to try civilians not connected with the armed forces, "for Hawaii since annexation has been held by and loyal to the United States." In his strongly worded concurring opinion, Justice Murphy brushed aside as untenable the army's argument that the civil courts were not swift enough to meet military needs:

But experience has demonstrated that such time is well spent. It is the only method we have of insuring the protection of constitutional rights and of guarding against oppression. The swift trial and punishment which the military desires is precisely what the Bill of Rights outlaws. We would be false to our trust if we allowed the time it takes to give effect to constitutional rights to be used as the very reason for taking away those rights.

The court's majority avoided the national security arguments which the army and the minority opinion stressed. In a sonorously worded decision, the majority, relying on lofty principles, criticized the army for seeking to defend the nation's liberties by temporarily curbing the liberties of the Hawaiian people. The court gave its decision five months after the overwhelming victory in the Pacific. On February 27, 1946, when informed of the court's action, Governor Stainback released the six prisoners still held under provost court sentences.

In retrospect, it is clear that the army had its way. Throughout the war it prevailed in its insistence on military justice in Hawaii as essential to the successful prosecution of the war. Criticized by cabinet officers who placed constitutional guaranties above pragmatic strategy, the army did not relinquish this power until in its opinion the battlefield situation warranted revocation.

The *Ex parte Milligan* dictum of 1866 stated: "Martial law cannot arise from a threatened invasion. The necessity must be actual and present; the invasion real, such as effectually closes the courts and deposes the civil administration." Not even the enormously destructive attack on Pearl Harbor closed the courts. On paper, therefore, it appeared that the Milligan rule should apply. In fact it did not; the counterargument being that it was not adequate in the face of a real emergency imposed by twentieth-century warfare. After the war the Supreme Court in *Duncan* reiterated the *Milligan* position, reestablishing it as a constitutional landmark, tarnished, however, because again the intervention of the court came only after the emergency had passed.

3

1945 to 1960: An Era of Conformity

As World War Two neared its end people everywhere hoped for a new era of peace guaranteed by cooperation among the world's powers. But such hopes were quickly dashed as the United States and Russia each rushed to fill the power vacuum left by the collapse of Germany. A grim cold war dominated the era, wherein the two major powers became locked in a corrosive struggle, each regarding the other as the embodiment of evil. The cold war delimited diplomatic opportunities, threatened civil liberties, and created a gigantic peacetime military establishment. In America a whole generation grew up considering Russia the Great Enemy, fearing internal communist subversion, and living in the shadow of possible atomic warfare. The demagogery of Senator Joseph McCarthy and the lives he injured by his irresponsible tactics were but the most overt manifestation of a noxious foreign and domestic situation unique in American history.

Not surprising was the relatively conservative response of the age. President Harry Truman institutionalized the internationalism of the war years in a policy of containment, aimed at cautious parrying of possible Russian threats. His successor, President Dwight Eisenhower, performed a similar function in domestic policy by placing a conservative imprimatur on the New Deal program but failing to extend its scope. By the mid-fifties domestic and foreign stability had been achieved. The Russians had filled out their European empire without serious challenge as early as 1948, and communist forces in Asia had absorbed all they were to get by 1950, although it required a war in Korea to hold the line achieved then. A Republican President and a Democratic Congress presided over a domestic policy hammered out in the 1930's. The American people clearly decided that public affairs were well in hand and turned with a vengence to the private life. After a generation of crisis, they demanded a rest.

The age of Eisenhower has been described as "the bland leading the bland." Americans were busy with prosperity after a long age, first of depression and then of wartime lack of consumer goods. Millions moved to the suburbs, as a vast, unplanned, often ugly splurge of construction occurred to compensate for the lack of building in the thirties and forties and to accommodate the suddenly booming birth rate. Consumer spending and the generally high estimation in which business enterprise was held recalled the 1920's. Publicists and social scientists began to complain of a dull conformity settling over the land, with one place more and more like another, and human lives increasingly interchangeable. Writers complained of the overemphasis on the private side of life: sex rather than politics, second cars rather than good schools, the desires of the group rather than the values of the individual.

As the decade of the fifties progressed, the blandness of American life began to seem less and less a reality. The Supreme Court, entering its great period of activism and social conscience, reminded Americans of the needs of its black people when no other agency of public life did so. Dissenting voices, which exist in any age, began to acquire an audience again. In 1957 the Russians launched the first large space capsule; Sputnik persuaded millions of Americans that what publicists had been saying about the failures of American education was true. By 1958, many conservatives in Congress were retired, and younger faces that would mark the liberalism of the 1960's entered national life. Social critics like Michael Harrington and C. Wright Mills issued warnings that America had to change directions to help its poor or to preserve its freedom from a military-industrial complex—and surprisingly people began to listen. By the end of the decade, poverty in America had been "discovered" and the plight of the blacks was acknowledged as a moral wrong. Even Dwight Eisenhower, who more than any other man symbolized the mood of the fifties, as though realizing an era had ended, issued his famous warning against the uncontrolled growth of a military-industrial complex. The respite from public excitement had been brief indeed: the exigencies of the modern world scarcely allow a nation many such periods of rest.

~~~~~*17*

SAMUEL LUBELL

The Truman Myth

President Harry Truman enunciated a program called the Fair Deal that was to be an extension of Franklin Roosevelt's New Deal. The rhetoric of Truman's speeches, especially the inaugural address of 1949, promised much, and it is puzzling that the modern Democratic party no longer appears particularly progressive. Perhaps the reality of Truman's accomplishments did not match his rhetoric. Some centers of Democratic strength, notably the urban machines, seem to stand still rather to grow in social awareness. Did local leaders urge the administration to "go slow" because welfare laws jeopardized their organizations? One historian even asks if "the Democratic coalition had ceased to be a 'have-not' coalition and had become interested chiefly in maintaining earlier gains."

Samuel Lubell asks here much the same question about the Fair Deal that Paul K. Conkin asks of the New Deal, and he fashions a similar conclusion. According to Lubell, Truman was by nature a moderate, a border-state politico whose very essence was compromise, and he operated in a period of rapprochement between government and business. Therefore, the Fair Deal never moved off center in domestic politics. Is Lubell merely dramatizing the depth of his own commitment to reform, or is he right that Truman could have done much more? To question the possibilities of politics in the New Deal and Fair Deal is to ask about the possibilities of government today.

From pp. 26–39, THE FUTURE OF AMERICAN POLITICS, 3rd Edition Revised, by Samuel Lubell. Copyright © 1951, 1952, 1956, 1965 by Samuel Lubell. By permission of Harper & Row, Publishers.

1. THE TRUMAN RIDDLE

When the Seventy-fifth Congress reconvened in January, 1938, most of the Senators were dismayed to find that the first order of business before them was the antilynching bill. Particularly among those Senators whose constituencies straddled Northern and Southern prejudices the prospect of having to vote on the proposal stirred much anguish. As one of these Senators explained to a leader of the Southern opposition, "You know I'm against this bill, but if it comes to a vote I'll have to be for it."

This Senator went on to recall how a favorite uncle had served in the Confederate Army and how his mother still associated all Republicans with the "redleg" abolitionists who had helped make the Kansas-Missouri border a guerrilla battlefield during the Civil War period. "All my sympathies are with you," the Senator fervently declared, "but the Negro vote in Kansas City and St. Louis is too important."

Turning to go, Senator Harry S Truman added almost wistfully, "Maybe the thing for me to be doing is to be playing poker this afternoon. Perhaps you fellows can call a no quorum."

This episode is related here for the first time in print, not to raise doubts about President Truman's sincerity in the matter of civil rights—of that more later—but because it brings into focus so clearly the essential political qualities which made Truman President and which remained the key to his whole administration. Few Presidents have seemed more erratic and puzzling to their contemporaries; yet few occupants of the White House have run more consistently true to form.

Truman was commonly pictured as "a little man" hopelessly miscast for the "biggest job in the world." Yet how many of our Presidents gave the historians more to write about? Almost any one of a number of his actions would have made his Presidency memorable—the dropping of the first atomic bomb, the Truman Doctrine of resistance to communism, the Marshall Plan, the Berlin Airlift, his spectacular election triumph in 1948, his abandonment of the tradition of "no entangling alliances" with the signing of the North Atlantic Defense Treaty, our armed intervention in Korea, the firing of General Douglas MacArthur.

The strange thing about these precedent-shattering actions is how basically unchanged things were left. After seven years of Truman's hectic, even furious, activity the nation seemed to be about on the same general spot as when he first came to office.

Consider the three principal conflicts which dominated the Truman years and whose interweavings form the fabric of our times:

Domestically, our economy still trembles with the alternating fevers and chills of threatened inflation and threatened depression, even as it did when World War Two ended. The cold war with Russia continues to pursue its malarial course, now and then sinking into endemic concealment, only to flare up in blood-letting recurrence, with no end in sight. Although both the Wallaceites and Dixiecrats were discredited in 1948, the civil war inside the Democratic party raged on relentlessly through Truman's entire administration.

Nowhere in the whole Truman record can one point to a single, decisive break-through. All his more important policies reduced themselves to one thing —to buying time for the future. Far from seeking decision, he sought to put off any possible showdown, to perpetuate rather than break the prevailing stalemate.

The mystery of where Truman was heading can be answered simply. All his skills and energies—and he was among our hardest-working Presidents— were directed to standing still.

This persistent irresolution can hardly be blamed on a lack of personal courage. A less courageous—or less stubborn—man, in fact, would not have been so resolutely indecisive. It took courage to order American troops into Korea. It also took courage to dismiss General MacArthur at a time when the Republicans were howling so furiously for Secretary of State Dean Acheson's English mustache. Characteristically, both these moves, each so bold in itself, neatly neutralized themselves into a policy of limited action.

This faculty for turning two bold steps into a halfway measure—no mean trick—was Truman's political hallmark. If it applied solely to our relations with the Soviets one might conclude that it was the only shrewd course left between an inability to make peace and an unwillingness to go to war. But the same middle touch could be seen in Truman's handling of domestic political and economic problems. When he took vigorous action in one direction it was axiomatic that he would contrive soon afterward to move in the conflicting direction. In the end he managed to work himself back close to the center spot of indecision from which he started.

In the fight against inflation, for example, Truman warned again and again of the calamitous consequences of uncontrolled price rises and, just as repeatedly, he followed these warnings with actions which aggravated the dangers of inflation. When World War Two ended, he eloquently called for holding the line against inflation to avoid another boom and collapse such as followed World War One. Still, despite the enormous backlog of spending power left over from wartime savings and profits, Truman supported repeal of the excess profits tax, wage increases and liberal credit policies, all of which pumped still more money into the economy.

Again, when Truman called a special session to enact the Marshall Plan, he demanded legislation to control prices. When the Korean War broke out, however, he pointedly refrained from requesting price control powers, even while asking for the broadest authority to mobilize the economy. Why did he seek price control in 1948 but not in 1950? Could it have been that in 1948 he requested legislation which he knew would not be enacted so he could blame the Republican-controlled Congress for whatever happened, while in 1950 he feared that price powers *would* be given him, leaving him no alibi for failing to check the rise in living costs?

Even after Congress forced price control powers on him, Truman delayed acting for several months, while wholesale prices leaped 14 percent and the real value of every defense dollar was cut by one fifth. By the spring of 1951, with the renewal of price control at issue, Truman had once again donned the armor of the champion of the voting consumer.

There is a good deal more behind this curious jerkiness which character-ized Truman's administration than the politician's common desire to face both ways at the same time. Partly it can be attributed to Truman's personality. Where Franklin Roosevelt radiated serene self-confidence, Truman seemed afflicted by an inner sense of inferiority. It might have been an outgrowth of the shyness forced on him as a child because of nearsightedness, or of the financial failures of his father who lost the family farm speculating on the grain market and was reduced to the job of night watchman, or of Truman's own business reverses and his lateness in getting into politics. Thirty-eight years old when he ran for his first political office, he was fifty when he won his seat in the U.S. Senate. On reaching Washington he felt his inadequacy so keenly that he an-nounced he intended to go to law school at night.

Whatever the psychological reason, Truman's personality seemed to de-mand that he alternate between crafty caution and asserting himself boldly, even brashly, as if proving something to himself. His usual instinct appeared to be to play things close to his vest, but periodically he had to unbutton his vest and thump his chest.

Many of his explosive flare-ups probably were forced by his irresolution in allowing situations to build up until drastic action became unavoidable. With the RFC and Internal Revenue Bureau frauds for example, he let matters drift for months until it became clear that a major scandal was in the offing and only then instituted his own "shake-up."

The real key to Truman's determined indecision, however, is the fact that he was the product of political deadlock. It was because stalemate fitted his nature so snugly that he became President. Truman can be considered a "politi-cal accident" in the sense that Roosevelt's death brought him to the White House. But there was nothing accidental about his being in the line of succes-sion. Only a man exactly like Truman politically, with both his limitations and strong points, could have been the Democratic choice for Roosevelt's successor.

2. HOW PRESIDENTS ARE MADE

The ruthless, Darwinian process of natural selection which Truman had to undergo to reach the White House was provided by the fierce struggle between the President and Congress which burst into the open early in 1937 with Roosevelt's proposal to pack the Supreme Court and which has continued to the present.

Roosevelt's winning a third and fourth term has obscured the fact that the last major measure of a New Deal nature which he was able to get through Congress was the Wages and Hours Law in mid-1938. With the failure of the attempted purge of the more conservative Democratic Senators and the Repub-lican gains in the 1938 Congressional election, the anti-New Deal coalition came into undisputed control on Capitol Hill. After that Roosevelt never could work his will with Congress. Through the power of veto, he usually could hold the rebellious Congress in check. Congress, for its part, was able to block any Roosevelt proposal it disliked.

That this President-Congress deadlock did not paralyze the effective functioning of the government can be credited largely to the development of a new profession in Washington—that of the so-called "border-state" politician, who undertook to act as political brokers between the White House and Capitol Hill.

Although many members of this bloc actually came from the border states, the label really represented a state of mind. In favor of Roosevelt's foreign policy, the border Democrats were middle of the roaders on domestic issues. They leaned more toward the farmer than toward labor, but still were not antilabor. In fact, they consciously made a point of remaining acceptable to both the liberals and conservatives, to both the isolationists and interventionists.

Theirs was the balance of compromise, which they employed to mediate between the Democratic extremes, being careful never to throw their influence finally on one side or the other. Probably the most effective single member of the group, until his elevation to the Supreme Court, was South Carolina's Jimmy Byrnes, whose talents were admirably suited to cloakroom negotiation.

In many ways this border-state bloc, which included Senators like Dick Russell of Georgia and Carl Hatch of New Mexico, constituted the real locus of political power in Washington. Roosevelt soon learned what Truman discovered, that to get any proposal through Congress required the approval of these middle-of-the-road Democrats. Throughout Truman's administration whenever the border-state Democrats swung their influence against the Administration it got beaten.

By political geography and personal temperament, Truman was a typical border-state Senator. Campaign biographies usually describe him as having been one of Roosevelt's most faithful supporters and in his first year in the Senate Truman did go down the line for every New Deal measure. But in the struggle within the Democratic party, which developed during Roosevelt's second term, Truman had a way of straying in and out of both camps.

He backed the resolution introduced early in 1937 by Byrnes condemning sit-down strikes. Although supporting Roosevelt on packing the Supreme Court, Truman voted for Pat Harrison of Mississippi for Senate majority leader against Alben Barkley, the White House choice. A regular member of John Garner's convivial "Board of Education," Truman supported the Vice-President's efforts to block a third term.

Garner had calculated that a majority of the 1936 convention delegates consisted of postmasters, marshals, internal revenue collectors, and other federal officeholders, plus their relatives. Hoping to deprive Roosevelt of this support, Garner contrived the Hatch Act, which barred federal officeholders from political activity. Truman supported the Hatch Act. Early in 1940 he issued a statement, "I am not for anyone for a third term."

Nor was Roosevelt especially friendly toward Truman. Several times Truman complained to James A. Farley, then Democratic National Chairman, of being treated unfairly on patronage matters. Roosevelt preferred to consult with Missouri's Governor Lloyd Stark, who was planning to oppose Truman for the

Senate. Late in 1939 Roosevelt tried to get Truman to withdraw in Stark's favor by offering him a $10,000-a-year appointment to the Interstate Commerce Commission.

Truman has described the 1940 Democratic primary as the crucial battle of his entire political career. With Boss Pendergast in jail, the Kansas City organization could not be counted upon for its usual ingenious vote. Truman had no funds of his own for campaign purposes—he couldn't even prevent the family farm from being foreclosed.

One noon at lunch in the office of Edward Halsey, then secretary of the Senate, Truman complained of his difficulties in raising funds for radio talks and political advertising. Byrnes was at the same table. In 1938 Byrnes had taken the lead in opposing Roosevelt's efforts to purge some of the more conservative Senators like Walter George, Bennett Clark, Millard Tydings, Pat McCarran and Guy Gillette. Although Truman was not being openly purged by Roosevelt, Byrnes still felt that no President should interfere in Democratic primary contests. Byrnes sought out Bernard M. Baruch, who had helped finance the fight against the purge, and interested him in Truman's behalf.

Up to this time, Bennett Clark, then senior Senator from Missouri and now a federal judge, had been on the fence taking no active part in the campaign. When Clark decided to support Truman, he also went to Baruch for campaign funds. Again, Baruch contributed generously.

Truman's biographers have made much of his loyalty to those who stuck with him in 1940, like Harry Vaughan and Secretary of the Treasury John Snyder. Yet, during the 1948 campaign, when Baruch refused to join a Democratic fund-raising committee, explaining that he never had accepted such a post before, Truman upbraided Baruch with the taunt that politics was not a one-way street. That action hardly jibes with the legend of Truman's code of unswerving loyalty to his political friends.

It was Baruch, moreover, who sparked the idea which inspired Truman's successful 1948 campaign strategy. Shortly after the Republican Convention, Baruch suggested to Truman that he call the Republican-controlled Congress back into special session, thus providing an arena in which the Republican performance could be matched against the newly drafted Republican platform. Truman was so enthusiastic over this suggestion that he sent Clark Clifford to New York City to discuss the idea more fully with Baruch on the eve of the latter's departure for Europe.

That Baruch should have been interested in Truman by Byrnes, who has become a leader of the anti-Truman opposition within the Democratic party, must surely rate as one of the more ironic footnotes in American political history. The irony deepens in view of how the famous Truman Defense Investigating Committee came to be set up.

Early in 1941 Representative Eugene Cox of Georgia, an uncompromising Roosevelt foe, began demanding an investigation of defense spending. The prospect of an inquiry headed by Cox, a zealot by nature, sent shivers through the heads of the defense agencies. One day Roosevelt explained the concern of the Army and Navy to Byrnes, without referring to Cox by name. "I can fix that by putting the investigation into friendly hands," Byrnes assured the President.

Under its rules, Byrnes explained, the House could not authorize an investigation for a week but the Senate could act in a few hours.

. Some weeks earlier Truman had introduced a resolution for an investigation, which had been referred to the Committee on Audit and Control which Byrnes headed. Calling Truman to his office, Byrnes asked him why had he introduced the resolution? Truman explained that some Missouri contractors were complaining that the big companies were getting all the defense construction contracts. A little pressure on the War Department, he felt, would be a good thing.

"What would you do if the resolution were reported out?" Byrnes asked.

"I know there isn't a chance in the world of your reporting it out," Truman replied. "But if you did I wouldn't conduct the investigation in a way that would hurt defense. You could count on me for that."

Shortly afterward the resolution was reported out and, although no one dreamed it, a new President was in the making.

Truman's able management of the Defense Investigating Committee transformed him into a figure of national importance, earning him a reputation for honesty and fearlessness. What was not widely appreciated was how adroitly Truman appealed to both Democratic factions. Since his Committee's reports were sharply critical of the defense agencies the conservative Democrats were pleased, as were the Republicans. Since the "military" was a favorite committee target the New Dealers also were gratified. An informal understanding existed between the Truman Committee staff and Donald Nelson, the chairman of the War Production Board. Whenever Nelson ran into particular difficulty with the War or Navy departments, he would "leak" his troubles to the Truman Committee, which would then bring pressure on the military.

While the Truman Committee was conducting its able investigations, the attrition of the wartime "Battle of Washington" was steadily shifting the political balance against Roosevelt in favor of Congress. A variety of factors entered into this—the off-year Republican gains in 1942; the vengeful fury of the isolationists who, although supporting the war, drummed constantly with criticism of home front bungling; the failure to bring prices and wages under control; the feuding and squabbling among the government administrators; also the rising resistance in various quarters to wartime restrictions.

In the case of the rubber crisis, the rumbling resentment on Capitol Hill broke through with the passage of a bill which would have disrupted the whole mobilization machinery by setting up a separate rubber administrator independent of Donald Nelson. Roosevelt vetoed the measure. But, confronted with the likelihood that his veto would be overridden, he called upon Baruch, Harvard president James B. Conant, and Karl Compton, then president of the Massachusetts Institute of Technology, to investigate the situation. Their report, unsparing in criticizing the administrative irresponsibility, saved Roosevelt's veto.

The following month Roosevelt pulled Byrnes off the Supreme Court and made him "assistant president" with an office in the White House. The political significance of this action was largely overlooked. It meant that Congress had gained the ascendancy in Washington. After that, the overhanging political question facing the administration became how to come to terms with the dominant coalition in Congress.

Significantly, all of the new administrators Byrnes brought in either had served in Congress or were acceptable on the Hill. Scrappy Leon Henderson gave way as price administrator to Prentiss Brown, a former Senator. Marvin Jones, a former Congressman, was appointed Food Administrator, Fred Vinson, later to become Chief Justice of the Supreme Court, was brought off the Court of Appeals and named Director of Economic Stabilization.

It was hoped that Vinson, who had been a highly popular member of the House Ways and Means Committee, would be able to charm Congress into accepting a stiff tax bill. When Vinson appeared to request $10,500,000,000 in additional taxes, his former colleagues listened to him with obvious good humor. They laughed at his jokes and chuckled when, in his colloquial way, he took out his lead pencil to do some figuring. But when it came time to write the tax bill they ignored everything Vinson had said.

Only about two billion dollars in new taxes were voted. When Roosevelt vetoed the bill, condemning it a bit too pungently perhaps, the Senate rose in front page revolt. Barkley resigned as majority leader, rebuking the President who made hasty amends. Ironically, few of Roosevelt's actions were more conservative in the true meaning of the term or more justified in the national interest than this veto of so obviously inadequate a tax bill. The Senate, though, was less concerned with the merits of its tax position than with showing Roosevelt who was boss.

Further weakening Roosevelt's influence with Congress were the victories of American arms abroad. That may sound like a paradox. But since a two-thirds vote of the Senate would be needed to approve any peace treaty, Roosevelt had to edge closer to the views of Senator George and Senator Arthur Vandenberg, the Republican leader, who headed the conservative coalition in the Senate. Also, with the war's end in prospect, the struggle over who was to control the political destinies of postwar America broke forth in savage earnestness.

To make sure that the future of America would be shaped without benefit of New Deal planning, the Senate killed the National Resources Planning Board. Instead it created its own Postwar Planning Committee, vigilantly headed by George and Vandenberg, which was determined to stamp "conservative" on every postwar policy.

But the problems of war and peace could not be separated so cleanly. Since war contracts were already being canceled, reconversion policies had to be laid down while the war was still on. The Senate, though, bristled jealously at any suggestion of Administration action. Searching for some means of bridging the paralyzing deadlock of suspicion, Roosevelt asked Baruch to prepare a report on reconversion policies. In formulating some of the policies, as in the contract termination law, what Baruch and his associate, John M. Hancock, really did was to negotiate a treaty of peace between Congress and the Executive, as if they were foreign powers.

By the time the 1944 Democratic convention opened in Chicago, the balance of Washington power had shifted so strongly that Roosevelt's running mate had to be acceptable to the conservative Democrats in the Senate. Henry

Wallace, on whom Roosevelt had soured before the end of the 1940 campaign, was never really in the running. He served as a stalking-horse behind whom labor and the big city delegates could hold their votes and bargaining power. The logistics of the Battle of Washington required that the Vice-Presidency go to one of the border-state Democrats who had made a veritable profession of reconciling the warring Democratic wings. The real choice lay between Byrnes and Truman, who had gone to Chicago to nominate Byrnes.

Three principal objections were raised to Byrnes. Negro leaders opposed him as a Southerner. Ed Flynn, the Democratic boss closest to Roosevelt, argued that Byrnes would "hurt the ticket" since he had been converted from Catholicism. Then, as "assistant president," Byrnes had been too forceful for the liking of some labor leaders.

Truman's record, by contrast, could hardly have been more shrewdly tailored to the needs of a compromise candidate. Usually a safe administration vote, he enjoyed the asset of having been opposed for re-election by Roosevelt, which reassured the more conservative Democrats. He had supported Roosevelt in the World Court and neutrality battles, yet two of the Senate's leading isolationists, Burton Wheeler and Bennett Clark, were the men Truman usually looked to for political guidance. Although acceptable to labor, Truman had opposed the sit-down strikes and had voted for the Smith-Connally antistrike act, but not to override Roosevelt's veto of it.

Truman had voted for price control but against the wartime limitation of $25,000 a year on salaries. He had favored all relief appropriations but had helped kill the WPA theater project.

In nominating Truman the embattled Democrats actually were voting to keep the line of succession to the Presidency from passing to either the Northern or Southern Democrats. The 1948 convention found the deadlocked Democrats in the same plight—with the same result. When the Philadelphia convention opened, the clamor to ditch Truman was joined in by such factional rivals as Dixiecrat Southerners and the Americans for Democratic Action, by James Roosevelt and big city bosses like Jacob Arvey of Chicago and Frank Hague of Jersey City. Their unanimity in desiring to get rid of Truman was surpassed only by their inability to agree on anyone to take his place.

This same necessity to preserve the precarious balance within the party dictated the nomination of Barkley, another border-state Senator, as Vice-President.

3. THE RED QUEEN

Compromise made Truman President and—despite the controversies he stirred, the officials he fired and the terrible-tempered letters he wrote—compromise remained the unanswering objective of his Presidency. If this has been obscured it is because of a failure to appreciate that the only form of compromise possible in Truman's administration was stalemate.

Broadly speaking, any middle-of-the-road politician faces one of two prospects. He can allow himself to be torn in two by the forces he is attempting to conciliate. Or he can draw strength from both irreconcilable extremes by playing one off against the other. In view of Truman's Senate record it is not surprising that he followed the latter course.

His role was to raise all issues but to settle none. He repeatedly pressed vigorous recommendations on Congress knowing they would be rejected—not only on inflation control but on civil rights and repeal of the Taft-Hartley Law. During the 1948 campaign he would think of sending Justice Vinson to Moscow on a "peace mission," not long after he had publicly denounced the Soviet leaders as men whose word could not be trusted. One doesn't have to question Truman's sincerity to observe that he appeared happiest when able to make a dramatic show of activity, secure in the knowledge that nothing much was going to happen.

Harsh as that estimate may sound it was Truman's only claim to greatness. There is much to be said, after all, for the mariner who, knowing that he cannot quiet the storm, contrives somehow to stay afloat until the storm has died down of itself. The major problems Truman grappled with were mainly inherited. All were fearfully difficult, perhaps impossible of harmonious solution. As the President of the last center of hope in the world, Truman could hardly confess helplessness. Unable either to reconcile or to ignore the forces in conflict, he tried to stall them off hoping that time would make decision unnecessary.

The contradictions in Truman's actions vanish when one appreciates that actually he dreaded moving too far in any direction, of doing too much or too little. Even his acrobatic economics find their consistency in the fact that he was afraid of both rising and falling prices. When prices went up, Truman wanted them to come down. When they started down, as in 1949, he would become frightened of a possible recession and start up the government's inflationary credit engines. Truman's apologists may contend that this is what is known as a "managed economy"—but the motivating force was to put off politically painful economic adjustments.

Similarly, in foreign affairs Truman would lash out boldly when his hand was forced, as in Korea. When it came to seeing things through, however, he would drag action, as if hoping for something to turn up to make it unnecessary to go too far. Not for two years after the North Atlantic Defense Pact was signed was anything much done to implement it, although in the interval the Soviets exploded their first atomic bomb. So leisurely was the timetable for mobilization laid down in 1950, that it really represented a gamble that the Soviet Union did not intend to go to war. Our slow rate of rearming could be justified only on the basis of faith in Stalin's desire for peace.

If over the course of his Presidency Truman's personal standing rocketed up and down like a roller coaster, it was not because he, himself, was so erratic, but because of changes in the stresses and strains of the forces in conflict.

As the costs and frustrations of continued stalemate grew more burdensome the middle ground on which Truman pitched his political tent tended to crack and crumble. The tensions of office told on him personally as, like Alice's Red Queen, he had to run ever faster in order to stand still. In the glaring light of threatened showdown, all his weaknesses became mercilessly exposed—the wavering evasions, the lack of any policy for achieving decision.

But if that was the source of his weakness, it also explains his astonishing recoveries from the abysmally low levels of public esteem to which he fell at times. The choices of action which Truman tried to evade were all extremely difficult ones, such as splitting the Democratic party or letting the economy run loose to find its natural level, or precipitating a showdown with the Soviets which might cause them to back down but could also bring on war. Truman's constant gamble was that the American public, when confronted with the unpleasant implications of decisive action, would prefer to continue with his policy of calculated drift.

The secret of Truman's political vitality was that he shrewdly planted himself on the furiously dead center of stalemate to which irreconcilables must repair if they are to make a bargain. Whenever the balance of the raging conflict shifted in favor of conciliation, Truman inherited the situation. But could the stalemated forces be held at arm's length indefinitely? Eventually wouldn't they wrench apart whoever stood in the middle?

There we have the essential drama of Truman's Presidency. It was the drama of a man fighting stubbornly and, yes, courageously, to avoid decision. Whether, in standing against these pressures, Truman was a pitiful or heroic figure cannot be answered fully today. Whatever the judgment of the future, it should be clear that Truman was incapable of breaking the stalemate which gripped us and was probably even unwilling to try. Deadlock was the essence of the man. Stalemate was his Midas touch.

LIONEL TRILLING

Sex and Science: The Kinsey Report

According to David Riesman's famous book The Lonely Crowd, *modern man has changed from "inner-directed," or responsive to the authority of his own mind and conscience, to "other-directed," or dependent on external authorities. The change to an economy that no longer rewards individual enterprise and zeal, the compulsions of the mass media, and many other factors have combined to make scarce the inner-directed man.*

In this world of "other direction," where interpersonal relations are crucial to identity, sexuality becomes increasingly important. The open discussion of sexual habits clearly marks off modern man from his forefathers. With the decline of religion in American life, sexual matters passed from under the aegis of the church to the nonnormative world of modern science. Clergymen studied "pastoral psychology." Science had become supreme—and it was a "science of statistics and not of ideas." The price modern man has paid for empirically defined sexual liberty is the subject of Lionel Trilling's widely discussed essay.

By virtue both of its intrinsic nature and its dramatic reception, the Kinsey Report, as it has come to be called, is an event of great importance in our culture.[1] As such an event it is significant in two separate ways, as symptom and as therapy. The therapy lies in the large permissive effect the Report is likely to have, the long way it goes toward establishing the *community* of sexuality. The symptomatic significance lies in the fact that the Report was felt to be needed at all, that the community of sexuality requires now to be established in explicit quantitative terms. Nothing shows more clearly the extent to which modern

[1] *Sexual Behavior in the Human Male.* By Alfred C. Kinsey, Wardell B. Pomeroy, and Clyde E. Martin. Saunders. $6.50.

society has atomized itself than the sexual isolation in ignorance which exists among us. We have censored the folk knowledge of the most primal things and have systematically dried up the social affections which might naturally seek to enlighten and release. Many cultures, the most primitive and the most complex, have entertained sexual fears of an irrational sort, but probably our culture is unique in strictly isolating the individual in the fears that society has devised. Now, having become somewhat aware of what we have perpetrated at great cost and with little gain, we must assure ourselves by statistical science that the solitude is imaginary. The Report will surprise one part of the population with some facts and another part with other facts, but really all that it says to society as a whole is that there is an almost universal involvement in the sexual life and therefore much variety of conduct. This was taken for granted in any comedy that Aristophanes put on the stage.

There is a further diagnostic significance to be found in the fact that our society makes this effort of self-enlightenment through the agency of science. Sex is inextricably involved with morality, and hitherto it has been dealt with by those representatives of our cultural imagination that have been committed to morality—it has been dealt with by religion, ethical philosophy, and literature. But now science seems to be the only one of our institutions which has the authority to speak decisively on the matter. Nothing in the Report is more suggestive in a large cultural way than the insistent claims it makes for its strictly scientific nature, its announcement of divorce from all questions of morality at the same time that it patently intends a moral effect. Nor will any science do for the job—it must be a science as simple and materialistic as the subject can possibly permit. It must be a science of statistics and not of ideas. The way for the Report was prepared by Freud, but Freud, in all the years of his activity, never had the currency or authority with the public that the Report has achieved in a matter of weeks.

The scientific nature of the Report must be taken in conjunction with the manner of its publication. The Report says of itself that it is only a "preliminary survey," a work intended to be the first step in a larger research; that it is nothing more than an "accumulation of scientific fact," a collection of "objective data," a "report on what people do, which raises no question of what they should do," and it is fitted out with a full complement of charts, tables, and discussions of scientific method. A work conceived and executed in this way is usually presented only to an audience of professional scientists; and the publishers of the Report, a medical house, pay their ritual respects to the old tradition which held that not all medical or quasi-medical knowledge was to be made easily available to the general lay reader, or at least not until it had been subjected to professional debate; they tell us in a foreword for what limited professional audience the book was primarily intended—physicians, biologists and social scientists and "teachers, social workers, personnel officers, law enforcement groups and others concerned with the direction of human behavior." And yet the book has been so successfully publicized that at the present writing it stands fourth on the national non-fiction best-seller list.

This way of bringing out a technical work of science is a cultural phenomenon that ought not to pass without some question. The public which receives this technical report, this merely preliminary survey, this accumulation of data, has never, even on its upper educational levels, been properly instructed in the most elementary principles of scientific thought. With this public, science is authority. It has been trained to accept heedlessly "what science says," which it conceives to be a unitary utterance. To this public nothing is more valuable, more precisely "scientific" and more finally convincing, than raw data without conclusions; no disclaimer of conclusiveness can mean anything to it—it has learned that the disclaimer is simply the hallmark of the scientific attitude, science's way of saying "thy unworthy servant."

So that if the Report were really, as it claims to be, only an accumulation of objective data, there would be some question of the cultural wisdom of dropping it in a lump on the general public. But in point of fact, it is full of assumption and conclusion; it makes very positive statements on highly debatable matters and it editorializes very freely. This preliminary survey gives some very conclusive suggestions to a public that is quick to obey what science says, no matter how contradictory science may be, which is most contradictory indeed. This is the public that, on scientific advice, ate spinach in one generation and avoided it in the next; that in one decade trained its babies to rigid Watsonian schedules and believed that affection corrupted the infant character, only to learn in the next decade that rigid discipline was harmful and that cuddling was as scientific as induction.

Then there is the question of whether the Report does not do harm by encouraging people in their commitment to mechanical attitudes toward life. The tendency to divorce sex from the other manifestations of life is already a strong one. This truly absorbing study of sex in charts and tables, in data and quantities, may have the effect of strengthening the tendency still more with people who are by no means trained to invert the process of abstraction and to put the fact back into the general life from which it has been taken. And the likely mechanical implications of a statistical study are in this case supported by certain fully formulated attitudes which the authors strongly hold.

These, I believe, are valid objections to the book's indiscriminate circulation. And yet I also believe that there is something good about the manner of publication, something honest and right. Every complex society has its agencies which are "concerned with the direction of human behavior," but we today are developing a new element in that old activity, the element of scientific knowledge. Whatever the Report claims for itself, the social sciences in general no longer insist that they merely describe what people do; they now have the clear consciousness of their power to manipulate and adjust. First for industry and then for government, sociology has shown its instrumental nature. A government which makes use of social knowledge still suggests benignity; and in an age that daily brings the proliferation of government by police methods it may suggest the very spirit of rational liberalism. Yet at least one sociologist has expressed the fear that sociology may become the instrument of a bland tyranny —it is the same fear that Dostoevsky gave immortal expression to in "The Grand Inquisitor." And indeed there is something repulsive in the idea of men being studied for their own good. The paradigm of what repels us is to be found in the common situation of the child who is *understood* by its parents, hemmed in, anticipated and lovingly circumscribed, thoroughly taped, finding it easier and easier to conform internally and in the future to the parents' own interpretation of the external acts of the past, and so, yielding to understanding as never to coercion, does not develop the mystery and wildness of spirit which it is still our grace to believe is the mark of full humanness. The act of understanding becomes an act of control.

If, then, we are to live under the aspect of sociology, let us at least all be sociologists together—let us broadcast what every sociologist knows, and let us all have a share in observing each other. The general indiscriminate publication of the Report makes sociology a little less the study of many men by a few men and a little more man's study of himself. There is something right in turning loose the Report on the American public—it turns the American public loose on the Report. It is right that the Report should be sold in stores that never before sold books and bought by people who never before bought books, and passed from hand to hand and talked about and also snickered at and giggled over and generally submitted to humor: American popular culture has surely been made the richer by the Report's gift of a new folk hero—he already is clearly the hero of the Report—the "scholarly and skilled lawyer" who for thirty years has had an orgasmic frequency of thirty times a week.

As for the objection to the involvement of sex with science, it may be said that if science, through the Report, serves in any way to free the physical and even the "mechanical" aspects of sex, it may by that much have acted to free the emotions it might seem to deny. And perhaps only science could effectively undertake the task of freeing sexuality from science itself. Nothing has so reinforced moralistic or religious prohibitions as the concepts of science. At some point in the history of Europe, some time in the Reformation, masturbation ceased to be thought of as merely a sexual sin which could be dealt with like any other sexual sin and, perhaps by analogy with the venereal diseases with which the sexual mind of Europe was obsessed, came to be thought of as the specific cause of mental and physical disease, of madness and decay.[2] The prudery of Victorian England went forward with scientific hygiene; and both in Europe and in America the sexual mind was haunted by the idea of *degeneration,* apparently by analogy with the second law of thermodynamics—here is enlightened liberal opinion in 1896: "The effects of venereal disease have been treated at length, but the amount of vitality burned out through lust has never been and, perhaps, never can be adequately measured" (Article "Degeneration" in *The Encyclopedia of Social Reform*). The very word *sex,* which we now utter so casually, came into use for scientific reasons, to replace *love,* which had once been indiscriminately used but was now to be saved for ideal purposes, and *lust,* which came to seem both too pejorative and too human: *sex* implied scientific neutrality, then vague devaluation, for the word which neutralizes the mind of the observer also neuterizes the men and women who are being observed. Perhaps the Report is the superfetation of neutrality and objectivity which, in the dialectic of culture, was needed before sex could be free of their cold dominion.

Certainly it is a great merit of the Report that it brings to mind the earliest and best commerce between sex and science—the best thing about the Report is the quality that makes us remember Lucretius. The dialectic of culture has its

[2] See Abram Kardiner, *The Psychological Frontiers of Society,* p. 32 and p. 441 n.

jokes, and *alma Venus* having once been called to preside protectively over science, the situation is now reversed. The Venus of the Report does not, like the Venus of *De Rerum Natura,* shine in the light of the heavenly signs, nor does the earth put forth flowers for her. She is rather fusty and hole-in-the-corner and no doubt it does not help her charm to speak of her in terms of mean frequencies of 3.2. No *putti* attend her: although Dr. Gregg in his Preface refers to sex as the reproductive instinct, there is scarcely any further indication in the book that sex has any connection with propagation. Yet clearly all things still follow where she leads, and somewhere in the authors' assumptions is buried the genial belief that still without her "nothing comes forth into the shining borders of light, nothing joyous and lovely is made." Her pandemic quality is still here—it is one of the great points of the Report how much of every kind of desire there is, how early it begins, how late it lasts. Her well-known jealousy is not abated, and prodigality is still her characteristic virtue: the Report assures us that those who respond to her earliest continue latest. The Lucretian flocks and herds are here too. Professor Kinsey is a zoologist and he keeps us always in mind of our animal kinship, although he draws some very illogical conclusions from it; and those who are honest will have to admit that their old repulsion by the idea of human-animal contacts is somewhat abated by the chapter on this subject, which is, oddly, the tenderest chapter in the book. This large, recognizing, Lucretian sweep of the Report is the best thing about it and it makes up for much that is deficient and confused in its ideas.

But the Report is something more than a public and symbolic act of cultural revision in which, while the Heavenly Twins brood benignly over the scene in the form of the National Research Council and the Rockefeller Foundation, Professor Kinsey and his coadjutors drag forth into the light all the hidden actualities of sex so that they may lose their dark power and become domesticated among us. It is also an early example of science undertaking to deal head-on with a uniquely difficult matter that has traditionally been involved in valuation and morality. We must ask the question very seriously, How does science conduct itself in such an enterprise?

Certainly it does not conduct itself the way it says it does. I have already suggested that the Report overrates its own objectivity. The authors, who are enthusiastically committed to their method and to their principles, make the mistake of believing that, being scientists, they do not deal in assumptions, preferences, and conclusions. Nothing comes more easily to their pens than the criticism of the subjectivity of earlier writers on sex, yet their own subjectivity is sometimes extreme. In the nature of the enterprise, a degree of subjectivity was inevitable. Intellectual safety would then seem to lie not in increasing the number of mechanical checks or in more rigorously examining those assumptions which had been brought to conscious formulation, but rather in straightforwardly admitting that subjectivity was bound to appear and inviting the reader to be on the watch for it. This would not have guaranteed an absolute objectivity, but it would have made for a higher degree of relative objectivity. It would have done a thing even more important—it would have taught the readers of the Report something about the scientific processes to which they submit their thought.

The first failure of objectivity occurs in the title of the Report, *The Sexual Behavior of the Human Male*. That the behavior which is studied is not that of the human male but only that of certain North American males has no doubt been generally observed and does not need further comment.[3] But the intention of the word *behavior* requires notice. By *behavior* the Report means behavioristic behavior, only that behavior which is physical. "To a large degree the present study has been confined to securing a record of the individual's overt sexual experiences." This limitation is perhaps forced on the authors by considerations of method, because it will yield simpler data and more manageable statistics; but it is also a limitation which suits their notion of reality and its effect is to be seen throughout the book.

The Report, then, is a study of sexual behavior insofar as it can be quantitatively measured. This is certainly very useful. But, as we might fear, the sexuality that is measured is taken to be the definition of sexuality itself. The authors are certainly not without interest in what they call attitudes but they believe that attitudes are best shown by "overt sexual experiences." We want to know, of course, what they mean by an experience and we want to know by what principles of evidence they draw their conclusions about attitudes.

We are led to see that their whole definition of a sexual experience is comprised by the physical act and that their principles of evidence are entirely quantitative. Quality is not integral to what they mean by experience. As I have suggested, the Report is partisan with sex, it wants people to have a good sexuality. But by good it means nothing else but frequent. "It seems safe to assume that daily orgasm would be within the capacity of the average human male and that the more than daily rates which have been observed for some primate species could be matched by a large portion of the human population if sexual activity were unrestricted." The Report never suggests that a sexual experience is anything but the discharge of specifically sexual tension and therefore seems to conclude that frequency is always the sign of a robust sexuality. Yet masturbation in children may be and often is the expression not of sexuality only, but of anxiety. In the same way, adult intercourse may be the expression of anxiety, its frequency may not be so much robust as compulsive.

The Report is by no means unaware of the psychic conditions of sexuality, yet it uses the concept almost always under the influence of its quantitative assumption. In a summary passage (p. 159) it describes the different intensities of orgasm and the various degrees of satisfaction, but disclaims any intention of taking these variations into account in its record of behavior. The Report holds out the hope to respectable males that they might be as frequent in performance as underworld characters if they were as unrestrained as this group. But before the respectable males aspire to this unwonted freedom they had better ascertain in how far the underworld characters are ridden by anxiety and in how far their sexuality is to be correlated with other ways of dealing with anxiety, such as dope, and in how far it is actually enjoyable. The Report's own data suggest that there may be no direct connection between, on the one hand, lack of restraint and frequency, and, on the other hand, psychic health; they tell

[3] The statistical method of the report lies, necessarily, outside my purview. Nor am I able to assess with any confidence the validity of the interviewing methods that were employed.

us of men in the lower social levels who in their sexual careers have intercourse with many hundreds of girls but who despise their sexual partners and cannot endure relations with the same girl more than once.

But the Report, as we shall see, is most resistant to the possibility of making any connection between the sexual life and the psychic structure. This strongly formulated attitude of the Report is based on the assumption that the real reality of sex is anatomical and physiological; the emotions are dealt with very much as if they were a "superstructure." "The subject's awareness of the [erotic] situation is summed up by this statement that he is 'emotionally' aroused; but the material sources of the emotional disturbance are rarely recognized, either by laymen or scientists, both of whom are inclined to think in terms of passion, or natural drive, or a libido, which partakes of the mystic [4] more than it does of solid anatomy and physiologic function." Now there is of course a clear instrumental advantage in being able to talk about psychic or emotional phenomena in terms of physiology, but to make a disjunction between the two descriptions of the same event, to make the anatomical and physiological description the "source" of the emotional and then to consider it as the more real of the two is simply to commit not only the Reductive Fallacy but also what William James called the Psychologist's Fallacy. It must bring under suspicion any subsequent generalization which the Report makes about the nature of sexuality.[5]

The emphasis on the anatomical and physiologic nature of sexuality is connected with the Report's strong reliance on animal behavior as a norm. The italics in the following quotation are mine. *"For those who like the term* it is clear that there is a sexual drive which cannot be set aside for any large portion of the population, by any sort of social convention. *For those who prefer to think in simpler terms of action and reaction,* it is a picture of an animal who, however civilized or cultured, continues to respond to the constantly present sexual stimuli, albeit with some social and physical restraints." The Report obviously finds the second formulation to be superior to the first.

Now there are several advantages in keeping in mind our own animal nature and our family connection with the other animals. The advantages are

---

[4] We must observe how the scientific scorn of the "mystic" quite abates when the "mystic" suits the scientist's purpose. The Report is explaining why the interviews were not checked by means of narcosynthesis, lie-detectors, etc.: "In any such study which needs to secure quantities of data from human subjects, there is no way except to win their voluntary cooperation through the establishment of that intangible thing known as rapport." This intangible thing is established by looking the respondent squarely in the eye. It might be asked why a thing which is intangible but real enough to assure scientific accuracy should not be real enough to be considered as having an effect in sexual behavior.

[5] The implications of the Reductive Fallacy may be seen by means of a paraphrase of the sentence: "Professor Kinsey's awareness of the [intellectual] situation is summed up by his statement that he 'has had an idea' or 'has come to a conclusion'; but the material sources of his intellectual disturbances are rarely recognized, either by laymen or scientists, both of whom are inclined to think in terms of 'thought' or 'intellection' or 'cognition', which partakes of the mystic more than it does of solid anatomy or physiologic function." The Psychologist's Fallacy is what James calls "the confusion of his own standpoint with that of the mental fact about which he is making a report." "Another variety of the psychologist's fallacy is the assumption that the mental fact studied must be conscious of itself as the psychologist is conscious of it." *Principles of Psychology,* vol. I, pp. 196–7.

instrumental, moral, and poetic—I use the last word for want of a better to suggest the mere pleasure in finding kinship with some of the animals. But perhaps no idea is more difficult to use than this one. In the Report it is used to establish a dominating principle of judgment, which is the Natural. As a concept of judgment this is notoriously deceptive and has been belabored for generations, but the Report knows nothing of its dangerous reputation and uses it with the naivest confidence. And although the Report directs the harshest language toward the idea of the Normal, saying that it has stood in the way of any true scientific knowledge of sex, it is itself by no means adverse to letting the idea of the Natural develop quietly into the idea of the Normal. The Report has in mind both a physical normality—as suggested by its belief that under optimal conditions men should be able to achieve the orgasmic frequency of the primates—and a moral normality, the acceptability, on the authority of animal behavior, of certain usually taboo practices.

It is inevitable that the concept of the Natural should haunt any discussion of sex. It is inevitable that it should make trouble, but most of all for a scientific discussion that bars judgments of value. Thus, in order to show that homosexuality is not a neurotic manifestation, as the Freudians say it is, the Report adduces the homosexual behavior of rats. But the argument *de animalibus* must surely stand by its ability to be inverted and extended. Thus, in having lost sexual periodicity, has the human animal lost naturalness? Again, the female mink, we learn, fiercely resists intercourse and must be actually coerced into submission. Is it she who is unnatural or is her defense of her chastity to be taken as a comment on the females, animal or human, who willingly submit or who merely play at escape? Professor Kinsey is like no one so much as Sir Percival in Malory who, seeing a lion and a serpent in battle with each other, decided to help the lion, "for he was the more natural beast of the two."

This awkwardness in the handling of ideas is characteristic of the Report. It is ill at ease with any idea that is in the least complex and it often tries to get rid of such an idea in favor of another that has the appearance of not going beyond the statement of physical fact. We see this especially in the handling of certain Freudian ideas. The Report acknowledges its debt to Freud with the generosity of spirit that marks it in other connections and it often makes use of Freudian concepts in a very direct and sensible way. Yet nothing could be clumsier than its handling of Freud's idea of pre-genital generalized infantile sexuality. Because the Report can show, what is interesting and significant, that infants are capable of actual orgasm, although without ejaculation, it concludes that infantile sexuality is not generalized but specifically genital. But actually it has long been known, though the fact of orgasm had not been established, that infants can respond erotically to direct genital stimulation; and this knowledge does not contradict the Freudian idea that there is a stage in infant development in which sexuality is generalized throughout the body rather than specifically centered in the genital area—the fact of infant orgasm must be interpreted in conjunction with other and more complex manifestations of infant sexuality.[6]

[6] The Report also handles the idea of sublimation in a very clumsy way. It does not represent accurately what the Freudian theory of sublimation is. For this, however, there is some excuse in the change of emphasis and even of meaning in Freud's use of the word.

The Report, we may say, has an extravagant fear of all ideas that do not seem to it to be, as it were, immediately dictated by simple physical fact. Another way of saying this is that the Report is resistant to any idea that seems to refer to a specifically human situation. An example is the position it takes on the matter of male potency. The folk feeling, where it is formulated on the question, and certainly where it is formulated by women, holds that male potency is not to be measured, as the Report measures it, merely by frequency, but by the ability to withhold orgasm long enough to bring the woman to climax. This is also the psychoanalytic view, which holds further that the inability to sustain intercourse is the result of unconscious fear. This view is very strongly controverted by the Report. The denial is based on mammalian behavior —"in many species" (but not in all?) ejaculation follows almost immediately upon intromission; in chimpanzees ejaculation in ten to twenty seconds. The Report therefore concludes that the human male who ejaculates immediately upon intromission "is quite normal [here the word becomes suddenly permissible] among mammals and usual among his own species." Indeed, the Report finds it odd that the term "impotent" should be applied to such rapid responses. "It would be difficult to find another situation in which an individual who was quick and intense in his responses was labeled anything but superior, and that in most instances is exactly what the rapidly ejaculating male probably is, however inconvenient and unfortunate his qualities may be from the standpoint of the wife in the relationship."

But by such reasoning the human male who is quick and intense in his leap to the lifeboat is natural and superior, however inconvenient and unfortunate his speed and intensity may be to the wife he leaves standing on the deck, as is also the man who makes a snap judgment, who bites his dentist's finger, who kicks the child who annoys him, who bolts his—or another's food—who is incontinent of his feces. Surely the problem of the natural in the human was solved four centuries ago by Rabelais, and in the simplest naturalistic terms; and it is sad to have the issue all confused again by the naivety of men of science. Rabelais' solution lay in the simple perception of the *natural* ability and tendency of man to grow in the direction of organization and control. The young Gargantua in his natural infancy had all the quick and intense responses just enumerated; had his teachers confused the traits of his natural infancy with those of his natural manhood, he would not have been the more natural but the less; he would have been a monster.

In considering the Report as a major cultural document, we must not underestimate the significance of its petulant protest against the inconvenience to the male of the unjust demand that is made upon him. This protest is tantamount to saying that sexuality is not to be involved in specifically human situations or to be connected with desirable aims that are conceived of in specifically human terms. We may leave out of account any ideal reasons which would lead a man to solve the human situation of the discrepancy—arising from conditions of biology or of culture or of both—between his own orgasmic speed and that of his mate, we can consider only that it might be hedonistically desirable for him to do so, for advantages presumably accrue to him in the woman's accessibility and responsiveness. Advantages of this kind, however, are precisely the matters of quality in experience that the Report does not consider.[7]

And its attitude on the question of male potency is but one example of the Report's insistence on drawing sexuality apart from the general human context. It is striking how small a role woman plays in *The Sexual Behavior of the Human Male*. We learn nothing about the connection of sex and reproduction; the connection, from the sexual point of view, is certainly not constant yet it is of great interest. The pregnancy or possibility of pregnancy of his mate has a considerable effect, sometimes one way, sometimes the other, on the sexual behavior of the male; yet the index gives but one entry under *Pregnancy*— *"fear of."* Again, the contraceptive devices which *Pregnancy, fear of* requires have a notable influence on male sexuality; but the index lists only *Contraception, techniques*. Or again, menstruation has an elaborate mythos which men take very seriously; but the two indexed passages which refer to menstruation give no information about its relation to sexual conduct.

Then too the Report explicitly and stubbornly resists the idea that sexual behavior is involved with the whole of the individual's character. In this it is strangely inconsistent. In the conclusion of its chapter on masturbation, after saying that masturbation does no physical harm and, if there are no conflicts, no mental harm, it goes on to raise the question of the effect of adult masturbation on the ultimate personality of the individual. With a certain confusion of cause and effect which we need not dwell on, it says: "It is now clear that masturbation is relied upon by the upper [social] level primarily because it has insufficient outlet through heterosexual coitus. This is, to a degree, an escape from reality, and the effect upon the ultimate personality of the individual is something that needs consideration." The question is of course a real one, yet the Report strenuously refuses to extend the principle of it to any other sexual activity. It summarily rejects the conclusions of psychoanalysis which make the sexual conduct an important clue to, even the crux of, character. It finds the psychoanalytical view unacceptable for two reasons (1) The psychiatric practitioner misconceives the relation between sexual aberrancy and psychic illness because only those sexually aberrant people who are ill seek out the practitioner, who never learns about the large incidence of health among the aberrant. (2) The emotional illness which sends the sexually aberrant person to find psychiatric help is the result of no flaw in the psyche itself that is connected with the aberrancy, but is only the result of the fear of social disapproval of his sexual conduct. And the Report instances the many men who are well adjusted socially and who yet show, among them, the whole range of taboo conduct.

The quality of the argument which the Report advances is as significant as the wrong conclusions it reaches. "It is not possible," the Report says, "to insist that any departure from the sexual mores, or any participation in socially

---

[7] It is hard not to make a connection between the Report's strong stand against any delay in the male orgasm and its equally strong insistence that there is no difference for the woman between a clitoral and vaginal orgasm, a view which surely needs more investigation before it is as flatly put as the Report puts it. The conjunction of the two ideas suggests the desirability of a sexuality which uses a minimum of sexual apparatus.

taboo activities, always, or even usually, involves a neurosis or psychosis, for the case histories abundantly demonstrate that most individuals who engage in taboo activities make satisfactory social adjustments." In this context either "neuroses and psychoses" are too loosely used to stand for all psychic malad-justment, or "social adjustment" is too loosely used to stand for emotional peace and psychic stability. When the Report goes on to cite the "socially and intel-lectually significant persons," the "successful scientists, educators, physicians," etc., who have among them "accepted the whole range of the so-called ab-normalities," we must keep in mind that very intense emotional disturbance, known only to the sufferer, can go along with the efficient discharge of social duties; and that the psychoanalyst could counter with as long a list of distin-guished and efficient people who consult him.

Then no one except a straw man would insist that *any* departure from sexual mores, or *any* participation in sexually taboo activities, involves a neuro-sis or a psychosis. It is just at this point that distinctions are needed of a sort which the Report seems not to want to make. For example: the Report comes out in a bold and simple way for the naturalness and normality and therefore the desirability of mouth-genital contacts in heterosexual love-making. This is a form of sexual expression which is officially taboo enough, yet to say that its practice indicated a neurosis or psychosis would be impossible to any psycho-analyst. But a person who disliked or was unable to practice any other form of contact would justify the conclusion that there was a neurotic streak in his psychic constitution. His social adjustment, in the rather crude terms which the Report conceives of it, might not be impaired, but certainly the chances are that his psychic life would show signs of disturbance, not from the practice itself but from the psychic needs which make him insist on it. It is not the breaking of the taboo but the emotional circumstance of the breaking of the taboo that is significant.

The Report handles in the same oversimplified way and with the same con-fusing use of absolute concepts the sexual aberrancy which is, I suppose, the most complex and the most important in our cultural life, homosexuality. It rejects the view that homosexuality is innate and that "no modification of it may be expected." But then it goes on also to reject the view that homosexuality provides evidence of a "psychopathic personality." "Psychopathic personality" is a very strong term which perhaps few analysts would wish to use in this con-nection. Perhaps even the term "neurotic" would be extreme in a discussion which takes "social adjustment," as indicated by status, to be the limit of its analysis of character. But this does not leave the discussion where the Report seems to want to leave it—at the idea that homosexuality is to be accepted as a form of sexuality like another and that it is as "natural" as heterosexuality, a judgment to which the Report is led in part because of the surprisingly large incidence of homosexuality it finds in the population. Nor does the practice of "an increasing proportion of the most skilled psychiatrists who make no attempt to re-direct behavior, but who devote their attention to helping an individual ac-cept himself" imply what the Report seems to want it to, that these psychiatrists have thereby judged homosexuality to be an unexceptionable form of sexuality; it is rather that, in many cases, they are able to effect no change in the psychic disposition and therefore do the sensible and humane next best thing. Their opinion of the etiology of homosexuality as lying in some warp—as our culture judges it—of the psychic structure has not, I believe, changed. And I think that they would say that the condition that produced the homosexuality also produces other character traits on which judgment could be passed. This judgment need by no means be totally adverse; as passed upon individuals it need not be adverse at all; but there can be no doubt that a society in which homosexuality was dominant or even accepted would be different in the nature and quality of its life from a society in which homosexuality was censured.

The refusal of the Report to hold such a view leads us at this point to take into account what seem to be certain motives that animate the work. And when we do, we see how very characteristically American a document it is.

In speaking of its motives, I have in mind chiefly the impulse toward acceptance and liberation, the broad and generous desire for others not to be harshly judged. Much in the Report is to be understood as a recoil from the crude and often brutal rejection which society has made of the persons it calls aberrant. The Report has the intention of habituating its readers to the idea of sexuality in all its manifestations, to establish, as it were, a democratic pluralism of sexuality.

This good impulse shows itself very clearly in certain parts of our intellectual life, often in the more or less official parts. It is, for example, far more established in the universities than most of us, with our habits of criticism of America, particularly of American universities, easily admit. This generosity of mind is to be much admired, yet it is often associated with an almost willed intellectual weakness, with a preference for not making intellectual distinctions, perhaps out of fear that they may turn out to be social discriminations. Somehow the democratic virtues are inclined, in the intellectual life, to lead from the large acceptance of the facts of society to the belief that any use of these facts which perceives values and demonstrates consequences is dangerous.

One result of this set of mind is the worship of the factuality of the fact. There seem to be two criteria for factuality. One is the material physicality of the fact and its relative removal from idea and ideal, from complication and modification. The other is the numerical strength of the fact. As the first criterion is used in the Report it has the effect, ironic in a work that is so clearly directed to democratic values, of removing the human subject from its human implications. As the second criterion is used in the Report it has the effect, equally ironic in a democratic and instrumental document, of preventing the consideration of the consequences of certain forms of human conduct. The two criteria taken together have the effect of suggesting a most ineffectual standard of social behavior—that is, social behavior as it exists. Yet this is contradicted at any number of points and the Report is quite willing to judge among behaviors by various manipulations of its factual criteria. It is impossible to say of the Report that it does not bring light, and necessary to say of it that it spreads confusion.

~~~~~19

IRVING KRISTOL

McCarthyism and Civil Liberties

*Senator Joseph R. McCarthy of Wisconsin flourished during a time
of frenzied international suspicion and rivalry. Russia had survived
World War Two with her economy impaired and her taste for
international adventure soured. She had lowered her seemingly
impenetrable iron curtain. But indigenous communist movements,
from the northern Mediterranean to distant Asia, seemed to be losing for America the world it had fought so hard to preserve. The
uncertain blends of nationalism, ideology, and economic deprivation
that typified the world's troubles were too complex for most
Americans to comprehend. After the war the American imagination,
having exhausted the defeated Fascists and Japanese as the embodiment of evil, settled on the Bolsheviks. The Cold War had begun
in earnest.*

*During these post-World War Two years a search began for
the domestic presence of the foreign foe. A similar Red hunt had
engaged the national attention after the First World War. Concrete evidence of communist influence sparked both movements: in
1919 at least some segments of American labor drew inspiration
from the Bolshevik revolution as did certain anarchists who settled
on May Day as a symbolic date for exploding real bombs; and in
the late forties a young California congressman, Richard Nixon,
exposed at least one probably bona fide American communist, Alger
Hiss. Hiss's stunning rise in government service, capped by an advisory role in the American delegation at Yalta, worked upon receptive imaginations, and a picture evolved of the wily Hiss charming
the ailing F.D.R. into handing eastern Europe to Stalin at Yalta. The
influence of Hiss at Yalta was minor, and America never had eastern
Europe to give away; but in such ways during both postwar eras that
frustration and concern begot distortion and hysteria.*

*The Red hunt after 1918 was violent but short-lived, while
following World War Two international tensions, the loss of China,*

and particularly the Korean War gave continued life to anti-communist fears. The meteoric rise of Senator McCarthy paralleled and outlasted even the Korean conflict. He brilliantly employed the political smear, always linking his antagonists, however remotely, with international communism. Innuendo, guilt by association—any effective charge, often regardless of its truth or falsity—were commonly used by McCarthy to magnify the national hysteria and destroy his enemies. He was as blatant a demogogue as any in America's history; that he at one time commanded wide support in America is a mark against democracy itself.

This essay by Irving Kristol considers the reaction of liberals to McCarthyism; specifically it criticizes several pieces of protest writing that appeared. It is necessary to consider not only the particular points where Kristol catches his adversaries in a logical fallacy, but also to understand the background conditioning of the times. Anyone writing in the early fifties was influenced by the widespread institutional support for the notion of a communist threat. In 1950 few people anywhere in the United States dissented from the view that Russia was bent on world conquest. Men such as George Kennan, a diplomat skilled in deciphering Russian intentions, argued forcefully for containment of Soviet aggression. Only very recently has a contrary picture, finding good and evil on both sides, been drawn by reputable historians.

> Heard ye not lately of a man
> That went beside his witt,
> And naked through the citty rann
> Wrapt in a frantique fitt?

The above tantalizing bit of 17th-century verse was quoted recently in the London *Times Literary Supplement,* in the same issue in which there appeared, elsewhere in its pages, a review of the English edition of Alan Barth's *The Loyalty of Free Men.* This fortuitous juxtaposition was not without its ironic relevance, Mr. Barth's book having been provoked by the "frantique fitt" of McCarthyism, beneath which he saw a cool and calculating assault on the American democracy, and his defense being couched in a cool and calculating eloquence that turns out, upon close examination, to be not nearly the exercise in pure reason it seems.

A close examination, however, Mr. Barth's book and others of its kind have not received. It was hardly to be expected from Senator McCarthy and his friends, who are less famous for their habits of meticulous reading than for their preference for arguing in the large, while the more scholarly sections of American opinion have been so delighted to see the Senator get his, and so soothed by the cadences of a familiar tone, that they have not so much read these books as permitted themselves to be enchanted by them. This enchantment has had its political sequel, for as a result of it there has been drawn a line of battle. On the one side are the men of intellect and sensibility, fair-minded and generous-hearted and confessedly not infallible: the Alan Barths, the Henry Steele Commagers, the Zechariah Chafees, the Howard Mumford Joneses, the Ralph Barton Perrys, the William O. Douglases, and, rather more tentatively committed, the Francis Biddles. On the other side are the mindless men, the kind who get elected to office when the spirit of the age reverts to primitivism, and who wish, under cover of fighting Communism, to squeeze the nation into a Know-Nothing straitjacket.

The line is drawn—and those liberals who have rallied to their positions on the left of it find themselves ever more pressed against the outer walls of the city. The ready quotations from Jefferson about the trees of liberty and the blood of tyrants, the sonorous repetition of Justice Holmes' dissenting opinions, the schoolmaster's measured accents alternating with prophetic indignation—the whole battery has failed significantly to make an impression on the dominant American mood. Senator McCarthy remains blithely on the offensive and his critics give ground before him. It is a most exasperating and melancholy situation for liberals to be in; yet in proportion as they fail in strength, they gain in their sense of petulant righteousness.

Is it conceivable that the line was incorrectly drawn in the first place? The liberals are loath to weigh the possibility lest it give comfort to the enemy; Senator McCarthy for his part has no cause for dissatisfaction with things as they are; but those of us who are the displaced persons of this war might reflect on this question to our advantage. Perhaps it is a calamitous error to believe that because a vulgar demagogue lashes out at both Communism and liberalism as identical, it is necessary to protect Communism in order to defend liberalism. This way of putting the matter will surely shock liberals, who are convinced that it is only they who truly understand Communism and who thoughtfully oppose it. They are nonetheless mistaken, and it is a mistake on which McCarthyism waxes fat. For there is one thing that the American people know about Senator McCarthy: he, like them, is unequivocally anti-Communist. About the spokesmen for American liberalism, they feel they know no such thing. And with some justification.

With what justification, can be seen from an illustrative incident involving Professor Henry Steele Commager, a distinguished historian who never was a Communist and never will be. In the May 1947 issue of *Harper's,* Professor Commager wrote a spirited article that began as follows:

"On May 6 a Russian-born girl, Mrs. Shura Lewis, gave a talk to the students of the Western High School of Washington, D.C. She talked about Russia —its school system, its public health program, the position of women, of the aged, of the workers, the farmers, and the professional classes—and compared, superficially and uncritically, some American and Russian institutions. . . . Mrs. Lewis said nothing that had not been said a thousand times, in speeches, in newspapers, magazines and books. She said nothing that any normal person could find objectionable."

What greatly disturbed Professor Commager was that this inoffensive speech did give rise to a furor in Washington. Congressmen bellowed that our schools were being subverted, the principal of the school came forward with a humble apology, the superintendent of schools for the nation's capital swore it would never happen again, and the speech itself was reprinted (after some discussion of the wisdom of exposing the public to inflammation) in the Congressional Record as a horrible example. Professor Commager saw in this a reflection of an anti-Communist hysteria that threatened to engulf all civil liberties, and he pleaded earnestly that reason control the anti-Communist passion, lest we find ourselves saddled with an anti-Communist orthodoxy no less reprehensible than the Communist one. His article was hailed as a kind of liberal manifesto, and was reprinted—alongside John Stuart Mill and John Milton—in Howard Mumford Jones' *Primer of Intellectual Freedom* (1949). Evil won a transient victory in the seats of power and Good won a permanent niche in the anthologies—a familiar tale.

Familiar, that is, until one goes to the Congressional Record and reads through this speech that no "normal person could find objectionable." Mrs. Lewis' English was broken, but her sentiments were whole:

"They call it collective farm—the peasants farm and divide up products according to work put in by each individual during the years. As a result of planning, unemployment is completely wiped out. . . .

"In Russia right now people absolutely do not worry about today or tomorrow. They never think 'All of a sudden I lose a job.' That fear doesn't exist among Russian people. . . .

"No matter where you live you have to work. What the Russian people have, they are more secure about this. They work. They need not worry much about losing the job. They are free to travel from one place to another, and each person must work 25 years for after that he is able to get a pension. No matter where you work—in this plant or another, 25 years and then you get 50% of your salary and live the rest of your life. . . .

"I never appreciated the life in Russia until I live here. Here you have to work hard in order to live, use all your courage not to die. . . .

"I read all the papers here and occasionally I go to the Library of Congress and read all papers printed in Moscow. It is very interesting, and when I read these papers always you can see here evidence of press where people talk all the time about having a war, to throw the atomic bomb on Russia, to destroy because they have a system which is very prideful. At the present time Russians are busy to restore all those houses, all those cities, all those towns. Russian people make streets, plants, produce new style of shoes, new fashion of dress, new production, and never they talk about having a war."

The echoes this awakened in Congress may have been exaggerated, but they were not factitious or beside the point. Obviously, Professor Commager can argue that it will not harm American school children to encounter an occasional Communist apologist in the flesh; one may even go further and say it would do them good. However, in the first place, Mrs. Lewis was not introduced as a Communist apologist but as an informed reporter, and, in the second place, everything she said should have been objectionable to every normal person, and especially to a historian like Professor Commager—for the good and sufficient reason that it was a tissue of lies. For Professor Commager to defend the rights of Communists to free speech is one thing, for him to assert that there is nothing objectionable in mendacious pleading in support of Communism is quite another. The conclusion "any normal person" will draw from such behavior is that, for whatever reason, his critical faculties are less alert when he looks out of the left corner of his eye.

Indeed, the heart of the matter is exactly that he looks at Communism out of the *left* corner of his eye. Professor Commager seems to be seduced by the insidious myth according to which Communism is a political trend continuous with liberalism and democratic socialism, only more impatient and inclined to the fanatical, only more "radical" than its companions who are not quite so "left." It is a myth that Senator McCarthy, for his own ends, is happy to accept, since it allows him to tag a New Dealer as being by nature an embryonic Communist. Neither the Professor nor the Senator is concerned to see that the antithesis of "left" and "right" no longer suits the political realities; that measured by the ideals of the French or even Russian Revolution, Communism today is as counter-revolutionary as Louis XVI or Kolchak ever was; that if one wishes to defend the civil liberties of Communists (as the Senator does not), one must do so on the same grounds that one defends the civil liberties of Nazis and fascists—no more, no less.

Professor Commager might retort that he knows all this full well, and that he is for civil liberties for everyone, fascist, Communist, or what-have-you. But if a Nazi had, in 1938, addressed a high-school audience in this country, extolling the accomplishments of Hitler's regime, presenting a thoroughly fictitious account of life in Nazi Germany, never once mentioning the existence of concentration camps—would Professor Commager find in such a speech "nothing that any normal person could find objectionable"? It is doubtless an injustice to him even to conceive of the possibility.

This notion of Communism as "left" and therefore at an opposite pole from fascism, which is "right," appears to have become intrinsic to the liberal outlook. It is imbedded in the meretricious historical analogies, in the rolling phrases about "the forces of freedom and those of fear," beneath which there lies the gross metaphysic of the liberal Manichee, apportioning the universe to "forward-looking" and "backward-looking" demiurges. It helps explain how Professor Commager can permit himself to write: "After all, it is no accident that the nations dedicated to freedom won the two great wars of the 20th century and those committed to totalitarianism went under"—when it is not only no accident, it is not even a fact. The same notion is evidenced in Zechariah Chafee's explanation (in his essay in the recent symposium *Civil Liberties Under Attack*) of the origin of Communist fronts: "It is inevitable that the membership of organizations formed to bring about change should include some persons who want a great deal of change"—as if Professor Chafee and the Communists were agreed on the direction of the change, quarreling only over the measure. It is the presupposition from which Ralph Barton Perry (in his new book *The Citizen Decides*) can deduce that Communism is "democratic" by virtue of being a revolt of the "masses" against the "classes," that the Soviet regime is a government "for the people with the consent of the people" though not by the people, and that the Chinese Communist leaders are "hostages" of a popular revolution.

Moreover, after staring out of the left corner of the eye for any length of time, there comes an irrepressible inclination to wink. How else explain, for instance, the attitude Alan Barth takes toward the Hiss-Chambers affair? He can begin a sentence: "Insofar as Chambers may be credited with having told the truth. . . ."; or: "whatever the guilt of Alger Hiss and whatever the utility of exposing it and punishing it a decade later. . . ." About Whittaker Chambers and the Communist "informer" in general, he is no longer judiciously bland but is knowingly tart: "The ex-Communists, conscious of their betrayal of American values, wanted the comfort of company; they had to show that many others, even many who were highly respected, had been as recreant as they." In other words, Chambers in telling the truth is a man of malice, Hiss in denying it is his defenseless victim. Hiss's guilt is problematic and, in any case, not important; Chambers' wickedness is certain.

On Owen Lattimore, there is liberal unanimity: he got a raw deal. Professor Commager believes (in his contribution to *Civil Liberties Under Attack*) that the attack on Lattimore was an attack on "independence and non-conformity." Professor Chafee laments: "Owen Lattimore did his own thinking and look how his services were appreciated." Alan Barth is casually positive: "Dr. Lattimore's ordeal was, of course, only the most spectacular instance of legislative punishment of teachers for expressing their opinions." About the worst that can be said for such arrant nonsense is that it is uttered in all sincerity. For the incontrovertible facts of the case are, "of course," that Owen Lattimore did *not* do his own thinking; that his "ordeal" was the public demonstration of this fact, that he was a faithful and enormously influential fellow-traveler who for more than a decade followed the Communist line as if magnetized by it, including a docile zig-zag during the Stalin-Hitler pact. Is it really no legitimate concern of Congress that such a man was appointed advisor to Chiang Kai-shek, that he accompanied Vice-President Wallace during his tour of Asia, that he was admired and listened to by important people in the State Department?

In his denunciation of Lattimore's pro-Communist record and in hurling unsubstantiated charges against him (chief of Soviet espionage, etc.), Senator McCarthy may well have been aiming a blow against independence of mind and nonconformity of spirit. For Messrs. Commager, Barth, and Chafee to defend Lattimore's pro-Communist record in order to defend such independence and nonconformity, is for them to play the Senator's game, on the losing side.

It is equally futile for liberals to try to match Senator McCarthy's irresponsible declamations with a crafty rhetoric of their own, especially when this rhetoric, while not designedly pro-Communist, is compelled by the logic of disingenuousness and special pleading to become so in effect. The need for disingenuousness arises out of a refusal to see Communism for what it is: a movement guided by conspiracy and aiming at totalitarianism, rather than merely another form of "dissent" or "nonconformity." Hence the liberal argument runs askew of reality and must clothe itself with neat obfuscation.

Once again, Professor Commager obliges with a superior specimen:

"The House Un-American Activities Committee has launched an attack on the Lawyers' Guild as a pro-Communist or 'subversive' organization. The chief basis for this attack is, as far as we know, that the Guild has proffered its services to the defense of Communists under indictment for violation of the Smith Act. We need not inquire into the accuracy of this charge or into the degree of zeal displayed by the Lawyers' Guild. Let us ask rather what are the logical conclusions to be drawn by the position which the House Committee has adopted? They are two: that certain criminals are so despicable that they are not entitled to counsel, and that a lawyer who defends a criminal is himself sympathetic to crime."

That phrase in the second sentence, "as far as we know," is curious. It implies strongly that the only conceivable explanation of the Committee's attitude is the action of the Guild in providing lawyers to defend indicted Communists, and that there is no public information which gives plausibility to the Committee's belief that the Guild is a "front" organization, controlled and run by Communists. On the contrary, however, "as far as we know," and we know much further than Professor Commager suggests, the Lawyers' Guild is a Communist creation that, as A. A. Berle stated when he resigned from it in 1940, "is not prepared to take any stand which conflicts with the Communist party line." Moreover, the House Committee on Un-American Activities has collected and published sufficient evidence to demonstrate this beyond cavil—which leads one to think that if Professor Commager spent nearly as much time reading the records of Congressional hearings as he does denouncing them, we should all be better off.

The entire third sentence is even more curious: "We need not inquire into the accuracy of this charge or into the degree of zeal displayed by the Lawyers' Guild." If we take "zeal" to mean pro-Communism (in the context, that is all it can mean), then the degree of this zeal and the accuracy of the charge of pro-Communism are precisely what we *do* need to inquire into. How can we know whether to sanction or condemn the Committee's investigation of the Guild as a pro-Communist organization unless we make an effort to find out if the Guild is or is not, in fact, a pro-Communist organization? Even Professor Commager surreptitiously ignores his own disclaimer, as the last two sentences of his paragraph show. Obviously, the two "logical conclusions" flow, not from the Committee's premise, but his own: namely, that the Lawyers' Guild is neither pro-Communist nor subversive. From the Committee's own premise, quite other logical conclusions may be inferred—one of them being that the Committee is engaged in showing up Communist fronts for what they are. Professor Commager's "logic" is a sleight-of-hand whereby premises that are prejudiced in favor of the Communist interpretation of affairs are made to pass for natural conclusions.

In the same vein, there is a liberal rhetoric of insinuation that works under cover of a high moral posture. Its net effect is to give a backhanded credence to the Communist assertion that it is impossible to oppose Communism vigorously without walking into the arms of Black Reaction. It is the kind of thing represented in the following observation of Alan Barth's:

"In the New York trial of eleven Communist Party leaders in 1949, a number of FBI undercover operatives who had joined the party appeared as prosecution witnesses. How widely such agents have been dispersed in labor unions, in lawful voluntary associations, and in political groups is a matter of mere conjecture. But it is certainly a matter of legitimate concern to Americans who care about preservation of the traditional rights of privacy."

A noble sentiment, and the unwary reader assents—who is against the right to privacy, and who is not prepared to be concerned with its violation? Only the exceptionally attentive will note that the supposed threat to "the traditional rights of privacy" is "a matter of mere conjecture." Whose conjecture? We are not told. Is there any ground for such a conjecture? We are not told that either. Is Mr. Barth against the use of undercover agents in principle? He does not say so. Is he against the use of undercover agents in Communist organizations? He does not say this, either. He would seem to be against dispersing FBI agents in bona fide labor unions, lawful voluntary associations, and political groups, and reminds us of the consequences. But who is for it? The answer, which he does not bother to give, is: nobody—and that is why the FBI is doing no such thing and why the whole business is a "matter of mere conjecture." In the course of Mr. Barth's innuendoes, however, the onus has been neatly shifted from the Communist conspirators to the FBI agents who identified them.

The same technique of persuasion is at work in such a statement as this one by Professor Commager: "It will be useful to determine, a generation from now, whether those universities that have purged their faculties are actually stronger than they were before the purges occurred—stronger in those essentials that go to make a univesity." This has about it so trembling an air of bitter-sweet wisdom that it seems positively boorish to ask: just which universities would Professor Commager describe as "purged"? Surely Columbia is not one of them, for Professor Commager is not the kind of man who would retain his post on a "purged" faculty. Is it Yale? Princeton? Harvard? University of Chicago? The list could be extended indefinitely, and never provoke an affirmative response, for there is not a single university in the United States that can be said to have been, in any meaningful sense of the word, "purged." There has been no more than a handful of cases where Communist college teachers have been dismissed, and less than a handful of cases where non-Communists have been unjustly fired as "Reds." To call this a "purge"—even regardless of whether or not one thinks Communists have a right to teach in colleges—is to echo Communist propaganda.

Perhaps Professor Commager had in mind the University of California, where several dozen (out of a total of more than a thousand) teachers found the idea of a special loyalty oath—the content of which was irrelevant to their action—so offensive and intolerable that they exercised their constitutional right to refuse to swear it, and consequently had to seek other employment. Granting that the notion of a special oath for teachers is obnoxious, and even conceding that this minority was correct and courageous in its particular reaction to it—is it the part of sobriety to insist, as Professor Commager goes on to do, that the philosophy behind the actions of California's Board of Trustees does not differ "in any essentials" from the philosophy behind the totalitarian control of university teaching? One swallow does not make a spring, or one injustice an apocalypse.

Despite their fondness for clichés of Communist manufacture, all these liberal spokesmen are sincerely anti-Communist—otherwise, what they have to say would be of little interest to anyone. But their rejection of Communism has all the semblance of a preliminary gesture, a repudiation aiming to linger in the memory as a floating credential. It has little relation to all the ensuing scenes of the political drama, where bad conscience and stubborn pride join to guide the liberal through his role.

Did not the major segment of American liberalism, as a result of joining hands with the Communists in a Popular Front, go on record as denying the existence of Soviet concentration camps? Did it not give its blessing to the "liquidation" of millions of Soviet "kulaks"? Did it not apologize for the mass purges of 1936–38, and did it not solemnly approve the grotesque trials of the Old Bolsheviks? Did it not applaud the massacre of the non-Communist left by the GPU during the Spanish Civil War? All this carries no weight with Alan Barth who knows that, though a man repeat the Big Lie, so long as he is of a liberal intention he is saved. On the participation of non-Communists in Communist fronts during the 30's, he writes: "In the main, their participation, while it lasted, was not only innocent but *altogether* praiseworthy." (My italics.)

Even Francis Biddle, who is generally cautious, remarks in his book *The Fear of Freedom:* "What makes an organization subversive? If a vast majority of its members are Communists but its conduct has always been exemplary, advocating desirable social reforms which Communists usually back, it can hardly fit the description."

One surmises that Mr. Biddle is not really so politically naive as this statement, on the face of it, would lead one to believe. He must know what it means to be "subversive," since it was he who, as Attorney General, sent eighteen members of a minuscule Trotskyist sect to jail in 1942 for being just that; he must know how Communists work, how front organizations act as an ancillary to the Communist party apparatus, since this is a matter of common knowledge and Mr. Biddle is uncommonly literate and intelligent. No, it was no elevated unsophistication that urged him on, but rather a sense of shame and cowardliness to confess that shame. Mr. Biddle, like Mr. Barth, refuses to admit what is now apparent: that a generation of earnest reformers who helped give this country a New Deal should find themselves in retrospect stained with the guilt of having lent aid and comfort to Stalinist tyranny. This is, to be sure, a truth of hindsight, an easy truth. But it is the truth nonetheless, and might as well be owned up to. If American liberalism is not willing to discriminate between its achievements and its sins, it only disarms itself before Senator McCarthy, who is eager to have it appear that its achievements *are* its sins.

There is a false pride, by which liberals persuade themselves that no matter what association a man has had with a Communist enterprise, he is absolutely guiltless of the crimes that Communism has committed so long as he was moved to this association by a generous idealism. There is a political mythology, by which liberals locate Communism over on the "left," in a zone exempt from the unsparing verdict directed against the totalitarian "right." There is also a fear, a fear that the American democracy in an excess of anti-Communism will gather its abundant energy into a wave of "conformism" that will drown all free thought. This pride, this mythology, this fear all unite for a liberal prejudgment of issues (e.g., the cases of Alger Hiss, Owen Lattimore, William Remington, Harry Dexter White) which is not easy to explain on a purely rational view. It is what stimulates a flood of irrelevant and gaudy prose about loyalty in the abstract ("like love it must be given freely," etc.) while it shuns a careful discussion of Communist disloyalty in the concrete.

Of the three factors, the fear of "conformism" or "orthodoxy" is probably the most influential in its appeal, for it is founded in some degree on objective fact. Alexis de Tocqueville and John Stuart Mill, both friendly critics of the egalitarian trend, pointed out long ago that in every democratic society there is an inherent tendency toward a "despotism of public opinion"; where the majority makes the laws, it may also wish—especially in feverish and unsettled times—to make opinion, lauding the popular and extirpating the unpopular. In America, where the people are more powerful than elsewhere, and where there is, too, a significant tradition of vigilante-ism, the danger of despotism of public opinion is proportionately greater. When the State Department is forced to suspend an exhibition abroad of modern American art because some Congressmen denounce it as "Communistic," the danger of such a despotism seems more than academic, and many otherwise sensible people are led to reprehend any attempt to unveil Communist activities or Communist beliefs as a malignant form of "punishment by publicity," which will soon be extended to all opinions that illiterate and narrow-minded Congressmen detest.

What these people do not see is that Communism, because it is a conspiratorial movement, has not the faintest interest in any genuine resistance to the despotism of public opinion. These martyrs whose testament is—"I refuse to answer on the grounds that it might incriminate me"! These "intellectuals" of Hollywood and radio who are outraged at a Congressman's insistence that they say what they actually believe, and who wail that they are in danger of—being excluded from well-paying jobs! Is this the vibrant voice of "nonconformity" and "dissent"? Are these the American rebels of today? Oddly enough, the majority of American liberals seem to think so: they have been moved to indignation by the questions, but never moved to disgust by the answers. Presumably, this is what they think a dissenter looks like, and no sadder commentary is possible on the corruption they have inflicted on themselves. And not only on themselves—for this image of a dissenter happens to coincide with the image held by Joseph McCarthy and Pat McCarran, for whom the dissenter is *per se* a scheming subversive. No greater spur to the despotism of public opinion can be imagined than this identification of free thought with underground conspiracy.

There is only one way the despotism of public opinion can be resisted. That is for a person with unpopular views to express himself, loudly, brazenly, stubbornly, in disregard of the consequences. Such a person may have to suffer for his convictions, as others have suffered before him, and as others will suffer after. But the responsibility for the mind's freedom in a democracy lies with the intransigent thinker, with his courage to shout the truth in the face of the mob, with his faith that truth will win out, and with his maddening commitment to the truth, win or lose. Yet, during all the occasions of the past several years, not a single liberal voice was to say to these strange "victims": "Speak up and damn the consequences! Let them take your job—as they certainly will anyway; tell the truth—you have nothing to lose and honor to gain!" Instead, there were erudite essays on the "right to a job" that would have corroborated William James in his mournful conviction that "the prevalent fear of poverty among our educated classes is the worst moral disease from which our civilization suffers."

Still, unworthy as these "victims" are, may they not, despite themselves, represent the right of the individual to hold whatever opinions he pleases without having to give a public accounting of them? Even if these Communists and Communist sympathizers are despicable, don't they have the right to believe privately anything they please? This is the way the question is frequently put, and it reveals a total misapprehension as to what Communism really is.

Communism is an idea, beyond question. Indeed, it is an Idea, and it is of the essence of this Idea that it is also a conspiracy to subvert every social and political order it does not dominate. It is, furthermore, an Idea that has ceased to have any intellectual status but has become incarnate in the Soviet Union and the official Communist parties, to whose infallible directives unflinching devotion is owed. A person who is captive to this idea can, at any time, in any place, be called upon to do whatever the Idea, i.e., the Party, thinks necessary. Since this is so, it is of considerably more than private interest if a person is held by the Idea—he is, all appearances to the contrary, a person with different loyalties, and with different canons of scrupulousness, from ours. To grant him an "immunity by silence" is to concede the right to conspiracy, a concession no government has ever made or ever will make.

This sounds exaggerated, as it must, being so foreign to the nature of American political experience. Many of us have known Communists, and most of them conveyed no impression of being conspirators. But then, some of us have known Nazis too, and they conveyed no immediate association with gas chambers. It is quite impossible to judge a political movement by the personality of an individual member. Roosevelt certainly didn't see in Stalin any symptoms of blood lust. Hermann Goering in jail struck one as a clever clown. And there are still plenty of people who can't believe that Alger Hiss ever did any such thing.

No doubt there are some present members of the Communist party who would, in a showdown, break free of the Idea and rally to the democratic cause. Unfortunately, we have no way of knowing who they are. No doubt there are some present members and fellow-travelers of the Communist party who would sooner or later get disillusioned with Communism if they were permitted to hold down their present jobs as teachers, civil service workers, etc., whereas they are likely to harden in the face of persecution. Unfortunately, it is quite as impossible to tell the citizens of Oshkosh, some of whom have suffered personal loss as a result of the war in Korea, that there is no harm in having their children taught the three R's by a Communist, as it would have been to persuade the citizens of Flatbush in 1939 that there was no cause for excitement in their children being taught by a Nazi, or to convince a businessman that it is smart practice for him to pay a handsome salary to someone pledged to his "liquidation." No doubt some of these people became Communists after having suffered during the depression, or during a labor conflict, or as a result of race prejudice, and society must bear its share of the blame. Unfortunately, as Fitzjames Stephens remarked many decades ago: "It does not follow that because society caused a fault it is not to punish it. A man who breaks his arm when he is drunk may have to cut it off when he is sober."

The problem of fighting Communism while preserving civil liberties is no simple one, and there is no simple solution. A prerequisite for any solution, however, is, firstly, a proper understanding of Communism for what it is, and secondly, a sense of proportion. So long as liberals agree with Senator McCarthy that the fate of Communism involves the fate of liberalism, and that we must choose between complete civil liberties for everyone and a disregard for civil liberties entirely, we shall make no progress except to chaos. So long as one is either for or against "guilt by association," it is hopeless to try to distinguish between a sober and silly definition of that concept—sober when it is taken to mean, as for instance the Canwell Committee of the State of Washington took it to mean, that anyone who is a member of three or more organizations officially declared subversive is to be considered a Communist; silly when it is taken to mean, as many government loyalty boards take it to mean, that if you have a friend or a relation who is sympathetic to Communism, you are a "bad security risk." So long as Senator McCarthy and the liberals agree that the right of a Communist to teach or be a government employee is a matter of principle, we shall remain distant from that intelligent discrimination between one case and another, and one situation and another, which alone can give us our true bearings. And so long as Senator McCarthy and the liberals are enmeshed in this confusion, the Senator will grow the stronger, for such confusion is the sap of his political life.

Inevitably, liberals will disagree among themselves about the appropriateness of specific actions with regard to Communism and Communists. Inevitably, too, there will always be a basic division and antagonism between liberalism (which is solicitous of freedom) and McCarthyism (which is not). But if a liberal wishes to defend the civil liberties of Communists or of Communist fellow-travelers, he must enter the court of American opinion with clean hands and a clear mind. He must show that he knows the existence of an organized subversive movement such as Communism is a threat to the consensus on which civil society and its liberties are based. He must bluntly acknowledge Communists and fellow-travelers to be what they are, and then, if he so desires, defend the expediency in particular circumstances of allowing them the right to be what they are. He must speak as one of *us,* defending *their* liberties. To the extent he insists that they are on our side, that we can defend our liberties only by uncritically defending theirs, he will be taken as speaking as one of them.

DWIGHT MACDONALD

Masscult and Midcult

A game of one-upmanship can be played with the categories de-lineated in Dwight Macdonald's essay on mass culture. Name brands of practically any commodity can be placed on a scale beginning with mass culture, rising to middlebrow or midcult, and finally to highbrow. That taste delineates class better than income or educa-tion is one of Macdonald's themes, but such factors as age, ethnic background, or individual sensibility can throw the scale askew. Many familiar products have a fairly stable place. Whether a person reads Confidential, The National Enquirer, *or* The New Yorker, *drinks Thunderbird wine, Manischewitz, or can translate* Wachenheimer Gerümpel Riesling Trockenbeerenauslese, *or listens to country and western music, the Hollywood strings, or chamber music will determine where he fits on the scale.*

In the years since Macdonald wrote, mass culture has taken remarkable turns. Popular music, thought unbearable in the early and middle nineteen fifties, is now often a delight; the Beatles' music is everywhere respected. Popular culture has entered the arts. Whatever our doubts about Andy Warhol's soup cans, he and others have succeeded in bringing a freshness and vitality into the realm Macdonald set against the humanist tradition. The following essay is, however, more than a period piece. Philistinism is still much in evidence—and a militantly anti-philistine snobbery is simply its transcendent form.

For about two centuries Western culture has in fact been two cultures: the traditional kind—let us call it High Culture—that is chronicled in the textbooks, and a novel kind that is manufactured for the market. This latter may be called Mass Culture, or better Masscult, since it really isn't culture at all. Masscult is a parody of High Culture. In the older forms, its artisans have long been at work. In the novel, the line stretches from the eighteenth-century "servant-girl romances" to Edna Ferber, Fannie Hurst and such current ephemera as Burdick, Drury, Michener, Ruark and Uris; in music, from Hearts and Flowers to Rock 'n Roll; in art, from the chromo to Norman Rockwell; in architecture, from Victorian Gothic to ranch-house moderne; in thought, from Martin Tupper's *Proverbial Philosophy* ("Marry not without means, for so shouldst thou tempt Providence;/But wait not for more than enough, for marriage is the DUTY of most men.") to Norman Vincent Peale. (Thinkers like H. G. Wells, Stuart Chase, and Max Lerner come under the head of Midcult rather than Masscult.) And the enormous output of such new media as the radio, television and the movies is almost entirely Masscult.

This is something new in history. It is not that so much bad art is being produced. Most High Culture has been undistinguished, since talent is always rare —one has only to walk through any great art museum or try to read some of the forgotten books from past centuries. Since only the best works still have currency, one thinks of the past in their terms, but they were really just a few plums in a pudding of mediocrity.

Masscult is bad in a new way: it doesn't even have the theoretical possibility of being good. Up to the eighteenth century, bad art was of the same nature as good art, produced for the same audience, accepting the same standards. The difference was simply one of individual talent. But Masscult is something else. It is not just unsuccessful art. It is non-art. It is even anti-art.

> There is a novel of the masses but no Stendhal of the masses; a music for the masses but no Bach or Beethoven, whatever people say . . . [André Malraux observes in "Art, Popular Art and the Illusion of the Folk"—(*Partisan Review,* September–October, 1951).] It is odd that no word . . . designates the common character of what we call, separately, bad painting, bad architecture, bad music, etc. The word "painting" only designates a domain in which art is possible. . . . Perhaps we have only one word because bad painting has not existed for very long. There is no bad Gothic painting. Not that all Gothic painting is good. But the difference that separates Giotto from the most mediocre of his immitators is not of the same kind as that which separates Renoir from the caricaturists of *La Vie Parisienne.* . . . Giotto and the Gaddi are separated by talent, Degas and Bonnat by a schism, Renoir and "suggestive" painting by what? By the fact that this last, totally subjected to the spectator, is a form of advertising which aims at selling itself. If there exists only one word . . . it is because there was a time when the distinction between them had no point. Instruments played real music then, for there was no other.

But now we have pianos playing Rock 'n Roll and *les sanglots longs des violons* accompanying torch singers.

Masscult offers its customers neither an emotional catharsis nor an aesthetic experience, for these demand effort. The production line grinds out a uniform product whose humble aim is not even entertainment, for this too implies life and hence effort, but merely distraction. It may be stimulating or narcotic, but it must be easy to assimilate. It asks nothing of its audience, for it is "totally subjected to the spectator." And it gives nothing.[1]

Some of its producers are able enough. Norman Rockwell is technically skilled, as was Meissonier—though Degas was right when he summed up the cavalry charge in *Friedland, 1806:* "Everything is steel except the breastplates." O. Henry could tell a story better than many contributors to our Little Magazines. But a work of High Culture, however inept, is an expression of feelings, ideas, tastes, visions that are idiosyncratic and the audience similarly responds to them as individuals. Furthermore, both creator and audience accept certain standards. These may be more or less traditional; sometimes they are so much less so as to be revolutionary, though Picasso, Joyce and Stravinsky knew and respected past achievements more than did their academic contemporaries; their works may be seen as a heroic breakthrough to earlier, sounder foundations that had been obscured by the fashionable gim-crackery of the academies. But Masscult is indifferent to standards. Nor is there any communication between individuals. Those who consume Masscult might as well be eating ice-cream sodas, while those who fabricate it are no more expressing themselves than are the "stylists" who design the latest atrocity from Detroit.

The difference appears if we compare two famous writers of detective stories, Mr. Erle Stanley Gardner and Mr. Edgar Allan Poe. It is impossible to find any personal note in Mr. Gardner's enormous output—he has just celebrated his centenary, the hundredth novel under his own name (he also has knocked off several dozen under pseudonyms). His prose style varies between the incompetent and the nonexistent; for the most part, there is just no style, either good or bad. His books seem to have been manufactured rather than composed; they are assembled with the minimum expenditure of effort from identical parts that are shifted about just enough to allow the title to be changed from *The Case of the Curious Bride* to *The Case of the Fugitive Nurse.* Mr. Gardner obviously has the production problem licked—he has rated his "native abilities" as Very Good as a lawyer, Good as a business analyst, and Zero as a writer, the last realistic estimate being the clue to his production-line fertility—and his popularity indicates he has the problem of distribution well in hand. He is marketing a standard product, like Kleenex, that precisely because it is not related to any individual needs on the part of either the producer or the consumer appeals to the widest possible audience. The obsession of our fact-minded culture with the processes of the law is probably the lowest common denominator that has made Mr. Gardner's unromantic romances such dependable commodities.

Like Mr. Gardner, Mr. Poe was a money-writer. (That he didn't make any is irrelevant.) The difference, aside from the fact that he was a good writer, is that, even when he was turning out hack work, he had an extraordinary

---

[1] "Distraction is bound to the present mode of production, to the rationalized and mechanized process of labor to which . . . the masses are subject. . . . People want to have fun. A fully concentrated and conscious experience of art is possible only to those whose lives do not put such a strain on them that in their spare time they want relief from both boredom and effort simultaneously. The whole sphere of cheap commercial entertainment reflects this dual desire."—T. W. Adorno: *On Popular Music.*

ability to use the journalistic forms of his day to express his own peculiar personality, and indeed, as Marie Bonaparte has shown in her fascinating study, to relieve his neurotic anxieties. (It is simply impossible to imagine Mr. Gardner afflicted with anything as individual as a neurosis.) The book review, the macabre-romantic tale, the magazine poem, all served his purposes, and he even invented a new one, the detective story, which satisfied the two chief and oddly disparate drives in his psychology—fascination with horror (*The Murders in the Rue Morgue*) and obsession with logical reasoning or, as he called it, "ratiocination" (*The Purloined Letter*). So that while his works are sometimes absurd, they are rarely dull.

It is important to understand that the difference between Mr. Poe and Mr. Gardner, or between High Culture and Masscult, is not mere popularity. From *Tom Jones* to the films of Chaplain, some very good things have been popular; *The Education of Henry Adams* was the top nonfiction best seller of 1919. Nor is it that Poe's detective stories are harder to read than Gardner's, though I suppose they are for most people. The difference lies in the qualities of Masscult already noted: its impersonality and its lack of standards, and "total subjection to the spectator." The same writer, indeed the same book or even the same chapter, may contain elements of both Masscult and High Culture. In Balzac, for instance, the most acute psychological analysis and social observation is bewilderingly interlarded with the cheapest, flimsiest kind of melodrama. In Dickens, superb comedy alternates with bathetic sentimentality, great descriptive prose with the most vulgar kind of theatricality. All these elements were bound between the same covers, sold to the same mass audience, and, it may well be, considered equally good by their authors—at least I know of no evidence that either Dickens or Balzac was aware of when he was writing down and when he was writing up. Masscult is a subtler problem than is sometimes recognized.

"What is a poet?" asked Wordsworth. "He is a man speaking to men . . . a man pleased with his own passions and volitions, and one who rejoices more than other men in the spirit of life that is in him." It is this human dialogue that Masscult interrupts, this spirit of life that it exterminates. Evelyn Waugh commented on Hollywood, after a brief experience there: "Each book purchased for motion pictures has some individual quality, good or bad, that has made it remarkable. It is the work of a great array of highly paid and incompatible writers to distinguish this quality, separate it and obliterate it." This process is called "licking the book"—i.e., licking it into shape, as mother bears were once thought to lick their amorphous cubs into real bears; though here the process is reversed and the book is licked not into but out of shape. The other meaning of "licked" also applies; before a proper Hollywood film can be made, the work of art has to be defeated.

The question of Masscult is part of the larger question of the masses. The tendency of modern industrial society, whether in the USA or the USSR, is to transform the individual into the mass man. For the masses are in historical time what a crowd is in space: a large quantity of people unable to express their human qualities because they are related to each other neither as individuals nor as members of a community. In fact, they are not related *to each other* at all but only to some impersonal, abstract, crystallizing factor. In the case of crowds, this can be a football game, a bargain sale, a lynching; in the case of the masses, it can be a political party, a television program, a system of industrial production. The mass man is a solitary atom, uniform with the millions of other atoms that go to make up "the lonely crowd," as David Riesman well calls our society. A community, on the contrary, is a group of individuals linked to each other by concrete interests. Something like a family, each of whose members has his or her special place and function while at the same time sharing the group's economic aims (family budget), traditions (family history), sentiments (family quarrels, family jokes), and values ("That's the way we do it in *this* family!"). The scale must be small enough so that it "makes a difference" what each person does—this is the first condition for human, as against mass, existence. Paradoxically, the individual in a community is both more closely integrated into the group than is the mass man and at the same time is freer to develop his own special personality. Indeed, an individual can only be defined in relation to a community. A single person in nature is not an individual but an animal; Robinson Crusoe was saved by Friday. The totalitarian regimes, which have consciously tried to create the mass man, have systematically broken every communal link—family, church, trade union, local and regional loyalties, even down to ski and chess clubs—and have reforged them so as to bind each atomized individual directly to the center of power.

The past cultures I admire—Periclean Greece, the city-states of the Italian Renaissance, Elizabethan England, are examples—have mostly been produced by communities, and remarkably small ones at that. Also remarkably heterogeneous ones, riven by faction, stormy with passionate antagonisms. But this diversity, fatal to that achievement of power over other countries that is the great aim of modern statecraft, seems to have been stimulating to talent. (What could be more deadly than the usual post-Marx vision of socialism as equality and agreement? Fourier was far more perceptive when he based his Utopia on cabals, rivalry, and every kind of difference including what he called "innocent mania.") A mass society, like a crowd, is inchoate and uncreative. Its atoms cohere not according to individual liking or traditions or even interests but in a purely mechanical way, as iron filings of different shapes and sizes are pulled toward a magnet working on the one quality they have in common. Its morality sinks to the level of the most primitive members—a crowd will commit atrocities that very few of its members would commit as individuals—and its taste to that of the least sensitive and the most ignorant.

Yet this collective monstrosity, "the masses," "the public," is taken as a human norm by the technicians of Masscult. They at once degrade the public by treating it as an object, to be handled with the lack of ceremony of medical students dissecting a corpse, and at the same time flatter it and pander to its taste and ideas by taking them as the criterion of reality (in the case of the questionnaire-sociologists) or of art (in the case of the Lords of Masscult). When one hears a questionnaire-sociologist talk about "setting-up" an investigation, one realizes that he regards people as mere congeries of conditioned reflexes, his concern being which reflex will be stimulated by which question. At the same time, of necessity, he sees the statistical majority as the great Reality, the secret of life he is trying to unriddle. Like a Lord of Masscult, he is—professionally —without values, willing to take seriously any idiocy if it is held by many people (though, of course, *personally* . . .). The aristocrat's approach to the masses is less degrading to them, as it is less degrading to a man to be shouted at than to be treated as nonexistent. But the *plebs* have their dialectical revenge: indifference to their human quality means prostration before their statistical quantity, so that a movie magnate who cynically "gives the public what it wants"—i.e., assumes it wants trash—sweats with anxiety if the box-office returns drop 5 percent.

Whenever a Lord of Masscult is reproached for the low quality of his products, he automatically ripostes, "But that's what the public wants, what can I do?" A simple and conclusive defense, at first glance. But a second look reveals that (1) to the extent the public "wants" it, the public has been conditioned to some extent by his products, and (2) his efforts have taken this direction because (a) he himself also "wants" it—never underestimate the ignorance and vulgarity of publishers, movie producers, network executives and other architects of Masscult—and (b) the technology of producing mass "entertainment" (again, the quotes are advised) imposes a simplistic, repetitious pattern so that it is easier to say the public wants this than to say the truth which is that the public gets this and so wants it. The March Hare explained to Alice that "I like what I get" is not the same thing as "I get what I like," but March Hares have never been welcome on Madison Avenue.

For some reason, objections to the giving-to-the-public-what-it-wants line are often attacked as undemocratic and snobbish. Yet it is precisely because I do believe in the potentialities of ordinary people that I criticize Masscult. For the masses are not people, they are not The Man in the Street or The Average Man, they are not even that figment of liberal condescension, The Common Man. The masses are, rather, man as non-man, that is man in a special relationship to other men that makes it impossible for him to function as man (one of the human functions being the creation and enjoyment of works of art). "Mass man," as I use the term, is a theoretical construction, an extreme toward which we are being pushed but which we shall never reach. For to become wholly a mass man would mean to have no private life, no personal desires, hobbies, aspirations, or aversions that are not shared by everybody else. One's behavior would be entirely predictable, like a piece of coal, and the sociologists could at last make up their tables confidently. It is still some time to 1984 but it looks unlikely that Orwell's anti-Utopia will have materialized by then, or that it will ever materialize. Nazism and Soviet Communism, however, show us how far things can go in politics, as Masscult does in art. And let us not be too smug in this American temperate zone, unravaged by war and ideology. "It seems to me that nearly the whole Anglo-Saxon race, especially of course in America, have lost the power to be individuals. They have become social insects like bees and ants." So Roger Fry wrote years ago, and who will say that we have become less apian?

Like the early capitalism Marx and Engels described in *The Communist Manifesto,* Masscult is a dynamic, revolutionary force, breaking down the old barriers of class, tradition, and taste, dissolving all cultural distinctions. It mixes, scrambles everything together, producing what might be called homogenized culture, after another American achievement, the homogenization process that distributes the globules of cream evenly throughout the milk instead of allowing them to float separately on top. The interesting difference is that whereas the cream is still in the homogenized milk, somehow it disappears from homogenized culture. For the process destroys all values, since value-judgments require discrimination, an ugly word in liberal-democratic America. Masscult is very, very democratic; it refuses to discriminate against or between anything or anybody. All is grist to its mill and all comes out finely ground indeed.

Life is a typical homogenized magazine, appearing on the mahogany library tables of the rich, the glass cocktail tables of the middle class, and the oilcloth kitchen tables of the poor. Its contents are thoroughly homogenized as its circulation. The same issue will present a serious exposition of atomic energy followed by a disquisition on Rita Hayworth's love life; photos of starving children picking garbage in Calcutta and of sleek models wearing adhesive brassières; an editorial hailing Bertrand Russell's eightieth birthday (A GREAT MIND IS STILL ANNOYING AND ADORNING OUR AGE) across from a full-page photo of a matron arguing with a baseball umpire (MOM GETS THUMB); nine color pages of Renoir paintings followed by a picture of a roller-skating horse; a cover announcing in the same size type two features: A NEW FOREIGN POLICY, BY JOHN FOSTER DULLES and KERIMA: HER MARATHON KISS IS A MOVIE SENSATION.[2] Somehow these scramblings together seem to work all one way, degrading the serious rather than elevating the frivolous. Defenders of our Masscult society like Professor Edward Shils of the University of Chicago—he is, of course, a sociologist—see phenomena like *Life* as inspiriting attempts at popular education—just think, nine pages of Renoirs! But that roller-skating horse comes along, and the final impression is that both Renoir and the horse were talented.

The historical reasons for the rise of Masscult are well known. There could obviously be no mass culture until there were masses, in our modern sense. The industrial revolution produced the masses. It uprooted people from their agrarian communities and packed them into factory cities. It produced goods in such unprecedented abundance that the population of the Western world has increased more in the last two centuries than in the preceding two millennia—poor Malthus, never has a brilliantly original theorist been so speedily refuted by history! And it subjected them to a uniform discipline whose only precedent was the "slave socialism" of Egypt. But the Egypt of the Pharaohs produced no Masscult any more than did the great Oriental empires or the late Rome of the proletarian rabble, because the masses were passive, inert, submerged far below the level of political or cultural power. It was not until the end of the eighteenth century in Europe that the majority of people began to play an active part in either history or culture.

Up to then, there was only High Culture and Folk Art. To some extent,

---

[2] The advertisements provide even more scope for the editors' homogenizing talents, as when a full-page photo of a ragged Bolivian peon grinningly drunk on cocoa leaves (which Mr. Luce's conscientious reporters tell us he chews to narcotize his chronic hunger pains) appears opposite an ad of a pretty, smiling, well-dressed American mother with her two pretty, smiling, well-dressed children (a boy and a girl, of course—children are always homogenized in our ads) looking raptly at a clown on a TV set, the whole captioned in type big enough to announce the Second Coming: RCA VICTOR BRINGS YOU A NEW KIND OF TELEVISION—SUPER SETS WITH "PICTURE POWER." The peon would doubtless find the juxtaposition piquant if he could afford a copy of *Life,* which, luckily for the Good Neighbor Policy, he cannot.

Masscult is a continuation of Folk Art, but the differences are more striking than the similarities. Folk Art grew mainly from below, an autochthonous product shaped by the people to fit their own needs, even though it often took its cue from High Culture. Masscult comes from above. It is fabricated by technicians hired by businessmen. They try this and try that and if something clicks at the box office, they try to cash in with similar products, like consumer-researchers with a new cereal, or like a Pavlovian biologist who has hit on a reflex he thinks can be conditioned. It is one thing to satisfy popular tastes, as Robert Burns's poetry did, and quite another to exploit them, as Hollywood does. Folk Art was the people's own institution, their private little kitchen-garden walled off from the great formal park of their masters.[3] But Masscult breaks down the wall, integrating the masses into a debased form of High Culture and thus becoming an instrument of domination. If one had no other data to go on, Masscult would expose capitalism as a class society rather than the harmonious commonwealth that, in election years, both parties tell us it is.

The same goes even more strongly for the Soviet Union. Its Masscult is both worse and more pervasive than ours, a fact which is often not recognized because in form Soviet Masscult is just the opposite, aiming at propaganda and pedogogy rather than distraction. But like ours, it is imposed from above and it exploits rather than satisfies the needs of the masses—though, of course, for political rather than commercial reasons. Its quality is even lower. Our Supreme Court building is tasteless and pompous but not to the lunatic degree of most Soviet architecture; post-1930 Soviet films, with a few exceptions, are far duller and cruder than our own; the primitive level of *serious* Soviet periodicals devoted to matters of art or philosophy has to be read to be believed, and as for the popular press, it is as if Hearst or Colonel McCormick ran every periodical in America. Furthermore, while here individuals can simply turn their back on Masscult and do their own work, there no such escape is possible; the official cultural bodies control all outlets and a *Doctor Zhivago* must be smuggled out for foreign publication. . . .

Since in a mass society people are related not to each other but to some abstract organizing principle, they are often in a state of exhaustion, for this lack of contact is unnatural. So Masscult attempts to provide distraction for the tired businessman—or the tired proletarian. This kind of art is necessarily at a distance from the individual since it is specifically designed to affect not what differentiates him from everybody else—that is what is of liveliest interest to *him*—but rather to work on the reflexes he shares with everybody else. So he is at a distance.

But people feel a need to be related to other people. The simplest way of

[3] And if it was often influenced by High Culture, it did change the forms and themes into its own style. The only major form of Folk Art that still persists in this country is jazz, and the difference between Folk Art and Masscult may be most readily perceived by comparing the kind of thing heard at the annual Newport Jazz Festivals to Rock 'n Roll. The former is musically interesting and emotionally real; the latter is—not. The amazing survival of jazz despite the exploitative onslaughts of half a century of commercial enterpreneurs, is in my opinion, due to its folk quality. And as the noble and the peasant understood each other better than either understood the bourgeois, so it seems significant that jazz is the only art form that appeals to both the intelligentsia and the common people. As for the others, let them listen to *South Pacific*.

bridging this distance, or rather of pretending to bridge it, is by emphasizing the personality of the artist; the individual buried in the mass audience can relate himself to the individual in the artist, since they are, after all, both persons. So while Masscult is in one sense extremely impersonal, in another it is extremely personal. The artist is thus charismatic and his works become the expression of this charisma rather than, as in the past, objective creations.

In his alcoholic last years, John Barrymore gave an extreme illustration of this principle.

> Six months ago [ran a story in *Time* of November 6, 1939] a ham show opened in Chicago. Last week it was still running there. It had become a civic institution. It had played to 150,000 people and grossed over $250,000. The theater was sold out three weeks in advance. . . .
>
> The answer was . . . that the leading man [was] the great John Barrymore—sometimes ill, sometimes tight, but always a trouper. . . . "Yep," says the doorman, "he arrives every night, dead or alive." . . . He says anything that comes into his head. When he is well wound up, *My Dear Children* may bumble on till after midnight. Once a fire engine sounded in the street. Sang out Barrymore: "I hope they get to the fire in time." Once he saw Ned Sparks in the audience. Walking to the footlights, Barrymore shouted: "There's that old bastard Ned Sparks." Once he couldn't hear the prompter in the wings, yelled: "Give those cues louder!" [etc.] Once, unable to stand up, he played the whole show sitting down. Another time, when he couldn't even issue from the dressing room to stage, he said: "Get me a wheel chair—I'll play Lionel."
>
> Audiences eat it up. They complain to the box office only on those rare occasions when Barrymore plays his part straight.

Barrymore was not, by this time, exploiting his romantic personality; he was not even burlesquing it, since the *ad libs*—except for the crack about Lionel— were not funny. He was living on his capital, selling his gilt-edge bonds (his romantic reputation) and when he had liquidated them all (when the public began to think of him not as "the great John Barrymore" of the past but as the drunken cut-up of the present) he would have been bankrupt. Luckily, he died before that happened.

For their part, the mass public liked him in this final stage of disintegration precisely because it showed them he was no better than they were, in fact he was a good deal worse. In the "genius" act of the Masscult period, there is a strange ambivalence. The masses put an absurdly high value on the personal genius, the charisma, of the performer, but they also demand a secret rebate: he must play the game—*their* game—must distort his personality to suit their taste. Bryon did it when he wore an open collar and made sure that his hyacinthine locks were properly disordered. Robert Frost did it when he called a press conference, not so long ago, on moving into his office at the Library of Congress as Consultant on Poetry, and told the assembled reporters that his job might be called "Poet in Waiting" and further confided that he wanted some good paintings to hang in his office: "I want to get the place out of the small-potatoes class." Even the staid *New York Times* was stimulated to headline its story: POET IN WAITING BIDS FOR A RATING. That Frost is a fine poet isn't relevant here; he is also a natural showman, and the relevant question is why our most distinguished poet feels it desirable to indulge this minor talent, clowning around like another Carl Sandburg. Bernard Shaw is the most interesting case of all, combining arrogance and subservience in the most dazzling way, as in the postcards he wrote to his admirers explaining why he couldn't possibly be bothered to reply.

In Masscult (and in its bastard, Midcult) everything becomes a commodity, to be mined for $$$$, used for something it is not, from Davy Crockett to Picasso. Once a writer becomes a Name, that is, once he writes a book that for good or bad reasons catches on, the Masscult (or Midcult) mechanism begins to "build him up," to package him into something that can be sold in identical units in quantity. He can coast along the rest of his life on momentum; publishers will pay him big advances just to get his Name on their list; his charisma becomes such that people will pay him $250 and up to address them (really just to *see* him); editors will reward him handsomely for articles on subjects he knows nothing about. Artists and writers have always had a tendency to repeat themselves, but Masscult (and Midcult) make it highly profitable to do so and in fact penalize those who don't. Some years ago, I'm told, a leading abstract artist complained to a friend that he was tired of the genre that had made him famous and wanted to try something else; but his gallery insisted such a shift would be commercially disastrous and, since he had children to send through college, he felt obliged to comply. . . .

Let us, finally, consider Masscult first from the standpoint of consumption and then from that of production.

As a marketable commodity, Masscult has two great advantages over High Culture. The post-1750 public, lacking the taste and knowledge of the old patron class, is not only satisfied with shoddy mass-produced goods but in general feels more at home with them (though on unpredictable occasions, they will respond to the real thing, as with Dickens' novels and the movies of Chaplin and Griffith). This is because such goods are standardized and so are easier to consume since one knows what's coming next—imagine a Western in which the hero loses the climactic gun fight or an office romance in which the mousy stenographer loses out to the predatory blonde. But standardization has a subtler aspect, which might be called The Built-In Reaction. As Clement Greenberg noted in "Avant-garde and *Kitsch*" many years ago in *Partisan Review,* the special aesthetic quality of *Kitsch*—a term which includes both Masscult and Midcult—is that it "predigests art for the spectator and spares him effort, provides him with a shortcut to the pleasures of art that detours what is necessarily difficult in the genuine art" because it includes the spectator's reactions in the work itself instead of forcing him to make his own responses. That standby of provincial weddings, "I love You Truly," is far more "romantic" than the most beautiful of Schubert's songs because its wallowing, yearning tremolos and glissandos make it clear to the most unmusical listener that something very tender indeed is going on. It does his feeling for him; or, as T. W. Adorno has observed of popular music, "The composition hears for the listener." Thus Liberace is a much more "musical" pianist than Serkin, whose piano is not adorned with antique candelabra and whose stance at it is as businesslike as Liberace's is "artistic." So, too, our Collegiate Gothic, which may be seen in its most resolutely picturesque (and expensive) phase at Yale, is more relentlessly Gothic than Chartres, whose builders didn't even know they *were* Gothic and so missed many chances for quaint effects.[4] And so, too, Boca Raton, the millionaires' suburb that Addison Mizener designed in Palm Beach during the Great Bull Market of the 'twenties, is so aggressively Spanish Mission that a former American ambassador to Spain is said to have murmured in awe, "It's more Spanish than anything I ever saw in Madrid." The same Law of the Built-In Reaction also insures that a smoothly air-brushed pin-up girl by Petty is more "sexy" than a real naked woman, the emphasis of breasts and thighs corresponding to the pornographically exaggerated Gothic details of Harkness. More *sexy* but not more *sexual,* the relation between the terms being similar to that of *sentimentality* to *sentiment* or *modernistic* to *modern,* or *arty* to *art.*

The production of Masscult is a subtler business than one might think. We have already seen in the case of Poe than a serious writer will produce art even when he is trying to function as a hack, simply because he cannot help putting himself into his work. The unhappy hero of James's story, "The Next Time," tried again and again to prostitute his talents and write a best seller to support his family, but each time he created another unprofitable masterpiece; with the best will in the world, he was simply unable to achieve a low enough standard. The reverse is also true: a hack will turn out hack stuff even when he tries to be serious. Most of these examples will come later under Midcult, but Masscult also has its little tragedies. When I was in Hollywood recently, I was told by one of the most intelligent younger directors, Stanley Kubrick: "The reason movies are often so bad out here isn't because the people who make them are cynical money hacks. Most of them are doing the very best they can; they really want to make good movies. The trouble is with their heads, not their hearts." This was borne out by the film I was there to write about, a mawkish travesty of Nathanael West's *Miss Lonelyhearts* that was written and produced by Dore Schary with the noblest intentions.

There seem to be two main conditions for the successful production of *Kitsch.* One is that the producer must believe in what he is doing. A good example is Norman Rockwell, who since 1916 has painted over three hundred covers for the *Saturday Evening Post.* When a fellow illustrator remarked that their craft was just a way to make a living—"You do your job, you get your check, and nobody thinks it's art"—Rockwell was horrified. "Oh no no no. How can you say that? No man with a conscience can just bat out illustrations.

---

[4] When I lived in Harkness Memorial Quadrangle some thirty years ago, I noticed a number of cracks in the tiny-paned windows of my room that had been patched with picturesquely wavy strips of lead. Since the place had just been built, I thought this peculiar. Later I found that after the windows has been installed, a special gang of artisans had visited them; one craftsman had delicately cracked every tenth or twentieth pane with a little hammer and another had then repaired the cracks. In a few days, the windows of Harkness had gone through an evolution that in backward places like Oxford had taken centuries. I wonder what they do in Harkness when a window is broken by accident.

He's got to put all of his talent, all of his feelings into them." Having just seen a most interesting exhibition of Rockwell's techniques at a local bank, I think he was telling the truth. He makes dozens of careful, highly competent pencil sketches, plus oil renderings of details, for just one *Post* cover; if genius were really "an infinite capacity for taking pains," Norman Rockwell would be a genius. The trouble is that the final result of all this painstaking craftsmanship is just—a *Post* cover, as slick and cliché in execution as in content. "There's this magazine cover," says the comedian Mort Sahl, "and it shows this kid getting his first haircut you know and a dog licking his hand and his mother is crying and it's Saturday night in the old home town and people are dancing outside in the streets and the Liberty Bell is ringing and, uh, did I miss anything?" But Rockwell is sincere, so much so that he constantly wonders whether he is living up to his talents. In the 'twenties, according to a profile in the *Post,* he went through a crisis as comic as it was pathetic:

> Professional friends, dabbling in modernism, told him he ought to learn something about dynamic symmetry, and their arguments worried him. . . . Rockwell packed up and went to Paris. He attended lectures and bought Picassos to hang in his studio for inspiration. On his return he set about applying what he had learned to *Post* covers. When editor George Horace Lorimer examined the first new Rockwell offerings, he laid them aside and gave the artist a paternal lecture on the value of being one's self, pointing out in passing that it was conceivably better to have one's work displayed on the *Post's* covers than embalmed in art museums. Chastened, Rockwell agreed and went back to being himself. He now refers to his temporary aberration as "my James-Joyce-Gertrude-Stein period."

Lorimer's missionary work was completed by a Stanford girl Rockwell married a few years later, a nice, sensible young bride who in good American fashion "helped get him back on the beam and keep him there." In this not exactly Herculean task, she appears to have succeeded. He was positively defiant some years ago when he was being interviewed for a *New Yorker* profile:

> My creed is that painting pictures of any kind is a definite form of expression and that illustration is the principal pictorial form of conveying ideas and telling funny stories. The critics say that any proper picture should be primarily a series of technical problems of light, shadow, proportion, color and voids. I say that if you can tell a story in a picture and if a reasonable number of people like your work, it is art. Maybe it isn't the highest form of art, but it's art nevertheless and it's what I love to do. I feel that I am doing something when I paint a picture that appeals to most people. This is a democracy, isn't it?

To which last the reply is, in terms of Rockwell's covers, "Yep, sure is." Yet, despite this credo, which every popular artist should have printed in red and black and hung over his drawing board alongside Kipling's "If," Rockwell still keeps worrying. He had another crisis a couple of years ago, at sixty-five, when he again wondered what he might have done "if I hadn't gone commercial" and again began to talk of Picasso as "the greatest"; he took a year off to do some Serious painting (except for a mere six *Post* covers), with results unknown to me. He also wrote his autobiography. It is being serialized in the *Post*.

The other condition for success in Masscult is that the writer, artist, editor, director or entertainer must have a good deal of the mass man in himself, as was the case with Zane Grey, Howard Chandler Christy, Mr. Lorimer of the *Post,* Cecil B. DeMille, and Elvis Presley. This is closely related to sincerity— how can he take his work seriously if he doesn't have this instinctive, this built-in vulgar touch? Like Rockwell, he may know that art is good and honor-able and worthy of respect, and he may pay tribute to it. But knowing it is one thing and feeling it is another. A journalistic entrepreneur like Henry Luce— by no means the worst—has the same kind of idle curiosity about the Facts and the same kind of gee-whiz excitement about rather elementary ideas (see *Life* editorials passim) as his millions of readers have. When I worked for him on *Fortune* in the early 'thirties, I was struck by three qualities he had as an editor: his shrewdness as to what was and what was not "a story," his high dedication to his task, and his limited cultural background despite, or perhaps because of, his having attended Yale College. All three are closely interrelated in his suc-cess: a more sophisticated editor would have gotten out of step with his millions of readers, a less idealistic one would have lacked the moral oomph to attract them, and he knew a "story" when he saw one because what interested them interested him.[5]

As I have already noted in this essay, the separation of Fo!k Art and High Culture in fairly watertight compartments corresponded to the sharp line once drawn between the common people and the aristocracy. The blurring of this line, however desirable politically, has had unfortunate results culturally. Folk Art had its own authentic quality, but Masscult is at best a vulgarized reflection

---

[5] An episode in my six years at *Fortune* is to the point here. In 1931–1932 I was active on a literary magazine (along with two friends who in 1938 were to become, with me, editors of *Partisan Review:* F. W. Dupee and George L. K. Morris) which had a circulation of about 600. Thinking Luce would be pleased, and interested, by this evidence of cultural enterprise on the part of one of his writers, I sent him up an issue of *The Miscellany,* as it was dismally called. His reaction was that I had be-trayed Time, Inc. "But Henry," I said—in those days, long before *Sports Illustrated* or even *Life,* manners were still pastorally simple at Time, Inc., and Luce was merely *primus inter pares*—"But Henry, you can't expect *Fortune* to be my only interest. I give it a good day's work from nine to five, that's what you pay me for, and it's my business what I do in my spare time." This argument affected Luce much as his cynical colleague's did Norman Rockwell. With his usual earnestness—he was and I'm sure is a decent and honorable man, not at all the ogre the liberal press portrays —Luce expounded quite a different philosophy: *Fortune* was not just a job, it was a vocation worthy of a man's whole effort, and pay and time schedules weren't the point at all. "Why, the very name *Fortune* was thought up by so-and-so [one of my fellow editors] late one night on the West Side subway between the Seventy-second and the Seventy-ninth street stations [Luce was a *Time* man always]. This is a twenty-four-hour profession, you never know when you may get an idea for us, and if you're all the time thinking about some damn little magazine . . ." "But Henry . . ." It was an impasse, since I looked on *Fortune* as a means and he as an end, nor had it been resolved when I left the magazine four years later.

of High Culture and at worst a cultural nightmare, a *Kulturkatzenjammer.* And while High Culture could formerly address itself only to the *cognoscenti,* now it must take the *ignoscenti* into account even when it turns its back on them. For Masscult is not merely a parallel formation to High Culture, as Folk Art was; it is a competitor. The problem is especially acute in this country because class lines are especially weak here. If there were a clearly defined cultural elite here, then the masses could have their *Kitsch* and the classes could have their High Culture, with everybody happy. But a significant part of our population is chronically confronted with a choice between looking at TV or old masters, between reading Tolstoy or a detective story; i.e., the pattern of their cultural lives is "open" to the point of being porous. For a lucky few, this openness of choice is stimulating. But for most, it is confusing and leads at best to that middlebrow compromise called Midcult.

The turning point in our culture was the Civil War, whose aftermath destroyed the New England tradition almost as completely as the October Revolution broke the continuity of Russian culture. (Certain disturbing similarities between present-day American and Soviet Russian culture and society may be partly due to these seismic breaks, much more drastic than anything in European history, including the French Revolution.) The New England culture was simply pushed aside by history, dwindling to provincial gentility, and there was no other to take its place; it was smothered by the growth of mass industry, by westward expansion, and above all by the massive immigration from non-English-speaking countries. The great metaphor of the period was the melting pot; the tragedy was that it melted so thoroughly. A pluralistic culture might have developed, enriched by the contributions of Poles, Italians, Serbs, Greeks, Jews, Finns, Croats, Germans, Swedes, Hungarians, and all the other peoples that came here from 1870 to 1910. It is with mixed feelings one reads Emma Lazarus' curiously condescending inscription on the Statue of Liberty:

> Give me your tired, your poor,
> Your huddled masses yearning to breathe free,
> The wretched refuse of your teeming shore,
> Send these, the homeless, tempest-tossed, to me:
> I lift my lamp beside the golden door.

For indeed these *were* the poor and tempest-tossed, the bottom-dogs of Europe, and for just this reason they were all too eager to give up their old-world languages and customs, which they regarded as marks of inferiority. Uprooted from their own traditions, offered the dirtiest jobs at the lowest pay, the masses from Europe were made to feel that their only hope of rising was to become "Americanized," which meant being assimilated at the lowest cultural (as well as economic) level. They were ready-made consumers of *Kitsch.* A half-century ago, when the issue was still in the balance, Randolph Bourne wrote:

> What we emphatically do not want is that these distinctive qualities should be washed out into a tasteless, colorless fluid of uniformity. Already we have far too much of this insipidity—masses of

people who are half-breeds. . . . Our cities are filled with these half-breeds who retain their foreign names but have lost the foreign savor. This does not mean that . . . they have been really Americanized. It means that, letting slip from them whatever native culture they had, they have substituted for it only the most rudimentary American—the American culture of the cheap newspaper, the movies, the popular song, the ubiquitous automobile. . . .

Just so surely as we tend to disintegrate these nuclei of nationalistic culture do we tend to create hordes of men and women without a spiritual country, cultural outlaws without taste, without standards but those of the mob. We sentence them to live on the most rudimentary planes of American life.[6]

Bourne's fears were realized. The very nature of mass industry and of its offshoot, Masscult, made a pluralistic culture impossible. The melting pot produced merely "the tasteless, colorless fluid of uniformity." This much can be said for the dominant Anglo-Saxon Americans: they didn't ask the immigrants to accept anything they themselves were unwilling to accept. One recalls Matthew Josephson's vignette of Henry Clay Frick sitting on a Renaissance chair under a Rembrandt reading the *Saturday Evening Post*. They were preoccupied with building railroads, settling the West, expanding industry, perfecting monopolies and other practical affairs. Pioneers, O Pioneers! And the tired pioneer preferred Harold Bell Wright to Henry James.

We are now in a more sophisticated period. The West has been won, the immigrants melted down, the factories and railroads built to such effect that since 1929 the problem has been consumption rather than production. The work week has shrunk, real wages have risen, and never in history have so many people attained such a high standard of living as in this country since 1945. College enrollment is now well over four million, three times what it was in 1929. Money, leisure and knowledge, the prerequisites for culture, are more plentiful and more evenly distributed than ever before.

In these more advanced times, the danger to High Culture is not so much from Masscult as from a peculiar hybrid bred from the latter's unnatural intercourse with the former. A whole middle culture has come into existence and it threatens to absorb both its parents. This intermediate form—let us call it Midcult—has the essential qualities of Masscult—the formula, the built-in reaction, the lack of any standard except popularity—but it decently covers them with a cultural figleaf. In Masscult the trick is plain—to please the crowd by

---

[6] From "Trans-National America." Of course the immigrants were not all "huddled masses." Many, especially the Jews, were quite aware of the inferior quality of American cultural life. In *The Spirit of the Ghetto* (1902), Hutchins Hapgood quotes a Jewish immigrant: "In Russia, a few men, really cultivated and intellectual, give the tone and everybody follows them. But in America the public gives the tone and the literary man simply expresses the public. So that really intellectual Americans do not express as good ideas as less intellectual Russians. The Russians all imitate the best. The Americans imitate what the mass of the people want." A succinct definition of Masscult.

any means. But Midcult has it both ways: it pretends to respect the standards of High Culture while in fact it waters them down and vulgarizes them.[7]

The enemy outside the walls is easy to distinguish. It is its ambiguity that makes Midcult alarming. For it presents itself as part of High Culture. Not that coterie stuff, not those snobbish inbred so-called intellectuals who are only talking to themselves. Rather the great vital mainstream, wide and clear though perhaps not so deep. You, too, can wade in it for a mere $16.70 pay nothing now just fill in the coupon and receive a full year six hard-cover lavishly illustrated issues of *Horizon: A Magazine of the Arts,* "probably the most beautiful magazine in the world . . . seeks to serve as guide to the long cultural advance of modern man, to explore the many mansions of the philosopher, the painter, the historian, the architect, the sculptor, the satirist, the poet . . . to build bridges between the world of scholars and the world of intelligent readers. It's a good buy. Use the coupon *now.*" *Horizon* has some 160,000 subscribers, which is more than the combined circulations, after many years of effort, of *Kenyon, Hudson, Sewanee, Partisan, Art News, Arts, American Scholar, Dissent, Commentary,* and half a dozen of our other leading cultural-critical magazines.

Midcult is not, as might appear at first, a raising of the level of Masscult. It is rather a corruption of High Culture which has the enormous advantage over Masscult that while also in fact "totally subjected to the spectator," in Malraux's phrase, it is able to pass itself off as the real thing. Midcult is the Revised Standard Version of the Bible, put out several years ago under the aegis of the Yale Divinity School, that destroys our greatest monument of English prose, the King James Version, in order to make the text "clear and meaningful to people today," which is like taking apart Westminster Abbey to make Disneyland out of the fragments. Midcult is the Museum of Modern Art's film department paying tribute to Samuel Goldwyn because his movies are alleged to be (slightly) better than those of other Hollywood producers—though why they are called "producers" when their function is to prevent the production of art (cf., the fate in Hollywood of Griffith, Chaplin, von Stroheim, Eisenstein and Orson Welles) is a semantic puzzle. Midcult is the venerable and once venerated *Atlantic*—which in the last century printed Emerson, Lowell, Howells, James, and Mark Twain—putting on the cover of a recent issue a huge photograph of Dore Schary, who has lately transferred his high-minded sentimentality from Hollywood to Broadway and who is represented in the issue by a homily, "To A Young Actor," which synthesizes Jefferson, Polonius and Dr. Norman Vincent Peale, concluding: "Behave as citizens not only of your profession but of the full world in which you live. Be indignant with injustice, be gracious with success, be courageous with failure, be patient with opportunity, and be resolute with faith and honor." Midcult is the Book-of-the-Month

---

[7] It's not done, of course, as consciously as this suggests. The editors of the *Saturday Review* or *Harper's* or the *Atlantic* would be honestly indignant at this description of their activities, as would John Steinbeck, J. P. Marquand, Pearl Buck, Irwin Shaw, Herman Wouk, John Hersey and others of that remarkably large group of Midcult novelists we have developed. One of the nice things about Zane Grey was that it seems never to have occurred to him that his books had anything to do with literature.

Club, which since 1926 has been supplying its members with reading matter of which the best than can be said is that it could be worse, i.e., they get John Hersey instead of Gene Stratton Porter. Midcult is the transition from Rodgers and Hart to Rodgers and Hammerstein, from the gay tough lyrics of *Pal Joey,* a spontaneous expression of a real place called Broadway, to the folk-fakery of *Oklahoma!* and the orotund sentimentalities of *South Pacific.*[8] Midcult is or was, "Omnibus," subsidized by a great foundation to raise the level of television, which began its labors by announcing it would "be aimed straight at the average American audience, neither highbrow nor lowbrow, the audience that made the *Reader's Digest, Life,* the *Ladies' Home Journal,* the audience which is the solid backbone of any business as it is of America itself" and which then proved its good faith by programming Gertrude Stein and Jack Benny, Chekhov and football strategy, Beethoven and champion ice skaters. "Omnibus" failed. The level of television, however, was not raised, for some reason. . . .

What is to be done? Conservatives like Ortega y Gasset and T. S. Eliot argue that since "the revolt of the masses" has led to the horrors of totalitarianism and of California roadside architecture, the only hope is to rebuild the old class walls and bring the masses once more under aristocratic control. They think of the popular as synonomous with the cheap and vulgar, Marxian radicals and liberal sociologists, on the other hand, see the masses as intrinsically healthy but as the dupes and victims of cultural exploitation—something like Rousseau's "noble savage." If only the masses were offered good stuff instead of *Kitsch,* how they would eat it up! How the level of Masscult would rise! Both these diagnoses seem to me fallacious because they assume that Masscult is (in the conservative view) or could be (in the liberal view) an expression of *people,* like Folk Art, whereas actually it is, as I tried to show earlier in this essay, an expression of *masses,* a very different thing.

The conservative proposal to save culture by restoring the old class lines has a more solid historical basis than the liberal-cum-Marxian hope for a new democratic, classless culture. Politically, however, it is without meaning in a world dominated by the two great mass nations, the USA and the USSR, and a

---

[8] An interesting Midcult document is the editorial the *New York Times* ran August 24, 1960, the day after the death of Oscar Hammerstein 2nd:

. . . The theatre has lost a man who stood for all that is decent in life. . . . The concern for racial respect in *South Pacific,* the sympathy and respect for a difficult though aspiring monarch in *The King and I,* the indomitable faith that runs through *Carousel* were not clever bits of showmanship. They represented Mr. Hammerstein's faith in human beings and their destiny. . . .

Since he was at heart a serious man, his lyrics were rarely clever. Instead of turning facetious phrases he made a studious attempt to write idiomatically in the popular tradition of the musical theatre, for he was a dedicated craftsman. But the style that was apparently so artless has brought glimpses of glory into our lives. "There's a bright, golden haze on the meadow," sings Curly in *Oklahoma!* and the gritty streets of a slatternly city look fresher. "June is bustin' out all over," sing Carrie and Nettie in *Carousel* and the harshness of our winter vanishes. . . . To us it is gratifying that he had the character to use his genius with faith and scruple.

The contrast of faith (good) with cleverness (bad) is typical of Midcult, as is the acceptance of liberalistic moralizing as a satisfactory substitute for talent. Indeed, talent makes the midbrow uneasy: "Since he was a serious man, his lyrics were rarely clever." The death of Mr. Hart did not stimulate the *Times* to editorial elegy.

world that is becoming more industrialized and mass-ified all the time. The only practical thing along those lines would be to revive the spirit of the old avant-garde, that is to re-create a cultural—as against a social, political or economic—elite as a countermovement to both Masscult and Midcult. It may be possible, in a more modest and limited sense than in the past—I shall return to this point later—but it will be especially difficult in this country where the blurring of class lines, the lack of a continuous tradition and the greater facilities for the manufacturing and distribution of *Kitsch,* whether Masscult or Midcult, all work in the other direction. Unless this country goes either fascist or communist, there will continue to be islands above the flood for those determined enough to reach them and live on them; as Faulkner has shown, a writer can use Hollywood instead of being used by it, if his purpose be firm enough. But islands are not continents.

The alternative proposal is to raise the level of our culture in general. Those who advocate this start off from the assumption that there has already been a great advance in the diffusion of culture in the last two centuries—Edward Shils is sure of this, Daniel Bell thinks it is probably the case—and that the main problem is how to carry this even further; they tend to regard such critics of Masscult as Ernest van den Haag, Leo Lowenthal or myself as either disgruntled Left romantics or reactionary dreamers or both. Perhaps the most impressive—and certainly the longest—exposition of this point of view appears in Gilbert Seldes' *The Great Audience.* Mr. Seldes blames the present sad state of our Masscult on (1) the stupidity of the Lords of *Kitsch* (who underestimate the mental age of the public), (2) the arrogance of the intellectuals (who make the same mistake and so snobbishly refuse to try to raise the level of the mass media), and (3) the passivity of the public itself (which doesn't insist on better Masscult). This diagnosis seems to me superficial because it blames everything on subjective, moral factors: stupidity (the Lords of *Kitsch*), perversity (the intellectuals), or failure of will (the public). My own notion is that—as in the case of the "responsibility" of the German (or Russian) people for the horrors of Nazism (or of Soviet Communism)—it is unjust and unrealistic to blame large social groups for such catastrophes. Burke was right when he said you cannot indict a people. Individuals are caught up in the workings of a mechanism that forces them into its own pattern; only heroes can resist, and while one can hope that everybody will be a hero, one cannot demand it.

I see Masscult—and its recent offspring, Midcult—as a reciprocating engine, and who is to say, once it has been set in motion, whether the stroke or the counterstroke is responsible for its continued action? The Lords of *Kitsch* sell culture to the masses. It is a debased, trivial culture that avoids both the deep realities (sex, death, failure, tragedy) and also the simple, spontaneous pleasures, since the realities would be too real and the pleasures too lively to induce what Mr. Seldes calls "the mood of consent": a narcotized acceptance of Masscult-Midcult and of the commodities it sells as a substitute for the unsettling and unpredictable (hence unsalable) joy, tragedy, wit, change, originality and beauty of real life. The masses—and don't let's forget that this term includes the well-educated fans of *The Old Man and the Sea, Our Town, J.B.,* and *John Brown's Body*—who have been debauched by several generations of this sort of thing, in turn have come to demand such trivial and comfortable cultural products. Which came first, the chicken or the egg, the mass demand or its satisfaction (and further stimulation), is a question as academic as it is un-answerable. The engine is reciprocating and shows no signs of running down.

"Our fundamental want today in the United States," Walt Whitman wrote in 1871, "is of a class and the clear idea of a class, of native authors, literatures, far different, far higher in grade than any yet known, sacerdotal, modern, fit to cope with our occasions, lands, permeating the whole mass of American mentality, taste, belief, breathing into it a new life, giving it decision, affecting politics far more than the popular superficial suffrage. . . . For know you not, dear, earnest reader, that the people of our land may all read and write, and may all possess the right to vote—and yet the main things may be entirely lacking? . . . The priest departs, the divine literatus comes."

The divine literatus is behind schedule. Masscult and Midcult have so per-vaded the land that Whitman's hope for a democratic culture shaped by a sacerdotal class at once so sublime and so popular that they can swing elections —that this noble vision now seems absurd. But a more modest aspiration is still open, one adumbrated by Whitman's idea of a new cultural class and his warn-ing that "the main things may be entirely lacking" even though everybody knows how to read, write and vote. This is to recognize that two cultures have developed in this country and that it is to the national interest to keep them separate. The conservatives are right when they say there has never been a broadly democratic culture on a high level. This is not because the ruling class forcibly excluded the masses—this is Marxist melodrama—but quite simply be-cause the great majority of people at any given time (including most of the ruling class for the matter) have never cared enough about such things to make them an important part of their lives. So let the masses have their Masscult, let the few who care about good writing, painting, music, architecture, philos-ophy, etc., have their High Culture, and don't fuzz up the distinction with Midcult.

Whitman would have rejected this proposal as undemocratic, which it is. But his own career is a case in point: he tried to be a popular bard but the masses were not interested, and his first recognition, excepting Emerson's lonely voice, came from the English pre-Raphaelites, a decadent and precious group if ever there was one. If we would create a literature "fit to cope with our occasions," the only public the writer or artist or composer or philosopher or critic or architect should consider must be that of his peers. The informed, interested minority—what Stendhal called "We Happy Few." Let the majority eavesdrop if they like, but their tastes should be firmly ignored.

There is a compromise between the conservative and liberal proposals which I think is worth considering—neither an attempt to re-create the old avant-garde nor one to raise the general level of Masscult and Midcult. It is based on the recent discovery—since 1945—that there is not One Big Audience but rather a number of smaller, more specialized audiences that may still be commercially profitable. (I take it for granted that the less differentiated the audience, the less chance there is of something original and lively creeping in, since the principle of the lowest common denominator applies.) This discovery has in fact resulted in the sale of "quality" paperbacks and recordings and the growth of "art" cinema houses, off-Broadway theatres, concert orchestras and art museums and galleries. The mass audience is divisible, we have discovered —and the more it is divided, the better. Even television, the most senseless and routinized expression of Masscult (except for the movie newsreels), might be improved by this approach. One possibility is pay-TV, whose modest concept is that only those who subscribe could get the program, like a magazine; but, also like a magazine, the editors would decide what goes in, not the advertisers; a small gain but a real one. The networks oppose this on philanthropic grounds —they don't see why the customer should pay for what he now gets free. But perhaps one would rather pay for bread than get stones for nothing.

As long as our society is "open" in Karl Popper's sense—that is unless or until it is closed by a mass revolution stimulated by the illusion of some "total solution" such as Russian-type Communism or Hitler-type Fascism, the name doesn't really matter—there will always be happy accidents because of the stubbornness of some isolated creator. But if we are to have more than this, it will be because our new public for High Culture becomes conscious of itself and begins to show some *esprit de corps,* insisting on higher standards and setting itself off—joyously, implacably—from most of its fellow citizens, not only from the Masscult depths but also from the agreeable ooze of the Midcult swamp.

~~~~~*21*

ARTHUR SCHLESINGER, Jr.

Origins of the Cold War

In the years following the McCarthy era, official Washington's view of Russia became infinitely more complicated in response to changes within Russia after the death of Stalin in 1953 (changes which were manifested in Premier Khrushchev's visit to the United States in 1959). The open break within the communist world further clouded the picture. In the nineteen sixties analysts of Russian behavior much revised the history of postwar Russian-American relations. Under the spur of revisionist historians, even such staunch anti-communist liberals as Arthur Schlesinger, Jr., conceded points to the argument that mutual suspicion and a mutual failure to gauge intentions heightened international tension.

Schlesinger was the epitome of American liberalism in the nineteen fifties. A Harvard professor and a leader of Americans for Democratic Action, he served for years as the favorite target of conservatives. In "Origins of the Cold War," he ironically became one of the Old Guard. For here he defends the received truth of the fifties, that Russia deserves almost the entire blame for precipitating and continuing the Cold War. The essay is perhaps the most reasoned brief statement of that point of view.

The Cold War in its original form was a presumably mortal antagonism, arising in the wake of the Second World War, between two rigidly hostile blocs, one led by the Soviet Union, the other by the United States. For nearly two somber and dangerous decades this antagonism dominated the fears of mankind; it may even, on occasion, have come close to blowing up the planet. In recent years, however, the once implacable struggle has lost its familiar clarity of outline. With the passing of old issues and the emergence of new conflicts and contestants, there is a natural tendency, especially on the part of the generation

Reprinted by special permission from FOREIGN AFFAIRS, October, 1967. © Copyright by the Council on Foreign Relations, Inc., New York. Reprinted by permission of the author.

which grew up during the Cold War, to take a fresh look at the causes of the great contention between Russia and America.

Some exercises in reappraisal have merely elaborated the orthodoxies promulgated in Washington or Moscow during the boom years of the Cold War. But others, especially in the United States (there are no signs, alas, of this in the Soviet Union), represent what American historians call "revisionism" —that is, a readiness to challenge official explanations. No one should be surprised by this phenomenon. Every war in American history has been followed in due course by skeptical reassessments of supposedly sacred assumptions. So the War of 1812, fought at the time for the freedom of the seas, was in later years ascribed to the expansionist ambitions of Congressional war hawks; so the Mexican War became a slaveholders' conspiracy. So the Civil War has been pronounced a "needless war," and Lincoln has even been accused of manœuvring the rebel attack on Fort Sumter. So too the Spanish-American War and the First and Second World Wars have, each in its turn, undergone revisionist critiques. It is not to be supposed that the Cold War would remain exempt.

In the case of the Cold War, special factors reinforce the predictable historiographical rhythm. The outburst of polycentrism in the communist empire has made people wonder whether communism was ever so monolithic as official theories of the Cold War supposed. A generation with no vivid memories of Stalinism may see the Russia of the forties in the image of the relatively mild, seedy and irresolute Russia of the sixties. And for this same generation the American course of widening the war in Viet Nam—which even non-revisionists can easily regard as folly—has unquestionably stirred doubts about the wisdom of American foreign policy in the sixties which younger historians may have begun to read back into the forties.

It is useful to remember that, on the whole, past exercises in revisionism have failed to stick. Few historians today believe that the war hawks caused the War of 1812 or the slaveholders the Mexican War, or that the Civil War was needless, or that the House of Morgan brought America into the First World War or that Franklin Roosevelt schemed to produce the attack on Pearl Harbor. But this does not mean that one should deplore the rise of Cold War revisionism.[1] For revisionism is an essential part of the process by which history, through the posing of new problems and the investigation of new possibilities, enlarges its perspectives and enriches its insights.

More than this, in the present context, revisionism expresses a deep, legitimate and tragic apprehension. As the Cold War has begun to lose its purity of definition, as the moral absolutes of the fifties become the moralistic clichés of the sixties, some have begun to ask whether the appalling risks which humanity ran during the Cold War were, after all, necessary and inevitable; whether more restrained and rational policies might not have guided the energies of man from the perils of conflict into the potentialities of collaboration. The fact that such questions are in their nature unanswerable does not mean that it is not right and useful to raise them. Nor does it mean that our sons and daughters are not entitled to an accounting from the generation of Russians and Americans who produced the Cold War.

[1] As this writer somewhat intemperately did in a letter to *The New York Review of Books,* October 20, 1966.

The orthodox American view, as originally set forth by the American government and as reaffirmed until recently by most American scholars, has been that the Cold War was the brave and essential response of free men to communist aggression. Some have gone back well before the Second World War to lay open the sources of Russian expansionism. Geopoliticians traced the Cold War to imperial Russian strategic ambitions which in the nineteenth century led to the Crimean War, to Russian penetration of the Balkans and the Middle East and to Russian pressure on Britain's "lifeline" to India. Ideologists traced it to the Communist Manifesto of 1848 ("the violent overthrow of the bourgeoisie lays the foundation for the sway of the proletariat"). Thoughtful observers (a phrase meant to exclude those who speak in Dullese about the unlimited evil of godless, atheistic, militant communism) concluded that classical Russian imperialism and Pan-Slavism, compounded after 1917 by Leninist messianism, confronted the West at the end of the Second World War with an inexorable drive for domination.[2]

The revisionist thesis is very different.[3] In its extreme form, it is that, after

[2] Every student of the Cold War must acknowledge his debt to W. H. McNeill's remarkable account, "America, Britain and Russia: Their Cooperation and Conflict, 1941–1946" (New York, 1953) and to the brilliant and indispensable series by Herbert Feis: "Churchill, Roosevelt, Stalin: The War They Waged and the Peace They Sought" (Princeton, 1957); "Between War and Peace: The Potsdam Conference" (Princeton, 1960); and "The Atomic Bomb and the End of World War II" (Princeton, 1966). Useful recent analyses include André Fontaine, "Histoire de la Guerre Froide" (2 v., Paris, 1965, 1967); N. A. Graebner, "Cold War Diplomacy, 1945–1960" (Princeton, 1962); L. J. Halle, "The Cold War as History" (London, 1967); M. F. Herz, "Beginnings of the Cold War " (Bloomington, 1966) and W. L. Neumann, "After Victory: Churchill, Roosevelt, Stalin and the Making of the Peace" (New York, 1967).

[3] The fullest statement of this case is to be found in D. F. Fleming's voluminous "The Cold War and Its Origins" (New York, 1961). For a shorter version of this argument, see David Horowitz, "The Free World Colossus" (New York, 1965); the most subtle and ingenious statements come in W. A. Williams' "The Tragedy of American Diplomacy" (rev. ed., New York, 1962) and in Gar Alperowitz's "Atomic Diplomacy: Hiroshima and Potsdam" (New York, 1965) and in subsequent articles and reviews by Mr. Alperowitz in *The New York Review of Books*. The fact that in some aspects the revisionist thesis parallels the official Soviet argument must not, of course, prevent consideration of the case on its merits, nor raise questions about the motives of the writers, all of whom, so far as I know, are independent-minded scholars.

I might further add that all these books, in spite of their ostentatious display of scholarly apparatus, must be used with caution. Professor Fleming, for example, relies heavily on newspaper articles and even columnists. While Mr. Alperowitz bases his case on official documents or authoritative reminiscences, he sometimes twists his material in a most unscholarly way. For example, in describing Ambassador Harriman's talk with President Truman on April 20, 1945, Mr. Alperowitz writes, "He argued that a reconsideration of Roosevelt's policy was necessary" (p. 22, repeated on p. 24). The citation is to p. 70–72 in President Truman's "Years of Decision." What President Truman reported Harriman as saying was the exact opposite: "Before leaving, Harriman took me aside and said, 'Frankly, one of the reasons that made me rush back to Washington was the fear that you did not understand, as I had seen Roosevelt understand, that Stalin is breaking his agreements.' " Similarly, in an appendix (p. 271) Mr. Alperowitz writes that the Hopkins and Davies missions of May 1945 "were opposed by the 'firm' advisers." Actually the Hopkins mission was proposed by Harriman and Charles E. Bohlen, who Mr. Alperowitz elsewhere suggests the death of Franklin Roosevelt and the end of the Second World War, the United States deliberately abandoned the wartime policy of collaboration and, exhilarated by the possession of the atomic bomb, undertook a course of aggression of its own designed to expel all Russian influence from Eastern Europe and to establish democratic-capitalist states on the very border of the Soviet Union. As the revisionists see it, this radically new American policy—or rather this resumption by Truman of the pre-Roosevelt policy of insensate anti-communism—left Moscow no alternative but to take measures in defense of its own borders. The result was the Cold War.

These two views, of course, could not be more starkly contrasting. It is therefore not unreasonable to look again at the half-dozen critical years between June 22, 1941, when Hitler attacked Russia, and July 2, 1947, when the Russians walked out of the Marshall Plan meeting in Paris. Several things should be borne in mind as this reëxamination is made. For one thing, we have thought a great deal more in recent years, in part because of writers like Roberta Wohlstetter and T. C. Schelling, about the problems of communication in diplomacy—the signals which one nation, by word or by deed, gives, inadvertently or intentionally, to another. Any honest reappraisal of the origins of the Cold War requires the imaginative leap—which should in any case be as instinctive for the historian as it is prudent for the statesman—into the adversary's viewpoint. We must strive to see how, given Soviet perspectives, the Russians might conceivably have misread our signals, as we must reconsider how intelligently we read theirs.

For another, the historian must not overindulge the man of power in the illusion cherished by those in office that high position carries with it the easy ability to shape history. Violating the statesman's creed, Lincoln once blurted out the truth in his letter of 1864 to A. G. Hodges: "I claim not to have controlled events, but confess plainly that events have controlled me." He was not asserting Tolstoyan fatalism but rather suggesting how greatly events limit the capacity of the statesman to bend history to his will. The physical course of the Second World War—the military operations undertaken, the position of the respective armies at the war's end, the momentum generated by victory and the vacuums created by defeat—all these determined the future as much as the character of individual leaders and the substance of national ideology and purpose.

Nor can the historian forget the conditions under which decisions are made, especially in a time like the Second World War. These were tired, overworked, aging men: in 1945, Churchill was 71 years old, Stalin had governed his country for 17 exacting years, Roosevelt his for 12 years nearly as exacting. During the war, moreover, the importunities of military operations

---

were the firmest of the firm—and was proposed by them precisely to impress on Stalin the continuity of American policy from Roosevelt to Truman. While the idea that Truman reversed Roosevelt's policy is tempting dramatically, it is a myth. See, for example, the testimony of Anna Rosenberg Hoffman, who lunched with Roosevelt on March 24, 1945, the last day he spent in Washington. After luncheon, Roosevelt was handed a cable. "He read it and became quite angry. He banged his fists on the arms of his wheelchair and said, 'Averell is right; we can't do business with Stalin. He has broken every one of the promises he made at Yalta.' He was very upset and continued in the same vein on the subject."

had shoved postwar questions to the margins of their minds. All—even Stalin, behind his screen of ideology—had became addicts of improvisation, relying on authority and virtuosity to conceal the fact that they were constantly surprised by developments. Like Eliza, they leaped from one cake of ice to the next in the effort to reach the other side of the river. None showed great tactical consistency, or cared much about it; all employed a certain ambiguity to preserve their power to decide big issues; and it is hard to know how to interpret anything any one of them said on any specific occasion. This was partly because, like all princes, they designed their expressions to have particular effects on particular audiences; partly because the entirely genuine intellectual difficulty of the questions they faced made a degree of vacillation and mind-changing eminently reasonable. If historians cannot solve their problems in retrospect, who are they to blame Roosevelt, Stalin and Churchill for not having solved them at the time?

Peacemaking after the Second World War was not so much a tapestry as it was a hopelessly raveled and knotted mess of yarn. Yet, for purposes of clarity, it is essential to follow certain threads. One theme indispensable to an understanding of the Cold War is the contrast between two clashing views of world order: the "universalist" view, by which all nations shared a common interest in all the affairs of the world, and the "sphere-of-influence" view, by which each great power would be assured by the other great powers of an acknowledged predominance in its own area of special interest. The universalist view assumed that national security would be guaranteed by an international organization. The sphere-of-interest view assumed that national security would be guaranteed by the balance of power. While in practice these views have by no means been incompatible (indeed, our shaky peace has been based on a combination of the two), in the abstract they involved sharp contradictions.

The tradition of American thought in these matters was universalist—*i.e.* Wilsonian. Roosevelt had been a member of Wilson's subcabinet; in 1920, as candidate for Vice President, he had campaigned for the League of Nations. It is true that, within Roosevelt's infinitely complex mind, Wilsonianism warred with the perception of vital strategic interests he had imbibed from Mahan. Moreover, his temperamental inclination to settle things with fellow princes around the conference table led him to regard the Big Three—or Four—as trustees for the rest of the world. On occasion, as this narrative will show, he was beguiled into flirtation with the sphere-of-influence heresy. But in principle he believed in joint action and remained a Wilsonian. His hope for Yalta, as he told the Congress on his return, was that it would "spell the end of the system of unilateral action, the exclusive alliances, the spheres of influence, the balances of power, and all the other expedients that have been tried for centuries—and have always failed."

Whenever Roosevelt backslid, he had at his side that Wilsonian fundamentalist, Secretary of State Cordell Hull, to recall him to the pure faith. After his visit to Moscow in 1943, Hull characteristically said that, with the Declaration of Four Nations on General Security (in which America, Russia, Britain and China pledged "united action . . . for the organization and maintenance of peace and security"), "there will no longer be need for spheres of influence, for alliances, for balance of power, or any other of the special arrangements through which, in the unhappy past, the nations strove to safeguard their security or to promote their interests."

Remembering the corruption of the Wilsonian vision by the secret treaties of the First World War, Hull was determined to prevent any sphere-of-influence nonsense after the Second World War. He therefore fought all proposals to settle border questions while the war was still on and, excluded as he largely was from wartime diplomacy, poured his not inconsiderable moral energy and frustration into the promulgation of virtuous and spacious general principles.

In adopting the universalist view, Roosevelt and Hull were not indulging personal hobbies. Sumner Welles, Adolf Berle, Averell Harriman, Charles Bohlen—all, if with a variety of nuances, opposed the sphere-of-influence approach. And here the State Department was expressing what seems clearly to have been the predominant mood of the American people, so long mistrustful of European power politics. The Republicans shared the true faith. John Foster Dulles argued that the great threat to peace after the war would lie in the revival of sphere-of-influence thinking. The United States, he said, must not permit Britain and Russia to revert to these bad old ways; it must therefore insist on American participation in all policy decisions for all territories in the world. Dulles wrote pessimistically in January 1945, "The three great powers which at Moscow agreed upon the 'closest coöperation' about European questions have shifted to a practice of separate, regional responsibility."

It is true that critics, and even friends, of the United States sometimes noted a discrepancy between the American passion for universalism when it applied to territory far from American shores and the preëminence the United States accorded its own interests nearer home. Churchill, seeking Washington's blessing for a sphere-of-influence initiative in Eastern Europe, could not forbear reminding the Americans, "We follow the lead of the United States in South America"; nor did any universalist of record propose the abolition of the Monroe Doctrine. But a convenient myopia prevented such inconsistencies from qualifying the ardency of the universalist faith.

There seem only to have been three officials in the United States Government who dissented. One was the Secretary of War, Henry L. Stimson, a classical balance-of-power man, who in 1944 opposed the creation of a vacuum in Central Europe by the pastoralization of Germany and in 1945 urged "the settlement of all territorial acquisitions in the shape of defense posts which each of these four powers may deem to be necessary for their own safety" in advance of any effort to establish a peacetime United Nations. Stimson considered the claim of Russia to a preferred position in Eastern Europe as not unreasonable: as he told President Truman, "he thought the Russians perhaps were being more realistic than we were in regard to their own security." Such a position for Russia seemed to him comparable to the preferred American position in Latin America; he even spoke of "our respective orbits." Stimson was therefore skeptical of what he regarded as the prevailing tendency "to hang on to exaggerated views of the Monroe Doctrine and at the same time butt into every question that comes up in Central Europe." Acceptance of spheres of influence seemed to him the way to avoid "a head-on collision."

A second official opponent of universalism was George Kennan, an eloquent advocate from the American Embassy in Moscow of "a prompt and clear recognition of the division of Europe into spheres of influence and of a policy based on the fact of such division." Kennan argued that nothing we could do would possibly alter the course of events in Eastern Europe; that we were deceiving ourselves by supposing that these countries had any future but Russian domination; that we should therefore relinquish Eastern Europe to the Soviet Union and avoid anything which would make things easier for the Russians by giving them economic assistance or by sharing moral responsibility for their actions.

A third voice within the government against universalism was (at least after the war) Henry A. Wallace. As Secretary of Commerce, he stated the sphere-of-influence case with trenchancy in the famous Madison Square Garden speech of September 1946 which led to his dismissal by President Truman:

> On our part, we should recognize that we have no more business in the *political* affairs of Eastern Europe than Russia has in the *political* affairs of Latin America, Western Europe, and the United States. . . . Whether we like it or not, the Russians will try to socialize their sphere of influence just as we try to democratize our sphere of influence. . . . The Russians have no more business stirring up native Communists to political activity in Western Europe, Latin America, and the United States than we have in interfering with the politics of Eastern Europe and Russia.

Stimson, Kennan and Wallace seem to have been alone in the government, however, in taking these views. They were very much minority voices. Meanwhile universalism, rooted in the American legal and moral tradition, overwhelmingly backed by contemporary opinion, received successive enshrinements in the Atlantic Charter of 1941, in the Declaration of the United Nations in 1942 and in the Moscow Declaration of 1943.

The Kremlin, on the other hand, thought *only* of spheres of interest; above all, the Russians were determined to protect their frontiers, and especially their border to the west, crossed so often and so bloodily in the dark course of their history. These western frontiers lacked natural means of defense—no great oceans, rugged mountains, steaming swamps or impenetrable jungles. The history of Russia had been the history of invasion, the last of which was by now horribly killing up to twenty million of its people. The protocol of Russia therefore meant the enlargement of the area of Russian influence. Kennan himself wrote (in May 1944), "Behind Russia's stubborn expansion lies only the age-old sense of insecurity of a sedentary people reared on an exposed plain in the neighborhood of fierce nomadic peoples," and he called this "urge" a "permanent feature of Russian psychology."

In earlier times the "urge" had produced the tsarist search for buffer states and maritime outlets. In 1939 the Soviet-Nazi pact and its secret protocol had enabled Russia to begin to satisfy in the Baltic states, Karelian Finland and Poland, part of what it conceived as its security requirements in Eastern Europe.

But the "urge" persisted, causing the friction between Russia and Germany in 1940 as each jostled for position in the area which separated them. Later it led to Molotov's new demands on Hitler in November 1940—a free hand in Finland, Soviet predominance in Rumania and Bulgaria, bases in the Dardanelles—the demands which convinced Hitler that he had no choice but to attack Russia. Now Stalin hoped to gain from the West what Hitler, a closer neighbor, had not dared yield him.

It is true that, so long as Russian survival appeared to require a second front to relieve the Nazi pressure, Moscow's demand for Eastern Europe was a little muffled. Thus the Soviet government adhered to the Atlantic Charter (though with a significant if obscure reservation about adapting its principles to "the circumstances, needs, and historic peculiarities of particular countries"). Thus it also adhered to the Moscow Declaration of 1943, and Molotov then, with his easy mendacity, even denied that Russia had any desire to divide Europe into spheres of influence. But this was guff, which the Russians were perfectly willing to ladle out if it would keep the Americans, and especially Secretary Hull (who made a strong personal impression at the Moscow conference) happy. "A declaration," as Stalin once observed to Eden, "I regard as algebra, but an agreement as practical arithmetic. I do not wish to decry algebra, but I prefer practical arithmetic."

The more consistent Russian purpose was revealed when Stalin offered the British a straight sphere-of-influence deal at the end of 1941. Britain, he suggested, should recognize the Russian absorption of the Baltic states, part of Finland, eastern Poland and Bessarabia; in return, Russia would support any special British need for bases or security arrangements in Western Europe. There was nothing specifically communist about these ambitions. If Stalin achieved them, he would be fulfilling an age-old dream of the tsars. The British reaction was mixed. "Soviet policy is amoral," as Anthony Eden noted at the time; "United States policy is exaggeratedly moral, at least where non-American interests are concerned." If Roosevelt was a universalist with occasional leanings toward spheres of influence and Stalin was a sphere-of-influence man with occasional gestures toward universalism, Churchill seemed evenly poised between the familiar realism of the balance of power, which he had so long recorded as an historian and manipulated as a statesman, and the hope that there must be some better way of doing things. His 1943 proposal of a world organization divided into regional councils represented an effort to blend universalist and sphere-of-interest conceptions. His initial rejection of Stalin's proposal in December 1941 as "directly contrary to the first, second and third articles of the Atlantic Charter" thus did not spring entirely from a desire to propitiate the United States. On the other hand, he had himself already reinterpreted the Atlantic Charter as applying only to Europe (and thus not to the British Empire), and he was, above all, an empiricist who never believed in sacrificing reality on the altar of doctrine.

So in April 1942 he wrote Roosevelt that "the increasing gravity of the war" had led him to feel that the Charter "ought not to be construed so as to deny Russia the frontiers she occupied when Germany attacked her." Hull, however, remained fiercely hostile to the inclusion of territorial provisions in the Anglo-Russian treaty; the American position, Eden noted, "chilled me with

Wilsonian memories." Though Stalin complained that it looked "as if the Atlantic Charter was directed against the U.S.S.R.," it was the Russian season of military adversity in the spring of 1942, and he dropped his demands.

He did not, however, change his intentions. A year later Ambassador Standley could cable Washington from Moscow: "In 1918 Western Europe attempted to set up a *cordon sanitaire* to protect it from the influence of bolshevism. Might not now the Kremlin envisage the formation of a belt of pro-Soviet states to protect it from the influences of the West?" It well might; and that purpose became increasingly clear as the war approached its end. Indeed, it derived sustenance from Western policy in the first area of liberation.

The unconditional surrender of Italy in July 1943 created the first major test of the Western devotion to universalism. America and Britain, having won the Italian war, handled the capitulation, keeping Moscow informed at a distance. Stalin complained:

> The United States and Great Britain made agreements but the Soviet Union received information about the results . . . just as a passive third observer. I have to tell you that it is impossible to tolerate the situation any longer. I propose that the [tripartite military-political commission] be established and that Sicily be assigned . . . as its place of residence.

Roosevelt, who had no intention of sharing the control of Italy with the Russians, suavely replied with the suggestion that Stalin send an officer "to General Eisenhower's headquarters in connection with the commission." Unimpressed, Stalin continued to press for a tripartite body; but his Western allies were adamant in keeping the Soviet Union off the Control Commission for Italy, and the Russians in the end had to be satisfied with a seat, along with minor Allied states, on a meaningless Inter-Allied Advisory Council. Their acquiescence in this was doubtless not unconnected with a desire to establish precedents for Eastern Europe.

Teheran in December 1943 marked the high point of three-power collaboration. Still, when Churchill asked about Russian territorial interests, Stalin replied a little ominously, "There is no need to speak at the present time about any Soviet desires, but when the time comes we will speak." In the next weeks, there were increasing indications of a Soviet determination to deal unilaterally with Eastern Europe—so much so that in early February 1944 Hull cabled Harriman in Moscow:

> Matters are rapidly approaching the point where the Soviet Government will have to choose between the development and extension of the foundation of international cooperation as the guiding principle of the postwar world as against the continuance of a unilateral and arbitrary method of dealing with its special problems even though these problems are admittedly of more direct interest to the Soviet Union than to other great powers.

As against this approach, however, Churchill, more tolerant of sphere-of-influence deviations, soon proposed that, with the impending liberation of the Balkans, Russia should run things in Rumania and Britain in Greece. Hull strongly opposed this suggestion but made the mistake of leaving Washington for a few days; and Roosevelt, momentarily free from his Wilsonian conscience, yielded to Churchill's plea for a three-months' trial. Hull resumed the fight on his return, and Churchill postponed the matter.

The Red Army continued its advance into Eastern Europe. In August the Polish Home Army, urged on by Polish-language broadcasts from Moscow, rose up against the Nazis in Warsaw. For 63 terrible days, the Poles fought valiantly on, while the Red Army halted on the banks of the Vistula a few miles away, and in Moscow Stalin for more than half this time declined to coöperate with the Western effort to drop supplies to the Warsaw Resistance. It appeared a calculated Soviet decision to let the Nazis slaughter the anti-Soviet Polish underground; and, indeed, the result was to destroy any substantial alternative to a Soviet solution in Poland. The agony of Warsaw caused the most deep and genuine moral shock in Britain and America and provoked dark forebodings about Soviet postwar purposes.

Again history enjoins the imaginative leap in order to see things for a moment from Moscow's viewpoint. The Polish question, Churchill would say at Yalta, was for Britain a question of honor. "It is not only a question of honor for Russia," Stalin replied, "but one of life and death. . . . Throughout history Poland had been the corridor of attack on Russia." A top postwar priority for any Russian régime must be to close that corridor. The Home Army was led by anti-communists. It clearly hoped by its action to forestall the Soviet occupation of Warsaw and, in Russian eyes, to prepare the way for an anti-Russian Poland. In addition, the uprising from a strictly operational viewpoint was premature. The Russians, it is evident in retrospect, had real military problems at the Vistula. The Soviet attempt in September to send Polish units from the Red Army across the river to join forces with the Home Army was a disaster. Heavy German shelling thereafter prevented the ferrying of tanks necessary for an assault on the German position. The Red Army itself did not take Warsaw for another three months. None the less, Stalin's indifference to the human tragedy, his effort to blackmail the London Poles during the ordeal, his sanctimonious opposition during five precious weeks to aerial resupply, the invariable coldness of his explanations ("the Soviet command has come to the conclusion that it must dissociate itself from the Warsaw adventure") and the obvious political benefit to the Soviet Union from the destruction of the Home Army—all these had the effect of suddenly dropping the mask of wartime comradeship and displaying to the West the hard face of Soviet policy. In now pursuing what he grimly regarded as the minimal requirements for the postwar security of his country, Stalin was inadvertently showing the irreconcilability of both his means and his ends with the Anglo-American conception of the peace.

Meanwhile Eastern Europe presented the Alliance with still another crisis that same September. Bulgaria, which was not at war with Russia, decided to surrender to the Western Allies while it still could; and the English and Americans at Cairo began to discuss armistice terms with Bulgarian envoys. Moscow, challenged by what it plainly saw as a Western intrusion into its own zone of vital interest, promptly declared war on Bulgaria, took over the surrender negotiations and, invoking the Italian precedent, denied its Western Allies any role in the Bulgarian Control Commission. In a long and thoughtful cable, Ambassador Harriman meditated on the problems of communication with the Soviet Union. "Words," he reflected, "have a different connotation to the Soviets than they have to us. When they speak of insisting on 'friendly governments' in their neighboring countries, they have in mind something quite different from what we would mean." The Russians, he surmised, really believed that Washington accepted "their position that although they would keep us informed they had the right to settle their problems with their western neighbors unilaterally." But the Soviet position was still in flux: "the Soviet Government is not one mind." The problem, as Harriman had earlier told Harry Hopkins, was "to strengthen the hands of those around Stalin who want to play the game along our lines." The way to do this, he now told Hull, was to

> be understanding of their sensitivity, meet them much more than half way, encourage them and support them wherever we can, and yet oppose them promptly with the greatest of firmness where we see them going wrong. . . . The only way we can eventually come to an understanding with the Soviet Union on the question of non-interference in the internal affairs of other countries is for us to take a definite interest in the solution of the problems of each individual country as they arise.

As against Harriman's sophisticated universalist strategy, however, Churchill, increasingly fearful of the consequences of unrestrained competition in Eastern Europe, decided in early October to carry his sphere-of-influence proposal directly to Moscow. Roosevelt was at first content to have Churchill speak for him too and even prepared a cable to that effect. But Hopkins, a more rigorous universalist, took it upon himself to stop the cable and warn Roosevelt of its possible implications. Eventually Roosevelt sent a message to Harriman in Moscow emphasizing that he expected to "retain complete freedom of action after this conference is over." It was now that Churchill quickly proposed —and Stalin as quickly accepted—the celebrated division of southeastern Europe: ending (after further haggling between Eden and Molotov) with 90 percent Soviet predominance in Rumania, 80 percent in Bulgaria and Hungary, fifty-fifty in Jugoslavia, 90 percent British predominance in Greece.

Churchill in discussing this with Harriman used the phrase "spheres of influence." But he insisted that these were only "immediate wartime arrangements" and received a highly general blessing from Roosevelt. Yet, whatever Churchill intended, there is reason to believe that Stalin construed the percentages as an agreement, not a declaration; as practical arithmetic, not algebra. For Stalin, it should be understood, the sphere-of-influence idea did not mean that he would abandon all efforts to spread communism in some other nation's sphere; it did mean that, if he tried this and the other side cracked down, he could not feel he had serious cause for complaint. As Kennan wrote to Harriman at the end of 1944:

As far as border states are concerned the Soviet government has never ceased to think in terms of spheres of interest. They expect us to support them in whatever action they wish to take in those regions, regardless of whether that action seems to us or to the rest of the world to be right or wrong. . . . I have no doubt that this position is honestly maintained on their part, and that they would be equally prepared to reserve moral judgment on any actions which we might wish to carry out, i.e., in the Caribbean area.

In any case, the matter was already under test a good deal closer to Moscow than the Caribbean. The communist-dominated resistance movement in Greece was in open revolt against the effort of the Papandreou government to disarm and disband the guerrillas (the same Papandreou whom the Greek colonels have recently arrested on the claim that he is a tool of the communists). Churchill now called in British Army units to crush the insurrection. This action produced a storm of criticism in his own country and in the United States; the American Government even publicly dissociated itself from the intervention, thereby emphasizing its detachment from the sphere-of-influence deal. But Stalin, Churchill later claimed, "adhered strictly and faithfully to our agreement of October, and during all the long weeks of fighting the Communists in the streets of Athens not one word of reproach came from *Pravda* or *Izvestia*," though there is no evidence that he tried to call off the Greek communists. Still, when the communist rebellion later broke out again in Greece, Stalin told Kardelj and Djilas of Jugoslavia in 1948, "The uprising in Greece must be stopped, and as quickly as possible."

No one, of course, can know what really was in the minds of the Russian leaders. The Kremlin archives are locked; of the primary actors, only Molotov survives, and he has not yet indicated any desire to collaborate with the Columbia Oral History Project. We do know that Stalin did not wholly surrender to sentimental illusion about his new friends. In June 1944, on the night before the landings in Normandy, he told Djilas that the English "find nothing sweeter than to trick their allies. . . . And Churchill? Churchill is the kind who, if you don't watch him, will slip a kopeck out of your pocket. Yes, a kopeck out of your pocket! . . . Roosevelt is not like that. He dips in his hand only for bigger coins." But whatever his views of his colleagues it is not unreasonable to suppose that Stalin would have been satisfied at the end of the war to secure what Kennan has called "a protective glacis along Russia's western border," and that, in exchange for a free hand in Eastern Europe, he was prepared to give the British and Americans equally free hands in their zones of vital interest, including in nations as close to Russia as Greece (for the British) and, very probably—or at least so the Jugoslavs believe—China (for the United States). In other words, his initial objectives were very probably not world conquest but Russian security.

It is now pertinent to inquire why the United States rejected the idea of stabilizing the world by division into spheres of influence and insisted on an East European strategy. One should warn against rushing to the conclusion that it was all a row between hard-nosed, balance-of-power realists and starry-eyed Wilsonians. Roosevelt, Hopkins, Welles, Harriman, Bohlen, Berle, Dulles and other universalists were tough and serious men. Why then did they rebuff the sphere-of-influence solution?

The first reason is that they regarded this solution as containing within itself the seeds of a third world war. The balance-of-power idea seemed inherently unstable. It had always broken down in the past. It held out to each power the permanent temptation to try to alter the balance in its own favor, and it built this temptation into the international order. It would turn the great powers of 1945 away from the objective of concerting common policies toward competition for postwar advantage. As Hopkins told Molotov at Teheran, "The President feels it essential to world peace that Russia, Great Britain and the United States work out this control question in a manner which will not start each of the three powers arming against the others." "The greatest likelihood of eventual conflict," said the Joint Chiefs of Staff in 1944 (the only conflict which the J.C.S., in its wisdom, could then glimpse "in the forseeable future" was between Britain and Russia), ". . . would seem to grow out of either nation initiating attempts to build up its strength, by seeking to attach to herself parts of Europe to the disadvantage and possible danger of her political adversary." The Americans were perfectly ready to acknowledge that Russia was entitled to convincing assurance of her national security—but not this way. "I could sympathize fully with Stalin's desire to protect his western borders from future attack," as Hull put it. "But I felt that this security could best be obtained through a strong postwar peace organization."

Hull's remark suggests the second objection: that the sphere-of-influence approach would, in the words of the State Department in 1945, "militate against the establishment and effective functioning of a broader system of general security in which all countries will have their part." The United Nations, in short, was seen as the alternative to the balance of power. Nor did the universalists see any necessary incompatibility between the Russian desire for "friendly governments" on its frontier and the American desire for self-determination in Eastern Europe. Before Yalta the State Department judged the general mood of Europe as "to the left and strongly in favor of far-reaching economic and social reforms, but not, however, in favor of a left-wing totalitarian regime to achieve these reforms." Governments in Eastern Europe could be sufficiently to the left "to allay Soviet suspicions" but sufficiently representative "of the center and *petit bourgeois* elements" not to seem a prelude to communist dictatorship. The American criteria were therefore that the government "should be dedicated to the preservation of civil liberties" and "should favor social and economic reforms." A string of New Deal states—of Finlands and Czechoslovakias—seemed a reasonable compromise solution.

Third, the universalists feared that the sphere-of-interest approach would be what Hull termed "a haven for the isolationists," who would advocate America's participation in Western Hemisphere affairs on condition that it did not participate in European or Asian affairs. Hull also feared that spheres of interest would lead to "closed trade areas or discriminatory systems" and thus defeat his cherished dream of a low-tariff, freely trading world.

Fourth, the sphere-of-interest solution meant the betrayal of the principles for which the Second World War was being fought—the Atlantic Charter, the Four Freedoms, the Declaration of the United Nations. Poland summed up the problem. Britain, having gone to war to defend the independence of Poland from the Germans, could not easily conclude the war by surrendering the independence of Poland to the Russians. Thus, as Hopkins told Stalin after Roosevelt's death in 1945, Poland had "become the symbol of our ability to work out problems with the Soviet Union." Nor could American liberals in general watch with equanimity while the police state spread into countries which, if they had mostly not been real democracies, had mostly not been tyrannies either. The execution in 1943 of Ehrlich and Alter, the Polish socialist trade union leaders, excited deep concern. "I have particularly in mind," Harriman cabled in 1944, "objection to the institution of secret police who may become involved in the persecution of persons of truly democratic convictions who may not be willing to conform to Soviet methods."

Fifth, the sphere-of-influence solution would create difficult domestic problems in American politics. Roosevelt was aware of the six million or more Polish votes in the 1944 election; even more acutely, he was aware of the broader and deeper attack which would follow if, after going to war to stop the Nazi conquest of Europe, he permitted the war to end with the communist conquest of Eastern Europe. As Archibald MacLeish, then Assistant Secretary of State for Public Affairs, warned in January 1945, "The wave of disillusionment which has distressed us in the last several weeks will be increased if the impression is permitted to get abroad that potentially totalitarian provisional governments are to be set up without adequate safeguards as to the holding of free elections and the realization of the principles of the Atlantic Charter." Roosevelt believed that no administration could survive which did not try everything short of war to save Eastern Europe, and he was the supreme American politician of the century.

Sixth, if the Russians were allowed to overrun Eastern Europe without argument, would that satisfy them? Even Kennan, in a dispatch of May 1944, admitted that the "urge" had dreadful potentialities: "If initially successful, will it know where to stop? Will it not be inexorably carried forward, by its very nature, in a struggle to reach the whole—to attain complete mastery of the shores of the Atlantic and the Pacific?" His own answer was that there were inherent limits to the Russian capacity to expand—"that Russia will not have an easy time in maintaining the power which it has seized over the people in Eastern and Central Europe unless it receives both moral and material assistance from the West." Subsequent developments have vindicated Kennan's argument. By the late forties, Jugoslavia and Albania, the two East European states farthest from the Soviet Union and the two in which communism was imposed from within rather than from without, had declared their independence of Moscow. But, given Russia's success in maintaining centralized control over the international communist movement for a quarter of a century, who in 1944 could have had much confidence in the idea of communist revolts against Moscow?

Most of those involved therefore rejected Kennan's answer and stayed with his question. If the West turned its back on Eastern Europe, the higher probability, in their view, was that the Russians would use their security zone, not just for defensive purposes, but as a springboard from which to mount an attack on Western Europe, now shattered by war, a vacuum of power awaiting its master. "If the policy is accepted that the Soviet Union has a right to penetrate her immediate neighbors for security," Harriman said in 1944, "penetration of the next immediate neighbors becomes at a certain time equally logical." If a row with Russia were inevitable, every consideration of prudence dictated that it should take place in Eastern rather than Western Europe.

Thus idealism and realism joined in opposition to the sphere-of-influence solution. The consequence was a determination to assert an American interest in the postwar destiny of all nations, including those of Eastern Europe. In the message which Roosevelt and Hopkins drafted after Hopkins had stopped Roosevelt's initial cable authorizing Churchill to speak for the United States at the Moscow meeting of October 1944, Roosevelt now said, "There is in this global war literally no question, either military or political, in which the United States is not interested." After Roosevelt's death Hopkins repeated the point to Stalin: "The cardinal basis of President Roosevelt's policy which the American people had fully supported had been the concept that the interests of the U.S. were worldwide and not confined to North and South America and the Pacific Ocean."

For better or worse, this was the American position. It is now necessary to attempt the imaginative leap and consider the impact of this position on the leaders of the Soviet Union who, also for better or for worse, had reached the bitter conclusion that the survival of their country depended on their unchallenged control of the corridors through which enemies had so often invaded their homeland. They could claim to have been keeping their own side of the sphere-of-influence bargain. Of course, they were working to capture the resistance movements of Western Europe; indeed, with the appointment of Oumansky as Ambassador to Mexico they were even beginning to enlarge underground operations in the Western Hemisphere. But, from their viewpoint, if the West permitted this, the more fools they; and, if the West stopped it, it was within their right to do so. In overt political matters the Russians were scrupulously playing the game. They had watched in silence while the British shot down communists in Greece. In Jugoslavia Stalin was urging Tito (as Djilas later revealed) to keep King Peter. They had not only acknowledged Western preëminence in Italy but had recognized the Badoglio régime; the Italian Communists had even voted (against the Socialists and the Liberals) for the renewal of the Lateran Pacts.

They would not regard anti-communist action in a Western zone as a *casus belli;* and they expected reciprocal license to assert their own authority in the East. But the principle of self-determination was carrying the United States into a deeper entanglement in Eastern Europe than the Soviet Union claimed as a right (whatever it was doing underground) in the affairs of Italy, Greece or China. When the Russians now exercised in Eastern Europe the same brutal control they were prepared to have Washington exercise in the American sphere of influence, the American protests, given the paranoia produced alike by Russian history and Leninist ideology, no doubt seemed not only an act of hypocrisy but a threat to security. To the Russians, a stroll into the neighborhood easily became a plot to burn down the house: when, for example, damaged American planes made emergency landings in Poland and Hungary, Moscow took this as attempts to organize the local resistance. It is not unusual to suspect one's adversary of doing what one is already doing oneself. At the same time, the cruelty with which the Russians executed their idea of spheres of influence—in a sense, perhaps, an unwitting cruelty, since Stalin treated the East Europeans no worse than he had treated the Russians in the thirties—discouraged the West from accepting the equation (for example, Italy = Rumania) which seemed so self-evident to the Kremlin.

So Moscow very probably, and not unnaturally, perceived the emphasis on self-determination as a systematic and deliberate pressure on Russia's western frontiers. Moreover, the restoration of capitalism to countries freed at frightful cost by the Red Army no doubt struck the Russians as the betrayal of the principles for which *they* were fighting. "That they, the victors," Isaac Deutscher has suggested, "should now preserve an order from which they had experienced nothing but hostility, and could expect nothing but hostility . . . would have been the most miserable anti-climax to their great 'war of liberation.' " By 1944 Poland was the critical issue; Harriman later said that "under instructions from President Roosevelt, I talked about Poland with Stalin more frequently than any other subject." While the West saw the point of Stalin's demand for a "friendly government" in Warsaw, the American insistence on the sovereign virtues of free elections (ironically in the spirit of 1917 Bolshevik decree of peace, which affirmed "the right" of a nation "to decide the forms of its state existence by a free vote, taken after the complete evacuation of the incorporating or, generally, of the stronger nation") created an insoluble problem in those countries, like Poland (and Rumania) where free elections would almost certainly produce anti-Soviet governments.

The Russians thus may well have estimated the Western pressures as calculated to encourage their enemies in Eastern Europe and to defeat their own minimum objective of a protective glacis. Everything still hung, however, on the course of military operations. The wartime collaboration had been created by one thing, and one thing alone: the threat of Nazi victory. So long as this threat was real, so was the collaboration. In late December 1944, von Rundstedt launched his counter-offensive in the Ardennes. A few weeks later, when Roosevelt, Churchill and Stalin gathered in the Crimea, it was in the shadow of this last considerable explosion of German power. The meeting at Yalta was still dominated by the mood of war.

Yalta remains something of an historical perplexity—less, from the perspective of 1967, because of a mythical American deference to the sphere-of-influence thesis than because of the documentable Russian deference to the universalist thesis. Why should Stalin in 1945 have accepted the Declaration on Liberated Europe and an agreement on Poland pledging that "the three governments will jointly" act to assure "free elections of governments responsive to the will of the people"? There are several probable answers: that the war was not over and the Russians still wanted the Americans to intensify their military effort in the West; that one clause in the Declaration premised action on "the opinion of the three governments" and thus implied a Soviet veto, though the Polish agreement was more definite; most of all that the universalist algebra of the Declaration was plainly in Stalin's mind to be construed in terms of the practical arithmetic of his sphere-of-influence agreement with Churchill the previous October. Stalin's assurance to Churchill at Yalta that a proposed Russian amendment to the Declaration would not apply to Greece makes it clear that Roosevelt's pieties did not, in Stalin's mind, nullify Churchill's percentages. He could well have been strengthened in this supposition by the fact that *after* Yalta, Churchill himself repeatedly reasserted the terms of the October agreement as if he regarded it, despite Yalta, as controlling.

Harriman still had the feeling before Yalta that the Kremlin had "two approaches to their postwar policies" and that Stalin himself was "of two minds." One approach emphasized the internal reconstruction and development of Russia; the other its external expansion. But in the meantime the fact which dominated all political decisions—that is, the war against Germany—was moving into its final phase. In the weeks after Yalta, the military situation changed with great rapidity. As the Nazi threat declined, so too did the need for coöperation. The Soviet Union, feeling itself menaced by the American idea of self-determination and the borderlands diplomacy to which it was leading, skeptical whether the United Nations would protect its frontiers as reliably as its own domination in Eastern Europe, began to fulfill its security requirements unilaterally.

In March Stalin expressed his evaluation of the United Nations by rejecting Roosevelt's plea that Molotov come to the San Francisco conference, if only for the opening sessions. In the next weeks the Russians emphatically and crudely worked their will in Eastern Europe, above all in the test country of Poland. They were ignoring the Declaration of Liberated Europe, ignoring the Atlantic Charter, self-determination, human freedom and everything else the Americans considered essential for a stable peace. "We must clearly recognize," Harriman wired Washington a few days before Roosevelt's death, "that the Soviet program is the establishment of totalitarianism, ending personal liberty and democracy as we know and respect it."

At the same time, the Russians also began to mobilize communist resources in the United States itself to block American universalism. In April 1945 Jacques Duclos, who had been the Comintern official responsible for the Western communist parties, launched in *Cahiers du Communisme* an uncompromising attack on the policy of the American Communist Party. Duclos sharply condemned the revisionism of Earl Browder, the American Communist leader, as "expressed in the concept of a long-term class peace in the United States, of the possibility of the suppression of the class struggle in the postwar period and of establishment of harmony between labor and capital." Browder was specifically rebuked for favoring the "self-determination" of Europe "west of the Soviet Union" on a bourgeois-democratic basis. The excommunication of Browderism was plainly the Politburo's considered reaction to the impending defeat of Germany; it was a signal to the communist parties of the West that they should recover their identity; it was Moscow's alert to communists everywhere that they should prepare for new policies in the postwar world.

The Duclos piece obviously could not have been planned and written much later than the Yalta conference—that is, well before a number of events which revisionists now cite in order to demonstrate American responsibility for the Cold War: before Allen Dulles, for example, began to negotiate the surrender of the German armies in Italy (the episode which provoked Stalin to charge Roosevelt with seeking a separate peace and provoked Roosevelt to denounce the "vile misrepresentations" of Stalin's informants); well before Roosevelt died; many months before the testing of the atomic bomb; even more months before Truman ordered that the bomb be dropped on Japan. William Z. Foster, who soon replaced Browder as the leader of the American Communist Party and embodied the new Moscow line, later boasted of having said in January 1944, "A post-war Roosevelt administration would continue to be, as it is now, an imperialist government." With ancient suspicions revived by the American insistence on universalism, this was no doubt the conclusion which the Russians were reaching at the same time. The Soviet canonization of Roosevelt (like their present-day canonization of Kennedy) took place after the American President's death.

The atmosphere of mutual suspicion was beginning to rise. In January 1945 Molotov formerly proposed that the United States grant Russia a $6 billion credit for postwar reconstruction. With characteristic tact he explained that he was doing this as a favor to save America from a postwar depression. The proposal seems to have been diffidently made and diffidently received. Roosevelt requested that the matter "not be pressed further" on the American side until he had a chance to talk with Stalin; but the Russians did not follow it up either at Yalta in February (save for a single glancing reference) or during the Stalin-Hopkins talks in May at Potsdam. Finally the proposal was renewed in the very different political atmosphere of August. This time Washington inexplicably mislaid the request during the transfer of the records of the Foreign Economic Administration to the State Department. It did not turn up again until March 1946. Of course this was impossible for the Russians to believe; it is hard enough even for those acquainted with the capacity of the American government for incompetence to believe; and it only strengthened Soviet suspicions of American purposes.

The American credit was one conceivable form of Western contribution to Russian reconstruction. Another was lend-lease, and the possibility of reconstruction aid under the lend-lease protocol had already been discussed in 1944. But in May 1945 Russia, like Britain, suffered from Truman's abrupt termination of lend-lease shipments—"unfortunate and even brutal," Stalin told Hopkins, adding that, if it was "designed as pressure on the Russians in order to soften them up, then it was a fundamental mistake." A third form was German reparations. Here Stalin in demanding $10 billion in reparations for the Soviet Union made his strongest fight at Yalta. Roosevelt, while agreeing essentially with Churchill's opposition, tried to postpone the matter by accepting the Soviet figure as a "basis for discussion"—a formula which led to future misunderstanding. In short, the Russian hope for major Western assistance in postwar reconstruction foundered on three events which the Kremlin could well have interpreted respectively as deliberate sabotage (the loan request), blackmail (lend-lease cancellation) and pro-Germanism (reparations).

Actually the American attempt to settle the fourth lend-lease protocol was generous and the Russians for their own reasons declined to come to an agreement. It is not clear, though, that satisfying Moscow on any of these financial scores would have made much essential difference. It might have persuaded some doves in the Kremlin that the U.S. government was genuinely friendly; it might have persuaded some hawks that the American anxiety for Soviet friendship was such that Moscow could do as it wished without inviting challenge from the United States. It would, in short, merely have reinforced both sides of the Kremlin debate; it would hardly have reversed deeper tendencies toward the deterioration of political relationships. Economic deals were surely subordinate to the quality of mutual political confidence; and here, in the months after Yalta, the decay was steady.

The Cold War had now begun. It was the product not of a decision but of a dilemma. Each side felt compelled to adopt policies which the other could not but regard as a threat to the principles of the peace. Each then felt compelled to undertake defensive measures. Thus the Russians saw no choice but to consolidate their security in Eastern Europe. The Americans, regarding Eastern Europe as the first step toward Western Europe, responded by asserting their interest in the zone the Russians deemed vital to their security. The Russians concluded that the West was resuming its old course of capitalist encirclement; that it was purposefully laying the foundation for anti-Soviet régimes in the area defined by the blood of centuries as crucial to Russian survival. Each side believed with passion that future international stability depended on the success of its own conception of world order. Each side, in pursuing its own clearly indicated and deeply cherished principles, was only confirming the fear of the other that it was bent on aggression.

Very soon the process began to acquire a cumulative momentum. The impending collapse of Germany thus provoked new troubles: the Russians, for example, sincerely feared that the West was planning a separate surrender of the German armies in Italy in a way which would release troops for Hitler's eastern front, as they subsequently feared that the Nazis might succeed in surrendering Berlin to the West. This was the context in which the atomic bomb now appeared. Though the revisionist argument that Truman dropped the bomb less to defeat Japan than to intimidate Russia is not convincing, this thought unquestionably appealed to some in Washington as at least an advantageous side-effect of Hiroshima.

So the machinery of suspicion and counter-suspicion, action and counter-action, was set in motion. But, given relations among traditional national states, there was still no reason, even with all the postwar jostling, why this should not have remained a manageable situation. What made it unmanageable, what caused the rapid escalation of the Cold War and in another two years completed the division of Europe, was a set of considerations which this account has thus far excluded.

Up to this point, the discussion has considered the schism within the wartime coalition as if it were entirely the result of disagreements among national states. Assuming this framework, there was unquestionably a failure of communication between America and Russia, a misperception of signals and, as time went on, a mounting tendency to ascribe ominous motives to the other side. It seems hard, for example, to deny that American postwar policy created genuine difficulties for the Russians and even assumed a threatening aspect for them. All this the revisionists have rightly and usefully emphasized.

But the great omission of the revisionists—and also the fundamental explanation of the speed with which the Cold War escalated—lies precisely in the fact that the Soviet Union was *not* a traditional national state.[4] This is where the "mirror image," invoked by some psychologists, falls down. For the Soviet Union was a phenomenon very different from America or Britain: it was a totalitarian state, endowed with an all-explanatory, all-consuming ideology, committed to the infallibility of government and party, still in a somewhat messianic mood, equating dissent with treason, and ruled by a dictator who, for all his quite extraordinary abilities, had his paranoid moments.

Marxism-Leninism gave the Russian leaders a view of the world according to which all societies were inexorably destined to proceed along appointed roads by appointed stages until they achieved the classless nirvana. Moreover, given the resistance of the capitalists to this development, the existence of any non-communist state was *by definition* a threat to the Soviet Union. "As long as capitalism and socialism exist," Lenin wrote, "we cannot live in peace: in the end, one or the other will triumph—a funeral dirge will be sung either over the Soviet Republic or over world capitalism."

Stalin and his associates, whatever Roosevelt or Truman did or failed to do, were bound to regard the United States as the enemy, not because of this deed or that, but because of the primordial fact that America was the leading capitalist power and thus, by Leninist syllogism, unappeasably hostile, driven by the logic of its system to oppose, encircle and destroy Soviet Russia. Nothing the United States could have done in 1944–45 would have abolished this mistrust, required and sanctified as it was by Marxist gospel—nothing short of the conversion of the United States into a Stalinist despotism; and even this would not have sufficed, as the experience of Jugoslavia and China soon showed, unless it were accompanied by total subservience to Moscow. So long as the United States remained a capitalist democracy, no American policy, given Moscow's theology, could hope to win basic Soviet confidence, and every American action was poisoned from the source. So long as the Soviet Union remained a messianic state, ideology compelled a steady expansion of communist power.

It is easy, of course, to exaggerate the capacity of ideology to control events. The tension of acting according to revolutionary abstractions is too much for most nations to sustain over a long period: that is why Mao Tse-tung has launched his Cultural Revolution, hoping thereby to create a permanent revolutionary mood and save Chinese communism from the degeneration which, in his view, has overtaken Russian communism. Still, as any revolution grows older, normal human and social motives will increasingly reassert themselves. In due course, we can be sure, Leninism will be about as effective in governing the daily lives of Russians as Christianity is in governing the daily lives of Americans. Like the Ten Commandments and the Sermon on the Mount, the Leninist verities will increasingly become platitudes for ritual observance, not

[4] This is the classical revisionist fallacy—the assumption of the rationality, or at least of the traditionalism, of states where ideology and social organization have created a different range of motives. So the Second World War revisionists omit the totalitarian dynamism of Nazism and the fanaticism of Hitler, as the Civil War revisionists omit the fact that the slavery system was producing a doctrinaire closed society in the American South. For a consideration of some of these issues, see "The Causes of the Civil War: A Note on Historical Sentimentalism" in my "The Politics of Hope" (Boston, 1963).

guides to secular decision. There can be no worse fallacy (even if respectable people practiced it diligently for a season in the United States) than that of drawing from a nation's ideology permanent conclusions about its behavior.

A temporary recession of ideology was already taking place during the Second World War when Stalin, to rally his people against the invader, had to replace the appeal of Marxism by that of nationalism. ("We are under no illusions that they are fighting for us," Stalin once said to Harriman. "They are fighting for Mother Russia.") But this was still taking place within the strictest limitations. The Soviet Union remained as much a police state as ever; the régime was as infallible as ever; foreigners and their ideas were as suspect as ever. "Never, except possibly during my later experience as ambassador in Moscow," Kennan has written, "did the insistence of the Soviet authorities on isolation of the diplomatic corps weigh more heavily on me . . . than in these first weeks following my return to Russia in the final months of the war. . . . [We were] treated as though we were the bearers of some species of the plague"—which, of course, from the Soviet viewpoint, they were: the plague of skepticism.

Paradoxically, of the forces capable of bringing about a modification of ideology, the most practical and effective was the Soviet dictatorship itself. If Stalin was an ideologist, he was also a pragmatist. If he saw everything through the lenses of Marxism-Leninism, he also, as the infallible expositor of the faith, could reinterpret Marxism-Leninism to justify anything he wanted to do at any given moment. No doubt Roosevelt's ignorance of Marxism-Leninism was inexcusable and led to grievous miscalculations. But Roosevelt's efforts to work on and through Stalin were not so hopelessly naïve as it used to be fashionable to think. With the extraordinary instinct of a great political leader, Roosevelt intuitively understood that Stalin was the *only* lever available to the West against the Leninist ideology and the Soviet system. If Stalin could be reached, then alone was there a chance of getting the Russians to act contrary to the prescriptions of their faith. The best evidence is that Roosevelt retained a certain capacity to influence Stalin to the end; the nominal Soviet acquiescence in American universalism as late as Yalta was perhaps an indication of that. It is in this way that the death of Roosevelt was crucial—not in the vulgar sense that his policy was then reversed by his successor, which did not happen, but in the sense that no other American could hope to have the restraining impact on Stalin which Roosevelt might for a while have had.

Stalin alone could have made any difference. Yet Stalin, in spite of the impression of sobriety and realism he made on Westerners who saw him during the Second World War, was plainly a man of deep and morbid obsessions and compulsions. When he was still a young man, Lenin had criticized his rude and arbitrary ways. A reasonably authoritative observer (N. S. Khrushchev) later commented, "These negative characteristics of his developed steadily and during the last years acquired an absolutely insufferable character." His paranoia, probably set off by the suicide of his wife in 1932, led to the terrible purges of the mid-thirties and the wanton murder of thousands of his Bolshevik comrades. "Everywhere and in everything," Khrushchev says of this period, "he saw 'enemies,' 'double-dealers' and 'spies.' " The crisis of war evidently steadied him in some way, though Khrushchev speaks of his "nervousness and hysteria . . . even after the war began." The madness, so rigidly controlled for a time, burst out with new and shocking intensity in the postwar years. "After the war," Khrushchev testifies,

> the situation became even more complicated. Stalin became even more capricious, irritable and brutal; in particular, his suspicion grew. His persecution mania reached unbelievable dimensions. . . . He decided everything, without any consideration for anyone or anything.
>
> Stalin's wilfulness showed itself . . . also in the international relations of the Soviet Union. . . . He had completely lost a sense of reality; he demonstrated his suspicion and haughtiness not only in relation to individuals in the USSR, but in relation to whole parties and nations.

A revisionist fallacy has been to treat Stalin as just another Realpolitik states-man, as Second World War revisionists see Hitler as just another Stresemann or Bismarck. But the record makes it clear that in the end nothing could satisfy Stalin's paranoia. His own associates failed. Why does anyone suppose that any conceivable American policy would have succeeded?

An analysis of the origins of the Cold War which leaves out these factors —the intransigence of Leninist ideology, the sinister dynamics of a totalitarian society and the madness of Stalin—is obviously incomplete. It was these factors which made it hard for the West to accept the thesis that Russia was moved only by a desire to protect its security and would be satisfied by the control of Eastern Europe; it was these factors which charged the debate between univer-salism and spheres of influence with apocalyptic potentiality.

Leninism and totalitarianism created a structure of thought and behavior which made postwar collaboration between Russia and America—in any normal sense of civilized intercourse between national states—inherently im-possible. The Soviet dictatorship of 1945 simply could not have survived such a collaboration. Indeed, nearly a quarter-century later, the Soviet régime, though it has meanwhile moved a good distance, could still hardly survive it without risking the release inside Russia of energies profoundly opposed to communist despotism. As for Stalin, he may have represented the only force in 1945 capable of overcoming Stalinism, but the very traits which enabled him to win absolute power expressed terrifying instabilities of mind and temperament and hardly offered a solid foundation for a peaceful world.

The difference between America and Russia in 1945 was that some Americans fundamentally believed that, over a long run, a modus vivendi with Russia was possible; while the Russians, so far as one can tell, believed in no more than a short-run modus vivendi with the United States.

Harriman and Kennan, this narrative has made clear, took the lead in warning Washington about the difficulties of short-run dealings with the Soviet Union. But both argued that, if the United States developed a rational policy and stuck to it, there would be, after long and rough passages, the prospect of eventual clearing. "I am, as you know," Harriman cabled Washington in early April, "a most earnest advocate of the closest possible understanding with the Soviet Union so that what I am saying relates only to how best to attain such understanding." Kennan has similarly made it clear that the function of his containment policy was "to tide us over a difficult time and bring us to the point where we could discuss effectively with the Russians the dangers and drawbacks this status quo involved, and to arrange with them for its peaceful replacement by a better and sounder one." The subsequent careers of both men attest to the honesty of these statements.

There is no corresponding evidence on the Russian side that anyone seriously sought a modus vivendi in these terms. Stalin's choice was whether his long-term ideological and national interests would be better served by a short-run truce with the West or by an immediate resumption of pressure. In October 1945 Stalin indicated to Harriman at Sochi that he planned to adopt the second course—that the Soviet Union was going isolationist. No doubt the succession of problems with the United States contributed to this decision, but the basic causes most probably lay elsewhere: in the developing situations in Eastern Europe, in Western Europe and in the United States.

In Eastern Europe, Stalin was still for a moment experimenting with techniques of control. But he must by now have begun to conclude that he had underestimated the hostility of the people to Russian dominion. The Hungarian elections in November would finally convince him that the Yalta formula was a road to anti-Soviet governments. At the same time, he was feeling more strongly than ever a sense of his opportunities in Western Europe. The other half of the Continent lay unexpectedly before him, politically demoralized, economically prostrate, militarily defenseless. The hunting would be better and safer than he had anticipated. As for the United States, the alacrity of postwar demobilization must have recalled Roosevelt's offhand remark at Yalta that "two years would be the limit" for keeping American troops in Europe. And, despite Dr. Eugene Varga's doubts about the imminence of American economic breakdown, Marxist theology assured Stalin that the United States was heading into a bitter postwar depression and would be consumed with its own problems. If the condition of Eastern Europe made unilateral action seem essential in the interests of Russian security, the condition of Western Europe and the United States offered new temptations for communist expansion. The Cold War was now in full swing.

It still had its year of modulations and accommodations. Secretary Byrnes conducted his long and fruitless campaign to persuade the Russians that America only sought governments in Eastern Europe "both friendly to the Soviet Union and representative of all the democratic elements of the country." Crises were surmounted in Trieste and Iran. Secretary Marshall evidently did not give up hope of a modus vivendi until the Moscow conference of foreign secretaries of March 1947. Even then, the Soviet Union was invited to participate in the Marshall Plan.

The point of no return came on July 2, 1947, when Molotov, after bringing 89 technical specialists with him to Paris and evincing initial interest in the project for European reconstruction, received the hot flash from the Kremlin, denounced the whole idea and walked out of the conference. For the next fifteen years the Cold War raged unabated, passing out of historical ambiguity into the realm of good versus evil and breeding on both sides simplifications, stereotypes and self-serving absolutes, often couched in interchangeable phrases. Under the pressure even America, for a deplorable decade, forsook its pragmatic and pluralist traditions, posed as God's appointed messenger to ignorant and sinful man and followed the Soviet example in looking to a world remade in its own image.

In retrospect, if it is impossible to see the Cold War as a case of American aggression and Russian response, it is also hard to see it as a pure case of Russian aggression and American response. "In what is truly tragic," wrote Hegel, "there must be valid moral powers on both the sides which come into collision. . . . Both suffer loss and yet both are mutually justified." In this sense, the Cold War had its tragic elements. The question remains whether it was an instance of Greek tragedy—as Auden has called it, "the tragedy of necessity," where the feeling aroused in the spectator is "What a pity it had to be this way" —or of Christian tragedy, "the tragedy of possibility," where the feeling aroused is "What a pity it was this way when it might have been otherwise."

Once something has happened, the historian is tempted to assume that it had to happen; but this may often be a highly unphilosophical assumption. The Cold War could have been avoided only if the Soviet Union had not been possessed by convictions both of the infallibility of the communist word and of the inevitability of a communist world. These convictions transformed an impasse between national states into a religious war, a tragedy of possibility into one of necessity. One might wish that America had preserved the poise and proportion of the first years of the Cold War and had not in time succumbed to its own forms of self-righteousness. But the most rational of American policies could hardly have averted the Cold War. Only today, as Russia begins to recede from its messianic mission and to accept, in practice if not yet in principle, the permanence of the world of diversity, only now can the hope flicker that this long, dreary, costly contest may at last be taking on forms less dramatic, less obsessive and less dangerous to the future of mankind.

22

CHRISTOPHER LASCH

The Cold War—Revisited and Revisioned

Christopher Lasch, in his response to the previous essay by Arthur Schlesinger, Jr., surveys Cold War history and concludes that the blame for the conflict can be divided between Russia and America. Some of the revisionist historians believe that the United States has taken on global responsibilities to mold other nations in its capitalist image; that it is and always has been an imperialist nation—one that will freely intervene in such diverse areas as Vietnam, the Dominican Republic, Cuba, Guatemala, and Lebanon.

Whether American ambitions have ever been this blatant is doubtful. But most assuredly the nation has been wrong time and time again about the capacities and intentions of Soviet Russia. America did not anticipate the Bolshevik revolution, and when the revolution broke out, did not think it would succeed. America thought socialism would be abandoned; it was not, and the nation sought not to recognize the new Soviet state. When America eventually did, the Germans had invaded Russia, and again the nation believed Russia would not last. She not only did but recovered quickly and overcame her technological deficiency to build missiles and atomic weapons. No doubt America underestimated Russia, thinking her atheistic and anti-capitalist—or, evil, and hence unable to prosper. When the nation finally realized that the Russian economy was strong and growing, it compensated by overestimating Soviet ambitions. The apocalyptic hysteria of the early fifties led, for example, to a suggestion by one major American newspaper that America use atomic weapons against Russia before Russia used them first.

The Soviet action against Czechoslovakia in 1968 seemed a throwback to the Stalin era in the eyes of those who had accepted the existence of a new Russia. Conservatives viewed it simply as fresh evidence of brutal totalitarianism. It may be, however, that the Russians would not have done what they did had not the United States intervened in Vietnam. Perhaps international relations may be described as a counterpoint of action and response; the arms and missile race are clear examples of this.

More than a year has passed since Arthur Schlesinger, Jr., announced that the time had come "to blow the whistle before the current outburst of revisionism regarding the origins of the cold war goes much further." Yet the outburst of revisionism shows no signs of subsiding. On the contrary, a growing number of historians and political critics, judging from such recent books as Ronald Steel's *Pax Americana* and Carl Oglesby's and Richard Shaull's *Containment and Change,* are challenging the view, once so widely accepted, that the cold war was an American response to Soviet expansionism, a distasteful burden reluctantly shouldered in the face of a ruthless enemy bent on our destruction, and that Russia, not the United States, must therefore bear the blame for shattering the world's hope that two world wars in the 20th century would finally give way to an era of peace.

"Revisionist" historians are arguing instead that the United States did as much as the Soviet Union to bring about the collapse of the wartime coalition. Without attempting to shift the blame exclusively to the United States, they are trying to show, as Gar Alperovitz puts it, that "the cold war cannot be understood simply as an American response to a Soviet challenge, but rather as the insidious interaction of mutual suspicions, blame for which must be shared by all."

Not only have historians continued to re-examine the immediate origins of the cold war—in spite of attempts to "blow the whistle" on their efforts—but the scope of revisionism has been steadily widening. Some scholars are beginning to argue that the whole course of American diplomacy since 1898 shows that the United States has become a counterrevolutionary power committed to the defense of a global status quo. Arno Mayer's monumental study of the Conference of Versailles, *Politics and Diplomacy of Peacemaking,* which has recently been published by Knopf and which promises to become the definitive work on the subject, announces in its subtitle what a growing number of historians have come to see as the main theme of American diplomacy: *Containment and Counterrevolution.*

Even Schlesinger has now admitted, in a recent article in *Foreign Affairs,* that he was "somewhat intemperate," a year ago, in deploring the rise of cold-war revisionism. Even though revisionist interpretations of earlier wars "have failed to stick," he says, "revisionism is an essential part of the process by which history . . . enlarges its perspectives and enriches its insights." Since he goes on to argue that "postwar collaboration between Russia and America [was] . . . inherently impossible" and that "the most rational of American policies could hardly have averted the cold war," it is not clear what Schlesinger thinks revisionism has done to enlarge our perspective and enrich our insights; but it is good to know, nevertheless, that revisionists may now presumably continue their work (inconsequential as it may eventually prove to be) without fear of being whistled to a stop by the referee.

The orthodox interpretation of the cold war, as it has come to be regarded, grew up in the late forties and early fifties—years of acute international tension, during which the rivalry between the United States and the Soviet Union repeatedly threatened to erupt in a renewal of global war. Soviet-American relations had deteriorated with alarming speed following the defeat of Hitler. At Yalta, in February, 1945, Winston Churchill had expressed the hope that world peace was nearer the grasp of the assembled statesmen of the great powers "than at any time in history." It would be "a great tragedy," he said, "if they, through inertia or carelessness, let it slip from their grasp. History would never forgive them if they did."

Yet the Yalta agreements themselves, which seemed at the time to lay the basis of postwar cooperation, shortly provided the focus of bitter dissension, in which each side accused the other of having broken its solemn promises. In Western eyes, Yalta meant free elections and parliamentary democracies in Eastern Europe, while the Russians construed the agreements as recognition of their demand for governments friendly to the Soviet Union.

The resulting dispute led to mutual mistrust and to a hardening of positions on both sides. By the spring of 1946 Churchill himself, declaring that "an iron curtain has descended" across Europe, admitted, in effect, that the "tragedy" he had feared had come to pass. Europe split into hostile fragments, the eastern half dominated by the Soviet Union, the western part sheltering nervously under the protection of American arms. NATO, founded in 1949 and countered by the Russian-sponsored Warsaw Pact, merely ratified the existing division of Europe.

From 1946 on, every threat to the stability of this uneasy balance produced an immediate political crisis—Greece in 1947, Czechoslovakia and the Berlin blockade in 1948—each of which, added to existing tensions, deepened hostility on both sides and increased the chance of war. When Bernard Baruch announced in April, 1947, that "we are in the midst of a cold war," no one felt inclined to contradict him. The phrase stuck, as an accurate description of postwar political realities.

Many Americans concluded, moreover, that the United States was losing the cold war. Two events in particular contributed to this sense of alarm—the collapse of Nationalist China in 1949, followed by Chiang Kai-shek's flight to Taiwan, and the explosion of an atomic bomb by the Russians in the same year. These events led to the charge that American leaders had deliberately or unwittingly betrayed the country's interests. The Alger Hiss case was taken by some people as proof that the Roosevelt Administration had been riddled by subversion.

Looking back to the wartime alliance with the Soviet Union, the American Right began to argue that Roosevelt, by trusting the Russians, had sold out the cause of freedom. Thus Nixon and McCarthy, aided by historians like Stefan J. Possony, C. C. Tansill and others, accused Roosevelt of handing Eastern Europe to the Russians and of giving them a preponderant interest in China which later enabled the Communists to absorb the entire country.

The liberal interpretation of the cold war—what I have called the orthodox interpretation—developed partly as a response to these charges. In liberal eyes, the right-wingers made the crucial mistake of assuming that American actions had been decisive in shaping the postwar world. Attempting to rebut this devil theory of postwar politics, liberals relied heavily on the argument that the shape of postwar politics had already been dictated by the war itself, in which the Western democracies had been obliged to call on Soviet help in defeating Hitler. These events, they maintained, had left the Soviet Union militarily dominant in Eastern Europe and generally occupying a position of much greater power, relative to the West, than the position she had enjoyed before the war.

In the face of these facts, the United States had very little leeway to influence events in what were destined to become Soviet spheres of influences, particularly since Stalin was apparently determined to expand even if it meant ruthlessly breaking his agreements—and after all it was Stalin, the liberals emphasized, and not Roosevelt or Truman, who broke the Yalta agreement on Poland, thereby precipitating the cold war.

These were the arguments presented with enormous charm, wit, logic and power in George F. Kennan's *American Diplomacy* (1951), which more than any other book set the tone of cold-war historiography. For innumerable historians, but especially for those who were beginning their studies in the fifties, Kennan served as the model of what a scholar should be—committed yet detached—and it was through the perspective of his works that a whole generation of scholars came to see not only the origins of the cold war, but the entire history of 20th century diplomacy.

It is important to recognize that Kennan's was by no means an uncritical perspective—indeed, for those unacquainted with Marxism, it seemed the only critical perspective that was available in the fifties. While Kennan insisted that the Russians were primarily to blame for the cold war, he seldom missed an opportunity to criticize the excessive moralism, the messianic vision of a world made safe for democracy, which he argued ran "like a red skein" through American diplomacy.

As late as 1960, a radical like Staughton Lynd could still accept the general framework of Kennan's critique of American idealism while noting merely that Kennan had failed to apply it to the specific events of the cold war and to the policy of containment which he had helped to articulate. "Whereas in general he counseled America to 'admit the validity and legitimacy of power realities and aspirations . . . and to seek their point of maximum equilibrium rather than their reform or their repression'—'reform or repression' of the Soviet system were the very goals which Kennan's influential writings of those years urged."

Even in 1960, however, a few writers had begun to attack not the specific applications of the principles of *Realpolitik* but the principles themselves, on the ground that on many occasions they served simply as rationalizations for American (not Soviet) expansionism. And whereas Lynd in 1960 could still write that the American demand for freedom in Eastern Europe, however misguided, "expressed a sincere and idealistic concern," some historians had already begun to take a decidedly more sinister view of the matter—asking, for instance, whether a country which demanded concessions in Eastern Europe that it was not prepared to grant to the Russians in Western Europe could really be accused, as the "realist" writers had maintained, of an excess of good-natured but occasionally incompetent altruism.

Meanwhile the "realist" interpretation of the cold war inspired a whole series of books—most notably, Herbert Feis's series (*Churchill-Roosevelt-Stalin; Between War and Peace; The Atomic Bomb and the End of World War II*); William McNeill's *America, Britain and Russia: Their Cooperation and Conflict;* Norman Graebner's *Cold War Diplomacy;* Louis J. Halle's *Dream and Reality* and *The Cold War as History;* and M. F. Herz's *Beginnings of the Cold War.*

Like Kennan, all of these writers saw containment as a necessary response to Soviet expansionism and to the deterioration of Western power in Eastern Europe. At the same time, they were critical, in varying degrees of the legalistic-moralistic tradition which kept American statesmen from looking at foreign relations in the light of balance-of-power considerations.

Some of them tended to play off Churchillian realism against the idealism of Roosevelt and Cordell Hull, arguing for instance, that the Americans should have accepted the bargain made between Churchill and Stalin in 1944, whereby Greece was assigned to the Western sphere of influence and Rumania, Bulgaria and Hungary to the Soviet sphere, with both liberal and Communist parties sharing in the control of Yugoslavia.

These criticisms of American policy, however, did not challenge the basic premise of American policy, that the Soviet Union was a ruthlessly aggressive power bent on world domination. They assumed, moreover, that the Russians were in a position to realize large parts of this program, and that only counter-pressure exerted by the West, in the form of containment and the Marshall Plan, prevented the Communists from absorbing all of Europe and much of the rest of the world as well.

It is their criticism of these assumptions that defines the revisionist historians and distinguishes them from the "realists." What impresses revisionists is not Russia's strength but her military weakness following the devastating war with Hitler, in which the Russians suffered much heavier losses than any other member of the alliance.

Beginning with Carl Marzani's *We Can Be Friends: Origins of the Cold War* (1952), revisionists have argued that Russia's weakness dictated, for the moment at least, a policy of postwar cooperation with the West. Western leaders' implacable hostility to Communism, they contend, prevented them from seeing this fact, a proper understanding of which might have prevented the cold war. This argument is spelled out in D. F. Fleming's two-volume study, *The Cold War and Its Origins* (1961); in David Horowitz's *The Free World Colossus* (1965), which summarizes and synthesizes a great deal of revisionist writing; in Gar Alperovitz's *Atomic Diplomacy: Hiroshima and Potsdam* (1965); and in the previously mentioned *Containment and Change.*

But the historian who has done most to promote a revisionist interpretation of the cold war, and of American diplomacy in general is William Appleman Williams of the University of Wisconsin, to whom most of the writers just mentioned owe a considerable debt. Williams's works, particularly *The Tragedy of American Diplomacy* (1959), not only challenge the orthodox interpretation of the cold war, they set against it an elaborate counterinterpretation which, if valid, forces one to see American policy in the early years of the cold war as part of a larger pattern of American globalism reaching as far back as 1898.

According to Williams, American diplomacy has consistently adhered to the policy of the "open door"—that is, to a policy of commercial, political and cultural expansion which seeks to extend American influence into every corner of the earth. This policy was consciously and deliberately embarked upon,

Williams argues, because American statesmen believed that American capitalism needed ever-expanding foreign markets in order to survive, the closing of the frontier having put an end to its expansion on the continent of North America. Throughout the 20th century, the makers of American foreign policy, he says, have interpreted the national interest in this light.

The cold war, in Williams' view, therefore has to be seen as the latest phase of a continuing effort to make the world safe for democracy—read liberal capitalism, American-style—in which the United States finds itself increasingly cast as the leader of a world-wide counterrevolution.

After World War II, Williams maintains, the United States had "a vast proportion of actual as well as potential power vis-à-vis the Soviet Union." The United States "cannot with any real warrant or meaning claim that it has been *forced* to follow a certain approach or policy." (Compare this with a statement by Arthur Schlesinger: "The cold war could have been avoided only if the Soviet Union had not been possessed by convictions both of the infallibility of the Communist word and of the inevitability of a Communist world.")

The Russians, by contrast, Williams writes, "viewed their position in the nineteen-forties as one of weakness, not offensive strength." One measure of Stalin's sense of weakness, as he faced the enormous task of rebuilding the shattered Soviet economy, was his eagerness to get a large loan from the United States. Failing to get such a loan—instead, the United States drastically cut back lend-lease payments to Russia in May, 1945—Stalin was faced with three choices, according to Williams:

He could give way and accept the American peace program at every point —which meant, among other things, accepting governments in Eastern Europe hostile to the Soviet Union.

He could follow the advice of the doctrinaire revolutionaries in his own country who argued that Russia's best hope lay in fomenting world-wide revolution.

Or he could exact large-scale economic reparations from Germany while attempting to reach an understanding with Churchill and Roosevelt on the need for governments in Eastern Europe not necessarily Communist but friendly to the Soviet Union.

His negotiations with Churchill in 1944 according to Williams, showed that Stalin had already committed himself, by the end of the war, to the third of these policies—a policy, incidentally, which required him to withdraw support from Communist revolutions in Greece and in other countries which under the terms of the Churchill-Stalin agreement had been conceded to the Western sphere of influence.

But American statesmen, the argument continues, unlike the British, were in no mood to compromise. They were confident of America's strength and Russia's weakness (although later they and their apologists found it convenient to argue that the contrary had been the case). Furthermore, they believed that "we cannot have full employment and prosperity in the United States without the foreign markets," as Dean Acheson told a special Congressional committee on postwar economic policy and planning in November, 1944. These considerations led to the conclusion, as President Truman put it in April, 1945, that the United States should "take the lead in running the world in the way that the world ought to be run"; or more specifically, in the words of Foreign Economic Administrator Leo Crowley, that "if you create good governments in foreign countries, automatically you will have better markets for ourselves." Accordingly, the United States pressed for the "open door" in Eastern Europe and elsewhere.

In addition to these considerations, there was the further matter of the atomic bomb, which first became a calculation in American diplomacy in July, 1945. The successful explosion of an atomic bomb in the New Mexican desert, Williams argues, added to the American sense of omnipotence and led the United States "to overplay its hand"—for in spite of American efforts to keep the Russians out of Eastern Europe, the Russians refused to back down.

Nor did American pressure have the effect, as George Kennan hoped, of promoting tendencies in the Soviet Union "which must eventually find their outlet in either the break-up or the gradual mellowing of Soviet power." Far from causing Soviet policy to mellow, American actions, according to Williams, stiffened the Russians in their resistance to Western pressure and strengthened the hand of those groups in the Soviet Union which had been arguing all along that capitalist powers could not be trusted.

Not only did the Russians successfully resist American demands in Eastern Europe, they launched a vigorous counterattack in the form of the Czechoslovakian coup of 1948 and the Berlin blockade. Both East and West thus found themselves committed to the policy of cold war, and for the next 15 years, until the Cuban missile crisis led to a partial detente, Soviet-American hostility was the determining fact of international politics.

Quite apart from his obvious influence on other revisionist historians of the cold war and on his own students in other areas of diplomatic history, Williams has had a measurable influence on the political radicals of the sixties, most of whom now consider it axiomatic that American diplomacy has been counter-revolutionary and that this fact reflects, not a series of blunders and mistakes as some critics have argued, but the basically reactionary character of American capitalism.

Some radicals now construe these facts to mean that American foreign policy therefore cannot be changed unless American society itself undergoes a revolutionary change. Carl Oglesby, for instance, argues along these lines in *Containment and Change.* From Oglesby's point of view, appeals to conscience or even to enlightened self-interest are useless; the cold war cannot end until the "system" is destroyed.

Williams thought otherwise. At the end of the 1962 edition of *The Tragedy of American Diplomacy,* he noted that "there is at the present time no radicalism in the United States strong enough to win power, or even a very significant influence, through the processes of representative government"—and he took it for granted that genuinely democratic change could come about only through representative processes. This meant, he thought, that "the well-being of the United States depends—*in the short-run but only in the short-run*—upon the extent to which calm and confident and enlightened conservatives can see and bring themselves to act upon the validity of a radical analysis."

In an essay in *Ramparts* last March, he makes substantially the same point in commenting on the new radicals' impatience with conservative critics of

American diplomacy like Senator Fulbright. Fulbright, Williams says, attracted more support for the position of more radical critics than these critics had attracted through their own efforts. "He hangs tough over the long haul, and that is precisely what American radicalism has never done in the 20th century."

As the New Left becomes more and more beguiled by the illusion of its own revolutionary potential, and more and more intolerant of radicals who refuse to postulate a revolution as the only feasible means of social change, men like Williams will probably become increasingly uncomfortable in the presence of a movement they helped to create. At the same time, Williams' radicalism, articulated in the fifties before radicalism came back into fashion, has alienated the academic establishment and prevented his works from winning the widespread recognition and respect they deserve. In scholarly journals, many reviews of Williams' work—notably a review by Oscar Handlin of *The Contours of American History* in the *Mississippi Valley Historical Review* a few years ago—have been contemptuous and abusive in the extreme. The result is that Williams' books on diplomatic history are only beginning to pass into the mainstream of scholarly discourse, years after their initial publication.

Next to Williams' *Tragedy of American Diplomacy,* the most important attack on the orthodox interpretation of the cold war is Alperovitz's *Atomic Diplomacy.* A young historian trained at Wisconsin, Berkeley and King's College, Cambridge, and currently a research fellow at Harvard, Alperovitz adds very little to the interpretation formulated by Williams, but he provides Williams' insights with a mass of additional documentation. By doing so, he has made it difficult for conscientious scholars any longer to avoid the challenge of revisionist interpretations. Unconventional in its conclusions, *Atomic Diplomacy* is thoroughly conventional in its methods. That adds to the book's persuasiveness. Using the traditional sources of diplomatic history—official records, memoirs of participants, and all the unpublished material to which scholars have access—Alperovitz painstakingly reconstructs the evolution of American policy during the six-month period March to August, 1945. He proceeds with a thoroughness and caution which, in the case of a less controversial work, would command the unanimous respect of the scholarly profession. His book is no polemic. It is a work in the best—and most conservative—traditions of historical scholarship. Yet the evidence which Alperovitz has gathered together challenges the official explanation of the beginnings of the cold war at every point.

What the evidence seems to show is that as early as April, 1945, American officials from President Truman on down had decided to force a "symbolic showdown" with the Soviet Union over the future of Eastern Europe. Truman believed that a unified Europe was the key to European recovery and economic stability, since the agricultural southeast and the industrial northwest depended on each other. Soviet designs on Eastern Europe, Truman reasoned, threatened to disrupt the economic unity of Europe and therefore had to be resisted. The only question was whether the showdown should take place immediately or whether it should be delayed until the bargaining position of the United States has improved.

At first it appeared to practically everybody that delay would only weaken the position of the United States. Both of its major bargaining counters, its armies in Europe and its lend-lease credits to Russia, could be more effectively employed at once, it seemed, than at any future time. Accordingly, Truman tried to "lay it on the line" with the Russians. He demanded that they "carry out their [Yalta] agreements" by giving the pro-Western elements in Poland an equal voice in the Polish Government (although Roosevelt, who made the Yalta agreements, believed that "we placed, as clearly shown in the agreement, somewhat more emphasis" on the Warsaw [pro-Communist] Government than on the pro-Western leaders). When Stalin objected that Poland was "a country in which the U.S.S.R. is interested first of all and most of all," the United States tried to force him to give in by cutting back lend-lease payments to Russia.

At this point, however—in April, 1945—Secretary of War Henry L. Stimson convinced Truman that "we shall probably hold more cards in our hands later than now." He referred to the atomic bomb, and if Truman decided to postpone the showdown with Russia, it was because Stimson and other advisers persuaded him that the new weapon would "put us in a position," as Secretary of State James F. Byrnes argued, "to dictate our own terms at the end of the war."

To the amazement of those not privy to the secret, Truman proceeded to take a more conciliatory attitude toward Russia, an attitude symbolized by Harry Hopkins's mission to Moscow in June, 1945. Meanwhile, Truman twice postponed the meeting with Churchill and Stalin at Potsdam. Churchill complained, "Anyone can see that in a very short space of time our armed power on the Continent will have vanished."

But when Truman told Churchill that an atomic bomb had been successfully exploded at Alamogordo, exceeding all expectations, Churchill immediately understood and endorsed the strategy of delay. "We were in the presence of a new factor in human affairs," he said, "and possessed of powers which were irresistible." Not only Germany but even the Balkans, which Churchill and Roosevelt had formerly conceded to the Russian sphere, now seemed amenable to Western influence. That assumption, of course, had guided American policy (though not British policy) since April, but it could not be acted upon until the bombing of Japan provided the world with an unmistakable demonstration of American military supremacy.

Early in September, the foreign ministers of the Big Three met in London. Byrnes—armed, as Stimson noted, with "the presence of the bomb in his pocket, so to speak, as a great weapon to get through" the conference—tried to press the American advantage. He demanded that the Governments of Bulgaria and Rumania reorganize themselves along lines favorable to the West. In Bulgaria, firmness won a few concessions; in Rumania, the Russians stood firm. The American strategy had achieved no noteworthy success. Instead —as Stimson, one of the architects of that strategy, rather belatedly observed— it had "irretrievably embittered" Soviet-American relations.

The revisionist view of the origins of the cold war, as it emerges from the works of Williams, Alperovitz, Marzani, Fleming, Horowitz, and others, can be summarized as follows. The object of American policy at the end of World War II was not to defend Western or even Central Europe but to force the Soviet Union out of Eastern Europe. The Soviet menace to the "free world," so often cited as the justification of the containment policy, simply did not exist in the minds of American planners. They believed themselves to be negotiating not from weakness but from almost unassailable superiority.

Nor can it be said that the cold war began because the Russians "broke their agreements." The general sense of the Yalta agreements—which were in any case very vague—was to assign to the Soviet Union a controlling influence in Eastern Europe. Armed with the atomic bomb, American diplomats tried to take back what they had implicitly conceded at Yalta.

The assumption of American moral superiority, in short, does not stand up under analysis.

The opponents of this view have yet to make a very convincing reply. Schlesinger's recent article in *Foreign Affairs,* referred to at the outset of this article, can serve as an example of the kind of arguments which historians are likely to develop in opposition to the revisionist interpretation. Schlesinger argues that the cold war came about through a combination of Soviet intransigence and misunderstanding. There were certain "problems of communication" with the Soviet Union, as a result of which "the Russians might conceivably have misread our signals." Thus the American demand for self-determination in Poland and other East European countries "very probably" appeared to the Russians "as a systematic and deliberate pressure on Russia's western frontiers."

Similarly, the Russians "could well have interpreted" the American refusal of a loan to the Soviet Union, combined with cancellation of lend-lease, "as deliberate sabotage" of Russia's postwar reconstruction or as "blackmail." In both cases, of course, there would have been no basis for these suspicions; but "we have thought a great deal more in recent years," Schlesinger says, ". . . about the problems of communication in diplomacy," and we know how easy it is for one side to misinterpret what the other is saying.

This argument about difficulties of "communications" at no point engages the evidence uncovered by Alperovitz and others—evidence which seems to show that Soviet officials had good reason to interpret American actions exactly as they did: as attempt to dictate American terms.

In reply to the assertion that the refusal of a reconstruction loan was part of such an attempt, Schlesinger can only argue weakly that the Soviet request for a loan was "inexplicably mislaid" by Washington during the transfer of records from the Foreign Economic Administration to the State Department! "Of course," he adds, "this was impossible for the Russians to believe." It is impossible for some Americans to believe. As William Appleman Williams notes, Schlesinger's explanation of the "inexplicable" loss of the Soviet request "does not speak to the point of how the leaders could forget the request even if they lost the document."

When pressed on the matter of "communications," Schlesinger retreats to a second line of argument, namely that none of these misunderstandings "made much essential difference," because Stalin suffered from "paranoia" and was "possessed by convictions both of the infallibility of the Communist word and of the inevitability of a Communist world."

The trouble is that there is very little evidence which connects either Stalin's paranoia or Marxist-Leninist ideology or what Schlesinger calls "the sinister dynamics of a totalitarian society" with the actual course of Soviet diplomacy during the formative months of the cold war. The only piece of evidence that Schlesinger has been able to find is an article by the Communist theoretician Jacques Duclos in the April, 1945, issue of *Cahiers du communisme,* the journal of the French Communist party, which proves, he argues, that Stalin had already abandoned the wartime policy of collaboration with the West and had returned to the traditional Communist policy of world revolution.

Even this evidence, however, can be turned to the advantage of the revisionists. Alperovitz points out that Duclos did not attack electoral politics or even collaboration with bourgeois governments. What he denounced was precisely the American Communists' decision, in 1944, to withdraw from electoral politics. Thus the article, far from being a call to world revolution, "was one of many confirmations that European Communists had decided to abandon violent revolutionary struggle in favor of the more modest aim of electoral success." And while this decision did not guarantee world peace, neither did it guarantee 20 years of cold war.

Schlesinger first used the Duclos article as a trump card in a letter to the *New York Review of Books,* Oct. 20, 1966, which called forth Alperovitz's rejoinder. It is symptomatic of the general failure of orthodox historiography to engage the revisionist argument that Duclos's article crops up again in Schlesinger's more recent essay in *Foreign Affairs,* where it is once again cited as evidence of a "new Moscow line," without any reference to the intervening objections raised by Alperovitz.

Sooner or later, however, historians will have to come to grips with the revisionist interpretation of the cold war. They cannot ignore it indefinitely. When serious debate begins, many historians, hitherto disposed to accept without much question the conventional account of the cold war, will find themselves compelled to admit its many inadequacies. On the other hand, some of the ambiguities of the revisionist view, presently submerged in the revisionists' common quarrel with official explanations, will begin to force themselves to the surface. Is the revisionist history of the cold war essentially an attack on "the doctrine of historical inevitability," as Alperovitz contends? Or does it contain an implicit determinism of its own?

Two quite different conclusions can be drawn from the body of revisionist scholarship. One is that American policy-makers had it in their power to choose different policies from the ones they chose. That is, they could have adopted a more conciliatory attitude toward the Soviet Union, just as they now have the choice of adopting a more conciliatory attitude toward Communist China and toward nationalist revolutions elsewhere in the Third World.

The other is that they have no such choice, because the inner requirements of American capitalism force them to pursue a consistent policy of economic and political expansion. "For matters to stand otherwise," writes Carl Oglesby, "the Yankee free-enterpriser would . . . have to . . . take sides against himself. . . . He would have to change entirely his style of thought and action. In a word, he would have to become a revolutionary Socialist whose aim was the destruction of the present American hegemony."

Pushed to what some writers clearly regard as its logical conclusion, the revisionist critique of American foreign policy thus becomes the obverse of the cold-war liberals' defense of that policy, which assumes that nothing could have modified the character of Soviet policy short of the transformation of the Soviet Union into a liberal democracy—which is exactly the goal the containment policy sought to promote. According to a certain type of revisionism, American policy has all the rigidity the orthodox historians attribute to the U.S.S.R., and this inflexibility made the cold war inevitable.

Moreover, Communism really did threaten American interests, in this view. Oglesby argues that, in spite of its obvious excesses, the "theory of the International Communist Conspiracy is not the hysterical old maid that many leftists seem to think it is." If there is no conspiracy, there is a world revolution and it "does aim itself at America"—the America of expansive corporate capitalism.

Revisionism, carried to these conclusions, curiously restores cold-war anti-Communism to a kind of intellectual respectability, even while insisting on its immorality. After all, it concludes, the cold warriors were following the American national interest. The national interest may have been itself corrupt, but the policy-makers were more rational than their critics may have supposed.

23

EMMET JOHN HUGHES

Eisenhower: An Evaluation

A fairly prevalent interpretation of the Eisenhower administration weighs one presidential term of creditable achievement against one of failure. According to this view, Ike, as the father of a country yearning for stability and rest, performed three welcome services during his first years in office: he ended the Korean War on conditions that might have been unacceptable under Truman; he made palatable and acceptable to almost everyone the reforms of the New Deal and thereby restored confidence in the national government; and by ignoring Senator Joe McCarthy he allowed that ruthless but sometimes witless demagogue to destroy himself. In Eisenhower's second term the economy lagged; foreign relations plummeted toward disaster in Asia and fragmented in Europe; Russia's success in launching Sputnik in 1957 and the U-2 affair on the eve of the 1960 summit conference exacerbated matters; and vacillation on civil rights completed the image of decline.

This reconstruction of the Eisenhower administration has partial truth, but Emmet John Hughes's attempt to see it whole better records the continuities of the President's policies and contributes to a sharper understanding of them.

Dwight David Eisenhower, the man of many paradoxes, left the office of the presidency as the most widely popular—and the most sharply criticized—citizen of his nation. By almost unanimous consensus of all political leaders of both parties, only the constitutional bar to a third term kept him from inflicting upon John Fitzgerald Kennedy an electoral rout as severe and complete as those twice suffered by Adlai Stevenson. By almost equally unanimous consensus of the national community of intellectuals and critics—journalists and academicians, pundits and prophets—his conduct of the presidency was unskillful and his definition of it inaccurate. And these fiercely contradictory judgments inspired two images: the profile acidly etched by his detractors, the portrait warmly painted by his idolators.

The caricature was—as always—easier to draw.

Here, in this vignette, was a weak and irresolute man, surrounded by vastly stronger men, their vision small but their will powerful. To them, this man delegated the powers of the presidency slackly and carelessly. To the role of national leader, he came unequipped by experience, by knowledge, by temperament, or even by taste for politics. To the role of military responsibility, he brought the prejudices of a professional life that had effectively ended before the advent of nuclear weapons. To the role of world statesman, he brought a genial and gregarious disposition, undisciplined and unsophisticated, never holding promise of a diplomacy more profound than a rather maudlin kind of global sociability. On the world scene, he sought to check the power of Soviet Communism by complacent citation of the "spiritual" superiority of American life; and he thereby showed a blindness to national danger reminiscent of a Stanley Baldwin of the 1930s, assuring the people of Great Britain of their serene immunity to the menace of Nazi power. On the national scene, he persisted, too, in facile exhortations on "spiritual" and "moral" values—even while he practiced an aloof neutralism toward the struggle for civil rights that seemed, to many of his citizens, the most pure and urgent moral issue to confront his presidency. As a politician, he set forth to remake the blurred image of the Republican party, but he merely ended by suffering himself to be remade in *its* image. As an intellectual, he bestowed upon the games of golf and bridge all the enthusiasm and perseverance that he withheld from books and ideas. As a President, he sought to affirm the dignity of his high office by the simple device of reducing its complex functions to the circumspect discharge of its ceremonial obligations. As the leader of the world's greatest democracy—charting its flight through all the clouds and storms of the mid-twentieth century, on toward the mysteries and perils of the Age of Space—he elected to leave his nation to fly on automatic pilot.

The appreciative portrait was—as almost always—not so easy to draw.

Here, by this portrait, was a man of selfless and serious patriotism. Physically, he gave of himself unstintingly, in bearing the burden of the presidency, despite three illnesses that would have crippled weaker men. Morally, he gave uncompromising scorn to all temptations of expediency, despite knowing full well the easy accolades to be won at almost any instant—by publicly chastising a McCarthy, by blaming congressional leadership for failures, by wrathfully denouncing a Faubus, by combating recession with tax reduction or government deficit, by appeasing critics with the replacement of a Dulles or a Benson, or, most dramatically, by proclaiming himself the soldier-champion of gigantic military programs to assure American supremacy in the Age of Space. Whatever the crisis or the clamor, he stayed defiantly faithful to the policy—or to the man—as honest conviction decreed. As a national leader, he avoided, through the greater part of a perilous decade, his and his people's two greatest fears—war in the world and depression at home. As a partisan leader, he steered Republicanism toward new historic ground, far from its isolationist traditions; and, for all the conservatism of his economics, he left the policies of the New Deal and the Fair Deal intact and secure after eight years of a Republican Administration. Personally, he led his party to two successive and smashing national triumphs, after it had endured twenty years of failure and rebuff. He brought to the White House itself a personal sense of dignity and honor that could only elevate the office of the presidency in the eyes of his people. When he entered this office, the political air of the nation was sulphurous with bitterness, recrimination, and frustration. And when he left office, this air was clean of all such rancor, fresh with good will and good feeling.[1]

The two portraits of the man deny and taunt each other. It is easy and obvious to note—as I believe—that each contains some pieces and fractions of the whole truth. It is less easy—but more important—to discern that both suffer from the same flaws and tricks. Both confuse the plausible with the actual, the logic with the reality. Both ignore the capricious and imponderable and the elusive in history. And so, by the neat fancy of fitting every event to some intent, they contrive the most seductive distortions: the happy occurrence confers credit, where none may be due, and the mourned occasion decrees guilt, where blame may be impossible.

A few instances may give warning. Thus, for example . . .

The hugeness of a President's popularity may be consoling or alarming, according to the viewer's prejudice, but it is of little relevance to a historian's judgment. Through the years, the upward graph of Eisenhower's popularity seemed a fact of formidable meaning. Yet almost immediately upon his departure from office, the significance of this fact seemed drastically to depreciate, for his successor in the presidency—a man with a wholly different concept of the office and with a record of only mingled successes and reverses—scaled even higher peaks in the favor of opinion polls. The generosity of such popular tributes to both men suggests that these accolades may reveal not much about either of the men, but more about the temper of the nation. For the awareness of national peril seems inevitably to inspire an anxious sense of dependence upon the presidency, unbridled by the strict appraisal of logic or fact. And this sense—of both danger and dependence—may be greatly quickened, in fact, by a manifest lapse in presidential leadership. Thus the humiliation suffered by Eisenhower on his Far Eastern journey, in the summer of 1960, only brought forth new signs of popular acclaim. At such moments of national stress, partisans cannot rejoice and critics cannot gloat—and a Chief Executive's political error or diplomatic defeat can acquire a weirdly self-nullifying quality. In a democracy—whose very life may depend upon the clarity and courage of its faculties for self-criticism—this could be an alarming sign of intellectual slackness. It cannot be confused, in any event, with a true estimate of the merit or the vigor of a President's leadership.

And the national political scene, quite as much as the world scene, carries its own warnings against the too simple and sweeping judgment. An indictment

---

[1] Nine months after leaving the presidency, Eisenhower cited this as the first item, when asked to enumerate "your greatest achievements." In his words: "When I came to the presidency the country was rather in an unhappy state. There was bitterness and there was quarreling . . . in Washington and around the country. I tried to create an atmosphere of greater serenity and mutual confidence, and I think that it . . . was noticeable over those eight years that that was brought about." ("Eisenhower on the Presidency," CBS telecast with Walter Cronkite, October 12, 1961.)

of Eisenhower, for example, for allowing himself to be a meek creature of traditional Republican conservatism, rather than a bold creator of a new Republican liberalism, must start from the premise that Eisenhower was not, in fact, a conservative. The passage of years proved this premise largely false. Initially, the reality was obscured by Eisenhower's *foreign* policies, for his stands on mutual security or reciprocal trade invited the label of "liberal," even as they invited the hostility of most Republican traditionalists. But Eisenhower, after leaving the presidency, candidly compared himself and Robert Taft: "I found him to be more liberal in his support of some policies even than I was. . . . I laughed at him one day, and I said, 'How did you ever happen to be known as a conservative and me as a liberal?'" [2] The progress of his presidency brought a more and more heavily conservative accent to Eisenhower's policies and pronouncements. But this was not a matter of slow acquiescence to new political pressures: it meant a gradual reaffirmation of old political persuasions. And to appreciate this, one need only imagine the personal politics of a Dwight David Eisenhower from Abilene, Kansas, who never served in World War II; who passed no memorable years in Europe, there to become the comrade of a Churchill or a De Gaulle; and who became known to the political annals of the 1950s as the quite predictable congressman from the Fourth District of his native Kansas.

For like reasons, there is some unrealism in any tribute to Eisenhower for ratifying or consolidating the social gains of New Deal and Fair Deal. Eight years of a Republican Administration did leave intact all such laws and measures. Yet it is hardly accurate to ascribe this to presidential statesmanship, liberalism, or even choice. The Administration was not required to defend these measures against challenge, but merely to accept their immutability, as a matter of political necessity. And even with this tacit act of acceptance, the President himself held an antipathy toward TVA—and at least a tolerance toward right-to-work laws—scarcely reminiscent of the basic social attitudes of the New Deal. There was exceedingly little here, then, to suggest the labor of a President who was *trying* to be a farsighted consolidator of past social legislation. And it is not easy to assign historic credit to a man for achievements he never attempted.

All these cautions and qualifications bring some light to the question of the final fate of one of the supreme objectives of the Eisenhower presidency.

This purpose was the invigoration and the rejuvenation of the Republican party.

This purpose ended in defeat.

The size of the defeat was easy to measure. The loss of Executive power in the 1960 elections, despite all advantages enjoyed by the incumbent Administration, could not be ascribed, harshly or entirely, to popular distaste for the personality of Richard Nixon. For the signs of Republican weakness and ineptitude were visible almost everywhere across the political landscape. The Republican party that in 1930 claimed governorships in thirty states could boast of merely sixteen in 1960. Of the nation's forty-one major urban centers, the Democrats in 1960 swept a total of twenty-seven. Through all the Eisenhower

2 Ibid.

Years, in fact, the total polling strength of the GOP had steadily declined despite the President's personal electoral triumphs—from 49 percent in 1950, to 47 percent in 1954, finally to 43 percent in 1958. In the Congress convening as Eisenhower left the presidency, the GOP was outnumbered three to two in the House of Representatives and two to one in the Senate. Such a stark reckoning more than sufficed, in short, to justify Eisenhower's own unhappy query to Sherman Adams: "What happened . . . ?"

The answer clearly lay, in great part, with the man who asked the question. The very definition he imposed upon his roles as President and party leader approached a political philosophy of self-denial. Months after leaving office, for example, he was asked if he had "ever sort of turned the screw on Congress to get something done . . . saying you'll withhold an appointment or something like that." And with disarming accuracy, Eisenhower answered: "No, never. I took very seriously the matter of appointments and [their] qualifications. . . . Possibly I was not as shrewd and as clever in this matter as some of the others, but I never thought that any of these appointments should be used for bringing pressure upon the Congress." [3] The President proudly forswearing the use of "pressure," of course, comes close to brusquely renouncing power itself. And such smothering of his own voice must have two inescapable consequences: the floundering of his legislative program in the halls of the Congress, and the blurring of his party's image in the eyes of the electorate.

As he treated the political present, so, too, Eisenhower faced the future: he served as a passive witness, rather than an aggressive judge, in the choice of leadership to follow him. It is reasonable to accept the sincerity of his belief— by 1960—that "experience" significantly qualified Richard Nixon for the presidency. It is no less certain, however, that—before 1960—Eisenhower constantly reviewed and privately discussed many alternatives to a successor whom he regarded as less than ideal. Along with such personal favorites as Robert Anderson or Alfred Gruenther, he faced—after the 1958 elections—the far more serious political possibility of a Nelson Rockefeller. Even if all calculations of simple political success were disregarded—including John Fitzgerald Kennedy's own calm judgment that his defeat could have been easy—the striking fact is that Eisenhower did nothing to encourage his party to weigh such alternatives, even while he pondered them within himself.

The conclusion must be that—for the Republican party under the leadership of Eisenhower—the 1950s essentially were a lost decade. Let the measure be the growth of the party in popular vote or popular confidence. Let it be the record of specific legislative achievements. Let it be the less specific but more meaningful matter of clear commitment to abiding principles or exhilarating purposes, relevant to an age of revolution. By all criteria, the judgment must be the same. And it darkly suggests no political truth more modern, perhaps, than the venerable warning of Edmund Burke: "The only thing necessary for the triumph of evil is for good men to do nothing."

And yet, there can be no just criticism of a political leader, obviously, without full reference to the political circumstances. And of the Republican party itself, the serious question must be asked: would some other kind of presidential leadership, more vigorous and more creative, have cleanly prevailed

[3] Ibid., Part II, November 23, 1961.

over this party's capacity to resist change? The chance of revitalizing a major political organization depends critically upon the nature of the material with which the work must begin. And, in this instance, the circumstances confronting Eisenhower might at least be called mitigating.

For the full half-century since the historic struggle of 1912 between Theodore Roosevelt and William Howard Taft, the Republican party has been known to the nation, of course, as the citadel of conservative orthodoxy. In this span of time, it summoned from its own ranks no President who could lay serious historic claim to greatness. It collectively offered no leadership that could be hailed, by a grateful nation, as imaginative, bold, or memorable. For thirty of those years, the party could not win a presidential election except under the leadership of a war hero. Over this same thirty-year period, it held control of the Congress for a meager total of four years. All this added up to a distinction of the most unwanted kind.

Yet, behind this near-barren half-century, there lies a Republican tradition of a vastly different fiber. This was, almost instantly upon birth, the party that abolished slavery. Throughout the decades of frenetically expanding capitalism—and the lawless acquisitiveness of "the robber barons"—this was the party that conceived and wrote the national laws most vital to the public good and welfare. These included: the first laws of civil service, the anti-trust legislation, the control of the railways, the first federal regulation of food and drugs, the first acts to conserve the nation's natural resources. And throughout this full and rich earlier life, the Republican party logically was both the home and the hope—rather than the enemy and the despair—of the American intellectual.

The third half-century of the story of the Republican party has now just begun. The party, quite obviously, still does not know which of its two selves to *be* in the years immediately ahead. And Dwight David Eisenhower—by his own austere and negative prescription for the role of party leader—could not help it to make up its deeply divided mind.

I have witnessed closely some of this party's recent inner travail. I confess to frequent and sharp dismay at the pettiness of its calculations and narrowness of its vision. And yet, I presume to believe that the choice before it, as it faces its *third* half-century of life, is as clear as it is historic.

It must, if it is to be a live and generous force in American politics, stir with the energy of enduring convictions, rather than appeal for saving moments to the popularity of a new hero or the plausibility of an ancient shibboleth. It must comprehend and assimilate, in its own mind and spirit, some of the political and intellectual qualities that have enabled British conservatism to hold power for a full decade and that have animated Christian Democratic parties on the European continent ever since World War II. It must honor, too, its own very origin as a party—by conscientious leadership in the struggle for civil rights. It must learn to use political power in some exercise other than the reflexes of opposition and denunciation. It must forswear the charades of hysterical duels with the imagined menaces of "socialism" and "totalitarianism." It must learn to assess its own political worth by some arithmetic more elevated than the facile addition of its own congressional votes to those of southern Democrats, to contrive the frustration of a fairly impressive number of Executive actions in any congressional session. It must attain a self-respecting sense of identity—and sense of purpose—that can turn cold and confident scorn upon the tawdry political temptations proffered by a Senator Joseph McCarthy or a John Birch Society. And—with these and a host of kindred acts—it might begin to celebrate each political year, each session of the Congress in Washington, by offering the nation a modest minimum of one proud sign of imaginative political action, dedicated unabashedly to the common weal.

To inspire and to lead—indeed, to *re-create*—such a Republican party can only be, still, a patient and painful labor.

To this labor, there was, perhaps, not a great deal that such a President as Eisenhower could bring. This was not only because of the nature of the Republican party long before he encountered it. It was also because of the nature of the man long before the party encountered him. For he appeared upon the national scene as the political father of a phenomenon called "modern Republicanism." Yet his economic and social views could not convincingly be described as "modern." And his political behavior could not, with rare exception, be described as militantly and passionately "Republican." The fact is that the President who was supposed to lead the Republican party toward new, high ground —both "liberal" and "modern"—could not seriously be distinguished from a conservative Democrat.

If this suggests some kind of political paradox about the man, it suggests a more profound paradox about the system of political parties by which America governs itself in the middle of the twentieth century.

And it suggests the final reason why Dwight Eisenhower left the Republican party—politically and intellectually—where first he found it. . . .

> O! it is excellent
> To have a giant's strength, but it is tyrannous
> To use it like a giant.
> *Measure for Measure*

The man who, for these several years, entered his office each morning to nod approvingly at the legend on his desk—"Gentle in manner, strong in deed" —would have commended Shakespeare's admonition on "a giant's strength" as an admirable definition of the proper use of power in the presidency of the United States. Because he so believed, he would be charged—quite justly—with refusal to give vigorous leadership even to cherished purposes. And he would also be condemned—not at all justly—for wholly lacking any concept of presidential leadership.

The Eisenhower who rose to fame in the 1940s, under the wartime presidency of Franklin Roosevelt, brought to the White House of the 1950s a view of the presidency so definite and so durable as to seem almost a studied retort and rebuke to a Roosevelt. Where Roosevelt had sought and coveted power, Eisenhower distrusted and discounted it: one man's appetite was the other man's distaste. Where Roosevelt had avidly grasped and adroitly manipulated the abundant authorities of the office, Eisenhower fingered them almost hesitantly and always respectfully—or generously dispersed them. Where Roosevelt had challenged Congress, Eisenhower courted it. Where Roosevelt had been an extravagant partisan, Eisenhower was a tepid partisan. Where Roosevelt had trusted no one and nothing so confidently as his own judgment and his own instinct, Eisenhower trusted and required a consensus of Cabinet or staff to shape the supreme judgments and determinations. Where Roosevelt had sought to goad and taunt and prod the processes of government toward the new and untried, Eisenhower sought to be both guardian of old values and healer of old wounds.

The contrast was quite as blunt in the case of an earlier—and a Republican—Roosevelt. For the Eisenhower who so deeply disliked all struttings of power, all histrionics of politics, would have found the person and the presidency of Theodore Roosevelt almost intolerable. He would have applied to this Roosevelt, too, the homely phrase of derision that he reserved for politicians of such verve and vehemence: they were "the desk-pounders." Echoing back across the decades would have come the lusty answer of T. R.—exulting in the presidency as the "bully pulpit." And it is hard to imagine a concept of the presidency more alien to Eisenhower: to preach and to yell.

A yet more exact and intimate insight into the Eisenhower presidency was revealed by his particular tribute to the Abraham Lincoln of his admiration. He was asked, on one occasion, to describe this Lincoln. And he chose these adjectives: "dedicated, selfless, so modest and humble." He made no mention or suggestion of such possible attributes as: imagination, tenacity, single-mindedness, vision. Pressed gently by his interrogator as to whether Lincoln were not something of a "desk-pounder," Eisenhower denied such a notion and spontaneously related the one episode of Lincoln's life that surged to the surface of memory . . .

> Oh no. Lincoln was noted both for his modesty and his humility. For example, one night he wanted to see General McClellan. He walked over to General McClellan's house . . . but General McClellan was out. He . . . waited way late in the evening. But when the general came in, he told an aide . . . he was tired and was going to bed, and he would see the President the next day. And when criticized later . . . someone told Mr. Lincoln he ought to have been more arbitrary about this. He said: "I would hold General McClellan's horse if he would just win the Union a victory." [4]

The Eisenhower appreciation of Lincoln, in short, reflected one sovereign attitude: all esteemed qualities of the founder of Republicanism were personal and individual, and not one was political or historical. And if the logic of such an estimate were carried coldly to its extreme, it would end in the unspoken implication that the highest national office should be sought and occupied less as an exercise of political power than as a test of personal virtue. To excel in this test, the man would live not *with* the office but *within* it—intact and independent, proudly uncontaminated by power, essentially uninvolved with it. Rather than a political life, this would be a life in politics. Its supreme symbol would not be the sword of authority but the shield of rectitude.

While this self-conscious kind of idealism sprang from deep within the man who was Eisenhower, it found reinforcement—and rationalization—in his

---

[4] Eisenhower on the Presidency," October 12, 1961.

explicit theory of political leadership. This theory was profoundly felt and emphatically argued. It claimed even to bespeak a sense of responsibility more serious than the conventional shows of leadership. And no words of Eisenhower stated this theory more succinctly than these:

> I am not a . . . leader. I don't want you to follow me or anything else. If you are looking for a Moses to lead you out of the . . . wilderness, you will stay right where you are. I would not lead you into this promised land if I could, because if I could lead you in, someone else could lead you out.

These words might have been spoken by Dwight David Eisenhower—at almost any moment in the years from 1952 to 1960—to the Republican party or, indeed, to the American people at large. They were actually spoken, however, by one of the great leaders of American labor, Eugene V. Debs, more than half a century earlier. And they are worthy of note here as simple evidence that, quite apart from all impulses of personal character, the political posture assumed by Eisenhower toward the challenge of national leadership could not, in fact, be curtly described as negligent, eccentric, or even entirely original.

This posture *was* Eisenhower—remarkably and unshakably—because it was prescribed for him by *both* the temper of the man and the tenets of his politics. In any President, or in any political leader, these two need not necessarily coincide: they may fiercely clash. A man of vigorous and aggressive spirit, restless with the urge for action and accomplishment, may fight frantically against the limits of a political role calling for calm, composure, and self-effacement. Or a man of easy and acquiescent temper, content to perform the minimal duties of his office, may strain pathetically and vainly to fill the vastness of a political role demanding force, boldness, and self-assurance. Eisenhower suffered neither kind of conflict. The definition of the office perfectly suited and matched the nature of the man. And neither critical argument nor anxious appeal could persuade him to question, much less to shed, an attire of leadership so appropriate, so form-fitting, so comfortable.

The want and the weakness in all this was not a mere matter of indecision. The man—and the President—was never more decisive than when he held to a steely resolve *not* to do something that he sincerely believed wrong in itself or alien to his office. The essential flaw, rather, was one that had been suggested a full half-century ago—when the outrageously assertive Theodore Roosevelt had occupied the White House—and Woodrow Wilson had then prophesied that "more and more" the presidency would demand *"the sort of action that makes for enlightenment."* [5] The requisite for such action, however, is not merely a stout sense of responsibility, but an acute sense of history—a discerning, even intuitive, appreciation of the elusive and cumulative force of every presidential word and act, shaped and aimed to reach final goals, unglimpsed by all but a few. And as no such vision ever deeply inspired the Eisenhower presidency, there could be no true "enlightenment" to shine forth from its somber acts of prudence or of pride.

[5] Woodrow Wilson, *Constitutional Government in the United States,* p. 81.

This is not to say that the record of the Administration wholly lacked zeal —of a kind. It is doubtful if the leadership of any great nation can endure for nearly a decade without at least the flickering of some such flame of commitment. The man who came closest to a display of such fervor in these years, however, was not the President but his Secretary of State. This man possessed at least his own understanding of what Theodore Roosevelt meant when he spoke of a "pulpit." And yet, this particular ardor of John Foster Dulles could not be enough. For this kind of zeal was neither creative nor impassioned. It was austere, constrained, and cerebral. And in lieu of fire, it offered ice.

Ultimately, all that Eisenhower did, and refused to do, as a democratic leader was rigorously faithful to his understanding of democracy itself. When the record of his presidency was written and done, he could look back upon it and soberly reflect: "One definition of democracy that I like is merely the opportunity for self-discipline." [6] He lived by this definition. And by all acts of eight years of his presidency, he urged its acceptance by the people of his nation.

The implications of this simple political credo could not instantly be dismissed as shallow. Forbearance and constraint, patience and discipline—those are not virtues for a democracy to deride. They can be fatefully relevant to the ways of free men.

And yet, by the year 1960, they did not seem to serve or to suffice, as full statement of either the nation's purpose or a President's policy.

What was so wrong or wanting in them?

Perhaps one might have caught some hint of the answer, if one were listening attentively, on Inauguration Day in 1961. The provocative moment came shortly before John Fitzgerald Kennedy took his oath of office. At this moment, there stood at the lectern of the Inaugural platform on Capitol Hill not a politician but a poet. His white hair was whipped by the chill January wind. His fingers fumbled clumsily with his text. He was eighty-six years of age—old enough to forget some of his own written lines. But the voice of Robert Frost was strong, and his meaning was clear . . .

> Something we were withholding left us weak
> Until we found it was ourselves
> We were withholding from our land of living
> And forthwith found salvation in surrender.

[6] "Eisenhower on the Presidency," October 12, 1961.

24

ALEXANDER BICKEL

The Warren Court

Instead of celebrating the accomplishments of the Supreme Court under Chief Justice Earl Warren—the school desegregation decision of 1954, the one-man, one-vote reapportionment cases, or decisions on Bible reading in the schools—Alexander Bickel charges that the Warren Court has intervened in extralegal fashion in matters of social policy, matters that rightly belong to the political process instead of to the judiciary. More important, he argues that the Court has little power to force social views on a populace not ready to accept them; the result will be, and already has been, nullification of judicial decisions by the American public. Finally, Bickel believes that the Warren Court's decisions have lacked coherence and consistency.

This article fits a pattern emerging in scholarly and intellectual circles that might be called "post-liberal." It is based on fears of domination, inefficiency, instability, and inhumanity in a centralized national government. Post-liberals want to extend liberal policy to bureaucratic procedure, making it more humane and less arbitrary. Some of their anti-centralist concerns relate post-liberals to traditional conservatism, but the social and economic goals they seek are the goals of New Deal liberalism.

"When eras die," runs a verse by Clarence Day, "their legacies/Are left to strange police./Professors in New England guard/The glory that was Greece." Professors in New England—and elsewhere, to be sure—parse the glories of the Warren Court, criticize its syllogisms, reduce its purported logic to absurd consequences, disprove its factual assertions, answer the unavoidable questions it managed to leave unasked, and most often conclude by regretting its failures of method, while either welcoming its results or professing detachment from them. Historians a generation or two hence, however—other professors in New England—may barely note, and care little about, method, logic, or intellectual coherence, and may assess results in hindsight—only results, and by their own future lights.

Past historians have so dealt with the Court, as do many—outside the profession, most—contemporary observers,[1] and one sensed that this was what the Justices of the Warren Court expected, and that they were content to take their chances.[2] They relied on events for vindication more than on the method of reason for contemporary validation. They were thoroughly conscious of the condemnation that has been visited on certain of their predecessors, who exalted rights of property, but responded with insufficient vigor to other claims, and they admired the generally admired force and vision of John Marshall, who is forgiven for his attachment to the rights of property. Like Marshall, who had, of course, the advantage of a clean slate, they bet on the future, even if to do so they had to wield, on their slate, eraser as well as chalk.

The eraser was used selectively, however, if often. For what informed the enterprise was the idea of progress. There was, therefore, discontinuity—open or disguised—in specifics, but it was sustained by an aspiration to a transcendent consistency with a preferred past, a striving for fidelity to a true line of progress. And so the Warren Court, as Namier said we all do, "imagine[d] the past and remember[ed] the future." The cast of mind is perhaps nowhere more saliently, more ingenuously—or more succinctly—exhibited than in a decisive remark of Mr. Justice Douglas, speaking for the Warren Court in one of the reapportionment cases. Said Justice Douglas: "The conception of political equality from the Declaration of Independence to Lincoln's Gettysburg Address, to the Fifteenth, Seventeenth, and Nineteenth Amendments can mean only one thing—one person, one vote." The key word is *can,* and the sentence is further notable for its references to documents not commonly taken as having legal effect, and to the extralegal significance of provisions that do have strictly legal, but circumscribed, application.

The Justices of the Warren Court thus ventured to identify a goal. It was necessarily a grand one—if we had to give it a single name, that name, as

---

[1] See, *e.g.*: "Only history will know whether the Warren Court has struck the balance right. For myself, I am confident that historians will write that the trend of decisions during the 1950's and 1960's was in keeping with the mainstream of American history—a bit progressive but also moderate, a bit humane but not sentimental, a bit idealistic but seldom doctrinaire and in the long run essentially pragmatic—in short, in keeping with the true genius of our institutions." Archibald Cox, *The Warren Court,* 133–34 (1968).

[2] Strictly speaking, the Justices of the Warren Court, in addition to the Chief Justice, were: Hugo L. Black, Stanley F. Reed, Felix Frankfurter, William O. Douglas, Robert H. Jackson, Harold H. Burton, Tom C. Clark, Sherman Minton, John M. Harlan, William J. Brennan, Jr., Charles E. Whittaker, Potter Stewart, Byron R. White, Arthur J. Goldberg, Abe Fortas, and Thurgood Marshall. In my usage, the terms "Warren Court" and "Justices of the Warren Court" refer to the dominant majority that gave the Court its character. That majority consisted over the years of the Chief Justice and Justices Black, Douglas, Brennan, Goldberg, Fortas, and Marshall. Of course, the majority was no monolith. There were defections, if that is the right word, in one or another case—on Justice Black's part, with increasing frequency toward the end—and the majority would now and then draw to itself a member of the opposition, if that, again, is the right word, such as Justice Stewart or Justice White. And in Brown v. Board of Education and a number of other racial cases, the Court was unanimous.

Professor Kurland has suggested, would be the Egalitarian Society. And the Justices steered by this goal, as Marshall did by his vision of a nation, in the belief that progress, called history, would validate their course, and that another generation, remembering its own future, would imagine them favorably. Such a faith need not conflict with, but it overrides standards of analytical reason and scientific inquiry as warrantors of the validity of judgment. . . .

A broadly-conceived egalitarianism was the main theme in the music to which the Justices of the Warren Court marched. It was evident, of course, in the racial cases, in decisions leveling qualifications for voting, and in those decreeing equal apportionment on a one-man, one-vote basis. And the egalitarian melody was strong in procedural decisions, chiefly criminal, seeking to minimize the disadvantages to which the poor are subject. Two accompanying themes were the enlargement of the dominion of law and the centralization in national institutions of the law-giving function.

The Warren Court was quick to impose the same norms on state and national governments alike. In dealing with the obscenity problem, for example, the Court would not heed Mr. Justice Harlan's plea that separate rules might be made applicable to the federal government and to state and local governments. Yet the dangers of national censorship are not the same as the dangers of local suppression. The federal government is apt to impose the standards of Dubuque on Greenwich Village, whereas Dubuque can impose them only on Dubuque. Again, in its decisions on criminal procedure—decisions concerning, for example, unreasonable searches and seizures—the Warren Court sought to enforce national uniformity in every detail, without regard, so to speak, to varieties of criminal experience.

In pursuit of the ideal of equality, the Warren Court all too often assimilated private behavior to government action; it not only forbade, of course, as had its predecessors, discrimination at the hands of the state, or of any unit of government, but was keen to detect the hand of the state in private discriminations. In the Warren era, moreover, as to a degree also in the heyday of the old faith at the turn of the century and after, a general tendency was noticeable to circumscribe and displace private ordering, to legalize the society, to rationalize it in the sense of which the great industrial consolidators spoke of rationalizing the economy, to impose order on the market of norms, values, and institutions. There was evidence, particularly in the subordinate federal courts, of an imperfectly bridled managerial drive.

A certain habit of command, an impatience to take charge of unruly affairs and impose a solution that seems apt, comes as readily to judges as to other able men of good intentions who are in a position to work their will. It came readily enough to the judges of the early decades of this century, who intervened routinely in labor disputes, for example, and in controversies concerning rates and services between public utilities and various states and municipalities. Rebuking—as it rarely did—a somewhat overzealous judge in such a case in 1910, the Supreme Court quoted the remark of an English Vice-Chancellor: "I am not sitting here as a Committee of Public Safety, armed with arbitrary power to prevent what it is said will be a great injury not to Birmingham only but to the whole of England; that is not my function." But it is a function that judges are prone to assume, and to which they were increasingly encouraged by the reach the Warren Court gave to law, and by the expectations that were thus induced. . . .

The Warren Court's tendency to disenthrall itself from jurisdictional fetters is a function of this conception of law. The Court has not by any means taken on all that has been pressed on it. It has declined opportunities to pass on the constitutionality of the President's actions in Vietnam. It has not dispensed with the need for a lawsuit; it is still, unlike the President or the Congress, a passive body that must wait for a litigant to move it to action. But in such decisions as *Flast* v. *Cohen* and *South Carolina* v. *Katzenbach,* the Court has substantially loosened the definition of a lawsuit, it has opened the door wider to more litigants, and has indeed come near to making the lawsuit something of a formality, still an expensive one, but within the reach of just about all who can afford it, at just about any time of their choice.

In assuming the power, like a legislature, to set an arbitrary date for the coming into effect of its decisions, the Warren Court further enlarged its freedom to address an ever-widening range of the society's problems, and to pronounce applicable law. The Court assumed this power, as we have seen, with respect to a number of its decisions concerning criminal procedure, which it did not allow to be, as is unusual, wholly retroactive, but which it did not announce for solely prospective application either. To have announced them altogether prospectively would have run the risk of stemming the flow of litigation, the Court said, since "the incentive of counsel to advance contentions requiring a change in the law" might have been decreased. Without running this risk, then—a telling and characteristic precaution—the Court liberated itself from the restraint naturally imposed by the retroactivity of decisions, which can work out inequitably, or otherwise in alarming fashion, and hence gives pause.

Another of the principal themes of the Warren Court, related to the egalitarian, legalitarian, and centralizing themes, was majoritarianism. The Court found the essence of political democracy in the power of a majority to impose its wishes through an election, except, to be sure, as the sway of the majority is limited by law. This is the meaning of the one-man, one-vote rule of the apportionment cases. It is the meaning also, in part, of the decisions enlarging the electorate and leveling qualifications for voting, as is shown by Justice Douglas' citation of the apportionment cases in *Harper* v. *Virginia Board of Elections,* the poll-tax decision.

The main statement of the Court's position came in *Reynolds* v. *Sims.* Chief Justice Warren's opinion for the Court spoke of individual equality. One man's vote ought not to be worth more than another's. But there was great emphasis also, in *Reynolds* v. *Sims* and in the rest of the apportionment cases, on a statistical showing that malapportionment enabled a minority of voters to control a legislature, or under the Georgia county-unit system, elect a governor. The Chief Justice proclaimed: "Legislators represent people, not trees or acres. Legislators are elected by voters, not farms or cities or economic interest. . . . Logically, in a society ostensibly grounded on representative government, it would seem reasonable that a majority of the people of a State could elect a majority of that State's legislators. To conclude differently, and to sanction minority control of state legislative bodies, would appear to deny majority rights in a way that far surpasses any possible denial of minority rights that might otherwise be thought to result. Since legislatures are responsible for enacting laws by which all citizens are to be governed, they should be bodies which are collectively responsive to the popular will." And the Chief Justice laid it down explicitly that "economic or other sorts of group interests" were not factors that could constitutionally be taken into account in apportioning a legislature. "Citizens, not history or economic interests, cast votes," he said. In Colorado, a substantial majority of the voters had by referendum approved a departure from the one-man, one-vote standard. Even the majority itself, the Court held, cannot deprive itself of the right to rule as a majority.

Populist majoritarianism, not some complex checked and balanced Madisonian adjustment among countervailing groups and factions, leading to rule by minorities . . . —populist majoritarianism was the principle of the apportionment cases. . . .

Majoritarianism is heady stuff. It is, in truth, a tide, flowing with the swiftness of a slogan—whether popular sovereignty, as in the past, or one man, one vote, as in the Warren Court's formulation. The tide is apt to sweep over all institutions, seeking its level everywhere. Now that the Warren Court has released it again, it bids fair, for example, to engulf the Electoral College, even though on a less simplistic view of political arrangements, on a less obtrusively chaste view, that peculiar institution may be seen as performing a valuable function. The tide could well engulf the Court itself also.

Analytically, supreme judicial autonomy is not easily reconciled with any theory of political democracy, Madisonian or majoritarian. Judicial autonomy is sustained, not by a self-consistent theory, but by an ambivalent practical accommodation, and by a rhetorical tradition. The tradition, however, is Madisonian in tenor. It will be difficult to evolve a rhetoric of survival in a climate of uncompromising majoritarianism—as difficult for the judges as for the Electoral College. The Court fared rather ill with the Populists and other majoritarian political reformers of the Progressive Era. In times when Madisonian theory is in favor, it is at least rhetorically possible to defend the power of the judges by pointing to all manner of checks and balances, to the limited nature of all power, which signifies the intended inability of any group, including a majority, always to get everything it wants, and the intended ability of many groups, all of them minorities, to exercise vetoes; and by declaiming that our government is, after all, republican, not in the majoritarian sense democratic. It is not so easy to say all this when populist slogans are the order of the day, as the Warren Court's one-man, one-vote decisions have caused them to be. Thoroughgoing majoritarians, the Court may discover, are no more reliable a constituency for judges than revolutionaries, and the Court-induced reapportionment revolution may turn into an ironic triumph.

The Warren Court achieved a certain symmetry in its deployment of the majoritarian principle and of a concept of centralized and pervasive law; and it mistook this symmetry for theoretical consistency. (The symmetrical arrangement I speak of has at least the virtue of bypassing—even though, unfortunately, quite without disowning—the sophistry of arguments that the supremacy of the judges is consistent with democratic theory so long as the judges enhance the democratic process rather than restricting it, which is supposedly what they do in First Amendment and apportionment cases.)

The Warren Court's implicit model of a government at once majoritarian and judicial had it that when individuals and groups are unsuccessful in attaching themselves to the ruling majority in a given constituency, or in getting satisfaction from it, they may appeal to the larger majority in the national constituency. This recourse the Court encouraged by enlarging the power of Congress under the Fourteenth Amendment, as for example in *Katzenbach* v. *Morgan.* If no remedy is forthcoming even from the central majoritarian legislature, then the losers in the political process may appeal to the Court, which was consequently concerned to make itself more readily available than it had been in the past. As early as the argument of *Brown* v. *Board of Education,* the late Justice Robert H. Jackson, stating a fact rather than his own preference, remarked that the plaintiffs were in court because Congress would not act.

Unmistakably the Warren Court considered itself under a special duty to act when recourse to Congress had failed or was likely to fail; and not unnaturally, for in a polity arranged on the majoritarian principle, and hence inescapably on the assumption that an identifiable majority exists at all times on most issues, and is coherent and relatively stable, the political process cannot be assumed to be accessible to all groups. In the Madisonian model, and one might say in purposefully malapportioned legislatures, most identifiable groups and interests in the society have access, and are likely to be able to maneuver for enough bargaining power to achieve at least some portion of their objectives. No such presumption is sensible in a more strictly majoritarian system.

It can be said, therefore, that the Warren Court's imposition of majoritarianism as the operative principle of political organization, and its conception of its own function were congruent. They met in the premise that the majoritarian process must, and perhaps if it works correctly will, produce certain results, which are given *a priori.* When it does not at the level of one constituency, it should be tried again at the higher level of another one. And when it doesn't at all, the Court will supply the deficiency. Madisonian theory also posits the possible miscarriage of the majoritarian process in a not dissimilar sense, and also has recourse to enlargement of the constituency. But it guards against miscarriages by diffusing and limiting power through the introduction of a series of non-majoritarian devices, and enlarges the constituency to this end. What the Warren Court crucially omitted to explain was why its model, unlike the Madisonian one, allowed for only a single locus of power countervailing that of the majority—the Court itself—and by reliance on the majoritarian principle forbade all others the Court could reach.

I am attempting now to identify and orchestrate the Warren Court's major themes; I am not now dealing with fragments of the music in one or another case, and not—to pursue a figure of Professor Kurland—with techniques of piano playing.[3] My object is not to formulate and defend the grounds

---

[3] "It behooves any critic of the Court's performance to close on a note reminiscent of the wall plaque of frontier times: 'Don't shoot the piano player. He's do-

of my own approval or disapproval—intellectual, moral, esthetic—although I should say that in my view the Court's majoritarianism is ill-conceived, egalitarianism is a worthy ideal but not in all circumstances a self-evident virtue, and centralized, unmitigatedly legalitarian government bears the seed of tyranny. But this is an assertion of ultimates put forward for revelatory rather than forensic purposes. And it is a parenthesis. My endeavor is to see whether the Warren Court's themes, whatever their worth as ultimates, were in harmony with each other, and whether they harmonized with so much of the future as contemporary history allows us to glimpse.

There are heard in the society dissonant themes; not voices of opposition or resistance to the Court's law, albeit there are those, but in increasing volume notes that amount to another tune. There is in being a reaction to the steady unification and nationalization of recent years, a movement toward a decentralization and a diversity of which the as yet unacknowledged prophet—due, I should suppose, for a revival—is Brandeis. "The great America for which we long," wrote Brandeis in 1920, "is unattainable unless that individuality of communities becomes far more highly developed and becomes a common American phenomenon. For a century our growth has come through national expansion and the increase of the functions of the Federal Government. The growth of the future—at least of the immediate future—must be in quality and spiritual value. And that can come only through the concentrated, intensified striving of smaller groups. The field of special effort shall now be the State, the city, the village—and each should be led to seek to excel in something peculiar to it. If ideals are developed locally —the national ones will come pretty near to taking care of themselves."

Diversity implies less rather than more law, and certainly less centralized, national law. A striving for diversity is not necessarily in express conflict with the goal of an egalitarian society, but it connotes a different order of priorities. In politics, even as the Warren Court's virtually irresistible slogan—one man, one vote—may still be mouthed on all sides, the cry is for a group participation which presupposes, whether it knows it or not, the Madisonian more than the majoritarian model, and for a process calculated to heed the expression not only of desires and preferences, but of intensities that no ballot can register. These are all indications that the society of the rather near future may be forming beyond the horizon on which the Warren Court's gaze was fixed, that it may be taking on shapes the Court did not perceive and its law cannot accommodate; that, in sum, the society may not be conforming to the Warren Court's vision. . . .

---

ing his best.' It is still possible, however, to wish that he would stick to the piano and not try to be a one-man band. It is too much to ask that he take piano lessons." P. B. Kurland, "Foreword: 'Equal in Origin and Equal in Title to the Legislative Branches of the Government,'" 78 *Harvard Law Review*, 143, 176 (1964).

MICHAEL HARRINGTON

The Other America

Some Americans condemn the poor as shiftless. In a country where individual initiative and pride of ownership are enshrined as national virtues, the impoverished have not easily found understanding or compassion—not to mention assistance. But studies of the relationship between environment and social attitudes prohibit moral condemnation here. Some Americans romanticize the poor. Instructed in part by the Christian heritage, they see poverty as ennobling, a special strain of purity. But statistics on the relationship between crime and poverty mock this notion. Another mistaken view of the poor is that they lead simple, happy lives. College students, when asked about the social background of the mentally ill, generally respond that they are upper middle class or rich. But ample evidence shows that it is the poor who lapse most frequently into paranoid delusions or senility. This is predictable, for they are the dispossessed; they must somehow escape the squalor of their surroundings.

Michael Harrington is concerned with a phenomenon in America uncommon to most nations of the world: poverty in the midst of great affluence, being poor where most people are not. Harrington deserves much of the credit for arousing a whole generation to the existence of poverty. His work and that of others led to the Economic Opportunity Act of 1964 and the subsequent war on poverty.

The millions who are poor in the United States tend to become increasingly invisible. Here is a great mass of people, yet it takes an effort of the intellect and will even to see them.

I discovered this personally in a curious way. After I wrote my first article on poverty in America, I had all the statistics down on paper. I had proved to my satisfaction that there were around 50,000,000 poor in the country. Yet, I realized I did not believe my own figures. The poor existed in the Government

Reprinted with permission of The Macmillan Company from THE OTHER AMERICA by Michael Harrington. © 1962 by Michael Harrington.

reports; they were percentages and numbers in long, close columns, but they were not part of my experience. I could prove that the other America existed, but I had never been there.

My response was not accidental. It was typical of what is happening to an entire society, and it reflects profound social changes in this nation. The other America, the America of poverty, is hidden today in a way that it never was before. Its millions are socially invisible to the rest of us. No wonder that so many misinterpreted Galbraith's title and assumed that "the affluent society" meant that everyone had a decent standard of life. The misinterpretation was true as far as the actual day-to-day lives of two-thirds of the nation were concerned. Thus, one must begin a description of the other America by understanding why we do not see it.

There are perennial reasons that make the other America an invisible land.

Poverty is often off the beaten track. It always has been. The ordinary tourist never left the main highway, and today he rides interstate turnpikes. He does not go into the valleys of Pennsylvania where the towns look like movie sets of Wales in the thirties. He does not see the company houses in rows, the rutted roads (the poor always have bad roads whether they live in the city, in towns, or on farms), and everything is black and dirty. And even if he were to pass through such a place by accident, the tourist would not meet the unemployed men in the bar or the women coming home from a runaway sweatshop.

Then, too, beauty and myths are perennial masks of poverty. The traveler comes to the Appalachians in the lovely season. He sees the hills, the streams, the foliage—but not the poor. Or perhaps he looks at a run-down mountain house and, remembering Rousseau rather than seeing with his eyes, decides that "those people" are truly fortunate to be living the way they are and that they are lucky to be exempt from the strains and tensions of the middle class. The only problem is that "those people," the quaint inhabitants of those hills, are undereducated, underprivileged, lack medical care, and are in the process of being forced from the land into a life in the cities, where they are misfits.

These are normal and obvious causes of the invisibility of the poor. They operated a generation ago; they will be functioning a generation hence. It is more important to understand that the very development of American society is creating a new kind of blindness about poverty. The poor are increasingly slipping out of the very experience and consciousness of the nation.

If the middle class never did like ugliness and poverty, it was at least aware of them. "Across the tracks" was not a very long way to go. There were forays into the slums at Christmas time; there were charitable organizations that brought contact with the poor. Occasionally, almost everyone passed through the Negro ghetto or the blocks of tenements, if only to get downtown to work or to entertainment.

Now the American city has been transformed. The poor still inhabit the miserable housing in the central area, but they are increasingly isolated from contact with, or sight of, anybody else. Middle-class women coming in from Suburbia on a rare trip may catch the merest glimpse of the other America on the way to an evening at the theater, but their children are segregated in suburban schools. The business or professional man may drive along the fringes of the slums in a car or bus, but it is not an important experience to him. The failures, the unskilled, the disabled, the aged, and the minorities are right there, across the tracks, where they have always been. But hardly anyone else is.

In short, the very development of the American city has removed poverty from the living, emotional experience of millions upon millions of middle-class Americans. Living out in the suburbs, it is easy to assume that ours is, indeed, an affluent society.

This new segregation of poverty is compounded by a well-meaning ignorance. A good many concerned and sympathetic Americans are aware that there is much discussion of urban renewal. Suddenly, driving through the city, they notice that a familiar slum has been torn down and that there are towering, modern buildings where once there had been tenements or hovels. There is a warm feeling of satisfaction, of pride in the way things are working out: the poor, it is obvious, are being taken care of.

The irony in this . . . is that the truth is nearly the exact opposite to the impression. The total impact of the various housing programs in postwar America has been to squeeze more and more people into existing slums. More often than not, the modern apartment in a towering building rents at $40 a room or more. For, during the past decade and a half, there has been more subsidization of middle- and upper-income housing than there has been of housing for the poor.

Clothes make the poor invisible too: America has the best-dressed poverty the world has ever known. For a variety of reasons, the benefits of mass production have been spread much more evenly in this area than in many others. It is much easier in the United States to be decently dressed than it is to be decently housed, fed, or doctored. Even people with terribly depressed incomes can look prosperous.

This is an extremely important factor in defining our emotional and existential ignorance of poverty. In Detroit the existence of social classes became much more difficult to discern the day the companies put lockers in the plants. From that moment on, one did not see men in work clothes on the way to the factory, but citizens in slacks and white shirts. This process has been magnified with the poor throughout the country. There are tens of thousands of Americans in the big cities who are wearing shoes, perhaps even a stylishly cut suit or dress, and yet are hungry. It is not a matter of planning, though it almost seems as if the affluent society had given out costumes to the poor so that they would not offend the rest of society with the sight of rags.

Then, many of the poor are the wrong age to be seen. A good number of them (over 8,000,000) are sixty-five years of age or better; an even larger number are under eighteen. The aged members of the other America are often sick, and they cannot move. Another group of them live out their lives in loneliness and frustration: they sit in rented rooms, or else they stay close to a house in a neighborhood that has completely changed from the old days. Indeed, one of the worst aspects of poverty among the aged is that these people are out of sight and out of mind, and alone.

The young are somewhat more visible, yet they too stay close to their neighborhoods. Sometimes they advertise their poverty through a lurid tabloid story about a gang killing. But generally they do not disturb the quiet streets of the middle class.

And finally, the poor are politically invisible. It is one of the cruelest ironies of social life in advanced countries that the dispossessed at the bottom of society are unable to speak for themselves. The people of the other America do not, by far and large, belong to unions, to fraternal organizations, or to political parties. They are without lobbies of their own; they put forward no legislative program. As a group, they are atomized. They have no face; they have no voice.

Thus, there is not even a cynical political motive for caring about the poor, as in the old days. Because the slums are no longer centers of powerful political organizations, the politicians need not really care about their inhabitants. The slums are no longer visible to the middle class, so much of the idealistic urge to fight for those who need help is gone. Only the social agencies have a really direct involvement with the other America, and they are without any great political power.

To the extent that the poor have a spokesman in American life, that role is played by the labor movement. The unions have their own particular idealism, an ideology of concern. More than that, they realize that the existence of a reservoir of cheap, unorganized labor is a menace to wages and working conditions throughout the entire economy. Thus, many union legislative proposals—to extend the coverage of minimum wage and social security, to organize migrant farm laborers—articulate the needs of the poor.

That the poor are invisible is one of the most important things about them. They are not simply neglected and forgotten as in the old rhetoric of reform; what is much worse, they are not seen. . . .

Forty to 50,000,000 people are becoming increasingly invisible. This is a shocking fact. But there is a second basic irony of poverty that is equally important: if one is to make the mistake of being born poor, he should choose a time when the majority of the people are miserable too.

J. K. Galbraith develops this idea in *The Affluent Society,* and in doing so defines the "newness" of the kind of poverty in contemporary America. The old poverty, Galbraith notes, was general. It was the condition of life of an entire society, or at least of that huge majority who were without special skills or the luck of birth. When the entire economy advanced, a good many of these people gained higher standards of living. Unlike the poor today, the majority poor of a generation ago were an immediate (if cynical) concern of political leaders. The old slums of the immigrants had the votes; they provided the basis for labor organizations; their very numbers could be a powerful force in political conflict. At the same time the new technology required higher skills, more education, and stimulated an upward movement for millions.

Perhaps the most dramatic case of the power of the majority poor took place in the 1930's. The Congress of Industrial Organizations literally organized millions in a matter of years. A labor movement that had been declining and confined to a thin stratum of the highly skilled suddenly embraced masses of men and women in basic industry. At the same time this acted as a pressure upon the Government, and the New Deal codified some of the social gains in laws like the Wagner Act. The result was not a basic transformation of the American system, but it did transform the lives of an entire section of the population.

In the thirties one of the reasons for these advances was that misery was general. There was no need then to write books about unemployment and poverty. That was the decisive social experience of the entire society, and the apple sellers even invaded Wall Street. There was political sympathy from middle-class reformers; there were an élan and spirit that grew out of a deep crisis.

Some of those who advanced in the thirties did so because they had unique and individual personal talents. But for the great mass, it was a question of being at the right point in the economy at the right time in history, and utilizing that position for common struggle. Some of those who failed did so because they did not have the will to take advantage of new opportunities. But for the most part the poor who were left behind had been at the wrong place in the economy at the wrong moment in history.

These were the people in the unorganizable jobs, in the South, in the minority groups, in the fly-by-night factories that were low on capital and high on labor. When some of them did break into the economic mainstream—when, for instance, the CIO opened up the way for some Negroes to find good industrial jobs—they proved to be as resourceful as anyone else. As a group, the other Americans who stayed behind were not originally composed primarily of individual failures. Rather, they were victims of an impersonal process that selected some for progress and discriminated against others.

Out of the thirties came the welfare state. Its creation had been stimulated by mass impoverishment and misery, yet it helped the poor least of all. Laws like unemployment compensation, the Wagner Act, the various farm programs, all these were designed for the middle third in the cities, for the organized workers, and for the upper third in the country, for the big market farmers. If a man works in an extremely low-paying job, he may not even be covered by social security or other welfare programs. If he receives unemployment compensation, the payment is scaled down according to his low earnings.

One of the major laws that was designed to cover everyone, rich and poor, was social security. But even here the other Americans suffered discrimination. Over the years social security payments have not even provided a subsistence level of life. The middle third have been able to supplement the Federal pension through private plans negotiated by unions, through joining medical insurance schemes like Blue Cross, and so on. The poor have not been able to do so. They lead a bitter life, and then have to pay for that fact in old age.

Indeed, the paradox that the welfare state benefits those least who need help most is but a single instance of a persistent irony in the other America. Even when the money finally trickles down, even when a school is built in a poor neighborhood, for instance, the poor are still deprived. Their entire environment, their life, their values, do not prepare them to take advantage of the new opportunity. The parents are anxious for the children to go to work; the pupils are pent up, waiting for the moment when their education has complied with the law.

Today's poor, in short, missed the political and social gains of the thirties. They are, as Galbraith rightly points out, the first minority poor in history, the first poor not to be seen, the first poor whom the politicians could leave alone.

The first step toward the new poverty was taken when millions of people proved immune to progress. When that happened, the failure was not individual and personal, but a social product. But once the historic accident takes place, it begins to become a personal fate.

The new poor of the other America saw the rest of society move ahead. They went on living in depressed areas, and often they tended to become depressed human beings. In some of the West Virginia towns, for instance, an entire community will become shabby and defeated. The young and the adventurous go to the city, leaving behind those who cannot move and those who lack the will to do so. The entire area becomes permeated with failure, and that is one more reason the big corporations shy away.

Indeed, one of the most important things about the new poverty is that it cannot be defined in simple, statistical terms. Throughout this book a crucial term is used: aspiration. If a group has internal vitality, a will—if it has aspiration—it may live in dilapidated housing, it may eat an inadequate diet, and it may suffer poverty, but it is not impoverished. So it was in those ethnic slums of the immigrants that played such a dramatic role in the unfolding of the American dream. The people found themselves in slums, but they were not slum dwellers.

But the new poverty is constructed so as to destroy aspiration; it is a system designed to be impervious to hope. The other America does not contain the adventurous seeking a new life and land. It is populated by the failures, by those driven from the land and bewildered by the city, by old people suddenly confronted with the torments of loneliness and poverty, and by minorities facing a wall of prejudice. . . .

Finally, one might summarize the newness of contemporary poverty by saying: These are the people who are immune to progress. But then the facts are even more cruel. The other Americans are the victims of the very inventions and machines that have provided a higher living standard for the rest of the society. They are upside-down in the economy, and for them greater productivity often means worse jobs; agricultural advance becomes hunger.

In the optimistic theory, technology is an undisguised blessing. A general increase in productivity, the argument goes, generates a higher standard of living for the whole people. And indeed, this has been true for the middle and upper thirds of American society, the people who made such striking gains in the last two decades. It tends to overstate the automatic character of the process, to omit the role of human struggle. (The CIO was organized by men in conflict, not by economic trends.) Yet it states a certain truth—for those who are lucky enough to participate in it.

But the poor, if they were given to theory, might argue the exact opposite. They might say: Progress is misery.

As the society became more technological, more skilled, those who learn to work the machines, who get the expanding education, move up. Those who miss out at the very start find themselves at a new disadvantage. A generation ago in American life, the majority of the working people did not have high-school educations. But at that time industry was organized on a lower level of skill and competence. And there was a sort of continuum in the shop: the youth who left school at sixteen could begin as a laborer, and gradually pick up skill as he went along.

Today the situation is quite different. The good jobs require much more academic preparation, much more skill from the very outset. Those who lack a high-school education tend to be condemned to the economic underworld—to low-paying service industries, to backward factories, to sweeping and janitorial duties. If the fathers and mothers of the contemporary poor were penalized a generation ago for their lack of schooling, their children will suffer all the more. The very rise in productivity that created more money and better working conditions for the rest of the society can be a menace to the poor.

But then this technological revolution might have an even more disastrous consequence: it could increase the ranks of the poor as well as intensify the disabilities of poverty. At this point it is too early to make any final judgment, yet there are obvious danger signals. There are millions of Americans who live just the other side of poverty. When a recession comes, they are pushed onto the relief rolls. (Welfare payments in New York respond almost immediately to any economic decline.) If automation continues to inflict more and more penalties on the unskilled and the semiskilled, it could have the impact of permanently increasing the population of the other America.

Even more explosive is the possibility that people who participated in the gains of the thirties and the forties will be pulled back down into poverty. Today the mass-production industries where unionization made such a difference are contracting. Jobs are being destroyed. In the process, workers who had achieved a certain level of wages, who had won working conditions in the shop, are suddenly confronted with impoverishment. This is particularly true for anyone over forty years of age and for members of minority groups. Once their job is abolished, their chances of ever getting similar work are very slim.

It is too early to say whether or not this phenomenon is temporary, or whether it represents a massive retrogression that will swell the numbers of the poor. To a large extent, the answer to this question will be determined by the political response of the United States in the sixties. If serious and massive action is not undertaken, it may be necessary for statisticians to add some old-fashioned, pre-welfare-state poverty to the misery of the other America.

Poverty in the 1960's is invisible and it is new, and both these factors make it more tenacious. It is more isolated and politically powerless than ever before. It is laced with ironies, not the least of which is that many of the poor view progress upside-down, as a menace and a threat to their lives.

Beauty can be a mask for ugliness. That is what happens in the Appalachians.

Driving through this area, particularly in the spring or the fall, one perceives the loveliness, the openness, the high hills, streams, and lush growth. Indeed, the people themselves are captivated by their mountain life. They cling to their patches of land and their way of living. Many of them refuse to act "reasonably"; they stay even though misery is their lot.

It is not just the physical beauty that blinds the city man to the reality of these hills. The people are mountain folk. They are of old American stock, many of them Anglo-Saxon, and old traditions still survive among them. Seeing in them a romantic image of mountain life as independent, self-reliant, and athletic, a tourist could pass through these valleys and observe only quaintness. But not quite: for suddenly the mountain vista will reveal slashed, scarred hills and dirty little towns living under the shadow of decaying mining buildings.

The irony is deep, for everything that turns the landscape into an idyl for the urban traveler conspires to hold the people down. They suffer terribly at the hands of beauty.

Though the steep slopes and the narrow valleys are a charming sight, they are also the basis of a highly unproductive agriculture. The very geography is an anachronism in a technological society. Even if the farmers had the money, machines would not make much difference. As it is, the people literally scratch their half-livings from the difficult soil.

The seasons are vivid here. The tourist perceives this in the brilliance of spring, the bracing air of fall, the lush charm of summer. The tourist will not, of course, come here in the winter. Yet the intensity of the weather also means a short growing season. The land is resistant, and even unapproachable for great portions of the year.

But, the traveler may say, granted that there is a low level of income, isn't it still true that these folk have escaped the anxiety and the rigors of industrialism? Perhaps this myth once held a real truth. Now it is becoming more false every day. Increasingly, these are a beaten people, sunk in their poverty and deprived of hope. In this, they are like the slum dwellers of the city.

During the decade of the fifties, 1,500,000 people left the Appalachians. They were the young, the more adventurous, those who sought a new life. As a result of their exile, they made colonies of poverty in the city. One newspaper in Cincinnati talked of "our 50,000 refugees." Those who were left behind tended to be the older people, the less imaginative, the defeated. A whole area, in the words of a Maryland State study, became suffused with a "mood of apathy and despair."

This, for example, is how one reporter saw the independent yeomanry, the family farmers, and the laid-off industrial workers in the Appalachians: "Whole counties are precariously held together by a flour-and-dried-milk paste of surplus foods. The school lunch program provides many children with their only decent meals. Relief has become a way of life for a once proud and aggressively independent mountain people. The men who are no longer needed in the mines and the farmers who cannot compete with the mechanized agriculture of the Midwest have themselves become surplus commodities in the mountains."

Perhaps the most dramatic statistical statement of the plight of these men and women occurred in a study produced in Kentucky: that, as the sixties begin, 85 percent of the youth in this area would have to leave or else accept a life of grinding poverty. And a place without the young is a place without hope, without future.

Indeed, it is difficult to find any basis for optimism in this area. And yet, the various states of the Appalachians have come up with a program to offer some basic relief for the incredible plight of these people. Still, the very candor of their analysis defeats much of their purpose. One study, for instance, estimated that the Appalachians would need slightly more than one million new jobs if the area were to begin catching up with the rest of America. As of now, the vicious circle is at work making such a development unlikely: the mountains are beautiful and quaint and economically backward; the youth are leaving; and because of this poverty modern industry hesitates to come in and agriculture becomes even more marginal.

The roads are bad. Less than half of the population has had more than one or two years of high school. There is no human backlog of ready skills. The industrial incentive is for the low-paying, manpower-exploiting sharp operator. In the Appalachians this has meant the coming of textiles and apparels plants. (This is the classic association of low-paying industry with low-paying agriculture.)

Some things could be done. The roads could be improved and brought up to the standards required by modern industry—but only with Federal grants. Education and the cultural life of the area could be improved. There could be regional planning. (Significantly, the Kennedy Task Force on depressed areas recommended only one regional planning commission specifically and by name: for the Appalachians.) The whole structure of backwardness and decay, including bad public facilities, lack of water control, and the struggle with soil erosion, could be dealt with.

But such a program would be truly massive. It would require a basic commitment from the Federal Government. As the sixties began, the nation cheered a Depressed-Areas law which provided that the bulk of the funds should be spent in the South. Yet even its proponents admitted that the money for bringing in industry was minimal, and the allocation for retraining and education almost miniscule. It seems likely that the Appalachians will continue going down, that its lovely mountains and hills will house a culture of poverty and despair, and that it will become a reservation for the old, the apathetic, and the misfits.

For the city traveler driving through the mountains, the beauty will persist. So too, probably, will the myth about the sturdy, happy, and uncomplicated mountain folk. But behind all this charm, nestled on the steep hills and in the plunging valleys, lies an incredible social ugliness.

One of the most distinctive things about most American cities is that it is not easy to distinguish social class on the streets. Clothes are cheap and increasingly standardized. The old "proletarian" dress—the cloth hat, the work clothes—either disappeared or else was locked up at the shop.

But when you enter Stockton, California, a center of migrant labor, this generalization fails. The field hands are obvious. All wear broad-brimmed hats; all are tanned, sometimes to a mahogany color; and all are in levis and work clothes. The middle class, the shopkeepers, and practically everybody else, are familiar Americans from any place, city dwellers. The migrants around Stockton are heavily "Anglo" (both white and not Mexican), yet it is almost as if one were looking at two different races. The field hands wear their calling like a skin.

Stockton is a town of about 90,000 permanent residents. At high tide of the migrant invasion, there are more pickers than regular inhabitants. Almost a hundred thousand of them are in the area. They sleep where they can, some in the open. They eat where they can (and sometimes when they can).

California agriculture is the richest in the nation, and its agricultural suffering is perhaps the most spectacular. People work ten-, eleven-, and twelve-hour days in temperatures over one hundred degrees. Sometimes there is no drinking water; sometimes big common barrels of it are used. Women and children work on ladders and with hazardous machinery. (The Industrial Welfare Commission was told in 1961 that 500 children are maimed each year.) Babies are brought to the fields and are placed in "cradles" of wood boxes.

In the Stockton area about a third of the migrants are "Anglos," another third, Mexican-American. Around 15 percent are Filipinos, and the rest are Negroes. (On the East Coast the migrants are much more heavily Negro.) And everywhere, threatening the American workers, are the Braceros, the imported Mexican laborers.

I drove past the fields with an organizer from the Agricultural Workers Organizing Committee of the AFL-CIO. He had grown up in this area and had known the fields as a child. As we passed each farm, he told me who was working there. Whenever he saw a group of Braceros, his voice became sharp.

"They are poor people," he said. "That is why they come here, and work for so little. The growers get them cheap, and they know that the union can't organize them. So that keeps the rates down for the American workers. We don't want to hurt these poor people; they are like us. But it is no way to help them to hurt us. Let the Government work out some kind of a deal with Mexico for aid, or something like that. But let the American farm workers have a decent living without having to hate other poor people."

In Stockton, as in most of the migrant centers in the area, the workers "shape up" at three o'clock in the morning. There is a milling mass of human beings down by skid row, and they are there to sell themselves in the market place. The various hiring men chant out piece-work prices or hourly rates. In some of these places in California, there is a regular exchange with a voice rasping over the public-address system, announcing the going rate for a hundred-weight or a basket of fruit.

Once the worker is taken on, he is driven to the field where he will work. The trucks are packed; safety regulations are often non-existent; and there is no pay for the time spent en route. South from Stockton, along the Riviera coast near Santa Barbara, I remember seeing a most incredible contrast: the lush line of beach, coastal mountains, and rich homes, and, passing by, a truckload of stolid-faced Mexican-Americans coming back from work.

The statistics of migrant wages are low enough—they will be described shortly—yet they conceal some of the misery of this life. They pay is often according to piece rates. The good fruit picker might even make a good sum on one of his better days. But behind him are women and children who may be toiling for $0.50 an hour or less, who receive for ten hours in the hot, broiling sun less than $5.00. In 1960 and 1961, union pressure around Stockton drove the rates up somewhat, but the gain was relative. The workers are low paid, and in competition with themselves on piece rates.

These indignities are not, of course, confined to the fields. In Stockton many of the Anglos live in cheap skid-row hotels (which is better than being out in the open, but still miserable enough). They eat at the Missions. When a flood of Braceros come in and there is a layoff, it is common for men to go without food for two or three days.

Far to the South, in the Imperial Valley of California, the living is, if anything, more terrible than in Stockton. A friend of mine wrote me of some of the people there. One family he described lives in a shack and sleeps on flattened pasteboard boxes on the floor. There is no heat, and since the man of the house has been driven out of the fields by Braceros there is often no food. The mother is breastfeeding her infant—and her four-year-old as well, since that is the only way he will eat. (In this detail there is an eerie echo of the occasion in *The Grapes of Wrath* when the young girl breastfeeds a starving Oakie man. That scene was set almost thirty years ago.)

Or there is the fruit tramp in southern California who was hired to pick tangerines. He works in a gang that includes Braceros, but the pickings were slim in his section of the grove. His job kept him on a ladder all day. He and his wife are charged $18 a week for a one-room shack, with the sink stopped up, and a community stand-in-line privy. The store from which he and the other workers buy their food is owned by the grower.

And yet, incredibly enough, one occasionally encounters a pride of métier, a spirit of loving the land, among some of the migrants. I talked to one of the Filipino workers in Stockton, and he told me of his community which had been there for some years. The Filipinos work together in crews, and have developed speed and efficiency. As a result, they make much more money than the rest of the workers. They are, to be sure, a minority group and suffer discrimination. (The Filipino field hand and I ate in a cheap Chinese restaurant in Stockton; there is a sort of alliance between the minorities.) But, as so often happens at the bottom of society, they look down upon the other workers, and think of them as careless and irresponsible.

Or there was an Anglo worker who lived the year round in Stockton. I asked him why he stayed there, and he said: "It just gets in your blood. I been quitting for twelve years now."

Still, the impression of the California migrants is not one of romance and élan. It is, rather, a sight of near medieval poverty in the midst of lush abundance.

Every Negro ghetto in America is different.

In Atlanta on a soft evening, everyone sits out on the porches of the rooming houses and on the stoops. There is an excited, persistent hum of voices. In Los Angeles, the Negro slum sprawls like everything else. The only obvious thing about it is that the streets, like the streets of the poor everywhere, are badly paved. It takes a little while to learn that the innocent, individual houses are often as rotten inside as any tenement. In Chicago, on the South Side, there is the unmistakable feeling of the great metropolitan ghetto: high buildings, honky tonks, and on the fringes, a sense of tension in one of the most explosive racial situations in the country.

Harlem is different. It is not the solidest or the best organized Negro community (in Chicago, Negro political representation came a full decade before that in New York). It is not the most depressed, even in the New York area. That honor belongs to Bedford-Stuyvesant. But Harlem is the Negro capital, much as New York is an unofficial American capital. It is big, teeming, and brassy. It is where Marcus Garvey established the center of his Empire in Exile, where Joe Louis was cheered after he knocked out Max Schmeling, and where Fidel Castro stayed.

Yet Harlem is essentially the same as any other Negro ghetto. It exists in the midst of a city where liberal rhetoric is required for election to practically every public office. There is no legal segregation; there are a Fair Employment

Practices Law, a State Commission Against Discrimination, a municipal Open Occupancy Law. And yet the white man is still way ahead, and in this Harlem is like any community of Negroes in the United States.

To live in Harlem is to be a Negro; to be a Negro is to participate in a culture of poverty and fear that goes far deeper than any law for or against discrimination. In this sense Harlem could well be a warning: that after the racist statutes are all struck down, after legal equality has been achieved in the schools and in the courts, there remains the profound institutionalized and abiding wrong that white America has worked on the Negro for so long.

Harlem has a discriminatory economy, a discriminatory psychology, a discriminatory society. Like the young Negroes of *The Cool World,* it watches all the wonderful movies about America with a certain bitter cynicism.

> If the population density in some of Harlem's worst blocks obtained in the rest of New York City, the entire population of the United States could fit into three of New York's boroughs.
> CIVIL RIGHTS COMMISSION, 1959

Negro poverty is unique in every way. It grows out of a long American history, and it expresses itself in a subculture that is built up on an interlocking base of economic and racial injustice. It is a fact imposed from without, from white America.

And yet, there is the uniqueness of Negro poverty as an impression, as a walk through the streets of the ghetto will reveal. Here one sees the faces and attitudes behind the statistics: the fear, the food, the religion, the politics of Negro poverty. Looking at this surface of Negro life first, one gains a human perspective on the grim economic figures and occupational data that lie behind it.

Still, a few statistics are necessary for even the most impressionistic description of Harlem, and these can be dealt with briefly. In the mid-fifties (the last point when figures were available), there were almost 1,000,000 Negroes in New York. In this group, 50 percent of the families had incomes under $4,000 a year (as compared with 20 percent of the white families). On Home Relief and Aid to Dependent Children, Negroes formed the majority—and they were 40 percent of all the people who received public assistance. Negro unemployment in the city was somewhat more than double that of the whites, and wages were around half of what white workers got. This affected every other aspect of life: in 1959 the infant mortality rate in central Harlem was 45.3 per thousand (the white district with the lowest rate had 15.4 per thousand).

The statistics could be piled on and on, but the point is obvious: Harlem, as well as every other Negro ghetto, is a center of poverty, of manual work, of sickness, and of every typical disability which America's underdeveloped areas suffer. It is on this very real and material base that the ghetto builds its unique culture.

There is, on the very surface of Harlem life, the imminence of the Man.

The Man is white. He has many guises: as policeman, as judge, as rent collector—as authority made tangible. He is to be feared and hated, for the law is especially swift and hard upon the crimes and vices that grow within these crowded, littered streets. Ultimately, he becomes anyone with a white skin. ("Offay," the old Negro slang term for a white, is foe in pig Latin.) Because of this, Harlem is a place that is suspicious of all outsiders from the world of white America. It is stunted and sick, and the bread of its poverty has the taste of hatred and fear.

When I was doing research for this book in Harlem, I was walking around with a notebook. I stopped on Lenox Avenue to take down some prices in the window of a barbecue joint. When I looked up, everyone was watching me. I knew what they thought, and turned to the two men nearest me and said, "I'm not a cop." When I walked over and started to tell them that I was a writer, one accepted the story. The other listened for a moment, and then said, "I still think he's from the police." Then they were gone.

Part of the reason for this attitude is that there is more obvious crime in Harlem. The numbers game remains a community pastime; streetwalking still flourishes on 125th Street; and marijuana is easy to get. These things are not, of course, "natural" to the Negro. They are the by-products of a ghetto which has little money, much unemployment, and a life to be lived in the streets. Because of them, and because the white man is so ready to believe crime in the Negro, fear is basic to the ghetto. It gives Negro poverty a quality of psychological depth and torment that is unique among all the impoverished people in the United States.

So it is that Malcolm X, Harlem's Muslim leader, can boast that he can assemble a couple of hundred followers within a few minutes after any act of racial violence (or of alleged racial violence). Harlem, for all its brashness, for all the ubiquitous rhythms of rock 'n' roll, is afraid. And for good reason. The white has been the Man, and in many cases he still is.

Another aspect of this fear is the way the Negro in Harlem is a second-class citizen in his own neighborhood. Walking down 125th Street, one of the most obvious, surface impressions is that Harlem's economy is white. Practically all the stores are presided over by white men, and this has been true for years. (The situation is not nearly so extreme in other Negro ghettos, for instance in Chicago). During the riot in the forties, the rage of the people was directed against these shops—so much so that a legendary Chinese is alleged to have put up a sign, "Me Colored Too." When the proprietor (or salesman, rent agent, or other contact) is Jewish as well as white, this has been a source of Harlem anti-Semitism. The most recent variations on this theme are played by Muslim orators who relate it to a pro-Arab, anti-Israel political line.

This aspect of the Negro ghetto is also unique. In the Puerto Rican section, which borders on Harlem, the situation is quite different. Almost as soon as the Puerto Ricans arrive, Spanish-speaking shops dot the avenue. And this was true even before the big migration of Puerto Ricans in the postwar period. Writing of Harlem in 1940, Claude McKay traced the pattern all the way back to the twenties, when the Puerto Ricans were only a fringe of Harlem.

Why is this so? The sociologist Nathan Glazer has suggested that the Negro suffers from being in, but not of, American society. There are no traditions of the "old country" that bind Harlem as a Ghetto. This is the home of America's internal aliens. The people participate in the consumption cult of the white world—the Negro is an "exaggerated American" Myrdal said, and Harlem is

Hollywood carried to its logical conclusion the poet Thomas Merton wrote—
yet the Negroes are poor. They do not huddle together around a language and
a common memory from overseas, saving, planning, waiting for the breakthrough, isolated from the lures of easy life in the magazines and on television.

That is part of it. Another part is that Harlem is quite literally the center
of a migration (as every ghetto is). In 1950 almost two-thirds of the nonwhite
Americans moved (as compared to a rate of 13 percent for the entire nation).
The Negro in Harlem, as Ralph Ellison has written of him, is often "shot up
from the South into the busy city like wild jacks-in-the-box broken loose from
our springs—so sudden that our gait becomes like that of deep-sea divers suffering from the bends."

A white welfare worker tells of the children when they first begin school.
They show off their books; they are interested and friendly. But then, in a few
years, they learn. Their schools are crowded; the instruction is inferior; and the
neighborhood is omnipresent and more powerful than the classroom.

These are only some of the factors, but they all point in the same direction:
Harlem is not only afraid; more than that, Harlem does not even own itself;
the Negro is not master even when he has retreated into the ghetto far from
white eyes. The Man is still with him.

If all the discriminatory laws in the United States were immediately repealed, race would still remain as one of the most pressing moral and political
problems in the nation. Negroes and other minorities are not simply the victims
of a series of iniquitous statutes. The American economy, the American society,
the American unconscious are all racist. If all the laws were framed to provide
equal opportunity, a majority of the Negroes would not be able to take full
advantage of the change. There would still be a vast, silent, and automatic system directed against men and women of color.

To belong to a racial minority is to be poor, but poor in a special way. The
fear, the lack of self-confidence, the haunting, these have been described. But
they, in turn, are the expressions of the most institutionalized poverty in the
United States, the most vicious of the vicious circles. In a sense, the Negro
is classically the "other" American, degraded and frustrated at every turn and
not just because of laws.

There are sympathetic and concerned people who do not understand how
deeply America has integrated racism into its structure. Given time, they argue,
the Negroes will rise in the society like the Irish, the Jews, the Italians, and all
the rest. But this notion misses two decisive facts: that the Negro is colored,
and no other group in the United States has ever faced such a problem, and
that the Negro of today is an internal migrant who will face racism wherever
he goes, who cannot leave his oppression behind as if it were a czar or a potato
famine. To be equal, the Negro requires something much more profound than
a way "into" the society; he needs a transformation of some of the basic institutions of the society.

The Negro is poor because he is black; that is obvious enough. But, perhaps more importantly, the Negro is black because he is poor. The laws against
color can be removed, but that will leave the poverty that is the historic and
institutionalized consequence of color. As long as this is the case, being born a

Negro will continue to be the most profound disability that the United States imposes upon a citizen.

Perhaps the quickest way to point up the racism of the American economy is to recall a strange case of jubilation.

Late in 1960 the Department of Labor issued a study, "The Economic Situation of Negroes in the United States." It noted that in 1939, nonwhite workers earned, on the average, 41 percent as much as whites, and that by 1958 their wages had climbed to 58 percent of that of whites. Not a little elation greeted this announcement. Some of the editorialists cited these statistics as indicating that slow and steady progress was being made. (At this rate, the Negro would reach parity with the white some time well after the year 2000.)

To begin with, the figures were somewhat more optimistic than the reality. Part of the Negro gain reflected the shift of rural Negroes to cities and Southern Negroes to the North. In both cases, the people involved increased their incomes by going into a more prosperous section of the country. But within each area their relative position remained the same: at the bottom. Then, the statistics take a depression year (1939) as a base for comparison, and contrast it to a year of recession (1958). This tended to exaggerate the advance because Negroes in 1939 were particularly victimized.

Another important aspect of the problem was obscured by the sweeping comparisons most editorialists made between the 1939 and 1958 figures. Even the Department of Labor statistics themselves indicate that the major gain was made during World War II (the increase from 1939 to 1947 was from 41.4 percent to 54.3 of the white wage). In the postwar period the rate of advance slowed to a walk. Moreover, most of the optimism was based upon figures for Negro men. When the women are included, and when one takes a median family income from the Current Population Reports, Negroes rose from 51 percent of white family income in 1947 to 57 percent in 1952—and then declined back to the 1947 level by 1959.

But even without these qualifications, the fact is stark enough: the United States found cause for celebration in the announcement that Negro workers had reached 58 percent of the wage level of their white co-workers. This situation is deeply imbedded in the very structure of American society.

Negroes in the United States are concentrated in the worst, dirtiest, lowest-paying jobs. A third continue to live in the rural South, most of them merely subsisting within a culture of poverty and a society of open terror. A third live in Southern cities and a third in Northern cities, and these have bettered their lot compared to the sharecroppers. But they are still the last hired and the first fired, and they are particularly vulnerable to recessions.

Thus, according to the Department of Labor in 1960, 4 percent of Negro employees were "professional, technical and kindred workers" (compared to 11.3 percent for the whites); 2.7 percent were "managers, officials and proprietors" (the white figure is 14.6 percent). In short, at the top of the economic structure there were 6.7 percent of the Negroes—and 25.9 percent of the whites. And this, in itself, represented considerable *gains* over the past two decades.

Going down the occupational scale, Negroes are primarily grouped in the bottom jobs. In 1960, 20 percent of the whites had high-skill industrial jobs, while the Negro share of this classification was 9 percent. Semiskilled mass production workers and laborers constituted around 48 percent of the Negro male population (and 25.3 percent of the white males). Negro women are the victims of a double discrimination. According to a New York State study, Negro female income as a percentage of white actually declined between 1949 and 1954 (and, in 1960, over a third of Negro women were still employed as domestics).

In part, this miserable structure of the Negro work force is an inheritance of the past. It reflects what happens to a people who have been systematically oppressed and denied access to skill and opportunity. If this completely defined the problem, there would be a basis for optimism. One could assume that the Negro would leave behind the mess of pottage bequeathed him by white America and move into a better future. But that is not the case. For the present position of the Negro in the economy has been institutionalized. Unless something basic is done, it will reproduce itself for years to come.

Take, as an example, the problem of automation. This has caused "structural" unemployment through the American work force, that is, the permanent destruction of jobs rather than cyclical layoffs. When this happens, the blow falls disproportionately upon the Negro. As the last significant group to enter the factory, the Negroes have low seniority (if they are lucky enough to be in union occupations), and they are laid off first. As one of the least skilled groups in the work force, they will have the hardest time getting another job. The "older" Negro (over forty) may well be condemned to job instability for the rest of his life.

All of this is immediate and automatic. It is done without the intervention of a single racist, yet it is a profound part of racism in the United States.

However, more is involved than the inevitable working of an impersonal system. The Negro lives in the other America of poverty for many reasons, and one of them is conscious racism reinforcing institutional patterns of the economy. In 1960, according to the report of Herbert Hill, Labor Secretary of the National Association for the Advancement of Colored People, Negroes made up only 1.69 percent of the total number of apprentices in the economy. The exact figure offered by Hill has been disputed; the shocking fact which he describes is agreed upon by everyone. This means that Negroes are denied access precisely to those jobs that are not low-paying and vulnerable to recession.

The main cause of this problem is the attitude of management, which fundamentally determines hiring policy. But in the case of apprenticeship programs, the labor movement and the Federal and state agencies involved also bear part of the responsibility. In the AFL-CIO, it is the politically conservative unions from the building trades who are the real stumbling block; the mass-production unions of the CIO have some bad areas, but on the whole they pioneered in bringing Negroes into the plants and integrating local organizations.

With the companies, one of the real difficulties in dealing with this structure of racism is that it is invisible. Here is a huge social fact, yet no one will accept responsibility for it. When questioned as to why there are no Negroes in sales, or in the office, the personnel man will say that he himself has nothing against Negroes. The problem, he will claim, is with subordinates who would revolt if Negroes were brought into their department, and with superiors who impose the policy. This response is standard up and down the line. The subordinates and the superiors make the same assertion.

Indeed, one of the difficulties in fighting against racist practices in the American economy is the popularity of a liberal rhetoric. Practically no one, outside of convinced white supremacists in the South, will admit to discriminatory policies. So it is that the Northern Negro has, in one sense, a more personally frustrating situation than his Southern brother. In Dixie, Jim Crow is personified, an actual living person who speaks in the accents of open racism. In the rest of the country, everybody is against discrimination for the record, and Jim Crow is a vast impersonal system that keeps the Negro down.

~~~~~4

The 1960's:
Discord and Progress

The advent of the Kennedy administration suggested that a changed public mood had replaced the already shaken complacency of the previous decade. At the very start of the decade, the civil rights movement began its activist phase with the first sit-ins at Greensboro, North Carolina, and the nation faced new foreign policy challenges in Laos, the Congo, and Cuba. The engaging rhetoric of President Kennedy raised expectations for the future as the nation faced fresh demands in almost all areas of national life.

Many of the issues of the Cold War that had frozen American diplomacy for a generation were resolved in the sixties. After the near Armageddon of the Cuban missile crisis, the détente between the United States and the Soviet Union was the most important trend in international affairs, marked by a broad range of agreements on nuclear armaments, cultural exchange, and trade relations. The two powers successfully avoided direct confrontation and turned instead to a competition for the loyalties of the emerging third world. The Russians promised to sponsor "wars of national liberation," which America prepared to extinguish by a thoroughgoing updating of its military forces. The new army stressed flexibility and rapid response to guerrilla challenges instead of reliance on nuclear capacity.

By a process which is still the subject of violent controversy, the United States soon found its new military capacities put to the test in Vietnam. In response to an essentially civil war in which the contending forces received supplies from outside powers, America eventually committed half a million of the finest trained and equipped soldiers in human history to an apparent endless war of counterinsurgency. Vietnam became the first military stalemate that the nation had endured since the War of 1812. But whereas stalemate in 1812 was a form of victory, in the 1960's it was clearly a *defeat, and the nation, unused to reverses on the battlefield, reeled under the impact.*

The Vietnamese war increased disruption in a society already under stress earlier in the decade. President Kennedy's assassination in November, 1963, signaled a new age of militancy to replace the emphasis on nonviolent change manifested in the civil rights movement and the Kennedy New Frontier program of the early sixties. The first years of the Johnson administration embraced enormous achievement but also mounting social disorder and intergroup tension. To a sense of dislocation was added a feeling of moral unease over whether the most powerful nation in history should forcefully impose its anti-communist ideology on a small southeast Asian country. A rich harvest of domestic legistlation in public health, education, welfare, and civil rights resulted from a short-lived liberal coalition under Johnson's powerful leadership. But the ghettos erupted in 1964, the "white backlash" began to emerge, and the Republican National Convention was a scene of ugly division and barely hidden racism—a scandalous occasion, yet nowhere near as horrifying as what was to follow in the Democratic conclave in Chicago only four years later.

Into this cauldron of social tensions, the Vietnamese war added a nightly horror show on the television news, a daily roll of killed and wounded, and a painful inflation. Events reached their bitter climax in 1968, one of the most confusing years in American history, when assassinations, new political movements, presidential turnabouts, and massive political violence led to the anticlimactic election of a moderately conservative President who promised the beginning of the end of the Vietnamese involvement. In retrospect it was clear that in the sixties had come one of the realignments of political coalitions recurring each generation throughout the history of the republic; such realignments had always come at the price of violence and social crisis. At the end of the decade Americans were also left in the strange position of being able to look to the stars with more assurance than they could look about them.

26

NORMAN MAILER

Kennedy—The Existential Hero

*It was the great strength of John Kennedy that he was at once a
toughly realistic politician and a man who inspired idealism and
dedication, especially among young people. Combining strength and
sensitivity as he did, he was a perfect symbolic head of state for an
America of growing strength and culture, of "power and poetry," as
Robert Frost put it at the Kennedy inaugural. He had his faults, of
course, including perhaps a tendency to rely too much on his ad-
visors—at least early in his administration. Nevertheless, Kennedy's
thousand days were rich in promise and full of grace.*

*The time to catch Kennedy is at the 1960 convention. Smiling,
hatless, jesting, he comes alive again in this journalistic-literary essay
by Norman Mailer. For Mailer it was important that Kennedy was
young and handsome, that his wife was attractive and bright.
"Image" is a much-worked term, but it covers something of what
the Kennedy administration was about.*

The afternoon he arrived at the convention from the airport, there was of
course a large crowd on the street outside the Biltmore, and the best way to
get a view was to get up on an outdoor balcony of the Biltmore, two flights
above the street, and look down on the event. One waited thirty minutes, and
then a honking of horns as wild as the getaway after an Italian wedding
sounded around the corner, and the Kennedy cortege came into sight, circled
Pershing Square, the men in the open and leading convertibles sitting back-
wards to look at their leader, and finally came to a halt in a space cleared for
them by the police in the crowd. The television cameras were out, and a
Kennedy band was playing some circus music. One saw him immediately. He
had the deep orange-brown suntan of a ski instructor, and when he smiled at
the crowd his teeth were amazingly white and clearly visible at a distance of
fifty yards. For one moment he saluted Pershing Square, and Pershing Square

saluted him back, the prince and the beggars of glamour staring at one another across a city street, one of those very special moments in the underground history of the world, and then with a quick move he was out of the car and by choice headed into the crowd instead of the lane cleared for him into the hotel by the police, so that he made his way inside surrounded by a mob, and one expected at any moment to see him lifted to its shoulders like a matador being carried back to the city after a triumph in the plaza. All the while the band kept playing the campaign tunes, sashaying circus music, and one had a moment of clarity, intense as a *déjà vu,* for the scene which had taken place had been glimpsed before in a dozen musical comedies; it was the scene where the hero, the matinee idol, the movie star comes to the palace to claim the princess, or what is the same, and more to our soil, the football hero, the campus king, arrives at the dean's home surrounded by a court of open-singing students to plead with the dean for his daughter's kiss and permission to put on the big musical that night. And suddenly I saw the convention, it came into focus for me, and I understood the mood of depression which had lain over the convention, because finally it was simple: the Democrats were going to nominate a man who, no matter how serious his political dedication might be, was indisputably and willy-nilly going to be seen as a great box-office actor, and the consequences of that were staggering and not at all easy to calculate.

Since the First World War Americans have been leading a double life, and our history has moved on two rivers, one visible, the other underground; there has been the history of politics which is concrete, factual, practical and unbelievably dull if not for the consequences of the actions of some of these men; and there is a subterranean river of untapped, ferocious, lonely and romantic desires, that concentration of ecstasy and violence which is the dream life of the nation.

The twentieth century may yet be seen as that era when civilized man and underprivileged man were melted together into mass man, the iron and steel of the nineteenth century giving way to electronic circuits which communicated their messages into men, the unmistakable tendency of the new century seeming to be the creation of men as interchangeable as commodities, their extremes of personality singed out of existence by the psychic fields of force the communicators would impose. This loss of personality was a catastrophe to the future of the imagination, but billions of people might first benefit from it by having enough to eat—one did not know—and there remained citadels of resistance in Europe where the culture was deep and roots were visible in the architecture of the past.

Nowhere, as in America, however, was this fall from individual man to mass man felt so acutely, for America was at once the first and most prolific creator of mass communications, and the most rootless of countries, since almost no American could lay claim to the line of a family which had not once at least severed its roots by migrating here. But, if rootless, it was then the most vulnerable of countries to its own homogenization. Yet America was also the country in which the dynamic myth of the Renaissance—that every man was potentially extraordinary—knew its most passionate persistence. Simply, America was the land where people still believed in heroes: George Washington; Billy the Kid; Lincoln, Jefferson; Mark Twain, Jack London, Hemingway; Joe Louis, Dempsey, Gentleman Jim; America believed in athletes, rum-runners, aviators; even lovers, by the time Valentino died. It was a country which had grown by the leap of one hero past another—is there a county in all of our ground which does not have its legendary figure? And when the West was filled, the expansion turned inward, became part of an agitated, overexcited, super-heated dream life. The film studios threw up their searchlights as the frontier was finally sealed, and the romantic possibilities of the old conquest of land turned into a vertical myth, trapped within the skull, of a new kind of heroic life, each choosing his own archetype of a neo-renaissance man, be it Barry-more, Cagney, Flynn, Bogart, Brando or Sinatra, but it was almost as if there were no peace unless one could fight well, kill well (if always with honor), love well and love many, be cool, be daring, be dashing, be wild, be wily, be re-sourceful, be a brave gun. And this myth, that each of us was born to be free, to wander, to have adventure and to grow on the waves of the violent, the per-fumed, and the unexpected, had a force which could not be tamed no matter how the nation's regulators—politicians, medicos, policemen, professors, priests, rabbis, ministers, *idéologues,* psychoanalysts, builders, executives and endless communicators—would brick-in the modern life with hygiene upon sanity, and middle-brow homily over platitude; the myth would not die. Indeed a quarter of the nation's business must have depended upon its existence. But it stayed alive for more than that—it was as if the message in the labyrinth of the genes would insist that violence was locked with creativity, and adventure was the secret of love.

Once, in the Second World War and in the year or two which followed, the underground river returned to earth, and the life of the nation was intense, of the present, electric; as a lady said, "That was the time when we gave parties which changed people's lives." The Forties was a decade when the speed with which one's own events occurred seemed as rapid as the history of the battle-fields, and for the mass of people in America a forced march into a new jungle of emotion was the result. The surprises, the failures, and the dangers of that life must have terrified some nerve of awareness in the power and the mass, for, as if stricken by the orgiastic vistas the myth had carried up from underground, the retreat to a more conservative existence was disorderly, the fear of communism spread like an irrational hail of boils. To anyone who could see, the excessive hysteria of the Red wave was no preparation to face an enemy, but rather a terror of the national self: free-loving, lust-looting, atheistic implac-able—absurdity beyond absurdity to label communism so, for the moral products of Stalinism had been Victorian sex and a ponderous machine of material theology.

Forced underground again, deep beneath all *Reader's Digest* hospital dress-ings of Mental Health in Your Community, the myth continued to flow, fed by television and the film. The fissure in the national psyche widened to the danger point. The last large appearance of the myth was the vote which tricked the polls and gave Harry Truman his victory in '48. That was the last. Came the Korean War, the shadow of the H-bomb, and we were ready for the Gen-eral. Uncle Harry gave way to Father, and security, regularity, order, and the life of no imagination were the command of the day. If one had any doubt of this, there was Joe McCarthy with his built-in treason detector, furnished by God, and the damage was done. In the totalitarian wind of those days, anyone who worked in Government formed the habit of being not too original, and many a mind atrophied from disuse and private shame. At the summit there was benevolence without leadership, regularity without vision, security without safety, rhetoric without life. The ship drifted on, that enormous warship of the United States, led by a Secretary of State whose cells were seceding to cancer, and as the world became more fantastic—Africa turning itself upside down, while some new kind of machine man was being made in China—two events occurred which stunned the confidence of America into a new night: the Russians put up their Sputnik, and Civil Rights—that reluctant gift to the American Negro, granted for its effect on foreign affairs—spewed into real life at Little Rock. The national Ego was in shock: the Russians were now in some ways our technological superiors, and we had an internal problem of subject populations equal conceivably in its difficulty to the Soviet and its satellites. The fatherly calm of the General began to seem like the uxorious mellifluences of the undertaker.

Underneath it all was a larger problem. The life of politics and the life of myth had diverged too far, and the energies of the people one knew everywhere had slowed down. Twenty years ago a post-Depression generation had gone to war and formed a lively, grousing, by times inefficient, carousing, pleasure-seeking, not altogether inadequate army. It did part of what it was supposed to do, and many, out of combat, picked up a kind of private life on the fly, and had their good time despite the yaws of the military system. But today in America the generation which respected the code of the myth was Beat, a horde of half-begotten Christs with scraggly beards, heroes none, saints all, weak before the strong, empty conformisms of the authority. The sanction for finding one's growth was no longer one's flag, one's career, one's sex, one's adventure, not even one's booze. Among the best in this newest of the generations, the myth had found its voice in marijuana, and the joke of the underground was that when the Russians came over they could never dare to occupy us for long because America was too Hip. Gallows humor. The poorer truth might be that America was too Beat, the instinct of the nation so separated from its public mind that apathy, schizophrenia, and private beatitudes might be the pride of the welcoming committee any underground could offer.

Yes, the life of politics and the life of the myth had diverged too far. There was nothing to return them to one another, no common danger, no cause, no desire, and, most essentially, no hero. It was a hero America needed, a hero central to his time, a man whose personality might suggest contradictions and mysteries which could reach into the alienated circuits of the underground, because only a hero can capture the secret imagination of a people, and so be good for the vitality of his nation; a hero embodies the fantasy and so allows each private mind the liberty to consider its fantasy and find a way to grow. Each mind can become more conscious of its desire and waste less strength in hiding from itself. Roosevelt was such a hero, and Churchill, Lenin and De Gaulle; even Hitler, to take the most odious example of this thesis, was a hero, the hero-as-monster, embodying what had become the monstrous fantasy of a people, but the horror upon which the radical mind and liberal temperament foundered was that he gave outlet to the energies of the Germans and so presented the twentieth century with an index of how horrible had become the secret heart of its desire. Roosevelt is of course a happier example of the hero; from his paralytic leg to the royal elegance of his geniality he seemed to contain the country within himself; everyone from the meanest starving cripple to an ambitious young man could expand into the optimism of an improving future because the man offered an unspoken promise of a future which would be rich. The sexual and the sex-starved, the poor, the hard-working and the imaginative well-to-do could see themselves in the President, could believe him to be like themselves. So a large part of the country was able to discover its energies because not as much was wasted in feeling that the country was a poisonous nutrient which stifled the day.

Too simple? No doubt. One tries to construct a simple model. The thesis is after all not so mysterious; it would merely nudge the notion that a hero embodies his time and is not so very much better than his time, but he is larger than life and so is capable of giving direction to the time, able to encourage a nation to discover the deepest colors of its character. At bottom the concept of the hero is antagonistic to impersonal social progress, to the belief that social ills can be solved by social legislating, for it sees a country as all-but-trapped in its character until it has a hero who reveals the character of the country to itself. The implication is that without such a hero the nation turns sluggish. Truman for example was not such a hero, he was not sufficiently larger than life, he inspired familiarity without excitement, he was a character but his proportions came from soap opera: Uncle Harry, full of salty common-sense and small-minded certainty, a storekeeping uncle.

Whereas Eisenhower has been the anti-Hero, the regulator. Nations do not necessarily and inevitably seek for heroes. In periods of dull anxiety, one or more is likely to look for security than a dramatic confrontation, and Eisenhower could stand as a hero only for that large number of Americans who were most proud of their lack of imagination. In American life, the unspoken war of the century has taken place between the city and the small town: the city which is dynamic, orgiastic, unsettling, explosive and accelerating to the psyche; the small town which is rooted, narrow, cautious and planted in the life-logic of the family. The need of the city is to accelerate growth; the pride of the small town is to retard it. But since America has been passing through a period of enormous expansion since the war, the double-four years of Dwight Eisenhower could not retard the expansion, it could only denude it of color, character, and the development of novelty. The small-town mind is rooted—it is rooted in the small town—and when it attempts to direct history the results are disastrously colorless because the instrument of world power which is used by the smalltown mind is the committee. Committees do not create, they merely proliferate, and the incredible dullness wreaked upon the American landscape in Eisenhower's eight years has been the triumph of the corporation. A tasteless, sexless, odorless sanctity in architecture, manners, modes, styles has been the result. Eisenhower embodied half the needs of the nation, the needs of the timid, the petrified, the sanctimonious, and the sluggish. What was even worse, he did not divide the nation as a hero might (with a dramatic dialogue as the result); he merely excluded one part of the nation from the other. The result was an alienation of the best minds and bravest impulses from the faltering history which was made. America's need in those years was to take an existential turn, to walk into the nightmare, to face into that terrible logic of history which demanded that the country and its people must become more extraordinary and more adventurous, or else perish, since the only alternative was to offer a false security in the power and panacea of organized religion, family, and the FBI, a totalitarianization of the psyche by the stultifying techniques of the mass media which would seep into everyone's most private associations and so leave the country powerless against the Russians even if the denouement were to take fifty years, for in a competition between totalitarianisms the first maxim of the prizefight manager would doubtless apply: "Hungry fighters win fights."

Some part of these thoughts must have been in one's mind at the moment there was that first glimpse of Kennedy entering the Biltmore Hotel; and in the days which followed, the first mystery—the profound air of depression which hung over the convention—gave way to a second mystery which can be answered only by history. The depression of the delegates was understandable: no one had too much doubt that Kennedy would be nominated, but if elected he would be not only the youngest President ever to be chosen by voters, he would be the most conventionally attractive young man ever to sit in the White House, and his wife—some would claim it—might be the most beautiful first lady in our history. Of necessity the myth would emerge once more, because America's politics would now be also America's favorite movie, America's first soap opera, America's best-seller. One thinks of the talents of writers like Taylor Caldwell or Frank Yerby, or is it rather *The Fountainhead* which would contain such a fleshing of the romantic prescription? Or is it indeed one's own work which is called into question? "Well, there's your first hipster," says a writer one knows at the convention, "Sergius O'Shaugnessy born rich," and the temptation is to nod, for it could be true, a war hero, and the heroism is bonafide, even exceptional, a man who has lived with death, who, crippled in the back, took on an operation which would kill him or restore him to power, who chose to marry a lady whose face might be too imaginative for the taste of a democracy which likes its first ladies to be executives of home-management, a man who courts political suicide by choosing to go all out for a nomination four, eight, or twelve years before his political elders think he is ready, a man who announces a week prior to the convention that the young are better fitted to direct history than the old. Yes, it captures the attention. This is no routine candidate calling every shot by safety's routine book. ("Yes," Nixon said, naturally but terribly tired an hour after his nomination, the TV cameras and lights and microphones bringing out a sweat of fatigue on his face, the words coming very slowly from the tired brain, somber, modest, sober, slow, slow enough so that one could touch emphatically the cautions behind each word, "Yes, I want to say," said Nixon, "that whatever abilities I have, I got from my mother." A tired pause . . . dull moment of warning, ". . . and my father." The connection now made, the rest comes easy, ". . . and my school and my church." Such men are capable of anything.)

One had the opportunity to study Kennedy a bit in the days that followed. His style in the press conferences was interesting. Not terribly popular with the reporters (too much a contemporary, and yet too difficult to understand, he received nothing like the rounds of applause given to Eleanor Roosevelt, Stevenson, Humphrey, or even Johnson), he carried himself nonetheless with a cool grace which seemed indifferent to applause, his manner somehow similar to the poise of a fine boxer, quick with his hands, neat in his timing, and two feet away from his corner when the bell ended the round. There was a good lithe wit to his responses, a dry Harvard wit, a keen sense of proportion in disposing of difficult questions—invariably he gave enough of an answer to be formally satisfactory without ever opening himself to a new question which might go further than the first. Asked by a reporter, "Are you for Adlai as vice-president?" the grin came forth and the voice turned very dry, "No, I cannot say we have considered *Adlai* as a vice-president." Yet there was an elusive detachment to everything he did. One did not have the feeling of a man present in the room with all his weight and all his mind. Johnson gave you all of himself, he was a political animal, he breathed like an animal, sweated like one, you knew his mind was entirely absorbed with the compendium of political fact and maneuver; Kennedy seemed at times like a young professor whose manner was adequate for the classroom, but whose mind was off in some intricacy of the Ph.D. thesis he was writing. Perhaps one can give a sense of the discrepancy by saying that he was like an actor who had been cast as the candidate, a good actor, but not a great one—you were aware all the time that the role was one thing and the man another—they did not coincide, the actor seemed a touch too aloof (as, let us say, Gregory Peck is usually too aloof) to become the part. Yet one had little sense of whether to value this elusiveness, or to beware of it. One could be witnessing the fortitude of a superior sensivity or the detachment of a man who was not quite real to himself. And his voice gave no clue. When Johnson spoke, one could separate what was fraudulent from what was felt, he would have been satisfying as an actor the way Broderick Crawford or Paul Douglas are satisfying; one saw into his emotions, or at least had the illusion that one did. Kennedy's voice, however, was only a fair voice, too reedy, near to strident, it had the metallic snap of a cricket in it somewhere, it was more impersonal than the man, and so became the least-impressive quality in a face, a body, a selection of language, and a style of movement which made up a better-than-decent presentation, better than one had expected.

With all of that, it would not do to pass over the quality in Kennedy which is most difficult to describe. And in fact some touches should be added to this hint of a portrait, for later (after the convention), one had a short session alone with him, and the next day, another. As one had suspected in advance the interviews were not altogether satisfactory, they hardly could have been. A man running for President is altogether different from a man elected President: the hazards of the campaign make it impossible for a candidate to be as interesting as he might like to be (assuming he has such a desire). One kept advancing the argument that this campaign would be a contest of personalities, and Kennedy kept returning the discussion to politics. After a while one recognized this was an inevitable caution for him. So there would be not too much point to reconstructing the dialogue since Kennedy is hardly inarticulate about his political attitudes and there will be a library vault of text devoted to it in the newspapers. What struck me most about the interview was a passing remark whose importance was invisible on the scale of politics, but was altogether meaningful to my particular competence. As we sat down for the first time, Kennedy smiled nicely and said that he had read my books. One muttered one's pleasure. "Yes," he said, "I've read . . ." and then there was a short pause which did not last long enough to be embarrassing in which it was yet obvious no title came instantly to his mind, an omission one was not ready to mind altogether since a man in such a position must be obliged to carry a hundred thousand facts and names in his head, but the hesitation lasted no longer than three seconds or four, and then he said, "I've read *The Deer Park* and . . . the others," which startled me for it was the first time in a hundred similar situations, talking to someone whose knowledge of my work was casual, that the sentence did not come out, "I've read *The Naked and the Dead* . . . and the others." If one is to take the worst and assume that Kennedy was briefed for this interview (which is most doubtful), it still speaks well for the striking instincts of his advisers.

What was retained later is an impression of Kennedy's manners which were excellent, even artful, better than the formal good manners of Choate and Harvard, almost as if what was creative in the man had been given to the manners. In a room with one or two people, his voice improved, became low-pitched, even pleasant—it seemed obvious that in all these years he had never become a natural public speaker and so his voice was constricted in public, the symptom of all orators who are ambitious, throttled, and determined.

His personal quality had a subtle, not quite describable intensity, a suggestion of dry pent heat perhaps, his eyes large, the pupils grey, the whites prominent, almost shocking, his most forceful feature: he had the eyes of a mountaineer. His appearance changed with his mood, strikingly so, and this made him always more interesting than what he was saying. He would seem at one moment older than his age, forty-eight or fifty, a tall, slim, sunburned professor with a pleasant weathered face, not even particularly handsome; five minutes later, talking to a press conference on his lawn, three microphones before him, a television camera turning, his appearance would have gone through a metamorphosis, he would look again like a movie star, his coloring vivid, his manner rich, his gestures strong and quick, alive with that concentration of vitality a successful actor always seems to radiate. Kennedy had a dozen faces. Although they were not at all similar as people, the quality was reminiscent of someone like Brando whose expression rarely changes, but whose appearance seems to shift from one person into another as the minutes go by, and one bothers with this comparison because, like Brando, Kennedy's most characteristic quality is the remote and private air of a man who has traversed some lonely terrain of experience, of loss and gain, of nearness to death, which leaves him isolated from the mass of others.

> The next day while they waited in vain for rescuers, the wrecked half of the boat turned over in the water and they saw that it would soon sink. The group decided to swim to a small island three miles away. There were other islands bigger and nearer, but the Navy officers knew that they were occupied by the Japanese. On one island, only one mile to the south, they could see a Japanese camp. McMahon, the engineer whose legs were disabled by burns, was unable to swim. Despite his own painfully crippled back, Kennedy swam the three miles with a breast stroke, towing behind

him by a life-belt strap that he held between his teeth the helpless
McMahon . . . it took Kennedy and the suffering engineer five
hours to reach the island.

The quotation is from a book which has for its dedicated unilateral title,
The Remarkable Kennedys, but the prose is by one of the best of the war reporters, the former *Yank* editor, Joe McCarthy, and so presumably may be
trusted in such details as this. Physical bravery does not of course guarantee a
man's abilities in the White House—all too often men with physical courage
are disappointing in their moral imagination—but the heroism here is remarkable for its tenacity. The above is merely one episode in a continuing saga
which went on for five days in and out of the water, and left Kennedy at one
point "miraculously saved from drowning (in a storm) by a group of Solomon
Island natives who suddenly came up beside him in a large dugout canoe."
Afterward, his back still injured (that precise back injury which was to put him
on crutches eleven years later, and have him search for "spinal-fusion surgery"
despite a warning that his chances of living through the operation were "extremely limited") afterward, he asked to go back on duty and became so bold
in the attacks he made with his PT boat "that the crew didn't like to go out with
him because he took so many chances."

It is the wisdom of a man who senses death within him and gambles that
he can cure it by risking his life. It is the therapy of the instinct, and who is so
wise as to call it irrational? Before he went into the Navy, Kennedy had been
ailing. Washed out of Freshman year at Princeton by a prolonged trough of
yellow jaundice, sick for a year at Harvard, weak already in the back from an
injury at football, his trials suggest the self-hatred of a man whose resentment
and ambition are too large for his body. Not everyone can discharge their furies
on an analyst's couch, for some angers can be relaxed only by winning power,
some rages are sufficiently monumental to demand that one try to become a
hero or else fall back into that death which is already within the cells. But if
one succeeds, the energy aroused can be exceptional. Talking to a man who
had been with Kennedy in Hyannis Port the week before the convention, I
heard that he was in a state of deep fatigue.

"Well, he didn't look tired at the convention," one commented.

"Oh, he had three days of rest. Three days of rest for him is like six
months for us."

One thinks of that three-mile swim with the belt in his mouth and Mc-
Mahon holding it behind him. There are pestilences which sit in the mouth
and rot the teeth—in those five hours how much of the psyche must have been
remade, for to give vent to the bite in one's jaws and yet use that rage to save a
life: it is not so very many men who have the apocalyptic sense that heroism
is the First Doctor.

If one had a profound criticism of Kennedy it was that his public mind was
too conventional, but that seemed to matter less than the fact of such a man in
office because the law of political life had become so dreary that only a conventional mind could win an election. Indeed there could be no politics which
gave warmth to one's body until the country had recovered its imagination, its
pioneer lust for the unexpected and incalculable. It was the changes that might

come afterward on which one could put one's hope. With such a man in office the myth of the nation would again be engaged, and the fact that he was Catholic would shiver a first existential vibration of consciousness into the mind of the White Protestant. For the first time in our history, the Protestant would have the pain and creative luxury of feeling himself in some tiny degree part of a minority, and that was an experience which might be incommensurable in its value to the best of them.

As yet we have said hardly a word about Stevenson. And his actions must remain a puzzle unless one dares a speculation about his motive, or was it his need?

So far as the people at the convention had affection for anyone, it was Stevenson, so far as they were able to generate any spontaneous enthusiasm, their cheers were again for Stevenson. Yet it was obvious he never had much chance because so soon as a chance would present itself he seemed quick to dissipate the opportunity. The day before the nominations, he entered the Sports Arena to take his seat as a delegate—the demonstration was spontaneous, noisy and prolonged; it was quieted only by Governor Collins' invitation for Stevenson to speak to the delegates. In obedience perhaps to the scruple that a candidate must not appear before the convention until nominations are done, Stevenson said no more than: "I am grateful for this tumultuous and moving welcome. After getting in and out of the Biltmore Hotel and this hall, I have decided I know whom you are going to nominate. It will be the last survivor." This dry reminder of the ruthlessness of politics broke the roar of excitement for his presence. The applause as he left the platform was like the dying fall-and-moan of a baseball crowd when a home run curves foul. The next day, a New York columnist talking about it said bitterly, "If he'd only gone through the motions, if he had just said that now he wanted to run, that he would work hard, and he hoped the delegates would vote for him. Instead he made that lame joke." One wonders. It seems almost as if he did not wish to win unless victory came despite himself, and then was overwhelming. There are men who are not heroes because they are too good for their time, and it is natural that defeats leave them bitter, tired, and doubtful of their right to make new history. If Stevenson had campaigned for a year before the convention, it is possible that he could have stopped Kennedy. At the least, the convention would have been enormously more exciting, and the nominations might have gone through half-a-dozen ballots before a winner was hammered into shape. But then Stevenson might also have shortened his life. One had the impression of a tired man who (for a politician) was sickened unduly by compromise. A year of maneuvering, broken promises, and detestable partners might have gutted him for the election campaign. If elected, it might have ruined him as a President. There is the possibility that he sensed his situation exactly this way, and knew that if he were to run for president, win and make a good one, he would first have to be restored, as one can indeed be restored, by an exceptional demonstration of love—love, in this case, meaning that the Party had a profound desire to keep him as their leader. The emotional truth of a last-minute victory for Stevenson over the Kennedy machine might have given him new energy; it would certainly have given him new faith in a country and a party whose good motives he was possibly beginning to doubt. Perhaps the fault he saw with his candidacy was that he attracted only the nicest people to himself and there were not enough of them. (One of the private amusements of the convention was to divine some of the qualities of the candidates by the style of the young women who put on hats and clothing and politicked in the colors of one presidential gent or another. Of course, half of them must have been hired models, but someone did the hiring and so it was fair to look for a common denominator. The Johnson girls tended to be plump, pie-faced, dumb sexy Southern; the Symingteeners seemed a touch mulish, stubborn, good-looking pluggers; the Kennedy ladies were the handsomest; healthy, attractive, tough, a little spoiled—they looked like the kind of girls who had gotten all the dances in high school and/or worked for a year as an airline hostess before marrying well. But the Stevenson girls looked to be doing it for no money; they were good sorts, slightly horsy-faced, one had the impression they played field hockey in college.) It was indeed the pure, the saintly, the clean-living, the pacifistic, the vegetarian who seemed most for Stevenson, and the less humorous in the Kennedy camp were heard to remark bitterly that Stevenson had nothing going for him but a bunch of Goddamn Beatniks. This might even have had its sour truth. The demonstrations outside the Sports Arena for Stevenson seemed to have more than a fair proportion of tall, emaciated young men with thin, wry beards and three-string guitars accompanied (again in undue proportion) by a contingent of ascetic, face-washed young Beat ladies in sweaters and dungarees. Not to mention all the Holden Caulfields one could see from here to the horizon. But of course it is unfair to limit it so, for the Democratic gentry were also committed half en masse for Stevenson, as well as a considerable number of movie stars, Shelley Winters for one: after the convention she remarked sweetly, "Tell me something nice about Kennedy so I can get excited about him."

What was properly astonishing was the way this horde of political half-breeds and amateurs came within distance of turning the convention from its preconceived purpose, and managed at least to bring the only hour of thoroughgoing excitement the convention could offer.

But then nominating day was the best day of the week and enough happened to suggest that a convention out of control would be a spectacle as extraordinary in the American scale of spectator values as a close seventh game in the World Series or a tied fourth quarter in a professional-football championship. A political convention is after all not a meeting of a corporation's board of directors; it is a fiesta, a carnival, a pig-rooting, horse-snorting, band-playing, voice-screaming medieval get-together of greed, practical lust, compromised idealism, career-advancement, meeting, feud, vendetta, conciliation, of rabble-rousers, fist fights (as it used to be), embraces, drunks (again as it used to be) and collective rivers of animal sweat. It is a reminder that no matter how the country might pretend it has grown up and become tidy in its manners, bodiless in its legislative language, hygienic in its separation of high politics from private life, that the roots still come grubby from the soil, and that politics in America is still different from politics anywhere else because the politics has arisen out of the immediate needs, ambitions, and cupidities of the people, that our politics still smell of the bedroom and the kitchen, rather than having descended to us from the chill punctilio of aristocratic negotiation.

So. The Sports Arena was new, too pretty, of course, tasteless in its design—it was somehow pleasing that the acoustics were so bad for one did not wish the architects well; there had been so little imagination in their design, and this arena would have none of the harsh grandeur of Madison Square Garden when it was aged by spectators' phlegm and feet over the next twenty years. Still it had some atmosphere; seen from the streets, with the spectators moving to the ticket gates, the bands playing, the green hot-shot special editions of the Los Angeles newspapers being hawked by the newsboys, there was a touch of the air of promise that precedes a bullfight, not something so good as the approach to the Plaza Mexico, but good, let us say, like the entrance into El Toreo of Mexico City, another architectural monstrosity, also with seats painted, as I remember, in rose-pink, and dark, milky sky-blue.

Inside, it was also different this nominating day. On Monday and Tuesday the air had been desultory, no one listened to the speakers, and everybody milled from one easy chatting conversation to another—it had been like a tepid Kaffeeklatsch for fifteen thousand people. But today there was a whip of anticipation in the air, the seats on the floor were filled, the press section was working, and in the gallery people were sitting in the aisles.

Sam Rayburn had just finished nominating Johnson as one came in, and the rebel yells went up, delegates started filing out of their seats and climbing over seats, and a pullulating dance of bodies and bands began to snake through the aisles, the posters jogging and whirling in time to the music. The dun color of the floor (faces, suits, seats and floor boards), so monotonous the first two days, now lit up with life as if an iridescent caterpillar had emerged from a fold of wet leaves. It was more vivid than one had expected, it was right, it felt finally like a convention, and from up close when one got down to the floor (where your presence was illegal and so consummated by sneaking in one time as demonstrators were going out, and again by slipping a five-dollar bill to a guard) the nearness to the demonstrators took on high color, that electric vividness one feels on the side lines of a football game when it is necessary to duck back as the ballcarrier goes by, his face tortured in the concentration of the moment, the thwomp of his tackle as acute as if one had been hit oneself.

That was the way the demonstrators looked on the floor. Nearly all had the rapt, private look of a passion or a tension which would finally be worked off by one's limbs, three hundred football players, everything from seedy delegates with jowl-sweating shivers to livid models, paid for their work that day, but stomping out their beat on the floor with the hypnotic adulatory grimaces of ladies who had lived for Lyndon these last ten years.

Then from the funereal rostrum, whose color was not so rich as mahogany nor so dead as a cigar, came the last of the requests for the delegates to take their seats. The seconding speeches began, one minute each; they ran for three and four, the minor-league speakers running on the longest as if the electric antenna of television was the lure of the Sirens, leading them out. Bored cheers applauded their concluding Götterdämmerungen and the nominations were open again. A favorite son, a modest demonstration, five seconding speeches, tedium.

Next was Kennedy's occasion. Governor Freeman of Minnesota made the speech. On the second or third sentence his television prompter jammed, an accident. Few could be aware of it at the moment; the speech seemed merely flat and surprisingly void of bravura. He was obviously no giant of extempore. Then the demonstration. Well-run, bigger than Johnson's, jazzier, the caliber of the costumes and decorations better chosen: the placards were broad enough, "Let's Back Jack," the floats were garish, particularly a papier-mâché or plastic balloon of Kennedy's head, six feet in diameter, which had nonetheless the slightly shrunken, over-red, rubbery look of a toy for practical jokers in one of those sleezy off-Times Square magic-and-gimmick stores; the band was suitably corny; and yet one had the impression this demonstration had been designed by some hands-to-hip interior decorator who said, "Oh, joy, let's have fun, let's make this *true* beer hall."

Besides, the personnel had something of the Kennedy *élan,* those paper hats designed to look like straw boaters with Kennedy's face on the crown, and small photographs of him on the ribbon, those hats which had come to symbolize the crack speed of Kennedy's team, that Madison Avenue cachet which one finds in bars like P. J. Clarke's, the elegance always giving its subtle echo of the Twenties so that the raccoon coats seem more numerous than their real count, and the colored waistcoats are measured by the charm they would have drawn from Scott Fitzgerald's eye. But there, it occurred to one for the first time that Kennedy's middle name was just that, Fitzgerald, and the tone of his crack lieutenants, the unstated style, was true to Scott. The legend of Fitzgerald had an army at last, formed around the self-image in the mind of every superior Madison Avenue opportunist that he was hard, he was young, he was In, his conversation was lean as wit, and if the work was not always scrupulous, well the style could aspire. If there came a good day . . . he could meet the occasion.

The Kennedy snake dance ran its thirty lively minutes, cheered its seconding speeches, and sat back. They were so sure of winning, there had been so many victories before this one, and this one had been scouted and managed so well, that hysteria could hardly be the mood. Besides, everyone was waiting for the Stevenson barrage which should be at least diverting. But now came a long tedium. Favorite sons were nominated, fat mayors shook their hips, seconders told the word to constituents back in Ponderwaygot County, treacly demonstrations tried to hold the floor, and the afternoon went by; Symington's hour came and went, a good demonstration, good as Johnson's (for good cause —they had pooled their demonstrators). More favorite sons, Governor Docking of Kansas declared "a genius" by one of his lady speakers in a tense go-back-to-religion voice. The hours went by, two, three, four hours, it seemed forever before they would get to Stevenson. It was evening when Senator Eugene McCarthy of Minnesota got up to nominate him.

The gallery was ready, the floor was responsive, the demonstrators were milling like bulls in their pen waiting for the *toril* to fly open—it would have been hard not to wake the crowd up, not to make a good speech. McCarthy made a great one. Great it was by the measure of convention oratory, and he held the crowd like a matador, timing their *oles!,* building them up, easing them back, correcting any sag in attention, gathering their emotion, discharging it, creating new emotion on the wave of the last, driving his passes tighter and tighter as he readied for the kill. "Do not reject this man who made us all proud to be called Democrats, do not leave this prophet without honor in his own party." One had not heard a speech like this since 1948 when Vito Marcantonio's voice, his harsh, shrill, bitter, street urchin's voice screeched through the loud-speakers at Yankee Stadium and lashed seventy thousand people into an uproar.

"There was only one man who said let's talk sense to the American people," McCarthy went on, his muleta furled for the *naturales*. "There was only one man who said let's talk sense to the American people," he repeated. "He said the promise of America is the promise of greatness. This was his call to greatness. . . . Do not forget this man. . . . Ladies and Gentlemen, I present to you not the favorite son of one state, but the favorite son of the fifty states, the favorite son of every country he has visited, the favorite son of every country which has not seen him but is secretly thrilled by his name." Bedlam. The kill. "Ladies and Gentlemen, I present to you Adlai Stevenson of Illinois." Ears and tail. Hooves and bull. A roar went up like the roar one heard the day Bobby Thompson hit his home run at the Polo Grounds and the Giants won the pennant from the Dodgers in the third playoff game of the 1951 season. The demonstration cascaded onto the floor, the gallery came to its feet, the Sports Arena sounded like the inside of a marching drum. A tidal pulse of hysteria, exaltation, defiance, exhilaration, anger and roaring desire flooded over the floor. The cry which had gone up on McCarthy's last sentence had not paused for breath in five minutes, and troop after troop of demonstrators jammed the floor (the Stevenson people to be scolded the next day for having collected floor passes and sent them out to bring in new demonstrators) and still the sound mounted. One felt the convention coming apart. There was a Kennedy girl in the seat in front of me, the Kennedy hat on her head, a dimpled healthy brunette; she had sat silently through McCarthy's speech, but now, like a woman paying her respects to the power of natural thrust, she took off her hat and began to clap herself. I saw a writer I knew in the next aisle; he had spent a year studying the Kennedy machine in order to write a book on how a nomination is won. If Stevenson stampeded the convention, his work was lost. Like a reporter at a mine cave-in I inquired the present view of the widow. "Who can think," was the answer, half frantic, half elated, "just watch it, that's all." I found a cool one, a New York reporter, who smiled in rueful respect. "It's the biggest demonstration I've seen since Wendell Willkie's in 1940," he said, and added, "God, if Stevenson takes it, I can wire my wife and move the family on to Hawaii."

"I don't get it."

"Well, every story I wrote said it was locked up for Kennedy."

Still it went on, twenty minutes, thirty minutes, the chairman could hardly be heard, the demonstrators refused to leave. The lights were turned out, giving a sudden theatrical shift to the sense of a crowded church at midnight, and a new roar went up, louder, more passionate than anything heard before. It was the voice, the passion, if one insisted to call it that, of everything in America which was defeated, idealistic, innocent, alienated, outside and Beat, it was the potential voice of a new third of the nation whose psyche was ill from cultural malnutrition, it was powerful, it was extraordinary, it was larger than the decent, humorous, finicky, half-noble man who had called it forth, it was a cry from the Thirties when Time was simple, it was a resentment of the slick technique, the oiled gears, and the superior generals of Fitzgerald's Army; but it was also—and for this reason one could not admire it altogether, except with one's excitement—it was also the plea of the bewildered who hunger for simplicity again, it was the adolescent counterpart of the boss's depression before the unpredictable dynamic of Kennedy as President, it was the return to the sentimental dream of Roosevelt rather than the approaching nightmare of history's oncoming night, and it was inspired by a terror of the future as much as a revulsion of the present.

Fitz's army held; after the demonstration was finally down, the convention languished for ninety minutes while Meyner and others were nominated, a fatal lapse of time because Stevenson had perhaps a chance to stop Kennedy if the voting had begun on the echo of the last cry for him, but in an hour and a half depression crept in again and emotions spent, the delegates who had wavered were rounded into line. When the vote was taken, Stevenson had made no gains, The brunette who had taken off her hat was wearing it again, and she clapped and squealed when Wyoming delivered the duke and Kennedy was in. The air was sheepish, like the mood of a suburban couple who forgive each other for cutting in and out of somebody else's automobile while the country club dance is on. Again, tonight, no miracle would occur. In the morning the papers would be moderate in their description of Stevenson's last charge.

27

Summary of the Report of the National Advisory Commission on Civil Disorders, 1968

The President's Commission on Civil Disorders was appointed to examine the causes of riots in black ghettos. When on March 1, 1968, the Commission made its report charging widespread white racism, it was greeted by an avalanche of protests. Few readers agreed that the American middle class was racist. The very word conjured up Mississippi rednecks with guns and hemp.

But white racism may also be something else—a kind of reflex action, a social conditioning to be found in most American whites, and a characteristic of American political, social, and economic life. White racism means many things. It covers the range of pressures and restraints on the black community. For most white Americans it represents not the direct result of a consciously sustained attitude in the community as a whole, but rather the variety of injuries that are ultimately traceable, directly or indirectly, to racism itself. If a white man refuses to hire a black man, it may be that the applicant is educationally unqualified; the educational system for blacks in this country is markedly inferior to that for whites.

The indignation with which many whites greeted the report was both understandable and misplaced: understandable because the indignant were possibly not themselves racist, or they had brought their racism under some kind of control; misplaced, because the term is a shorthand that refers particular facts to their ultimate cause.

Are conditions in the black ghettos improving? A report of the Urban League, issued one year to the day after the Commission document appeared, holds that they are worsening.

INTRODUCTION

The summer of 1967 again brought racial disorders to American cities, and with them shock, fear and bewilderment to the nation.

The worst came during a two-week period in July, first in Newark and then in Detroit. Each set off a chain reaction in neighboring communities.

On July 28, 1967, the President of the United States established this Commission and directed us to answer three basic questions:

What happened?

Why did it happen?

What can be done to prevent it from happening again?

To respond to these questions, we have undertaken a broad range of studies and investigations. We have visited the riot cities; we have heard many witnesses; we have sought the counsel of experts across the country.

This is our basic conclusion: Our nation is moving toward two societies, one black, one white—separate and unequal.

Reaction to last summer's disorders has quickened the movement and deepened the division. Discrimination and segregation have long permeated much of American life; they now threaten the future of every American.

This deepening racial division is not inevitable. The movement apart can be reversed. Choice is still possible. Our principal task is to define that choice and to press for a national resolution.

To pursue our present course will involve the continuing polarization of the American community and, ultimately, the destruction of basic democratic values.

The alternative is not blind repression or capitulation to lawlessness. It is the realization of common opportunities for all within a single society.

This alternative will require a commitment to national action—compassionate, massive and sustained, backed by the resources of the most powerful and the richest nation on this earth. From every American it will require new attitudes, new understanding, and, above all, new will.

The vital needs of the nation must be met; hard choices must be made, and, if necessary, new taxes enacted.

Violence cannot build a better society. Disruption and disorder nourish repression, not justice. They strike at the freedom of every citizen. The community cannot—it will not—tolerate coercion and mob rule.

Violence and destruction must be ended—in the streets of the ghetto and in the lives of people.

Segregation and poverty have created in the racial ghetto a destructive environment totally unknown to most white Americans.

What white Americans have never fully understood—but what the Negro can never forget—is that white society is deeply implicated in the ghetto. White institutions created it, white institutions maintain it, and white society condones it.

It is time now to turn with all the purpose at our command to the major unfinished business of this nation. It is time to adopt strategies for action that will produce quick and visible progress. It is time to make good the promises of American democracy to all citizens—urban and rural, white and black, Spanish-surname, American Indian, and every minority group.

Our recommendations embrace three basic principles:

To mount programs on a scale equal to the dimension of the problems:

To aim these programs for high impact in the immediate future in order to close the gap between promise and performance;

To undertake new initiatives and experiments that can change the system of failure and frustration that now dominates the ghetto and weakens our society.

These programs will require unprecedented levels of funding and performance, but they neither probe deeper nor demand more than the problems which called them forth. There can be no higher priority for national action and no higher claim on the nation's conscience.

We issue this Report now, four months before the date called for by the President. Much remains that can be learned. Continued study is essential.

As Commissioners we have worked together with a sense of the greatest urgency and have sought to compose whatever differences exist among us. Some differences remain. But the gravity of the problem and the pressing need for action are too clear to allow further delay in the issuance of this Report.

PART I—WHAT HAPPENED?

Chapter 1—Profiles of Disorder

The report contains profiles of a selection of the disorders that took place during the summer of 1967. These profiles are designed to indicate how the disorders happened, who participated in them, and how local officials, police forces, and the National Guard responded. Illustrative excerpts follow:

NEWARK

. . . It was decided to attempt to channel the energies of the people into a nonviolent protest. While Lofton promised the crowd that a full investigation would be made of the Smith incident, the other Negro leaders began urging those on the scene to form a line of march toward the city hall.

Some persons joined the line of march. Others milled about in the narrow street. From the dark grounds of the housing project came a barrage of rocks. Some of them fell among the crowd. Others hit persons in the line of march. Many smashed the windows of the police station. The rock throwing, it was believed, was the work of youngsters; approximately 2,500 children lived in the housing project.

Almost at the same time, an old car was set afire in a parking lot. The line of march began to disintegrate. The police, their heads protected by World War I-type helmets, sallied forth to disperse the crowd. A fire engine, arriving on the scene, was pelted with rocks. As police drove people away from the station, they scattered in all directions.

A few minutes later a nearby liquor store was broken into. Some persons, seeing a caravan of cabs appear at city hall to protest Smith's arrest, interpreted this as evidence that the disturbance had been organized, and generated rumors to that effect.

However, only a few stores were looted. Within a short period of time, the disorder appeared to have run its course. . . .

. . . On Saturday, July 15 [Director of Police Dominick] Spina received a report of snipers in a housing project. When he arrived he saw approximately 100 National Guardsmen and police officers crouching behind vehicles, hiding in corners and lying on the ground around the edge of the courtyard.

Since everything appeared quiet and it was broad daylight, Spina walked directly down the middle of the street. Nothing happened. As he came to the last building of the complex, he heard a shot. All around him the troopers jumped, believing themselves to be under sniper fire. A moment later a young Guardsman ran from behind a building.

The Director of Police went over and asked him if he had fired the shot. The soldier said yes, he had fired to scare a man away from a window; that his orders were to keep everyone away from windows.

Spina said he told the soldier: "Do you know what you just did? You have now created a state of hysteria. Every Guardsman up and down this street and every state policeman and every city policeman that is present thinks that somebody just fired a shot and that it is probably a sniper."

A short time later more "gunshots" were heard. Investigating, Spina came upon a Puerto Rican sitting on a wall. In reply to a question as to whether he knew "where the firing is coming from?" the man said:

"That's no firing. That's fireworks. If you look up to the fourth floor, you will see the people who are throwing down these cherry bombs."

By this time four truckloads of National Guardsmen had arrived and troopers and policemen were again crouched everywhere looking for a sniper. The Director of Police remained at the scene for three hours, and the only shot fired was the one by the Guardsmen.

Nevertheless, at six o'clock that evening two columns of National Guardsmen and state troopers were directing mass fire at the Hayes Housing Project in response to what they believed were snipers. . . .

DETROIT

. . . A spirit of carefree nihilism was taking hold. To riot and destroy appeared more and more to become ends in themselves. Late Sunday afternoon it appeared to one observer that the young people were "dancing amidst the flames."

A Negro plainclothes officer was standing at an intersection when a man threw a Molotov cocktail into a business establishment at the corner. In the heat of the afternoon, fanned by the 20 to 25 m.p.h. winds of both Sunday and Monday, the fire reached the home next door within minutes. As residents uselessly sprayed the flames with garden hoses, the fire jumped from roof to roof of adjacent two- and three-story buildings. Within the hour the entire block was in flames. The ninth house in the burning row belonged to the arsonist who had thrown the Molotov cocktail. . . .

. . . Employed as a private guard, 55-year-old Julius L. Dorsey, a Negro, was standing in front of a market when accosted by two Negro men and a woman. They demanded he permit them to loot the market. He ignored their demands. They began to berate him. He asked a neighbor to call the police. As the argument grew more heated, Dorsey fired three shots from his pistol into the air.

The police radio reported: "Looters, they have rifles." A patrol car driven by a police officer and carrying three National Guardsmen arrived. As the looters fled, the law enforcement personnel opened fire. When the firing ceased, one person lay dead.

He was Julius L. Dorsey. . . .

. . . As the riot alternately waxed and waned, one area of the ghetto remained insulated. On the northeast side the residents of the some 150 square blocks inhabited by 21,000 persons had, in 1966, banded together in the Positive Neighborhood Action Committee (PNAC). With professional help from the Institute of Urban Dynamics, they had organized block clubs and made plans for the improvement of the neighborhood. . . .

When the riot broke out, the residents, through the block clubs, were able to organize quickly. Youngsters, agreeing to stay in the neighborhood, participated in detouring traffic. While many persons reportedly sympathized with the idea of a rebellion against the "system," only two small fires were set—one in an empty building. . . .

. . . According to Lt. Gen. Throckmorton and Col. Bolling, the city, at this time, was saturated with fear. The National Guardsmen were afraid, the residents were afraid, and the police were afraid. Numerous persons, the majority of them Negroes, were being injured by gunshots of undetermined origin. The general and his staff felt that the major task of the troops was to reduce the fear and restore an air of normalcy.

In order to accomplish this, every effort was made to establish contact and rapport between the troops and the residents. The soldiers—20 percent of whom were Negro—began helping to clean up the streets, collect garbage, and trace persons who had disappeared in the confusion. Residents in the neighborhoods responded with soup and sandwiches for the troops. In areas where the National Guard tried to establish rapport with the citizens, there was a smaller response.

NEW BRUNSWICK

. . . A short time later, elements of the crowd—an older and rougher one than the night before—appeared in front of the police station. The participants wanted to see the mayor.

Mayor [Patricia] Sheehan went out onto the steps of the station. Using a bullhorn, she talked to the people and asked that she be given an opportunity to correct conditions. The crowd was boisterous. Some persons challenged the mayor. But, finally, the opinion, "She's new! Give her a chance!" prevailed.

A demand was issued by people in the crowd that all persons arrested the previous night be released. Told that this already had been done, the people were suspicious. They asked to be allowed to inspect the jail cells.

It was agreed to permit representatives of the people to look in the cells to satisfy themselves that everyone had been released.

The crowd dispersed. The New Brunswick riot had failed to materialize.

Chapter 2—Patterns of Disorder

The "typical" riot did not take place. The disorders of 1967 were unusual, irregular, complex and unpredictable social processes. Like most human events, they did not unfold in an orderly sequence. However, an analysis of our survey information leads to some conclusions about the riot process.

In general:

The civil disorders of 1967 involved Negroes acting against local symbols of white American society, authority and property in Negro neighborhoods—rather than against white persons.

Of 164 disorders reported during the first nine months of 1967, eight (5 percent) were major in terms of violence and damage; 33 (20 percent) were serious but not major; 123 (75 percent) were minor and undoubtedly would not have received national attention as "riots" had the nation not been sensitized by the more serious outbreaks.

In the 75 disorders studied by a Senate subcommittee, 83 deaths were reported. Eighty-two percent of the deaths and more than half the injuries occurred in Newark and Detroit. About 10 percent of the dead and 38 percent of the injured were public employees, primarily law officers and firemen. The overwhelming majority of the persons killed or injured in all the disorders were Negro civilians.

Initial damage estimates were greatly exaggerated. In Detroit, newspaper damage estimates at first ranged from $200 million to $500 million; the highest recent estimate is $45 million. In Newark, early estimates ranged from $15 to $25 million. A month later damage was estimated at $10.2 million, over 80 percent in inventory losses.

In the 24 disorders in 23 cities which we surveyed:

The final incident before the outbreak of disorder, and the initial violence itself, generally took place in the evening or at night at a place in which it was normal for many people to be on the streets.

Violence usually occurred almost immediately following the occurrence of the final precipitating incident, and then escalated rapidly. With but few exceptions, violence subsided during the day, and flared rapidly again at night. The night-day cycles continued through the early period of the major disorders.

Disorder generally began with rock and bottle throwing and window breaking. Once store windows were broken, looting usually followed.

Disorder did not erupt as a result of a single "triggering" or "precipitating" incident. Instead, it was generated out of an increasingly disturbed social atmosphere, in which typically a series of tension-heightening incidents over a period of weeks or months became linked in the minds of many in the Negro community with a reservoir of underlying grievances. At some point in the mounting tension, a further incident—in itself often routine or trivial—became the breaking point and the tension spilled over into violence.

"Prior" incidents, which increased tensions and ultimately led to violence, were police actions in almost half the cases; police actions were "final" incidents before the outbreak of violence in 12 of the 24 surveyed disorders.

No particular control tactic was successful in every situation. The varied effectiveness of control techniques emphasizes the need for advance training, planning, adequate intelligence systems, and knowledge of the ghetto community.

Negotiations between Negroes—including your militants as well as older Negro leaders—and white officials concerning "terms of peace" occurred during virtually all the disorders surveyed. In many cases, these negotiations involved discussion of underlying grievances as well as the handling of the disorder by control authorities.

The typical rioter was a teenager or young adult, a lifelong resident of the city in which he rioted, a high school dropout; he was, nevertheless, somewhat better educated than his nonrioting Negro neighbor, and was usually underemployed or employed in a menial job. He was proud of his race, extremely hostile to both whites and middle-class Negroes and, although informed about politics, highly distrustful of the political system.

A Detroit survey revealed that approximately 11 percent of the total residents of two riot areas admitted participation in the rioting, 20 to 25 percent identified themselves as "bystanders," over 16 percent identified themselves as "counter-rioters" who urged rioters to "cool it," and the remaining 48 to 53 percent said they were at home or elsewhere and did not participate. In a survey of Negro males between the ages of 15 and 35 residing in the disturbance area in Newark, about 45 percent identified themselves as rioters, and about 55 percent as "noninvolved."

Most rioters were young Negro males. Nearly 53 percent of arrestees were between 15 and 24 years of age; nearly 81 percent between 15 and 35.

In Detroit and Newark about 74 percent of the rioters were brought up in the North. In contrast, of the noninvolved, 36 percent in Detroit and 52 percent in Newark were brought up in the North.

What the rioters appeared to be seeking was fuller participation in the social order and the material benefits enjoyed by the majority of American citizens. Rather than rejecting the American system, they were anxious to obtain a place for themselves in it.

Numerous Negro counter-rioters walked the streets urging rioters to "cool it." The typical counter-rioter was better educated and had higher income than either the rioter or the noninvolved.

The proportion of Negroes in local government was substantially smaller than the Negro proportion of population. Only three of the 20 cities studied had more than one Negro legislator; none had ever had a Negro mayor or city manager. In only four cities did Negroes hold other important policy-making positions or serve as heads of municipal departments.

Although almost all cities had some sort of formal grievance mechanism for handling citizen complaints, this typically was regarded by Negroes as ineffective and was generally ignored.

Although specific grievances varied from city to city, at least 12 deeply held grievances can be identified and ranked into three levels of relative intensity:

First Level of Intensity

1. Police practices
2. Unemployment and underemployment
3. Inadequate housing

Second Level of Intensity

4. Inadequate education
5. Poor recreation facilities and programs
6. Ineffectiveness of the political structure and grievance mechanisms

Third Level of Intensity

7. Disrespectful white attitudes
8. Discriminatory administration of justice
9. Inadequacy of federal programs

10. Inadequacy of municipal services
11. Discriminatory consumer and credit practices
12. Inadequate welfare programs

The results of a three-city survey of various federal programs—manpower, education, housing, welfare and community action—indicate that, despite substantial expenditures, the number of persons assisted constituted only a fraction of those in need.

The background of disorder is often a complex and difficult to analyze as the disorder itself. But we find that certain general conclusions can be drawn:

Social and economic conditions in the riot cities constituted a clear pattern of severe disadvantage for Negroes compared with whites, whether the Negroes lived in the area where the riot took place or outside it. Negroes had completed fewer years of education and fewer had attended high school. Negroes were twice as likely to be unemployed and three times as likely to be in unskilled and service jobs. Negroes averaged 70 percent of the income earned by whites and were more than twice as likely to be living in poverty. Although housing cost Negroes relatively more, they had worse housing—three times as likely to be overcrowded and substandard. When compared to white suburbs, the relative disadvantage is even more pronounced.

A study of the aftermath of disorder leads to disturbing conclusions. We find that, despite the institution of some post-riot programs:

Little basic change in the conditions underlying the outbreak of disorder has taken place. Actions to ameliorate Negro grievances have been limited and sporadic; with but few exceptions, they have not significantly reduced tensions.

In several cities, the principal official response has been to train and equip the police with more sophisticated weapons.

In several cities, increasing polarization is evident, with continuing break-down of inter-racial communication, and growth of white segregationist or black separatist groups.

Chapter 3—Organized Activity

The President directed the Commission to investigate "to what extent, if any, there has been planning or organization in any of the riots."

To carry out this part of the President's charge, the Commission established a special investigative staff supplementing the field teams that made the general examination of the riots in 23 cities. The unit examined data collected by federal agencies and congressional committees, including thousands of documents supplied by the Federal Bureau of Investigation, gathered and evaluated information from local and state law enforcement agencies and officials, and conducted its own field investigation in selected cities.

On the basis of all the information collected, the Commission concludes that:

> The urban disorders of the summer of 1967 were not caused by, nor were they the consequence of, any organized plan or "conspiracy."

Specifically, the Commission has found no evidence that all or any of the disorders or the incidents that led to them were planned or directed by any organization or group, international, national or local.

Militant organizations, local and national, and individual agitators, who repeatedly forecast and called for violence, were active in the spring and summer of 1967. We believe that they sought to encourage violence, and that they helped to create an atmosphere that contributed to the outbreak of disorder.

We recognize that the continuation of disorders and the polarization of the races would provide fertile ground for organized exploitation in the future.

Investigations of organized activity are continuing at all levels of government, including committees of Congress. These investigations relate not only to the disorders of 1967 but also to the actions of groups and individuals, particularly in schools and colleges, during this last fall and winter. The Commission has cooperated in these investigations. They should continue.

PART II—WHY DID IT HAPPEN?

Chapter 4—The Basic Causes

In addressing the question "Why did it happen?" we shift our focus from the local to the national scene, from the particular events of the summer of 1967 to the factors within the society at large that created a mood of violence among many urban Negroes.

These factors are complex and interacting; they vary significantly in their effect from city to city and from year to year; and the consequences of one disorder, generating new grievances and new demands, become the causes of the next. Thus was created the "thicket of tension, conflicting evidence and extreme opinions" cited by the President.

Despite these complexities, certain fundamental matters are clear. Of these, the most fundamental is the racial attitude and behavior of white Americans toward black Americans.

Race prejudice has shaped our history decisively; it now threatens to affect our future.

White racism is essentially responsible for the explosive mixture which has been accumulating in our cities since the end of World War II. Among the ingredients of this mixture are:

Pervasive discrimination and segregation in employment, education and housing, which have resulted in the continuing exclusion of great numbers of Negroes from the benefits of economic progress.

Black in-migration and white exodus, which have produced the massive and growing concentrations of impoverished Negroes in our major cities, creating a growing crisis of deteriorating facilities and services and unmet human needs.

The black ghettos where segregation and poverty converge on the young to destroy opportunity and enforce failure. Crime, drug addiction, dependency on welfare, and bitterness and resentment against society in general and white society in particular are the result.

At the same time, most whites and some Negroes outside the ghetto have prospered to a degree unparalleled in the history of civilization. Through television and other media, this affluence has been flaunted before the eyes of the Negro poor and the jobless ghetto youth.

Yet these facts alone cannot be said to have caused the disorders. Recently, other powerful ingredients have begun to catalyze the mixture:

Frustrated hopes are the residue of the unfulfilled expectations aroused by the great judicial and legislative victories of the Civil Rights Movement and the dramatic struggle for equal rights in the South.

A climate that tends toward approval and encouragement of violence as a form of protest has been created by white terrorism directed against nonviolent protest; by the open defiance of law and federal authority by state and local officials resisting desegregation; and by some protest groups engaging in civil disobedience who turn their backs on nonviolence, go beyond the constitutionally protected rights of petition and free assembly, and resort to violence to attempt to compel alteration of laws and policies with which they disagree.

The frustrations of powerlessness have led some Negroes to the conviction that there is no effective alternative to violence as a means of achieving redress of grievances, and of "moving the system." These frustrations are reflected in alienation and hostility toward the institutions of law and government and the white society which controls them, and in the reach toward racial consciousness and solidarity reflected in the slogan "Black Power."

A new mood has sprung up among Negroes, particularly among the young, in which self-esteem and enhanced racial pride are replacing apathy and submission to "the system."

The police are not merely a "spark" factor. To some Negroes police have come to symbolize white power, white racism and white repression. And the fact is that many police do reflect and express these white attitudes. The atmosphere of hostility and cynicism is reinforced by a widespread belief among Negroes in the existence of police brutality and in a "double standard" of justice and protection—one for Negroes and one for whites. . . .

To this point, we have attempted to identify the prime components of the "explosive mixture." In the chapters that follow we seek to analyze them in the perspective of history. Their meaning, however, is clear:

In the summer of 1967, we have seen in our cities a chain reaction of racial violence. If we are heedless, none of us shall escape the consequences.

Chapter 5—Rejection and Protest: An Historical Sketch

The causes of recent racial disorders are embedded in a tangle of issues and circumstances—social, economic, political and psychological—which arise out of the historic pattern of Negro-white relations in America.

In this chapter we trace the pattern, identify the recurrent themes of Negro protest and, most importantly, provide a perspective on the protest activities of the present era.

We describe the Negro's experience in America and the development of slavery as an institution. We show his persistent striving for equality in the face of rigidly maintained social, economic and educational barriers, and re-peated mob violence. We portray the ebb and flow of the doctrinal tides—accommodation, separatism, and self-help—and their relationship to the cur-rent theme of Black Power. We conclude:

> The Black Power advocates of today consciously feel that they are the most militant group in the Negro protest movement. Yet they have retreated from a direct confrontation with American society on the issue of integration and, by preaching separatism, uncon-sciously function as an accommodation to white racism. Much of their economic program, as well as their interest in Negro history, self-help, racial solidarity and separation, is reminiscent of Booker T. Washington. The rhetoric is different, but the ideas are remark-ably similar.

Chapter 6—The Formation of the Racial Ghettos [1]

Throughout the 20th century the Negro population of the United States has been moving steadily from rural areas to urban and from South to North and West. In 1910, 91 percent of the nation's 9.8 million Negroes lived in the South and only 27 percent of American Negroes lived in cities of 2,500 persons or more. Between 1910 and 1966 the total Negro population more than doubled, reaching 21.5 million, and the number living in metropolitan areas

---

[1] The term "ghetto" as used in this report refers to an area within a city char-acterized by poverty and acute social disorganization, and inhabited by members of a racial or ethnic group under conditions of involuntary segregation.

rose more than five-fold (from 2.6 million to 14.8 million). The number outside the South rose eleven-fold (from 880,000 to 9.7 million).

Negro migration from the South has resulted from the expectation of
thousands of new and highly paid jobs for unskilled workers in the North and
the shift to mechanized farming in the South. However, the Negro migration
is small when compared to earlier waves of European immigrants. Even between 1960 and 1966, there were 1.8 million immigrants from abroad compared
to the 613,000 Negroes who arrived in the North and West from the South.

As a result of the growing number of Negroes in urban areas, natural
increase has replaced migration as the primary source of Negro population
increase in the cities. Nevertheless, Negro migration from the South will continue unless economic conditions there change dramatically.

Basic data concerning Negro urbanization trends indicate that:

Almost all Negro population growth (98 percent from 1950 to 1966) is
occurring within metropolitan areas, primarily within central cities.[2]

The vast majority of white population growth (78 percent from 1960 to
1966) is occurring in suburban portions of metropolitan areas. Since 1960,
white central-city population has declined by 1.3 million.

As a result, central cities are becoming more heavily Negro while the
suburban fringes around them remain almost entirely white.

The twelve largest central cities now contain over two-thirds of the Negro
population outside the South, and one-third of the Negro total in the
United States.

Within the cities, Negroes have been excluded from white residential
areas through discriminatory practices. Just as significant is the withdrawal
of white families from, or their refusal to enter, neighborhoods where Negroes
are moving or already residing. About 20 percent of the urban population of
the United States changes residence every year. The refusal of whites to move
into "changing" areas when vacancies occur means that most vacancies
eventually are occupied by Negroes.

The result, according to a recent study, is that in 1960 the average
segregation index for 207 of the largest United States cities was 86.2. In
other words, to create an unsegregated population distribution, an average of
over 86 percent of all Negroes would have to change their place of residence
within the city.

Chapter 7—Unemployment, Family Structure, and Social Disorganization

Although there have been gains in Negro income nationally, and a decline in
the number of Negroes below the "poverty level," the condition of Negroes in
the central city remains in a state of crisis. Between 2 and 2.5 million Negroes

[2] A "central city" is the largest city of a standard metropolitan statistical area,
that is, a metropolitan area containing at least one city of 50,000 or more inhabitants.

—16 to 20 percent of the total Negro population of all central cities—live in squalor and deprivation in ghetto neighborhoods.

Employment is a key problem. It not only controls the present for the Negro American but, in a most profound way, it is creating the future as well. Yet, despite continuing economic growth and declining national unemployment rates, the unemployment rate for Negroes in 1967 was more than double that for whites.

Equally important is the undesirable nature of many jobs open to Negroes and other minorities. Negro men are more than three times as likely as white men to be in low-paying, unskilled or service jobs. This concentration of male Negro employment at the lowest end of the occupational scale is the single most important cause of poverty among Negroes.

In one study of low-income neighborhoods, the "subemployment rate," including both unemployment and underemployment, was about 33 percent, or 8.8 times greater than the overall unemployment rate for all United States workers.

Employment problems, aggravated by the constant arrival of new unemployed migrants, many of them from depressed rural areas, create persistent poverty in the ghetto. In 1966, about 11.9 percent of the nation's whites and 40.6 percent of its nonwhites were below the "poverty level" defined by the Social Security Administration (currently $3,335 per year for an urban family of four). Over 40 percent of the nonwhites below the poverty level live in the central cities.

Employment problems have drastic social impact in the ghetto. Men who are chronically unemployed or employed in the lowest status jobs are often unable or unwilling to remain with their families. The handicap imposed on children growing up without fathers in an atmosphere of poverty and deprivation is increased as mothers are forced to work to provide support.

The culture of poverty that results from unemployment and family breakup generates a system of ruthless, exploitative relationships within the ghetto. Prostitution, dope addiction, and crime create an environmental "jungle" characterized by personal insecurity and tension. Children growing up under such conditions are likely participants in civil disorder.

Chapter 8—Conditions of Life in the Racial Ghetto

A striking difference in environment from that of white, middle-class Americans profoundly influences the lives of residents of the ghetto.

Crime rates, consistently higher than in other areas, create a pronounced sense of insecurity. For example, in one city one low-income Negro district had 35 times as many serious crimes against persons as a high-income white district. Unless drastic steps are taken, the crime problems in poverty areas are likely to continue to multiply as the growing youth and rapid urbanization of the population outstrip police resources.

Poor health and sanitation conditions in the ghetto result in higher mortality rates, a higher incidence of major diseases, and lower availability and utilization of medical services. The infant mortality rate for nonwhite babies under the age of one month is 58 percent higher than for whites; for one to 12 months it is almost three times as high. The level of sanitation in the ghetto is far below that in high income areas. Garbage collection is often inadequate. Of an estimated 14,000 cases of rat bite in the United States in 1965, most were in ghetto neighborhoods.

Ghetto residents believe they are "exploited" by local merchants; and evidence substantiates some of these beliefs. A study conducted in one city by the Federal Trade Commission showed that distinctly higher prices were charged for goods sold in ghetto stores than in other areas.

Lack of knowledge regarding credit purchasing creates special pitfalls for the disadvantaged. In many states garnishment practices compound these difficulties by allowing creditors to deprive individuals of their wages without hearing or trial.

Chapter 9—Comparing the Immigrant and Negro Experience

In this chapter, we address ourselves to a fundamental question that many white Americans are asking: why have so many Negroes, unlike the European immigrants, been unable to escape from the ghetto and from poverty. We believe the following factors play a part:

The Maturing Economy: When the European immigrants arrived, they gained an economic foothold by providing the unskilled labor needed by industry. Unlike the immigrant, the Negro migrant found little opportunity in the city. The economy, by then matured, had little use for the unskilled labor he had to offer.

The Disability of Race: The structure of discrimination has stringently narrowed opportunities for the Negro and restricted his prospects. European immigrants suffered from discrimination, but never so pervasively.

Entry into the Political System: The immigrants usually settled in rapidly growing cities with powerful and expanding political machines, which traded economic advantages for political support. Ward-level grievance machinery, as well as personal representation, enabled the immigrant to make his voice heard and his power felt.

By the time the Negro arrived, these political machines were no longer so powerful or so well equipped to provide jobs or other favors, and in many cases were unwilling to share their influence with Negroes.

Cultural Factors: Coming from societies with a low standard of living and at a time when job aspirations were low, the immigrants sensed little deprivation in being forced to take the less desirable and poorer-paying jobs. Their large and cohesive families contributed to total income. Their vision of the future—one that led to a life outside of the ghetto—provided the incentive necessary to endure the present.

Although Negro men worked as hard as the immigrants, they were unable to support their families. The entrepreneurial opportunities had vanished. As a result of slavery and long periods of unemployment, the Negro family structure had become matriarchal; the males played a secondary and marginal family role—one which offered little compensation for their hard and unrewarding labor. Above all, segregation denied Negroes access to good jobs and the opportunity to leave the ghetto. For them, the future seemed to lead only to a dead end.

Today, whites tend to exaggerate how well and quickly they escaped from poverty. The fact is that immigrants who came from rural backgrounds, as many Negroes do, are only now, after three generations, finally beginning to move into the middle class.

By contrast, Negroes began concentrating in the city less than two generations ago, and under much less favorable conditions. Although some Negroes have escaped poverty, few have been able to escape the urban ghetto.

PART III—WHAT CAN BE DONE?

Chapter 10—The Community Response

Our investigation of the 1967 riot cities establishes that virtually every major episode of violence was foreshadowed by an accumulation of unresolved grievances and by widespread dissatisfaction among Negroes with the unwillingness or inability of local government to respond.

Overcoming these conditions is essential for community support of law enforcement and civil order. City governments need new and more vital channels of communication to the residents of the ghetto; they need to improve their capacity to respond effectively to community needs before they become community grievances; and they need to provide opportunity for meaningful involvement of ghetto residents in shaping policies and programs which affect the community.

The Commission recommends that local governments:

Develop Neighborhood Action Task Forces as joint community-government efforts through which more effective communication can be achieved, and the delivery of city services to ghetto residents improved.

Establish comprehensive grievance-response mechanisms in order to bring all public agencies under public scrutiny.

Bring the institutions of local government closer to the people they serve by establishing neighborhood outlets for local, state and federal administrative and public service agencies.

Expand opportunities for ghetto residents to participate in the formulation of public policy and the implementation of programs affecting them through improved political representation, creation of institutional channels for community action, expansion of legal services, and legislative hearings on ghetto problems.

In this effort, city governments will require state and federal support. The Commission recommends:

State and federal assistance for mayors and city councils to support the research, consultants, staff and other resources needed to respond effectively to federal program initiatives.

State cooperation in providing municipalities with the jurisdictional tools needed to deal with their problems; a fuller measure of financial aid to urban areas; and the focusing of the interests of suburban communities on the physical, social and cultural environment of the central city.

Chapter 11—Police and the Community

The abrasive relationship between the police and the minority communities has been a major—and explosive—source of grievance, tension and disorder. The blame must be shared by the total society.

The police are faced with demands for increased protection and service in the ghetto. Yet the aggressive patrol practices thought necessary to meet these demands themselves create tension and hostility. The resulting grievances have been further aggravated by the lack of effective mechanisms for handling complaints against the police. Special programs for bettering police-community relations have been instituted, but these alone are not enough. Police administrators, with the guidance of public officials, and the support of the entire community, must take vigorous action to improve law enforcement and to decrease the potential for disorder.

The Commission recommends that city government and police authorities:

Review police operations in the ghetto to ensure proper conduct by police officers, and eliminate abrasive practices.

Provide more adequate police protection to ghetto residents to eliminate their high sense of insecurity, and the belief of many Negro citizens in the existence of a dual standard of law enforcement.

Establish fair and effective mechanisms for the redress of grievances against the police, and other municipal employees.

Develop and adopt policy guidelines to assist officers in making critical decisions in areas where police conduct can create tension.

Develop and use innovative programs to ensure widespread community support for law enforcement.

Recruit more Negroes into the regular police force, and review promotion policies to ensure fair promotion for Negro officers.

Establish a "Community Service Officer" program to attract ghetto youths between the ages of 17 and 21 to police work. These junior officers would perform duties in ghetto neighborhoods, but would not have full police authority. The federal government should provide support equal to 90 percent of the costs of employing CSOs on the basis of one for every ten regular officers.

Chapter 12—Control of Disorder

Preserving civil peace is the first responsibility of government. Unless the rule of law prevails, our society will lack not only order but also the environment essential to social and economic progress.

The maintenance of civil order cannot be left to the police alone. The police need guidance, as well as support, from mayors and other public officials. It is the responsibility of public officials to determine proper police policies, support adequate police standards for personnel and performance, and participate in planning for the control of disorders.

To maintain control of incidents which could lead to disorders, the Commission recommends that local officials:

Assign seasoned, well-trained policemen and supervisory officers to patrol ghetto areas, and to respond to disturbances.

Develop plans which will quickly muster maximum police manpower and highly qualified senior commanders at the outbreak of disorders.

Provide special training in the prevention of disorders, and prepare police for riot control and for operation in units, with adequate command and control and field communication for proper discipline and effectiveness.

Develop guidelines governing the use of control equipment and provide alternatives to the use of lethal weapons. Federal support for research in this area is needed.

Establish an intelligence system to provide police and other public officials with reliable information that may help to prevent the outbreak of a disorder and to institute effective control measures in the event a riot erupts.

Develop continuing contacts with ghetto residents to make use of the forces for order which exist within the community.

Establish machinery for neutralizing rumors, and enabling Negro leaders and residents to obtain the facts. Create special rumor details to collect, evaluate, and dispel rumors that may lead to a civil disorder.

The Commission believes there is a grave danger that some communities may resort to the indiscriminate and excessive use of force. The harmful effects of overreaction are incalculable. The Commission condemns moves to equip police departments with mass destruction weapons, such as automatic rifles, machine guns and tanks. Weapons which are designed to destroy, not to control, have no place in densely populated urban communities.

The Commission recognizes the sound principle of local authority and responsibility in law enforcement, but recommends that the federal government share in the financing of programs for improvement of police forces, both in their normal law enforcement activities as well as in their response to civil disorders.

To assist government authorities in planning their response to civil disorder, this report contains a Supplement on Control of Disorder. It deals with specific problems encountered during riot-control operations, and includes:

> Assessment of the present capabilities of police, National Guard and Army forces to control major riots, and recommendations for improvement;

> Recommended means by which the control operations of those forces may be coordinated with the response of other agencies, such as fire departments, and with the community at large;

> Recommendations for review and revision of federal, state and local laws needed to provide the framework for control efforts and for the call-up and interrelated action of public safety forces.

Chapter 13—The Administration of Justice Under Emergency Conditions

In many of the cities which experienced disorders last summer, there were recurring breakdowns in the mechanisms for processing, prosecuting and protecting arrested persons. These resulted mainly from long-standing structural deficiencies in criminal court systems, and from the failure of communities to anticipate and plan for the emergency demands of civil disorders.

In part, because of this, there were few successful prosecutions for serious crimes committed during the riots. In those cities where mass arrests occurred many arrestees were deprived of basic legal rights.

The Commission recommends that the cities and states:

> Undertake reform of the lower courts so as to improve the quality of justice rendered under normal conditions.

> Plan comprehensive measures by which the criminal justice system may be supplemented during civil disorders so that its deliberative functions are protected, and the quality of justice is maintained.

> Such emergency plans require broad community participation and dedicated leadership by the bench and bar. They should include:

> Laws sufficient to deter and punish riot conduct.

> Additional judges, bail and probation officers, and clerical staff.

Arrangements for volunteer lawyers to help prosecutors and to represent riot defendants at every stage of proceedings.

Policies to ensure proper and individual bail, arraignment, pre-trial, trial and sentencing proceedings.

Procedures for processing arrested persons, such as summons and release, and release on personal recognizance, which permit separation of minor offenders from those dangerous to the community, in order that serious offenders may be detained and prosecuted effectively.

Adequate emergency processing and detention facilities.

Chapter 14—Damages: Repair and Compensation

The Commission recommends that the federal government:

Amend the Federal Disaster Act—which now applies only to natural disasters—to permit federal emergency food and medical assistance to cities during major civil disorders, and provide long-term economic assistance afterwards.

With the cooperation of the states, create incentives for the private insurance industry to provide more adequate property-insurance coverage in inner-city areas.

The Commission endorses the report of the National Advisory Panel on Insurance in Riot-Affected Areas: "Meeting the Insurance Crisis of our Cities."

Chapter 15—The News Media and the Disorders

In his charge to the Commission, the President asked: "What effect do the mass media have on the riots?"

The Commission determined that the answer to the President's question did not lie solely in the performance of the press and broadcasters in reporting the riots. Our analysis had to consider also the overall treatment by the media of the Negro ghettos, community relations, racial attitudes, and poverty—day by day and month by month, year in and year out.

A wide range of interviews with government officials, law enforcement authorities, media personnel and other citizens, including ghetto residents, as well as a quantitative analysis of riot coverage and a special conference with industry representatives, leads us to conclude that:

Despite instances of sensationalism, inaccuracy and distortion, newspapers, radio and television tried on the whole to give a balanced, factual account of the 1967 disorders.

Elements of the news media failed to portray accurately the scale and character of the violence that occurred last summer. The overall effect was, we believe, an exaggeration of both mood and event.

Important segments of the media failed to report adequately on the causes and consequences of civil disorders and on the underlying problems of race relations. They have not communicated to the majority of their audience—which is white—a sense of the degradation, misery and hopelessness of life in the ghetto.

These failings must be corrected, and the improvement must come from within the industry. Freedom of the press is not the issue. Any effort to impose governmental restrictions would be inconsistent with fundamental constitutional precepts.

We have seen evidence that the news media are becoming aware of and concerned about their performance in this field. As that concern grows, coverage will improve. But much more must be done, and it must be done soon.

The Commission recommends that the media:

Expand coverage of the Negro community and of race problems through permanent assignment of reporters familiar with urban and racial affairs, and through establishment of more and better links with the Negro community.

Integrate Negroes and Negro activities into all aspects of coverage and content, including newspaper articles and television programming. The news media must publish newspapers and produce programs that recognize the existence and activities of Negroes as a group within the community and as a part of the larger community.

Recruit more Negroes into journalism and broadcasting and promote those who are qualified to positions of significant responsibility. Recruitment should begin in high schools and continue through college; where necessary, aid for training should be provided.

Improve coordination with police in reporting riot news through advance planning, and cooperate with the police in the designation of police information officers, establishment of information centers, and development of mutually acceptable guidelines for riot reporting and the conduct of media personnel.

Accelerate efforts to ensure accurate responsible reporting of riot and racial news, through adoption by all news gathering organizations of stringent internal staff guidelines.

Cooperate in the establishment of a privately organized and funded Institute of Urban Communications to train and educate journalists in urban affairs, recruit and train more Negro journalists, develop methods for improving police-press relations, review coverage of riots and racial issues, and support continuing research in the urban field.

Chapter 16—The Future of the Cities

By 1985, the Negro population in central cities is expected to increase by 72 percent to approximately 20.8 million. Coupled with the continued exodus of white families to the suburbs, this growth will produce majority Negro populations in many of the nation's largest cities.

The future of these cities, and of their burgeoning Negro populations, is grim. Most new employment opportunities are being created in suburbs and outlying areas. This trend will continue unless important changes in public policy are made.

In prospect, therefore, is further deterioration of already inadequate municipal tax bases in the face of increasing demands for public services, and continuing unemployment and poverty among the urban Negro population:

Three choices are open to the nation:

We can maintain present policies, continuing both the proportion of the nation's resources now allocated to programs for the unemployed and the disadvantaged, and the inadequate and failing effort to achieve an integrated society.

We can adopt a policy of "enrichment" aimed at improving dramatically the quality of ghetto life while abandoning integration as a goal.

We can pursue integration by combining the ghetto "enrichment" with policies which will encourage Negro movement out of central city areas.

The first choice, continuance of present policies, has ominous consequences for our society. The share of the nation's resources now allocated to programs for the disadvantaged is insufficient to arrest the deterioration of life in central city ghettos. Under such conditions, a rising proportion of Negroes may come to see in the deprivation and segregation they experience, a justification for violent protest, or for extending support to now isolated extremists who advocate civil disruption. Large-scale and continuing violence could result, followed by white retaliation, and, ultimately, the separation of the two communities in a garrison state.

Even if violence does not occur, the consequences are unacceptable. Development of a racially integrated society, extraordinarily difficult today, will be virtually impossible when the present black ghetto population of 12.5 million has grown to almost 21 million.

To continue present policies is to make permanent the division of our country into two societies; one, largely Negro and poor, located in the central cities; the other, predominantly white and affluent, located in the suburbs and in outlying areas.

The second choice, ghetto enrichment coupled with abandonment of integration, is also unacceptable. It is another way of choosing a permanently divided country. Moreover, equality cannot be achieved under conditions of nearly complete separation. In a country where the economy, and particularly the resources of employment, are predominantly white, a policy of separation can only relegate Negroes to a permanently inferior economic status.

We believe that the only possible choice for America is the third—a policy which combines ghetto enrichment with programs designed to encourage integration of substantial numbers of Negroes into the society outside the ghetto.

Enrichment must be an important adjunct to integration, for no matter how ambitious or energetic the program, few Negroes now living in central cities can be quickly integrated. In the meantime, large-scale improvements in the quality of ghetto life is essential.

But this can be no more than an interim strategy. Programs must be developed which will permit substantial Negro movement out of the ghettos. The primary goal must be a single society, in which every citizen will be free to live and work according to his capabilities and desires, not his color.

Chapter 17—Recommendations For National Action

INTRODUCTION

No American—white or black—can escape the consequences of the continuing social and economic decay of our major cities.

Only a commitment to national action on an unprecedented scale can shape a future compatible with the historic ideals of American society.

The great productivity of our economy, and a federal revenue system which is highly responsive to economic growth, can provide the resources.

The major need is to generate new will—the will to tax ourselves to the extent necessary to meet the vital needs of the nation.

We have set forth goals and proposed strategies to reach those goals. We discuss and recommend programs not to commit each of us to specific parts of such programs but to illustrate the type and dimension of action needed.

The major goal is the creation of a true union—a single society and a single American identity. Toward that goal, we propose the following objectives for national action:

> Opening up opportunities to those who are restricted by racial segregation and discrimination, and eliminating all barriers to their choice of jobs, education and housing.

> Removing the frustration of powerlessness among the disadvantaged by providing the means for them to deal with the problems that affect their own lives and by increasing the capacity of our public and private institutions to respond to these problems.

> Increasing communication across racial lines to destroy stereotypes, to halt polarization, end distrust and hostility, and create common ground for efforts toward public order and social justice.

We propose these aims to fulfill our pledge of equality and to meet the fundamental needs of a democratic and civilized society—domestic peace and social justice.

EMPLOYMENT

Pervasive unemployment and underemployment are the most persistent and serious grievances in minority areas. They are inextricably linked to the problem of civil disorder.

Despite growing federal expenditures for manpower development and training programs, and sustained general economic prosperity and increasing demands for skilled workers, about two million—white and nonwhite—are permanently unemployed. About ten million are underemployed, of whom 6.5 million work full time for wages below the poverty line.

The 500,000 "hard-core" unemployed in the central cities who lack a basic education and are unable to hold a steady job are made up in large part of Negro males between the ages of 18 and 25. In the riot cities which we surveyed, Negroes were three times as likely as whites to hold unskilled jobs, which are often part time, seasonal, low-paying and "dead end."

Negro males between the ages of 15 and 25 predominated among the rioters. More than 20 percent of the rioters were unemployed, and many who were employed held intermittent, low status, unskilled jobs which they regarded as below their education and ability.

The Commission recommends that the federal government:

Undertake joint efforts with cities and states to consolidate existing manpower programs to avoid fragmentation and duplication.

Take immediate action to create 2,000,000 new jobs over the next three years—one million in the public sector and one million in the private sector—to absorb the hard-core unemployed and materially reduce the level of underemployment for all workers, black and white. We propose 250,000 public sector and 300,000 private sector jobs in the first year.

Provide on-the-job training by both public and private employers with reimbursement to private employers for the extra costs of training the hardcore unemployed, by contract or by tax credits.

Provide tax and other incentives to investment in rural as well as urban poverty areas in order to offer to the rural poor an alternative to migration to urban centers.

Take new and vigorous action to remove artificial barriers to employment and promotion, including not only racial discrimination but, in certain cases, arrest records or lack of a high school diploma. Strengthen those agencies such as the Equal Employment Opportunity Commission, charged with eliminating discriminatory practices, and provide full support for Title VI of the 1964 Civil Rights Act allowing federal grant-in-aid funds to be withheld from activities which discriminate on grounds of color or race.

The Commission commends the recent public commitment of the National Council of the Building and Construction Trades Unions, AFL-CIO, to encourage and recruit Negro membership in apprenticeship programs. This commitment should be intensified and implemented.

EDUCATION

Education in a democratic society must equip children to develop their potential and to participate fully in American life. For the community at large, the schools have discharged this responsibility well. But for many minorities, and particularly for the children of the ghetto, the schools have failed to provide the educational experience which could overcome the effects of discrimination and deprivation.

This failure is one of the persistent sources of grievance and resentment within the Negro community. The hostility of Negro parents and students toward the school system is generating increasing conflict and causing disruption within many city school districts. But the most dramatic evidence of the relationship between educational practices and civil disorders lies in the high incidence of riot participation by ghetto youth who have not completed high school.

The bleak record of public education for ghetto children is growing worse. In the critical skills—verbal and reading ability—Negro students are falling further behind whites with each year of school completed. The high unemployment and underemployment rate for Negro youth is evidence, in part, of the growing educational crisis.

We support integration as the priority education strategy; it is essential to the future of American society. In this last summer's disorders we have seen the consequences of racial isolation at all levels, and of attitudes toward race, on both sides, produced by three centuries of myth, ignorance and bias. It is indispensable that opportunities for interaction between the races be expanded.

We recognize that the growing dominance of pupils from disadvantaged minorities in city school populations will not soon be reversed. No matter how great the effort toward desegregation, many children of the ghetto will not, within their school careers, attend integrated schools.

If existing disadvantages are not to be perpetuated, we must drastically improve the quality of ghetto education. Equality of results with all-white schools must be the goal.

To implement these strategies, the Commission recommends:

Sharply increased efforts to eliminate de facto segregation in our schools through substantial federal aid to school systems seeking to desegregate either within the system or in cooperation with neighboring school systems.

Elimination of racial discrimination in Northern as well as Southern schools by vigorous application of Title VI of the Civil Rights Act of 1964.

Extension of quality early childhood education to every disadvantaged child in the country.

Efforts to improve dramatically schools serving disadvantaged children through substantial federal funding of year-round compensatory education programs, improved teaching, and expanded experimentation and research.

Elimination of illiteracy through greater federal support for adult basic education.

Enlarged opportunities for parent and community participation in the public schools.

Reoriented vocational education emphasizing work-experience training and the involvement of business and industry.

Expanded opportunities for higher education through increased federal assistance to disadvantaged students.

Revision of state aid formulas to assure more per student aid to districts having a high proportion of disadvantaged school-age children.

THE WELFARE SYSTEM

Our present system of public welfare is designed to save money instead of people, and tragically ends up doing neither. This system has two critical deficiencies:

First, it excludes large numbers of persons who are in great need, and who, if provided a decent level of support, might be able to become more productive and self-sufficient. No federal funds are available for millions of men and women who are needy but neither aged, handicapped nor the parents of minor children.

Second, for those included, the system provides assistance well below the minimum necessary for a decent level of existence, and imposes restrictions that encourage continued dependency on welfare and undermine self-respect.

A welter of statutory requirements and administrative practices and regulations operate to remind recipients that they are considered untrustworthy, promiscuous and lazy. Residence requirements prevent assistance to people in need who are newly arrived in the state. Regular searches of recipients' homes violate privacy. Inadequate social services compound the problems.

The Commission recommends that the federal government, acting with state and local governments where necessary, reform the existing welfare system to:

Establish uniform national standards of assistance at least as high as the annual "poverty level" of income, now set by the Social Security Administration at $3,335 per year for an urban family of four.

Require that all states receiving federal welfare contributions participate in the Aid to Families with Dependent Children—Unemployed Parents program (AFDC-UP) that permits assistance to families with both father and mother in the home, thus aiding the family while it is still intact.

Bear a substantially greater portion of all welfare costs—at least 90 percent of total payments.

Increase incentives for seeking employment and job training, but remove restrictions recently enacted by the Congress that would compel mothers of young children to work.

Provide more adequate social services through neighborhood centers and family-planning programs.

Remove the freeze placed by the 1967 welfare amendments on the percentage of children in a state that can be covered by federal assistance. Eliminate residence requirements.

As a long-range goal, the Commission recommends that the federal government seek to develop a national system of income supplementation based strictly on need with two broad and basic purposes:

To provide, for those who can work or who do work, any necessary supplements in such a way as to develop incentives for fuller employment;

To provide, for those who cannot work and for mothers who decide to remain with their children, a minimum standard of decent living, and to aid in the saving of children from the prison of poverty that has held their parents.

A broad system of supplementation would involve substantially greater federal expenditures than anything now contemplated. The cost will range widely depending on the standard of need accepted as the "basic allowance" to individuals and families, and on the rate at which additional income above this level is taxed. Yet if the deepening cycle of poverty and dependence on welfare can be broken, if the children of the poor can be given the opportunity to scale the wall that now separates them from the rest of society, the return on this investment will be great indeed.

HOUSING

After more than three decades of fragmented and grossly underfunded federal housing programs, nearly six million substandard housing units remain occupied in the United States.

The housing problem is particularly acute in the minority ghettos. Nearly two-thirds of all non-white families living in the central cities today live in neighborhoods marked with substandard housing and general urban blight. Two major factors are responsible.

First: Many ghetto residents simply cannot pay the rent necessary to support decent housing. In Detroit, for example, over 40 percent of the non-white occupied units in 1960 required rent of over 35 percent of the tenants' income.

Second: Discrimination prevents access to many non-slum areas, particularly the suburbs, where good housing exists. In addition, by creating a "back pressure" in the racial ghettos, it makes it possible for landlords to break up apartments for denser occupancy, and keeps prices and rents of deteriorated ghetto housing higher than they would be in a truly free market.

To date, federal programs have been able to do comparatively little to provide housing for the disadvantaged. In the 31-year history of subsidized federal housing, only about 800,000 units have been constructed, with recent production averaging about 50,000 units a year. By comparison, over a period only three years longer, FHA insurance guarantees have made possible the construction of over ten million middle and upper-income units.

Two points are fundamental to the Commission's recommendations:

First: Federal housing programs must be given a new thrust aimed at overcoming the prevailing patterns of racial segregation. If this is not done, those programs will continue to concentrate the most impoverished and dependent segments of the population into the central-city ghettos where there is already a critical gap between the needs of the population and the public resources to deal with them.

Second: The private sector must be brought into the production and financing of low and moderate rental housing to supply the capabilities and capital necessary to meet the housing needs of the nation.

The Commission recommends that the federal government:

Enact a comprehensive and enforceable federal open housing law to cover the sale or rental of all housing, including single family homes.

Reorient federal housing programs to place more low and moderate income housing outside of ghetto areas.

Bring within the reach of low and moderate income families within the next five years six million new and existing units of decent housing, beginning with 60,000 units in the next year.

To reach this goal we recommend:

Expansion and modification of the rent supplement program to permit use of supplements for existing housing, thus greatly increasing the reach of the program.

Expansion and modification of the below-market interest rate program to enlarge the interest subsidy to all sponsors and provide interest-free loans to nonprofit sponsors to cover pre-construction costs, and permit sale of projects to nonprofit corporations, cooperatives, or condominiums.

Creation of an ownership supplement program similar to present rent supplements, to make home ownership possible for low-income families.

Federal writedown of interest rates on loans to private builders constructing moderate-rent housing.

Expansion of the public housing program, with emphasis on small units on scattered sites, and leasing and "turnkey" programs.

Expansion of the Model Cities program.

Expansion and reorientation of the urban renewal program to give priority to projects directly assisting low-income households to obtain adequate housing.

CONCLUSION

One of the first witnesses to be invited to appear before this Commission was Dr. Kenneth B. Clark, a distinguished and perceptive scholar. Referring to the reports of earlier riot commissions, he said:

> I read that report . . . of the 1919 riot in Chicago, and it is as if I were reading the report of the investigating committee on the Harlem riot of '35, the report of the investigating committee on the Harlem riot of '43, the report of the McCone Commission on the Watts riot.
>
> I must again in candor say to you members of this Commission —it is a kind of Alice in Wonderland—with the same moving picture re-shown over and over again, the same analysis, the same recommendations, and the same inaction.

These words come to our minds as we conclude this report.

We have provided an honest beginning. We have learned much. But we have uncovered no startling truths, no unique insights, no simple solutions. The destruction and the bitterness of racial disorder, the harsh polemics of black revolt and white repression have been seen and heard before in this country.

It is time now to end the destruction and the violence, not only in the streets of the ghetto but in the lives of people.

28

NORMAN PODHORETZ

My Negro Problem—and Ours

Norman Podhoretz's essay, published five years before the report of the National Advisory Commission on Civil Disorders, demonstrates that racism can be both a subtle and a pervading part of our upbringing. By stressing the unconscious and involuntary nature of racism, he makes the conclusions of the Report far more meaningful if not more acceptable.

Podhoretz writes about feelings toward blacks learned at an early age, long before one comprehends social relationships and social problems. Because this understanding can never fully overcome the damage wrought by childhood experience, many whites find that their commitment to the "movement" breaks down under direct confrontation. For Podhoretz, growing up in what he calls the provinces of New York City, Negroes represented an always present threat. They were tougher, better athletes, and more ruthless than the Jews and Italians. Negro boys possessed greater freedom from social control than whites. And so was born envy, fear, hatred of them. How much worse than Podhoretz's situation must be that of anyone who grew up in a family where Negroes were openly detested.

Certainly blacks have distinct feelings toward whites, feelings of hatred toward their jailers. Whites also have special feelings about blacks. "We White Americans," writes Podhoretz, "are . . . so twisted and sick in our feelings about Negroes that I despair of the present push toward integration." As an alternative, Podhoretz recommends racial intermarriage as a way of destroying racial identity.

If we—and . . . I mean the relatively conscious whites and the relatively conscious blacks, who must, like lovers, insist on, or create, the consciousness of the others—do not falter in our duty now, we may be able, handful that we are, to end the racial night-mare, and achieve our country, and change the history of the world.

James Baldwin

Two ideas puzzled me deeply as a child growing up in Brooklyn during the 1930's in what today would be called an integrated neighborhood. One of them was that all Jews were rich; the other was that all Negroes were persecuted. These ideas had appeared in print; therefore they must be true. My own experience and the evidence of my senses told me they were not true, but that only confirmed what a day-dreaming boy in the provinces—for the lower-class neighborhoods of New York belong as surely to the provinces as any rural town in North Dakota—discovers very early: *his* experience is unreal and the evidence of his senses is not to be trusted. Yet even a boy with a head full of fantasies incongruously synthesized out of Hollywood movies and English novels cannot altogether deny the reality of his own experience—especially when there is so much deprivation in that experience. Nor can he altogether gainsay the evidence of his own senses—especially such evidence of the senses as comes from being repeatedly beaten up, robbed, and in general hated, terrorized, and humiliated.

And so for a long time I was puzzled to think that Jews were supposed to be rich when the only Jews I knew were poor, and that Negroes were supposed to be persecuted when it was the Negroes who were doing the only persecuting I knew about—and doing it, moreover, to *me*. During the early years of the war, when my older sister joined a left-wing youth organization, I remember my astonishment at hearing her passionately denounce my father for thinking that Jews were worse off than Negroes. To me, at the age of twelve, it seemed very clear that Negroes were better off than Jews—indeed, than *all* whites. A city boy's world is contained within three or four square blocks, and in my world it was the whites, the Italians and Jews, who feared the Negroes, not the other way around. The Negroes were tougher than we were, more ruthless, and on the whole they were better athletes. What could it mean, then, to say that they were badly off and that we were more fortunate? Yet my sister's opinions, like print, were sacred, and when she told me about exploitation and economic forces I believed her. I believed her, but I was still afraid of Negroes. And I still hated them with all my heart.

It had not always been so—that much I can recall from early childhood. When did it start, this fear and this hatred? There was a kindergarten in the local public school, and given the character of the neighborhood, at least half of the children in my class must have been Negroes. Yet I have no memory of being aware of color differences at that age, and I know from observing my own children that they attribute no significance to such differences even when they begin noticing them. I think there was a day—first grade? second grade?—when my best friend Carl hit me on the way home from school and announced that he wouldn't play with me any more because I had killed Jesus. When I ran home to my mother crying for an explanation, she told me not to pay any attention to such foolishness, and then in Yiddish she cursed the *goyim* and the *schwartzes,* the *schwartzes* and the *goyim.* Carl, it turned out, was a *schwartze,* and so was added a third to the categories into which people were mysteriously divided.

Sometimes I wonder whether this is a true memory at all. It is blazingly vivid, but perhaps it never happened: can anyone really remember back to the age of six? There is no uncertainty in my mind, however, about the years that followed. Carl and I hardly ever spoke, though we met in school every day up through the eighth or ninth grade. There would be embarrassed moments of catching his eye or of his catching mine—for whatever it was that had attracted us to one another as very small children remained alive in spite of the fantastic barrier of hostility that had grown up between us, suddenly and out of nowhere. Nevertheless, friendship would have been impossible, and even if it had been possible, it would have been unthinkable. About that, there was nothing anyone could do by the time we were eight years old.

Item: The orphanage across the street is torn down, a city housing project begins to rise in its place, and on the marvelous vacant lot next to the old orphanage they are building a playground. Much excitement and anticipation as Opening Day draws near. Mayor LaGuardia himself comes to dedicate this great gesture of public benevolence. He speaks of neighborliness and borrowing cups of sugar, and of the playground he says that children of all races, colors, and creeds will learn to live together in harmony. A week later, some of us are swatting flies on the playground's inadequate little ball field. A gang of Negro kids, pretty much our own age, enter from the other side and order us out of the park. We refuse, proudly and indignantly, with superb masculine fervor. There is a fight, they win, and we retreat, half whimpering, half with bravado. My first nauseating experience of cowardice. Any my first appalled realization that there are people in the world who do not seem to be afraid of anything, who act as though they have nothing to lose. Thereafter the playground becomes a battleground, sometimes quiet, sometimes the scene of athletic competition between Them and Us. But rocks are thrown as often as baseballs. Gradually we abandon the place and use the streets instead. The streets are safer, though we do not admit this to ourselves. We are not, after all, sissies—that most dreaded epithet of an American boyhood.

Item: I am standing alone in front of the building in which I live. It is late afternoon and getting dark. That day in school the teacher had asked a surly Negro boy named Quentin a question he was unable to answer. As usual I had waved my arm eagerly ("Be a good boy, get good marks, be smart, go to college, become a doctor") and, the right answer bursting from my lips, I was held up lovingly by the teacher as an example to the class. I had seen Quentin's face—a very dark, very cruel, very Oriental-looking face—harden, and there had been enough threat in his eyes to make me run all the way home for fear that he might catch me outside.

Now, standing idly in front of my own house, I see him approaching from the project accompanied by his little brother who is carrying a baseball bat and wearing a grin of malicious anticipation. As in a nightmare, I am trapped. The surroundings are secure and familiar, but terror is suddenly present and there is no one around to help. I am locked to the spot. I will not cry out or run away like a sissy, and I stand there, my heart wild, my throat clogged. He walks up, hurls the familiar epithet ("Hey, mo'f——r"), and to my surprise only pushes me. It is a violent push, but not a punch. A push is not as serious as a punch. Maybe I can still back out without entirely losing my dignity. Maybe I can still say, "Hey, c'mon Quentin, whaddya wanna do *that* for. I dint do nothin' to *you*," and walk away, not too rapidly. Instead, before I can stop myself, I push him back—a token gesture—and I say, "Cut that out, I don't wanna fight, I ain't got nothin' to fight about." As I turn to walk back into the building, the corner of my eye catches the motion of the bat his little brother has handed him. I try to duck, but the bat crashes colored lights into my head.

The next thing I know, my mother and sister are standing over me, both of them hysterical. My sister—she who was later to join the "progressive" youth organization—is shouting for the police and screaming imprecations at those dirty little black bastards. They take me upstairs, the doctor comes, the police come. I tell them that the boy who did it was a stranger, that he had been trying to get money from me. They do not believe me, but I am too scared to give them Quentin's name. When I return to school a few days later, Quentin avoids my eyes. He knows that I have not squealed, and he is ashamed. I try to feel proud, but in my heart I know that it was fear of what his friends might do to me that had kept me silent, and not the code of the street.

Item: There is an athletic meet in which the whole of our junior high school is participating. I am in one of the seventh-grade rapid-advance classes, and "segregation" has now set in with a vengeance. In the last three or four years of the elementary school from which we have just graduated, each grade had been divided into three classes, according to "intelligence." (In the earlier grades the divisions had either been arbitrary or else unrecognized by us as having anything to do with brains.) These divisions by IQ, or however it was arranged, had resulted in a preponderance of Jews in the "1" classes and a corresponding preponderance of Negroes in the "3's," with the Italians split unevenly along the spectrum. At least a few Negroes had always made the "1's," just as there had always been a few Jewish kids among the "3's" and more among the "2's" (where Italians dominated). But the junior high's rapid-advance class of which I am now a member is overwhelmingly Jewish and entirely white—except for a shy lonely Negro girl with light skin and reddish hair.

The athletic meet takes place in a city-owned stadium far from the school. It is an important event to which a whole day is given over. The winners are to get those precious little medallions stamped with the New York City emblem that can be screwed into a belt and that prove the wearer to be a distinguished personage. I am a fast runner, and so I am assigned the position of anchor man on my class's team in the relay race. There are three other seventh-grade teams in the race, two of them all Negro, as ours is all white. One of the all-Negro teams is very tall—their anchor man waiting silently next to me on the line looks years older than I am, and I do not recognize him. He is the first to get the baton and crosses the finishing line in a walk. Our team comes in second, but a few minutes later we are declared the winners, for it has been discovered that the anchor man on the first-place team is not a member of the class. We are awarded the medallions, and the following day our home-room teacher makes a speech about how proud she is of us for being superior athletes as well as superior students. We want to believe that we deserve the praise, but we know that we could not have won even if the other class had not cheated.

That afternoon, walking home, I am waylaid and surrounded by five Negroes, among whom is the anchor man of the disqualified team. "Gimme my medal, mo'f——r," he grunts. I do not have it with me and I tell him so. "Anyway, it ain't yours," I say foolishly. He calls me a liar on both counts and pushes me up against the wall on which we sometimes play handball. "Gimme my mo'f——n' medal," he says again. I repeat that I have left it home. "Le's search the li'l mo'f——r," one of them suggests, "he prolly got it *hid* in his mo'f——n' *pants.*" My panic is now unmanageable. (How many times had I been surrounded like this and asked in soft tones, "Len' me a nickle, boy." How many times had I been called a liar for pleading poverty and pushed around, or searched, or beaten up, unless there happened to be someone in the marauding gang like Carl who liked me across that enormous divide of hatred and who would therefore say, "Aaah, c'mon, le's git someone else, *this* boy ain't got no money on 'im.") I scream at them through tears of rage and self-contempt, "Keep your f——n' filthy lousy black hands offa me! I swear I'll get the cops." This is all they need to hear, and the five of them set upon me. They bang me around, mostly in the stomach and on the arms and shoulders, and when several adults loitering near the candy store down the block notice what is going on and begin to shout, they run off and away.

I do not tell my parents about the incident. My team-mates, who have also been waylaid, each by a gang led by his opposite number from the disqualified team, have had their medallions taken from them, and they never squeal either. For days, I walk home in terror, expecting to be caught again, but nothing happens. The medallion is put away into a drawer, never to be worn by anyone.

Obviously experiences like these have always been a common feature of childhood life in working-class and immigrant neighborhoods, and Negroes do not necessarily figure in them. Wherever, and in whatever combination, they have lived together in the cities, kids of different groups have been at war, beating up and being beaten up: micks against kikes against wops against spicks against polacks. And even relatively homogeneous areas have not been spared the warring of the young: one block against another, one gang (called in my day, in a pathetic effort at gentility, an "S.A.C.," or social-athletic club) against another. But the Negro-white conflict had—and no doubt still has —a special intensity and was conducted with a ferocity unmatched by intra-mural white battling.

In my own neighborhood, a good deal of animosity existed between the Italian kids (most of whose parents were immigrants from Sicily) and the Jewish kids (who came largely from East European immigrant families). Yet everyone had friends, sometimes close friends, in the other "camp," and we often visited one another's strange-smelling houses, if not for meals, then for glasses of milk, and occasionally for some special event like a wedding or a wake. If it happened that we divided into warring factions and did battle, it would invariably be half-hearted and soon patched up. Our parents, to be sure, had nothing to do with one another and were mutually suspicious and hostile. But we, the kids, who all spoke Yiddish or Italian at home, were Americans, or New Yorkers, or Brooklyn boys: we shared a culture, the culture of the street, and at least for a while this culture proved to be more powerful than the opposing cultures of the home.

Why, *why* should it have been so different as between the Negroes and us? How was it borne in upon us so early, white and black alike, that we were enemies beyond any possibility of reconciliation? Why did we hate one another so?

I suppose if I tried, I could answer those questions more or less adequately from the perspective of what I have since learned. I could draw upon James Baldwin—what better witness is there?—to describe the sense of entrapment that poisons the soul of the Negro with hatred for the white man whom he knows to be his jailer. On the other side, if I wanted to understand how the white man comes to hate the Negro, I could call upon the psychologists who have spoken of the guilt that white Americans feel toward Negroes and that turns into hatred for lack of acknowledging itself as guilt. These are plausible answers and certainly there is truth in them. Yet when I think back upon my own experience of the Negro and his of me, I find myself troubled and puzzled, much as I was as a child when I heard that all Jews were rich and all Negroes persecuted. How could the Negroes in my neighborhood have regarded the whites across the street and around the corner as jailers? On the whole, the whites were not so poor as the Negroes, but they were quite poor enough, and the years were years of Depression. As for white hatred of the Negro, how could guilt have had anything to do with it? What share had these Italian and Jewish immigrants in the enslavement of the Negro? What share had they—down-trodden people themselves breaking their own necks to eke out a living—in the exploitation of the Negro?

No, I cannot believe that we hated each other back there in Brooklyn because they thought of us as jailers and we felt guilty toward them. But does it matter, given the fact that we all went through an unrepresentative confrontation? I think it matters profoundly, for if we managed the job of hating each other so well without benefit of the aids to hatred that are supposedly at the root of this madness everywhere else, it must mean that the madness is not yet properly understood. I am far from pretending that I understand it, but I would insist that no view of the problem will begin to approach the truth unless it can account for a case like the one I have been trying to describe. Are the elements of any such view available to us?

At least two, I would say, are. One of them is a point we frequently come upon in the work of James Baldwin, and the other is a related point always stressed by psychologists who have studied the mechanisms of prejudice. Baldwin tells us that one of the reasons Negroes hate the white man is that the white man refuses to *look* at him: the Negro knows that in white eyes all Negroes are alike; they are faceless and therefore not altogether human. The psychologists, in their turn, tell us that the white man hates the Negro because he tends to project those wild impulses that he fears in himself onto an alien group which he then punishes with his contempt. What Baldwin does *not* tell us, however, is that the principle of facelessness is a two-way street and can operate in both directions with no difficulty at all. Thus, in my neighborhood in Brooklyn, *I* was as faceless to the Negroes as they were to me, and if they hated me because I never looked at them, I must also have hated them for never looking at *me*. To the Negroes, my white skin was enough to define me as the enemy, and in a war it is only the uniform that counts and not the person.

So with the mechanism of projection that the psychologists talk about: it too works in both directions at once. There is no question that the psychologists are right about what the Negro represents symbolically to the white man. For me as a child the life lived on the other side of the playground and down the block on Ralph Avenue seemed the very embodiment of the values of the street—free, independent, reckless, brave, masculine, erotic. I put the word "erotic" last, though it is usually stressed above all others, because in fact it came last, in consciousness as in importance. What mainly counted for me about Negro kids of my own age was that they were "bad boys." There were plenty of bad boys among the whites—this was, after all, a neighborhood with a long tradition of crime as a career open to aspiring talents—but the Negroes were *really* bad, bad in a way that beckoned to one, and made one feel inadequate. *We* all went home every day for a lunch of spinach-and-potatoes; *they* roamed around during lunch hour, munching on candy bars. In winter *we* had to wear itchy woolen hats and mittens and cumbersome galoshes; *they* were bare-headed and loose as they pleased. *We* rarely played hookey, or got into serious trouble in school, for all our street-corner bravado; *they* were defiant, forever staying out (to do what delicious things?), forever making disturbances in class and in the halls, forever being sent to the principal and returning uncowed. But most important of all, they were *tough;* beautifully, enviably tough, not giving a damn for anyone or anything. To hell with the teacher, the truant officer, the cop; to hell with the whole of the adult world that held *us* in its grip and that we never had the courage to rebel against except sporadically and in petty ways.

This is what I saw and envied and feared in the Negro: this is what finally made him faceless to me, though some of it, of course, was actually there. (The psychologists also tell us that the alien group which becomes the object of a projection will tend to respond by trying to live up to what is expected of them.) But what, on his side, did the Negro see in me that made me faceless to *him?* Did he envy me my lunches of spinach-and-potatoes and my itchy woolen caps and my prudent behavior in the face of authority, as I envied him his noon-time candy bars and his bare head in winter and his magnificent rebelliousness? Did those lunches and caps spell for him the prospect of power and riches in the future? Did they mean that there were possibilities open to me that were denied to him? Very likely they did. But if so, one also supposes that he feared the impulses within himself toward submission to authority no less powerfully than I feared the impulses in myself toward defiance. If I represented the jailer to him, it was not because I was oppressing him or keeping him down: it was because I symbolized for him the dangerous and probably pointless temptation toward greater repression, just as he symbolized for me the equally perilous tug toward greater freedom. I personally was to be rewarded for this repression with a new and better life in the future, but how many of my friends paid an even higher price and were given only gall in return.

We have it on the authority of James Baldwin that all Negroes hate whites. I am trying to suggest that on their side all whites—all American whites, that is—are sick in their feelings about Negroes. There are Negroes, no doubt, who would say that Baldwin is wrong, but I suspect them of being less honest than he is, just as I suspect whites of self-deception who tell me they have no special feeling toward Negroes. Special feelings about color are a contagion to which white Americans seem susceptible even when there is nothing in their background to account for the susceptibility. Thus everywhere we look today in the North, we find the curious phenomenon of white middle-class liberals with no previous personal experience of Negroes—people to whom Negroes have always been faceless in virtue rather than faceless in vice—discovering that their abstract commitment to the cause of Negro rights will not stand the test of a direct confrontation. We find such people fleeing in droves to the suburbs as the Negro population in the inner city grows; and when they stay in the city we find them sending their children to private school rather than to the "integrated" public school in the neighborhood. We find them resisting the demand that gerrymandered school districts be re-zoned for the purpose of overcoming de facto segregation; we find them judiciously considering whether the Negroes (for their own good, of course) are not perhaps pushing too hard; we find them clucking their tongues over Negro militancy; we find them speculating on the question of whether there may not, after all, be something in the theory that the races are biologically different; we find them saying that it will take a very long time for Negroes to achieve full equality, no matter what anyone does; we find them deploring the rise of black nationalism and expressing the solemn hope that the leaders of the Negro community will discover ways of containing the impatience and incipient violence within the Negro ghettos.[1]

But that is by no means the whole story; there is also the phenomenon of what Kenneth Rexroth once called "crow-jimism." There are the broken-down white boys like Vivaldo Moore in Baldwin's *Another Country* who go to Harlem in search of sex or simply to brush up against something that looks like primitive vitality, and who are so often punished by the Negroes they meet for crimes that they would have been the last ever to commit and of which they themselves have been as sorry victims as any of the Negroes who take it out on them. There are the writers and intellectuals and artists who romanticize Negroes and pander to them, assuming a guilt that is not properly theirs. And there are all the white liberals who permit Negroes to blackmail them into adopting a double standard of moral judgment, and who lend themselves—again assuming the responsibility for crimes they never committed—to cunning and contemptuous exploitation by Negroes they employ or try to befriend.

And what about me? What kind of feelings do I have about Negroes to-

---

[1] For an account of developments like these, see "The White Liberal's Retreat" by Murray Friedman in the January 1963 *Atlantic Monthly*.

day? What happened to me, from Brooklyn, who grew up fearing and envying and hating Negroes? Now that Brooklyn is behind me, do I fear them and envy them and hate them still? The answer is yes, but not in the same proportions and certainly not in the same way. I now live on the upper west side of Manhattan, where there are many Negroes and many Puerto Ricans, and there are nights when I experience the old apprehensiveness again, and there are streets that I avoid when I am walking in the dark, as there were streets that I avoided when I was a child. I find that I am not afraid of Puerto Ricans, but I cannot restrain my nervousness whenever I pass a group of Negroes standing in front of a bar or sauntering down the street. I know now, as I did not know when I was a child, that power is on my side, that the police are working for me and not for them. And knowing this I feel ashamed and guilty, like the good liberal I have grown up to be. Yet the twinges of fear and the resentment they bring and the self-contempt they arouse are not to be gainsaid.

But envy? Why envy? And hatred? Why hatred? Here again the intensities have lessened and everything has been complicated and qualified by the guilts and the resulting over-compensations that are the heritage of the enlightened middle-class world of which I am now a member. Yet just as in childhood I envied Negroes for what seemed to me their superior masculinity, so I envy them today for what seems to me their superior physical grace and beauty. I have come to value physical grace very highly, and I am now capable of aching with all my being when I watch a Negro couple on the dance floor, or a Negro playing baseball or basketball. They are on the kind of terms with their own bodies that I should like to be on with mine, and for that precious quality they seem blessed to me.

The hatred I still feel for Negroes is the hardest of all the old feelings to face or admit, and it is the most hidden and the most overlarded by the conscious attitudes into which I have succeeded in willing myself. It no longer has, as for me it once did, any cause or justification (except, perhaps, that I am constantly being denied my right to an honest expression of the things I earned the right as a child to feel). How, then, do I know that this hatred has never entirely disappeared? I know it from the insane rage that can stir in me at the thought of Negro anti-Semitism; I know it from the disgusting prurience that can stir in me at the sight of a mixed couple; and I know it from the violence than can stir in me whenever I encounter that special brand of paranoid touchiness to which many Negroes are prone.

This, then, is where I am; it is not exactly where I think all other white liberals are, but it cannot be so very far away either. And it is because I am convinced that we white Americans are—for whatever reason, it no longer matters—so twisted and sick in our feelings about Negroes that I despair of the present push toward integration. If the pace of progress were not a factor here, there would perhaps be no cause for despair: time and the law and even the international political situation are on the side of the Negroes, and ultimately, therefore, victory—of a sort, anyway—must come. But from everything we have learned from observers who ought to know, pace has become as important to the Negroes as substance. They want equality and they want it *now,* and the white world is yielding to their demand only as much and as fast as it is absolutely being compelled to do. The Negroes know this in the most concrete terms imaginable, and it is thus becoming increasingly difficult to buy them off with rhetoric and promises and pious assurances of support. And so within the Negro community we find more and more people declaring—as Harold R. Isaacs recently put it in these pages [2]—that they want *out:* people who say that integration will never come, or that it will take a hundred or a thousand years to come, or that it will come at too high a price in suffering and struggle for the pallid and sodden life of the American middle class that at the very best it may bring.

The most numerous, influential, and dangerous movement that has grown out of Negro despair with the goal of integration is, of course, the Black Muslims. This movement, whatever else we may say about it, must be credited with one enduring achievement: it inspired James Baldwin to write an essay [3] which deserves to be placed among the classics of our language. Everything Baldwin has ever been trying to tell us is distilled here into a statement of overwhelming persuasiveness and prophetic magnificence. Baldwin's message is and always has been simple. It is this: "Color is not a human or personal reality; it is a political reality." And Baldwin's demand is correspondingly simple: color must be forgotten, lest we all be smited with a vengeance "that does not really depend on, and cannot really be executed by, any person or organization, and that cannot be prevented by any police force or army: historical vengeance, a cosmic vengeance based on the law that we recognize when we say, 'Whatever goes up must come down.'" The Black Muslims Baldwin portrays as a sign and a warning to the intransigent white world. They come to proclaim how deep is the Negro's disaffection with the white world and all its works, and Baldwin implies that no American Negro can fail to respond somewhere in his being to their message: that the white man is the devil, that Allah has doomed him to destruction, and that the black man is about to inherit the earth. Baldwin of course knows that this nightmare inversion of the racism from which the black man has suffered can neither win nor even point to the neighborhood in which victory might be located. For in his view the neighborhood of victory lies in exactly the opposite direction: the transcendence of color through love.

Yet the tragic fact is that love is not the answer to hate—not in the world of politics, at any rate. Color is indeed a political rather than a human or a personal reality and if politics (which is to say power) has made it into a human and a personal reality, then only politics (which is to say power) can unmake it once again. But the way of politics is slow and bitter, and as impatience on the one side is matched by a setting of the jaw on the other, we move closer and closer to an explosion and blood may yet run in the streets.

Will this madness in which we are all caught never find a resting-place? Is there never to be an end to it? In thinking about the Jews I have often wondered whether their survival as a distinct group was worth one hair on the head of a single infant. Did the Jews have to survive so that six million in-

---

[2] "Integration and the Negro Mood," December 1962.
[3] Originally published in the *New Yorker* under the title "Letter From a Region in My Mind," it has been reprinted (along with a new introduction) by Dial Press under the title *The Fire Next Time* (128 pp., $3.50).

nocent people should one day be burned in the ovens of Auschwitz? It is a terrible question and no one, not God himself, could ever answer it to my satisfaction. And when I think about the Negroes in America and about the image of integration as a state in which the Negroes would take their rightful place as another of the protected minorities in a pluralistic society, I wonder whether they really believe in their hearts that such a state can actually be attained, and if so *why* they should wish to survive as a distinct group. I think I know why the Jews once wished to survive (though I am less certain as to why we still do): they not only believed that God had given them no choice, but they were tied to a memory of past glory and a dream of imminent redemption. What does the American Negro have that might correspond to this? His past is a stigma, his color is a stigma, and his vision of the future is the hope of erasing the stigma by making color irrelevant, by making it disappear as a fact of consciousness.

I share this hope, but I cannot see how it will ever be realized unless color does *in fact* disappear: and that means not integration, it means assimilation, it means—let the brutal word come out—miscegenation. The Black Muslims, like their racist counterparts in the white world, accuse the "so-called Negro leaders" of secretly pursuing miscegenation as a goal. The racists are wrong, but I wish they were right, for I believe that the whole-sale merging of the two races is the most desirable alternative for everyone concerned. I am not claiming that this alternative can be pursued programmatically or that it is immediately feasible as a solution; obviously there are even greater barriers to its achievement than to the achievement of integration. What I am saying, however, is that in my opinion the Negro problem can be solved in this country in no other way.

I have told the story of my own twisted feelings about Negroes here, and of how they conflict with the moral convictions I have since developed, in order to assert that such feelings must be acknowledged as honestly as possible so that they can be controlled and ultimately disregarded in favor of the convictions. It is *wrong* for a man to suffer because of the color of his skin. Beside that clichéd proposition of liberal thought, what argument can stand and be respected? If the arguments are the arguments of feeling, they must be made to yield; and one's own soul is not the worst place to begin working a huge social transformation. Not so long ago, it used to be asked of white liberals, "Would you like your sister to marry one?" When I was a boy and my sister was still unmarried, I would certainly have said no to that question. But now I am a man, my sister is already married, and I have daughters. If I were to be asked today whether I would like a daughter of mine "to marry one," I would have to answer: "No, I wouldn't *like* it at all. I would rail and rave and rant and tear my hair. And then I hope I would have the courage to curse myself for raving and ranting, and to give her my blessing. How dare I withhold it at the behest of the child I once was and against the man I now have a duty to be?"

JAMES BALDWIN

The Fire Next Time

A good part of Baldwin's case against the establishment liberals seems to be that the real injury to the blacks has not been simply the result of brutality, but the result of a situation in which everything was the whites' to give or to withhold. Establishment civil rights is simply the most recent instance of this: the last gracious gift, or an impudent notion that the blacks may now be allowed to integrate with the whites. Baldwin seeks to remove this insult from civil rights. He wishes to show that it is a matter of whether the blacks are willing to accept the whites. Baldwin's moral position is such that he refrains from demanding commitment to a special means or a specific institution of change. The difficult problem of the liberals is to commit themselves to definite techniques and institutions which nevertheless sustain their moral position.

The section reprinted here from Baldwin's The Fire Next Time *is perhaps the most powerful single statement that has been made on black and white identity in America. Like Norman Podhoretz's piece, it deals with currents of emotion and thought that underlie racial attitudes. But it also transcends the hatred that divides the races and poetically evokes common bonds that unite human beings.*

During a recent Muslim rally, George Lincoln Rockwell, the chief of the American Nazi party, made a point of contributing about twenty dollars to the cause, and he and Malcolm X decided that, racially speaking, anyway, they were in complete agreement. The glorification of one race and the consequent debasement of another—or others—always has been and always will be a recipe for murder. There is no way around this. If one is permitted to treat any group of people with special disfavor because of their race or the color of their skin, there is no limit to what one will force them to endure, and, since the entire race has been mysteriously indicted, no reason not to attempt to destroy it root and branch. This is precisely what the Nazis attempted. Their only originality lay in the means they used. It is scarcely worthwhile to attempt remembering how many times the sun has looked down on the slaughter of the innocents. I am very much concerned that American Negroes achieve their freedom here in the United States. But I am also concerned for their dignity, for the health of their souls, and must oppose any attempt that Negroes may make to do to others what has been done to them. I think I know—we see it around us every day—the spiritual wasteland to which that road leads. It is so simple a fact and one that is so hard, apparently, to grasp: *Whoever debases others is debasing himself.* That is not a mystical statement but a most realistic one, which is proved by the eyes of any Alabama sheriff—and I would not like to see Negroes ever arrive at so wretched a condition.

Now, it is extremely unlikely that Negroes will ever rise to power in the United States, because they are only approximately a ninth of this nation. They are not in the position of the Africans, who are attempting to reclaim their land and break the colonial yoke and recover from the colonial experience. The Negro situation is dangerous in a different way, both for the Negro qua Negro and for the country of which he forms so troubled and troubling a part. The American Negro is a unique creation; he has no counterpart anywhere, and no predecessors. The Muslims react to this fact by referring to the Negro as "the so-called American Negro" and substituting for the names inherited from slavery the letter "X." It is a fact that every American Negro bears a name that originally belonged to the white man whose chattel he was. I am called Baldwin because I was either sold by my African tribe or kidnapped out of it into the hands of a white Christian named Baldwin, who forced me to kneel at the foot of the cross. I am, then, both visibly and legally the descendant of slaves in a white, Protestant country, and this is what it means to be an American Negro, this is who he is—a kidnapped pagan, who was sold like an animal and treated like one, who was once defined by the American Constitution as "three-fifths" of a man, and who, according to the Dred Scott decision, had no rights that a white man was bound to respect. And today, a hundred years after his technical emancipation, he remains—with the possible exception of the American Indian—the most despised creature in his country. Now, there is simply no possibility of a real change in the Negro's situation without the most radical and far-reaching changes in the American political and social structure. And it is clear that white Americans are not simply unwilling to effect these changes; they are, in the main, so slothful have they become, unable even to envision them. It must be added that the Negro himself no longer believes in the good faith of white Americans—if, indeed, he ever could have. What the Negro *has* discovered, and on an international level, is that power to intimidate which he has always had privately but hitherto could manipulate only privately—for private ends often, for limited ends always. And therefore when the country speaks of a "new" Negro, which it has been doing every hour on the hour for decades, it is not really referring to a change in the Negro, which, in any case, it is quite incapable of assessing, but only to a new difficulty in keeping him in his place, to the fact that it encounters him (again! again!) barring yet another door to its spiritual and social ease. This is probably, hard and odd as it may sound, the most important thing that one human being can do for another—it is certainly *one* of the most important things; hence the torment and necessity of love—and this is the enormous contribution that the Negro has made to this otherwise shapeless and undiscovered country. Consequently, white Americans are in nothing more deluded than in supposing that Negroes could ever have imagined that white people would "give" them anything. It is rare indeed that people give. Most people guard and keep; they suppose that it is they themselves and what they identify with themselves that they are guarding and keeping, whereas what they are actually guarding and keeping is their system of reality and what they assume themselves to be. One can give nothing whatever without giving oneself—that is to say, risking oneself. If one cannot risk oneself, then one is simply incapable of giving. And, after all, one can give freedom only by setting someone free. This, in the case of the Negro, the American republic has never become sufficiently mature to do. White Americans have contented themselves with gestures that are now described as "tokenism." For hard example, white Americans congratulate themselves on the 1954 Supreme Court decision outlawing segregation in the schools; they suppose, in spite of the mountain of evidence that has since accumulated to the contrary, that this was proof of a change of heart—or, as they like to say, progress. Perhaps. It all depends on how one reads the word "progress." Most of the Negroes I know do not believe that this immense concession would ever have been made if it had not been for the competition of the Cold War, and the fact that Africa was clearly liberating herself and therefore had, for political reasons, to be wooed by the descendants of her former masters. Had it been a matter of love or justice, the 1954 decision would surely have occurred sooner; were it not for the realities of power in this difficult era, it might very well not have occurred yet. This seems an extremely harsh way of stating the case—ungrateful, as it were—but the evidence that supports this way of stating it is not easily refuted. I myself do not think that it can be refuted at all. In any event, the sloppy and fatuous nature of American good will can never be relied upon to deal with hard problems. These have been dealt with, when they have been dealt with at all, out of necessity—and in political terms, anyway, necessity means concessions made in order to stay on top. I think this is a fact, which it serves no purpose to deny, *but, whether it is a fact or not, this is what the black population of the world, including black Americans, really believe.* The word "independence" in Africa and the word "integration" here are almost equally meaningless; that is, Europe has not yet left Africa, and black men here are not yet free. And both of these last statements are undeniable facts, related facts, containing the gravest implications for us all. The Negroes of this country may never be able to rise to power, but they are very well placed indeed to precipitate chaos and ring down the curtain on the American dream.

This has everything to do, of course, with the nature of that dream and with the fact that we Americans, of whatever color, do not dare examine it and are far from having made it a reality. There are too many things we do not wish to know about ourselves. People are not, for example, terribly anxious to be equal (equal, after all, to what and to whom?) but they love the idea of being superior. And this human truth has an especially grinding force here, where identity is almost impossible to achieve and people are perpetually attempting to find their feet on the shifting sands of status. (Consider the history of labor in a country in which, spiritually speaking, there are no workers, only candidates for the hand of the boss's daughter.) Furthermore, I have met only a very few people—and most of these were not Americans—who had any real desire to be free. Freedom is hard to bear. It can be objected that I am speaking of political freedom in spiritual terms, but the political institutions of any nation are always menaced and are ultimately controlled by the spiritual state of that nation. We are controlled here by our confusion, far more than we know, and the American dream has therefore become something much more closely resembling a nightmare, on the private, domestic, and international levels. Privately, we cannot stand our lives and dare not examine them; domestically, we take no responsibility for (and no pride in) what goes on in our country; and, internationally, for many millions of people, we are an unmitigated disaster. Whoever doubts this last statement has only to open his ears, his heart, his mind, to the testimony of—for example—any Cuban peasant or any Spanish poet, and ask himself what *he* would feel about us if *he* were the victim of our performance in pre-Castro Cuba or in Spain. We defend our curious role in Spain by referring to the Russian menace and the necessity of protecting the free world. It has not occurred to us that we have simply been mesmerized by Russia, and that the only real advantage Russia has in what we think of as a struggle between the East and the West is the moral history of the Western world. Russia's secret weapon is the bewilderment and despair and hunger of millions of people of whose existence we are scarcely aware. The Russian Communists are not in the least concerned about these people. But our ignorance and indecision have had the effect, if not of delivering them into Russian hands, of plunging them very deeply in the Russian shadow, for which effect—and it is hard to blame them—the most articulate among them, and the most oppressed as well, distrust us all the more. Our power and our fear of change help bind these people to their misery and bewilderment, and insofar as they find this state intolerable we are intolerably menaced. For if they find their state intolerable, but are too heavily oppressed to change it, they are simply pawns in the hands of larger powers, which, in such a context, are always unscrupulous, and when, eventually, they do change their situation—as in Cuba—we are menaced more than ever, by the vacuum that succeeds all violent upheavals. We should certainly know by now that it is one thing to overthrow a dictator or repel an invader and quite another thing really to achieve a revolution. Time and time again, the people discover that they have merely betrayed themselves into the hands of yet another Pharaoh, who, since he was necessary to put the broken country together, will not let them go. Perhaps, people being the conundrums that they are, and having so little desire to shoulder the burden of their lives, this is what will always happen. But at the bottom of my heart I do not believe this. I think that people can be better than that, and I know that people can be better than they are. We are capable of bearing a great burden, once we discover that the burden is reality and arrive where reality is. Anyway, the point here is that we are living in an age of revolution, whether we will or no, and that America is the only Western nation with both the power and, as I hope to suggest, the experience that may help to make these revolutions real and minimize the human damage. Any attempt we make to oppose these outbursts of energy is tantamount to signing our death warrant.

Behind what we think of as the Russian menace lies what we do not wish to face, and what white Americans do not face when they regard a Negro: reality —the fact that life is tragic. Life is tragic simply because the earth turns and the sun inexorably rises and sets, and one day, for each of us, the sun will go down for the last, last time. Perhaps the whole root of our trouble, the human trouble, is that we will sacrifice all the beauty of our lives, will imprison ourselves in totems, taboos, crosses, blood sacrifices, steeples, mosques, races, armies, flags, nations, in order to deny the fact of death, which is the only fact we have. It seems to me that one ought to rejoice in the *fact* of death—ought to decide, indeed, to *earn* one's death by confronting with passion the conundrum of life. One is responsible to life: It is the small beacon in that terrifying darkness from which we come and to which we shall return. One must negotiate this passage as nobly as possible, for the sake of those who are coming after us. But white Americans do not believe in death, and this is why the darkness of my skin so intimidates them. And this is also why the presence of the Negro in this country can bring about its destruction. It is the responsibility of free men to trust and to celebrate what is constant—birth, struggle, and death are constant, and so is love, though we may not always think so—and to apprehend the nature of change, to be able and willing to change. I speak of change not on the surface but in the depths—change in the sense of renewal. But renewal becomes impossible if one supposes things to be constant that are not—safety, for example, or money, or power. One clings then to chimeras, by which one can only be betrayed, and the entire hope—the entire possibility—of freedom disappears. And by destruction I mean precisely the abdication by Americans of any effort really to be free. The Negro can precipitate this abdication because white Americans have never, in all their long history, been able to look on him as a man like themselves. This point need not be labored; it is proved over and over again by the Negro's continuing position here, and his indescribable struggle to defeat the stratagems that white Americans have used, and use, to deny him his humanity. America could have used in other ways the energy that both groups have expended in this conflict. America, of all the Western nations, has been best placed to prove the uselessness and the obsolescence of the concept of color. But it has not dared to accept this opportunity, or even to conceive of it as an opportunity. White Americans have thought of it as their shame, and have envied those more civilized and elegant European nations that were untroubled by the presence of black men on their shores. This is because white Americans have supposed "Europe" and "civilization" to be synonyms—which they are not—and have been distrustful of other standards and other sources of vitality, especially those produced in America itself, and have attempted to behave in all matters as though what was east for Europe was also east for them. What it comes to is that if we, who can scarcely be considered a white nation, persist in thinking of ourselves as one, we condemn ourselves, with the truly white nations, to sterility and decay, whereas if we could accept ourselves *as we are,* we might bring new life to the Western achievements, and transform them. The price of this transformation is the unconditional freedom of the Negro; it is not too much to say that he, who has been so long rejected, must now be embraced, and at no matter what psychic or social risk. He is *the* key figure in his country, and the American future is precisely as bright or as dark as his. And the Negro recognizes this, in a negative way. Hence the question: Do I really *want* to be integrated into a burning house?

White Americans find it as difficult as white people elsewhere do to divest themselves of the notion that they are in possession of some intrinsic value that black people need, or want. And this assumption—which, for example, makes the solution to the Negro problem depend on the speed with which Negroes accept and adopt white standards—is revealed in all kinds of striking ways, from Bobby Kennedy's assurance that a Negro can become President in forty years to the unfortunate tone of warm congratulation with which so many liberals address their Negro equals. It is the Negro, of course, who is presumed to have become equal—an achievement that not only proves the comforting fact that perseverance has no color but also overwhelmingly corroborates the white man's sense of his own value. Alas, this value can scarcely be corroborated in any other way; there is certainly little enough in the white man's public or private life that one should desire to imitate. White men, at the bottom of their hearts, know this. Therefore, a vast amount of the energy that goes into what we call the Negro problem is produced by the white man's profound desire not to be judged by those who are not white, not to be seen as he is, and at the same time a vast amount of the white anguish is rooted in the white man's equally profound need to be seen as he is, to be released from the tyranny of his mirror. All of us know, whether or not we are able to admit it, that mirrors can only lie, that death by drowning is all that awaits one there. It is for this reason that love is so desperately sought and so cunningly avoided. Love takes off the masks that we fear we cannot live without and know we cannot live within. I use the word "love" here not merely in the personal sense but as a state of being, or a state of grace—not in the infantile American sense of being made happy but in the tough and universal sense of quest and daring and growth. And I submit, then, that the racial tensions that menace Americans today have little to do with real antipathy—on the contrary, indeed—and are involved only symbolically with color. These tensions are rooted in the very same depths as those from which love springs, or murder. The white man's unadmitted—and apparently, to him, unspeakable—private fears and longings are projected onto the Negro. The only way he can be released from the Negro's tyrannical power over him is to consent, in effect, to become black himself, to become a part of that suffering and dancing country that he now watches wistfully from the heights of his lonely power and, armed with spiritual traveller's checks, visits surreptitiously after dark. How can one respect, let alone adopt, the values of a people who do not, on any level whatever, live the way they say they do, or the way they say they should? I cannot accept the proposition that the four-hundred-year travail of the American Negro should result merely in his attainment of the present level of the American civilization. I am far from convinced that being released from the African witch doctor was worthwhile if I am now—in order to support the moral contradictions and the spiritual aridity of my life—expected to become dependent on the American psychiatrist. It is a bargain I refuse. The only thing white people have that black people need, or should want, is power—and no one holds power forever. White people cannot, in the generality, be taken as models of how to live.

Rather, the white man is himself in sore need of new standards, which will release him from his confusion and place him once again in fruitful communion with the depths of his own being. And I repeat: The price of the liberation of the white people is the liberation of the blacks—the total liberation, in the cities, in the towns, before the law, and in the mind. Why, for example— especially knowing the family as I do—I should *want* to marry your sister is a great mystery to me. But your sister and I have every right to marry if we wish to, and no one has the right to stop us. If she cannot raise me to her level, perhaps I can raise her to mine.

In short, we, the black and the white, deeply need each other here if we are really to become a nation—if we are really, that is, to achieve our identity, our maturity, as men and women. To create one nation has proved to be a hideously difficult task; there is certainly no need now to create two, one black and one white. But white men with far more political power than that possessed by the Nation of Islam movement have been advocating exactly this, in effect, for generations. If this sentiment is honored when it falls from the lips of Senator Byrd, then there is no reason it should not be honored when it falls from the lips of Malcolm X. And any Congressional committee wishing to investigate the latter must also be willing to investigate the former. They are expressing exactly the same sentiments and represent exactly the same danger. There is absolutely no reason to suppose that white people are better equipped to frame the laws by which I am to be governed than I am. It is entirely unacceptable that I should have no voice in the political affairs of my own country, for I am not a ward of America; I am one of the first Americans to arrive on these shores.

This past, the Negro's past, of rope, fire, torture, castration, infanticide, rape; death and humiliation; fear by day and night, fear as deep as the marrow of the bone; doubt that he was worthy of life, since everyone around him denied it; sorrow for his women, for his kinfolk, for his children, who needed his protection, and whom he could not protect; rage, hatred, and murder, hatred for white men so deep that it is often turned against him and his own, and made all love, all trust, all joy impossible—this past, this endless struggle to achieve and reveal and confirm a human identity, human authority, yet contains, for all its horror, something very beautiful. I do not mean to be sentimental about suffering—enough is certainly as good as a feast—but people who cannot suffer can never grow up, can never discover who they are. That man who is forced each day to snatch his manhood, his identity, out of the fire of human cruelty that rages to destroy it knows, if he survives his effort, and even if he does not survive it, something about himself and human life that no school on earth—and, indeed, no church—can teach. He achieves his own authority, and that is unshakable. This is because, in order to save his life, he is forced to look beneath appearances, to take nothing for granted, to hear the meaning behind the words. If one is continually surviving the worst that life can bring, one eventually ceases to be controlled by a fear of what life can bring; whatever it brings must be borne. And at this level of experience one's bitterness begins to be palatable, and hatred becomes too heavy a sack to carry. The apprehension of life here so briefly and inadequately sketched has been the experience of generations of Negroes, and it helps to explain how they have endured and how they have been able to produce children of kinder-garten age who can walk through mobs to get to school. It demands great force and great cunning continually to assault the mighty and indifferent fortress of white supremacy, as Negroes in this country have done so long. It demands great spiritual resilience not to hate the hater whose foot is on your neck, and an even greater miracle of perception and charity not to teach your child to hate. The Negro boys and girls who are facing mobs today come out of a long line of improbable aristocrats—the only genuine aristocrats this country has produced. I say "this country" because their frame of reference was totally American. They were hewing out of the mountain of white supremacy the stone of their individuality. I have great respect for that unsung army of black men and women who trudged down back lanes and entered back doors, saying "Yes, sir" and "No, Ma'am" in order to acquire a new roof for the schoolhouse, new books, a new chemistry lab, more beds for the dormitories, more dormitories. They did not like saying "Yes, sir" and "No, Ma'am," but the country was in no hurry to educate Negroes, these black men and women knew that the job had to be done, and they put their pride in their pockets in order to do it. It is very hard to believe that they were in any way inferior to the white men and women who opened those back doors. It is very hard to believe that those men and women, raising their children, eating their greens, crying their curses, weeping their tears, singing their songs, making their love, as the sun rose, as the sun set, were in any way inferior to the white men and women who crept over to share these splendors after the sun went down. But we must avoid the Euro-pean error; we must not suppose that, because the situation, the ways, the per-ceptions of black people so radically differed from those of whites, they were racially superior. I am proud of these people not because of their color but because of their intelligence and their spiritual force and their beauty. The country should be proud of them, too, but, alas, not many people in this country even know of their existence. And the reason for this ignorance is that a knowledge of the role these people played—and play—in American life would reveal more about America to Americans than Americans wish to know.

The American Negro has the great advantage of having never believed that collection of myths to which white Americans cling: that their ancestors were all freedom-loving heroes, that they were born in the greatest country the world has ever seen, or that Americans are invincible in battle and wise in peace, that Americans have always dealt honorably with Mexicans and Indians and all other neighbors or inferiors, that American men are the world's most direct and virile, that American women are pure. Negroes know far more about white Americans than that; it can almost be said, in fact, that they know about white Americans what parents—or, anyway, mothers—know about their children, and that they very often regard white Americans that way. And perhaps this attitude, held in spite of what they know and have endured, helps to explain why Negroes, on the whole, and until lately, have allowed themselves to feel so little hatred. The tendency has really been, insofar as this was possible, to dismiss white people as the slightly mad victims of their own brain-washing. One watched the lives they led. One could not be fooled about that; one watched the things they did and the excuses that they gave themselves, and if a white man was really in trouble, deep trouble, it was to the Negro's door that he came. And one felt that if one had had that white man's worldly advantages, one would never have become as bewildered and as joyless and as thoughtlessly cruel as he. The Negro came to the white man for a roof or for five dollars or for a letter to the judge; the white man came to the Negro for love. But he was not often able to give what he came seeking. The price was too high; he had too much to lose. And the Negro knew this, too. When one knows this about a man, it is impossible for one to hate him, but unless he becomes a man—becomes equal—it is also impossible for one to love him. Ultimately, one tends to avoid him, for the universal characteristic of children is to assume that they have a monopoly on trouble, and therefore a monopoly on *you*. (Ask any Negro what he knows about the white people with whom he works. And then ask the white people with whom he works what they know about *him*.)

How can the American Negro past be used? It is entirely possible that this dishonored past will rise up soon to smite all of us. There are some wars, for example (if anyone on the globe is still mad enough to go to war) that the American Negro will not support, however many of his people may be coerced —and there is a limit to the number of people any government can put in prison, and a rigid limit indeed to the practicality of such a course. A bill is coming in that I fear America is not prepared to pay. "The problem of the twentieth century," wrote W. E. B. Du Bois around sixty years ago, "is the problem of the color line." A fearful and delicate problem, which compromises, when it does not corrupt, all the American efforts to build a better world— here, there, or anywhere. It is for this reason that everything white Americans think they believe in must now be reëxamined. What one would not like to see again is the consolidation of peoples on the basis of their color. But as long as we in the West place on color the value that we do, we make it impossible for the great unwashed to consolidate themselves according to any other principle. Color is not a human or a personal reality; it is a political reality. But this is a distinction so extremely hard to make that the West has not been able to make it yet. And at the center of this dreadful storm, this vast confusion, stand the black people of this nation, who must now share the fate of a nation that has never accepted them, to which they were brought in chains. Well, if this is so, one has no choice but to do all in one's power to change that fate, and at no matter what risk—eviction, imprisonment, torture, death. For the sake of one's children, in order to minimize the bill that *they* must pay, one must be careful not to take refuge in any delusion—and the value placed on the color of the skin is always and everywhere and forever a delusion. I know that what I am asking is impossible. But in our time, as in every time, the impossible is the least that one can demand—and one is, after all, emboldened by the spectacle of human history in general, and American Negro history in particular, for it testifies to nothing less than the perpetual achievement of the impossible.

When I was very young, and was dealing with my buddies in those wine- and urine-stained hallways, something in me wondered, *What will happen to all that beauty?* For black people, though I am aware that some of us, black and white, do not know it yet, are very beautiful. And when I sat at Elijah's table and watched the baby, the women, and the men, and we talked about God's—or Allah's—vengeance, I wondered, when that vengeance was achieved,

What will happen to all that beauty then? I could also see that the intransigence and ignorance of the white world might make that vengeance inevitable—a vengeance that does not really depend on, and cannot really be executed by, any person or organization, and that cannot be prevented by any police force or army: historical vengeance, a cosmic vengeance, based on the law that we recognize when we say, "Whatever goes up must come down." And here we are, at the center of the arc, trapped in the gaudiest, most valuable, and most improbable water wheel the world has ever seen. Everything now, we must assume, is in our hands; we have no right to assume otherwise. If we—and now I mean the relatively conscious whites and the relatively conscious blacks, who must, like lovers, insist on, or create, the consciousness of the others—do not falter in our duty now, we may be able, handful that we are, to end the racial nightmare, and achieve our country, and change the history of the world. If we do not now dare everything, the fulfillment of that prophecy, re-created from the Bible in song by a slave, is upon us: *God gave Noah the rainbow sign, No more water, the fire next time!*

30

STOKELY CARMICHAEL and
CHARLES V. HAMILTON

Black Power

On the surface the origins of the Black Power movement seem to lie in the failure of the civil rights movements: the persistence of school and community segregation, the deterioration of the ghetto, and the failure of the American economy to accommodate the black man. Yet Black Power could just as easily be understood as resulting from the success of the civil rights movement, which broke the crust of the traditional white supremacy and black subordination and made it possible for an entirely new realm of possibilities to arise. The movement has been ambiguous in its definitions, which have ranged from the apocalyptic to the mild and practical.

There is also a larger ambiguity which touches on the precarious relationship of community to individuality in America. For Black Power, recognizing that the black American has traditionally been denied a place in society and therefore a full personal identity, seeks to provide a communal situation in which that identity may realize itself. Yet Black Power may, like any community or movement, stand surrogate for the individual will and therefore threaten the autonomy of its black members as much as the lack of a viable community denied autonomy to their Negro forebears.

It is fitting to reprint Stokely Carmichael's description of Black Power, for, as spokesman of the Student Nonviolent Coordinating Committee (SNCC), he first proclaimed it. There may, however, be a discrepancy between the actions of SNCC and the relatively mild program enunciated here by Carmichael.

"To carve out a place for itself in the politico-social order," V. O. Key, Jr. wrote in *Politics, Parties and Pressure Groups*, "a new group may have to fight for reorientation of many of the values of the old order" (p. 57). This is especially true when that group is composed of black people in the American society—a society that has for centuries deliberately and systematically excluded them from political participation. Black people in the United States must raise hard questions, questions which challenge the very nature of the society itself: its long-standing values, beliefs and institutions.

To do this, we must first redefine ourselves. Our basic need is to reclaim our history and our identity from what must be called cultural terrorism, from the depredation of self-justifying white guilt. We shall have to struggle for the right to create our own terms through which to define ourselves and our relationship to the society, and to have these terms recognized. This is the first necessity of a free people, and the first right that any oppressor must suspend. . . .

Black people must redefine themselves, and only *they* can do that. Throughout this country, vast segments of the black communities are beginning to recognize the need to assert their own definitions, to reclaim their history, their culture; to create their own sense of community and togetherness. There is a growing resentment of the word "Negro," for example, because this term is the invention of our oppressor; it is *his* image of us that he describes. Many blacks are now calling themselves African-Americans, Afro-Americans or black people because that is *our* image of ourselves. When we begin to define our own image, the stereotypes—that is, lies—that our oppressor has developed will begin in the white community and end there. The black community will have a positive image of itself that *it* has created. This means we will no longer call ourselves lazy, apathetic, dumb, good-timers, shiftless, etc. Those are words used by white America to define us. If we accept these adjectives, as some of us have in the past, then we see ourselves only in a negative way, precisely the way white America wants us to see ourselves. Our incentive is broken and our will to fight is surrendered. From now on we shall view ourselves as African-Americans and as black people who are in fact energetic, determined, intelligent, beautiful and peace-loving.

There is a terminology and ethos peculiar to the black community of which black people are beginning to be no longer ashamed. Black communities are the only large segments of this society where people refer to each other as brother—soul-brother, soul-sister. Some people may look upon this as *ersatz*, as make-believe, but it is not that. It is real. It is a growing sense of community. It is a growing realization that black Americans have a common bond not only among themselves, but with their African brothers. In *Black Man's Burden*, John O. Killens described his trip to ten African countries as follows:

> Everywhere I went people called me brother. . . . "Welcome, American brother." It was a good feeling for me, to be in Africa. To walk in a land for the first time in your entire life knowing within yourself that your color would not be held against you. No black man ever knows this in America [p. 160].

More and more black Americans are developing this feeling. They are becoming aware that they have a history which pre-dates their forced intro-

duction to this country. African-American history means a long history beginning on the continent of Africa, a history not taught in the standard textbooks
of this country. It is absolutely essential that black people know this history,
that they know their roots, that they develop an awareness of their cultural
heritage. Too long have they been kept in submission by being told that they
had no culture, no manifest heritage, before they landed on the slave auction
blocks in this country. If black people are to know themselves as a vibrant,
valiant people, they must know their roots. And they will soon learn that the
Hollywood image of maneating cannibals waiting for, and waiting on, the
Great White Hunter is a lie.

With redefinition will come a clearer notion of the role black Americans
can play in this world. This role will emerge clearly out of the unique, common experiences of Afro-Asians. Killens concludes:

> I believe furthermore that the American Negro can be the
> bridge between the West and Africa-Asia. We black Americans
> can serve as a bridge to mutual understanding. The one thing we
> black Americans have in common with the other colored peoples
> of the world is that we have all felt the cruel and ruthless heel of
> white supremacy. We have all been "niggerized" on one level or
> another. And all of us are determined to "deniggerize" the earth.
> To rid the world of "niggers" is the Black Man's Burden, human
> reconstruction is the grand objective [p. 176].

Only when black people fully develop this sense of community, of themselves,
can they begin to deal effectively with the problems of racism in *this* country.
This is what we mean by a new consciousness; this is the vital first step.

The next step is what we shall call the process of political modernization—
a process which must take place if the society is to be rid of racism. "Political
modernization" includes many things, but we mean by it three major concepts:
(1) questioning old values and institutions of the society; (2) searching for
new and different forms of political structure to solve political and economic
problems; and (3) broadening the base of political participation to include
more people in the decision-making process. These notions (we shall take up
each in turn) are central to our thinking throughout this book and to contemporary American history as a whole. As David Apter wrote in *The Politics
of Modernization*, ". . . the struggle to modernize is what has given meaning
to our generation. It tests our cherished institutions and our beliefs. . . . So
compelling a force has it become that we are forced to ask new questions of
our own institutions. Each country, whether modernized or modernizing,
stands in both judgment and fear of the results. Our own society is no exception" (p. 2).

The values of this society support a racist system; we find it incongruous
to ask black people to adopt and support most of those values. We also reject
the assumption that the basic institutions of this society must be preserved.
The goal of black people must *not* be to assimilate into middle-class America,
for that class—as a whole—is without a viable conscience as regards humanity.
The values of the middle class permit the perpetuation of the ravages of the

black community. The values of that class are based on material aggrandizement, not the expansion of humanity. The values of that class ultimately support cloistered little closed societies tucked away neatly in tree-lined suburbia. The values of that class do *not* lead to the creation of an open society. That class *mouths* its preference for a free, competitive society, while at the same time forcefully and even viciously denying to black people as a group the opportunity to compete.

We are not unmindful of other descriptions of the social utility of the middle class. Banfield and Wilson, in *City Politics,* concluded:

> The departure of the middle class from the central city is important in other ways. . . . The middle class supplies a social and political leavening in the life of a city. Middle-class people demand good schools and integrity in government. They support churches, lodges, parent-teacher associations, scout troops, better-housing committees, art galleries, and operas. It is the middle class, in short, that asserts a conception of the public interest. Now its activity is increasingly concentrated in the suburbs [p. 14].

But this same middle class manifests a sense of superior group position in regard to race. This class wants "good government" *for themselves;* it wants good schools *for its children.* At the same time, many of its members sneak into the black community by day, exploit it, and take the money home to their middle-class communities at night to support their operas and art galleries and comfortable homes. When not actually robbing, they will fight off the handful of more affluent black people who seek to move in; when they approve or even seek token integration, it applies only to black people like themselves—as "white" as possible. *This class is the backbone of institutional racism in this country.*

Thus we reject the goal of assimilation into middle-class America because the values of that class are in themselves anti-humanist and because that class as a social force perpetuates racism. We must face the fact that, in the past, what we have called the movement has not really questioned the middle-class values and institutions of this country. If anything, it has accepted those values and institutions without fully realizing their racist nature. Reorientation means an emphasis on the dignity of man, not on the sanctity of property. It means the creation of a society where human misery and poverty are repugnant to that society, not an indication of laziness or lack of initiative. The creation of new values means the establishment of a society based, as Killens expresses it in *Black Man's Burden,* on "free people," not "free enterprise" (p. 167). To do this means to modernize—*indeed, to civilize*—this country.

Supporting the old values are old political and economic structures; these must also be "modernized." We should at this point distinguish between "structures" and "system." By system, we have in mind the entire American complex of basic institutions, values, beliefs, etc. By structures, we mean the specific institutions (political parties, interest groups, bureaucratic administrations) which exist to conduct the business of that system. Obviously, the first is broader than the second. Also, the second assumes the legitimacy of the first.

Our view is that, given the illegitimacy of the system, we cannot then proceed to transform that system with existing structures.

The two major political parties in this country have become non-viable entities for the legitimate representation of the real needs of masses—especially blacks—in this country. Walter Lippmann raised the same point in his syndicated column of December 8, 1966. He pointed out that the party system in the United States developed before our society became as technologically complex as it is now. He says that the ways in which men live and define themselves are changing radically. Old ideological issues, once the subject of passionate controversy, Lippmann argues, are of little interest today. He asks whether the great urban complexes—which are rapidly becoming the centers of black population in the U.S.—can be run with the same systems and ideas that derive from a time when America was a country of small villages and farms. While not addressing himself directly to the question of race, Lippmann raises a major question about our political institutions; and the crisis of race in America may be its major symptom.

Black people have seen the city planning commissions, the urban renewal commissions, the boards of education and the police departments fail to speak to their needs in a meaningful way. We must devise new structures, new institutions to replace those forms or to make them responsive. There is nothing sacred or inevitable about old institutions; the focus must be on people, not forms.

Existing structures and established ways of doing things have a way of perpetuating themselves and for this reason, the modernizing process will be difficult. Therefore, timidity in calling into question the boards of education or the police departments will not do. They must be challenged forcefully and clearly. If this means the creation of parallel community institutions, then that must be the solution. If this means that black parents must gain control over the operation of the schools in the black community, then that must be the solution. The search for new forms means the search for institutions that will, for once, make decisions in the interest of black people. It means, for example, a building inspection department that neither winks at violations of building codes by absentee slumlords nor imposes meaningless fines which permit them to continue their exploitation of the black community.

Essential to the modernization of structures is a broadened base of political participation. More and more people must become politically sensitive and active (we have already seen this happening in some areas of the South). People must no longer be tied, by small incentives or handouts, to a corrupting and corruptible white machine. Black people will choose their own leaders and hold those leaders responsible to *them*. A broadened base means an end to the condition described by James Wilson in *Negro Politics,* whereby "Negroes tended to be the objects rather than the subjects of civic action. Things are often done for, or about, or to, or because of Negroes, but they are less frequently done *by* Negroes" (p. 133). Broadening the base of political participation, then, has as much to do with the quality of black participation as with the quantity. We are fully aware that the black vote, especially in the North, has been pulled out of white pockets and "delivered" whenever it was in the interest of white politicians to do so. That vote must no longer be controllable by those who have neither the interests nor the demonstrated concern of black people in mind.

As the base broadens, as more and more black people become activated, they will perceive more clearly the special disadvantages heaped upon them as a group. They will perceive that the larger society is growing more affluent while the black society is retrogressing, as daily life and mounting statistics clearly show. V. O. Key describes what often happens next, in *Politics, Parties and Pressure Groups:* "A factor of great significance in the setting off of political movements is an abrupt change for the worse in the status of one group relative to that of other groups in society. . . . A rapid change for the worse . . . in the relative status of any group . . . is likely to precipitate political action" (p. 24). Black people will become increasingly active as they notice that their retrogressive status exists in large measure because of values and institutions arraigned against them. They will begin to stress and strain and call the entire system into question. Political modernization will be in motion. We believe that it is now in motion. One form of that motion is Black Power.

The adoption of the concept of Black Power is one of the most legitimate and healthy developments in American politics and race relations in our time. The concept of Black Power speaks to all the needs mentioned in this chapter. It is a call for black people in this country to unite, to recognize their heritage, to build a sense of community. It is a call for black people to begin to define their own goals, to lead their own organizations and to support those organizations. It is a call to reject the racist institutions and values of this society.

The concept of Black Power rests on a fundamental premise: *Before a group can enter the open society, it must first close ranks.* By this we mean that group solidarity is necessary before a group can operate effectively from a bargaining position of strength in a pluralistic society. Traditionally, each new ethnic group in this society has found the route to social and political viability through the organization of its own institutions with which to represent its needs within the larger society. Studies in voting behavior specifically, and political behavior generally, have made it clear that politically the American pot has not melted. Italians vote for Rubino over O'Brien; Irish for Murphy over Goldberg, etc. This phenomenon may seem distasteful to some, but it has been and remains today a central fact of the American political system. There are other examples of ways in which groups in the society have remembered their roots and used this effectively in the political arena. Theodore Sorensen describes the politics of foreign aid during the Kennedy Administration in his book *Kennedy:*

> No powerful constituencies or interest groups backed foreign aid. The Marshall Plan at least had appealed to Americans who traced their roots to the Western European nations aided. But there were few voters who identified with India, Colombia or Tanganyika [p. 351].

The extent to which black Americans can and do "trace their roots" to Africa, to that extent will they be able to be more effective on the political scene.

A white reporter set forth this point in other terms when he made the following observation about white Mississippi's manipulation of the anti-poverty program:

> The war on poverty has been predicated on the notion that there is such a thing as a community which can be defined geographically and mobilized for a collective effort to help the poor. This theory has no relationship to reality in the deep South. In every Mississippi county there are two communities. Despite all the pious platitudes of the moderates on both sides, these two communities habitually see their interests in terms of conflict rather than cooperation. Only when the Negro community can muster enough political, economic and professional strength to compete on somewhat equal terms, will Negroes believe in the possibility of true cooperation and whites accept its necessity. En route to integration, the Negro community needs to develop a greater independence—a chance to run its own affairs and not cave in whenever "the man" barks—or so it seems to me, and to most of the knowledgeable people with whom I talked in Mississippi. To OEO, this judgment may sound like black nationalism. . . .

The point is obvious: black people must lead and run their own organizations. Only black people can convey the revolutionary idea—and it is a revolutionary idea—that black people are able to do things themselves. Only they can help create in the community an aroused and continuing black consciousness that will provide the basis for political strength. In the past, white allies have often furthered white supremacy without the whites involved realizing it, or even wanting to do so. Black people must come together and do things for themselves. They must achieve self-identity and self-determination in order to have their daily needs met.

Black Power means, for example, that in Lowndes County, Alabama, a black sheriff can end police brutality. A black tax assessor and tax collector and county board of revenue can lay, collect, and channel tax monies for the building of better roads and schools serving black people. In such areas as Lowndes, where black people have a majority, they will attempt to use power to exercise control. This is what they seek: control. When black people lack a majority, Black Power means proper representation and sharing of control. It means the creation of power bases, of strength, from which black people can press to change local or nation-wide patterns of oppression—instead of from weakness.

It does not mean *merely* putting black faces into office. Black visibility is not Black Power. Most of the black politicians around the country today are not examples of Black Power. The power must be that of a community, and emanate from there. The black politicians must start from there. The black politicians must stop being representatives of "downtown" machines, whatever the cost might be in terms of lost patronage and holiday handouts.

Black Power recognizes—it must recognize—the ethnic basis of American politics as well as the power-oriented nature of American politics. Black Power therefore calls for black people to consolidate behind their own, so that they can bargain from a position of strength. But while we endorse the *procedure* of group solidarity and identity for the purpose of attaining certain goals in the body politic, this does not mean that black people should strive for the same kind of rewards (i.e., end results) obtained by the white society. The ultimate values and goals are not domination or exploitation of other groups, but rather an effective share in the total power of the society.

Nevertheless, some observers have labeled those who advocate Black Power as racists; they have said that the call for self-identification and self-determination is "racism in reverse" or "black supremacy." This is a deliberate and absurd lie. There is no analogy—by any stretch of definition or imagination —between the advocates of Black Power and white racists. Racism is not merely exclusion on the basis of race but exclusion for the purpose of sub-jugating or maintaining subjugation. The goal of the racists is to keep black people on the bottom, arbitrarily and dictatorially, as they have done in this country for over three hundred years. The goal of black self-determination and black self-identity—Black Power—is full participation in the decision-making processes affecting the lives of black people, and recognition of the virtues in themselves as black people. The black people of this country have not lynched whites, bombed their churches, murdered their children and manipulated laws and institutions to maintain oppression. White racists have. Congressional laws, one after the other, have not been necessary to stop black people from oppress-ing others and denying others the full enjoyment of their rights. White racists have made such laws necessary. The goal of Black Power is positive and func-tional to a free and viable society. No white racist can make this claim.

A great deal of public attention and press space was devoted to the hysteri-cal accusation of "black racism" when the call for Black Power was first sounded. A national committee of influential black churchmen affiliated with the National Council of Churches, despite their obvious respectability and responsibility, had to resort to a paid advertisement to articulate their position, while anyone yapping "black racism" made front-page news. In their statement, published in the *New York Times* of July 31, 1966, the churchmen said:

> We, an informal group of Negro churchmen in America, are deeply disturbed about the crisis brought upon our country by his-toric distortions of important human realities in the controversy about "black power." What we see shining through the variety of rhetoric is not anything new but the same old problem of power and race which has faced our beloved country since 1619.
>
> . . . The conscience of black men is corrupted because having no power to implement the demands of conscience, the concern for justice in the absence of justice becomes a chaotic self-surrender. Powerlessness breeds a race of beggars. We are faced with a situa-tion where powerless conscience meets conscienceless power, threat-ening the very foundations of our Nation.
>
> We deplore the overt violence of riots, but we feel it is more important to focus on the real sources of these eruptions. These

sources may be abetted inside the Ghetto, but their basic cause lies in the silent and covert violence which white middle class America inflicts upon the victims of the inner city.

. . . In short, the failure of American leaders to use American power to create equal opportunity *in life* as well as *law,* this is the real problem and not the anguished cry for black power.

. . . Without the capacity to participate with power, i.e., to have some organized political and economic strength to really influence people with whom one interacts, integration is not meaningful.

. . . America has asked its Negro citizens to fight for opportunity as *individuals,* whereas at certain points in our history what we have needed most has been opportunity for the *whole group,* not just for selected and approved Negroes.

. . . We must not apologize for the existence of this form of group power, for we have been oppressed as a group and not as individuals. We will not find our way out of that oppression until both we and America accept the need for Negro Americans, as well as for Jews, Italians, Poles, and white Anglo-Saxon Protestants, among others, to have and to wield group power.

It is a commentary on the fundamentally racist nature of this society that the concept of group strength for black people must be articulated—not to mention defended. No other group would submit to being led by others. Italians do not run the Anti-Defamation League of B'nai B'rith. Irish do not chair Christopher Columbus Societies. Yet when black people call for black-run and all-black organizations, they are immediately classed in a category with the Ku Klux Klan. This is interesting and ironic, but by no means surprising: the society does not expect black people to be able to take care of their business, and there are many who prefer it precisely that way.

In the end, we cannot and shall not offer any guarantees that Black Power, if achieved, would be non-racist. No one can predict human behavior. Social change always has unanticipated consequences. If black racism is what the larger society fears, we cannot help them. We can only state what we hope will be the result, given the fact that the present situation is unacceptable and that we have no real alternative but to work for Black Power. The final truth is that the white society is not entitled to reassurances, even if it were possible to offer them.

We have outlined the meaning and goals of Black Power; we have also discussed one major thing which it is not. There are others of greater importance. The advocates of Black Power reject the old slogans and meaningless rhetoric of previous years in the civil rights struggle. The language of yesterday is indeed irrelevant: progress, non-violence, integration, fear of "white backlash," coalition. Let us look at the rhetoric and see why these terms must be set aside or redefined.

One of the tragedies of the struggle against racism is that up to this point there has been no national organization which could speak to the growing militancy of young black people in the urban ghettos and the black-belt South. There has been only a "civil rights" movement, whose tone of voice was adapted to an audience of middle-class whites. It served as a sort of buffer zone between that audience and angry young blacks. It claimed to speak for the needs of a community, but it did not speak in the tone of that community. None of its so-called leaders could go into a rioting community and be listened to. In a sense, the blame must be shared—along with the mass media—by those leaders for what happened in Watts, Harlem, Chicago, Cleveland and other places. Each time the black people in those cities saw Dr. Martin Luther King get slapped they became angry. When they saw little black girls bombed to death *in a church* and civil rights workers ambushed and murdered, they were angrier; and when nothing happened, they were steaming mad. We had nothing to offer that they could see, except to go out and be beaten again. We helped to build their frustration.

We had only the old language of love and suffering. And in most places —that is, from the liberals and middle class—we got back the old language of patience and progress. The civil rights leaders were saying to the country: "Look, you guys are supposed to be nice guys, and we are only going to do what we are supposed to do. Why do you beat us up? Why don't you give us what we ask? Why don't you straighten yourselves out?" For the masses of black people, this language resulted in virtually nothing. In fact, their objective day-to-day condition worsened. The unemployment rate among black people increased while that among whites declined. Housing conditions in the black communities deteriorated. Schools in the black ghettos continued to plod along on outmoded techniques, inadequate curricula, and with all too many tired and indifferent teachers. Meanwhile, the President picked up the refrain of "We Shall Overcome" while the Congress passed civil rights law after civil rights law, only to have them effectively nullified by deliberately weak enforcement. "Progress is being made," we were told.

Such language, along with admonitions to remain non-violent and fear the white backlash, convinced some that that course was the *only* course to follow. It misled some into believing that a black minority could bow its head and get whipped into a meaningful position of power. The very notion is absurd. The white society devised the language, adopted the rules and had the black community narcotized into believing that that language and those rules were, in fact, relevant. The black community was told time and again how *other* immigrants finally won *acceptance:* that is, by following the Protestant Ethic of Work and Achievement. They worked hard; therefore, they achieved. We were not told that it was by building Irish Power, Italian Power, Polish Power or Jewish Power that these groups got themselves together and operated from positions of strength. We were not told that "the American dream" wasn't designed for black people. That while today, to whites, the dream may *seem* to include black people, it cannot do so by the very nature of this nation's political and economic system, which imposes institutional racism on the black masses if not upon every individual black. A notable comment on that "dream" was made by Dr. Percy Julian, the black scientist and director of the Julian Research Institute in Chicago, a man for whom the dream seems to have come true. While not subscribing to "black power" as he understood it, Dr. Julian clearly understood the basis for it: "The false concept of basic Negro inferiority is one of the curses that still lingers. It is a problem created by the white man.

Our children just no longer are going to accept the patience we were taught by our generation. We were taught a pretty little lie—excel and the whole world lies open before you. *I obeyed the injunction and found it to be wishful thinking.*" (Authors' italics)

A key phrase in our buffer-zone days was non-violence. For years it has been thought that black people would not literally fight for their lives. Why this has been so is not entirely clear; neither the larger society nor black people are noted for passivity. The notion apparently stems from the years of marches and demonstrations and sit-ins where black people did not strike back and the violence always came from white mobs. There are many who still sincerely believe in that approach. From our viewpoint, rampaging white mobs and white night-riders must be made to understand that their days of free head-whipping are over. Black people should and must fight back. Nothing more quickly repels someone bent on destroying you than the unequivocal message: "O.K., fool, make your move, and run the same risk I run—of dying."

When the concept of Black Power is set forth, many people immediately conjure up notions of violence. The country's reaction to the Deacons for Defense and Justice, which originated in Louisiana, is instructive. Here is a group which realized that the "law" and law enforcement agencies would not protect people, so they had to do it themselves. If a nation fails to protect its citizens, then that nation cannot condemn those who take up the task themselves. The Deacons and all other blacks who resort to self-defense represent a simple answer to a simple question: what man would not defend his family and home from attack?

But this frightened some white people, because they knew that black people would now fight back. They knew that this was precisely what *they* would have long since done if *they* were subjected to the injustices and oppression heaped on blacks. Those of us who advocate Black Power are quite clear in our own minds that a "non-violent" approach to civil rights is an approach black people cannot afford and a luxury white people do not deserve. It is crystal clear to us—and it must become so with the white society—*that there can be no social order without social justice*. White people must be made to understand that they must stop messing with black people, or the blacks *will* fight back!

Next, we must deal with the term "integration." According to its advocates, social justice will be accomplished by "integrating the Negro into the mainstream institutions of the society from which he has been traditionally excluded." This concept is based on the assumption that there is nothing of value in the black community and that little of value could be created among black people. The thing to do is siphon off the "acceptable" black people into the surrounding middle-class white community.

The goals of integrationists are middle-class goals, articulated primarily by a small group of Negroes with middle-class aspirations or status. Their kind of integration has meant that a few blacks "make it," leaving the black community, sapping it of leadership potential and know-how. Those token Negroes —absorbed into a white mass—are of no value to the remaining black masses. They become meaningless show-pieces for a conscience-soothed white society. Such people will state that they would prefer to be treated "only as individuals, not as Negroes"; that they "are not and should not be preoccupied with race." This is a totally unrealistic position. In the first place, black people have not suffered as individuals but as members of a group; therefore, their liberation lies in group action. This is why SNCC—and the concept of Black Power—affirms that helping *individual* black people to solve their problems on an *individual* basis does little to alleviate the mass of black people. Secondly, while color blindness *may* be a sound goal ultimately, we must realize that race is an overwhelming fact of life in this historical period. Their is no black man in this country who can live "simply as a man." His blackness is an ever-present fact of this racist society, whether he recognizes it or not. It is unlikely that this or the next generation will witness the time when race will no longer be relevant in the conduct of public affairs and in public policy decision-making. To realize this and to attempt to deal with it does not make one a racist or overly preoccupied with race; it puts one in the forefront of a significant *struggle*. If there is no intense struggle today, there will be no meaningful results tomorrow.

"Integration" as a goal today speaks to the problem of blackness not only in an unrealistic way but also in a despicable way. It is based on complete acceptance of the fact that in order to have a decent house or education, black people must move into a white neighborhood or send their children to a white school. This reinforces, among both black and white, the idea that "white" is automatically superior and "black" is by definition inferior. For this reason, "integration" is a subterfuge for the maintenance of white supremacy. It allows the nation to focus on a handful of Southern black children who get into white schools at a great price, and to ignore the ninety-four percent who are left in unimproved all-black schools. Such situations will not change until black people become equal in a way that means something, and integration ceases to be a one-way street. Then integration does not mean draining skills and energies from the black ghetto into white neighborhoods. To sprinkle black children among white pupils in outlying schools is at best a stop-gap measure. The goal is not to take black children out of the black community and expose them to white middle-class values; the goal is to build and strengthen the black community.

"Integration" also means that black people must give up their identity, deny their heritage. We recall the conclusion of Killian and Grigg: "At the present time, integration as a solution to the race problem demands that the Negro foreswear his identity as a Negro." The fact is that integration, as traditionally articulated, would abolish the black community. The fact is that what must be abolished is not the black community, but the dependent colonial status that has been inflicted upon it.

The racial and cultural personality of the black community must be preserved and that community must win its freedom while preserving its cultural integrity. Integrity includes a pride—in the sense of self-acceptance, not chauvinism—in being black, in the historical attainments and contributions of black people. No person can be healthy, complete and mature if he must deny a part of himself; this is what "integration" has required thus far. This is the essential difference between integration as it is currently practiced and the concept of Black Power.

31

MARTIN HOFFMAN

Homosexuality and the Social Creation of Evil

While a subculture exists in partial isolation from society, it also receives the impress of society, which provides its opportunities, its limits, and even its assumptions about itself. Martin Hoffman, a social psychiatrist and lecturer at Berkeley, believes the homosexual is not emotionally ill except insofar as society forces the condition upon him by the employment of stereotypes. Hollywood movies, for example, seem to be acting out a dread of homosexuals, inevitably presenting them as sick, vicious, or insipid. Unless he is strong enough to resist the beliefs that the culture holds of him, the homosexual, so the argument runs, is compelled into role playing of the most destructive sort, as an identity is forced on him that may not be at all inevitable to his sexuality.

Hoffman's thesis may ask a larger question that is central to the study of modern America: at what point does a culture or subculture cease to enrich the individual within it and begin to deny him the personal identity that his private will, unfettered by public stereotypes, might attain? Or to the immediate subject, if the homosexual should no longer be considered only a homosexual and be recognized as having a moral life apart from his sexuality, could he not more easily achieve the complex selfhood open to the rest of men?

At the present time, the most fashionable view of a homosexually oriented object-choice is that it is a mental illness or a symptom of mental illness. Perhaps the most influential exponent of this view today is the New York psychoanalyst Irving Bieber. Bieber's book (1962) is a strange mixture of astute clinical observation and the worst kind of pseudoscience. He interviewed a group of his psychoanalytic colleagues and elicited from them reports about patients they had treated in psychoanalysis. He compared the case histories of 106 male homosexuals and 100 male heterosexuals treated by these colleagues.

Bieber starts out with the assumption that homosexuality is a mental illness and finds, perhaps not surprisingly, that his clinical findings support his assumption. . . .

The flaws in Bieber's method are twofold: first, any inquiry that seeks to use only one kind of data to the exclusion of other data in order to substantiate a preconceived conclusion is not scientific; second, such data which do seem to support the preconceived conclusion may also be used, and perhaps even more advantageously, to support many other conclusions which the investigator has rejected on no other grounds than his prejudice. That individuals who come to psychoanalysts for treatment are usually mentally ill is a tautology—unless we can offer another explanation for their presence. Given this fact, it is reasonable to assume that a competent psychiatrist will diagnose most of his clients in one way or another as mentally ill. One would, therefore, expect that all homosexuals treated by psychiatrists are found to be mentally ill. How a psychiatrist can conclude from this fact that *all* homosexuals are mentally ill remains something of a mystery, and yet it is done all the time. The Philadelphia psychiatrist Samuel B. Hadden recently published an article in *Harper's* (March, 1967) in which he wrote, "In my observation, homosexuals are deeply troubled people . . . from earliest childhood none of the homosexuals I have known have been truly psychologically healthy individuals" (pp. 107, 114). What always appears most curious to me is that psychiatrists such as Bieber and Hadden can write this kind of thing with a straight face. When Hadden tells us that none of the homosexuals he has known are mentally healthy, the logical conclusion is that he has never known any mentally healthy homosexuals. But this is not the conclusion *he* draws. Instead, he comes to the conclusion that there *are* no mentally healthy homosexuals—which is quite another matter. But since he is forming dogmatic conclusions on the basis of his clinical experience alone, one can only suggest to him that he has no idea of what scientific method is all about. To put it in more technical terminology, Bieber and Hadden are claiming representativeness for a particular sample of a certain social group which is, in fact, not necessarily representative of that group. Homosexuals seen in psychiatric treatment are no more representative of homosexuals in the general population than are Jews seen in psychiatric treatment representative of all Jews. If I had to judge solely from my own psychiatric practice, I would have come to the same conclusions as Bieber and Hadden. None of the homosexuals I have treated has been mentally healthy; they were all sick. What I have refused to do, however, is to assume that my patients were the only kind of homosexuals that there are. It seemed to me quite obvious that they were not a representative or random sample of the general homosexual population.

I do not claim to be the first one to make this methodological critique of psychiatric writings on homosexuality. The psychoanalyst Ernest van den Haag wrote the following:

> To be sure, homosexual behavior often is a symptom or part of illness; so is heterosexual behavior. (I am reminded of a colleague who reiterated "all my homosexual patients are quite sick" —to which I finally replied "so are all my heterosexual patients."

As our culture has absorbed analysis, analysts have become culture-bound. It seems a questionable gain.)

Many homosexuals are neurotic or psychotic and seek the help of analysts, as do many heterosexuals. It does not follow that homosexuality itself is an illness—that it is always associated with clinical symptoms . . . of disturbance. (1963, p. 297.)

I might only add that van den Haag and I are not alone in taking this position in opposition to a large number of our colleagues. In his famous letter to the mother of an American homosexual, written on April 9, 1935, Freud wrote that homosexuality cannot be classified as an illness. In one of the most influential books published during the twentieth century, *Three Essays on the Theory of Sexuality,* Freud wrote the following:

Inversion is found in people who exhibit no other serious devia-tions from the normal. It is similarly found in people whose effi-ciency is unimpaired, and who are indeed distinguished by specially high intellectual development and ethical culture. (1925, p. 17.)

One of the reasons that I decided to do an ethnographic, community, or non-clinical study of homosexuals was because I felt that the homosexuals whom I was seeing in treatment were not representative of the general homo-sexual population. In the course of this work, one of the questions I was interested in answering was: are there a significant number of homosexuals who, by reasonable clinical criteria, cannot be considered mentally ill? The answer which I have found to this question is unequivocally in the affirmative. I have interviewed numerous men (and in many cases have extensive corroborating data from their friends and associates) who simply cannot be diagnosed men-tally ill on the basis of any clinical psychiatric criteria known to me. My own observations, therefore, provide more evidence to support Freud's state-ments quoted above.

But the reader does not need to take my word, van den Haag's word, or even Freud's word on this matter. There are more rigorous studies recently made which come to the same conclusion. In an investigation reported in the *British Medical Journal* in 1957, two English psychiatrists, Desmond Curran and Denis Parr, studied 100 cases seen in consultation in their private psychi-atric practice. Of these 100 homosexual men, 30 came because of some diffi-culty with the law and 25 came because they were troubled by their propensity toward socially unacceptable behavior. The rest came for other reasons, includ-ing standard psychiatric problems. Curran and Parr found that only 49 percent of these homosexuals showed significant psychiatric abnormalities, and that the abnormalities manifested were usually minimal. This means that, if one were to examine a psychiatrist's initial psychiatric evaluations of a sample of all individuals who come to his attention, rather than to study those patients who have been placed in extensive psychiatric treatment, one would find that the majority of those who are homosexual (which, incidentally, Curran and Parr found to be 5 percent of all their male patients over the age of 16) "were con-sidered to be free from gross personality disorder, neurosis, or psychosis during their adult lives" (p. 797). If Bieber or Hadden had seen these patients, they would surely have diagnosed them as mentally ill, since they have already assumed that homosexuality is an illness. They would then have placed the patients in treatment and found a psychiatric label for them.

At this point we must raise very briefly the whole question of the nature of mental illness. This is a very large and difficult subject and one which itself has an extensive literature. What is, I think, clear is that the diagnosis of mental illness is the result of a process of social definition and that certain individuals in society, usually psychiatrists, are granted the prerogative of making this definition. The standard which the psychiatrist has to use is determined by the general consensus among the community of his colleagues. Thus, he can, as is presently the case, define homosexuality *per se* as a mental illness merely because a large number of his colleagues have agreed that it is so. On the other hand, since there is no universal agreement about the matter, it is possible to hold a minority point of view, such as the view I hold. I maintain that homosexuality in itself does not necessarily indicate mental illness. The question is partly definitional and partly empirical. The definitional question is: do we want to say that a sexual preference for one's own sex is, by itself, either a mental illness or a symptom of an illness? This is a question which cannot altogether be solved by adducing scientific evidence, since it is basically a matter of attaching a particular label (mental illness) to a particular kind of sexual object-choice (homosexual). For those who elect to attach this label, the sexual object-choice in itself is sufficient ground for doing so, and no other evidence need be adduced.

As a matter of fact, the people who write on this subject are generally unclear as to what they mean, and the reader is very often confused or misled when he is finished reading what they have to say. They make two separate claims: (1) that homosexual behavior or preference is *itself* an illness; and (2) that homosexual behavior or preference is always associated with *other* clinical symptoms. The first claim, as we have indicated, is a matter of definition. The second claim is capable of empirical test. It has actually been empirically refuted.

The classic study which has refuted this notion was done by U.C.L.A. psychologist Evelyn Hooker and published in 1957. Hooker found 30 homosexuals whom she felt were reasonably well adjusted and were not in treatment. She obtained these men, to a large extent, with the assistance of the Mattachine Society, "an organization which has as its stated purpose the development of a homosexual ethic in order to better integrate the homosexual into society" (Hooker, 1957, p. 19). She then obtained 30 heterosexual men who were matched for age, education, and IQ with the homosexual subjects. Hooker then gave these 60 men a battery of psychological tests, including the Rorschach, the TAT, and the MATS, and obtained considerable information on their life histories. She then submitted this material for analysis to several of her colleagues, who did not know which of the tests had been given to the homosexual men and which to the heterosexual men; therefore, they analyzed the tests "blind." Hooker's general conclusion from the results of these analyses, made by clinicians who did not know the sexual orientation of the subjects in the study, was that there is no inherent connection between homosexual orientation and clinical symptoms of mental illness. She stated that "Homosexuality as a clinical entity does not exist. Its forms are as varied as are those of heterosexuality. Homosexuality may be a deviation in sexual pattern which is in the normal range, psychologically" (*ibid.*, p. 30). This conclusion is based on the fact that the clinicians who read the tests were unable to distinguish between the two groups. Nor was there any evidence that the homosexual group had a higher degree of pathology than the heterosexual group. When a sensitive clinical instrument, such as the Rorschach, was used, the conclusions were the same as those reached by Curran and Parr, by Freud, by van den Haag, and by myself, namely, that there certainly exists a significant number of homosexual men who are not mentally ill by any clinical criteria. If all this evidence is not to be discounted, then it is clear that the overt male homosexual is not necessarily subject to clinical symptoms of illness, to neurotic or psychotic disturbance. . . .

What is fundamentally wrong with the conventional disease concept of homosexuality is not that there is no connection between homosexuality and pathology, for there is, in fact, such a link. What is incorrect is that all the phenomena of gay life are analyzed in terms of individual pathology, as if there were no social forces acting upon the homosexual. The problem of paired intimacy, which in my judgment is *the central problem* of the gay world, is a problem which cannot meaningfully be understood without considering the social context in which it occurs. It is this failure to consider the social milieu in which the gay world is situated, namely, the hostile character of the surrounding non-homosexual world, that accounts for the simplistic explanations of so much current analysis of the problem.

We are now beginning to realize that social forces have an influence on all kinds of phenomena which we have hitherto analyzed in individual terms. We are beginning to understand, for example, that even physical illness such as heart disease and cancer may be influenced by sociological factors and that such illnesses vary in different parts of the population, in different socioeconomic and ethnic groups. If this be the case, as is plainly indicated by recent studies, then it ought to be clear that the relationship of the homosexual to a larger hostile society must have profound effects on his life which go considerably beyond the legal and social dangers of exposure. It is certainly very clear that one of the reasons for promiscuity is that to some extent, and in many cases, it provides anonymity, for if the partner is not known, then no follow-up of the relationship is possible. If a prominent individual has sex with another man in the park and no non-sexual contact is made, then there is less likelihood that he may be found out. In other words, the need to manage information about one's deviant activity leads to much of the anonymous promiscuity of the gay world.

I want to take the analysis to a deeper level and indicate that actually embedded in the individual's concept of himself is the idea that his homosexual proclivities are bad and that to establish a relationship with another man is carrying these proclivities to a worse extreme. Thus, the instability of relationships which is frequently used as grounds for condemnation of homosexuals is, in fact, the very product of this condemnation. There is thus, to say the least, a strange irony in homosexuals being accused of not forming stable relationships, when it is the social prohibitions they suffer which largely prevent them from becoming involved in such relationships.

If the reader will grant that the analysis of the gay world presented in the foregoing pages is correct, he will most likely wonder as to the origins of this problem. The gay world, in many respects, is a bad scene, and it is so because of the way homosexuals and homosexuality are treated by the straight world. We could, of course, have spent a great many pages detailing accounts of frank persecution of homosexuals: rejection by their families, dismissals by employers, brutal treatment by law enforcement agencies, etc. The reason we have not done so is that we have had to assume, in an attempt to explore the more subtle aspects of the problems of the gay world, the reader would already be sophisticated enough about the ways in which an outcast group can be, and is being, persecuted, so that he would find a detailed accounting of gross inhumanity toward homosexuals to be unnecessary. Perhaps it was wrong to focus on the more subtle problem of relationships between homosexual men themselves; it seems, however, on the basis of my own research, that this is the central problem in the gay world and that it is therefore both scientifically the most interesting and socially the most significant question.

Nevertheless, as we have pointed out, the relation between this problem and the general persecution of homosexuals by society is a very intimate and inextricably connected one. The problem of intimacy between homosexual males is in very large part a product of that very same social repression which leads employers to fire certain of their workers when they discover, or even suspect, that they are gay.

What we are confronted with is a pervasive characteristic of contemporary Western culture, namely, a dread of homosexuality. This dread, which is in large part unconscious, is intimately tied to widely held notions about the nature of masculinity and to what males are and are not permitted in the way of behavior and feelings. When it comes to understanding this dread of homosexuality we owe a very great debt to Freud, for it is his explanation which makes the most sense. Freud held that all individuals had sexual feelings toward members of their same sex, but that these had to be repressed in our society. Therefore, the dread of homosexuality is a result of, and derives its tremendous force from, the wishes for homosexual expression which are present in our unconscious minds. In other words, the fear is intimately connected with the wish, and the wish is only repressed because of the dread which is conjured up by the social taboo. The price, in short, for the repression of homosexual feelings is a very high one.

This price is paid in a very tragic way by those males who *are* able to overcome the repression against homosexual feelings. They pay for it in their inability to mix love and sex, by their isolation of sex from the other parts of their lives, and by their own conscious and unconscious feelings of guilt about their sexual activities. As anyone who saw the play *Tea and Sympathy* will remember, this price is also paid by very many heterosexual males who go through terrible agonies concerning their own masculinity, simply because they are in some ways unable to live up to a stereotype of what a "he-man" ought to be like. (One of the real benefits that will hopefully be derived from

the "hippie" movement is that the stereotype of masculinity which has dominated American culture for so long and which has been the source of great
unhappiness for so many of those who are unable to live up to it—even though
they be basically heterosexual—will be considerably diminished, and a male's
sexual and personal identity will no longer be threatened if he likes flowers or
cares about the texture of his clothes or likes to wear his hair long, etc.)

In 1911, Freud wrote an analysis of the published memoirs of Dr. Daniel
Paul Schreber, who was formerly an appellate court judge in Dresden. Schreber's
book was published in 1903 as *Memoirs of a Neurotic,* and Freud based
his general theory of paranoid delusions upon the analysis of this case. It is
unnecessary for us to repeat the train of thought which led to Freud's conclusions, since Freud's article is widely available and the reader may review it for
himself. For our purposes, it will suffice to look at Freud's conclusions. Freud
held that delusions of persecution arise because of repressed homosexual wishes.
The mechanism by which Freud believed this to occur was the following: The
individual felt positive, sexually charged feelings toward another male—"I love
him." But this feeling he was unable to bear because of the homosexual dread
in the culture. By means of a combination of defense mechanisms, the individual turns this feeling upside down, into a more acceptable feeling—"I hate him."
But, in order to justify this and allow himself to feel that his antagonism is
soundly based, the individual projects the hate onto the other person and says
—"He hates me."

This phenomenon of homosexual dread is, as we have stated explicitly,
more of a problem for males than it is for females. The reason this is so is
that the prohibition against intimate feelings toward one's own sex is much
stronger for the male than for the female in our society. Males are supposed to
be independent, rugged; they are not supposed to show tenderness toward each
other; and when the stereotype is pushed toward its logical conclusion, they are
not even allowed to show too much tenderness toward women. One of the
factors accounting for the problem of intimacy between homosexual males is
that, to the extent to which they have incorporated this masculine stereotype,
they have also identified with a fear of dependency, so that neither of them
wishes to be dependent on another male. Both wish to take the dominant role
in the relationship and this leads to no end of conflict in any kind of attempt
to form a stable partnership. Women, on the other hand, are encouraged to take
a dependent role and so their egos are not threatened by becoming emotionally
dependent on another person. This makes it much easier for them to form
stable, enduring kinds of intimate associations with another member of the
same sex.

Associated with the American concept of masculinity is the age-old degradation of women in Western society. It is not really necessary for me to review the history of the role of women in our society, since this has been done
in innumerable books, but let me only remind the reader that Western women
have always played, and still continue to play, the role of second-class citizens.
In general, neither church nor state has admitted them to the highest position
of honor, nor are they even allowed to enter into certain professions connected
with the church. In our own country, it was only fairly recently that women
were even allowed to vote in public elections. They have traditionally been

relegated to the home, and assigned the role of mother and housekeeper. The crucial fact here is not that women have been assigned the role of rearing children, for this is not an unsuitable role for one who is physiologically capable of nursing the baby (although this role is not true for all known cultures). What *is* crucial is that this role has been considered a second-class role and that all the status and power in society have been given to males.

So much of what goes on in the gay world can be understood if we see the homosexual community as a minority group subject to the same kinds of problems which other minority groups experience. Negroes are much more concerned with their skin color than are whites. The reason for this is obvious, namely, that their skin color has been defined as a problem by the larger society. In an analogous way, homosexuals are much more concerned with their sexuality than are heterosexuals, for the same reason, namely, that their sexual feelings have been defined as a problem by the straight world, and they have been subject to sanctions which are not altogether dissimilar from those which are thrust upon Negroes because of their skin color.

The gay world may thus be seen as a kind of non-geographical ghetto. It is not directly located on the map in clearly marked-off areas the way Negro and Mexican-American ghettos are, but it is a ghetto nevertheless and its inhabitants are subject to many of the same kinds of problems that other minority groups face. As Evelyn Hooker pointed out (1965b), there is a striking parallel between certain of the traits of minority group members who have been victimized by the larger society and many of the phenomena seen in the gay world. Hooker cites a number of "traits due to victimization" which are described by Gordon Allport in his book *The Nature of Prejudice* (1954) and says, "It would be strange indeed if all the traits caused by victimization in minority groups were, in the homosexual, produced by inner dynamics of the personality, for he too is a member of an out-group subject to extreme penalties, involving, according to Kinsey, 'cruelties [which] have not often been matched, except in religious and racial persecutions.' . . ."

The homosexual is caught up in a world in which there are no guides for conduct. Homosexuality in America is an anomic situation. The individual doesn't know what to do; there are no structures of social rules to help govern his behavior. He is, as soon as his homosexuality becomes conscious to him, more or less cast adrift by society and left to fare on his own, with only the very unsatisfactory supports of the gay world to guide him in his actions. He is, of course, very often cast forth in a very tragic way by his family, his employers, and his friends.

Society deals with homosexuality as if it did not exist. Although the situation is changing, this subject was not even discussed and was not even the object of scientific investigation until a few decades ago. We just didn't speak about these things; they were literally unspeakable and so loathsome that nothing could be said in polite society, or even in medical circles, about them. Aside from a few scientific books—many of them replete with stereotypes and inaccuracies—which were kept in special locked cabinets in the libraries of medical schools, individuals who had sensed in themselves the development of a homosexual orientation had nowhere to look for guidance. Physicians were untrained in this area because the subject was considered too unpleasant by all except psychiatry departments, which have, until recently, been held in low prestige by their medical colleagues. The whole treatment of homosexuals by the courts reflects, in many ways, a state of anomie, for the courts very often act as if they wish they didn't have to be bothered by such unpleasant business as dealing with a homosexual arrest. In other words, society did not like the subject, did not want to discuss it, did not want to take intelligent social action toward it, did not want to help those afflicted with problems related to it. Society simply wanted to get rid of it, but it did not know how to do that.

We may note, in passing, what is undoubtedly the reason for the popularity of the disease concept of homosexuality, which we have attempted to show is a concept which is scientifically untenable. The reason for its popularity is simply that it offers a way out in conceptualizing the problem. People don't like to think of homosexuality as sinful any longer, because the whole concept of sin has gone out of Western culture. To describe homosexuality as morally evil is now unfashionable. And yet the alternative, considering it as a legitimate way of life for some people, is simply not palatable to very many. Hence, the popularity of the disease concept. If homosexuality is labeled an illness, we can avoid these other alternatives. We don't need to blame the homosexual, and yet we don't have to accept him. He is simply sick and hence what we really want to do is to find a way of curing him. A reading of Irving Bieber's book will make it very clear that its author implies that the problem of homosexuality can be solved by psychoanalytic treatment. This is so absurd a notion that I hesitate to take the reader's time to discuss it at any length. Is it really possible to conceive that a problem involving so many millions of men can be solved through individual treatment methods which were designed for an entirely different class of individuals, for neurotics, who felt a desire for a radical change in their life situation and who voluntarily sought psychiatric attention? When one looks at Bieber's colleagues' psychoanalyses, one finds that a great percentage of those who were persuaded to give up homosexuality were already bisexual in the first place, and that in order for this change to be effected, they typically had to undergo around 350 hours of psychoanalysis, which costs in the neighborhood of $10,000. If this were a logical solution to the homosexual problem, we might begin to ask the question whether it is a feasible solution in terms of (a) time, (b) personnel available, and (c) money available. But we don't even need to do this because the solution itself is not even reasonable, simply because most male homosexuals do not want to change their sexual orientation and will certainly not visit a psychoanalyst for the purpose of undergoing "treatment" for a sexual orientation that they don't want to alter. Hence the implied promise (of a general solution to the problem through psychotherapy) made by those psychiatrists who wish to define homosexuality as a disease makes absolutely no sense in any terms. It is not practical in any way, and its only real function is to permit us to avoid seeing the problem in its real light. Are we going to move toward a rational examination of this serious social problem, or are we going to continue, ostrich-like, with our heads in the sand and avoid thinking about what a rational solution to this problem would entail. . . ?

A compelling scientific analysis of any serious social problem will carry with it implications for social change. If my analysis of the problem of homosexuality has been meaningful and convincing to the reader, he will at once see what needs to be done. Society as a whole must significantly shift its attitudes toward homosexuals and homosexuality in American life.

At one time in the history of our civilization, it was thought that unless everyone adhered to the same set of religious beliefs, society would crumble. The attempt to enforce religious conformity upon the populace brought out the worst in man's nature—including torture, war, and famine—has led to some of the darkest pages in the history of man's treatment of his fellow human creatures. Finally, at least in the contemporary West, we have emerged from this abominable state of coercion, and the history of the origins of America is, in part, a history of the development of religious tolerance. Religious tolerance means that we accept the idea that a society does not require, in order for it to continue in existence, the suppression of world views and conceptions of reality other than those held by the individuals who control power in the state. The separation of church and state, which is written into our Constitution, means that there exists for every citizen a private sphere in which he can think for himself about religious matters and worship God in the way he wants—or not worship at all, for that matter. This private sphere is guaranteed to him by the state itself, which has been shown to be quite a viable institution even without a uniform state religion.

What I am saying now is that the best solution to the problem of homosexuality is one which is modeled on the solution to the problem of religious difference, namely, a *radical tolerance for homosexual object-choice,* whether as a segment of an individual's sexual existence or as a full commitment to homosexuality as a way of life.

I suggest that we view homosexuals as a minority group, and begin to seriously consider giving them the full legal rights and social privileges that we *have* finally given to some minority groups (e.g., Roman Catholics) and that we talk about giving to others. This means, among other things, we will have to: (1) abolish the penalties that now exist for certain kinds of sexual relations between consenting adults in private; (2) end police activity against homosexuals, in all its forms, including use of decoys and harassment of gay bars and other homosexual meeting places; (3) cease firing government employees (including members of the armed forces) because they are thought to be homosexual; (4) encourage private industry to cease similar treatment of homosexual employees.

Homosexual sexual activity should be subject to no more stringent regulation than heterosexual activity. If, and only if, it becomes a genuine annoyance to those who do not wish involvement should the activity be subject to legal sanction. For example, if non-homosexual men are frequently annoyed by promiscuous homosexuals in certain lavatories, it would be appropriate for the police to guarantee these non-homosexuals their right to use these facilities in peace and quiet. There is, however, absolutely no moral justification for the harassment of gay bars and baths by police agencies and the arrest of respectable citizens in such locales. As a matter of fact, such establishments should be allowed to publicly advertise and label themselves as catering to homosexuals. They should, in other words, be allowed to exist officially, so that homosexuals may feel less ashamed about going into these places, and also that heterosexuals may know beforehand to what kind of clientele they cater.

These specific changes would, to a large degree, need to be predicated upon and be associated with a real change in the overall public attitude toward homosexuality. Instead of viewing this form of object-choice as an unspeakable horror, or even as a mental disease, the public should be encouraged to see it as what it actually is, i.e., a variation in the sexual impulse, which is one of the possible outcomes of human sexual development, and—most significantly—one which need not do harm to anyone. If the social attitude could move in this direction, we would see the causal connection between homosexuality and psychopathology—which now exists in certain forms, as I have indicated— begin to recede. We would see homosexuals develop into better-adjusted persons and we would, in my judgment, see less sex fetishism and instability of relationships in the gay world.

To carry this analysis to its utopian conclusion, we would see the end of the gay world as a hidden, deviant subculture, lurking in the unhappy interstices of the larger society. Instead, we would simply see homosexuals and heterosexuals and bisexuals within our social world, all living their lives without having to endure persecution.

Is this all a utopian dream? Is it really possible? Frankly, I don't know. Our society, like most others, is very slow in changing social attitudes, especially ones which go as deep into the hearts of the populace as do feelings about sexuality. Still, changes *are* occurring. During the past decade both England and Illinois have abolished age-old statutes prohibiting homosexual men from having sexual relations in private. While such legal changes are only a beginning, they *are* a necessary beginning, and they do indicate a greater degree of tolerance in the society as a whole.

There are other encouraging signs. Homosexuality is now being discussed in popular magazines, on television, in the sex education courses that are developing in our schools. Many are discovering that homosexuals are real people, not rare oddities of fun, and that perhaps they should be treated with human dignity.

32

ARTHUR SCHLESINGER, Jr.

The Cuban Missile Crisis of 1962

The outstanding foreign policy crises in the Kennedy administra-
tion were the ill-fated Bay of Pigs invasion of April, 1961, and the
missile crisis of October, 1962. The first occurrence was a measure
of Kennedy's naivete and insecurity, of his reliance on advice from
the Central Intelligence Agency and on military information; the
second reflected a matured self-reliance.

When Kennedy came to office, he inherited from the Eisen-
hower administration the option of an exile attack on Fidel Castro's
regime. Allen Dulles' CIA advised him that a Cuban beachhead
would generate anti-Castro action behind the lines. The Joint Chiefs
of Staff, Secretary of Defense Robert McNamara, and Secretary of
State Dean Rusk all approved the plan. Senator William Fulbright,
United Nations Ambassador Adlai Stevenson, and Arthur Schles-
inger, Jr., thought it reckless, which indeed it was. After the pa-
thetically unsuccessful invasion, the New Frontier, in Schlesinger's
words, looked like a collection of "stupid, ineffectual imperialists."

It is hard to believe that the same President a year later
blended caution and firmness so skillfully in the missile crisis.
Schlesinger, a White House aide under Kennedy and a well-known
American historian, tells the dramatic story with an insider's
knowledge.

1. THE GAMBLE

On July 2, 1962, Raúl Castro, the Minister of the Armed Forces of Cuba, arrived in Moscow. Either before his arrival or very soon thereafter the Soviet and
Cuban governments arrived at a startling decision: that Soviet nuclear missiles
were to be secretly installed in Cuba in the fall.

The Soviet Union had never before placed nuclear missiles in any other
country—neither in the communist nations of Eastern Europe, nor, even in

the season of their friendship, in Red China. Why should it now send nuclear missiles to a country thousands of miles away, lying within the zone of vital interest of their main adversary, a land, moreover, headed by a willful leader of, from the Russian viewpoint, somewhat less than total reliability? Castro, with characteristic loquacity, later produced a confusion of explanations. He told a Cuban audience in January 1963 that sending the missiles was a Soviet idea; he repeated this to Claude Julien of *Le Monde* in March 1963; in May he described it to Lisa Howard of the American Broadcasting Company as "simultaneous action on the part of both governments"; then in October he told Herbert Matthews of the *New York Times* that it was a Cuban idea, only to tell Jean Daniel of *L'Express* in November that it was a Soviet idea; in January 1964, when Matthews called him about the Daniel story, Castro claimed again that it was a Cuban idea; and, when Cyrus Sulzberger of the *New York Times* asked him in October 1964, Castro, pleading that the question raised security problems, said cagily, "Both Russia and Cuba participated."

As for the Russians, Khrushchev told the Supreme Soviet in December 1962, "We carried weapons there at the request of the Cuban government . . . including the stationing of a couple of score of Soviet IRBMs [intermediate-range ballistic missiles] in Cuba. These weapons were to be in the hands of Soviet military men. . . . Our aim was only to defend Cuba." The presence of the missiles, Khrushchev continued, was designed to make the imperialists understand that, if they tried to invade Cuba, "the war which they threatened to start stood at their own borders, so that they would realize more realistically the dangers of thermonuclear war." This was all very noble, and the defense of Cuba was certainly a side effect of the Soviet action. But the defense of Cuba did not really require the introduction of long-range nuclear missiles. One may be sure that Khrushchev, like any other national leader, took *that* decision not for Cuban reasons but for Soviet reasons. Pending Khrushchev's reminiscences, one can only speculate as to what these Soviet reasons were.

In a general sense, the decision obviously represented the supreme Soviet probe of American intentions. No doubt a 'total victory' faction in Moscow had long been denouncing the government's 'no-win' policy and arguing that the Soviet Union could safely use the utmost nuclear pressure against the United States because the Americans were too rich or soft or liberal to fight. Now Khrushchev was prepared to give this argument its crucial test. A successful nuclearization of Cuba would make about sixty-four medium-range (around 1000 miles) and intermediate-range (1500–2000 miles) nuclear missiles effective against the United States and thereby come near to doubling Soviet striking capacity against American targets. Since this would still leave the United States with at least a 2 to 1 superiority in nuclear power targeted against the Soviet Union, the shift in the military balance of power would be less crucial than that in the political balance. Every country in the world, watching so audacious an action ninety miles from the United States, would wonder whether it could ever thereafter trust Washington's resolution and protection. More particularly, the change in the nuclear equilibrium would permit Khrushchev, who had been dragging out the Berlin negotiation all year, to reopen that question—perhaps in a personal appearance before the United Nations General Assembly in November—with half the United States lying within range of nuclear missiles poised for delivery across the small stretch of water from Florida. It was a staggering project—staggering in its recklessness, staggering in its misconception of the American response, staggering in its rejection of the ground rules for coexistence among the superpowers which Kennedy had offered in Vienna.

The decision having been made, the next problem was the development of a plan. Moscow evidently saw the operation in two stages—first, the augmentation of Cuban defensive capabilities by bringing in surface-to-air anti-aircraft (SAM) missiles and MIG-21 fighters; then, as soon as the SAMS were in place to protect the bases and deter photographic reconnaissance (a SAM had brought down the U-2 over Russia in 1960), sending in offensive weapons, both ballistic missiles and Ilyushin-28 jet aircraft able to deliver nuclear bombs. The first stage, involving only defensive weapons, required no special concealment. The second stage called for the most careful and complex program of deception. One can only imagine the provisions made in Moscow and Havana through the summer to ship the weapons, to receive them, unload them, assemble them, erect bases for them, install them on launching pads—all with a stealth and speed designed to confront the United States one day in November or December with a fully operational Soviet nuclear arsenal across the water in Cuba.

2. THE SURVEILLANCE

By late July the Soviet shipments began to arrive. Three weeks later CIA sent an urgent report to the President that "something new and different" was taking place in Soviet aid operations to Cuba. There were perhaps 5000 Soviet 'specialists' now in Cuba; military construction of some sort was going on; more ships were on their way with more specialists and more electronic and construction equipment. The data suggested that the Soviet Union was refurbishing the Cuban air defense system, presumably by putting up a network of SAM sites.

The intelligence community concluded that Moscow, having resolved after a time of indecision that it had a large stake in Castro's survival, had decided to insure the regime against external attack. It could thereby hope to secure the Soviet bridgehead in the western hemisphere, strengthen Castro's prestige in Latin America and show the world Washington's inability to prevent such things at its very doorstep. This all seemed logical enough. Obviously Moscow had calculated that the United States, with the Bay of Pigs still in the world's recollection, could not convincingly object to Castro's taking defensive precautions against another invasion. No one in the intelligence community (with one exception; for the thought flickered through the mind of John McCone) supposed that the Soviet Union would conceivably go beyond defensive weapons. The introduction of nuclear missiles, for example, would obviously legitimatize an American response, even possibly an invasion of Cuba. Our best Soviet experts in State and CIA considered Khrushchev too wary and Soviet foreign policy too rational to court a risk of this magnitude.

Nonetheless, when a U-2 flight on August 29 showed clear evidence of SAM sites under construction, the President decided to put Moscow on notice. On September 4, the Secretary of State brought over a draft of the warning. The President showed it to the Attorney General, who recommended stiffening it with an explicit statement that we would not tolerate the import of offensive weapons. The draft as revised read that, while we had no evidence of "significant offensive capability either in Cuban hands or under Soviet direction," should it be otherwise, "the gravest issues would arise."

On the same day the Soviet Ambassador In Washington gave the Attorney General an unusual personal message from Khrushchev for the President. The Soviet leader pledged in effect that he would stir up no incidents before the congressional elections in November. Then a week later, in the midst of a long and wearying disquisition on world affairs, Moscow said flatly that the "armaments and military equipment sent to Cuba are designed exclusively for defensive purposes." It added:

> There is no need for the Soviet Union to shift its weapons for the repulsion of aggression, for a retaliatory blow, to any other country, for instance Cuba. Our nuclear weapons are so powerful in their explosive force and the Soviet Union has so powerful rockets to carry these nuclear warheads, that there is no need to search for sites for them beyond the boundaries of the Soviet Union.

The statement continued truculently by accusing the United States of "preparing for aggression against Cuba and other peace-loving states," concluding that "if the aggressors unleash war our armed forces must be ready to strike a crushing retaliatory blow at the aggressor." The President responded calmly two days later at his press conference that the new shipments did not constitute a serious threat but that if at any time Cuba were to "become an offensive military base of significant capacity for the Soviet Union, then this country will do whatever must be done to protect its own security and that of its allies." In the meantime, he asked Congress for stand-by authority to call up the reserves.

He had also taken the precaution of doubling the frequency of the U-2 overflights of Cuba. The evidence from flights on September 5, 17, 26, and 29 and October 5 and 7, as well as from other sources, indicated a continuing military build-up large in its proportions but still defensive in its character. The government saw no reason as yet to believe that Khrushchev intended anything beyond this; he had not, so far as we knew, lost his mind. Only John McCone had his personal presentiment that he might be planning the installation of offensive missiles. However, given the prevailing complacency on this point, McCone himself did not take this thought seriously enough to prevent his going off now for a three weeks' honeymoon in Europe. The White House staff worried about this increasingly visible Soviet presence, but it seemed to me much more a political threat to Latin America than a military threat to the United States. I found myself, as I told the President on September 13, relatively a hard-liner and felt that the State Department should tell the Soviet Ambassador in cold and tough fashion that persistence in the arming of Cuba would cause both an increase in our defense budget and a surge of national indignation which would color every other issue between our two countries. But, when I advanced this view at the Bundy staff meeting, I was confronted with the wholly proper question: "OK, but how far would you carry it if they keep on doing what you object to?"

And, across the world, ships were sliding out of Black Sea harbors with nuclear technicians in their cabins and nuclear missiles in their hatches. Khrushchev, having done his best to lull Kennedy by public statements and private messages, now in early September put the second stage of his plan into operation. He could hope that the hurricane season might interfere with the U-2 overflights and that the fall political campaign might inhibit the administration from taking drastic action. Moreover, he had an advantage unknown to us: Soviet engineering had enormously reduced the time required for the erection of nuclear missile sites. As Roberta Wohlstetter, the searching analyst of both Pearl Harbor and the Cuba crisis, later wrote, "The rapidity of the Russians' installation was in effect a logistical surprise comparable to the technological surprise at the time of Pearl Harbor."

In the meantime, Washington had been receiving a flow of tales about nuclear installations through refugee channels. Such reports had been routine for eighteen months. No one could be sure whether the sources in Cuba could tell a surface-to-air from a surface-to-surface missile; moreover, this government recalled that it had been misled by Cuban refugees before. Lacking photographic verification, the intelligence community treated the information with reserve. In the meantime, it recommended on October 4 a U-2 flight over western Cuba. The recommendation was approved on October 10, and from the eleventh to the thirteenth the pilot and plane waited for the weather to break. Sunday the fourteenth dawned beautiful and cloudless.

Senator Kenneth Keating of New York had also been receiving the refugee reports, and he treated them with no reserve at all. At the end of August he began a campaign to force the government into some unspecified form of action. In October he began to talk about offensive missile bases. If he felt the national safety involved, Keating was plainly right to make his case with all the urgency at his command. Some, however, discerned other motives, especially with the approach of the fall election. As Roger Hilsman, Director of Intelligence and Research at the State Department, later wrote, "The charge that Keating was more interested in personal publicity than in his country's welfare may be extreme. But until the Senator comes forward with a better explanation than he has so far supplied, one of two possible conclusions is inescapable: Either Senator Keating was peddling someone's rumors for some purpose of his own, despite the highly dangerous international situation; or, alternatively, he had information the United States Government did not have that could have guided a U-2 to the missile sites before October 14, and at less risk to the pilot."

Now on the fourteenth the U-2 plane returned from its mission. The negatives went swiftly to the processing laboratories, then to the interpretation center, where specialists pored over the blown-up photographs frame by frame.

Late Monday afternoon, reading the obscure and intricate markings, they identified a launching pad, a series of buildings for ballistic missiles and even one missile on the ground in San Cristóbal.

3. THE EXECUTIVE COMMITTEE

About 8:30 that evening the CIA informed Bundy of the incredible discovery. Bundy reflected on whether to inform the President immediately, but he knew that Kennedy would demand the photographs and supporting interpretation in order to be sure the report was right and knew also it would take all night to prepare the evidence in proper form. Furthermore, an immediate meeting would collect officials from dinner parties all over town, signal Washington that something was up and end any hope of secrecy. It was better, Bundy thought, to let the President have a night's sleep in preparation for the ordeal ahead.

The President was having breakfast in his dressing gown at eight forty-five on Tuesday morning when Bundy brought the news. Kennedy asked at once about the nature of the evidence. As soon as he was convinced that it was conclusive, he said that the United States must bring the threat to an end: one way or another the missiles would have to be removed. He then directed Bundy to institute low-level photographic flights and to set up a meeting of top officials. Privately he was furious: if Khrushchev could pull this after all his protestations and denials, how could he ever be trusted on anything?

The meeting, beginning at eleven forty-five that morning, went on with intermissions for the rest of the week. The group soon became known as the Executive Committee, presumably of the National Security Council; the press later dubbed it familiarly ExCom, though one never heard that phrase at the time. It carried on its work with the most exacting secrecy: nothing could be worse than to alert the Russians before the United States had decided on its own course. For this reason its members—the President, the Vice-President, Rusk, McNamara, Robert Kennedy, General Taylor, McCone, Dillon, Adlai Stevenson, Bundy, Sorensen, Ball, Gilpatric, Llewellyn Thompson, Alexis Johnson, Edwin Martin, with others brought in on occasion, among them Dean Acheson and Robert Lovett—had to attend their regular meetings, keep as many appointments as possible and preserve the normalities of life. Fortunately the press corps, absorbed in the congressional campaign, was hardly disposed or situated to notice odd comings and goings. And so the President himself went off that night to dinner at Joseph Alsop's as if nothing had happened. After dinner the talk turned to the contingencies of history, the odds for or against any particular event taking place. The President was silent for a time. Then he said, "Of course, if you simply consider mathematical chances, the odds are even on an H-bomb war within ten years." Perhaps he added to himself, "or within ten days."

In the Executive Committee consideration was free, intent and continuous. Discussion ranged widely, as it had to in a situation of such exceptional urgency, novelty and difficulty. When the presence of the President seemed by virtue of the solemnity of his office to have a constraining effect, preliminary meetings were held without him. Every alternative was laid on the table for examination, from living with the missiles to taking them out by surprise attack, from making the issue with Castro to making it with Khrushchev. In effect, the members walked around the problem, inspecting it first from this angle, then found that, viewing it in a variety of perspectives. In the course of the long hours of thinking aloud, hearing new arguments, entertaining new considerations, they almost all found themselves moving from one position to another. "If we had had to act on Wednesday in the first twenty-four hours," the President said later, "I don't think probably we would have chosen as prudently as we finally did." They had, it was estimated, about ten days before the missiles would be on pads ready for firing. The deadline defined the strategy. It meant that the response could not, for example, be confided to the United Nations, where the Soviet delegate would have ample opportunity to stall action until the nuclear weapons were in place and on target. It meant that we could not even risk the delay involved in consulting our allies. It meant that the total responsibility had to fall on the United States and its President.

On the first Tuesday morning the choice for a moment seemed to lie between an air strike or acquiescence—and the President had made it clear that acquiescence was impossible. Listening to the discussion, the Attorney General scribbled a wry note: "I now know how Tojo felt when he was planning Pearl Harbor." Then he said aloud that the group needed more alternatives: surely there was some course in between bombing and doing nothing: suppose, for example, we were to bring countervailing pressure by placing nuclear missiles in Berlin? The talk continued, and finally the group dispersed for further reflection.

The next step was military preparation for Caribbean contingencies. A Navy-Marine amphibious exercise in the area, long scheduled for this week, provided a convenient cover for the build-up of an amphibious task force, soon including 40,000 Marines; there were 5000 more in Guantanamo. The Army's 82nd and 101st Airborne Divisions were made ready for immediate deployment; altogether the Army soon gathered more than 100,000 troops in Florida. SAC bombers left Florida airfields to make room for tactical fighter aircraft flown in from bases all over the country. Air defense facilities were stripped from places outside the range of the Cuban missiles and re-installed in the Southeast. As the days went by, 14,000 reservists were recalled to fly transport planes in the eventuality of airborne operations.

In the meantime, the Pentagon undertook a technical analysis of the requirements for a successful strike. The conclusion, as it evolved during the week, was that a 'surgical' strike confined to the nuclear missile bases alone would leave the airports and IL-28s untouched; moreover, we could not be sure in advance that we had identified or could destroy all the missile sites. A limited strike therefore might expose the United States to nuclear retaliation. Military prudence called for a much larger strike to eliminate all sources of danger; this would require perhaps 500 sorties. Anything less, the military urged, would destroy our credibility before the world and leave our own nation in intolerable peril. Moreover, this was a heaven-sent opportunity to get rid of the Castro regime forever and re-establish the security of the hemisphere.

It was a strong argument, urged by strong men. But there were arguments on the other side. The Soviet experts pointed out that even a limited strike would kill the Russians manning the missile sites and might well provoke the Soviet Union into drastic and unpredictable response, perhaps nuclear war. The Latin American experts added that a massive strike would kill thousands of innocent Cubans and damage the United States permanently in the hemisphere. The Europeanists said the world would regard a surprise attack as an excessive response. Even if it did not produce Soviet retaliation against the United States, it would invite the Russians to move against Berlin in circumstances where the blame would fall, not on them, but on us. It would thereby give Moscow a chance to shift the venue to a place where the stake was greater than Cuba and our position weaker. In the Caribbean, we had overwhelming superiority in conventional military force; the only recourse for the Soviet Union there would be to threaten the world with nuclear war. But in Berlin, where the Russians had overwhelming conventional superiority, it was the United States which would have to flourish nuclear bombs.

All these considerations encouraged the search for alternatives. When the Executive Committee met on Wednesday, Secretary McNamara advanced an idea which had been briefly mentioned the day before and from which he did not thereafter deviate—the conception of a naval blockade designed to stop the further entry of offensive weapons into Cuba and hopefully to force the removal of the missiles already there. Here was a middle course between inaction and battle, a course which exploited our superiority in local conventional power and would permit subsequent movement either toward war or toward peace.

As the discussion proceeded through Thursday, the supporters of the air strike marshaled their arguments against the blockade. They said that it would not neutralize the weapons already within Cuba, that it could not possibly bring enough pressure on Khrushchev to remove those weapons, that it would permit work to go ahead on the bases and that it would mean another Munich. The act of stopping and searching ships would engage us with Russians instead of Cubans. The obvious retort to our blockade of Cuba would be a Soviet blockade of Berlin. Despite such arguments, however, the majority of the Executive Committee by the end of the day was tending toward a blockade.

That afternoon, in the interests of normality, the President received the Soviet Foreign Minister Andrei Gromyko. It was one of the more extraordinary moments of an extraordinary week. Kennedy knew that there were Soviet nuclear missiles in Cuba. Gromyko unquestionably knew this too, but did not know that Kennedy knew it. His emphasis was rather grimly on Berlin, almost as if to prepare the ground for demands later in the autumn. When the talk turned to Cuba, Gromyko heavily stressed the Cuban fears of an American invasion and said with due solemnity that the Soviet aid had "solely the purpose of contributing to the defense capabilities of Cuba"; "if it were otherwise," the Russian continued, "the Soviet Government would never become involved in rendering such assistance." To dispel any illusion about possible American reactions, the President read the Foreign Minister the key sentences from his statement of September 13. He went no further because he did not wish to indicate his knowledge until he had decided on his course.

In the evening the President met with the Executive Committee. Listening again to the alternatives over which he had been brooding all week, he said crisply, "Whatever you fellows are recommending today you will be sorry about a week from now." He was evidently attracted by the idea of the blockade. It avoided war, preserved flexibility and offered Khrushchev time to reconsider his actions. It could be carried out within the framework of the Organization of American States and the Rio Treaty. Since it could be extended to non-military items as occasion required, it could become an instrument of steadily intensifying pressure. It would avoid the shock effect of a surprise attack, which would hurt us politically through the world and might provoke Moscow to an insensate response against Berlin or the United States itself. If it worked, the Russians could retreat with dignity. If it did not work, the Americans retained the option of military action. In short, the blockade, by enabling us to proceed one step at a time, gave us control over the future. Kennedy accordingly directed that preparations be made to put the weapons blockade into effect on Monday morning.

The next day the President, keeping to his schedule, left Washington for a weekend of political barnstorming in Ohio and Illinois. In Springfield, Illinois, after a speech at the State Fairgrounds, he paused to lay flowers on Lincoln's tomb.

4. THE DECISION

Kennedy left behind a curiously restless group of advisers. This became evident when they met at the State Department at eleven on Friday morning. Over Ted Sorensen's protest that a decision had been reached the night before and should not be reopened now, several began to re-argue the inadequacy of the blockade. Someone said: Why not confront the world with a *fait accompli* by taking out the bases in a clean and swift operation? It was a test of wills, another said, and the sooner there was a showdown, the better. Someone else said that it was now or never; we must hit the bases before they became operational. If we took a decision that morning, the planes could strike on Sunday. But, if we committed ourselves to a blockade, it would be hard, if not impossible, to move on thereafter to military action.

Secretary McNamara, however, firmly reaffirmed his opposition to a strike and his support for the blockade. Then Robert Kennedy, speaking with quiet intensity, said that he did not believe that, with all the memory of Pearl Harbor and all the responsibility we would have to bear in the world afterward, the President of the United States could possibly order such an operation. For 175 years we had not been that kind of country. Sunday-morning surprise blows on small nations were not in our tradition. Thousands of Cubans would be killed without warning, and hundreds of Russians too. We were fighting for something more than survival, and a sneak attack would constitute a betrayal of our heritage and our ideals. The blockade, the Attorney General concluded, would demonstrate the seriousness of our determination to get the missiles out of Cuba and at the same time allow Moscow time and room to pull back from its position of peril. It was now proposed that the committee break up into working groups to write up the alternative courses for the President—one to analyze the quarantine policy, the other to analyze the strike. Then everyone dispersed to meet again at four o'clock for a discussion of the competing scenarios.[1]

At the second meeting the balance of opinion clearly swung back to the blockade (though, since a blockade was technically an act of war, it was thought better to refer to it as a quarantine). In retrospect most participants regarded Robert Kennedy's speech as the turning point. The case was strengthened too when the military representatives conceded that a quarantine now would not exclude a strike later. There was brief discussion of a *démarche* to Castro, but it was decided to concentrate on Khrushchev. Then they turned to the problem of the missiles already in Cuba. Someone observed that the United States would have to pay a price to get them out; perhaps we should throw in our now obsolescent and vulnerable Jupiter missile bases in Italy and Turkey, whose removal the Joint Congressional Committee on Atomic Energy as well as the Secretary of Defense had recommended in 1961. After a couple of hours, Adlai Stevenson, who had had to miss the day's meetings because of UN commitments, arrived from New York. He expressed his preference for the quarantine over the strike but wondered whether it might not be better to try the diplomatic route also. We must, he said, start thinking about our negotiating position; for example, a settlement might include the neutralization of Cuba under international guarantees and UN inspection; demilitarization would, of course, include our own base at Guantanamo as well as the Soviet installations. The integrity of Cuba should be guaranteed. He also echoed the suggestion that we might want to consider giving up the Italian and Turkish bases now, since we were planning to do so eventually.

The President, still campaigning, received reports from his brother in Washington. The schedule now called for a speech to the nation on Sunday night. By Saturday morning, however, it was evident that preparations would not be complete in time, so it was decided to hold things for another twenty-four hours. Meanwhile, the President, pleading a cold, canceled the rest of his political trip and returned to Washington. Before leaving Chicago, he called Jacqueline and suggested that she and the children come back from Glen Ora, where they had gone for the weekend.

That afternoon he presided over the Executive Committee and its final debate. McNamara impressively presented the case for the blockade. The military, with some civilian support, argued for the strike. Stevenson spoke with force about the importance of a political program, the President agreeing in

---

[1] The Secretary of State took little part in these discussions. John M. Hightower, who covers the State Department for the Associated Press, wrote on August 22, 1965: "Criticism over his role in the missile crisis angered Rusk to the point that he heatedly defended it in talks with newsmen on one or two occasions. He said that the responsibility of the Secretary of State was to advise the President and he did not think he should commit himself before all the facts were in. Therefore he withdrew himself from the argument for several days though Under Secretary of State George Ball, instructed by Rusk to take a free hand, presented the State Department viewpoint."

principle but disagreeing with his specific proposals. A straw vote indicated eleven for the quarantine, six for the strike. The President observed that everyone should hope his plan was not adopted; there just was no clear-cut answer. When someone proposed that each participant write down his recommendation, Kennedy said he did not want people, if things went wrong, claiming that their plans would have worked. Then he issued orders to get everything ready for the quarantine. On Sunday morning a final conference with the military leaders satisfied him that the strike would be a mistake. His course was now firmly set.

5. THE CRISIS

I knew nothing about any of this until late Friday. October 19, when Adlai Stevenson phoned me, saying casually that he was in Washington and wondered when we could get together. He was staying at the house of his friend Dr. Paul Magnuson across the street from my own house in Georgetown, and we agreed to ride down to the State Department together the next day. When we met after breakfast on Saturday morning, he beckoned me into the Magnuson house. "I don't want to talk in front of the chauffeur," he said; and then in a moment, "Do you know what the secret discussions this week have been about?" I said I knew of no discussions; the President was out campaigning; I had presumed that everything was fine. Adlai, observing gravely that there was trouble and he had the President's permission to tell me about it, described the seesaw during the week between the diplomatic and military solutions. The quarantine, he now felt, was sure to win. He would have to make a speech early in the week at the Security Council, and he wanted me to help on it. He outlined the argument and, with due discretion, I set to work.

The secret had been superbly kept. But later in the day, when the President returned from the campaign and Rusk canceled a speech that night, a sense of premonitory excitement began to engulf Washington. Already those whose business it was to sniff things out were on the track. In the British Embassy, where a delegation of intelligence officers had come to Washington for a long-scheduled conference with the CIA, suspicions had been aroused early in the week when the meetings drew a diminishing American representation or were called off altogether. By process of elimination the 007s decided on Friday that it must be Cuba. The *New York Times,* noting the troop movements and other unusual activities, also deduced Cuba by the weekend and even speculated about nuclear missiles. James Reston wrote the story and checked it with the White House. The President himself called Orville Dryfoos, the publisher of the *Times,* to say that publication might confront him with a Moscow ultimatum before he had the chance to put his own plans into effect; once again, the *Times* killed a story about Cuba. By Saturday night the town was alive with speculation and anticipation. A good deal of the government found itself late that evening at a dance given by the James Rowes. Here the gap between the witting and the unwitting could almost be detected by facial expressions—on the one hand, anxiety tinged with self-satisfaction; on the other, irritation and frustration. Henry Brandon, the Washington correspondent of the London *Sunday Times,* who had just returned from a trip to Cuba, began to wonder when a succession of top officials asked him elaborately off-hand questions about the mood in Havana.

On Sunday Stevenson, contemplating the problems of gathering UN backing for the quarantine, wrote down his thoughts about our UN strategy. He saw no hope of mustering enough votes in the UN to authorize action against Cuba in advance; but the OAS offered an opportunity for multilateral support, and OAS approval could provide some protection in law and a great deal in public opinion. As for the UN, he said, we must seize the initiative, bringing our case to the Security Council at the same time we imposed the quarantine. In order to avert resolutions against the quarantine, he continued, we should be ready to propose a political path out of the military crisis. His negotiating program, following his remarks to the Executive Committee, centered on the removal of Soviet military equipment and personnel—i.e., missiles, installations and the several thousand Russian specialists—under UN observation and the introduction of UN influence into Cuba in the hope of ending communist domination of the Cuban government. He would throw a non-invasion guarantee and Guantanamo into the bargain to evidence our restraint and good faith. Exercising the prerogative freely employed that week by nearly all his colleagues, he now wrote that Turkey and Italy should not be included; this would only divert attention from the Cuban threat to the general issue of foreign bases. That problem might later be considered apart from Cuba in the context of general disarmament.

The President, however, rightly regarded any political program as premature. He wanted to concentrate on a single issue—the enormity of the introduction of the missiles and the absolute necessity for their removal. Stevenson's negotiating program was accordingly rejected. Stevenson, when I saw him that week-end, took this realistically; he felt he had done his job as the custodian of our UN interests in making the recommendation, and the decision was the President's. However, some of his colleagues on the Executive Committee felt strongly that the thought of negotiations at this point would be taken as an admission of the moral weakness of our case and the military weakness of our posture. They worried considerably over the weekend (and some of them vocally thereafter) whether, denied his political program, Stevenson would make the American argument with sufficient force in the UN debate.

I spent all day Sunday till well after midnight working at the State Department with Harlan Cleveland, Joseph Sisco and Thomas Wilson on the UN speech. At ten o'clock on Monday morning the President called me in to instruct me to go to New York and assist Stevenson on the UN presentation. He was in a calm and reflective mood. It was strange, he said, how no one in the intelligence community had anticipated the Soviet attempt to transform Cuba into a nuclear base; everyone had assumed that the Russians would not be so stupid as to offer us this pretext for intervention. I asked why he thought Khrushchev had done such an amazing thing. He said that, first, it might draw Russia and China closer together, or at least strengthen the Soviet position in the communist world, by showing that Moscow was capable of bold action in support of a communist revolution; second, that it would radically redefine the setting in which the Berlin problem could be reopened after the election; third, that it would deal the United States a tremendous political blow. When I remarked that the Russians must have supposed we would not respond, Kennedy said, "They thought they had us either way. If we did nothing, we would be dead. If we reacted, they hoped to put us in an exposed position, whether with regard to Berlin or Turkey or the UN."

I met with him again at eleven to go over the draft of the UN speech with Rusk, Robert Kennedy and others. The President suggested a few omissions, including a passage threatening an American strike if the Soviet build-up in Cuba continued; he preferred to leave that to Moscow's imagination. The Attorney General drew me aside to say, "We're counting on you to watch things in New York. . . . We will have to make a deal at the end, but we must stand absolutely firm now. Concessions must come at the end of negotiation, not at the beginning." Then, clutching the speech, I caught the first plane to New York.

In Washington everything awaited the President's television broadcast that night to the nation. Sorensen had been laboring over the draft since Friday. Kennedy himself was never more composed. At four o'clock he had an appointment with Prime Minister Milton Obote of Uganda. Wholly at ease, he talked for forty-five minutes about the problems of Africa and Uganda as if he had nothing on his mind and all the time in the world. Angier Biddle Duke of the State Department remarked to Obote on their way back to Blair House that a crisis of some sort was imminent; the Ugandan was incredulous and, when he heard Kennedy's speech that evening, forever impressed.

At five o'clock Kennedy saw the congressional leaders, many of whom had flown in from their home states in Air Force planes. He showed them the U-2 photographs and told them what he proposed to do. Senator Russell of Georgia disagreed; the quarantine, he said, would be too slow and too risky—the only solution was invasion. To the President's surprise, Fulbright, who had opposed invasion so eloquently eighteen months before, now supported Russell. The President listened courteously but was in no way shaken in his decision. (Kennedy told me later, "The trouble is that, when you get a group of senators together, they are always dominated by the man who takes the boldest and strongest line. That is what happened the other day. After Russell spoke, no one wanted to take issue with him. When you can talk to them individually, they are reasonable.")

Then at seven o'clock the speech: his expression grave, his voice firm and calm, the evidence set forth without emotion, the conclusion unequivocal—"The purpose of these bases can be none other than to provide a nuclear strike capability against the Western Hemisphere." He recited the Soviet assurances, now revealed as "deliberate deception," and called the Soviet action "a deliberately provocative and unjustified change in the status quo which cannot be accepted by this country, if our courage and our commitments are ever to be trusted again by either friend or foe." Our "unswerving objective," he continued, was to end this nuclear threat to the Americas. He then laid out what he called with emphasis his *initial* steps: a quarantine on all offensive military equipment under shipment to Cuba; an intensified surveillance of Cuba itself; a declaration that any missile launched from Cuba would be regarded as an attack by the Soviet

Union on the United States, requiring full retaliatory response upon the Soviet Union; an immediate convening of the Organization of American States to consider the threat to hemisphere security; an emergency meeting of the UN Security Council to consider the threat to world peace; and an appeal to Chairman Khrushchev "to abandon this course of world domination, and to join in an historic effort to end the perilous arms race and to transform the history of man."

He concluded with quiet solemnity. "My fellow citizens: let no one doubt that this is a difficult and dangerous effort. . . . No one can foresee precisely what course it will take or what costs or casualties will be incurred. . . . But the greatest danger of all would be to do nothing. . . . Our goal is not the victory of might, but the vindication of right—not peace at the expense of freedom, but both peace *and* freedom, here in this hemisphere, and, we hope, around the world. God willing, that goal will be achieved."

After the broadcast the President returned to the Mansion, sought out Caroline and told her stories until it was time for dinner. He dined alone with Jacqueline.

6. THE REACTION

We listened to the speech clustered around a television set in Stevenson's office in New York. I had found Adlai unperturbed in the midst of pandemonium. The Mission was a frenzy of activity in preparation for the Security Council. The UN had never seemed so much like a permanent political convention: so many people to be considered and cajoled, so many issues going at once, such an inherent unpredictability about the parliamentary sequence. From the moment of the President's statement, Stevenson had to talk so much to UN delegates from other nations that he had little time left for his own speeches and strategy. Through Monday evening and Tuesday morning he snatched moments to revise and edit his remarks for the Security Council. It was reminiscent of his presidential campaigns: the last part of his address was still in the typewriter at the Mission on Tuesday afternoon when he had already begun to speak across the street at the UN.

The speech began at four o'clock. The OAS had been meeting since nine that morning. Edwin Martin had done a splendid job briefing the OAS ambassadors the night before, and Secretary Rusk, invoking the security resolution of Punta del Este, was now offering a resolution authorizing the use of force, individually or collectively, to carry out the quarantine. No one could doubt the OAS sentiment, but a number of ambassadors had not yet received instructions from their governments. As a result, the resolution establishing the legal basis for United States action was not passed until Stevenson was well into his speech.[2]

Martin, by prior arrangement, notified Harlan Cleveland the moment the

[2] It was passed unanimously. Uruguay, still awaiting instructions, abstained on Tuesday but changed its vote to affirmative on Wednesday.

OAS acted, and Cleveland instantly called Sisco in New York. Watching Stevenson on television, Cleveland could see Sisco leave the chamber to take the call, then in a moment return and place the text of the resolution on the desk in front of Stevenson. Stevenson, absorbed in his speech, talked on, apparently unaware of the sheet of paper before him. At this moment Kennedy, with characteristic attention to detail, called Cleveland and asked whether Stevenson knew about the OAS action. Cleveland replied that he had sent a message but feared that Adlai had not seen it. Just then on the screen Stevenson reached for the paper. Kennedy, who was also watching television, said, "I guess he has it now."

In New York Stevenson, who had been speaking with extraordinary eloquence to a hushed chamber, now read the OAS resolution. In another moment he concluded: "Since the end of the Second World War, there has been no threat to the vision of peace so profound, no challenge to the world of the Charter so fateful. The hopes of mankind are concentrated in this room. . . . Let [this day] be remembered, not as the day when the world came to the edge of nuclear war, but as the day when men resolved to let nothing thereafter stop them in their quest for peace." The President immediately dictated a telegram:

> DEAR ADLAI: I WATCHED YOUR SPEECH THIS AFTERNOON WITH GREAT SATISFACTION. IT HAS GIVEN OUR CAUSE A GREAT START. . . . THE UNITED STATES IS FORTUNATE TO HAVE YOUR ADVOCACY. YOU HAVE MY WARM AND PERSONAL THANKS.

And now the tension was rising. In Cuba workmen were laboring day and night to complete the bases. Forty-two medium-range nuclear missiles were being unpacked and prepared for launching pads with desperate speed. IL-28 aircraft were being assembled. On the Atlantic at least seventy-five Soviet merchant ships, some no doubt loaded with intermediate-range missiles, were steaming toward Cuba, their courses thus far unaltered after the President's speech. Ninety ships of the American fleet, backed up by sixty-eight aircraft squadrons and eight aircraft carriers, were moving into position to intercept and search the onrushing ships. In Florida and neighboring states the largest United States invasion force since the Second World War was gathering. In Moscow, the Soviet government in a long and angry statement insisted that the weapons in Cuba were defensive, ignored the charges of nuclear missiles and savagely denounced the American quarantine.

The United Nations was only the first step in gaining world understanding of the American position. Africa now assumed vital strategic importance because Soviet flights to Cuba would have to refuel at African airports. Both Sékou Touré in Guinea and Ben Bella in Algeria sent Kennedy their assurances that they would deny Russian aircraft transit rights. (Touré later added that the problem must be kept in a Soviet-American context; if it became a Cuban-American problem, we would lose support in the uncommitted world.) Most African states, moved no doubt by their faith in the American President, indicated private sympathy.

In Western Europe support was general, though there were waverings in Britain and Italy. In Paris General de Gaulle received Dean Acheson, the President's special emissary, and, without waiting to see the aerial photographs Acheson had brought along, said, "If there is a war, I will be with you. But there will be no war." De Gaulle went on to wonder whether the quarantine would be enough, and so did Adenauer, but both strongly backed the American position. . . .

On Tuesday night Kennedy dined quietly at the White House with English friends. Cuba was hardly mentioned at the table; but after dinner he beckoned David Ormsby Gore out into the long central hall, where they quietly talked while the gaiety continued in the dining room. The British Ambassador, mentioning the dubious reaction in his own country, suggested the need for evidence: could not the aerial photographs be released? The President sent for a file, and together they went through them picking out the ones that might have the greatest impact on skeptics. In a while Robert Kennedy walked in, bleak, tired and disheveled. He had just been to see Ambassador Dobrynin in an effort to find out whether the Soviet ships had instructions to turn back if challenged on the high seas. The Soviet Ambassador, the Attorney General said, seemed very shaken, out of the picture and unaware of any instructions. This meant that the imposition of the quarantine the next day might well bring a clash.

The three old friends talked on. Ormsby Gore recalled a conversation with Defense Department officials who had declared it important to stop the Soviet ships as far out of the reach of the jets in Cuba as possible. The British Ambassador now suggested that Khrushchev had hard decisions to make and that every additional hour might make it easier for him to climb down gracefully; why not, therefore, make the interceptions much closer to Cuba and thereby give the Russians a little more time? If Cuban aircraft tried to interfere, they could be shot down. Kennedy, agreeing immediately, called McNamara and, over emotional Navy protests, issued the appropriate instruction. This decision was of vital importance in postponing the moment of irreversible action. They soon parted, looking forward with concern to the crisis of the morrow.

And so around the world emotions rose—fear, doubt, incertitude, apprehension. In the White House the President went coolly about his affairs, watching the charts with the Soviet ships steadily advancing toward Cuba, scrutinizing every item of intelligence for indications of Soviet purpose, reviewing the deployment of American forces. At one point the Air Force produced a photograph of planes lined wingtip to wingtip on a Cuban airfield, arguing that only a few bombs could wipe out the enemy air power. The President asked the Air Force to run similar reconnaissance over our own fields; to the Pentagon's chagrin, the photographs showed American planes also lined up row by row. In this manner he preserved a taut personal control over every aspect of the situation; the Bay of Pigs had not been in vain. He said to someone, "I guess this is the week I earn my salary."

He never had a more sober sense of his responsibility. It was a strange week; the flow of decision was continuous; there was no day and no night. In the intervals between meetings he sought out his wife and children as if the imminence of catastrophe had turned his mind more than ever to his family and, through them, to children everywhere in the world. This was the cruel question—the young people who, if things went wrong, would never have the chance to learn, to love, to fulfill themselves and serve their countries. One noon, swimming in the pool, he said to David Powers, "If it weren't for these people that haven't lived yet, it would be easy to make decisions of this sort."

In Buenos Aires Billy Graham preached to 10,000 people on "The End of the World."

7. WAITING ON KHRUSHCHEV

Within the Kremlin, so far as one could tell, there was confusion. The Russians had obviously anticipated neither the quick discovery of the bases nor the quick imposition of the quarantine. Their diplomats across the world were displaying all the symptoms of improvisation, as if they had been told nothing of the placement of the missiles and had received no instructions what to say about them. Ambassador Anatoly Dobrynin himself gave every indication of ignorance and confusion. As late as Wednesday a message to Robert Kennedy from Mikoyan repeated that Cuba was receiving no weapons capable of reaching the United States. Georgi Bolshakov, who transmitted the message and who had seemed to us all an honest fellow, assured the Attorney General that he believed this himself.

In New York on Wednesday Stevenson was continuing the battle for the American resolution in the United Nations. John J. McCloy, whom the President had summoned from a business trip to Germany to give the UN presentation a bipartisan flavor, was adding his weight to our councils. Then U Thant made an unexpected intervention, proposing that the Soviet Union suspend its arms shipments and the United States its quarantine to allow an interlude for negotiations. Khrushchev accepted this thought at once and with evident pleasure; but, from our viewpoint, it equated aggression and response, said nothing about the missiles already in Cuba, permitted work to go forward on the sites and contained no provisions for verification. Still, while New York and Washington agreed in rejecting U Thant's proposal, the manner of the rejection caused debate. Some in Washington appeared to fear any response which would 'entrap' us in a negotiating process; it seemed to us in New York that they must be bent to clear the road for an air strike and an invasion. Stevenson and McCloy strongly recommended a response to U Thant which would keep the diplomatic option alive.

On Wednesday night, as we were pondering these matters at the U.S. Mission in New York, I received a telephone call from Averell Harriman. Speaking with unusual urgency, he said that Khrushchev was desperately signaling a desire to cooperate in moving toward a peaceful solution. Harriman set forth the evidence: Khrushchev's suggestion of a summit meeting in his reply to Bertrand Russell; his well-publicized call on the American singer Jerome Hines the night before after a Moscow concert; his amiable if menacing talk with an American businessman, William Knox of Westinghouse International; the indications that afternoon that the nearest Soviet ships were slowing down and changing course. This was not the behavior of a man who wanted war,

Harriman said; it was the behavior of a man who was begging our help to get off the hook. Khrushchev had sent up similar signals after the U-2 affair in 1960, Harriman continued, and Eisenhower had made the mistake of ignoring him; we must not repeat that error now. "If we do nothing but get tougher and tougher, we will force him into countermeasures. The first incident on the high seas will engage Soviet prestige and infinitely reduce the chance of a peaceful solution." The key to it all, he went on, lay in Khrushchev's two remarks during the recent visit of Robert Frost and Stewart Udall to the Soviet Union—his observation to Frost that the democracies were too liberal to fight [3] and his observation to Udall that the Soviet Union must be treated as an equal. "We must give him an out," Harriman said again. "If we do this shrewdly, we can downgrade the tough group in the Soviet Union which persuaded him to do this. But if we deny him an out, then we will escalate this business into a nuclear war."

These words from the most experienced of all American diplomats seemed utterly convincing to me. I asked him whether he had made these points at the State Department. He said, "They never ask my advice about anything outside the Far East. I haven't been in on this at all." Accordingly I sent Harriman's views along to the President. Kennedy called him the next morning, and I imagine that Harriman's counsel may have strengthened his own inclination to go further along the diplomatic road. At any rate, his reply to U Thant on Thursday, while stressing that the "threat was created by the secret introduction of offensive weapons into Cuba, and the answer lies in the removal of such weapons," authorized Stevenson to continue discussions on whether satisfactory arrangements could be assured to this end. This was a second vital decision.

In Washington they had meanwhile been seeking to provide for every contingency the quarantine might create. By involving us directly with the Russians, it contained a great variety of potential risks; and the Executive Committee undertook the most intensive consideration of all possible gradations and configurations: where, when and how to stop ships, how much force to use, when to board, whether to disable the propeller and tow the ship to port. Soon they ascertained that Soviet submarines were following the ships: as quickly as possible, we put a destroyer on the tail of every submarine. It was all an amazing naval deployment, conducted with skill and efficiency. Among the destroyers to take part, apparently in the natural line of duty, was the *Joseph P. Kennedy, Jr.*

As they plotted the courses and studied the charts, Thursday seemed to confirm the encouraging signs of Wednesday and to justify Ormsby Gore's suggestion of Tuesday night that the line of interception be drawn closer to Cuba. Half the Soviet ships, the Executive Committee noted with a flood of relief, had put about and were heading home. Others were evidently waiting for further orders. Only one had entered the quarantine zone—a tanker, obviously not carrying nuclear weapons. In Washington some felt that we must react to this challenge with full military vigor; but the President decided to give Khrushchev more time and said that the tanker, once it had identified itself and thereby established the quarantine, should be permitted to proceed without boarding and search—a third vital decision.

[3] Actually Khrushchev never made this remark; it was Frost's interpretation in a New York press conference.

There were other portents, and to them our intelligence community turned like Roman haruspices to the entrails of a sacrificial victim. For the first time all that long week Soviet diplomatic behavior across the world was beginning to conform to a pattern; this indicated that Moscow had at last sent out instructions. For one thing—and very odd in view of our own and the British apprehension about Soviet reprisals in Berlin—the Russians appeared to be engaged in a studied effort to dissociate Berlin from Cuba. Gromyko, who spoke at Humboldt University in East Berlin on Tuesday, instead of using the occasion for implied threats, did not even mention Cuba. By Friday V. A. Zorin, the Soviet ambassador to the United Nations, was even assuring other UN diplomats that his government would not fall into the American "trap" of retaliatory action in Berlin.

But the essence of the emerging pattern seemed to be concern for a peaceful settlement. This was what the Soviet ambassadors in London and Bonn were saying to the British and West German governments. Nor was Moscow confining its efforts to orthodox channels. In London on Wednesday, for example, Captain Ivanov of the Soviet Embassy asked a demimondain doctor named Stephen Ward to use his influence to persuade the British government to invite Khrushchev and Kennedy to a summit meeting. Ward thereupon approached Lord Arran, a peer who wrote a column in the *Evening News,* and even sent a letter to Harold Wilson, whom he did not know. Thwarted in these efforts to solve the world's problems, he soon returned to the more relaxed company of Christine Keeler.

But despite these gestures the situation was still loaded with danger. Work continued on the sites; unless this was stopped, the missiles would soon be on their launching pads. Nor had the Soviet Union yet admitted the presence of nuclear missiles in Cuba at all. On Thursday evening at the UN Stevenson returned to the debate in the Security Council. He crisply dismissed the communist argument that the United States had created the threat to the peace: "This is the first time that I have ever heard it said that the crime is not the burglary, but the discovery of the burglar." As for those who thought the quarantine too extreme a remedy: "Were we to do nothing until the knife was sharpened? Were we to stand idly by until it was at our throats? . . . The course we have chosen seems to me perfectly graduated to meet the character of the threat."

Zorin made a cocky but evasive reply. Now Stevenson took the floor again. Ironically regretting that he lacked his opponent's "talent for obfuscation, for distortion, for confusing language and for double-talk," saying sternly "those weapons must be taken out of Cuba," he turned on the Russian with magnificent scorn:

> Do you, Ambassador Zorin, deny that the USSR has placed and is placing medium and intermediate-range missiles and sites in Cuba? Yes or no? Don't wait for the translation. Yes or no?

Zorin muttered something about not being in an American courtroom. Stevenson, cold and controlled:

> You are in the courtroom of world opinion. You have denied they
> exist, and I want to know if I understood you correctly. I am pre-
> pared to wait for my answer until hell freezes over. And I am also
> prepared to present the evidence in this room—now!

It was a moment of tremendous excitement. At Stevenson's order, aerial photographs were wheeled on easels into the council chamber, showing the transformation of San Cristóbal from a peaceful country spot into a grim nuclear
installation. Other pictures added further evidence. Zorin wanly denied the
authenticity of the display. Stevenson wondered savagely why the Soviet Union
did not test its denial by permitting a United Nations team to visit the sites.

Then, in a moment, Stevenson concluded: "We know the facts and so do
you, sir, and we are ready to talk about them. Our job here is not to score debating points. Our job, Mr. Zorin, is to save the peace. And if you are ready to
try, we are."

The Stevenson speech dealt a final blow to the Soviet case before world
opinion.

8. THE LETTERS

But on Friday work still continued on the sites. In Florida the American army
prepared for invasion. In Washington the pressure to attack mounted as each
passing moment brought the installations closer to operation. And in Moscow
there must have been deep anxiety and bitter debate.

Khrushchev had now evidently abandoned the effort to bring in more nuclear weapons. But some of the men around him—perhaps the Soviet military
—were apparently determined to make the missiles already there operational as
speedily as possible. Indeed, this group may have gone along with the pacific
gestures of Wednesday and Thursday precisely to gain time to complete
the sites. In any case, once the missiles were on launching pads, Moscow might
be able to drive a better bargain.

Khrushchev himself, however, seems to have reached a different position.
He knew by now that his essential gamble had failed. Whatever he had once
supposed, the Americans were ready to fight. His own options were narrowing
before his eyes. If he were to strike at Berlin, he would only expose the Soviet
Union to nuclear attack. If he did not compose matters quickly in the Caribbean, then the great army, massing so visibly in Florida, would descend on
Cuba; "on the morning of [Saturday] October 27," as he told the Supreme
Soviet in December, "we received information that the invasion would be carried out in the next two or three days." If an invasion began, Khrushchev either
would have to use the rockets he liked to boast about so jovially or else desert
the only communist state in the Americas and condemn himself as a *fainéant*
before the international communist movement. It was by now beyond the realm
of tactical maneuver: all roads led to the abyss. The Soviet Chairman and
the American President were the two men in the world with ultimate responsi-

bility for nuclear war. Like Kennedy, Khrushchev had peered into the abyss before. "Immediate action," as he later told the Supreme Soviet, "was needed to prevent an invasion of Cuba and to preserve peace."

At one-thirty on Friday John Scali, the State Department correspondent for the American Broadcasting Company, received a call from Aleksander Fomin, a counselor at the Soviet Embassy, insisting on an immediate meeting. Scali, who had lunched occasionally with Fomin in the past, joined him at once at the Occidental Restaurant. The usually phlegmatic Russian, now haggard and alarmed, said, "War seems about to break out. Something must be done to save the situation." Scali replied that they should have thought of that before they put the missiles in Cuba. The Russian sat in silence for a moment. Then he said. "There might be a way out. What would you think of a proposition whereby we would promise to remove our missiles under United Nations inspection, where Mr. Khrushchev would promise never to introduce such offensive weapons into Cuba again? Would the President of the United States be willing to promise publicly not to invade Cuba?" When Scali said he did not know, Fomin begged him to find out immediately from his State Department friends. Then, reaching for a pencil, he wrote down his home telephone number: "If I'm not at the Embassy, call me here. This is of vital importance."

Scali carried the proposal to Roger Hilsman at State, and Hilsman carried it to Rusk. After discussion with the Executive Committee, Rusk asked Scali to tell the Russian that we saw "real possibilities" for a negotiation but they must understand that time was short—no more than forty-eight hours. At seven-thirty Friday evening Scali passed this word along. They met this time in the coffee shop of the Statler Hilton. Fomin, once he had satisfied himself about the authenticity of Scali's message and after a brief attempt to introduce the idea of UN inspection of Florida as well as Cuba, rose and, in his haste to get the word back, tossed down a five-dollar bill for a thirty-cent check and speeded off without waiting for the change.

Two hours later a long letter from Khrushchev to the President began to come in by cable. The Soviet leader started by insisting that the weapons shipments were complete and that their purpose was defensive. Then he declared his profound longing for peace; let us, he said with evident emotion, not permit this situation to get out of hand. The enforcement of the quarantine would only drive the Soviet Union to take necessary measures of its own. But if the United States would give assurances that it would not invade Cuba nor permit others to do so and if it would recall its fleet from the quarantine, this would immediately change everything. Then the necessity for a Soviet presence in Cuba would disappear. This crisis, Khrushchev said, was like a rope with a knot in the middle: the more each side pulled, the more the knot would tighten, until finally it could be severed only by a sword. But if each side slackened the rope, the knot could be untied.

The letter was not, as subsequently described, hysterical. Though it pulsated with a passion to avoid nuclear war and gave the impression of having been written in deep emotion, why not? In general, it displayed an entirely rational understanding of the implications of the crisis. Together with the Scali proposal, it promised light at the end of the cave. And in New York on Friday we heard that Zorin had advanced the same proposal to U Thant, and that the

Cubans at the UN were beginning to hint to unaligned delegates that the bases might be dismantled and removed if the United States would guarantee the territorial integrity of Cuba. The President probably had his first good night's sleep for ten days; certainly the rest of us did.

But when the Executive Committee assembled on Saturday morning, prospects suddenly darkened. The Moscow radio began to broadcast a new Khrushchev letter containing, to everyone's consternation, an entirely different proposition from the one transmitted through Scali and embodied in Khrushchev's letter of the night before. The Soviet Union now said it would remove its missiles from Cuba and offer a non-aggression pledge to Turkey if the United States would remove its missiles from Turkey and offer a non-aggression pledge to Cuba. The notion of trading the Cuban and Turkish bases had been much discussed in England; Walter Lippmann and others had urged it in the United States. But Kennedy regarded the idea as unacceptable, and the swap was promptly rejected. This proposal was perplexing enough; but, far more alarming, word soon came that a U-2 was missing over Cuba, presumably shot down by the Russians (piloted, indeed, by the brave South Carolinian, Major Rudolph Anderson, Jr., who had first photographed the installations on October 14). American planes had thus far flown over the missile sites without interference. The Soviet action now, some felt, could only mean one thing: that the confrontation was entering its military phase. The bases were becoming operational, and the Russians were evidently determined to use force to maintain them. We had no choice, it was argued, but a military response; and our tactical analysis had already shown that strikes at the bases would be little use without strikes at the airfields, and strikes at the airfields of little use without further supporting action, so, once the process began, it could hardly stop short of invasion.

The President declined to be stampeded. Obviously, if they shot down U-2s, we would have to react—but not necessarily at once. Again he insisted that the Russians be given time to consider what they were doing before action and counteraction became irrevocable. There remained the Khrushchev letters, and the Executive Committee turned to them again with bafflement and something close to despair. It was noted that Defense Minister Rodion Malinovsky had mentioned Cuba and Turkey together as early as Tuesday, and that *Red Star,* the army paper, had coupled them again on Friday. Could the military have taken over in Moscow? Rusk called in Scali and asked him to find out anything he could from his Soviet contact. Scali, fearful that he had been used to deceive his own country, upbraided Fomin, accusing him of a double cross. The Russian said miserably that there must have been a cable delay, that the Embassy was waiting word from Khrushchev at any moment. Scali brought this report immediately to the President and the Executive Committee at the White House (where Pierre Salinger nearly had heart failure when, in the midst of the rigorous security precautions of the week, he suddenly saw the ABC reporter sitting at the door of the President's inner office).

In the meantime a new crisis: another U-2 on a routine air-sampling mission from Alaska to the North Pole had gone off course and was over the Soviet Union; it had already attracted the attention of Soviet fighters and was radioing Alaska for help. Would the Russians view this as a final reconnaissance in preparation for nuclear attack? What if they decided to strike first? Roger Hilsman brought the frightening news to the President. There was a moment of absolute grimness. Then Kennedy, with a brief laugh, said, "There is always some so-and-so who doesn't get the word." (The plane returned safely; but perhaps Khrushchev did interpret the flight exactly as Hilsman feared; perhaps this too, along with the invasion force massing in Florida and an unauthorized statement on Friday by the State Department press officer threatening "further action" if work continued on the bases, reinforced his determination to bring the crisis to an end.)

Later that afternoon the Executive Committee met again. Robert Kennedy now came up with a thought of breathtaking simplicity and ingenuity: why not ignore the second Khrushchev message and reply to the first? forget Saturday and concentrate on Friday? This suggestion may, indeed, have been more relevant than anyone could have known. For, as Henry Pachter has argued, the so-called second letter, from internal evidence, appears to have been initiated as the immediate follow-on of Khrushchev's reply to U Thant; it began with a reference to Kennedy's reply to U Thant on Thursday and took no note of events on Friday. Moreover, its institutional tone suggested that it was written in the Foreign Office. Might it not have been drafted in Moscow on Thursday and Friday with an eye to Saturday morning release in New York? Then the so-called first letter, which reflected the movement of events well beyond the U Thant proposal and which was clearly written by Khrushchev himself, may well have been composed late Friday night (Moscow time) and transmitted immediately to Kennedy while the 'second' letter was deep in the bureaucratic pipelines. Knowing heads of state and foreign office bureaucracies, one could take anything as possible.

At any rate, on October 27 Kennedy now wrote Khrushchev, "I have read your letter of October 26th with great care and welcomed the statement of your desire to seek a prompt solution." As soon as work stopped on the missile bases and the offensive weapons were rendered inoperable under UN supervision, Kennedy continued, he would be ready to negotiate a settlement along the lines Khrushchev had proposed. Then, in a sentence profoundly expressive of his desire to retrieve something out of crisis, he added: "If your letter signifies that you are prepared to discuss a detente affecting NATO and the Warsaw Pact, we are quite prepared to consider with our allies any useful proposals."

And so the message shot inscrutably into the night. Robert Kennedy carried a copy that evening to the Soviet Ambassador, saying grimly that, unless we received assurances in twenty-four hours, the United States would take military action by Tuesday. No one knew which Khrushchev letter superseded the other; no one knew whether Khrushchev was even still in power. "We all agreed in the end," Robert Kennedy said afterward, "that if the Russians were ready to go to nuclear war over Cuba, they were ready to go to nuclear war, and that was that. So we might as well have the showdown then as six months later." Saturday night was almost the blackest of all. Unless Khrushchev came through in a few hours, the meeting of the Executive Committee on Sunday night might well face the most terrible decisions.

Sunday, October 28, was a shining autumn day. At nine in the morning Khrushchev's answer began to come in. By the fifth sentence it was clear that he had thrown in his hand. Work would stop on the sites; the arms "which you described as offensive" would be crated and returned to the Soviet Union; negotiations would start at the UN. Then, no doubt to placate Castro, Khrushchev asked the United States to discontinue flights over Cuba. (As for the errant U-2 which had strayed over Russia the day before, he warned that "an intruding American plane could be easily taken for a nuclear bomber, which might push us to a fateful step.") Looking ahead, he said, "We should like to continue the exchange of views on the prohibition of atomic and thermonuclear weapons, general disarmament, and other problems relating to the relaxation of international tension."

It was all over, and barely in time. If word had not come that Sunday, if work had continued on the bases, the United States would have had no real choice but to take action against Cuba the next week. No one could discern what lay darkly beyond an air strike or invasion, what measures and countermeasures, actions and reactions, might have driven the hapless world to the ghastly consummation. The President saw more penetratingly into the mists and terrors of the future than anyone else. A few weeks later he said, "If we had invaded Cuba . . . I am sure the Soviets would have acted. They would have to, just as we would have to. I think there are certain compulsions on any major power." The compulsions opened up the appalling world of inexorability. The trick was to cut the chain in time. When Kennedy received Khrushchev's reply that golden October morning, he showed profound relief. Later he said, "This is the night to go to the theater, like Abraham Lincoln."

33

RICHARD HOFSTADTER

Goldwater and Pseudo-Conservative Politics

Was there a rationale for the candidacy of Barry Goldwater in 1964? His supporters believed that a fundamentalist minority existed apart from those committed to the standard politics, a group that normally participated in political life with reluctance, but might energetically engage in a right-wing campaign. In addition, they posited a man completely outside politics—a silent man not accommodated by the American system, one who could be brought into the political orbit if the "interest politics" of the nineteen sixties were abandoned in favor of direct appeals to simple values. Surveys reveal that many nonvoters are too authoritarian for the give and take of the present political system, but perhaps they would respond to a right-wing candidate. Since the Republican party seemed to have little chance to win the presidency in 1964, its conservative leaders were willing to risk going beyond ordinary opposition politics: they decided to add to the normal conservative Republican minority certain right-wing voters—whom they presumed to be largely working-class Democrats—and the nonvoters.

One reason this electorate never materialized in great body is that many Republicans sensed the essentially nonconservative character of the Goldwater forces. Those forces were of the radical right—a bit more so than the genial Senator himself; but in their proximity to totalitarianism, they were not far from the radical left. And if the voters at whom Goldwater aimed his appeal feared the left, they were not ready to sacrifice the comforts of interest politics for the uncharted visions of the right. What man with conservative instincts would risk replacing Social Security and crop subsidies with some undefined adventure against global communism?

Goldwater's capture of the Republican nomination was the triumphal moment of pseudo-conservatism in American politics. One may say that it was an accident, in that it was out of scale with right-wing Republican strength and could happen only because of a series of failures and misadventures among moderate Republicans which are not likely to recur. But in another sense it was far from accidental: it resulted from the chronic, frustrating impotence of the minority party and from the efficient organization that the right wing had quietly built up inside it.

If Goldwater is accepted on his own terms as a conservative, he baffles understanding, but if he is taken as a product of the pseudo-conservative revolt, his ideas fall into place. Questioning his conservatism may seem gratuitous, but there is more at stake here than an empty issue or a suitable label. What is at stake, as Robert J. Donovan puts it, is whether the Republican party can learn to make "a distinction between the conservatism represented by Senator Goldwater and his supporters and the conservatism that conserves." [1]

Unquestionably Goldwater's ideas do retain some shreds and scraps of genuine conservatism, but the main course of his career puts him closer to the right-wing ideologues who were essential to his success, who shaped his tactics, who responded to his line of argument, and whose extremism he chose to defend at the vital moment of his career. Without invoking these formative affiliations, how are we to explain the character of a "conservative" whose whole political life has been spent urging a sharp break with the past, whose great moment as a party leader was marked by a repudiation of our traditional political ways, whose followers were so notable for their destructive and divisive energies, and whose public reputation was marked not with standpattism or excessive caution but with wayward impulse and recklessness?

Goldwater's brand of conservatism has its most recognizable American roots in those thinkers, quite numerous in this country, who imagine conservatism to be almost identical with economic individualism. Here he has responded more fervently to the nostalgic reveries and the pronouncements of perennial truths that mark ideological conservatism than he has to the tradition of shrewd and subtle manipulation, concession, and conciliation that has characterized American conservatism in practice. Most conservatives are mainly concerned with maintaining a tissue of institutions for whose stability and effectiveness they believe the country's business and political elites hold responsibility. Goldwater thinks of conservatism as a system of eternal and unchanging ideas and ideals, whose claims upon us must be constantly asserted and honored in full.[2]

---

[1] *The Future of the Republican Party* (New York, 1964), p. 127.

[2] "The laws of God, and of nature, have no date-line. The principles on which the Conservative political position is based have been established by a process that has nothing to do with the social, economic, and political landscape that changes from decade to decade and from century to century. These principles are derived from the nature of man, and from the truths that God has revealed about His creation. Circumstances do change. So do the problems that are shaped by circumstances. But the principles that govern the solution of the problems do not. . . . The challenge is not to find new or different truths, but how to apply established truths to the problems of the contemporary world." Barry Goldwater: *The Conscience of a Conservative* (New York, Macfadden ed., 1960), "Foreword," p. 3. (It may be necessary to add, since Goldwater has been exceptionally candid about the extent to which his

The difference between conservatism as a set of doctrines whose validity is to be be established by polemics, and conservatism as a set of rules whose validity is to be established by their usability in government, is not a difference of nuance, but of fundamental substance.

It is instructive how far Goldwater's devotion to eternal truths brought him beyond the position of such a Republican predecessor as Eisenhower, and how far it took him even beyond the conservatism of Robert A. Taft. Many of Eisenhower's statements both before and after his presidency could lead one to conclude that his social thinking was more similar to Goldwater's than different. Eisenhower too spoke often for the old-fashioned prudential virtues and against growing federal bureaucracy, and his cabinet incorporated at least two members, George Humphrey and Ezra Taft Benson, who fully shared the right-wing philosophy. But in practice Eisenhower was faithful to the opportunistic traditions of American conservatism. Though a mediocre politician with little enthusiasm for the political game, he was nonetheless so intuitively an "insider" in the American political tradition that he instinctively took the working politician's approach to the split mentality of American conservatism. He knew that many conservatives yearn for the days of untrammeled enterprise, uncomplicated foreign problems, and negligible taxes, but also that they can usually recognize the complexity of the contemporary world, the difficult obligations the country has taken on, and the irreversibility of the historical process that has brought us from simple agrarian conditions to the complex conditions of modern urban life and corporate organization. When Eisenhower spoke in philosophical terms, therefore, he often gave voice to their wistfulness about old ideals, but in administrative practice he usually bowed to what he thought were the necessities of the hour.

Here the strategies of three of our leading politicians are instructive. Eisenhower believed, at least with half his mind, in the old pieties, but concluded, with whatever misgivings, that they could not be taken as rules for action. Goldwater not only believed in them, but believed that they ought to be followed unerringly. Lyndon Johnson presumably does not believe in them at all; but understands that since they are widely believed in by honest men, some symbolic gestures are desirable in order to show such men that he at least respects their values. His talk of economy, and his much-publicized gesture of turning out the lights in the White House to save money, are gestures of this sort. Among cynical men they are naturally taken to be cynical. But they may also be taken as a humane effort to give symbolic comfort to those to whom, in the nature of things, more substantial forms of comfort cannot be given.

In any case, to ultra-conservatives, for whom the old pieties are binding moral principles, the Eisenhower administration was worse than a disappointment, it was a betrayal. It did not repeal the New Deal reforms, do away with

---

books were ghost-written, that I have used them on the assumption that he read them carefully before he signed them, and that they do indeed represent his views as of the time that they were written.)

Again: "The basic problems are no different in our times than under Lincoln or Washington. . . . We have merely changed the horse for the tractor, the hand tools for a machine." A speech before the Utah State Convention of the Junior Chamber of Commerce in 1960, quoted in *The New Republic,* March 27, 1961, p. 14.

high taxes, kill foreign aid, or balance the budget. In fact, its primary historical function seemed to be to legitimate what had been done under Roosevelt and Truman: when it left certain domestic and foreign policies intact, it made them more generally acceptable by passing them, so to speak, through the purifying fire of eight years of Republicanism and thus confirming that they represented, after all, a bipartisan consensus. The right-wing minority saw all this not as a clue to the nature of our national problems but as further evidence that the conspiracy originally set in motion by the Democrats was being carried on by the Eastern Republicans behind Eisenhower. McCarthy, for example, had been quick to strike at Eisenhower and to change his slogan, "Twenty years of treason," to a more inflammatory one: "Twenty-one years of treason." Again, one of Eisenhower's budgets prompted Goldwater to brand his administration as "a dime-store New Deal." On a later occasion he said with fervor: "One Eisenhower in a generation is enough." [3]

Goldwater's deviation from Taft Republicanism also marks him off from the established moderate conservative wing of his party. Unlike Goldwater, Taft came from a family with long seasoning in public affairs; and, again unlike Goldwater, he took an active part on Capitol Hill in framing legislation. His brand of conservatism was modified by several concessions to the demands of expediency and responsibility. Though he had a profound dislike of change and a passionate bias toward fiscal conservatism and decentralized administration, Taft accepted the idea that the federal government should concern itself with "seeing that every family has a minimum standard of decent shelter," should "assist those states desiring to put a floor under essential services in relief, in medical care, in housing, and in education," should underwrite the states in providing "a basic minimum education to every child," sustain minimum-wage laws "to give the unorganized worker some protection" comparable to that given to organized workers by the unions, persist in a steeply graduated income tax, maintain minimum farm prices, and through its social security program (which he held to be woefully inadequate) "assure to every citizen 65 years of age and over a living wage."

These commitments, made in various speeches from 1943 to 1951, accept the reality of the welfare state. They stand in sharp contrast to Goldwater's notion that economic individualism can still be ruthlessly applied to American life. Before Goldwater found it necessary to modify a few of his positions for the sake of his primary and presidential campaigns in 1964, his beliefs came straight out of nineteenth-century laissez-faire doctrine and the strictest of strict constructionism. Governmental activities in "relief, social security, collective bargaining, and public housing," he thought, had caused "the weakening of the individual personality and of self-reliance." He asked for "prompt and final termination of the farm subsidy program," declared himself against "every form of federal aid to education," denounced the graduated income tax as "confiscatory," and asserted that the country had "no education problem which requires any form of Federal grant-in-aid programs to the states." The government, he said "must begin to withdraw from a whole series of programs that are "outside its constitutional mandate," including "social welfare programs, education, public power, agriculture, public housing, urban

[3] *Time,* July 24, 1964, p. 27.

renewal. . . ." [4] Collectively, such statements called for the dismantling of the welfare state. "My aim is not to pass laws but to repeal them," Goldwater once boasted, and on another occasion he said: "I fear Washington and centralized government more than I do Moscow." [5] These are the characteristic accents of the pseudo-conservative agitators, who are convinced that they live in a degenerate society and who see their main enemy in the power of their own government.

Goldwater's departure from the Republican pattern was compounded by his position on civil rights. One of the oldest, though hardly the most efficacious, of the traditions of many conservatives in the North—and even to a degree in the South as well—has been a certain persistent sympathy with the Negro and a disposition to help him in moderate ways to relieve his distress. This tradition goes back to the Federalist party; it was continued by the Whig gentry; it infused the early Republican party. By adopting "the Southern strategy," the Goldwater men abandoned this inheritance. They committed themselves not merely to a drive for a core of Southern states in the electoral college but to a strategic counterpart in the North which required the search for racist votes. They thought they saw a good mass issue in the white backlash, which they could indirectly exploit by talking of violence in the streets, crime, juvenile delinquency, and the dangers faced by our mothers and daughters.

Eisenhower, like Goldwater, had been unmoved by noble visions of progress toward racial justice, but he at least gave lip service to the ideal and thought it important to enforce the laws himself and to speak out for public compliance. But Goldwater arrived at the position, far from conservative in its implications, that the decisions of the Supreme Court are "not necessarily" the law of the land.[6] Of course, the decisions of the Court have always had political content and they have often been highly controversial; there is no reason why they should suddenly be regarded with whispered reverence. But it is only in our time, and only in the pseudo-conservative movement, that men have begun to hint that disobedience to the Court is not merely legitimate but is the essence of conservatism.

It is not the authority and legitimacy of the Court alone that the pseudo-conservative right calls into question. When it argues that we are governed largely by means of near-hypnotic manipulation (brainwashing), wholesale corruption, and betrayal, it is indulging in something more significant than the fantasies of indignant patriots: it is questioning the legitimacy of the political order itself. The two-party system, as it has developed in the United States, hangs on the common recognition of loyal opposition: each side accepts the ultimate good intentions of the other. The opponent's judgment may be held to be consistently execrable, but the legitimacy of his intent is not—that is, in

[4] *The Conscience of a Conservative,* p. 43; *Congressional Record,* 87th Cong., 1st sess. (June 21, 1961), p. 10971; ibid., 88th Cong., 1st sess. (September 3, 1963), p. 16222; statement to Senate Subcommittee on Education, Senate Committee on Labor and Public Welfare, April 30, 1963 (*Hearings,* I, 279).

[5] *Fortune,* May 1961, p. 139; *Look,* April 21, 1964; cf. *The Conscience of a Conservative,* p. 22.

[6] *The Conscience of a Conservative,* p. 37; cf. *The New York Times,* November 24, 1963.

popular terms, his Americanism is not questioned. One of the unspoken assumptions of presidential campaigns is that the leaders of both parties are patriots who, however serious their mistakes, must be accorded the right to govern. But an essential point in the pseudo-conservative world view is that our recent Presidents, being men of wholly evil intent, have conspired against the public good. This does more than discredit them: it calls into question the validity of the political system that keeps putting such men into office.

A man like Goldwater, who lives psychologically half in the world of our routine politics and half in the curious intellectual underworld of the pseudo-conservatives, can neither wholly accept nor wholly reject such a position. He disdains and repudiates its manifest absurdities (Eisenhower as a Communist agent), but he lives off the emotional animus that gives birth to them. This ambiguity makes it more understandable why, on the night of his defeat, he so flagrantly violated the code of decorum governing the conduct of losing presidential candidates. The code requires a message of congratulation, sent as soon as the result is beyond doubt, so worded that it emphasizes the stake of the whole nation in the successful administration of the victor, and reasserts the loser's acceptance of the public verdict. In withholding his congratulations until the morning after the election, and then in hinting at Johnson's incapacity to solve the acute problems gratuitously enumerated in his telegram, Goldwater did something more than show bad manners. By complying with the code, but grudgingly and tardily, he expressed his suspicion that the whole American political system, with its baffling ambiguities and compromises, is too soft and too equivocal for this carnivorous world.

Although the ultras usually speak with nostalgia about the supposed virtues of our remote past, they have a disposition to repudiate the more recent past, and it was in character for Goldwater to write off as unacceptable the Republican conservatism of recent years. But in return, he and his followers were unable to win acceptance from the major centers of genuinely conservative power. Businessmen, to be sure, gave Goldwater a narrow margin of support, but they gave him far less than any other Republican in recent history. The press also broke from its normal pattern: for the first time in memory a Democrat was favored by newspapers with an aggregate circulation much larger than those endorsing his opponent. Conservative chains like the Hearst and Scripps-Howard newspapers backed Johnson, as did establishment Republican papers like the New York *Herald Tribune.* Old centers of Republican conservatism such as rural New England turned their backs on Goldwater, and he became the first Republican presidential candidate to lose Vermont. The conservative voters of the normally Republican states of the wheat belt also deserted in large numbers. Repeatedly the pollsters who found Republican voters expressing doubt about Goldwater or open opposition to him noticed a recurrent explanation: "He's too radical for me." The American public is not notably sophisticated about ideological labels, and its use of the term "radical" rarely shows much precision; but this response registers a sounder sense of the situation than that of the highbrow conservatives who acclaimed the Arizonan as their own. Whatever tag Goldwater chose to wear, a large part of the public saw in him an excessively sharp deviation from the pattern of American politics and they found it frightening.

Goldwater's deviation is as much marked in his conduct as in his ideas. American politics is run mainly by professionals who have developed over a long span of time an ethos of their own, a kind of professional code. In emphasizing how completely Goldwater, and even more his followers, departed from the professional code, it is important to be clear that one is not making a substantive criticism of what they stood for but an attempt to compare their ways historically with our normal conservative practice. The professional code is not a binding moral imperative for anyone—not even for politicians. At one time or another most politicians have broken it. On occasion we admire them for breaking it in the interest of what they believe to be a higher principle. Finally, it should be conceded that Goldwater, at certain moments of his career, observed it handsomely, and that he too was victimized at times when the code was broken by others.[7]

The point, however, is that the professional code, for all its limitations, is an American institution embodying the practical wisdom of generations of politicians. It seems ironic that the most unqualified challenge ever made within a major party to this repository of the wisdom of our ancestors should have been made by a self-proclaimed conservative, and that Goldwater's advisers in 1964 brought him as close as any presidential candidate has ever come to subverting the whole pattern of our politics of coalition and consensus.

Professional politicians want, above all, to win, and their conduct is shaped by this pragmatic goal. Moreover, they know that if they win they have to govern; and their behavior in dealing with opposing factions in their own party, with the opposition party, and with the electorate is constantly molded and qualified by the understanding that they have to organize a government capable of coping with the problems of the moment. Both their ideas and their partisan passions are modified by the harsh corrective of reality. They are quite aware, for example, that their promises, which express rather what they think they should offer to do than what they think they can do, cannot be perfectly fulfilled. They are also aware that their denunciation of the opposing party in the conduct of election campaigns must be followed by the attempt to work with the opposition in Washington. Under the heated surface of our political rhetoric, therefore, there exists a certain sobriety born of experience, an understanding that what sounds good on the banquet circuit may not make feasible policy, that statements, manifestos, and polemics are very far from pragmatic programs; that these have to be *translated* into programs for the solution of our domestic and foreign problems; and that even then these programs have to undergo still further modification in the legislative mill before they can become reality.

Goldwater's career is distinguished by its lack of training for this code.

[7] For example, Goldwater observed the code conspicuously in his conduct toward Nixon in 1960 and again momentarily in 1964 when he expressed some sympathetic understanding for the position of Republicans who could not afford to be fully identified with him. His opponents broke it at the Cow Palace when they circulated the famous Scranton letter, which, in its denunciation of his ideas and alleged tactics, went far beyond the usual etiquette of intra-party dispute.

On the requirements of American coalition politics as they bear on convention behavior, and on their repudiation by the Goldwater forces, see my essay: "Goldwater and His Party," *Encounter,* XXIII (October 1964), 3–13.

Before his entry into national politics, his experience had given him responsibility for no national organization and had required an attention to administrative demands no more complex than those of his inherited department store. As a member of the Senate, he assumed no important role, involved himself with no legislation on major national problems. His main business there was simply to vote No. He made no outstanding contributions to debate or to the consideration of legislative details (as, for example, Taft had done); he was not prominent in committee work, and his busy speech-making program made him a frequent absentee. He did not, as a working senator, command the ear of fellow senators, not even of those who shared his views. In the framework of practical politics, he remained an "outsider," and as a presidential candidate he continued to make decisions that reflected the outsider's cast of mind.[8]

But to say this of Goldwater's legislative role is not to deny that he worked hard to earn his position in his party: it is simply that he rose to it not by making contributions to government but through his partisan activity, which for years was dedicated and tireless. He was chairman of the Republican Senatorial Campaign Committee. He was constantly available to fellow Republicans everywhere, giving substantial help to their campaign efforts and their fund-raising. His arduous round of speechmaking on the banquet circuit gave him a chance to bring his "conservative" message to thousands of rank-and-file party workers and to put many party leaders in his debt. His role, then, was that of the partisan exhorter and organizer, a speaker and ideologue for whom preaching a sound philosophy was more interesting than addressing himself to the problems of state. But in this role he was constantly speaking to audiences already largely or wholly converted to his point of view, unlike the legislator on Capitol Hill who must constantly deal with shrewd and informed men who differ with him. Resounding applause no doubt confirmed his conviction of the validity and importance of his "conservatism," and persuaded him that an irresistible conservative revival was astir in the country, but it did not enlarge his capacity to conciliate or persuade those who differed with him—still less to learn from an exchange of views. The habits of mind thus shaped were carried into his campaign, during which he once again brought salvation to the already converted.[9]

Goldwater, then, made up for his lack of stature as a legislative leader by his outstanding success as a partisan evangelist who particularly mobilized those Republicans whose discontent was keenest, whose ideological fervor was strongest, those most dissatisfied with the bland and circumspect Eisenhower legacy.

[8] For a shrewd statement of the differences between the political mentality of the outsider and that of the insider, see the contrast drawn by Eric L. McKitrick between Andrew Johnson and Abraham Lincoln in *Andrew Johnson and Reconstruction* (Chicago, 1960), esp. Ch. 4.

Oddly enough, the externals of John F. Kennedy's senatorial career correspond with Goldwater's. However, the difference in their cast of mind, not to speak of their intellectual caliber, was beyond reckoning. It was only one aspect of these differences that JFK was, by family training, education, and social position—one suspects also, as it were, by instinct—an insider.

[9] "With one exception, and that a slip-up apparently, he held no press conferences during the campaign. When he visited the cities he generally avoided the crowds, the slums, and the ghettos and appeared only in halls filled with militant conservatives who needed no persuasion by him. There was precious little effort on the senator's part to take his case to the unconvinced." Donovan: op. cit., p. 55.

At the grass roots large segments of the Republican party were taken over by dedicated enthusiasts, hitherto political amateurs, with a bent for unorthodox ideas and new departures. Reporters at San Francisco were impressed by the preponderance of unfamiliar faces among the Goldwater delegates.[10] Victory won with the help of these new-idea delegates was followed by the creation of a Goldwater staff in which professionals and cosmopolitans were entirely overshadowed by amateurs and provincials—a staff the press called "the Arizona Mafia."

Goldwater's advisers and enthusiasts, being new to major-party politics, found it easy to abandon the familiar rules of political conduct. Party workers raised on the professional code want above all to find winners, to get and keep office, to frame programs on which they can generally agree, to use these programs to satisfy the major interests in our society, and to try to solve its most acute problems. If they find that they have chosen a loser, they are quick to start looking for another leader. If they see that their program is out of touch with the basic realities, they grope their way toward a new one.

But Goldwater's zealots were moved more by the desire to dominate the party than to win the country, concerned more to express resentments and punish "traitors," to justify a set of values and assert grandiose, militant visions, than to solve actual problems of state. More important, they were immune to the pressure to move over from an extreme position toward the center of the political spectrum which is generally exerted by the professional's desire to win. Their true victory lay not in winning the election but in capturing the party —in itself no mean achievement—which gave them an unprecedented platform from which to propagandize for a sound view of the world.

Since the major parties in the United States have always been coalitions of disparate and even discordant elements, the professional leaders of major parties have always had to forge out of their experience the techniques of consensus politics that are adapted to holding such coalitions together and maintaining within them a workable degree of harmony. The art of consensus politics, in our system, has to be practiced not only in coping with the opposition party but internally, in dealing with one's partisans and allies. The life of an American major party is a constant struggle, in the face of serious internal differences, to achieve enough unity to win elections and to maintain it long enough to develop a program for government. Our politics has thus put a strong premium on the practical rather than the ideological bent of mind, on the techniques of negotiation and compromise rather than the assertion of divisive ideas and passions, and on the necessity of winning rather than the unqualified affirmation of principles, which is left to the minor parties.

---

[10] Robert D. Novak remarks that these were "not merely the run-of-the-mill party workers under the command and the bidding of regular party leaders. Here was a new breed of delegate, most of whom had never been to a national convention before. . . . They were going there for one purpose: to vote for Barry Goldwater. To woo them away to another candidate would be as difficult as proselytizing a religious zealot." *The Agony of the G.O.P. 1964* (New York, 1965), pp. 345–6.

Cf. Richard Rovere: "They are a new breed. It has been said—quite proudly— by the Goldwater people that this was the first Convention for more than half of them. . . . There was youth on every hand." "Letter from San Francisco," *The New Yorker,* July 25, 1964, p. 80.

The perennial task of coalition building has resulted in a number of rituals for party conventions, which Goldwater and his followers either ignored or deliberately violated at San Francisco. A candidate who enters a convention with the preponderant and controlling strength that Goldwater had in 1964 has at his disposal a number of effective devices to conciliate and incorporate the opposition. One is to write a conciliatory platform, which makes concessions to the defeated side or which hedges on disputed matters. Party platforms are often vague, they are usually long and tedious, and they remain unread; but their significance lies precisely in showing the ability of all factions and candidates to agree at least on a statement of policy. Their very vagueness proves that party leaders do not consider it necessary to fight issues out or to reach clear statements of principle and policy. Bitter or prolonged platform fights, such as those waged by the Democrats in 1896 and 1924, are always signs of a fatal absence of basic unity.

The winning candidate has other placatory devices available. One is the choice of a running mate: he may pick his leading opponent for this role, as Kennedy did in 1960, or he may turn to someone who represents the main opposing tendency in the party. He may go out of his way to arrive at an understanding, as Eisenhower did with Taft in 1952 or Nixon with Rockefeller in 1960. In his acceptance address he will almost invariably do the graceful thing and dwell upon conciliatory themes, stressing the commitments and sentiments that unite the party rather than those that divide it. In return, some corresponding rituals are expected of the loser: he, or one of his close associates, usually presents a motion to make the nomination unanimous. If he speaks, he minimizes the issues that have divided his party, denounces the opposition party with renewed vigor, and promises to support the victor with all his might. Normally he keeps this promise, as Goldwater himself did for Nixon in 1960.[11]

This traditional placatory ritual was flouted at every point by the Goldwater organization at San Francisco. To begin, their platform in effect repudiated many recent Republican policies. Then, proposed amendments endorsing civil rights, reasserting civilian control over nuclear weapons, and condemning extremist groups were crushed, and in the debate over the last of these, Governor Rockefeller was interrupted unmercifully by booing from the galleries. (The Goldwater managers, disturbed by this outburst, were able to prevent their delegates from persisting in the demonstration but could not stop their partisans in the galleries from giving vent to their feelings.) In the choice of a running mate, Goldwater again had an opportunity to soften the conflict by taking some eminent man from the large moderately conservative middle band of the party who would have been acceptable on all sides, but he settled on an obscure provincial, William E. Miller—professional enough, to be sure, but undistinguished except by belligerent partisanship. The effects of this choice were in no way mollified by the selection of his fellow Arizonan Dean Burch as national chairman—"a politician of limited experience who had never even been a

---

[11] Goldwater's break with the professional code in 1964 did not come from failure to understand its easily mastered general principles but from his constant gravitation toward the doctrinaires. "We are a big political party," he declared in a speech on September 11, 1963, "and there is all kinds of room for a difference of opinion. But in differing, we need not beat the hides off those we differ with." Novak: op. cit., p. 232. It was this message that got lost at San Francisco.

county chairman and who was a complete stranger to hundreds of eminent Republicans around the country." [12] Finally, to top it all, Goldwater's acceptance speech, far from sounding the conciliatory note so necessary after the acrimony of the proceedings, said that "those who do not care for our cause we don't expect to enter our ranks in any case," and flung his famous challenge: "I would remind you that extremism in the defense of liberty is no vice. And let me remind you also that moderation in the pursuit of justice is no virtue!"—a two-sentence manifesto approved by a dozen top members of his staff and written by a hard-core right-winger whom Goldwater found congenial and kept by his side as a speechwriter throughout the campaign.

Most presidential candidates try to look their best at the strategic moment when their party convention acclaims them. For Goldwater this was impossible. His moment of victory at the Cow Palace found him firmly in the hands of his ecstatic pseudo-conservative followers. For the past few years his own presidential prospects had done much to draw them into active politics, and it was their money and hard work which had built the Goldwater movement. In precinct after precinct and county after county they had fought and ousted old-line Republicans.[13] They were now prominent among his delegates—an official of the John Birch Society claimed that more than a hundred of the Goldwater delegates were Birchites. The Goldwater campaign had given focus to the right-wing movement, and had brought into prominence such exponents of the paranoid style as John A. Stormer and Phyllis Schlafly, whose books were sold and given away by the millions, and whose conspiratorial views articulated the mental heat behind pseudo-conservatism more fully than Goldwater's more equivocal utterances. Schlafly's *A Choice Not an Echo* expressed the animus of Midwestern Republicans against "the secret New York kingmakers" who had repeatedly stolen the Republican nomination "to insure control of the largest cash market in the world: the Executive Branch of the United States Government." It was reminiscent of the same bias which a few years earlier had inspired Goldwater to suggest that "this country would be better off if we could just saw off the Eastern Seaboard and let it float out to sea." Stormer's *None Dare Call It Treason*, which took its title from a couplet attributed to Sir John Harrington:

> Treason doth never prosper, what's the reason?
> For if it prosper, none dare call it treason,

was a masterful piece of folkish propaganda, which continued the McCarthyist and Birchite line of accusation without committing the bizarre verbal indiscretions that have caused people to make fun of Robert Welch. It drew up a

---

[12] Donovan: op. cit., p. 92.

[13] The procedure by which Goldwater and his followers conducted their campaign for delegates was not one calculated to develop their talents for conciliation. As Novak puts it, Goldwater repealed "the rule of preconvention politics that required a candidate to appease the uncommitted rather than titillate his own committed followers. . . . Rather than appease the uncommitted, Goldwater was destroying them. And this required keeping his own committed followers in a state of high titillation. . . . He was conquering, not convincing, the Republican party." Op. cit., p. 353.

thoroughgoing indictment of Eisenhower Republicanism without in so many words calling Eisenhower a traitor.[14]

To be fully faithful to this clientele, Goldwater had to be graceless to many fellow Republicans; yet it would have been graceless too to spurn the people whose work had won his victory. But, in fact, he saw nothing wrong with them. While he could hardly take Robert Welch seriously, he had said more than once that the John Birch Society was a fine organization,[15] and now he would neither repudiate nor offend its members. This meant that the path to the customary procedures of our politics was closed off, since the right-wingers scorned them. The convention showed the nation for the first time how well organized the right-wing movement was, but it also proved, as the subsequent campaign was to prove again, that the right wing, though brilliantly organized for *combat,* was not organized to conciliate or persuade. Having convinced themselves that the forces they were fighting were conspiratorial and sinister, not to say treasonous, they found it impossible to shake off the constricting mental framework of the paranoid style. The sudden and startling outburst of wild applause, the jeers and fist-shaking at the broadcast booths and press stands, which came when Eisenhower made a mildly hostile reference to some unidentified columnists, was a key to the prevailing mood. Animated by a profound resentment, and now at last on the verge of a decisive victory over their tormentors, the Goldwater zealots were filled with the desire to punish and humiliate, not to appease and pacify.[16] The acceptance speech showed that this desire extended upward into Goldwater's own staff.

The shock inflicted by San Francisco was so severe that some gesture seemed imperative; and for a moment it seemed that Goldwater would make the usual effort at rapprochement when the Hershey Conference was held in August. Indeed he did say there many of the expected things, and some in strong terms; but the damage had been done, and Goldwater's announcement to reporters at the close of the conference that "this is no conciliatory speech at all. It merely reaffirms what I've been saying all through the campaign,"

---

[14] Phyllis Schlafly: *A Choice Not an Echo* (Alton, Ill., 1964), p. 5; John A. Stormer: *None Dare Call It Treason* (Florissant, Mo., 1964), esp. pp. 33–53, 196–8, 224–5. These young writers represent the militant younger generation of conservatives that was attracted to Goldwater. Stormer was chairman of the Missouri Federation of Young Republicans, and Schlafly president of the Illinois Federation of Republican Women and a Goldwater delegate at the Cow Palace.

[15] "A lot of people in my home town have been attracted to the [Birch] society," Goldwater said in 1961, "and I am impressed by the type of people in it. They are the kind of people we need in politics." On another occasion he called them "the finest people in my community," and still later, when it had become clear that they might be a serious campaign liability, he stood by them, insisting that as a group they should not be called extremists. "They believe in the Constitution, they believe in God, they believe in Freedom." *Time,* April 7, 1961, p. 19; ibid., June 23, 1961, p. 16; *The New York Times,* July 18, 1964.

[16] Cf. Richard Rovere's report from San Francisco (p. 80). For the most part, he found the Goldwater delegates young and affluent, "smartly dressed, well organized, and well spoken. And they were as hard as nails. The spirit of compromise and accommodation was wholly alien to them. They did not come to San Francisco merely to nominate their man and then rally his former opponents behind him; they came for a total ideological victory and the total destruction of their critics. . . . They wished to punish as well as to prevail."

canceled much of the conciliatory effect. The wounds had been covered over, not healed, and although Goldwater won the dutiful support of a number of moderates, including his main opponent, Scranton, he went on to conduct a right-wing campaign in which they were inevitably out of key.[17] By now it was not altogether a matter of his being unwilling to offer reassurance. What had happened was that he had been so extreme so long that neither the Republican moderates nor a large, strategic segment of the electorate had confidence that further reassurances from him would have any meaning.

Overwhelming defeat in the election—a thing which the professional politician always takes as a spur to rethink his commitments and his strategy—had no such effect on the Goldwater camp. His enthusiasts were more disposed to see the event as further evidence of the basic unregeneracy of the country, or worse, of the conspiracy by which they had been thwarted all along. The old right-wing myth, that there was an enormous conservative "silent vote" that would pour out to the polls if the party would only nominate a proper right-winger, was exploded, but it seems to have been replaced by a new one: that Goldwater was defeated so badly largely because he was sabotaged by the party moderates and liberals.[18] It must be conceded that if one's underlying purpose is not to win elections or affect the course of government but to propagandize for a set of attitudes, the right-wing enterprise of 1964 can be considered something of a success. It was so taken by many Goldwater ideologues, and on the far right the post-election mood was one of cheer, if not elation. One of its spokesmen said that the election marked "the defeat not of conservatism but of the Republican party"—a clear confession that the fate of an ideology was taken as being far more important than the well-being of the institution; and Goldwater remarked in a revealing statement: "I don't feel the conservative cause has been hurt. Twenty-five million votes are a lot of votes and a lot of people dedicated to the concept of conservatism." [19]

If one accepts the point of view of political doctrinaires and amateurs, whose primary aim in politics is to make certain notions more popular, this statement has its validity: for a generation, no politician has been able to preach Goldwater's brand of ultra-right-wing individualism and aggressive nationalism

---

[17] It was impossible after San Francisco to put the pieces together again. Scranton made many strong campaign speeches, as the code required, for Goldwater, and acted as his host at a great rally in Pittsburgh near the end of the campaign. In his introduction he made a casual reference to the fact that he did not always agree with Goldwater. At this he was met by such a chorus of boos from the faithful that he hurried through to a perfunctory and cool conclusion. See Novak: op. cit., p. 5.

[18] As is often the case, there is a modest portion of truth in this myth: the battle with the moderates in the primaries and at San Francisco helped to fix an image of Goldwater in the public mind that was never erased. But after San Francisco, it was not true that Goldwater was a loser because the moderates deserted him, but rather that the moderates, with their survival in mind, had to desert him because he was a loser. After the Hershey Conference, most of them were prepared to obey the professional code (as, for example, Scranton handsomely did), but many of those who were running for office found it too dangerous to their chances. This effect was not confined to the moderates. The ultra-conservative senatorial candidate in California, George Murphy, also found it expedient to keep his distance from Goldwater, and this strategy may have been an element in his success.

[19] *The New York Times,* November 5, 1964. Goldwater's figure represented the current state of the vote count, which was not complete.

to so wide an audience from so exalted a platform. However, a practical conservative politician, more concerned with consequences than with doctrine, might see the matter in a different light. He would observe that Goldwater's overwhelming defeat and the consequent collapse of Republican party strength in Congress have smashed the legislative barriers that for more than twenty-five years have blocked major advances in the welfare state. He would note that the preponderance in Congress has been overwhelmingly shifted toward the liberals, that legislative seniority, the makeup of the House Rules Committee, the composition indeed of all the committees, were so changed that a new flood of welfare legislation of the kind so fervently opposed by Goldwater was made possible; that medicare, a major extension of federal aid to education, a new voting-rights bill, a wider coverage for the minimum-wage act, regional aid for the Appalachian states, and a general anti-poverty program—all policies which the Goldwater forces considered dangerous in the extreme—were brought much closer to enactment; and that beyond these lay the further improved chances of a new immigration act with quota changes, urban transportation measures, the creation of a national arts foundation, even repeal of the "right to work" section of the Taft-Hartley Act.

From this point of view, liberals could be grateful to Goldwater. No other Republican could have made such a startling contribution to the first really significant and general extension of the New Deal since the 1930's. It was his campaign that broke the back of our postwar practical conservatism.

Goldwater's views on foreign policy, which were more damaging to him than his views on domestic affairs, required even more strenuous efforts to undo the existing image of him as a reckless adventurer. In his opening speech at Prescott he used the word "peace" twenty times, and for his foreign-policy slogan he adopted the relatively inoffensive "Peace through strength." Many times during the campaign he reiterated that he did not *want* a general war—an assurance which even his critics should have credited but which it was dangerous for a politician to have to offer—and he frequently emphasized the argument that the Republican party had been the historic peace party rather than his own well-known dissatisfaction with some of its recent peaceful policies.

By the autumn of 1964, however, Goldwater was the prisoner of his previous utterances on foreign affairs. The views he had expressed went far beyond what might be called the "hard line" in the cold war. The hard line, which has always been arguable in theory and which has had some successes in practice, views the imperatives of the cold war as an ineluctable challenge, has encouraged a skeptical view of the limits of negotiation, and has placed its primary trust in ample reserves of strength. The pseudo-conservative line is distinguishable from this not alone in being more crusade-minded and more risk-oriented in its proposed policies but also in its conviction that those who place greater stress on negotiation and accommodation are either engaged in treasonable conspiracy (the Birch Society's view) or are guilty of well-nigh criminal failings in moral and intellectual fiber (Goldwater's).

The characteristic note in Goldwater's damaging pre-1964 statements was a certain robust impatience with negotiation and compromise, a resolution to do away with uncertainty and ambiguity, a readiness to believe that large and complex questions of state could somehow be swept off the board by some sudden and simple gesture of violent decision. It was this state of mind that had led him to declare that a policy of coexistence was wholly impossible, to urge on more than one occasion that we withdraw from the United Nations and break off diplomatic relations with Russia and that we flatly declare ourselves against disarmament, to suggest that nuclear defoliation might be considered as a tactic in Vietnam, and to vote against the test-ban treaty.

It can be argued that occasional indiscretions, which were finally qualified or repudiated, were used unfairly to Goldwater's disadvantage. Far more damaging than such indiscretions, however, was the militant conception of the cold war, never repudiated, but embodied in the argument and the title of Goldwater's book *Why Not Victory?* This book denies systematically and articulately a view of the situation that has gradually come to prevail in Washington and Moscow but not in Peking or Phoenix. The prevailing view assumes that in the thermonuclear age the losses in a general war, because it would destroy the peoples and societies on both sides of the Iron Curtain, are monstrously and unacceptably disproportionate to what could conceivably be gained by the military "victory" of either side; and that therefore both sides must conduct the cold war under restraints, both mutually imposed and self-imposed, and hardly less vital for being experimental and ill defined, which it is hoped will prevent conflict in limited theaters from escalating into a general conflict. What makes men circumspect today is their awareness that "victory" gained in such a conflict would be without meaning.

The hope of the peoples of the West has been that the uncomfortable but bearable equipoise made possible by this view will endure, at least until we have reached some less dangerous modus vivendi. And it was the basic message of Goldwater's philosophy of foreign policy that this hope is self-deceptive and cowardly. As he saw it, we are engaged in a relentless life-or-death struggle which makes coexistence meaningless. "Victory is the key to the whole problem," he wrote, "the only alternative is—obviously—defeat." The struggle against communism he saw not simply as the necessary and tragic burden of our time but as the great imperative of our existence; and there were passages in which he appeared to lament the time we find for other things. ("And yet, we still go about our everyday business, being good neighbors, providing comforts for our families, worshiping God, and stubbornly refusing to admit the enormity of the conspiracy which has been created to destroy us.") He was troubled by the thought that "the free world," frightened by nuclear war and too much influenced by unrealistic intellectuals, "is gradually accepting the notion that anything is better than fighting." "A craven fear of death is entering the American consciousness," he wrote in 1960, "so much so that many recently felt that honoring the chief despot himself was the price to pay to avoid nuclear destruction," and he followed this melancholy observation with a strange one-sentence affirmation of faith: "We want to stay alive, of course; but more than that we want to be free." He was among those, he said disquietingly in *Why Not Victory?*, who believe "that armed conflict *may* not be necessary to defeat communism"—the italics are mine.[20]

Goldwater's approach to the world-wide strategic problems of the United

[20] *Why Not Victory?* (New York, Macfadden ed., 1963), pp. 16, 19, 22; *The Conscience of a Conservative*, pp. 90, 94.

States went far beyond the old isolationism, which, arrogant and chauvinist though it could be, was also infused with a strong spirit of pacifism. To the isolationists, our withdrawal from a corrupt world was meant at least to serve the interests of our own peace. Goldwater, though taking a dim view of most kinds of foreign aid, stood for the broadest interpretation of our commitments outside our borders. As he once put it, he stood for neither isolationism nor internationalism but for "a new form of nationalism" which underwrites the resistance of free nations to communism and avows as a national goal a final victory over the Communists.[21] Thus far Goldwater was not remote from the American consensus, but his unyielding and unchanging conception of the cold war represented a breach of the continuity that had on the whole pervaded the administrations of Truman, Eisenhower, and Kennedy. Goldwater looked upon the cold war as a series of relentless confrontations between ourselves and the Communists on various fronts throughout the world. If we maintain superior strength we can emerge victorious from all these confrontations, and in time the whole Communist world (which should be treated uniformly as a bloc, whatever its apparent internal differences) will crack under the stress of repeated defeats. The goal of our policies cannot be limited to peace, security, and the extension of our influence, but must go on to ultimate total victory, the ideological and political extermination of the enemy. "Our objective must be the destruction of the enemy as an ideological force possessing the means of power. . . . We will never reconcile ourselves to the Communists' possession of power of any kind in any part of the world." [22] Thus to the pseudo-conservative the ambiguous world in which we have lived for twenty years is reduced to a fleeting illusion; what is ultimately real is total victory or total defeat, and it is this upon which we must insist. There can be no middle ground.[23] We are not merely preserving our own security; we are engaged in an attempt to stamp out an idea, in every corner of the globe, by the force of arms.

The question has been repeatedly raised whether the attempt to press every crisis to a victorious solution, especially with the avowed ultimate aim of the

[21] *Why Not Victory?,* pp. 90–1. It was significant that Goldwater, with a certain show of justice, should have denounced Johnson's acceptance speech to the 1964 Democratic convention as "isolationist" because of its failure to deal with the issues of foreign policy. It is also instructive to compare his views with those of Robert A. Taft, which were much affected by the older isolationism. Taft, while hardly deficient in nationalist enthusiasm, was always much more concerned with the prospect that war would completely destroy democracy, local self-government, and private enterprise in America. To the best of my knowledge, this concern has never been expressed by Goldwater in his significant statements on foreign policy. Taft's views, as they had developed to 1951, are stated in his book *A Foreign Policy for Americans* (New York, 1952); but for an excellent factual survey of his changing positions, see Vernon Van Dyke and Edward Lane Davis: "Senator Taft and American Security," *Journal of Politics,* XIV (May 1952), 177–202.

Although Taft's real fear of war and his understanding of its threat to free enterprise have disappeared from most right-wing thinking, there is also a strong point of continuity: Taft himself was among those Republicans who changed the debate on our foreign policy from an argument over political judgment to an argument over "treason." See Richard Rovere: "What's Happened to Taft?" *Harper's Magazine,* April 1952, pp. 38–44.

[22] *Why Not Victory?,* p. 118.

[23] For Goldwater's objection to the idea that total victory cannot be rendered meaningful in our time, see ibid., pp. 106–9.

utter ideological extermination of the enemy, might not bring on a general war. But to raise this question is felt by right-wingers to be tainted with an unforgivable lack of manhood. Goldwater's answer was to promise that the Soviets, faced with our superiority in weapons, will never strike. But of course this is a promise on which no American can deliver, and for whose fulfillment we must depend upon Moscow, and ultimately Peking. Moreover, there is a curious passage in *Why Not Victory?* in which Goldwater flatly admitted that such fulfillment is not to be expected. The Communist world, he said, is likely to resort to general war only under one of two conditions. One, of course, is if we invite their attack by political weakness and military disarmament. But the other is "if there is a decisive switch in world affairs to the point where it is obvious they are going to lose." [24] And it is, of course, precisely to this point that Goldwater has always urged that they be pushed. The central dilemma of total victory, as expounded by Goldwater, is thus made to seem more ominous and insoluble than the many perplexing dilemmas of coexistence.

It was his casual view of nuclear warfare, and not his occasional indiscretions, that made Goldwater seem dangerous to many conservative Americans. What had become clear by 1964, and what could not be undone in the campaign, was the public impression that Goldwater's imagination had never confronted the implications of thermonuclear war. For a man who was so gravely distressed by violence in the streets, he seemed strangely casual about the prospect of total destruction. The final spiritual Armageddon of the fundamentalists, their overarching moral melodrama, the dream of millennial crusading and decisive conflict, plainly stirred his mind, but the hard realities of the current world seemed more remote. He could no more recognize that nuclear weaponry had created a new age of diplomacy than he could admit that modern urban industrialism had created a new environment. "I do not subscribe to the theory," he wrote, "that nuclear weapons have changed everything. . . . We have in the nuclear bomb an advance in weaponry, and terrible though that advance is, it still is merely a more efficient means of destruction. In a historical and relative sense, it can be compared with the advance made in military operations by the invention and adaption [*sic*] of gunpowder to war-making and the development of aerial warfare and strategic bombing missions." [25]

As a concession to campaign opportunism, Goldwater sometimes softpedaled his approach to the problems of foreign policy, contenting himself mainly with appeals to the restlessness of the people over the inability of the country to resolve its foreign crises or maintain its prestige in the world: "Are you proud of our fight for freedom? Are you proud of Panama? Are you proud of the burned effigy in Greece? Are you proud when no country is too small to pull Uncle Sam's whiskers and get away with it? Are you proud of wheat deals with the destroyers of liberty?" An interesting aspect of this appeal, since it sheds light not simply on the pseudo-conservative mentality but on the dynamics of American politics today, is its resemblance to Kennedy's appeal in the campaign of 1960. Like Goldwater, Kennedy had protested that we were seriously underarmed—and his admirers remember the bogus "missile gap" issue with chagrin. Like Goldwater, Kennedy had stressed the theme that the United

24 Ibid., p. 82.
25 Ibid., pp. 83–4.

States had lost prestige abroad, and dwelled on the establishment of Castro in Cuba only ninety miles from our shores.

Thus the Kennedy and Goldwater campaigns were both vigorously nationalist, appealing to public uneasiness over the indecisiveness of the cold war. That two men so different in outlook should have had this much in common as campaigners underlines the force of a persistent issue that opposition candidates will find it hard to resist. Both campaigns signify the deep perplexity of the American public over our foreign policies. The weakness of the pseudo-conservative appeal is that it strikes at only one side of complex public feelings: it shows an utter lack of tenderness for the pervasive American desire to continue in peace. In its appeal to toughness and frontier hardihood and its call for a fundamentalist all-out struggle with absolute evil, it runs up against both the pacific yearnings and the basic hedonism of the public, for which pseudo-conservatives have an ill-concealed contempt. But the strength of the pseudo-conservative position lies in its appeal to the American bafflement before the ambiguities and compromises in our foreign dealings. The American public pays heavy taxes to maintain an immensely expensive military machine with vast and unprecedented powers of destruction and to sustain military and economic operations around the globe; and yet year by year it finds that its expenditures and efforts yield neither decisive victories nor final settlements. The roll of inconclusive negotiations, sorties, and stalemates, symbolized by the names of Yalta, Korea, Berlin, Cuba, and Vietnam, seems to stretch out indefinitely.

All attempts to explain that this frustrating situation is not simply the product of execrable statecraft—not to speak of treason—run up against a fundamental fact of American history and a basic fixture in the American imagination. Many years ago, in an illuminating essay, D. W. Brogan pointed to a state of mind which he called "the illusion of American omnipotence"—defined as "the illusion that any situation which distresses or endangers the United States can only exist because some Americans have been fools or knaves." [26] The best illustration, he suggested, was our response to the Chinese Revolution, toward which Americans had neither historical awe nor historical curiosity, preferring to regard it as no more than a problem in our foreign and domestic policy. The oldest civilization in existence, comprising about a fifth of the human race, situated six thousand miles from the Pacific coast of the United States and having a contiguous frontier with Russia, had taken a turn —presumably for reasons deeply rooted in its history and geography, its traditions and problems—which was understandably very unwelcome to Americans. Instead of concluding that this was a response to massive strategic and economic realities largely beyond our control, millions of Americans were apparently convinced that this enormous country had been in our pocket, and had been lost or stolen only because of the mistakes (or treachery) of Roosevelt, Marshall, and Acheson, mistakes which could easily have been rectified by greater statesmen like Walter Judd or Senator Jenner.[27] Roosevelt was anathematized

[26] "The Illusion of American Omnipotence," *Harper's Magazine,* December 1952, pp. 21–8.

[27] Cf. Stormer: "About 600-million Chinese were betrayed into communist slavery. It was all done by a handful of American traitors and their liberal dupes." Op. cit., p. 31.

for having "permitted" Russia to become a Pacific power at Yalta, although Russia had been a Pacific power before the United States existed. It was all too lightly assumed, Brogan prophetically remarked, that Russia had "taken over" China as she had taken over Poland. Moreover, the persistent faith that American intervention could have changed Chinese history was accompanied by the faith that this involved nothing more than the choice of a few sound alternative policies, without demanding of the American people the massive sacrifices necessary to sustain a major commitment in China.

The difficulty many Americans have in understanding that their power in the world is not unlimited—a difficulty shared by no other people—Brogan explained by observing that in one very real sense the Americans had only recently been confronted by a situation long since familiar to the rest of the human race. The trying responsibilities and insoluble problems now confronting the United States were, he remarked, "a new story for the United States but . . . an old one for Europe. What the American people are enduring now is what the French, the English, the Russian peoples, even the Spanish and Italian peoples, suffered in the process of extending or trying to retain their empires."

The American frame of mind was created by a long history that encouraged our belief that we have an almost magical capacity to have our way in the world, that the national will can be made entirely effective, as against other peoples, at a relatively small price. We began our existence without worldwide territorial aspirations or responsibilities, but as a continental power with basically continental aspirations. From the beginning of our national life, our power to attain national goals on which we were determined was in effect irresistible—*within* our chosen, limited continental theater of action. Our chief foes—Indians, Mexicans, the decaying Spanish Empire—were on the whole easily vanquished. It is true that in fighting the British in 1812 we became engaged with a vastly greater power, but at a time when the British were in mortal combat with Napoleon and their American effort was a sideshow. Even then, though we did rather badly—our invasions of Canada were repulsed, our capital was burned, and our shipping was bottled up—a curious stroke of luck at New Orleans made it possible for us to imagine that the stalemate peace we concluded represented some kind of victory.[28] The only time the American land was truly ravaged by the horrors of war was during our own Civil War when our wounds were self-inflicted. Europe's quarrels, which in the twentieth century have become an American problem, were during the nineteenth an American advantage. The achievement of independence with national boundaries stretching westward to the Mississippi, the bargain purchase of the enormous territory of Louisiana, the easy acquisition of the Floridas without war, the assertion of our place in the world's carrying trade, the annexation of Texas and the seizure of immense western territories from Mexico—all these were accomplished at the cost of troubled, preoccupied, or weak nations, and at a minimum expenditure of our blood and treasure. In our own hemisphere, which was our only center

[28] The smashing victory scored by the Americans under Jackson at New Orleans came only after the terms of peace, in which none of our demands was met, were already signed. The news of New Orleans, however, circulated about the country more or less simultaneously with the news of the peace—a fortunate conjuncture for the American imagination.

of territorial aspirations, our preponderance tempted Secretary of State Olney to say in 1895: "Today the United States is practically sovereign on this continent and its fiat is law on the subjects to which it confines its interposition." A few years later our entry into the imperial game of the nineteenth century came at the expense of a befuddled and bankrupt Spain, incapable of offering us serious opposition.[29]

While expansion was won so cheaply, the United States, thanks largely to its continental position, was enjoying, as C. Vann Woodward has pointed out, virtually free security—which, he suggests, should be given a place among the great shaping forces of our history alongside the free land of our continental interior.[30] Fenced in behind the Atlantic, Pacific, and Arctic oceans, the United States was in a position to spare itself expensive armies and elaborate chains of fortifications. Even naval protection came cheap, since the navy that policed and defended the Atlantic was maintained, to our considerable benefit, by the British. In 1861, as Woodward points out, the United States maintained the second-largest merchant marine in the world without having a battle fleet— there were only 7,600 men in our navy as compared with over ten times that number in the British navy. A luxurious penury also affected our military establishment. At the outbreak of the Civil War the United States army numbered only a few more than 16,000 men, occupied mainly at posts on the Indian frontier. Even by 1914, when the nation had been launched upon its imperial career and had reorganized its military establishment, the proportion of its military appropriations to national income was only one-fourth of that paid by the British people, about one-sixth of that paid by the French, Japanese, and Germans, and about one-eighth of that paid by the Russians.

Free security, easy expansion, inexpensive victories, decisive triumphs— such was almost our whole experience with the rest of the world down to the twentieth century. The First World War, which we entered triumphantly in its closing phases, gave us a glimpse, but only the glimpse of an outsider, of what the rest of the world endured. It was only after the major effort of the Second World War, when we found ourselves not presiding over a pacified and docile world, but engaged in a world-wide stalemate and a costly and indecisive struggle in Korea, that the American people first experienced the full reality of what all the other great nations have long known—the situation of limited power. The illusion of American omnipotence remained, but the reality of American preponderance was gone. It is this shock to the American consciousness to which Goldwater and others appealed when they cried: "Why not victory?" Why not, indeed, when one remembers all those facile triumphs? In this light it becomes possible to understand how Goldwater thought he could promise unremitting victories in the cold war along with balanced budgets and lower taxes.

"Until 1950," Goldwater wrote in *Why Not Victory?*, "America had never lost a shooting war," but within the next ten years we had suffered "repeated

[29] Goldwater, who is reported to read a good deal in the history and antiquities of Arizona, but not in world history, had a different version of this: "It was this independence—strong, virile, and unafraid—that led us to challenge a much mightier Spain and call her to her account for her tyranny over our Western Hemispheric neighbors." *Why Not Victory?*, p. 54. This is a delusion not shared by any American historian. Nor was it shared by informed American contemporaries.

[30] "This Age of Reinterpretation," *American Historical Review,* XLVI (October 1960), 2–8.

defeats." [31] This situation, in his view, is not to be accounted for by the fact that we now have world-wide aspirations going far beyond our early strategic goals or that our free security is gone because of technological changes; it is not because we are for the first time situated, as many peoples have been before us, in a position of limited power, or because we are counterposed to great and numerous peoples with a nuclear weaponry comparable to our own. It is because we have been ruled by the foolish and the incompetent, and perhaps, as his more ardent admirers boldly proclaim, by the treasonous as well. For those who conceive of history not as a sequence of related events but as a moral melodrama, such imputations seem plausible enough. And when one ponders how much the world position of America has changed within the past fifty years, what seems most remarkable is not that many should respond wholeheartedly to the pseudo-conservative interpretation of events, but that our statesmanship has been as restrained as it has usually been and that this restraint has won preponderant public support.

The right-wing enthusiasts were justified, I believe, in the elation they expressed, even in defeat, over the Goldwater campaign. They had less than nothing to show in practical results, but it is not practical results that they look for. They have demonstrated that the right wing is a formidable force in our politics and have given us reason to think that it is a permanent force. Writing in 1954, at the peak of the McCarthyist period, I suggested that the American right wing could best be understood not as a neo-fascist movement girding itself for the conquest of power but as a persistent and effective minority whose main threat was in its power to create "a political climate in which the rational pursuit of our well-being and safety would become impossible." [32] This still seems to be the true potential of the pseudo-conservative right; it is a potential that can be realized without winning the White House, even without again winning the Republican nomination.

That the right-wingers are actually increasing in numbers is doubtful; but their performance in 1964 shows how much leverage they can achieve, whatever their number, with dedication and organization. The tally of over 27 million votes for a candidate of pronounced right-wing views is delusive, but to them it is delusive in a heartening and invigorating way. A post-election poll suggested that at the most generous estimate only about 5.4 million Goldwater voters—or one-fifth of the whole—can be counted as hard-core Goldwater enthusiasts, a finding which fits roughly with his standing in the prenomination Gallup polls and with those primaries in which he was rated by Republican voters against the whole field of moderate and liberal candidates.[33] But so long as their zeal

[31] Pp. 23–4.

[32] See my *Paranoid Style in American Politics* (New York, 1965), p. 65.

[33] *The New York Times,* December 18, 1964; cf. the pre-election polls and primaries at various stages in the nomination fight, reported in Novak: op. cit., pp. 263, 325, 326, 332, 375, 379, 380, 389, 396. Louis H. Bean and Roscoe Drummond, however, estimate that only 2.5 to 3 million of Goldwater's votes were those of true believers and that the rest was simply a Republican party vote. They arrive at this estimate partly by measuring the proportion of Republicans who preferred Goldwater in polls to other Republicans against the total number of declared Republicans. They have checked this against his actual performance at the polls, as compared with more typical Republican candidates in the past. See "How Many Votes Does Goldwater Own?" *Look,* March 23, 1965, pp. 75–6.

and gifts for organization are as powerful as they have been in recent years, the right-wingers still stand in a position to make themselves effective far out of proportion to their numbers. The professionals who have already repossessed the party apparatus have not yet had a final reckoning with its right wing. Moreover, Goldwater's views, though far from predominant among the party's voters, were much more popular among its activist personnel—among those who do its hard work and supply its funds and who won him his delegates at the Cow Palace.

The largest single difficulty facing the right wing as a force within the Republican party is its inability to rear and sustain national leaders. Most Republican governors belong to the party's moderate wing. The roll call of the right wing's senatorial heroes is a list of the dead or the departed: Taft, McCarthy, Knowland, Bricker, Bridges, Jenner, and now Goldwater—and today not a single right-wing senator remains who is both secure in his seat and well known to the public. Although this is a serious liability in practical politics, it is less serious in the arena which the right wing regards as most important, the arena of "conservative education." At the level of party leadership, the right-wingers do well. In many parts of the country the most ardent Republicans are ultra-conservative. Often they are the heads of small businesses or independent professionals who can find the time and spend the money to make their views felt. Moderate Republicans are more likely to be officers or employees of large corporations whose positions leave them less time for partisan activity. Hence the party in some sections of the country has gravitated into the hands of a leadership that is considerably more conservative than its voters. The great middle band of the party, which is by far its largest portion, is conservative enough to be susceptible to some of the right-wing notions, even though it does not share the partisan rage and the conspiratorial suspicions of the Goldwaterites.

In the battle for public opinion, the right wing has ample funds at its disposal, and certain advantages that accrue from its rough-and-tumble tactics. The conservative label and the nationalist animus of the far right are handsome advantages: it can wrap itself in the symbols of respectability and Americanism, and yet it has no inhibitions about gaining what it can through intimidation, which it brings to bear with great effectiveness upon schoolteachers and school administrators, librarians, advertisers in the press and mass media, local merchants, and working politicians. It gets a bad press in the sophisticated national media which it so ardently resents, but the journalists and intellectuals in the cosmopolitan centers readily forget how frightening right-wing pressures can be in smaller communities.

Even the seemingly permanent minority position of the Republican party, which in one sense sets a limit to the operations of the far right, is in another sense one of its assets. Over the years the number of American voters who identify themselves in polls as Republicans has shrunk proportionately to a point at which it is now only half as large as the number of Democrats—a situation reflected quite precisely in the present ratio between the two parties in Congress. The Democratic party, with its broad centrist position, has come to embrace so large a part of the American political consensus that moderate Republican leaders find it all but impossible to discover a constructive issue upon which they can forge an independent identity and relieve themselves of the onus of "me-tooism" with which the right wing, on the whole quite correctly, charges them. The very destruction that Goldwater has wreaked within the party has its compensations for the right-wingers. It is true that this immediately cost them the control of the party; but so long as the party continues in its present helpless minority position, the possibility remains that, even without a repetition of the Goldwater takeover, the right-wingers can prevent the moderates from refurbishing the party as a constructive opposition.

But, above all, the far right has become a permanent force in the political order because the things upon which it feeds are also permanent: the chronic and ineluctable frustrations of our foreign policy, the opposition to the movement for racial equality, the discontents that come with affluence, the fevers of the culturally alienated who practice what Fritz Stern has called in another connection "the politics of cultural despair." As a movement, ironically enough, the far right flourishes to a striking degree on what it has learned from the radicals. Their forces, as men like Fred C. Schwarz and Stephen Shadegg have urged, have been bolshevized—staffed with small, quietly efficient cadres of zealots who on short notice can whip up a show of political strength greatly disproportionate to their numbers. The movement now uses the techniques it has taken from the radicals while it spends the money it gets from the conservatives. Finally, it moves in the uninhibited mental world of those who neither have nor expect to win responsibility. Its opponents, as men who carry the burdens of government, are always vulnerable to the discontents aroused by the manifold failures of our society. But the right-wingers, who are willing to gamble with the future, enjoy the wide-ranging freedom of the agitational mind, with its paranoid suspicions, its impossible demands, and its millennial dreams of total victory.

~~~~~~34

WILLIAM FULBRIGHT

The Arrogance of Power

*The leaders who committed the United States to the war in Vietnam
have already begun to insist in their memoirs that they made pragmatic decisions; these assertions are incredible to those who, from
the beginning, thought the war sheer madness. American critics observed very early that the enemy could match every troop increase;
that bombing their cities only strengthened their resolve to fight. To
most of the world, the moral shortcomings of the Vietcong seemed
unimportant compared to America's destruction of the people and
land with devastating firepower, its dropping of loathsome napalm,
and its support of a corrupt government.*

*Senator William Fulbright, the Democratic chairman of the
Foreign Relations Committee, has offered an essentially historical
explanation of why America went to war in Vietnam. A history of
victory, prosperity, and power gives Americans a dangerous sense
of omnipotence and self-righteousness, which, at its worst, can lead
to terrifying miscalculations like Vietnam.*

America is the most fortunate of nations—fortunate in her rich territory, fortunate in having had a century of relative peace in which to develop that territory,
fortunate in her diverse and talented population, fortunate in the institutions devised by the founding fathers and in the wisdom of those who have
adapted those institutions to a changing world.

For the most part America has made good use of her blessings, especially
in her internal life but also in her foreign relations. Having done so much
and succeeded so well, America is now at that historical point at which a great
nation is in danger of losing its perspective on what exactly is within the realm
of its power and what is beyond it. Other great nations, reaching this critical
juncture, have aspired to too much, and by overextension of effort have declined
and then fallen.

The causes of the malady are not entirely clear but its recurrence is one
of the uniformities of history: power tends to confuse itself with virtue and a

great nation is peculiarly susceptible to the idea that its power is a sign of God's favor, conferring upon it a special responsibility for other nations—to make them richer and happier and wiser, to remake them, that is, in its own shining image. Power confuses itself with virtue and tends also to take itself for omnipotence. Once imbued with the idea of a mission, a great nation easily assumes that it has the means as well as the duty to do God's work. The Lord, after all, surely would not choose you as His agent and then deny you the sword with which to work His will. German soldiers in the First World War wore belt buckles imprinted with the words *"Gott mit uns."* It was approximately under this kind of infatuation—an exaggerated sense of power and an imaginary sense of mission—that the Athenians attacked Syracuse and Napoleon and then Hitler invaded Russia. In plain words, they overextended their commitments and they came to grief.

I do not think for a moment that America, with her deeply rooted democratic traditions, is likely to embark upon a campaign to dominate the world in the manner of a Hitler or Napoleon. What I do fear is that she may be drifting into commitments which, though generous and benevolent in intent, are so far-reaching as to exceed even America's great capacities. At the same time, it is my hope—and I emphasize it because it underlies all of the criticisms and proposals to be made in these pages—that America will escape those fatal temptations of power which have ruined other great nations and will instead confine herself to doing only that good in the world which she *can* do, both by direct effort and by the force of her own example.

The stakes are high indeed: they include not only America's continued greatness but nothing less than the survival of the human race in an era when, for the first time in human history, a living generation has the power of veto over the survival of the next.

THE POWER DRIVE OF NATIONS

When the abstractions and subtleties of political science have been exhausted, there remain the most basic unanswered questions about war and peace and why nations contest the issues they contest and why they even care about them. As Aldous Huxley has written:

> There may be arguments about the best way of raising wheat in a cold climate or of re-afforesting a denuded mountain. But such arguments never lead to organized slaughter. Organized slaughter is the result of arguments about such questions as the following: Which is the best nation? The best religion? The best political theory? The best form of government? Why are other people so stupid and wicked? Why can't they see how good and intelligent *we* are? Why do they resist our beneficent efforts to bring them under our control and make them like ourselves.[1]

[1] Aldous Huxley, "The Politics of Ecology" (Santa Barbara: Center for the Study of Democratic Institutions, 1963), p. 6.

Many of the wars fought by man—I am tempted to say most—have been fought over such abstractions. The more I puzzle over the great wars of history, the more I am inclined to the view that the causes attributed to them—territory, markets, resources, the defense or perpetuation of great principles—were not the root causes at all but rather explanations or excuses for certain unfathomable drives of human nature. For lack of a clear and precise understanding of exactly what these motives are, I refer to them as the "arrogance of power"—as a psychological need that nations seem to have in order to prove that they are bigger, better, or stronger than other nations. Implicit in this drive is the assumption, even on the part of normally peaceful nations, that force is the ultimate proof of superiority—that when a nation shows that it has the stronger army, it is also proving that it has better people, better institutions, better principles, and, in general, a better civilization.

Evidence for my proposition is found in the remarkable discrepancy between the apparent and hidden causes of some modern wars and the discrepancy between their causes and ultimate consequences.

The precipitating cause of the Franco-Prussian War of 1870, for example, was a dispute over the succession to the Spanish throne, and the ostensible "underlying" cause was French resistance to the unification of Germany. The war was followed by the completion of German unification—which probably could have been achieved without war—but it was also followed by the loss of Alsace-Lorraine, the humiliation of France, and the emergence of Germany as the greatest power in Europe, which could not have been achieved without war. The peace treaty, incidentally, said nothing about the Spanish throne, which everyone apparently had forgotten. One wonders to what extent the Germans were motivated simply by the desire to cut those haughty Frenchmen down to size and have a good excuse to build another monument in Berlin.

The United States went to war in 1898 for the stated purpose of liberating Cuba from Spanish tyranny, but after winning the war—a war which Spain had been willing to pay a high price to avoid—the United States brought the liberated Cubans under an American protectorate and incidentally annexed the Philippines, because, according to President McKinley, the Lord told him it was America's duty "to educate the Filipinos, and uplift and civilize and Christianize them, and by God's grace do the very best we could by them, as our fellow-men for whom Christ also died." [2]

Isn't it interesting that the voice was the voice of the Lord but the words were those of Theodore Roosevelt, Henry Cabot Lodge, and Admiral Mahan, those "imperialists of 1898" who wanted America to have an empire just because a big, powerful country like the United States *ought* to have an empire? The spirit of the times was expressed by Albert Beveridge, soon thereafter to be elected to the United States Senate, who proclaimed Americans to be "a conquering race": "We must obey our blood and occupy new markets and if necessary new lands," he said, because "In the Almighty's infinite plan . . . debased civilizations and decaying races" must disappear "before the higher civilization of the nobler and more virile types of man." [3]

---

[2] Quoted in Samuel Flagg Bemis, *A Diplomatic History of the United States* (New York: Henry Holt, 1955), p. 472.

[3] Quoted in Barbara Tuchman, *The Proud Tower* (New York: Macmillan, 1966), p. 153.

In 1914 all Europe went to war, ostensibly because the heir to the Austrian throne had been assassinated at Sarajevo, but really because that murder became the symbolic focus of the incredibly delicate sensibilities of the great nations of Europe. The events of the summer of 1914 were a melodrama of abnormal psychology: Austria had to humiliate Serbia in order not to be humiliated herself but Austria's effort at recovering self-esteem was profoundly humiliating to Russia; Russia was allied to France, who had been feeling generally humiliated since 1871, and Austria in turn was allied to Germany, whose pride required that she support Austria no matter how insanely Austria behaved and who may in any case have felt that it would be fun to give the German Army another swing down the Champs-Élysées. For these ennobling reasons the world was plunged into a war which took tens of millions of lives, precipitated the Russian Revolution, and set in motion the events that led to another world war, a war which took tens of millions more lives and precipitated the worldwide revolutions of our time, revolutions whose consequences are beyond the foresight of any of us now alive.

The causes and consequences of war may have more to do with pathology than with politics, more to do with irrational pressures of pride and pain than with rational calculations of advantage and profit. There is a Washington story, perhaps apocryphal, that the military intellectuals in the Pentagon conducted an experiment in which they fed data derived from the events of the summer of 1914 into a computer and that, after weighing and digesting the evidence, the machine assured its users that there was no danger of war. What this "proves," if anything, is that computers are more rational than men; it also suggests that if there is a root cause of human conflict and of the power drive of nations, it lies not in economic aspirations, historical forces, or the workings of the balance of power, but in the ordinary hopes and fears of the human mind.

It has been said that buried in every woman's secret soul is a drum majorette; it might also be said that in all of our souls there is a bit of the missionary. We all like telling people what to do, which is perfectly all right except that most people do not like being told what to do. I have given my wife some splendid suggestions on household management but she has been so consistently ungrateful for my advice that I have stopped offering it. The phenomenon is explained by the Canadian psychiatrist and former Director-General of the World Health Organization, Brock Chisholm, who writes:

> . . . Man's method of dealing with difficulties in the past has always been to tell everyone else how they should behave. We've all been doing that for centuries.
>
> It should be clear by now that this no longer does any good. Everybody has by now been told by everybody else how he should behave. . . . The criticism is not effective; it never has been, and it never is going to be. . . .[4]

Ineffective though it has been, the giving—and enforcement—of all this unsolicited advice has at least until recently been compatible with the survival of the human race. Man is now, however, for the first time, in a situation in

[4] Brock Chisholm, *Prescription of Survival* (New York: Columbia University Press, 1957), p. 54.

which the survival of his species is in jeopardy. Other forms of life have been endangered and many destroyed by changes in their natural environment; man is menaced by a change of environment which he himself has wrought by the invention of nuclear weapons and ballistic missiles. Our power to kill has become universal, creating a radically new situation which, if we are to survive, requires us to adopt some radically new attitudes about the giving and enforcement of advice and in general about human and international relations.

The enormity of the danger of extinction of our species is dulled by the frequency with which it is stated, as if a familiar threat of catastrophe were no threat at all. We seem to feel somehow that because the hydrogen bomb has not killed us yet, it is never going to kill us. This is a dangerous assumption because it encourages the retention of traditional attitudes about world politics when our responsibility, in Dr. Chisholm's words, is nothing less than to "re-examine all of the attitudes of our ancestors and to select from those attitudes things which we, on our own authority in these present circumstances, with our knowledge, recognize as still valid in this new kind of world. . . ." [5]

The attitude above all others which I feel sure is no longer valid is the arrogance of power, the tendency of great nations to equate power with virtue and major responsibilities with a universal mission. The dilemmas involved are pre-eminently American dilemmas, not because America has weaknesses that others do not have but because America is powerful as no nation has ever been before, and the discrepancy between her power and the power of others appears to be increasing. One may hope that America, with her vast resources and democratic traditions, with her diverse and creative population, will find the wisdom to match her power; but one can hardly be confident because the wisdom required is greater wisdom than any great nation has ever shown before. It must be rooted, as Dr. Chisholm says, in the re-examination of "all of the attitudes of our ancestors."

It is a tall order. Perhaps one can begin to fill it by an attempt to assess the attitudes of Americans toward other peoples and some of the effects of America's power on small countries whom she has tried to help.

INNOCENTS ABROAD

There are signs of the arrogance of power in the way Americans act when they go to foreign countries. Foreigners frequently comment on the contrast between the behavior of Americans at home and abroad: in our own country, they say, we are hospitable and considerate, but as soon as we get outside our own borders something seems to get into us and wherever we are we become noisy and demanding and we strut around as if we owned the place. The British used to say during the war that the trouble with the Yanks was that they were "overpaid, oversexed, and over here." During a recent vacation in Mexico, I noticed in a small-town airport two groups of students on holiday, one group Japanese, the other American. The Japanese were neatly dressed and were talking and

[5] *Ibid.*, p. 9.

laughing in a manner that neither annoyed anybody nor particularly called attention to themselves. The Americans, on the other hand, were disporting themselves in a conspicuous and offensive manner, stamping around the waiting room in sloppy clothes, drinking beer, and shouting to each other as if no one else were there.

This kind of scene, unfortunately, has become familiar in many parts of the world. I do not wish to exaggerate its significance, but I have the feeling that just as there was once something special about being a Roman or a Spaniard or an Englishman, there is now something about the consciousness of being an American abroad, something about the consciousness of belonging to the biggest, richest country in the world, that encourages people who are perfectly well behaved at home to become boorish when they are in somebody else's country and to treat the local citizens as if they were not really there.

One reason Americans abroad may act as though they "own the place" is that in many places they very nearly do: American companies may dominate large segments of a country's economy; American products are advertised on billboards and displayed in shop windows; American hotels and snack bars are available to protect American tourists from foreign influence; American soldiers may be stationed in the country, and even if they are not, the population are probably well aware that their very survival depends on the wisdom with which America uses her immense military power.

I think that when any American goes abroad, he carries an unconscious knowledge of all this power with him and it affects his behavior, just as it once affected the behavior of Greeks and Romans, of Spaniards, Germans, and Englishmen, in the brief high noons of their respective ascendancies. It was the arrogance of their power that led nineteenth-century Englishmen to suppose that if they shouted at a foreigner loud enough in English he was bound to understand, or that now leads Americans to behave like Mark Twain's "innocents abroad," who reported on their travels in Europe that

> The people of those foreign countries are very, very ignorant. They looked curiously at the costumes we had brought from the wilds of America. They observed that we talked loudly at table sometimes. . . . In Paris they just simply opened their eyes and stared when we spoke to them in French! We never did succeed in making these idiots understand their own language.[6]

THE FATAL IMPACT

Reflecting on his voyages to Polynesia in the late eighteenth century, Captain Cook later wrote that "It would have been better for these people never to have known us." In a book on European explorations of the South Pacific, Alan Moorehead relates how the Tahitians and the Australian aborigines were corrupted

[6] Mark Twain, *The Innocents Abroad* (New York: The Thistle Press, 1962), p. 494.

by the white man's diseases, alcohol, firearms, laws, and concepts of morality, by what Moorehead calls "the long down-slide into Western civilization." The first missionaries to Tahiti, says Moorehead, were "determined to recreate the island in the image of lower-middle-class Protestant England. . . . They kept hammering away at the Tahitian way of life until it crumbled before them, and within two decades they had achieved precisely what they set out to do." [7] It is said that the first missionaries to Hawaii went for the purpose of explaining to the Polynesians that it was sinful to work on Sunday, only to discover that in those bountiful islands nobody worked on any day.

Even when acting with the best of intentions, Americans, like other Western peoples who have carried their civilizations abroad, have had something of the same "fatal impact" on smaller nations that European explorers had on the Tahitians and the native Australians. We have not harmed people because we wished to; on the contrary, more often than not we have wanted to help people and, in some very important respects, we have helped them. Americans have brought medicine and education, manufactures and modern techniques to many places in the world; but they have also brought themselves and the condescending attitudes of a people whose very success breeds disdain for other cultures. Bringing power without understanding, Americans as well as Europeans have had a devastating effect in less advanced areas of the world; without knowing they were doing it, they have shattered traditional societies, disrupted fragile economies and undermined peoples' self-confidence by the invidious example of their own power and efficiency. They have done this in many instances simply by being big and strong, by giving good advice, by intruding on people who have not wanted them but could not resist them.

The missionary instinct seems to run deep in human nature, and the bigger and stronger and richer we are, the more we feel suited to the missionary task, the more indeed we consider it our duty. Dr. Chisholm relates the story of an eminent cleric who had been proselyting the Eskimos and said: "You know, for years we couldn't do anything with those Eskimos at all; they didn't have any sin. We had to teach them sin for years before we could do anything with them." [8] I am reminded of the three Boy Scouts who reported to their scoutmaster that as their good deed for the day they had helped an old lady to cross the street.

"That's fine," said the scoutmaster, "but why did it take three of you?"

"Well," they explained, "she didn't want to go."

The good deed above all others that Americans feel qualified to perform is the teaching of democracy. Let us consider the results of some American good deeds in various parts of the world.

Over the years since President Monroe proclaimed his doctrine, Latin Americans have had the advantages of United States tutelage in fiscal responsibility, in collective security, and in the techniques of democracy. If they have fallen short in any of these fields, the thought presents itself that the fault may lie as much with the teacher as with the pupils.

When President Theodore Roosevelt announced his "corollary" to the

[7] Alan Moorehead, *The Fatal Impact* (New York: Harper & Row, 1966), pp. 61, 80–81.

[8] Chisholm, *op. cit.*, pp. 55–56.

Monroe Doctrine in 1905, he solemnly declared that he regarded the future interventions thus sanctified as a "burden" and a "responsibility" and an obligation to "international equity." Not once, so far as I know, has the United States regarded itself as intervening in a Latin American country for selfish or unworthy motives—a view not necessarily shared, however, by the beneficiaries. Whatever reassurance the purity of our motives may give must be shaken a little by the thought that probably no country in human history has ever intervened in another except for motives it regarded as excellent.

For all our noble intentions, the countries which have had most of the tutelage in democracy by United States Marines have not been particularly democratic. These include Haiti, which is under a brutal and superstitious dictatorship; the Dominican Republic, which languished under the brutal Trujillo dictatorship for thirty years and whose second elected government since the overthrow of Trujillo is threatened, like the first, by the power of a military oligarchy; and of course Cuba, which, as no one needs to be reminded, has replaced its traditional right-wing dictatorships with a communist dictatorship.

Maybe, in the light of this extraordinary record of accomplishment, it is time for us to reconsider our teaching methods. Maybe we are not really cut out for the job of spreading the gospel of democracy. Maybe it would profit us to concentrate on our own democracy instead of trying to inflict our particular version of it on all those ungrateful Latin Americans who stubbornly oppose their North American benefactors instead of the "real" enemies whom we have so graciously chosen for them. And maybe—just maybe—if we left our neighbors to make their own judgments and their own mistakes, and confined our assistance to matters of economics and technology instead of philosophy, maybe then they would begin to find the democracy and the dignity that have largely eluded them, and we in turn might begin to find the love and gratitude that we seem to crave.

Korea is another example. We went to war in 1950 to defend South Korea against the Russian-inspired aggression of North Korea. I think that American intervention was justified and necessary: we were defending a country that clearly wanted to be defended, whose army was willing to fight and fought well, and whose government, though dictatorial, was patriotic and commanded the support of the people. Throughout the war, however, the United States emphasized as one of its war aims the survival of the Republic of Korea as a "free society," something which it was not then and is not now. We lost 33,629 American lives in that war and have since spent $5.61 billion on direct military and economic aid and a great deal more on indirect aid to South Korea. The country, nonetheless, remained until recently in a condition of virtual economic stagnation and political unstability. Only now is economic progress being made, but the truly surprising fact is that having fought a war for three years to defend the freedom of South Korea, most Americans quickly lost interest in the state of the ward for whom they had sacrificed so much. It is doubtful that more than a handful of Americans now know or care whether South Korea is a "free society."

We are now engaged in a war to "defend freedom" in South Vietnam. Unlike the Republic of Korea, South Vietnam has an army which fights without notable success and a weak, dictatorial government which does not command the loyalty of the South Vietnamese people. The official war aims of the United States government, as I understand them, are to defeat what is regarded as North Vietnamese aggression, to demonstrate the futility of what the communists call "wars of national liberation," and to create conditions under which the South Vietnamese people will be able freely to determine their own future.

I have not the slightest doubt of the sincerity of the President and the Vice-President and the Secretaries of State and Defense in propounding these aims. What I do doubt, and doubt very much, is the ability of the United States to achieve these aims by the means being used. I do not question the power of our weapons and the efficiency of our logistics; I cannot say these things delight me as they seem to delight some of our officials, but they are certainly impressive. What I do question is the ability of the United States or any other Western nation to go into a small, alien, undeveloped Asian nation and create stability where there is chaos, the will to fight where there is defeatism, democracy where there is no tradition of it, and honest government where corruption is almost a way of life.

In the spring of 1966 demonstrators in Saigon burned American jeeps, tried to assault American soldiers, and marched through the streets shouting "Down with American imperialists," while a Buddhist leader made a speech equating the United States with the communists as a threat to South Vietnamese independence. Most Americans are understandably shocked and angered to encounter expressions of hostility from people who would long since have been under the rule of the Viet Cong but for the sacrifice of American lives and money. Why, we may ask, are they so shockingly ungrateful? Surely they must know that their very right to parade and protest and demonstrate depends on the Americans who are defending them.

The answer, I think, is that "fatal impact" of the rich and strong on the poor and weak. Dependent on it though the Vietnamese are, American strength is a reproach to their weakness, American wealth a mockery of their poverty, American success a reminder of their failures. What they resent is the disruptive effect of our strong culture upon their fragile one, an effect which we can no more avoid having than a man can help being bigger than a child. What they fear, I think rightly, is that traditional Vietnamese society cannot survive the American economic and cultural impact.

The evidence of that "fatal impact" is seen in the daily life of Saigon. A *New York Times* correspondent reported—and his information matches that of other observers on the scene—that many Vietnamese find it necessary to put their wives or daughters to work as bar girls or to peddle them to American soldiers as mistresses; that it is not unusual to hear a report that a Vietnamese soldier has committed suicide out of shame because his wife has been working as a bar girl; that Vietnamese have trouble getting taxicabs because drivers will not stop for them, preferring to pick up American soldiers who will pay outrageous fares without complaint; that as a result of the American influx bar girls, prostitutes, pimps, bar owners, and taxi drivers have risen to the higher levels of the economic pyramid; that middle-class Vietnamese families have difficulty renting homes because Americans have driven the rents beyond their reach, and some Vietnamese families have actually been evicted from houses and apartments by landlords who prefer to rent to the affluent Americans;

that Vietnamese civil servants, junior army officers, and enlisted men are unable to support their families because of the inflation generated by American spending and the purchasing power of the G.I.s. One Vietnamese explained to the *New York Times* reporter that "Any time legions of prosperous white men descend on a rudimentary Asian society, you are bound to have trouble." Another said: "We Vietnamese are somewhat xenophobe. We don't like foreigners, any kind of foreigners, so that you shouldn't be surprised that we don't like you." [9]

Sincere though it is, the American effort to build the foundations of freedom in South Vietnam is thus having an effect quite different from the one intended. "All this struggling and striving to make the world better is a great mistake," said George Bernard Shaw, "not because it isn't a good thing to improve the world if you know how to do it, but because striving and struggling is the worst way you could set about doing anything." [10]

One wonders how much the American commitment to Vietnamese freedom is also a commitment to American pride—the two seem to have become part of the same package. When we talk about the freedom of South Vietnam, we may be thinking about how disagreeable it would be to accept a solution short of victory; we may be thinking about how our pride would be injured if we settled for less than we set out to achieve; we may be thinking about our reputation as a great power, fearing that a compromise settlement would shame us before the world, marking us as a second-rate people with flagging courage and determination.

Such fears are as nonsensical as their opposite, the presumption of a universal mission. They are simply unworthy of the richest, most powerful, most productive, and best educated people in the world. One can understand an uncompromising attitude on the part of such countries as China or France: both have been struck low in this century and a certain amount of arrogance may be helpful to them in recovering their pride. It is much less comprehensible on the part of the United States—a nation whose modern history has been an almost uninterrupted chronicle of success, a nation which by now should be so sure of its own power as to be capable of magnanimity, a nation which by now should be able to act on the proposition that, as George Kennan said, "there is more respect to be won in the opinion of the world by a resolute and courageous liquidation of unsound positions than in the most stubborn pursuit of extravagant or unpromising objectives." [11]

The cause of our difficulties in Southeast Asia is not a deficiency of power but an excess of the wrong kind of power, which results in a feeling of impotence when it fails to achieve its desired ends. We are still acting like Boy Scouts dragging reluctant old ladies across streets they do not want to cross. We are trying to remake Vietnamese society, a task which certainly cannot be ac-

[9] Neil Sheehan, "Anti-Americanism Grows in Vietnam," *The New York Times,* April 24, 1966, p. 3.

[10] George Bernard Shaw, *Cashel Byron's Profession* (1886), Chapter 5.

[11] George F. Kennan, "Supplemental Foreign Assistance Fiscal Year 1966—Vietnam," *Hearings Before the Committee on Foreign Relations,* United States Senate, 89th Congress, 2nd Session on S. 2793, Part I (Washington: U.S. Government Printing Office, 1966), p. 335.

complished by force and which probably cannot be accomplished by any means available to outsiders. The objective may be desirable, but it is not feasible. As Shaw said: "Religion is a great force—the only real motive force in the world; but what you fellows don't understand is that you must get at a man through his own religion and not through yours." [12]

With the best intentions in the world the United States has involved itself deeply in the affairs of developing nations in Asia and Latin America, practicing what has been called a kind of "welfare imperialism." Our honest purpose is the advancement of development and democracy, to which end it has been thought necessary to destroy ancient and unproductive modes of life. In this latter function we have been successful, perhaps more successful than we know. Bringing skills and knowledge, money and resources in amounts hitherto unknown in traditional societies, the Americans have overcome indigenous groups and interests and become the dominant force in a number of countries. Far from being bumbling, wasteful, and incompetent, as critics have charged, American government officials, technicians, and economists have been strikingly successful in breaking down the barriers to change in ancient but fragile cultures.

Here, however, our success ends. Traditional rulers, institutions, and ways of life have crumbled under the fatal impact of American wealth and power but they have not been replaced by new institutions and new ways of life, nor has their breakdown ushered in an era of democracy and development. It has rather ushered in an era of disorder and demoralization because in the course of destroying old ways of doing things, we have also destroyed the self-confidence and self-reliance without which no society can build indigenous institutions. Inspiring as we have such great awe of our efficiency and wealth, we have reduced some of the intended beneficiaries of our generosity to a condition of dependency and self-denigration. We have done this for the most part inadvertently: with every good intention we have intruded on fragile societies, and our intrusion, though successful in uprooting traditional ways of life, has been strikingly unsuccessful in implanting the democracy and advancing the development which are the honest aims of our "welfare imperialism."

AMERICAN EMPIRE OR AMERICAN EXAMPLE?

Despite its dangerous and unproductive consequences, the idea of being responsible for the whole world seems to be flattering to Americans and I am afraid that it is turning our heads, just as the sense of universal responsibility turned the heads of ancient Romans and nineteenth-century British.

In 1965 Henry Fairlie, a British political writer for *The Spectator* and *The Daily Telegraph,* wrote what he called "A Cheer for American Imperialism." [13] An empire, he said, "has no justification except its own existence." It must never contract; it "wastes treasure and life"; its commitments "are without rhyme or

[12] George Bernard Shaw, *Getting Married* (1911).
[13] *The New York Times Magazine,* July 11, 1965.

reason." Nonetheless, according to Fairlie, the "American empire" is uniquely benevolent, devoted as it is to individual liberty and the rule of law, and having performed such services as getting the author released from a Yugoslav jail simply by his threatening to involve the American Consul, a service which he describes as "sublime."

What romantic nonsense this is. And what dangerous nonsense in the age of nuclear weapons. The idea of an "American empire" might be dismissed as the arrant imagining of a British Gunga Din except that it surely strikes a responsive chord in at least a corner of the usually sensible and humane American mind. It calls to mind the slogans of the past about the shot being fired at Concord being heard 'round the world, about "manifest destiny" and "making the world safe for democracy," and the demand for "unconditional surrender" in World War II. It calls to mind President McKinley taking counsel with the Supreme Being about his duty to the benighted Filipinos.

The "Blessings-of-Civilization Trust," as Mark Twain called it, may have been a "Daisy" in its day, uplifting for the soul and good for business besides, but its day is past. It is past because the great majority of the human race is demanding dignity and independence, not the honor of a supine role in an American empire. It is past because whatever claim America may make for the universal domain of her ideas and values is balanced by the communist counterclaim, armed like our own with nuclear weapons. And, most of all, it is past because it never should have begun, because we are not God's chosen saviour of mankind but only one of mankind's more successful and fortunate branches, endowed by our Creator with about the same capacity for good and evil, no more or less, than the rest of humanity.

An excessive preoccupation with foreign relations over a long period of time is more than a manifestation of arrogance; it is a drain on the power that gave rise to it, because it diverts a nation from the sources of its strength, which are in its domestic life. A nation immersed in foreign affairs is expending its capital, human as well as material; sooner or later that capital must be renewed by some diversion of creative energies from foreign to domestic pursuits. I would doubt that any nation has achieved a durable greatness by conducting a "strong" foreign policy, but many have been ruined by expending their energies in foreign adventures while allowing their domestic bases to deteriorate. The United States emerged as a world power in the twentieth century, not because of what it had done in foreign relations but because it had spent the nineteenth century developing the North American continent; by contrast, the Austrian and Turkish empires collapsed in the twentieth century in large part because they had so long neglected their internal development and organization.

If America has a service to perform in the world—and I believe she has— it is in large part the service of her own example. In our excessive involvement in the affairs of other countries we are not only living off our assets and denying our own people the proper enjoyment of their resources, we are also denying the world the example of a free society enjoying its freedom to the fullest. This is regrettable indeed for a nation that aspires to teach democracy to other nations, because, as Edmund Burke said, "Example is the school of mankind, and they will learn at no other." [14]

[14] Edmund Burke, "On a Regicide Peace" (1796).

The missionary instinct in foreign affairs may, in a curious way, reflect a deficiency rather than an excess of national self-confidence. In America's case the evidence of a lack of self-confidence is our apparent need for constant proof and reassurance, our nagging desire for popularity, our bitterness and confusion when foreigners fail to appreciate our generosity and good intentions. Lacking an appreciation of the dimensions of our own power, we fail to understand our enormous and disruptive impact on the world; we fail to understand that no matter how good our intentions—and they are, in most cases, decent enough—other nations are alarmed by the very existence of such great power, which, whatever its benevolence, cannot help but remind them of their own helplessness before it.

Those who lack self-assurance are also likely to lack magnanimity, because the one is the condition of the other. Only a nation at peace with itself, with its transgressions as well as its achievements, is capable of a generous understanding of others. Only when we Americans can acknowledge our own past aggressive behavior—in such instances, for example, as the Indian wars and the wars against Mexico and Spain—we will acquire some perspective on the aggressive behavior of others; only when we can understand the human implications of the chasm between American affluence and the poverty of most of the rest of mankind will we be able to understand why the American "way of life" which is so dear to us has few lessons and limited appeal to the poverty-stricken majority of the human race.

It is a curiosity of human nature that lack of self-assurance seems to breed an exaggerated sense of power and mission. When a nation is very powerful but lacking in self-confidence, it is likely to behave in a manner dangerous to itself and to others. Feeling the need to prove what is obvious to everyone else, it begins to confuse great power with unlimited power and great responsibility with total responsibility: it can admit of no error; it must win every argument, no matter how trivial. For lack of an appreciation of how truly powerful it is, the nation begins to lose wisdom and perspective and, with them, the strength and understanding that it takes to be magnanimous to smaller and weaker nations.

Gradually but unmistakably America is showing signs of that arrogance of power which has afflicted, weakened, and in some cases destroyed great nations in the past. In so doing we are not living up to our capacity and promise as a civilized example for the world. The measure of our falling short is the measure of the patriot's duty of dissent.

35

LESLIE A. FIEDLER

The New Mutants

Leslie Fiedler's social criticism generally begins with an assumption that the opposite of accepted opinion may be true. In an early book, for example, he dwelt on the self-deception of liberals in the Rosenberg and Hiss cases, concluding that many of them distort reality in order to accommodate their own points of view and their sometimes maudlin emotions. His purpose in writing, as he expressed it in a preface, is to produce "the difficult pleasure possible only to one recognizing a truth which involves a personal humiliation or the surrender of values long held."

Fiedler was perhaps the first American professor of literature to become a public personality. The photograph on his first book displayed a bearded, growling—or perhaps grinning—Fiedler in a heavy-textured black turtleneck. The image of an enfant terrible was effective enough for the nineteen fifties when almost any strong voice was a welcome one; and in the far different decade that followed, Fiedler came fully into his own. In a contretemps that reached the newspapers, the Buffalo police invaded his home in search of marijuana, which they allegedly found.

What is remarkable about Fiedler's most recent work is his ability to keep abreast of his times. Perhaps his disillusionment with Ernest Hemingway, whose suicide elicited a typically provocative Fiedlerian essay, brought him closer to more contemporary writers like William Burroughs and John Barth; and as the father of six children, he keeps an eye on the young. Whatever the reasons, "The New Mutants," which appeared in 1965, is able to catch the tone of a particular strain of the post-adolescent protest that acquired great prominence in the nineteen sixties.

Fiedler perceives that many young people find adult maturity, as defined by society, not merely hypocritical but repugnant. He understands the desire to experiment with alternative forms of experience through drugs and gives consideration to the idea of madness as a form of revelation. He appreciates passive resistance and

the need to redefine the terms by which sexual liaisons are made, in-
cluding the heterosexual male's rejection of self-consciously mascu-
line values. That this awareness should come from a man not under
thirty but over fifty, and one who has frequently dissociated himself
from "liberalism," speaks of Fiedler's ability to deal with change.

Nevertheless, for Fiedler the life style of the New Mutants
must be disconcerting. For what is happening among these young
people is not simply a fashion. In Fiedler's youth everyone was a
fierce rationalist growing up amidst the tensions and necessities of
work and money and masculinity. People read Marx and Freud and
talked of reason assaulting unreason; sharply defined sexual roles in
Fiedler's day were ways not only of understanding oneself but of
understanding the world. But today's young seem to insist on living
only in the present and deny the categories through which Fiedler's
generation seeks to understand them.

A realization that the legitimate functions of literature are bewilderingly, almost inexhaustibly various has always exhilarated poets and dismayed critics. And critics, therefore, have sought age after age to legislate limits to literature—legitimizing certain of its functions and disavowing others—in hope of insuring to themselves the exhilaration of which they have felt unjustly deprived, and providing for poets the dismay which the critics at least have thought good for them.

Such shifting and exclusive emphasis is not, however, purely the product of critical malice, or even of critical principle. Somehow every period is, to begin with, especially aware of certain functions of literature and especially oblivious to others: endowed with a special sensitivity and a complementary obtuseness, which, indeed, give to that period its characteristic flavor and feel. So, for instance, the Augustan Era is marked by sensitivity in regard to the uses of diction, obtuseness in regard to those of imagery.

What the peculiar obtuseness of the present age may be I find it difficult to say (being its victim as well as its recorder), perhaps toward the didactic or certain modes of the sentimental. I am reasonably sure, however, that our period is acutely aware of the sense in which literature, if not invents, at least collaborates in the invention of time. The beginnings of that awareness go back certainly to the beginnings of the Renaissance, to Humanism as a self-conscious movement; though a critical development occurred toward the end of the eighteenth century with the dawning of the Age of Revolution. And we may have reached a second critical point right now.

At any rate, we have long been aware (in the last decades uncomfortably aware) that a chief function of literature is to express and in part to create not only theories of time but also attitudes toward time. Such attitudes constitute, however, a politics as well as an esthetics; or, more properly perhaps, a necessary mythological substratum of politics—as, in fact, the conventional terms reactionary, conservative, revolutionary indicate: all involving stances toward the past.

It is with the past, then, that we must start, since the invention of the past seems to have preceded that of the present and the future; and since we are gathered in a university at whose heart stands a library—the latter, like the former, a visible monument to the theory that a chief responsibility of literature is to preserve and perpetuate the past. Few universities are explicitly (and none with any real degree of confidence) dedicated to this venerable goal any longer. The Great Books idea (which once transformed the University of Chicago and lives on now in provincial study groups) was perhaps its last desperate expression. Yet the shaky continuing existence of the universities and the building of new college libraries (with matching Federal funds) remind us not only of that tradition but of the literature created in its name: the neo-epic, for instance, all the way from Dante to Milton; and even the frantically nostalgic Historical Romance, out of the counting house by Sir Walter Scott.

Obviously, however, literature has a contemporary as well as a traditional function. That is to say, it may be dedicated to illuminating the present and the meaning of the present, which is, after all, no more given than the past. Certainly the modern or bourgeois novel was thus contemporary in the hands of its great inventors, Richardson, Fielding, Smollett and Sterne; and it became contemporary again—with, as it were, a sigh of relief—when Flaubert, having plunged deep into the Historical Romance, emerged once more into the present of Emma Bovary. But the second function of the novel tends to transform itself into a third: a revolutionary or prophetic or futurist function; and it is with the latter that I am here concerned.

Especially important for our own time is the sense in which literature first conceived the possibility of the future (rather than an End of Time or an Eternal Return, an Apocalypse or Second Coming); and then furnished that future in joyous or terrified anticipation, thus preparing all of us to inhabit it. Men have dreamed and even written down utopias from ancient times; but such utopias were at first typically allegories rather than projections: non-existent models against which to measure the real world, exploitations of the impossible (as the traditional name declares) rather than explorations or anticipations or programs of the possible. And, in any event, only recently have such works occupied a position anywhere near the center of literature.

Indeed, the movement of futurist literature from the periphery to the center of culture provides a clue to certain essential meanings of our times and of the art which best reflects it. If we make a brief excursion from the lofty reaches of High Art to the humbler levels of Pop Culture—where radical transformations in literature are reflected in simplified form—the extent and nature of the futurist revolution will become immediately evident. Certainly, we have seen in recent years the purveyors of Pop Culture transfer their energies from the Western and the Dracula-type thriller (last heirs of the Romantic and Gothic concern with the past) to the Detective Story especially in its hard-boiled form (final vulgarization of the realists' dedication to the present) to Science Fiction (a new genre based on hints in E. A. Poe and committed to "extrapolating" the future). This development is based in part on the tendency to rapid exhaustion inherent in popular forms; but in part reflects a growing sense of the irrelevance of the past and even of the present to 1965. Surely, there has never been a moment in which the most naïve as well as the most sophisticated have been so acutely aware of how the past threatens momentarily to disappear from the present, which itself seems on the verge of disappearing into the future.

And this awareness functions, therefore, on the level of art as well as entertainment, persuading quite serious writers to emulate the modes of Science Fiction. The novel is most amenable to this sort of adaptation, whose traces we can find in writers as various as William Golding and Anthony Burgess, William Burroughs and Kurt Vonnegut, Jr., Harry Mathews and John Barth—to all of whom young readers tend to respond with a sympathy they do not feel even toward such forerunners of the mode (still more allegorical than prophetic) as Aldous Huxley, H. G. Wells and George Orwell. But the influence of Science Fiction can be discerned in poetry as well, and even in the polemical essays of such polymath prophets as Wilhelm Reich, Buckminster Fuller, Marshall Mc-Luhan, perhaps also Norman O. Brown. Indeed, in Fuller the prophetic—Science-Fiction view of man is always at the point of fragmenting into verse:

> men are known as being six feet tall
> because that is their tactile limit;
> they are not known by how far we can hear them,
> e.g., as a one-half mile man
> and only to dogs are men known
> by their gigantic olfactoral dimensions. . . .

I am not now interested in analyzing, however, the diction and imagery which have passed from Science Fiction into post-Modernist literature, but rather in coming to terms with the prophetic content common to both: with the myth rather than the modes of Science Fiction. But that myth is quite simply the myth of the end of man, of the transcendence or transformation of the human—a vision quite different from that of the extinction of our species by the Bomb, which seems stereotype rather than archetype and consequently the source of editorials rather than poems. More fruitful artistically is the prospect of the radical transformation (under the impact of advanced technology and the transfer of traditional human functions to machines) of *homo sapiens* into something else: the emergence—to use the language of Science Fiction itself—of "mutants" among us.

A simpleminded prevision of this event is to be found in Arthur C. Clarke's *Childhood's End,* at the conclusion of which the mutated offspring of parents much like us are about to take off under their own power into outer space. Mr. Clarke believes that he is talking about a time still to come because he takes metaphor for fact; though simply translating "outer space" into "inner space" reveals to us that what he is up to is less prediction than description; since the post-human future is now, and if not we, at least our children, are what it would be comfortable to pretend we still only foresee. But what, in fact, are they: these mutants who are likely to sit before us in class, or across from us at the dinner table, or who stare at us with hostility from street corners as we pass?

Beatniks or hipsters, layabouts and drop-outs we are likely to call them with corresponding hostility—or more elegantly, but still without sympathy, passive onlookers, abstentionists, spiritual catatonics. There resides in all of these terms an element of truth, at least about the relationship of the young to what we have defined as the tradition, the world we have made for them; and if we turn to the books in which they see their own destiny best represented (*A Clockwork Orange,* say, or *On the Road* or *Temple of Gold*), we will find nothing to contradict that truth. Nor will we find anything to expand it, since the young and their laureates avoid on principle the kind of definition (even of themselves) for which we necessarily seek.

Let us begin then with the negative definition our own hostility suggests, since this is all that is available to us, and say that the "mutants" in our midst are non-participants in the past (though our wisdom assures us this is impossible), drop-outs from history. The withdrawal from school, so typical of their generation and so inscrutable to ours, is best understood as a lived symbol of their rejection of the notion of cultural continuity and progress, which our graded educational system represents in institutional form. It is not merely a matter of their rejecting what happens to have happened just before them, as the young do, after all, in every age; but of their attempting to disavow the very idea of the past, of their seeking to avoid recapitulating it step by step—up to the point of graduation into the present.

Specifically, the tradition from which they strive to disengage is the tradition of the human, as the West (understanding the West to extend from the United States to Russia) has defined it, Humanism itself, both in its bourgeois and Marxist forms; and more especially, the cult of reason—that dream of Socrates, redreamed by the Renaissance and surviving all travesties down to only yesterday. To be sure, there have long been anti-rational forces at work in the West, including primitive Christianity itself; but the very notion of literary culture is a product of Humanism, as the early Christians knew (setting fire to libraries), so that the Church in order to sponsor poets had first to come to terms with reason itself by way of Aquinas and Aristotle.

Only with Dada was the notion of an anti-rational anti-literature born; and Dada became Surrealism, i.e., submitted to the influence of those last neo-Humanists, those desperate Socratic Cabalists, Freud and Marx—dedicated respectively to contriving a rationale of violence and a rationale of impulse. The new irrationalists, however, deny all the apostles of reason, Freud as well as Socrates; and if they seem to exempt Marx, this is because they know less about him, have heard him evoked less often by the teachers they are driven to deny. Not only do they reject the Socratic adage that the unexamined life is not worth living, since for them precisely the unexamined life is the only one worth enduring at all. But they also abjure the Freudian one: "Where id was, ego shall be," since for them the true rallying cry is, "Let id prevail over ego, impulse over order," or—in negative terms—"Freud is a fink!"

The first time I heard this irreverent charge from the mouth of a student some five or six years ago (I who had grown up thinking of Freud as a revolutionary, a pioneer), I knew that I was already in the future; though I did not yet suspect that there would be no room in that future for the university system to which I had devoted my life. Kerouac might have told me so, or Ginsberg, or even so polite and genteel a spokesman for youth as J. D. Salinger, but I was too aware of what was wrong with such writers (their faults more readily apparent to my taste than their virtues) to be sensitive to the truths they told. It took, therefore, certain public events to illuminate (for me) the literature which might have illuminated them.

I am thinking, of course, of the recent demonstrations at Berkeley and elsewhere, whose ostensible causes were civil rights or freedom of speech or Vietnam, but whose not so secret slogan was all the time: *The Professor Is a Fink!* And what an array of bad anti-academic novels, I cannot help reminding myself, written by disgruntled professors, created the mythology out of which that slogan grew. Each generation of students is invented by the generation of teachers just before them; but how different they are in dream and fact—as different as self-hatred and its reflection in another. How different the professors in Jeremy Larner's *Drive, He Said* from those even in Randall Jarrell's *Pictures from an Institution* or Mary McCarthy's *Groves of Academe.*

To be sure, many motives operated to set the students in action, some of them imagined in no book, however good or bad. Many of the thousands who resisted or shouted on campuses did so in the name of naïve or disingenuous or even nostalgic politics (be careful what you wish for in your middle age, or your children will parody it forthwith!); and sheer ennui doubtless played a role along with a justified rage against the hypocrisies of academic life. Universities have long rivaled the churches in their devotion to institutionalizing hypocrisy; and more recently they have out-stripped television itself (which most professors affect to despise even more than they despise organized religion) in the institutionalization of boredom.

But what the students were protesting in large part, I have come to believe, was the very notion of man which the universities sought to impose upon them: that bourgeois-Protestant version of Humanism, with its view of man as justified by rationality, work, duty, vocation, maturity, success; and its concomitant understanding of childhood and adolescence as a temporarily privileged time of preparation for assuming those burdens. The new irrationalists, however, are prepared to advocate prolonging adolescence to the grave, and are ready to dispense with school as an outlived excuse for leisure. To them work is as obsolete as reason, a vestige (already dispensable for large numbers) of an economically marginal, pre-automated world; and the obsolescence of the two adds up to the obsolescence of everything our society understands by maturity.

Nor is it in the name of an older more valid Humanistic view of man that the new irrationalists would reject the WASP version; Rabelais is as alien to them as Benjamin Franklin. Disinterested scholarship, reflection, the life of reason, a respect for tradition stir (however dimly and confusedly) chiefly their contempt; and the Abbey of Theleme would seem as sterile to them as Robinson Crusoe's Island. To the classroom, the library, the laboratory, the office conference and the meeting of scholars, they prefer the demonstration, the sit-in, the riot: the mindless unity of an impassioned crowd (with guitars beating out the rhythm in the background), whose immediate cause is felt rather than thought out, whose ultimate cause is itself. In light of this, the Teach-in, often ill understood because of an emphasis on its declared political ends, can be seen as implicitly a parody and mockery of the real classroom: related to the actual business of the university, to real teaching only as the Demonstration Trial (of Dimitrov, of the Soviet Doctors, of Eichmann) to real justice or Demonstration Voting (for one party or a token two) to real suffrage.

At least, since Berkeley (or perhaps since Martin Luther King provided students with new paradigms for action) the choice has been extended beyond what the earlier laureates of the new youth could imagine in the novel: the nervous breakdown at home rather than the return to "sanity" and school, which was the best Salinger could invent for Franny and Holden; or Kerouac's way out for his "saintly" vagrants, that "road" from nowhere to noplace with homemade gurus at the way stations. The structure of those fictional vaudevilles between hard covers that currently please the young (*Catch 22, V., A Mother's Kisses*), suggest in their brutality and discontinuity, their politics of mockery something of the spirit of the student demonstrations; but only Jeremy Larner, as far as I know, had dealt explicitly with the abandonment of the classroom in favor of the dionysiac pack, the turning from *polis* to *thiasos*, from forms of social organization traditionally thought of as male to the sort of passionate community attributed by the ancients to females out of control.

Conventional slogans in favor of "Good Works" (pious emendations of existing social structures, or extensions of accepted "rights" to excluded groups) though they provide the motive power of such protests are irrelevant to their form and their final significance. They become their essential selves, i.e., genuine new forms of rebellion, when the demonstrators hoist (as they did in the final stages of the Berkeley protests) the sort of slogan which embarrasses not only fellow-travelers but even the bureaucrats who direct the initial stages of the revolt: at the University of California, the single four-letter word no family newspaper would reprint, though no member of a family who could read was likely not to know it.

It is possible to argue on the basis of the political facts themselves that the word "fuck" entered the whole scene accidentally (there were only four students behind the "Dirty Speech Movement," only fifteen hundred kids could be persuaded to demonstrate for it, etc., etc.). But the prophetic literature which anticipates the movement indicates otherwise, suggesting that the logic of their illogical course eventually sets the young against language itself, against the very counters of logical discourse. They seek an anti-language of protest as inevitably as they seek anti-poems and anti-novels, end with the ultimate anti-word, which the demonstrators at Berkeley disingenuously claimed stood for FREEDOM UNDER CLARK KERR.

Esthetics, however, had already anticipated politics in this regard; porno-poetry preceding and preparing the way for what Lewis Feuer has aptly called porno-politics. Already in 1963, in an essay entitled *"Phi Upsilon Kappa,"* the young poet Michael McClure was writing: "Gregory Corso has asked me to join with him in a project to free the word FUCK from its chains and strictures. I leap to make some new freedom. . . ." And McClure's own "Fuck Ode" is a product of this collaboration, as the very name of Ed Saunders' journal, *Fuck You,* is the creation of an analogous impulse. The aging critics of the young who have dealt with the Berkeley demonstrations in such journals as *Commentary* and the *New Leader* do not, however, read either Saunders' porno-pacifist magazine or *Kulchur,* in which McClure's manifesto was first printed—the age barrier separating readership in the United States more effectively than class, political affiliation or anything else.

Their sense of porno-esthetics is likely to come from deserters from their own camp, chiefly Norman Mailer, and especially his recent *An American Dream,* which represents the entry of anti-language (extending the tentative explorations of "The Time of Her Time") into the world of the middle-aged, both on the level of mass culture and that of yesterday's ex-Marxist, post-Freudian avant-garde. Characteristically enough, Mailer's book has occasioned in the latter quarter reviews as irrelevant, incoherent, misleading and fundamentally scared as the most philistine responses to the Berkeley demonstrations, Philip Rahv and Stanley Edgar Hyman providing two egregious examples. Yet elsewhere (in sectors held by those more at ease with their own conservatism, i.e., without defunct radicalisms to uphold) the most obscene forays of the young are being met with a disheartening kind of tolerance and even an attempt to adapt them to the conditions of commodity art.

But precisely here, of course, a disconcerting irony is involved; for after a while, there will be no Rahvs and Hymans left to shock—anti-language becoming mere language with repeated use and in the face of acceptance; so that all sense of exhilaration will be lost along with the possibility of offense. What to do then except to choose silence, since raising the ante of violence is ultimately self-defeating; and the way of obscenity in any case leads as naturally to silence as to further excess? Moreover, to the talkative heirs of Socrates, silence is the one offense that never wears out, the radicalism that can never become fashionable; which is why, after the obscene slogan has been hauled down, a blank placard is raised in its place.

There are difficulties, to be sure, when one attempts to move from the politics of silence to an analogous sort of poetry. The opposite number to the silent picketer would be the silent poet, which is a contradiction in terms; yet there are these days nonsingers of (perhaps) great talent who shrug off the temptation to song with the muttered comment, "Creativity is out." Some, however, make literature of a kind precisely at the point of maximum tension between the tug toward silence and the pull toward publication. Music is a better language really for saying what one would prefer not to say at all—and all the way from certain sorts of sufficiently cool jazz to Rock 'n' Roll (with its minimal lyrics that defy understanding on a first hearing), music is the preferred art of the irrationalists.

But some varieties of skinny poetry seem apt, too (as practiced, say, by Robert Creeley after the example of W. C. Williams), since their lines are three parts silence to one part speech:

> My lady
> fair with
> soft
> arms, what
> can I say to
> you—words, words . . .

And, of course, fiction aspiring to become Pop Art, say, *An American Dream* (with the experiments of Hemingway and Nathanael West behind it), works approximately as well, since clichés are almost as inaudible as silence itself. The point is not to shout, not to insist, but to hang cool, to baffle all mothers, cultural and spiritual as well as actual.

When the Town Council in Venice, California, was about to close down a particularly notorious beatnik cafe, a lady asked to testify before them, presumably to clinch the case against the offenders. What she reported, however, was that each day as she walked by the cafe and looked in its windows, she saw the unsavory types who inhabited it "just standing there, looking—nonchalant." And, in a way, her improbable adjective does describe a crime against her world; for non-chaleur ("cool," the futurists themselves would prefer to call it) is the essence of their life-style as well as of the literary styles to which they respond: the offensive style of those who are not so much *for* anything in particular, as "with it" in general.

But such an attitude is as remote from traditional "alienation," with its profound longing to end disconnection, as it is from ordinary forms of allegiance, with their desperate resolve not to admit disconnection. The new young celebrate disconnection—accept it as one of the necessary consequences of the industrial system which has delivered them from work and duty, of that welfare state which makes disengagement the last possible virtue, whether it call itself Capitalist, Socialist or Communist. "Detachment" is the traditional name for the stance the futurists assume; but "detachment" carries with it irrelevant religious, even specifically Christian overtones. The post-modernists are surely in some sense "mystics," religious at least in a way they do not ordinarily know how to confess, but they are not Christians.

Indeed, they regard Christianity, quite as the Black Muslim (with whom they have certain affinities) do, as a white ideology: merely one more method —along with Humanism, technology, Marxism—of imposing "White" or Western values on the colored rest of the world. To the new barbarian, however, that would-be post-Humanist (who is in most cases the white offspring of Christian forebears) his whiteness is likely to seem if not a stigma and symbol of shame, at least the outward sign of his exclusion from all that his Christian Humanist ancestors rejected in themselves and projected mythologically upon the colored man. For such reasons, his religion, when it becomes explicit, claims to be derived from Tibet or Japan or the ceremonies of the Plains Indians, or is composed out of the non-Christian sub-mythology that has grown up among Negro jazz musicians and in the civil rights movement. When the new barbarian speaks of "soul," for instance, he means not "soul" as in Heaven, but as in "soul music" or even "soul food."

It is all part of the attempt of the generation under twenty-five, not exclusively in its most sensitive members but especially in them, to become Negro, even as they attempt to become poor or pre-rational. About this particular form of psychic assimilation I have written sufficiently in the past (summing up what I had been long saying in chapters seven and eight of *Waiting for the End*), neglecting only the sense in which what starts as a specifically American movement becomes an international one, spreading to the *yé-yé* girls of France or the working-class entertainers of Liverpool with astonishing swiftness and ease.

What interests me more particularly right now is a parallel assimilationist attempt, which may, indeed, be more parochial and is certainly most marked at the moment in the Anglo-Saxon world, i.e., in those cultural communities most totally committed to bourgeois-Protestant values and surest that they are unequivocally "white." I am thinking of the effort of young men in England and the United States to assimilate into themselves (or even to assimilate themselves into) that otherness, that sum total of rejected psychic elements which the middle-class heirs of the Renaissance have identified with "woman." To become new men, these children of the future seem to feel, they must not only become more Black than White but more female than male. And it is natural that the need to make such an adjustment be felt with especial acuteness in post-Protestant highly industrialized societies, where the functions regarded as specifically male for some three hundred years tend most rapidly to become obsolete.

Surely, in America, machines already perform better than humans a large number of those aggressive-productive activities which our ancestors considered man's special province, even his *raison d'être*. Not only has the male's prerogative of making things and money (which is to say, of working) been preempted, but also his time-honored privilege of dealing out death by hand, which until quite recently was regarded as a supreme mark of masculine valor. While it seems theoretically possible, even in the heart of Anglo-Saxondom, to imagine a leisurely, pacific male, in fact the losses in secondary functions sustained by men appear to have shaken their faith in their primary masculine function as well, in their ability to achieve the conquest (as the traditional metaphor has it) of women. Earlier, advances in technology had detached the wooing and winning of women from the begetting of children; and though the invention of the condom had at least left the decision to inhibit fatherhood in the power of males, its replacement by the "loop" and the "pill" has placed paternity at the mercy of the whims of women.

Writers of fiction and verse registered the technological obsolescence of masculinity long before it was felt even by the representative minority who give to the present younger generation its character and significance. And literary critics have talked a good deal during the past couple of decades about the conversion of the literary hero into the non-hero or the anti-hero; but they have in general failed to notice his simultaneous conversion into the non- or anti-male. Yet ever since Hemingway at least, certain male protagonists of American literature have not only fled rather than sought out combat but have also fled rather than sought out women. From Jake Barnes to Holden Caulfield they have continued to run from the threat of female sexuality; and, indeed, there are models for such evasion in our classic books, where heroes still eager for the fight (Natty Bumppo comes to mind) are already shy of wives and sweethearts and mothers.

It is not absolutely required that the anti-male anti-hero be impotent or homosexual or both (though this helps, as we remember remembering Walt Whitman), merely that he be more seduced than seducing, more passive than active. Consider, for instance, the oddly "womanish" Herzog of Bellow's best seller, that Jewish Emma Bovary with a Ph.D., whose chief flaw is physical vanity and a taste for fancy clothes. Bellow, however, is more interested in summing up the past than in evoking the future; and *Herzog* therefore seems an end rather than a beginning, the product of nostalgia (remember when there were real Jews once, and the "Jewish Novel" had not yet been discovered!) rather than prophecy. No, the post-humanist, post-male, post-white, post-heroic world is a post-Jewish world by the same token, anti-Semitism as inextricably woven into it as into the movement for Negro rights; and its scriptural books are necessarily *goyish,* not least of all William Burroughs' *The Naked Lunch.*

Burroughs is the chief prophet of the post-male post-heroic world; and it is his emulators who move into the center of the relevant literary scene, for *The Naked Lunch* (the later novels are less successful, less exciting but relevant still) is more than it seems: no mere essay in heroin-hallucinated homosexual pornography—but a nightmare anticipation (in Science Fiction form) of post-Humanist sexuality. Here, as in Alexander Trocchi, John Rechy, Harry Mathews (even an occasional Jew like Allen Ginsberg, who has begun by inscribing properly anti-Jewish obscenities on the walls of the world), are clues to the new attitudes toward sex that will continue to inform our improbable novels of passion and our even more improbable love songs.

The young to whom I have been referring, the mythologically representative minority (who, by a process that infuriates the mythologically inert majority out of which they come, "stand for" their times), live in a community in which what used to be called the "Sexual Revolution," the Freudian-Laurentian revolt of their grandparents and parents, has triumphed as imperfectly and unsatisfactorily as all revolutions always triumph. They confront, therefore, the necessity of determining not only what meanings "love" can have in their new world, but—even more disturbingly—what significance, if any, "male" and "female" now possess. For a while, they (or at least their literary spokesmen recruited from the generation just before them) seemed content to celebrate a kind of *reductio* or *exaltatio ad absurdum* of their parents' once revolutionary sexual goals: The Reichian-inspired Cult of the Orgasm.

Young men and women eager to be delivered of traditional ideologies of love find especially congenial the belief that not union or relationship (much less offspring) but physical release is the end of the sexual act; and that, therefore, it is a matter of indifference with whom or by what method one pursues the therapeutic climax, so long as that climax is total and repeated frequently. And Wilhelm Reich happily detaches this belief from the vestiges of Freudian rationalism, setting it instead in a context of Science Fiction and witchcraft; but his emphasis upon "full genitality," upon growing up and away from infantile pleasures, strikes the young as a disguised plea for the "maturity" they have learned to despise. In a time when the duties associated with adulthood promise to become irrelevant, there seems little reason for denying oneself the joys of babyhood—even if these are associated with such regressive fantasies as escaping it all in the arms of little sister (in the Gospel according to J. D. Salinger) or flirting with the possibility of getting into bed with papa (in the Gospel according to Norman Mailer).

Only Norman O. Brown in *Life Against Death* has come to terms on the level of theory with the aspiration to take the final evolutionary leap and cast off adulthood completely, at least in the area of sex. His post-Freudian program for pan-sexual, nonorgasmic love rejects "full genitality" in favor of a species of indiscriminate bundling, a dream of unlimited sub-coital intimacy which Brown calls (in his vocabulary the term is an honorific) "polymorphous perverse." And here finally is an essential clue to the nature of the second sexual revolution, the post-sexual revolution, first evoked in literature by Brother

Antoninus more than a decade ago, in a verse prayer addressed somewhat improbably to the Christian God:

> Annul in me my manhood, Lord, and make
> Me woman sexed and weak. . .
> Make me then
> Girl-hearted, virgin-souled, woman-docile, maiden-meek . . .

Despite the accents of this invocation, however, what is at work is not essentially a homosexual revolt or even a rebellion against women, though its advocates seek to wrest from women their ancient privileges of receiving the Holy Ghost and pleasuring men; and though the attitudes of the movement can be adapted to the anti-female bias of, say, Edward Albee. If in *Who's Afraid of Virginia Woolf?* Albee can portray the relationship of two homosexuals (one in drag) as the model of contemporary marriage, this must be because contemporary marriage has in fact turned into something much like that parody. And it is true that what survives of bourgeois marriage and the bourgeois family is a target which the new barbarians join the old homosexuals in reviling, seeking to replace Mom, Pop and the kids with a neo-Whitmanian gaggle of giggling *camerados.* Such groups are, in fact, whether gathered in coffee houses, university cafeterias or around the literature tables on campuses, the peace-time equivalents, as it were, to the demonstrating crowd. But even their program of displacing Dick-Jane-Spot-Baby, etc., the WASP family of grade school primers, is not the fundamental motive of the post-sexual revolution.

What is at stake from Burroughs to Bellow, Ginsberg to Albee, Salinger to Gregory Corso is a more personal transformation: a radical metamorphosis of the Western male—utterly unforeseen in the decades before us, but visible now in every high school and college classroom, as well as on the paperback racks in airports and supermarkets. All around us, young males are beginning to retrieve for themselves the cavalier role once piously and class-consciously surrendered to women: *that of being beautiful and being loved.* Here once more the example to the Negro—the feckless and adorned Negro male with the blood of Cavaliers in his veins—has served as a model. And what else is left to young men, in any case, after the devaluation of the grim duties they had arrogated to themselves in place of the pursuit of loveliness?

All of us who are middle-aged and were Marxists, which is to say, who once numbered themselves among the last assured Puritans, have surely noticed in ourselves a vestigial roundhead rage at the new hair styles of the advanced or—if you please—delinquent young. Watching young men titivate their locks (the comb, the pocket mirror and the bobby pin having replaced the jackknife, catcher's mitt and brass knuckles), we feel the same baffled resentment that stirs in us when we realize that they have rejected work. A job and unequivocal maleness—these are two sides of the same Calvinist coin, which in the future buys nothing.

Few of us, however, have really understood how the Beatle hairdo is part of a syndrome, of which high heels, jeans tight over the buttocks, etc., are other aspects, symptomatic of a larger retreat from masculine aggressiveness to female allure—in literature and the arts to the style called "camp." And fewer still have realized how that style, though the invention of homosexuals, is now the possession of basically heterosexual males as well, a strategy in their campaign to establish a new relationship not only with women but with their own masculinity. In the course of that campaign, they have embraced certain kinds of gesture and garb, certain accents and tones traditionally associated with females or female impersonators; which is why we have been observing recently (in life as well as fiction and verse) young boys, quite unequivocally male, playing all the traditional roles of women: the vamp, the coquette, the whore, the icy tease, the pure young virgin.

Not only oldsters, who had envisioned and despaired of quite another future, are bewildered by this turn of events, but young girls, too, seem scarcely to know what is happening—looking on with that new, schizoid stare which itself has become a hallmark of our times. And the crop-headed jocks, those crew-cut athletes who represent an obsolescent masculine style based on quite other values, have tended to strike back blindly; beating the hell out of some poor kid whose hair is too long or whose pants are too tight—quite as they once beat up young Communists for revealing that their politics had become obsolete. Even heterosexual writers, however, have been slow to catch up, the revolution in sensibility running ahead of that in expression; and they have perforce permitted homosexuals to speak for them (Burroughs and Genet and Baldwin and Ginsberg and Albee and a score of others), even to invent the forms in which the future will have to speak.

The revolt against masculinity is not limited, however, to simple matters of coiffure and costume, visible even to athletes; or to the adaptation of certain campy styles and modes to new uses. There is also a sense in which two large social movements that have set the young in motion and furnished images of action for their books—movements as important in their own right as porno-politics and the pursuit of the polymorphous perverse—are connected analogically to the abdication from traditional maleness. The first of these is nonviolent or passive resistance, so oddly come back to the land of its inventor, that icy Thoreau who dreamed a love which ". . . has not much human blood in it, but consists with a certain disregard for men and their erections. . . ."

The civil rights movement, however, in which nonviolence has found a home, has been hospitable not only to the sort of post-humanist I have been describing; so that at a demonstration (Selma, Alabama, will do as an example) the true hippie will be found side by side with backwoods Baptists, nuns on a spiritual spree, boy bureaucrats practicing to take power, resurrected socialists, Unitarians in search of a God, and just plain tourists, gathered, as once at the Battle of Bull Run, to see the fun. For each of these, nonviolence will have a different sort of fundamental meaning—as a tactic, a camouflage, a passing fad, a pious gesture—but for each in part, and for the post-humanist especially, it will signify the possibility of heroism without aggression, effective action without guilt.

There have always been two contradictory American ideals: to be the occasion of maximum violence, and to remain absolutely innocent. Once, however, these were thought hopelessly incompatible for males (except, perhaps, as embodied in works of art), reserved strictly for women: the spouse of the wife-beater, for instance, or the victim of rape. But males have now assumed these classic roles; and just as a particularly beleaguered wife occasionally slipped over the dividing line into violence, so do the new passive protesters—leaving us to confront (or resign to the courts) such homey female questions as: *Did Mario Savio really bite that cop in the leg as he sagged limply toward the ground?*

The second social movement is the drug cult, more widespread among youth, from its squarest limits to its most beat, than anyone seems prepared to admit in public; and at its beat limit at least inextricably involved with the civil rights movement, as the recent arrests of Peter DeLissovoy and Susan Ryerson revealed even to the ordinary newspaper reader. "Police said that most of the recipients [of marijuana] were college students," the U.P. story runs. "They quoted Miss Ryerson and DeLissovoy as saying that many of the letter packets were sent to civil rights workers." Only fiction and verse, however, has dealt with the conjunction of homosexuality, drugs and civil rights, eschewing the general piety of the press which has been unwilling to compromise "good works" on behalf of the Negro by associating it with the deep radicalism of a way of life based on the ritual consumption of "pot."

The widespread use of such hallucinogens as peyote, marijuana, the "mexican mushroom," LSD, etc., as well as pep pills, goof balls, airplane glue, certain kinds of cough syrups and even, though in many fewer cases, heroin, is not merely a matter of a changing taste in stimulants but of the programmatic espousal of an anti-puritanical mode of existence—hedonistic and detached— one more strategy in the war on time and work. But it is also (to pursue my analogy once more) an attempt to arrogate to the male certain traditional privileges of the female. What could be more womanly, as Elémire Zolla was already pointing out some years ago, than permitting the penetration of the body by a foreign object which not only stirs delight but even (possibly) creates new life?

In any case, with drugs we have come to the crux of the futurist revolt, the hinge of everything else, as the young tell us over and over in their writing. When the movement was first finding a voice, Allen Ginsberg set this aspect of it in proper context in an immensely comic, utterly serious poem called "America," in which "pot" is associated with earlier forms of rebellion, a commitment to catatonia, and a rejection of conventional male potency:

> America I used to be a communist when I was a kid I'm not sorry.
> I smoke marijuana every chance I get.
> I sit in my house for days on end and stare at the roses in the closet.
> When I go to Chinatown I . . . never get laid . . .

Similarly, Michael McClure reveals in his essay, *"Phi Upsilon Kappa,"* that before penetrating the "cavern of Anglo-Saxon," whence he emerged with the slogan of the ultimate Berkeley demonstrators, he had been on mescalin. "I have emerged from a dark night of the soul; I entered it by Peyote." And by now, drug-taking has become as standard a feature of the literature of the young as oral-genital love-making. I flip open the first issue of yet another ephemeral San Francisco little magazine quite at random and read: "I tie up and the main pipe [the ante-cobital vein, for the clinically inclined] swells like a prideful beggar beneath the skin. Just before I get on it is always the worst."

Worse than the experience, however, is its literary rendering; and the badness of such confessional fiction, flawed by the sentimentality of those who desire to live "like a cunning vegetable," is a badness we older readers find it only too easy to perceive, as our sons and daughters find it only too easy to overlook. Yet precisely here the age and the mode define themselves; for not in the master but in the hacks new forms are established, new lines drawn.

Here, at any rate, is where the young lose us in literature as well as life, since here they pass over into real revolt, i.e., what we really cannot abide, hard as we try. The mother who has sent her son to private schools and on to Harvard to keep him out of classrooms overcrowded with poor Negroes, rejoices when he sets out for Mississippi with his comrades in SNCC, but shudders when he turns on with LSD; just as the ex-Marxist father, who has earlier proved radicalism impossible, rejoices to see his son stand up, piously and pompously, for CORE or SDS, but trembles to hear him quote Alpert and Leary or praise Burroughs. Just as certainly as liberalism is the LSD of the aging, LSD is the radicalism of the young.

If whiskey long served as an appropriate symbolic excess for those who chafed against Puritan restraint without finally challenging it—temporarily releasing them to socially harmful aggression and (hopefully) sexual self-indulgence, the new popular drugs provide an excess quite as satisfactorily symbolic to the post-Puritans—releasing them from sanity to madness by destroying in them the inner restrictive order which has somehow survived the dissolution of the outer. It is finally insanity, then, that the futurists learn to admire and emulate, quite as they learn to pursue vision instead of learning, hallucination rather than logic. The schizophrenic replaces the sage as their ideal, their new culture hero, figured forth as a giant schizoid Indian (his madness modeled in part on the author's own experiences with LSD) in Ken Kesey's *One Flew Over the Cuckoo's Nest.*

The hippier young are not alone, however, in their taste for the insane; we live in a time when readers in general respond sympathetically to madness in literature wherever it is found, in established writers as well as in those trying to establish new modes. Surely it is not the lucidity and logic of Robert Lowell or Theodore Roethke or John Berryman which we admire, but their flirtation with incoherence and disorder. And certainly it is Mailer at his most nearly psychotic, Mailer the creature rather than the master of his fantasies who moves us to admiration; while in the case of Saul Bellow, we endure the theoretical optimism and acceptance for the sake of the delightful melancholia, the fertile paranoia which he cannot disavow any more than the talent at whose root they lie. Even essayists and analysts recommend themselves to us these days by a certain redemptive nuttiness; at any rate, we do not love, say, Marshall McLuhan less because he continually risks sounding like the body-fluids man in *Dr. Strangelove.*

We have, moreover, recently been witnessing the development of a new form of social psychiatry (a psychiatry of the future already anticipated by the literature of the future) which considers some varieties of "schizophrenia" not diseases to be cured but forays into an unknown psychic world: random penetrations by bewildered internal cosmonauts of a realm that it will be the task of the next generations to explore. And if the accounts which the returning schizophrenics give (the argument of the apologists runs) of the "places" they have been are fantastic and garbled, surely they are no more so than, for example, Columbus' reports of the world he had claimed for Spain, a world bounded— according to his newly drawn maps—by Cathay on the north and Paradise on the south.

In any case, poets and junkies have been suggesting to us that the new world appropriate to the new men of the latter twentieth century is to be dis- covered only by the conquest of inner space: by an adventure of the spirit, an extension of psychic possibility, of which the flights into outer space—moon- shots and expeditions to Mars—are precisely such unwitting metaphors and analogues as the voyages of exploration were of the earlier breakthrough into the Renaissance, from whose consequences the young seek now so desperately to escape. The laureate of that new conquest is William Burroughs; and it is fitting that the final word be his:

> "This war will be won in the air. In the Silent Air with Image Rays.
> You were a pilot remember? Tracer bullets cutting the right wing
> you were free in space a few seconds before in blue space between
> eyes. Go back to Silence. Keep Silence. Keep Silence. K.S. K.S.
> . . . From Silence re-write the message that is you. You are the
> message I send to the Enemy. My Silent Message."
> The Naked Astronauts were free in space. . . .

36

THE NEW YORK TIMES

Lyndon Johnson Opts for Peace: The Foreign Policy Reversal of 1968

One of the greatest and least anticipated battles of the Vietnam War was fought in the American political arena. It drove one President from office, destroyed the chances of his Vice President to succeed him, and created a shift in the relative strength of the two parties that may have far-reaching results. As early as the 1966 congressional elections, it was plain that President Johnson's liberal coalition was breaking up. The confrontation on Vietnam between young people and the police at the Chicago Democratic Convention in 1968 shattered it beyond repair. For possibly the first time in our history an articulate minority has been willing openly to reject the traditional rhetoric and symbols of patriotism.

Vietnam is a blowup of many of our national flaws. The war demonstrated the weakness of what seemed to be a long and successful tradition of collective security and liberal evangelism. The momentum of past commitments and the need for one President to ratify the contingent planning of another played almost as large a part in Vietnam as in the Bay of Pigs fiasco. Moreover, American policy in Asia has always been hampered by the assumption that our native institutions like elections or our methods of political compromise can establish themselves in an alien culture.

The selection on President Lyndon Johnson's decision to de-escalate the Vietnam war was written by a team of New York Times *reporters who pooled their knowledge and insights about backstage maneuvers for power at the White House in 1968. At some point the realization dawned on the administration that the Vietnam war had opened the door for a Republican president. What influence this had on the President's decision is a matter of dispute. President Johnson, it should be noted, claims that there are major discrepancies in this analysis which he will presumably attempt to set right in his forthcoming memoirs.*

On the cold and cheerless early morning of Feb. 28, 1968, the Chairman of the Joint Chiefs of Staff, Gen. Earle G. Wheeler, landed at Andrews Air Force Base after an urgent mission to Saigon. Pausing only to change into a fresh uniform, he hurried through the rain to the White House to deliver a report and make a request.

The report was designed to encourage an anxious President and his beleaguered advisers, but it served only to shock them into extended debate.

The request—for more troops—was designed to bring military victory at last in the eight-year American military effort, but it led instead to a fateful series of decisions that stand in retrospect as one of the most remarkable turnabouts in United States foreign policy.

The month of March, 1968, became a watershed for a nation and a Government in turmoil. The Johnson Administration, by pulling back from the brink of deeper commitments and moving toward disengagement, set a new course that affects the daily decisions of the Nixon Administration.

Many of the ingredients of decision then—troop strength and what to do about bombing North Vietnam—are still live issues, and many of the principal actors involved a year ago are participants in yet another crucial policy debate on Vietnam.

On that day at the end of February, President Johnson and his closest aides assembled for breakfast around the Chippendale table in the elegant family dining room on the second floor of the Executive Mansion. Before rising from the table, they had set in motion the most intensive policy review of the Johnson Presidency—and one of the most agonizing of any Presidency.

The wrenching debate began almost by accident and then gained a momentum all its own. One dramatic record of its progress appeared in the 12 versions of a Presidential speech that evolved during the month—the last draft pointing in the opposite direction from the first.

The entire episode also provided a remarkable demonstration of how foreign policy is battled out, inch by inch, by negotiation rather than decision. The turnabout emerged through sharp confrontations and subtle, even conspiratorial, maneuvering—with compromises struck for bureaucratic purposes and with opponents in agreement for contrary reasons.

At the time of that breakfast meeting, President Johnson had been thinking for about two months about not seeking re-election. His principal advisers had little inkling of his thoughts, and the President himself had no expectation that the tensions in the Government would shatter the consensus of his inner circle.

Clark M. Clifford, appointed but not yet sworn in as Secretary of Defense, was to play the pivotal role in the Vietnam reassessment, but it was not a one-man show.

Mr. Clifford had to be persuaded. He immediately came under pressure from a faction of civilian dissenters at the Pentagon who believed the war was deadlocked, questioned American objectives and felt that time to salvage American policy was fast running out.

When the debate was over, the President had set the Government on the path toward peace negotiations and disengagement from the war. He had imposed a limit on the military commitment to South Vietnam, ordered a reduction in the bombing of North Vietnam, and offered to negotiate with the Hanoi regime. And he had coupled the offer with the announcement of his withdrawal from the 1968 political campaign.

The replacement of the quest for military victory with the search for compromise might have been reversed by North Vietnam if it had not—to almost everyone's surprise—responded favorably to Mr. Johnson's offer. Furthermore, the hawkish faction in the White House inner circle sought to resist the new trend until the Johnson Administration left office in January.

The catalytic event in the policy reappraisal—and the centerpiece of General Wheeler's vivid report—was the enemy's Lunar New Year offensive, which began Jan. 30, 1968, and swelled into coordinated assaults on 36 South Vietnamese cities and included, in Saigon, a bold penetration of the United States Embassy compound.

Confident and secure one day, Gen. William C. Westmoreland, then the American commander in Saigon, found himself on the next dealing with a vast battle the length of South Vietnam.

The psychological impact on Washington had outrun the event: The capital was stunned. But General Wheeler, with murals of the American Revolution behind him, offered a more reassuring picture to the White House breakfast on Feb. 28.

The Tet attacks had not caused a military defeat, he said. The enemy had been thrown back with heavy losses and had failed to spark a popular uprising against the South Vietnamese regime. Not only had the Government in Saigon and its army survived the hurricane, he continued, but the offensive has "scared the living daylights," out of non-Communists, and they were beginning to cooperate.

On the other hand, the general said that more—many more—American troops were needed because the allied forces were off balance and vulnerable to another offensive.

General Westmoreland felt, General Wheeler reported, that massive reinforcements would guard against a quick repetition of the Tet offensive and would allow the allies to regain the initiative, to exploit the enemy's losses and to "speed the course of the war to our objectives."

General Wheeler gave the Westmoreland request his personal endorsement. It added up to 206,000 more men.

General Westmoreland, who did not actually use the figure, regarded the proposal as a planning paper. But President Johnson and other officials, knowing that, as a matter of administrative technique, no request became formal until the President had decided how many troops would be sent, treated the Westmoreland paper as a request. Even without a precise total they sensed how much was being sought. The "shopping list" outlined by General Wheeler called for three more combat divisions, with sizable air, naval and land support.

Once the plan was fed through the Pentagon computers the precise number emerged. It became so secret that to this day some officials will not utter it—a reminder of the President's wrath when it did leak to the press during the March debate.

The sheer size of the request—a 40 percent increase in the 535,000-man force committed to Vietnam—stunned Mr. Johnson and the civilians around him, though the initial impulse was to see how the commander's needs might be filled.

"It was a hell of a serious breakfast," one participant recalled. "It was rough as a cob!"

Some of the participants believed that a substantial troop increase could well revive arguments for widening the war—for giving General Westmoreland permission to go after enemy sanctuaries on the ground in Cambodia and Laos, and perhaps even in North Vietnam.

The President was wary about a massive new commitment. Had he not gone to extraordinary lengths to send half a million men to Vietnam without calling up reserves or imposing economic controls? Every year the generals had come to him—sometimes more than once a year—with the plea for "a little bit more to get the job done." Now, with the nation sharply divided over the war, they were asking for mobilization.

They had confronted Mr. Johnson with a dilemma. The gist of the Wheeler-Westmoreland report, in the words of one breakfast guest, was blunt: "We've got to have a big infusion of troops or we can't achieve our objectives."

No one at the breakfast table that day advocated lowering objectives. It was a time, however, when many pressures for a change of course were converging on the White House.

The Tet offensive had punctured the heady optimism over the military progress reported to Congress by General Westmoreland and by Ellsworth Bunker, the Ambassador to South Vietnam, in November, 1967. Not only had the pool of disenchantment spread by late February to fence-sitters in Congress, to newspaper offices and to business organizations. It had also reached the upper echelons of the Government.

If tolerance of the war had worn thin, so had the nation's military resources—so thin, indeed, that there was almost nothing more to send to Vietnam without either mobilizing, enlarging draft calls, lengthening the 12-month combat tour or sending Vietnam veterans back for second tours of duty—all extremely unappealing.

Congress was in such ferment that the process of legislation was partly paralyzed. The dollar was being battered by the gold crisis in Europe and inflation at home.

More fundamentally, the nation was seriously divided. The fabric of public civility had begun to unravel as opinion on the war polarized.

President Johnson chose his long-time friend, Clark Clifford, to head a task force to advise him on the troop request. It quickly became a forum for debating the entire rationale for the war.

At 10:30 A.M. on Friday, March 1, in the East room of the White House, Mr. Clifford took the oath of office as the successor to Robert S. McNamara. Three hours later he gathered the task force around the oval oak table in the private Pentagon dining room of the Secretary of Defense.

Secretary of State Dean Rusk, for the first time in his seven years in office, went to the Defense Department for a formal meeting.

The others present were all, like Mr. Rusk, veterans of arguments on Vietnam policy—Walt W. Rostow, the President's assistant for national security affairs, Richard Helms, Director of Central Intelligence; General

Wheeler, General Maxwell D. Taylor, former Chairman of the Joint Chiefs of Staff, former Ambassador to Saigon and a Presidential adviser on Vietnam; Paul H. Nitze, Deputy Secretary of Defense; Under Secretary of State Nicholas deB. Katzenbach; Paul C. Warnke, Assistant Secretary of Defense for International Security Affairs; Phil G. Goulding, Assistant Secretary of Defense for Public Affairs; William P. Bundy, Assistant Secretary of State for East Asian Affairs, and, for financial advice, the Secretary of the Treasury, Henry H. Fowler.

None of the civilians present advocated a flat commitment of 206,000 more men, nor did they want to reject the request out of hand. Several insiders later suggested that a smaller request, for 30,000 to 50,000 men, would probably have been granted and the Administration crisis would have been avoided, or at least delayed.

Instead there was an early collision in the task force over war strategy and the possibilities of victory. There were, of course, shadings of viewpoint on most questions, but two broad coalitions emerged:

One favored continuation of General Westmoreland's strategy of wearing down the enemy by intense military pounding. The argument's assumption was that the Tet situation was less a setback than an opportunity. By boldly seizing the initiative, according to this view, the allies could decimate and demoralize the enemy and open the way to a favorable settlement.

The other group challenged the very premises of the old strategy. Its members urged a less aggressive ground war, called for new efforts to open negotiations and, implicitly, laid the groundwork for political compromise.

The exponents of continuity were Mr. Rusk and Mr. Rostow and Generals Wheeler and Taylor. Mr. Rusk, by then the stanchest defender of the war in public, patiently bore the heat of criticism. Tall, unbending, composed, he was, in his own words, "the iceman."

Mr. Rostow and General Taylor, who had gone to Vietnam early in 1961 as President Kennedy's personal envoys and who came back advocating intervention, were even more opposed to "letting up the pressure." Mr. Rostow, athletic and ebullient, funneled the news from Saigon to the President.

The advocates of change were Messrs. Nitze, Warnke, and Katzenbach, and later—most powerfully—Mr. Clifford. Mr. Helms, thoughtful and angular, was neutral on policy questions. The weight of his C.I.A. analysis called into question military judgments, past strategy and the quest for victory implicit in so many earlier decisions.

Although Mr. Clifford was never alone, his eventual role was remarkable because it was wholly unexpected.

He came into government with a reputation as a hawk, as a trusted, loyal "back-room" counselor to Mr. Johnson who had steadfastly supported Administration policy. In December, 1965, he had opposed the 36-day bombing pause then advocated by his predecessor. One man acquainted with the circumstances of the Clifford appointment said later:

"I am sure the President felt, 'Here is a good, strong, sturdy supporter of the war, and that's what I need.' McNamara was wobbling—particularly on the bombing issue. I think the President felt Clifford was strong and sturdy."

But Mr. Clifford had begun to have doubts during a trip in August, 1967, to Vietnam and allied countries contributing troops to the war. On his return he confided to the President that he was deeply uneasy at having discovered that the American view of the war was not fully shared by Australia, New Zealand, Thailand and the Philippines.

Disturbed he was, but he remained a supporter of Administration policy. He was encouraged by secret diplomatic efforts in August, 1967, and again in January, 1968, to get negotiations with Hanoi started on the basis of the so-called San Antonio formula.

That proposal, made public by President Johnson in a speech in the Texas city on September 30, 1967, offered to halt the bombing of North Vietnam provided it would lead promptly to productive talks and "assuming" that Hanoi would not take military advantage of the cessation.

At Mr. Clifford's Senate confirmation hearings on Jan. 25, 1968, he had added the important interpretation that this meant that the President would tolerate "normal" levels of infiltration from North to South Vietnam.

The President had not cleared Mr. Clifford's remarks in advance and, as a result, according to one informed source, "all hell broke loose at the White House and the State Department."

Secretary Rusk was said to have argued for two days with President Johnson against giving Administration endorsement to the interpretation. He was overruled. On Jan. 29 the State Department said Mr. Clifford's remarks represented United States policy.

He plunged into the minutiae of Vietnam like a lawyer taking a new case. He had private talks with Mr. McNamara, whose own misgivings had sharpened in his final months at the Pentagon.

As a newcomer with limited knowledge, Mr. Clifford had to rely on civilian subordinates more than had his brilliant and experienced predecessor. The large faction of dissenters from Administration policy was quick to seize the opportunity to press its views. The Tet offensive, recalled one dissenter, "gave us something we could hang our arguments on, something to contradict the beguiling upward curve on the progress charts" from Saigon.

With the lid off, the new Secretary discovered a nest of "hidden doves" at the Pentagon, including his deputy, Mr. Nitze; Assistant Secretaries Warnke, Alain C. Enthoven, Goulding and Alfred B. Fitt; the Under Secretaries of the Army, Navy and Air Force—David E. McGiffert, Charles F. Baird and Townsend W. Hoopes; a few younger generals and colonels and a score of young civilians brought in by Mr. McNamara, principally Dr. Morton H. Halperin, Dr. Leslie H. Gelb and Richard C. Steadman.

The men who clearly had the greatest impact on the new Secretary's thinking were Messrs. Nitze, Warnke and Goulding—perhaps Mr. Warnke more than the others.

"Warnke was deeply upset about Vietnam and he was persuasive," a colleague said. "His style and Mr. Clifford's meshed." As a measure of their mutual confidence, Mr. Clifford chose Mr. Warnke as a law partner when both left the Government.

When the Clifford task force got under way, a number of officials took the troop request as evidence of panic on General Westmoreland's part. But ranking officers who were in Saigon headquarters during and after the Tet offensive assert that there was no thought of asking for many more troops until shortly before General Wheeler's visit late in February.

"The President asked General Wheeler to go out to Vietnam to find out what General Westmoreland thought he could use," a Pentagon official said. Civilian officials were irritated by this approach. "It was a mistake to ask a damned-fool question like that," a State Department official remarked.

The Joint Chiefs of Staff had their own reasons for favoring a massive increase and a reserve call-up. For months they had been deeply concerned that the strategic reserve had been dangerously depleted and they had been looking for a chance to reconstitute it by persuading the President to mobilize National Guard units.

Another view was held by Ambassador Bunker, who never fully endorsed the troop request and who wanted first priority for re-equipping and expanding the South Vietnamese Army—a suggestion endorsed by Pentagon civilians.

The Wheeler-Westmoreland plan presented to the task force called for 206,000 men by June 30, 1969—roughly 100,000 within a few months and two later increments of about 50,000 men each. The first segment was to come from available active-duty units in the United States; the rest were to come from the reserves.

In the view of the Joint Chiefs, only the full number would assure victory. The implication was that with 206,000 more men, the war would "not be terribly long," as one Pentagon civilian put it—but there was no precise forecast.

At this point Mr. Warnke, in his nasal Massachusetts accent, read a paper that challenged the military thesis head on. Hanoi, he said, would match American reinforcements as it had in the past, and the result would simply be escalation and "a lot more killing" on both sides.

Besides, the task force was told, the financial costs would be immense. The proposed scale of reinforcements would add nearly $10-billion to a war already costing $30-billion a year.

As an alternative, Mr. Warnke urged a turn toward de-escalation—a pullback from General Westmoreland's aggressive search-and-destroy tactics and the abandonment of isolated outposts like the besieged Marine garrison at Khesanh. He said that American forces should be used as a mobile shield in and around population centers and that more should be demanded from the South Vietnamese Army.

The sheer complexity of the troop issue began to raise doubts in Mr. Clifford's mind.

"Part of it was Clark's intelligent questioning and part of it was his naiveté," a colleague recalled. "He asked about things that others more familiar with the details would not have asked.

"He just couldn't get the figures straight on troops. He drove Bus Wheeler mad. He would say, 'Now I understand you wanted 22,000 men for such and such,' and Wheeler would point out this didn't include the support elements, and if you added them, it would be 35,000 in all.

"This happened again and again every time Clark wanted to get the numbers down as low as possible, and it had a psychological impact on him," the source added.

The first weekend in March was consumed by a study of the papers drafted for the task force and by questions. "It was meet all day, sandwiches in for lunch, sandwiches in for dinner," a participant recalled.

Word was passed to President Johnson that the review "wasn't going well" and had hit a "discordant note." But Mr. Clifford's doubts had not hardened into convictions by the time he handed the President his first report on March 5.

A short, unsigned, four-or-five-page memorandum, it recommended giving General Westmoreland 50,000 more troops in the next three months and set out a schedule for readying the rest of the 206,000 men for dispatch over the next 15 months.

Characteristically, the President's advisers disagreed on the recommendation's significance. The Pentagon saw it as a move "to get the pipeline going" —general approval to the troop request; State Department officials viewed it as part of a process of "whittling down" the 206,000 figure.

Although Mr. Clifford had passed along the report, he was uneasy about it. He was worried that if the President approved the first batch of troops, that action would move him irrevocably toward the whole 206,000. But the Secretary did not challenge the report directly; he tried to stall, suggesting that the task force check General Westmoreland's reaction to be sure the "mix" of forces was right.

General Wheeler wanted to move ahead, but others, including Mr. Rusk and Mr. Rostow, were willing to have the issue studied further, so the task force carried on for several more days.

This seemed to suit Mr. Johnson's mood, too. His instinct, a White House aide explained later, was to delay implementing the plan. "He kept putting off making an initial decision," the aide said.

For the President had heard the grumbles in Congress over the danger to the dollar from the gold drain and from the rising costs of the war. Politicians were alarmed by the size of the troop request.

Old, trusted friends like Senator Richard B. Russell, the Georgia Democrat who headed the Armed Services Committee, were complaining tartly about General Westmoreland. Influential men like Senator John Stennis, the Mississippi Democrat, were privately warning the President to go slow on mobilizing reserves.

As the task force persisted, Secretary Clifford himself was putting more pointed questions. "What is our military plan for victory?" he asked. "How will we end the war?" He was not satisfied.

Then the bombing campaign came under his scrutiny. Mr. Hoopes wrote him a memorandum urging a halt, arguing that the bombing was not having significant results and that, because of Soviet and Chinese Communist aid, North Vietnam had become "on balance a stronger military power today than before the bombing began."

Mr. Hoopes contended that it was "a military fiction" that American combat casualties would rise if the bombing were halted. American losses, he said, were primarily a result of the aggressive ground strategy in the South.

Under the impact of such arguments, Mr. Clifford's doubts became convictions. He supported the President's previous restrictions on the war—no invasion of North Vietnam, no expansion of the ground war into Laos or Cambodia, no mining of the Haiphong harbor—and he became convinced that within those restrictions there was no military answer. He began the search for a path to disengagement.

The debate, by now in the White House, seesawed through the middle of March. At this time Mr. Clifford began to state his case for a fundamental change in American policy: It was time to emphasize peace, not a larger war.

He now challenged the task-force recommendation for more troops. "This isn't the way to go at all," he told the President. "This is all wrong."

With the nation bitterly divided over the war and in desperate need at home, he maintained, it would be immoral to consider enormous added investment in Vietnam—a "military sinkhole."

His outspoken challenge was deeply disturbing to President Johnson, who always preferred a consensus among his close advisers. Although he never turned his celebrated temper on Mr. Clifford, the argument chilled their personal relations and left the Defense Secretary, a friend for 30 years, feeling oddly frozen out of the White House at times.

Secretary Rusk apparently did not disagree with Mr. Clifford so sharply on troop numbers, but he was opposed to the long-run implications of Mr. Clifford's arguments—that in the end, the United States would have to settle for less. Mr. Rostow felt that the new Defense Secretary had fallen under the influence of "the professional pessimists" in the Defense Department.

At the Pentagon, morale was rising among civilian advocates of a new policy. "We used to ask," a former Pentagon civilian said of the Secretary, "is he one of us? Well, there was 'one of us' at the White House." He was Harry McPherson, the President's speech drafter, who, unknown to the Pentagon or the State Department, was already at work on a major Vietnam speech. The final version was Mr. Johnson's address to the nation on Sunday, March 31.

The speech was originally conceived late in February on the basis of Mr. Rostow's analysis that the Tet offensive had not been a real setback and that the allies should pull up their socks and hang on until the enemy came to his senses. While the discussions of troop strength were proceeding, Mr. McPherson was developing his draft.

Initially, it included an opened-ended commitment to the war—a willingness to carry on at whatever the cost. But as the internal debate over troop figures raged on and the numbers dwindled, the tone softened. But the President would not commit himself to any draft or any figure.

Then came a series of signal events: Senator Eugene J. McCarthy scored a stunning upset in the New Hampshire Democratic primary on March 1. American dead and wounded in Vietnam reached 139,801—exceeding over-all Korean-war losses. American and Western European bankers held an emergency meeting in Washington to stem the run of gold as the price soared. Senator Robert F. Kennedy announced on March 16 that he would seek the Democratic Presidential nomination.

All this formed the backdrop for the most delicate argument of all—that about the bombing.

On March 15, Arthur J. Goldberg, the American representative at the United Nations, sent an eight-page memo to the President urging him to halt the bombing to get negotiations started.

Others in the Administration favored such a step—Mr. Katzenbach and

Ambassador-at-Large W. Averell Harriman, among them—but it was Ambassador Goldberg, increasingly frustrated by his sense of powerlessness on the Vietnam issue, who dared brook the President's anger by raising the issue directly.

Advisers like Mr. Rostow opposed a halt, maintaining that it would look like a sign of weakness and would undermine the confidence of the Saigon regime. The military insisted that it would jeopardize American troops just south of the demilitarized zone.

Still others, including Assistant Secretary of State Bundy, favored waiting for several weeks on the ground that another enemy offensive might be near.

A day after the Goldberg memo arrived, the subject came up in Mr. Johnson's inner circle. The President, his patience sorely tested, sat up in his chair and said:

"Let's get one thing clear! I'm telling you now I am not going to stop the bombing. Now I don't want to hear any more about it. Goldberg has written me about the whole thing, and I've heard every argument. I'm not going to stop it. Now is there anybody here who doesn't understand that?"

No one misunderstood. The gathering in the gold and white Cabinet Room of the White House fell silent—but only temporarily. The dissenters from existing policy on Vietnam, who for two weeks had been battling against a request for massive troop reinforcements, chose to understand the President's pronouncement quite literally. They shifted tactics, and the argument flared up again.

In the administration, Secretary of Defense Clark M. Clifford, who had entered the government on March 1 as a moderate hawk but was now an active dissident, took the initiative. He proposed that the bombing be restricted to the Panhandle region of North Vietnam south of the 20th Parallel.

No one knew where Mr. Johnson stood on that issue. It was still two weeks before he would announce a major shift in the direction of his Vietnam policy —a shift toward de-escalation that is still having its impact on the daily decisions of the Nixon Administration.

At that time the pressures for change—political and economic—were mounting. The public was increasingly impatient with the war.

"Something had to be done to extend the lease on public support for the war," a high State Department official remarked. "We were focused on what we could do without significant military drawbacks to make clear to people we were serious about peace."

Secretary Clifford pleaded skillfully for the proposal that the bombing be restricted to the region south of the 20th Parallel. A cutback, he said, would not violate the President's insistence that there be no halt without matching restraint from Hanoi. He added that it would not, as the military feared in the case of a halt, jeopardize American troops in outposts just south of the demilitarized zone—Khesanh, Camp Carroll, the Rockpile and others.

The region south of the 20th Parallel contains many of the "meatiest" targets. All North Vietnamese troops and most of the supplies heading into South Vietnam have to pass through this region.

The proposal was also thought to offer a diplomatic opening: If Hanoi and Washington were not able to walk directly to the negotiating table, Mr. Clifford suggested, perhaps they could begin to "crawl."

This was not a new idea. In the spring of 1967, Mr. Clifford's predecessor as Defense Secretary, Robert S. McNamara, had his aides draft a similar proposal for cutting back to the 19th or 20th Parallel as a means of starting the process of tacit de-escalation. For many months, too, Secretary of State Dean Rusk had been developing a variety of plans for cutbacks.

The theory was that if Washington made the first move, Hanoi might match it and, step by step, they could begin scaling down the war even without negotiations.

President Johnson refused to accept the plan after it ran into heavy opposition from the Joint Chiefs of Staff. There were reports at the time that some senior generals would have resigned if it had been carried out.

Nonetheless, gingerly and indirect soundings of Hanoi were made at the time through what one diplomatic source called a "quasi-disavowable channel." The reaction from Hanoi, as read in Washington, was negative: Only a halt could produce talks. (The talks began in May, as it turned out, but the bombing did not come to a complete end until Nov. 1.)

Now, in March, 1968, the diplomatic experts thought that this was still a problem. Privately, the President had made no decision on the plan but publicly he was as stern as ever.

With Senator Robert F. Kennedy now in the race for the Democratic Presidential nomination and with the political tide apparently running against Mr. Johnson, he lashed back at his critics. In one of his pet phrases, he was "hunkering down like a Texas jackrabbit in a hailstorm."

On March 18 in Minneapolis, the President derided critics who would "tuck our tails and violate our commitments" in Vietnam. He raised the specter of appeasement in the Munich style. The Clifford camp took this as a counter-attack aimed at them by the hawkish faction of the Administration led by Walt W. Rostow, the President's adviser on national security affairs.

President Johnson ridiculed proposals for shifting to a less ambitious ground strategy in Vietnam, as the doves wanted. "Those of you who think you can save lives by moving the battlefield in from the mountains to the cities where the people live have another think coming," he said acidly.

That remark in a speech and two more addresses in a similar tone discouraged the doves. Mr. Clifford, exhausted by his first two intensive weeks in office—during which he was directing the reappraisal of policy on the war—and suffering renewed complications from a case of hepatitis picked up in Vietnam the year before, felt that he had lost the argument.

The bombing cutback seemed to have been brushed aside. The only hopeful sign, Mr. Clifford thought, was the fact that Mr. Johnson had still not approved the troop reinforcements for Gen. William C. Westmoreland. The request by the American commander in Vietnam, which amounted to 206,000 men, had precipitated the reappraisal when presented by Gen. Earle G. Wheeler, Chairman of the Joint Chiefs of Staff, on Feb. 28.

It was clear in the middle of March that despite his public declarations, President Johnson was deeply uneasy and undecided.

Late in the afternoon of March 20 he met in his oval office with Arthur J. Goldberg, the United States representative at the United Nations. It was their first meeting since Ambassador Goldberg, in a secret memo to the President on March 15, had proposed a bombing halt.

It was this proposal that had provoked the President's angry outburst at the White House meeting a day later. Mr. Goldberg had not been there and was unaware of Mr. Johnson's reaction. Now the two men met alone, and the President seemed interested in Ambassador Goldberg's position. He asked him to go through his arguments again, listening carefully and putting questions now and then. There were no angry words.

Before they parted, Mr. Johnson invited the silver-haired envoy to take part in a secret council of "wise men" that was to meet in Washington March 25. "I hope you'll put these same views to them there," he said.

The next hint of the President's thinking—though its significance was denied at the time—came on March 22. He announced that he was making General Westmoreland Army Chief of Staff, effective in July. He insisted that this did not necessarily foreshadow a change in strategy.

The White House explanation was that the shift had been in the mill for weeks and that the President was rewarding the general with the best job he could give him.

President Johnson was upset over the immediate speculation that, as an aide put it, he was "sacking Westy because of Tet," the costly Lunar New Year offensive the enemy had sprung in Vietnam on Jan. 30. To this day Mr. Johnson says privately as well as publicly that in his own heart that was not his motive. But some who know Lyndon Johnson extremely well believe that the shift came at this time—subconsciously, at least—as part of a gradual transition to a new policy.

Unknown to his political advisers, President Johnson was moving to settle the troop issue. He ordered General Wheeler to hold a secret rendezvous in the Pacific with General Westmoreland to learn if massive reinforcements were still needed. On March 24 the generals met alone for 90 minutes in 13th Air Force headquarters at Clark Air Force Base, in the Philippines.

General Westmoreland reported that the battlefield situation had improved —the crisis around the isolated Marine garrison at Khesanh had eased, the enemy seemed to have run out of steam and the South Vietnamese military forces were rebuilding their depleted ranks and moving back into the countryside.

Considering this trend, General Westmoreland said he would be satisfied if he could keep the two 5,000-man brigades rushed to Saigon early in February, at the peak of the enemy offensive, and if he were also given about 13,500 support troops for them.

General Wheeler flew back to report to the President. General Westmoreland sent a follow-up summary of his needs on March 28, three days before the President was to address the nation. No one was informed of the Pacific meeting.

By March 22, the inner circle in Washington had been informed that the President was going to give a Vietnam speech and they gathered in the family dining room of the White House to discuss it.

Present were the men who had shared the agony of Vietnam decisions with President Johnson—Secretary Rusk, Secretary Clifford, General Wheeler, press secretary, and Harry McPherson, a speech-writer.

The speech, conceived in the combative spirit after the Tet offensive, was still militant in tone. It deeply disturbed Mr. Clifford and others, who yearned to include some gesture of peace along with the scheduled reinforcements.

Once again Mr. Clifford urged the President to consider a bombing cutback on the ground that it would improve the Administration's position, internationally and domestically. Just two weeks before the crucial Democratic primary in Wisconsin, on April 2, most of the President's aides thought he needed a political shot in the arm. Vice President Humphrey believed that the bombing should be halted, not curtailed, if there was to be a change.

The discussion was exhaustive. How would a cutback affect Saigon? Would a bombing limitation to the 20th Parallel satisfy Hanoi? Were there other partial measures that made more sense?

After seven hours, Secretary Rusk gave a lucid summary. Mr. Rusk, who had himself raised the possibility of a bombing halt as early as March 3, said that there seemed to be a consensus that some step toward negotiations was desirable. But, according to one account, he cast doubt on whether a curtailment would satisfy the North Vietnamese.

"The feeling as we left," one participant recalled, "was that it would be nice if we could work it, but it wouldn't get anywhere."

The Administration doves had lost another round, but they did not relent.

The next morning Mr. McPherson, a bright, boyish-looking man, sent the President a memo that sought to strike a compromise between the general desire to make a peace gesture and the fear of rejection by Hanoi. The memo urged the President to stop the bombing north of the 20th Parallel and, simultaneously, to offer to stop the rest if Hanoi showed restraint at the demilitarized zone and left Saigon and other cities free from major attack.

The President sent the memo to Secretary Rusk, who later returned it with the comment that these were ideas that he had been working on and that they should be developed further. His reaction was favorable but, according to one account, he did not make any specific recommendation.

Mr. Johnson also asked Mr. McPherson for another copy to send to Ambassador Ellsworth Bunker in Saigon. The answer that came back mentioned some of the problems Washington had anticipated but apparently did not raise any fundamental objections.

The time for decision was drawing near, but still the President hesitated.

"It was one of those periods when the President had everybody thinking he was about to make up his mind when actually he wasn't," a former White House official commented. "He has a facility for keeping his innermost thoughts to himself. He could keep everybody else lathered up the whole time. He just kept slipping back the deadlines for decision."

President Johnson, canvassing more opinion, was reaching outside the administration to summon to Washington the secret council of trusted advisers he mentioned to Ambassador Goldberg. They had a special and surprising impact on the President.

The previous fall, almost without exception and with Mr. Clifford a participant, they had backed the President's policy. But in the wake of the Tet offensive several of these influential men had had a change of heart.

Mr. Clifford, in his new role as an advocate of change and looking for allies, encouraged the President to call them into council again in the hope that it would strengthen his argument.

They gathered at the State Department on Monday, March 25, with the President's address to the nation six days away. They constituted a "who's who" of the American foreign-policy establishment:

Dean Acheson, Secretary of State under President Truman; George W. Ball, Under Secretary of State in the Kennedy and Johnson Administrations; Gen. Omar N. Bradley, retired World War II commander; McGeorge Bundy, special assistant for national security affairs to Presidents Kennedy and Johnson; Arthur H. Dean, President Eisenhower's Korean war negotiator; Douglas Dillon, Secretary of the Treasury under President Kennedy.

Also Associate Justice Abe Fortas of the Supreme Court; Mr. Goldberg; Henry Cabot Lodge, twice Ambassador to Saigon; John J. McCloy, United States High Commissioner in West Germany under President Truman; Robert D. Murphy, ranking diplomat in the Truman-Eisenhower era; Gen. Matthew B. Ridgway, retired Korean war commander; Gen. Maxwell D. Taylor, former Chairman of the Joint Chiefs of Staff and a constant Presidential adviser on Vietnam, and Cyrus R. Vance, former Deputy Defense Secretary and President Johnson's trouble-shooter.

The wise men heard candid briefings, some of which bordered on pessimism, and then questioned Messrs. Rusk, Clifford and Rostow and others about the extent of the Tet disaster and the plans for the future. The discussion continued late that night and resumed the next morning at the White House.

For the first time President Johnson got the trend of their views. He was "deeply shaken," one aide said, by the change of temper of the wise men, who were deeply discouraged over the war after the exalted hopes of the previous fall.

The President was especially impressed by the fact that Mr. Acheson, McGeorge Bundy and to a lesser degree Mr. Vance had joined Mr. Ball and Mr. Goldberg in opposing further military commitments and advocating some way of getting out of the war. He was jolted when Mr. Bundy, one of the architects of intervention in the early sixties and of the bombing of North Vietnam in 1965, now took an opposite tack.

There was, to be sure, a faction that held firm in defense of the harder line —Justice Fortas, General Taylor and Mr. Murphy. Mr. Murphy wanted more bombing, not less.

Ambassador Lodge, now President Nixon's chief negotiator in Paris, left the other participants puzzled. Several found him hawkish, but at least one said he was "on all sides of the issue." Mr. McCloy leaned toward the hawkish group.

Mr. Dean, Mr. Dillion and Generals Bradley and Ridgway were now doubters. They were plainly war-weary if not yet ready to shift course dramatically. The waning public support of the war was a constant concern.

There was no consensus on the bombing issue. Mr. Goldberg and Mr. Ball advocated a halt as a way to negotiations. The others were uncertain but the impression left with Government sources was that the wise men as a group were saying: "We had better start looking for another way to get this war settled."

To the President and his senior advisers, one close observer said later, such shifts carried "more weight than something like the New Hampshire primary." Someone suggested that Mr. Johnson consider the impact of his Vietnam decisions on the coming election; he replied testily that the campaign was the least of his concerns.

Two days later, on March 28, Messrs. Rusk, Clifford, Rostow, McPherson and William Bundy met in Mr. Rusk's mahogany-paneled office on the seventh floor of the State Department to polish the President's speech.

It was still, in the words of one participant, a "teeth-clenched, see-it-through" speech, announcing that about 15,000 more troops would be sent to Vietnam. It made a pro-forma plea for peace at the negotiating table and said nothing about cutting back the bombing.

Secretary Clifford launched an impassioned plea against taking this approach.

"I can't do it—I can't go along with it," he said. "I can't be in the position of trying to polish a speech of this kind. This speech can't be polished. What's needed is a new speech. This one is irrevocably setting the President down the wrong road."

The others listened as he spoke for nearly an hour, using to enormous advantage his almost unique position of being able to speak for the views of many outside.

It would tear the country apart, the Defense Secretary argued, to hear a speech that promised only more war. What was needed, he said, was not a "war speech, but a peace speech—the issue is as sharp as the edge of an ax."

To Mr. Clifford's surprise, Mr. Rusk did not cut him short. The others chimed in. Mr. Rusk sent out for sandwiches. Mr. Clifford appealed for some compromise, and once again they debated the 20th Parallel idea.

By this time the military commanders were no longer raising strong objections. Some, like Adm. U.S. Grant Sharp, the Pacific Fleet commander, who had overall charge of the bombing, thought the cutback would fail. He fully expected that if it were tried, the President would order full bombing again in a month or so. Some officials thought this was Mr. Rostow's view also.

Secretary Rusk, eager to find some way to the negotiating table, still did not think the cutback would satisfy Hanoi. The month's arguments had had a cumulative effect on him.

At the end of the day—the meeting lasted until 5 P.M.—Mr. Rusk had agreed with Mr. Clifford that Mr. McPherson should prepare "an alternate draft." That night, while the President was showing Senator Mike Mansfield, the Democratic majority leader, a draft of the original hawkish speech, Mr. McPherson began writing alternate draft No. 1. Working through the night, he had it ready by morning.

He sent the draft, the first one containing the proposal for a bombing cutback to the 20th Parallel, to Mr. Johnson with a note saying that it seemed to reflect the sentiments of some of the President's leading advisers. He also offered to go back to the original version if that was Mr. Johnson's wish.

Later in the day the President called Mr. McPherson in to discuss changes in an item on "Page 3." He did not specify which draft, but it was clear that he was now working with the new speech. That was how he signaled a major break in the debate.

He had been deeply influenced by the shift in the public mood, as reflected in the wise men's meetings and his contacts on Capitol Hill. The country was in turmoil and the dollar was in danger.

He had been shaken by the change in his old friend, Mr. Clifford, and was finally persuaded to try a new tack by Mr. Clifford's sheer persistence. The mood of others had softened in the crucible of debate, too.

From then until 9 P.M. on the 31st, the speech went through five more drafts. None changed the new essence, though there was one important tug-of-war over the wording on the bombing cutback.

Under Secretary of State Nicholas deB. Katzenbach, drawn into the top-level discussions since Secretary Rusk was leaving for a Pacific meeting with the Vietnam allies, opposed naming the 20th Parallel as the cutoff point.

Mr. Katzenbach had long favored a halt. Now he wanted the northern limit to be the 19th Parallel rather than the 20th, but the military insisted on the 20th so they could hit Thanhhoa, a railroad switching point, and Route 7, leading into Laos—both just south of the 20th Parallel.

The Under Secretary, who suggested that it not be stated so baldly, was looking for a way to "winch" the limit further southward. And, like most Administration officials, he was operating under the mistaken assumption that one main purpose of the speech was to help President Johnson in the April 2 Democratic primary in Wisconsin.

Suggesting that the speech would have more public appeal if it emphasized that part of the bombing would be continued to protect American troops just south of the demilitarized zone, Mr. Katzenbach drafted a revision that said all bombing should stop "except in an area north of the demilitarized zone where the continuing enemy buildup directly threatens allied forward positions." His amendment specified that this would spare almost 90 percent of North Vietnam's population.

The President liked that language and accepted it. On Saturday he asked Mr. Rostow to telephone Mr. Katzenbach, now Acting Secretary, to persuade him to accept the 20th Parallel as the northern limit.

Reluctantly Mr. Katzenbach agreed, but with a caveat: "Don't make the first big raid at 19 degrees 59 minutes. Make sure the orders are consistent with the speech." Mr. Rostow replied that this would be done.

But they had different interpretations of what they had agreed on. Mr. Katzenbach thought he had won agreement on a plan that would let the bombing "roll northward" gradually from the buffer area as battlefield conditions dictated. Mr. Rostow felt he had Mr. Katzenbach's approval for military orders saying simply that bombing north of the 20th Parallel was forbidden after March 31.

On the Saturday a small group worked with President Johnson, who was in good spirits going over the text line by line until about 9 P.M. The speech had become progressively more dovish until, one official said, "it ended up 180 degrees from where it started."

Late the previous day Mr. Clifford had been concerned that the peroration, left over from original drafts, was still too militant, so Mr. McPherson was to draft a substitute.

When the Saturday session ended Mr. Johnson asked for the revised peroration. Mr. McPherson said he had not had time to rewrite it but would do so promptly.

The President, his shirt open and his tie down, muttered, "No need to—I may have one of my own." He winked at Mr. McPherson, who turned to Mr. Clifford and said: "My God? Do you think he is going to say sayonara?" Mr. Clifford responded with a strange and unbelieving grimace.

On Sunday the President had Horace Busby, another speech-writer, and Mr. Christian working on the withdrawal section. Mr. McPherson, still officially in the dark on the President's political plans, assumed that he did not want his ending.

But Mr. Johnson kept sending word that he did indeed want Mr. McPherson's peroration, obviously intending to deliver both.

Initially Mr. Johnson hesitated to make his withdrawal announcement with the policy declaration. But sometime near the end of March, as he became convinced of the need for a bombing cutback, he evidently concluded that it would be more effective if he made it clear that he was not just appealing for votes or pacifying domestic critics or serving some other personal interest.

The approach of the Wisconsin primary also served as a deadline for action, in the view of some of his political advisers. They thought his withdrawal would be more dignified and more effective if made before the primary rather than after the expected victory for Senator Eugene J. McCarthy of Minnesota.

By the eve of the speech the President's mind was made up.

He did not sleep particularly well that night, and he was up before dawn. In the afternoon, he began rehearsing the Vietnam portion of the speech. About 4 P.M. Mr. Busby gave him the revised ending on not seeking re-election. The President made a few final adjustments to insure that his motives would be understood.

At 8 P.M. the text was turned over to an Army Signal Corps man to put on prompter devices, and the President told his aides to begin informing members of the Cabinet of his intentions.

Secretary Clifford and his wife were invited to the Executive Mansion half an hour before the President was to go on nationwide television. Mr. Clifford already knew of the Vietnam decision—the bombing cutback to the 20th Parallel, 13,500 more troops for General Westmoreland and more equipment for the South Vietnamese Army at a cost of $2.5-billion a year.

After the wrenching tensions of the policy debate and the chill that had crept into their personal relations, the Secretary was warmed to learn that the President wanted to see him before delivering the speech. Upstairs in the family quarters, the Cliffords joined Mrs. Johnson and Jack Valenti, the President's former aide and an old Texas friend.

Mr. Johnson motioned Mr. Clifford into his bedroom and without a word handed him the last two paragraphs of the speech.

"With America's sons in the fields far away, with America's future under challenge right here at home, with our hopes and the world's hopes for peace in the balance every day," the President told the nation later, "I do not believe that I should devote an hour or a day of my time to any personal, partisan causes or to any duties other than the awesome duties of this office—the Presidency of your country.

"Accordingly, I shall not seek, and I will not accept, the nomination of my party for another term as your President."

EPILOGUE

The President's speech brought Washington—and the nation—the relief it feels when a breezy summer day breaks a sweltering heat wave. The bitterness of months had been lanced in a stroke. There was a rare moment of harmony. But it was only an instant.

Within 36 hours, while the world awaited Hanoi's response, Navy jets struck Thanhhoa, 210 miles north of the demilitarized zone, the very kind of raid that Mr. Katzenbach had wanted to prevent.

The enormous relief evaporated. The heat wave was back. The politicians, not knowing that the Russians and Hanoi had been privately told that the northern limit of the bombing was the 20th Parallel, complained that the public had been misled. State Department officials privately accused the military commanders of trying to sabotage the President's peace initiative.

With a new political storm mounting. Mr. Clifford persuaded President Johnson to pull the bombing back to the 19th parallel on the pretext that some American planes might have strayed over the 20th Parallel. It was a decision that Mr. Rostow, General Wheeler, General Westmoreland and others tried many times to reverse.

And so it went—all summer, all fall—the two coalitions in the Administration battling for the President's favor.

"It was like climbing the greasy pole," recalled an insider. "You wanted to continue climbing higher but you had to keep fighting to stay where you were."

In May, the hawks were urging escalation after enemy forces had launched their mini-Tet offensive.

General Westmoreland also wanted approval to launch B-52 raids and small ground forays against enemy supply dumps and base camps in remote areas of Cambodia, when enemy forces pulled back to these sanctuaries from assaults on American outposts. But President Johnson rejected this plan firmly.

In June, when enemy rockets were falling on Saigon, Ambassador Ellsworth Bunker was privately urging that the United States retaliate by bombing Hanoi. One official said the United States was "within two days" of stepping up the bombing of North Vietnam when the attacks on Saigon stopped.

Next it was the doves. During the prolonged summer battlefield lull W.

Averell Harriman and Cyrus R. Vance, the American negotiators in Paris, tried to talk the President into a total bombing halt.

They made their pitch at the end of July. It was strictly a ploy. They accepted the military estimate that the lull was not deliberate and that the enemy was merely regrouping and refitting his forces. But they suggested that President Johnson treat it as deliberate restraint anyway.

The proposal was to tell Hanoi that since it had de-escalated the war, the United States would end the bombing, but that to sustain this cessation, Hanoi would have to refrain from another offensive. The hope was to talk Hanoi into restraint.

Mr. Clifford and Vice President Humphrey promoted the idea. Mr. Katzenbach and Mr. Bundy were in Paris at this time, and simultaneously, The New York Times in a July 29 editorial advocated a similar tactic.

It was all too much for President Johnson. "He thought it was a conspiracy," said one high official. "There were so many coincidences that he thought it stank to high heaven." He rejected the plan out of hand.

In October, as in March, there was another debate. To all the complications of the earlier argument were added the intricacies—and miscalculations—of dealing with the South Vietnamese. Finally, on Oct. 31, the President stopped all the bombing of North Vietnam, but even that did not stop the inner wrangling.

The struggle for the President's mind persisted until the day he left office.

Selected Bibliography

1. GENERAL

George Mowry's excellent *The Urban Nation, 1920–1960* (1965) is the only textbook survey of modern American history, as the term is used in this anthology. Paul K. Conkin and David Burner are preparing an interpretive text covering the years from World War One to 1970, which will be published in 1971. Twentieth-century diplomatic studies include David Trask, *Victory Without Peace* (1968), Richard Leopold, *The Growth of American Foreign Policy* (rev. 1962), and George Kennan, *American Diplomacy* (1951).

2. WORLD WAR ONE TO THE GREAT DEPRESSION

The most recent historiographical article on American entry into World War One is Daniel Smith, "National Interest and American Intervention, 1917," *Journal of American History* (1965); an interesting group of early revisionists is examined in Warren I. Cohen, *The American Revisionists* (1967). Daniel Smith, *The Great Departure* (1965), is a general interpretation of the war. N. Gordon Levin, *Woodrow Wilson and World Politics* (1968), examines Wilson's postwar actions in the larger context of establishing world order, and Arno J. Mayer, in *Politics and the Diplomacy of Peacemaking* (1968), stresses fears of Bolshevism at Versailles. See also Arthur S. Link, *Wilson the Diplomatist* (rev. 1963).

Stanley Coben's *A. Mitchell Palmer* (1963) and his article reprinted in the present collection are keys to understanding the Red scare; see also Robert Murray, *Red Scare* (1955). David Burner, "1919—Prelude to Normalcy," John Braeman et al., *Change and Continuity in the Twentieth Century: The 1920's Revisited* (1968), is an introduction to the postwar reaction; the book also contains a number of interesting essays on the twenties. Three good surveys of the decade are William Leuchtenburg, *The Perils of Prosperity, 1914–1932* (1958), John D. Hicks, *Republican Ascendancy, 1921–1933.* (1960), and the contemporary account by Frederick Lewis Allen, *Only Yesterday* (1931). Arthur Schlesinger, Jr., *The Changing of the Old Order, 1919–33* (1957), looks retrospectively from the vantage point of Franklin Roosevelt's rise to national prominence. Paul Carter, *The Twenties in America* (1968), covers social and cultural trends and provides ample bibliography. Henry May, "Shifting Perspectives on the 1920's," *Mississippi Valley Historical Review* (1956), is an excellent if somewhat dated, effort at categorization.

The Republican Presidents are analyzed in three Harding books, Robert K. Murray, *The Harding Era* (1969), Francis Russell, *The Shadow on Blooming Grove* (1968), and Andrew Sinclair, *The Available Man* (1965); in Donald McCoy, *Calvin Coolidge* (1967), and the still-important account by a contemporary, William Allen White, *A Puritan in Babylon* (1938); and in Harris Warren, *Herbert Hoover and the Great Depression* (1959), Albert U. Romasco, *The Poverty of Abundance* (1965), Carl Degler, "The Ordeal of Herbert Hoover," *Yale Review* (1965), and Hoover's own *Memoirs* (1952). David Burner, *The Politics of Provincialism* (1968), covers the Democratic party in the twenties. J. Joseph Huthmacher, *Massachusetts People and Politics, 1919–33* (1959), is a pioneering study of the rise of Democratic ethnic groups. The best recent books on the Ku Klux Klan are David Chalmers, *Hooded Americanism* (1965), and Kenneth T. Jackson, *The Ku Klux Klan in the City, 1915–1930* (1968). Paul Murphy discusses the nativist theme in "Sources and Nature of Intolerance in the 1920's," *Journal of American History* (1964).

Arthur S. Link discusses the survival of progressivism in the twenties in "What Happened to the Progressive Movement in the 1920's?" *American Historical Review* (1959). Clark Chambers, *Seedtime of Reform* (1963), an examination of the social welfare movement, lends support to the Link thesis. Andrew Sinclair, *Era of Excess* (1962), is the best book on prohibition. Robert and Helen Lynd record the life of an Indiana community during the twenties in *Middletown* (1929). George Soule, *Prosperity Decade* (1947), surveys the economy, Irving Bernstein, *The Lean Years* (1960), is a labor history, and William Appleman Williams, "The Legend of Isolationism in the 1920's," *Science and Society* (1954), is an important essay on foreign policy. Other good monographs on the twenties include Arthur Mann, *La Guardia* (1959), Lawrence Levine, *Defender of the Faith: William Jennings Bryan, The Last Decade, 1915–1925* (1965), Preston Hubbard, *Origins of the T.V.A.* (1961), and Norman Furniss, *The Fundamentalist Controversy, 1918–1931* (1954). Selig Adler's *The Uncertain Giant* (1965) discusses foreign policy between the wars. Robert Ferrell studies *American Diplomacy in the Great Depression, 1929–1933* (1957).

3. THE GREAT DEPRESSION TO WORLD WAR TWO

There is no extended account of the Great Depression; John Kenneth Galbraith, *The Great Crash* (1955), is excellent but brief. An outstanding general survey of the 1930's is William Leuchtenburg, *Franklin D. Roosevelt and the New Deal, 1932–1940* (1963). Frank Freidel's multivolume biography of Franklin Roosevelt (1954–   ) brings his story up to 1932, and the beautifully written *Age of Roosevelt* (1957–   ) by Arthur Schlesinger, Jr., now reaches three volumes and comes up to about 1936. Schlesinger's important "Sources of the New Deal" may be found in Morton Keller, ed., *The New Deal* (1963). James MacGregor Burns, *Roosevelt: The Lion and the Fox* (1956), is a good one-volume biography. Rexford Tugwell, *The Democratic Roosevelt* (1957), and Raymond Moley, *After Seven Years* (1939), are important memoirs.

Richard Hofstadter has an enticing interpretation of the thirties in *The Age of Reform* (1955), and a portrait of Roosevelt in the *American Political Tradition* (1948). Paul K. Conkin's critical *The New Deal* (1967) is fascinating. Barton Bernstein makes a strong New Left argument in his chapter on the thirties in *Towards a New Past* (1968). Jerold Auerbach challenges revisionist interpretations in "New Deal, Old Deal, or Raw Deal: Some Thoughts on New Left Historiography," *Journal of Southern History* (1969).

Other important monographs on the thirties include Broadus Mitchell, *Depression Decade* (1947), an economic history; Ellis W. Hawley, *The New Deal and the Problem of Monopoly, 1933–39* (1965); Daniel Aaron, *Writers on the Left* (1961); James Patterson, *Congressional Conservatism and the New Deal* (1967); Otis L. Graham, Jr., *An Encore for Reform: The Old Progressives and the New Deal* (1967); and Sidney Fine, *The Automobile Under the Blue Eagle* (1963). Robert and Helen Lynd continued their study of Muncie, Indiana, in *Middletown in Transition* (1937). John Wiltz, *From Isolation to War, 1931–1941* (1968), surveys the diplomatic history of the thirties.

Key books on America's entry into World War Two are Robert A. Divine, *The Reluctant Belligerent* (1965), Paul Schroeder, *The Axis Alliance and Japanese-American Relations, 1941* (1958), Dorothy Borg, *The United States and the Far Eastern Crisis of 1933–1938* (1964), and Roberta Wohlstetter, *Pearl Harbor: Warning and Decision* (1962). Gaddis Smith, *American Diplomacy During the Second World War, 1941–1945* (1965), is a brief study; longer analyses are Herbert Feis, *Churchill, Roosevelt, Stalin* (1957), and W. H. McNeill, *America, Britain, and Roosevelt* (1953), Robert E. Sherwood's *Roosevelt and Hopkins* (1948), commands attention.

4. WORLD WAR TWO TO 1959

Good summaries of American foreign relations in this period include Paul Y. Hammond, *The Cold War Years* (1969), John Spanier, *American Foreign Policy Since World War II* (rev. 1965), and William G. Carleton, *The Revolution in American Foreign Policy* (1963). A heated debate has arisen concerning the origins of the Cold War. The Lasch article in the present anthology is a good survey of work criticizing the traditional view that Russia is largely to blame for the Cold War. An early statement of this point of view is D. F. Fleming, *The Cold War and Its Origins, 1917–1960* (2 vols., 1961); Walter La Feber makes a different argument, but in the same vein, in *America, Russia, and the Cold War, 1945–1960* (1967). Norman Graebner's *Cold War Diplomacy* (1962), is an excellent traditional account. George Kennan's classic statement of containment may be found in *Foreign Affairs* (1947). His *Memoirs, 1925–1950* appeared in 1967.

The years 1945 to 1960 are chronicled in Eric Goldman's *The Crucial Decade and After* (1961). President Truman's *Memoirs* (1955–6) can be supplemented by five interesting essays in Richard Kirkendall, ed., *The Truman Period as a Research Field* (1967). Eisenhower's memoirs are *The White House Years* (2 vols., 1963, 1965). The best brief essay on Eisenhower is Richard Rovere's "Eisenhower Over the Shoulder," *American Scholar* (1961); the best biography, Emmet John Hughes, *Ordeal of Power* (1963). Crucial for an understanding of politics in the fifties are Angus Campbell et al., *The American Voter* (1960), and Samuel Lubell, *The Revolt of the Moderates*

(1956). McCarthyism is the subject of Richard Rovere, *Senator Joseph R. McCarthy* (1959); a scholarly critique of McCarthy and his critics is Michael Paul Rogin, *McCarthyism and the Intellectuals* (1968). An essay on the Alger Hiss case is contained in Richard Morris, *Fair Trial* (1952).

Economic life is the subject of two important books by John Kenneth Galbraith, *The Affluent Society* (1958) and *American Capitalism* (1956). Alfred C. Kinsey *et al., Sexual Behavior in the Human Male* (1948) makes good reading. The interesting strain of social criticism is to be found in the fifties is illustrated by such titles as C. Wright Mills, *The Power Elite* (1959) and *White Collar* (1951), David Riesman, *The Lonely Crowd* (1950), and Arthur Bestor, *Educational Wastelands* (1953).

5. THE 1960'S

The politics of the sixties has already generated more than a score of studies, but few of them go beneath the surface of narrative events. The most notable exceptions are Arthur Schlesinger, Jr.'s analytical record of the Kennedy administration, *A Thousand Days* (1965), and Theodore J. Lowi's fascinating critique, *The End of Liberalism* (1969). Other memoirs on Kennedy include Theodore Sorensen, *Kennedy* (1966), and Pierre Salinger, *With Kennedy* (1966). James MacGregor Burns, *The Deadlock of Democracy* (1963), explains the congressional logjam of 1962–63. Tom Wicker's *JFK and LBJ* is good on LBJ, and Eric Goldman, *The Tragedy of Lyndon B. Johnson* (1968), offers an account of what it was like around the White House under Johnson. Rowland Evans and Robert Novak, *Lyndon B. Johnson: An Exercise in Power* (1966), is a mediocre book emphasizing Johnson's Senate career. Theodore White's books on the making of the President (1961, 1965, 1969) are well worth reading. *An American Melodrama* (1969), by a group of British journalists, surveys the 1968 campaign; Eugene McCarthy recounts his role in *The Year of the People* (1969). Good on Goldwater's strange campaign of 1964 are Richard Hofstadter, *The Paranoid Style in American Politics* (1965), and Richard Rovere, *The Goldwater Caper* (1965). The work of political scientists is of increasing importance for understanding contemporary American politics; essential are Angus Campbell *et al., The American Voter* (1960), and *Elections and the Political Order* (1966); Philip Converse *et al.,* "Stability and Change in 1960: A Reinstating Election," *American Political Science Review* (1961); and Walter Dean Burnham, "American Voting Behavior and the 1964 Election," *Midwest Journal of Political Science* (1966).

A good textbook survey of the years 1963 to 1968 is William E. Leuchtenburg's final chapter in S. E. Morison, H. S. Commager, and W. E. Leuchtenburg, *The Growth of the American Republic*, II (1969). There is as yet no good book on Nixon, but possible Republican strategy for 1972 is the subject of Kevin Phillips, *The Emerging Republican Majority* (1969). Vietnam is the subject of critical accounts by Bernard Fall, *Vietnam Witness, 1953–66* (1966), Arthur Schlesinger, Jr., *The Bitter Heritage* (1967), and William Fulbright, *The Arrogance of Power* (1967). *No More Vietnams,* edited by Richard M. Pfeffer (1968), is a superb collection of opinions. Frank M. Trager, *Why Vietnam?* (1966), is an early defense of the American role there; the decision to deescalate the war is analyzed in Townsend Hoopes, *The Limits of Inter-*

vention (1969). Samuel Lubell's *White and Black* (1964) is still perhaps the best book on black Americans in the sixties. *The Report of the National Advisory Commission on Civil Disorders* (1968) and the various reports of the President's commission on violence contain primary data and secondary critiques. Excellent on the economy is the last chapter of Robert Lekachman, *The Age of Keynes* (1966). Books of social criticism have been written by Ralph Nader, Michael Harrington, Fred Cooke, and many others. Summary views of the sixties, by Richard Rovere and Benjamin DeMott, are to be found in *The New York Times Magazine,* December 14, 1969.